D1603119

# JEWISH LIFE
# IN GERMANY

THE MODERN JEWISH EXPERIENCE

Paula Hyman and Deborah Dash Moore, *editors*

# JEWISH LIFE
# IN GERMANY

## *Memoirs from Three Centuries*

Edited by Monika Richarz

TRANSLATED BY STELLA P. ROSENFELD
AND SIDNEY ROSENFELD

*Sponsored by the Leo Baeck Institute*

*Indiana University Press*
BLOOMINGTON & INDIANAPOLIS

The paper used in this publication meets the minimum requirements of American
National Standard for Information Sciences—Permanence of Paper for Printed
Library Materials, ANSI Z39.48-1984.
∞ ™
Manufactured in the United States of America

**Library of Congress Cataloging-in-Publication Data**

Jüdisches Leben in Deutschland. English
    Jewish life in Germany : memoirs from three centuries, /
edited by Monika Richarz ; translated by Stella P. Rosenfeld and
Sidney Rosenfeld ; sponsored by the Leo Baeck Institute.
        p.   cm. — (The Modern Jewish experience)
    Translation of: Jüdisches Leben in Deutschland.
    "Translated, abridged version of an earlier three-volume edition"—
Translators' note.
    Includes indexes.
    ISBN 0-253-35024-7 (cloth)
    1. Jews—Germany—Biography. 2. Germany—Biography.
I. Richarz, Monika. II. Rosenfeld, Stella P.
III. Rosenfeld, Sidney. IV. Leo Baeck Institute. V. Title.
VI. Series: Modern Jewish experience (Bloomington, Ind.)
DS135.G5A14513      1991
943′.004924—dc20
                                                          90-38733
                                                             CIP

1 2 3 4 5 95 94 93 92 91

# CONTENTS

*Illustrations follow p. 290*

# Translators' Note

Translating is always a risky venture. How much more so when one must convey, in addition to meaning, the tone, diction, and rhythms of forty-six individual voices from a period of over 150 years. Only two of the memoirists in this volume, Paul Mühsam and Sammy Gronemann, were writers; of the others few would have claimed stylistic gifts. Many of them were plain, unassuming people, and more often than not their writing appeals through its very simplicity and lack of pretense. At times, to be sure, it may also appear naive or, for today's taste, overly sentimental. Some of the authors, for better or worse, emulated the "educated," that is, the dry, stilted style that was once typical for German academics and officials, and often unclear turns of phrase or awkward syntax frustrate the reader's understanding. Although we sometimes rewrote for the sake of smoother reading, we tried to preserve the stylistic qualities that were basic to the memoir.

Here and there we had to divine the meaning of an especially opaque expression or sentence, but otherwise we rarely sought to improve on the original. We hesitated to inject variety of diction where it was missing to start with, or to substitute a more or less refined expression for an everyday one. Nor did we attempt to reflect the quaintness of an older text by resorting to antiquated English idiom. Where a false sequence of tenses obscured the logic of events, we felt free to correct the imperfect construction. But our aim throughout was to respect the author's person by translating these historical documents as faithfully as possible into readable English.

The earlier memoirs confronted us with problems of transliteration and orthographical consistency. To preserve the flavor of Judeo-German (Western Yiddish)—for example, in given names and names of Jewish holidays, or in Hebrew words and expressions—we kept the original spellings. We feared that if we rendered the names "Bär" as "Ber," "Löb" as "Leib," or "Feibisch" as "Fayvel," to cite just these examples, we would be injecting the sounds or forms of (Eastern) Yiddish into the text. While these might be more familiar to the reader, at the same time they would falsify the original. Thus, we also kept such Hebrew terms and expressions as *Shavuot* ("Feast of Weeks"), *be shalom* ("peacefully") and *s'chorot* ("wares") in their Judeo-German versions (*Schwuaus*, *b'schaulem*, *s'chaures*), though today these forms have all but disappeared.

Consistency within individual memoirs sometimes required that we adhere to German spelling throughout. Thus, in some of the earlier texts, we retained German *j*, *sch*, *v*, and *w*, where English would have *y* (as in "yes"), *sh* (as in "shy") *f* (as in "far"), and *v* (as in "very"). As the use of Judeo-German diminished, we Anglicized the spelling of common words and terms, such as *Yom Kippur*, *kosher*, and others; but we retained (Western or Eastern) Yiddish forms, albeit in Anglicized spelling, whenever an author used them (e.g., *Shabbes*).

We wish to thank the following for their help in translating these memoirs: Monika Richarz (Cologne), the editor of the original three-volume German version, who through her profound knowledge of German-Jewish life and history provided us with valuable insights; Fred Grubel of the Leo Baeck Institute (New York), who has provided guidance to the memoir project since its beginning nearly two decades ago and who made the financial arrangements for the translation; and Robert Jacobs, also of the Leo Baeck Institute, whose close, patient reading of the manuscript led to many helpful suggestions for change. We also wish to thank Elliot Ginsberg and Sanford Margolis (Oberlin) for their readiness to answer our frequent questions on the intricacies of Hebrew and Yiddish usage. Not least, we acknowledge the Archive of the Leo Baeck Institute, to which the vast majority of the original memoirs are now entrusted, and we thank Inter Nationes (Bonn) for the grant that made our work possible.

If our translation helps to preserve and honor the memory of German Jewry, we will deem ourselves well rewarded.

# Editor's Preface

This volume contains a collection of autobiographical documents by German Jews who are unknown to the public. All of these texts, which are contributions to social history, come from the Archives of the Leo Baeck Institute in New York. Represented are Jews from all social strata, from city and country, from various professions and differing religious and political groupings. In almost every instance, the authors wrote these accounts solely for their own families. The selection primarily emphasizes two basic themes: the internal development of the Jewish social group and the changing situation of the Jews within the general society. The authors report vividly on childhood, school, and vocation, as well as on community life, religious practice, culture, and politics. These accounts from daily life testify to very diverse forms of Jewish identity and to the extraordinary variety of German Jewry. But they also illustrate the relationship between Jews and their environment, cultural and social rapprochement, as well as the denial of integration, and every level of antisemitic persecution. Thus, these texts enable the reader to gain a picture of the social life of German Jews in the one hundred and fifty years from the beginning of their emancipation to their expulsion and destruction.

This book is a translated, abridged version of an earlier three-volume edition of autobiographies of German Jews, which appeared under the title *Jüdisches Leben in Deutschland: Selbstzeugnisse zur Sozialgeschichte* (Stuttgart: Deutsche Verlags-Anstalt, 1976–1982). The original German edition, now out-of-print, contains 126 autobiographical accounts from the Archives of the Leo Baeck Institute, of which 51 have been included in the present volume. Almost all of the original autobiographies exist only in manuscript form.

The Leo Baeck Institute was founded in 1955 by emigrants from Germany as a research center for German-Jewish history, and it maintains branches in New York, London, and Jerusalem. An important division of the archives assembled in New York is the collection of memoirs and remembrances established by Max Kreutzberger. At present it contains some one thousand manuscripts and private printings, which were donated by Jews who had fled from Germany. About two-thirds of these manuscripts treat the period of the twentieth century and were thus written mainly after 1945. However, there are also numerous remembrances of the nineteenth century, which originated two or three generations ago, were handed down in the families, and were saved when their owners fled from Germany.

Who are the authors of these manuscripts? For the most part, they are men and women from the Jewish middle class who were unknown in public life. People with a university education are disproportionately represented, whereas authors from the social upper class and lower class, as well as East European Jews, are underrepresented, as are women. However, it was possible to correct this social imbalance when selecting the texts for inclusion. Many of the authors are people who had advanced socially, but who also describe the poorer or rural milieu of their childhood. The motivation for recording their earlier memories was not seldom pride in the social rise of the family. After the Holocaust entirely different reasons induced the authors to write: the conviction that they were obligated by history to bear witness, the intense mental pain because of their experiences, and the need to provide their children and grandchildren, who had grown up in another culture outside Germany, with an awareness of their family background.

The collection attempts to present as representative a social cross section as possible, even though this is something that can never completely be realized. The idea of writing memoirs is, after all, a middle-class notion. As regards the selection by period, the epochs of Emancipation (1780–1871), Imperial Germany (1871–1918), and the time of the Weimar Republic (1919–1933) and National Socialist persecution (1933–1945) were given almost equal weight. This may be surprising since today the period of National Socialism commands special interest. However, this volume is intended to document the rise, development, and destruction of German Jewry in like measure. For only thereby will a full picture of this destroyed culture and society emerge. Geographically, the documentation was limited to events within Germany. Thus, its final section ends with the beginning of emigration or deportation, and does not treat of life in exile or in the extermination camps. Exceptions to this are the concentration camps within Germany itself, in which Jews were imprisoned after the Pogrom of November 9/10, 1938. But the documentation does extend in time beyond the end of the mass deportations in 1943, since, contrary to National Socialist propaganda, tens of thousands of Jews were still living in Germany after that. For this reason, the last section has been devoted to the testimonies of those who went underground and whose depictions of life on the edge of death underscore this aspect of Jewish persecution.

The question of historical reliability always arises when memoirs are edited. All recollection is selective and in the course of time, due to forgetting, repressing, and reinterpretation, it is subject to further changes. The time of writing also influences the content of the memoirs. It makes a very distinct difference, for example, whether a manuscript was written with knowledge of the gas chambers at Auschwitz or not. Therefore, special effort was devoted to dating the undated manuscripts, mainly by questioning the families, and by examining their historical content—to the extent that this was possible. Errors were corrected without commentary only in the case of dates; otherwise, corrections appear in the notes. The Hebrew words in the text were often transcribed by the authors in keeping with the Ashkenazic pronunciation that was customary in Germany. This was not changed in favor of modern Hebrew. Parentheses in the text were inserted by the authors, square brackets by the editor.

This collection is intended as much for those interested in history and politics as for teachers and students seeking access to the history of German Jews. I have therefore provided the present abridged edition with an introductory essay, which summarizes the longer, scholarly introductions of the German edition and briefly outlines the social history of the Jews in Germany. It is based on the results of the historical research to date in this field, which especially in the last decade has become quite extensive internationally. The essay is without footnotes, which can be found in the original edition.

The three-volume edition upon which this abridged version is based was prepared during several years of work at the Leo Baeck Institute in New York, assisted by grants from the Deutsche Forschungsgemeinschaft. At the same time, I was a research associate in the Department of History at the Technical University of Berlin, where Professor Reinhard Rürup furthered the edition by gaining support from the Deutsche Forschungsgemeinschaft. The project originated as an idea of the Leo Baeck Institute and was then carried out through international cooperation. The board of directors and the staff of the Institute supported my work in New York in every imaginable way and fostered our working together in a manner that was as trusting as it was friendly. For this I am most grateful to the Institute and especially to its director, Fred Grubel.

Many scholars in New York gave me advice and help with individual questions. Among them I gratefully name Max Gruenewald, Ernest Hamburger, Ismar Schorsch, Marion Kaplan, Sybil Milton, Steven Lowenstein, and Robert Liberles. In Berlin my sincere thanks go to Reinhard Rürup for his friendly support and, for his advice, to E. G. Lowenthal, without whose private archive many footnotes would have been impossible. Not least, I thank Arnold Paucker (London) and Josef Walk (Jerusalem) for their help with my research in England and Israel.

Cologne, Spring 1989                                                                    Monika Richarz

# JEWISH LIFE IN GERMANY

# ❧ INTRODUCTION

The following autobiographical texts are historical documents of Jewish life in Germany. They can be understood fully only by readers who have a certain basic knowledge of the conditions under which these lives were lived. In the personal recollections themselves these conditions are either assumed to be familiar, or they were unknown even to the authors, since they became recognizable as basic structural paradigms only in historical retrospect. What appears to be strictly individual is frequently the expression of a general development. In the social history of the German Jews of the nineteenth century, phenomena such as social advancement, urbanization, and the decline in the birthrate were basic life patterns. Therefore, it is necessary to provide the reader with a historical survey of the circumstances and ways of life of the Jewish minority in German society. The following major sociohistorical themes will be treated: the evolution of the legal status of the Jews, demographic changes, changes in occupational patterns, social mobility, acculturation and education, family structure, changes in religious attitudes, community life and organization, political attitudes, and changes in the relations between Jews and their environment. For the period until 1933 each of these themes will be presented in its historical progression, while a separate section will be devoted to the period of National Socialism.

## Emancipation: From Protected Jew to Second-Class Citizen

The age of Jewish emancipation in Germany began in 1781 with the famous treatise by the Prussian State Councillor Christian Wilhelm Dohm, "Über die bürgerliche Verbesserung der Juden" (On the Betterment of the Civil Status of the Jews). It ended only with the constitution of the German Reich of 1871, which definitively declared the equal status of the Jews before the law, although this was not fully realized de facto in Imperial Germany. The age of emancipation simultaneously marked the epoch of the rise of bourgeois society in Germany, and both processes were closely interwoven. The emancipation of the Jews was but one of the basic social changes through which feudal society was dissolved and the ascendancy of the German bourgeoisie was made possible. The bourgeois-liberal movement, with its call for human rights, a constitution, and political self-determination, also had to speak up for the equality of the Jews if it did not wish to contradict itself. Bourgeois officials and elected representatives became advocates of Jewish emancipation. But unlike France, where the Jews received equality overnight, in Germany it was tied to the fulfillment of conditions, and thus the process of emancipation was drawn out over three generations. To the authorities the Jews never appeared sufficiently adapted for full emancipation, and thereby the emancipatory process itself permanently provided occasion for new discrimination. Thus, from the beginning the bourgeois movement and liberalism displayed an ambivalent attitude toward the

Jewish minority. Only when the Jews had advanced economically and entered the middle class in the course of industrialization were their legal disadvantages removed, since it was clear that they could no longer be discriminated against as poor and uneducated people.

But there soon arose in Imperial Germany a social antisemitism of unprecedented scale. Now, in contrast, it was precisely the education and unusual prosperity of the Jewish minority that served as a target of attack. Particularly the middle class refused the Jews social acceptance, excluded them from state positions and officer careers, and accused them of economic cheating and of imposing a foreign culture on the German people. Thus, at the time of their greatest economic success, German Jews remained in large measure socially isolated and became a German-Jewish middle class with its own character, which strove hard to adapt to its surroundings, but, despite considerable assimilation, also preserved Jewish traditions internally. To be sure, orthodox Judaism was greatly weakened, and only a small number of Jews still lived strictly according to religious law; yet the Jewish minority developed its own German-Jewish subculture, in which traditional Jewish elements combined with elements of German bourgeois culture. The much-discussed "German-Jewish symbiosis" was, then, less a social reality in the living-together of Jews and non-Jews than it was a cultural phenomenon within the Jewish group itself.

In the society of the Holy Roman Empire, which was divided according to the feudal system, during the eighteenth century Jews were legally no more than a tolerated and alien people who lived outside the common social order. As *Schutzjuden* (Protected Jews) they were directly subservient to the innumerable sovereigns and the Jews Laws decreed by them. Solely for reasons of economic and fiscal interest, the princes tolerated the members of the "Jewish Nation," as they were called. Because of the protection money and other special taxes that they were forced to pay to the princes, who were constantly in fiscal straits, the Jews represented a reliable source of income and, in addition, they enlivened the economy through their financial and trade connections. Thus, every sovereign sought to absorb only wealthy Jews into his state, while those Jews without means were often expelled and forced to rove from community to community as beggars.

Jews had no freedom of movement, nor were they entitled to practice a trade freely. By law, they were restricted to commercial occupations, and they could neither become guild craftsmen nor acquire land. The ruler even limited the number of Jewish children who were permitted to settle in his state to one or, upon sufficient payment, at most, two per family.

Regarded by the other subjects with distrust or religious hate, the Jews lived in their own corporate communities. In few places only, as for example in Frankfurt, was there a ghetto, but discrimination and differences in religion, culture, dress, and language created a strict social separation everywhere. For the most part, it was trade alone that brought Jews together with Christians. Internally, the Jewish communities possessed a certain autonomy. The ruler granted the right to practice religion and to establish synagogues and cemeteries, and the community heads regulated the religious and social affairs of their members. But the community heads needed confirmation by the ruler and were liable with all that they owned for the payment of the community taxes. Thus, they often belonged to the small number of Court Jews, who were used by the princes as tools of their economic policies and who had to satisfy the sovereign's constant need for credit, luxury goods, and army supplies. The Court Jews enjoyed certain privileges, and very early they showed signs of acculturation, i.e., acceptance of the surrounding culture, but they also served as spokesmen for their coreligionists.

Culturally, the Jewish masses lived in strict isolation. Torah and Talmud alone regulated their spiritual life, and until the end of the eighteenth century Jewish children learned to read and write only in Hebrew characters. The reading of German-language books was regarded with suspicion. The Jewish elementary schools, like the Talmud schools, imparted religious education, and occupation with the surrounding culture occurred only as an exception. The colloquial language of the Jews was the so-called Judendeutsch (Judeo-German), designated by modern philologists as Western Yiddish, which was written in Hebrew characters.

The Protected Jews show a distinct social stratification. One can assume that not even 2 percent belonged to the upper stratum of the Court Jews. Aside from a thin middle tier consisting of merchants with their own commercial capital, in the eighteenth century over three-fourths of the Jews lived in poverty. Most of them were petty traders of the most limited means or country peddlers, or they had to live as tradesman's helpers, without permission to marry and under the protection of a fellow Jew, if they themselves did not own a letter of protection. The lowest social stratum comprised the receivers of alms, who were found in every Jewish community, and the wandering beggar Jews (approximately 10 percent), who continually roamed from one place to another because they did not receive a residence permit anywhere.

This sketch ought not to awaken the impression that Jewish society was static. In the second half of the eighteenth century distinct changes in education and cultivation among Jews and in social relations between Jews and Christians occurred. In the case of individual Jews there was an awakening of interest in the surrounding culture, while at the same time, under the influence of the Enlightenment, readiness spread among the class of educated Christians to accept the "cultured" Jew as a human being and a potential fellow citizen. In this way there came about the encounter between a small number of cultivated Jews and Christians in scholarly circles and salons of the Enlightenment epoch. The Berlin philosopher Moses Mendelssohn, who achieved European renown, was the celebrated protagonist of this development. Jewish women such as Henriette Herz and Rahel Varnhagen became famous throughout Germany, thanks to their Berlin salons. As limited as the scope of this cultural encounter was, it still powerfully influenced the emergence and realization of the idea of Jewish emancipation.

When Christian Wilhelm Dohm, a friend of Mendelssohn, called for the civic equality of the Jews in 1781, it set off a public debate. Dohm's prime concern was to educate and "better" the Jews by drawing them away from trade and guiding them to the crafts and farming. In the following decades this idea of the necessity for education by the state was to greatly impede Jewish emancipation. The Edict of Tolerance decreed by Joseph II in 1782 for the Jews of Austria granted no civic rights, but rather introduced military duty, the steering to specific vocations, and state school reform for Jews. This influenced the discussion in the German states more strongly than did the immediate and unlimited equality for Jews enacted by the French National Assembly in 1791.

In reality, at the start only the Jews in the territories conquered by France enjoyed full equality, and it, too, was short-lived. When Napoleon was defeated, the Jews of the Rhine regions, in Westphalia, the Hanseatic cities, and Frankfurt, again lost these rights. In Prussia, the defeat of 1806 provided the impetus for a series of social reforms that were intended to remove the barriers of the estates society and promote the participation of the citizenry in national life. Part of this reform project was the Jews Edict of 1812, which granted the Jews Prussian citizenship, with all pertinent rights and duties, among which was military service. This eliminated the category of Protected Jew. Jews were free to choose their own occupations, but were not yet eligible to become public officials. This relatively progressive law, however, applied only to the radically reduced Prussia of 1812, and not until 1848 did it affect the rest of the Jews in Prussia, above all the masses of poorer Jews, who lived in the province of Posen. In contrast, the Jews of Bavaria were subjected to the rigorous Registration Law of 1813, which prohibited their increase beyond a set registration limit and thus caused vast emigration. In Bavaria, as well as in the two Hessian states, in Baden, and in Württemberg, the granting of citizens' rights was linked in the laws of emancipation with the practice of specified occupations, i.e., the state deliberately steered the choice of vocation. It was not until 1848 that this policy of education emancipated all of those Jews who, as peddlers, dealers in secondhand goods or mere trade intermediaries, and pawnbrokers, possessed only inconsiderable capital. This especially affected the large numbers of rural Jews in southern and western Germany.

If one surveys the process of Jewish emancipation, which was greatly complicated by the multitude of German states and step-by-step implementation, one can clearly distinguish several phases. The first phase comprised the period until 1815 and was marked by new Jews Laws that followed the model of either Austria or France. At the Congress of Vienna reactionary thinking won out on the "Jewish Question," too. Legislation and administrative practice in part placed new limits on the rights that had been granted. The Revolution of 1848 occasioned the decisive second phase of emancipatory legislation, even though a regressive movement occurred in the fifties, until in the sixties equality of rights was fully realized in almost all of the German states. Only at the end did the Jews receive municipal citizenship rights and, along with this, untaxed freedom of domicile. Even though the emancipation of the Jews, which was furthered by the liberal bourgeois movement, had proceeded but haltingly, after 1815 the effects of economic liberalism and the methods of capitalistic industrial production, in concert with the now visible social rise of the Jews, should have made special laws for Jews in a completely altered economic and social structure an anachronism.

Although the legal situation of the Jews in Imperial Germany corresponded to that of all other citizens, this still did not mean that society conceded them equal rights de facto. The prevalence of antisemitism among public officials, academics, and officers of Imperial Germany again and again resulted in the constitution being reduced to absurdity by social practice. While the Jews could now freely choose their occupations, every Jew knew, when faced with the choice of profession, that he had almost no prospect of becoming a civil servant, a teacher, a professor, a judge, or an officer. Legal discrimination had been replaced by social discrimination, the aim of which was above all to keep Jews out of positions of societal leadership.

## Changes in the Jewish Population

The legal emancipation of the Jews brought about their political integration into the municipalities and states in which they lived, and influenced their religious life and cultural development and, not least, their demographic patterns. It was typical during the time of the Protected Jews that the rulers tried to limit the growth of the Jewish population as much as possible; but at the start of the emancipatory period the laws that accomplished this were already abolished almost everywhere, except in Bavaria. It is not surprising, therefore, that between 1820 and 1871 the Jewish population, like the population at large, increased greatly. The general rate of increase was 63 percent, while among Jews it was 74 percent. In the German Reich of 1871 there were 512,000 Jews, who made up 1.2 percent of the population.

After 1871, the growth of the Jewish population began to slow. Between the censuses of 1871 and 1910 total population grew by 58 percent, whereas the Jewish population increased by only about 20 percent, to 615,000. How can this be explained? The social rise and the broad urbanization of the Jews had brought them into the urban middle class, a group that at the end of the nineteenth century had begun to limit the number of its children through birth control. Thus, the percentage of Jews among the Reich population sank, a development that was furthered by a large emigration overseas. Only the lower infant mortality rate and longer life expectancy among the Jews, and especially the migration to Germany of Jews from Eastern Europe, prevented an even greater loss in the Jewish population. Since most of these foreign Jews did not belong to the middle class, they had more children. Thus, by 1900 the German Jews already showed a negative growth balance.

The age structure of the Jewish minority soon differed clearly from that of the general population. Between 1871 and 1933 the proportion of Jewish children dropped by half. This negative demographic development was not noted by the German public. Because the Jews were concentrated in the large cities and in specific occupations, and because of Jewish migration from Eastern Europe, they had actually become more visible. The antisemites, Heinrich von Treitschke among them, even tried to awaken the impression that a mass migration of Jews was inundating the Reich. On the other hand, Jewish statisticians—above all, Felix Theilhaber in his *Untergang der deutschen Juden* (1911; The End of the German Jews)—warned of the negative development.

Table 1 provides an overview of Jewish growth trends in the Reich from 1871 to 1939. It must be taken into account that after the First World War the Reich was smaller in size, since it had lost territories on its eastern and western borders. The population figures for 1933, under the National Socialist regime, mirror the effects of the first flights, and for 1939 the result of forced mass emigration (all statistics from *Statistik des Deutschen Reichs*)

In addition to dropping birthrates and increasing longevity, two other factors determined the changes in Jewish population figures: immigration and emigration, along with mixed marriage and conversion. Throughout the nineteenth century there was Jewish emigration from Germany, particularly to the United States, but no exact statistics are available. According to estimates, between 1830 and 1910 as many as 200,000 German Jews emigrated overseas. Their percentage of the German emigration was

TABLE 1

|      | Jews    | Percent of Population |
|------|---------|-----------------------|
| 1871 | 512,153 | 1.25 |
| 1885 | 563,172 | 1.20 |
| 1900 | 586,833 | 1.04 |
| 1910 | 615,021 | 0.95 |
| 1925 | 564,379 | 0.90 |
| 1933 | 502,799 | 0.76 |
| 1939 | 213,930 | 0.31 |

certainly higher than their percentage in the population. The largest emigration was from Bavaria, where until 1862 it was spurred by the Registration Law, and from the other economically backward regions of southern Germany, as well as from the province of Posen. After 1880, as a result of the pogroms in Russia and the economic crisis of the Jews in Galicia, there began a relatively large Jewish immigration to Germany from Eastern Europe. To be sure, in comparison to the flood of over two million Jews from Eastern Europe to the United States this was only a trickle. Permanent residence in Germany was made difficult for East European Jews. They could almost never attain naturalization and nearly all of them were forced to remain aliens. Table 2 shows the immigration of foreign Jews and their percentage of the Jews in Germany.

TABLE 2

|      | Foreign-born Jews | As Percent of the Jews in Germany |
|------|-------------------|-----------------------------------|
| 1890 | 22,000  | 3.9  |
| 1910 | 78,746  | 12.8 |
| 1925 | 107,747 | 19.1 |
| 1933 | 98,747  | 19.8 |

During the First World War, Jewish workers were temporarily recruited from the areas of Tsarist Russia that were occupied by Germany. This led to increased immigration, and in the Weimar Republic the East European Jews comprised about a fifth of the Jews living in Germany. Most of them were petty traders or craftsmen and unskilled laborers; many of them belonged to the proletariat. They spoke Yiddish, practiced orthodoxy, or were socialists. In brief, they differed in every respect from the German Jews. Most of the East European Jews were concentrated in Berlin, as well as in Saxony and the Ruhr region, where in the large towns they lived apart from the German-Jewish middle class. In 1925 almost half of all foreign Jews in Germany came from Poland, the rest mainly from Austria and the Soviet Union; and 10 percent had become stateless as a result of the World War.

Population loss through conversion remained relatively slight. Jakob Toury estimates it at about 22,000 persons for the entire nineteenth century. Most of the con-

versions took place in Imperial Germany, when antisemitism became a systematic movement and religious indifference had also greatly increased among Jews. In the years 1918
and 1933 the baptism curve reached new peaks, which proves that conversions were
strongly influenced by the pressure of antisemitism.

Mixed marriages had more serious consequences than conversions for Jewish growth
trends. They were increasing in greater measure, and fewer than a quarter of the children
in such marriages were raised as Jews. For the period 1875–79, 4 percent of all Jewish
marriages in Prussia were mixed marriages; for 1901–04 the figure was 9 percent; and
for 1930–33 it was already 24 percent. In Hamburg the percentage of mixed marriages
of Jews and Christians before 1933 had reached 39 percent. This trend ran counter to
the tradition of in-group marriage, which had remained the strongest expression of
Jewish identity. In the long term, further increase of mixed marriages would have
jeopardized the continued existence of a separate Jewish social group and have led to
an absorption of the Jewish population.

For historical reasons, the geographic distribution of the Jews among the separate
German states before 1871 varied greatly. When full emancipation and the founding
of the Reich made unlimited mobility within Germany possible for Jews, their distribution steadily changed in favor of the more industrialized regions and the big cities.
Table 3 shows the distribution of the Jews among the various German states in 1871,
the year of the founding of the Reich.

TABLE 3

| Prussia | 325,587 | Hamburg | 13,796 |
|---|---|---|---|
| Bavaria | 50,648 | Württemberg | 12,245 |
| Alsace-Lorraine | 40,938 | Saxony | 3,346 |
| Baden | 25,703 | Thuringia | 3,309 |
| Hesse | 25,373 | Others | 11,208 |
| | | Total: | 512,153 |

Almost two-thirds of all German Jews were already living in Prussia (which had
the greatest industrialization), and by 1925 this figure had reached 72 percent. Within
Prussia there was a clear migration from the agrarian eastern provinces toward the capital
city of Berlin. But through industrialization and the growth of cities the Ruhr area,
too, attracted Jewish population. In the southern German states of Bavaria, Baden,
Württemberg, and Hesse the Jewish population changed very little, or there was a slight
emigration.

Given the rapid urbanization of the Jews in Imperial Germany, the large number
of Jews still living in rural areas at the end of the nineteenth century is often underestimated. In southern and western Germany the Jews were still settled predominately
in villages and rural towns, and this held true also for the Prussian Rhine province and
Westphalia. The kingdom of Württemberg, with 93 percent, showed the highest proportion of village Jews. Also in the Grand Duchy of Hesse, in 1871 half of all Jews
were still living in villages with fewer than 2,000 inhabitants. But then the rapid

migration of Jews from the villages and rural towns to the cities began throughout the Reich.

Urbanization, made possible by freedom of domicile, provides an important criterion for the economic and social rise of the German Jews. As the memoirs show again and again, it is the successful ones who migrate from the villages and small towns to the cities. Two factors for the move to the city are named most frequently: railroad connections and the Gymnasium. To an extent, both are vehicles for upward mobility. The development of modern transportation and the greater concentration of population and trade in individual cities now made it both vital and more convenient for the rural wholesale merchant to settle closer to his sales market or at least in a town with good railway connections. With the migration to the city, the wares and volume of the enterprise changed, which frequently resulted in a further move to the capital and royal seat. Thus, for example, new residence in Posen or Breslau was often only a stage on the way to Berlin. At the same time, urbanization offered the chance for considerably improved educational opportunities for the children, something that was greatly prized in traditional Jewish families. If the entire family was not yet able to move to the city, training there was still possible for the sons, which, as the example of Isidor Hirschfeld (24) shows, greatly promoted intergenerational mobility. The connection between social and geographic mobility was a special characteristic of Jewish social development and led to internal migration on the largest scale. In turn, this had radical consequences in the religious realm, for urbanization often caused a weakening of the traditional Jewish way of life.

The urbanization of the Jews took place quicker and to a far greater degree than that of the rest of the Reich population. In 1871, barely 20 percent of all Jews lived in cities; in 1910 the figure was already 58 percent; and in 1933 it was 67 percent. On the other hand, in 1871 only 5 percent of the total German population lived in cities, and in 1933, 27 percent. Behind these figures are concealed far-reaching differences in education and occupational patterns, but they also reflect the fact that amid the anonymity of the cities many Jews felt safe from antisemitism. Table 4 provides an overview of the growth of the seven largest Jewish communities, all of which were located in cities.

TABLE 4

|  | 1871 | Percent of Population | 1910 | Percent of Population | 1925 | Percent of Population |
|---|---|---|---|---|---|---|
| Berlin | 36,015 | 4.3 | 90,013 | 4.3 | 172,672 | 4.3 |
| Frankfurt | 10,009 | 7.1 | 26,228 | 6.3 | 29,385 | 6.3 |
| Breslau | 13,916 | 6.4 | 20,212 | 3.9 | 23,240 | 4.2 |
| Hamburg | 11,954 | 4.0 | 19,472 | 1.9 | 19,904 | 1.8 |
| Cologne | 3,172 | 2.4 | 12,393 | 2.0 | 16,093 | 2.3 |
| Leipzig | 1,739 | 1.1 | 9,434 | 1.6 | 12,540 | 1.8 |
| Munich | 2,884 | 1.8 | 11,083 | 1.9 | 10,068 | 1.5 |

In 1925, more than half of all German Jews lived in these seven communities. Most striking is the growth of the Berlin community, which itself accounted for almost a third of all German Jews after the incorporation of the western suburbs, a favored residential area of Jews. The economic and cultural opportunities in the Reich capital made it as much a magnet for both native and foreign Jews as did its intensive Jewish life. Jews from the entire Reich were drawn to Berlin, as were about half of all East European Jewish immigrants. As of 1918, more than 40,000 additional Jewish inhabitants came to Berlin from the relinquished eastern areas. While the poorer among the Jews and the East European Jews stayed in the center of Berlin, the Jewish middle class moved to the western suburbs, where they attained their greatest concentration in Wilmersdorf, constituting 13 percent of the population (1925).

Between 1910 and 1925, the Jewish communities on the Rhine and the Ruhr also increased greatly, thanks to good economic opportunities there. Likewise, the community in Leipzig expanded considerably, since this international trade-fair city, with its commerce to the east, particularly its fur trade, exercised a great attraction on East European Jews, who constituted about 80 percent of the Jewish community in 1933. On the other hand, Munich, as all of Bavaria, lost Jewish population, something that can be traced to the antisemitic policies of the Bavarian government, described by Philipp Löwenfeld (25) in his recollections.

The growth of the Jewish city population corresponded to a decline in the small towns and in the country. In southwestern Germany, which was less industrialized and had a large rural population, the process of concentration proceeded more slowly. From the beginning of the twentieth century the countryside showed ever more minimal communities, which were faced with great problems when the best taxpayers moved away, leaving behind the elderly and those without means. These communities no longer had the ten men (minyan) required for a prayer service, and finally they had to be dissolved.

In summary, it can be said that as a social group the Jews demonstrated a specific demographic pattern that increasingly differentiated them from the general population, but which reflected the demographic patterns of the middle class in many respects. The main factors behind this development were a sinking birthrate, greater longevity, great mobility, and extreme urbanization.

## Occupations and Social Advancement

Until emancipation, as a result of occupational restrictions about 90 percent of Jewish wage earners were engaged in commerce, the great majority of them as retail traders or peddlers. The remaining 10 percent worked either as slaughterers and nonguild craftsmen, or as employees of the Jewish community, which also included rabbis, teachers, and doctors. Since Jews were forbidden to own land almost everywhere, there were no Jewish peasants. And since most of the general population worked in agriculture, Jewish occupational patterns were fundamentally different from theirs.

Within the commercial sector there was a pronounced class structure among traders. The thin upper tier of Court Jews was occupied with commerce in money and luxury articles for the needs of the princes, and supplied their armies with horses and provisions. The likewise thin middle tier possessed some business capital and regular shops, while the greatest number of Jews eked out a minimal existence as peddlers, dealers in secondhand goods, and casual traders. In rural areas, the Jews mainly dealt in agrarian products such as cattle, grain, and wine, which they purchased from the peasants and sold at regional markets. On the other hand, Jewish peddlers brought manufactured goods such as textiles and metal wares from the towns to the peasants in the countryside. Until the mid-nineteenth century sources such as the memoirs of Isaac Thannhäuser (3) and Itzig Hamburger (11) tell again and again of the poverty and simplicity of these peddlers, who trudged with their bundles on their backs to the fairs and peasant households and often changed their wares as supply and demand required. Trade in secondhand goods such as rags and metals was also a typical Jewish occupation. Currency and credit dealing, which had been assigned them in the medieval period, was practiced by Jews of all social strata, from the court banker to the pawnbroker or cattle dealer who sold on credit. In particular, loans to the social lower class were left in large measure to Jews, since other creditors avoided the economic risk that the Jews had to accept in order to raise money for the protective tax. Under absolutism all of the Jews' rights depended ultimately on their ability to pay.

As a first step, the laws of emancipation eliminated the occupational limitations on Jews everywhere, so as to achieve the desired "normalization" of their occupational distribution. But the change in Jewish vocational patterns ran an entirely different course than the one that the emancipators had pictured. They had aimed for a steady and, as in southern Germany, also legally enforced adaptation to the general occupational distribution; but it soon turned out, in view of growing economic liberalism, that this notion was as antiquated as it was unrealistic. To draw the Jews away from trade, as an occupation considered unproductive, and to improve them morally and thus mold them as citizens was entirely an idea of the eighteenth century. Such a plan could not be reconciled with freedom of occupation, the growth of goods production, and the expansion of the commercial sector in the nineteenth century. With growing industrialization and efficiency in agriculture, the number of persons occupied in the crafts and agriculture decreased and their economic situation worsened, while at the same time the numbers of those employed in commerce were increased by the intensification of production and consumption. Thus, there was no necessity for Jews to turn to occupations that were alien to them and in decline. After all, commerce, at which they had centuries-long experience, offered better opportunities than ever.

For this reason, the attempts of the southern German governments between 1815 and 1848 to compel the Jews to become farmers and artisans for the most part achieved only temporary statistical gains. In order to acquire the right of residence and to marry earlier, young men did learn a craft, but often they later returned to trading. This is shown by two memoirs from Bavaria: the father of Eduard Silbermann (5) was a clothworker, but dealt in textiles, while Philipp Tuchmann (8), who had to learn tanning, became a hops dealer. Many rural Jews, who traded in cattle and grain, owned the requisite stables, barns, meadows, and fields, and some of them, like Eduard Silbermann, farmed as a second occupation. But it happened only rarely that Jews took up farming as their main occupation. The peasantry, after all, was still a socially closed group, into which one was born.

Even after they were granted freedom of occupation, the majority of Jews stuck to trading. For centuries, they had acquired experience under the most difficult external circumstances; they knew the methods of trade and promotion, had connections beyond their home regions, and knew the wares in various branches of trade. Thus, in the general transition to freedom of occupation they had the advantage of economic experience and mobility, and this contributed considerably to their advancement. It strikes one again and again in the memoirs how quickly new economic needs and opportunities were recognized and put to use, and how ready the entrepreneur was to constantly modernize and reorient his business. It was, above all, adaptation to the demands of an industrial economy that altered Jewish occupational patterns and paved the way to success, whereas the shift to other occupations played a comparatively minor role. This is reflected statistically in the fact that until the end of Jewish history in Germany between 50 and 60 percent of the Jewish salaried workers were employed in trade and business. Linked to this is the fact that among Jews the proportion of the self-employed was always much larger than that of those who worked for others. But the desire for independence was motivated not least by a constant feeling of threat from antisemitism.

A truly new feature in the Jewish occupational structure, on the other hand, was the growing number of Jews with a university education—a sign of their advancement into the educated class. However, compared to the occupational distribution of the general population, the greatest structural difference lay in the fact that only 1 percent of the Jews worked in agriculture, whereas in the mid-nineteenth century 70 percent of all Germans were still occupied in this sector. At the same time, almost 60 percent of the Jews in Prussia worked in the trading sector, as compared to only 2 percent of the population at large. Thus, the Jewish minority exhibited a very specific occupational pattern, which remained surprisingly stable. But would not a more even distribution across all occupational branches have stood in complete opposition to social cohesiveness and therewith to the idea of a minority? By definition, every minority is distinguished by its special occupational priorities. Once they cease to exist—as, for example, in the case of the descendants of the Huguenots in Germany—then the minority is absorbed by the majority.

Table 5 provides an overview of the percentile distribution of the total population and the Jews among the economic categories in Imperial Germany and the Republic. While the Jews remained concentrated in commerce, the involvement of the total population in business also grew. By 1933, the Jews made up only 2.4 percent of all persons employed in this area. However, this says nothing of their economic significance in the business sector, which would show only if the volume of all business enterprises could be determined. The slight decline in the number of Jews employed in commerce and business corresponded to their increase in the sectors of the free professions and public service. The number of people employed in domestic services decreased more among Jews than among the total population, which points to the attainment of middle-class status.

TABLE 5

|  | 1895 | | 1907 | | 1933 | |
|---|---|---|---|---|---|---|
|  | Total | Jews | Total | Jews | Total | Jews |
| Agriculture | 37.5 | 1.6 | 35.2 | 1.6 | 28.9 | 1.7 |
| Crafts and Industry | 37.5 | 22.5 | 40.0 | 26.5 | 40.4 | 23.1 |
| Commerce and Business | 10.6 | 65.2 | 12.4 | 61.4 | 18.4 | 61.3 |
| Public Services and Free Professions | 6.4 | 7.1 | 6.2 | 7.9 | 8.4 | 12.5 |
| Domestic Services | 8.0 | 3.6 | 6.2 | 2.6 | 3.9 | 1.4 |

Jewish employment showed a quite varied distribution among the individual branches of commerce, the crafts, and industry. Here, too, occupational traditions played a large role.

Because Jews were excluded from the guilds before emancipation, there were but few Jewish skilled workers. These were either butchers or bakers, who worked primarily to fill the needs of the Jewish community, or they were so-called nonguild craftsmen, such as gold embroiderers and seal engravers. Butchery was the oldest Jewish craft, and into the twentieth century the most widespread, for Jews could only take up residence where they received permission to practice ritual slaughtering. When Prussia acquired a large Jewish population through the division of Poland, about a quarter were skilled workers, since Jewish craftsmen were common in Poland and had their own guilds. It was a peculiarity of Jewish craftsmen that they preferred crafts with a pronounced commercial component, and thus they became mainly butchers, bakers, tailors, weavers, and shoemakers. These trades later allowed many to switch to factory production, as shown, for example, by the memoirs of Faibel Siegel (10), whose father and uncle began as weavers and by way of the cottage industry rose to become entrepreneurs in the textile industry.

While among the general population industrial workers made up the majority in the areas of crafts and industry, among Jews the craftsmen and owners of small factories predominated. In 1895 almost three-quarters of all Jewish wage earners in this sector were employed in the food and clothing trades. In no other branch of manufacturing were the Jews in Germany as strongly represented as in the textile industry; they played only an insignificant role in heavy industry, for example. Most of the Jewish textile factories arose from cottage industry, when handicraft and wholesale trade were combined and the profits gained thereby were invested early in mechanical production. Berlin, Württemberg, Swabia, and Silesia were centers of the Jewish textile industry. Its focal point was the ready-to-wear trade in Berlin. The manufacture of ready-made clothing in standardized sizes had already started at the beginning of the nineteenth century and was one of the new forms of production with a strong Jewish presence. In Imperial Germany, Jewish firms gained the greatest share in the production of outerwear, but were also strongly represented in the manufacture of linens, in the shoe industry, and in fur production, which had its center in Leipzig. East European Jewish immigrants, both male and female, were employed as skilled workers—as tailors and fur sewers—in the clothing industry, but they were also employed in the leather industry in Offenbach and in cigarette production in Berlin. In the Weimar Republic, 22,000 Jews, three quarters of whom were women or East European Jews, worked in the clothing trade. At the same time, 70 percent of the firms that made women's outerwear and 60 percent of those that made men's outerwear were Jewish-owned.

Outside of the textile industry Jews were represented as entrepreneurs in several other branches of production, above all in the food and leather industries, the chemical industry, the printing trade, and the electronics industry, while they played no role in heavy industry. Once the economic depression that followed the industrial expansion crash of 1873 had been overcome, total production in Germany between 1895 and 1913 doubled. This boom epoch was the period of the rise of heavy industry. With increasing economic integration and concentration, the number of business combines grew. The largest combine created by a Jewish industrialist was the AEG (General Electric Company), founded in 1887 by Emil Rathenau and taken over by his son Walther Rathenau in 1915. Together with the Siemens Combine, the AEG dominated the growing electronics industry. Isidor Loewe expanded the Ludwig Loewe Machine and Weapons Factory, Inc., one of Europe's leading manufacturers of firearms, into a combine that was also active in the electronics and automobile industries. In the metals trade, traditionally favored by Jews, the Frankfurt Metals Company, a Jewish creation, founded the Metallurgic Company, Inc., in 1897. It became an international combine in the metals manufacturing and metalworking industries. The metals combine of the metals trade firm of Ahron Hirsch was smaller. The Hirsch family remained orthodox Jews and, what is probably unique, set up a synagogue in its brass works near Berlin. As Henriette Hirsch reports (17), the Hirsch firm supported the Berlin orthodox rabbinical seminary from its profits.

The printing industry was a favored Jewish trade branch; for centuries there had been Jewish printers and printing presses for Hebrew books in Germany. In Imperial Germany Jews increasingly expanded from printing books to also publishing them. In the press and in book publishing the Berlin Jewish newspaper publishers Mosse and Ullstein, as well as the Societät Publishing House of Leopold Sonnemann in Frankfurt, attained outstanding rank. The *Berliner Tageblatt,* published by Mosse, and Sonnemann's *Frankfurter Zeitung* were among the newspapers favored by the liberal section of the bourgeoisie. As a publisher of modern literature, Samuel Fischer quickly made a name for himself through S. Fischer Publishers, which he founded in Berlin in 1886. These famous Jewish publishing houses were not only large business combines; in their publications they also reflected the cultural significance that Jews had gained in the press, in literature, and in the theater of Imperial Germany.

As has already been shown, over half of the Jews had always been employed in the trade sector. But in the nineteenth century, the manner and extent of Jewish trade changed fundamentally. The road led from the Jewish peddler and secondhand goods dealer to the middle-class Jewish merchant. Thus, an essential step in the process of restructuring and upward movement was taken *within* the trade sector. For example, in 1843 in Prussia 61 percent of all independent Jewish traders were still retailers, secondhand dealers, and peddlers without stores of their own. In 1861, this figure was only 51 percent, and it declined steadily. By the end of the nineteenth century, less than 3 percent of the Jews engaged in trade were still peddlers, while the number of Jewish store owners had increased correspondingly. Some of the peddlers, whose life Kurt Katsch (19) portrays so vividly, can be rediscovered in the new occupational group of commercial employees, as traveling salesmen and sales representatives with their samples cases.

In no branch of commerce did Jews occupy as strong a position as they did in the banking business. In 1882, 43 percent of all directors and owners of banking and credit houses in Prussia were Jews. This high representation is explained by the fact that the capital assets of the eighteenth-century Court Jews were augmented by the capital that Jews acquired through commerce and industry in the nineteenth century and likewise invested in the banking business. In addition to the well-known major banks of the Rothschilds, Mendelssohns, and Bleichröders, of the Warburgs and Oppenheims, there were many smaller private banks, whose owners continued to engage in wholesale commerce. Hirsch Oppenheimer (4) describes how such a private bank typically originated and developed. The major banks devoted themselves to dealing in government bonds and in growing measure to railway and industrial financing. In the stock exchange centers of Frankfurt, Berlin, and Hamburg, Jewish bankers had decisive economic influence, which, through dealings in government bonds, war loans, and railway shares, also extended into the political sphere. But with the founding of the corporate banks the significance of the Jewish private banks quickly diminished.

In wholesale commerce Jewish firms were most strongly represented in the textile and metals trades, as well as in the fur and leather businesses, but also in grain trade and in the cattle business. In 1913, 70 percent of all metal dealing firms had Jewish owners. Many of the wholesale trading companies had arisen directly from traditional Jewish trade with agricultural products, for example, from the hop and fodder trades. Into the twentieth century, three quarters of all cattle dealers in southern and western Germany were Jews. Thus, for a good while factors from the pre-emancipation period continued to affect the commercial sector, although on the other hand Jews introduced many modern methods into commerce, such as set prices and the mail-order business.

The most conspicuous innovation in retail trade was the department stores that began appearing in the nineties, with their palatial buildings, large-scale advertising, and special sales. In America, England, and France the department stores had already proved successful, but in Germany it was Jewish families like the Tietzs and Wertheims who first established them. Such department stores also created competition for the many Jewish ready-to-wear stores that could be found in every city. The sale of high-priced, fashionable ready-made clothing, as described by Isidor Hirschfeld (24), became a specialty of Jewish firms, which almost always combined sales with production. This also held true for the fur trade, which was centered in Leipzig, and for the numerous shoe firms with Jewish owners.

An unusual feature in wholesale trade was the Jewish army-suppliers, who played an important role not only in the Napoleonic wars, but also in times of peace, and later in the wars of 1866 and 1870–71, as well as in the First World War. They supplied the army mainly with horses, provisions, fodder, and uniforms, products from the traditionally Jewish branches of commerce. The wholesalers could rely on numerous Jewish subsuppliers of agricultural products and textiles and could thus assure quick supply at good value.

As statistics show, in addition to commerce and industry, only the professions that required academic training increasingly attracted Jews. But in Imperial Germany, too, despite the constitution, Jews were subject to career restrictions and rarely received civil service positions. They were mainly compelled to become private doctors, lawyers, and journalists, while most Christian university graduates found positions as clergymen, teachers, and judges. For many merchant families whose sons received a university education, this meant advancement into the ranks of the cultivated middle class: Around the middle of the nineteenth century the number of Jews among Prussian university students was twice their percentage in the population, and in 1886–87 their number was eight times larger. By no means was the prosperity of the parents a prerequisite for university study. Even young men from the countryside or from financially restricted circumstances, such as Conrad Rosenstein (16) and Samuel Spiro (20), attended the university.

In public service, before the First World War there were about nine hundred Jewish judges in the German Reich, but only thirteen Jewish full professors. Almost all of the Jewish teachers taught at Jewish schools.

In the Weimar Republic, when career opportunities for Jewish university graduates further improved, the number of Jews in the free professions and in public service increased to 12.5 percent of all Jewish salary earners. Table 6 gives an overview of Jews in professions requiring academic training in June 1933, when those Jews who were already forbidden to practice a profession were still registered by the census in their former occupational categories even though they were now unemployed. The percentage figure shows the proportion of Jews within the whole of their professional category. It was highest among lawyers and doctors.

TABLE 6

| | | |
|---|---|---|
| Lawyers, notaries | 3,030 | 16.2% |
| Judges | 286 | 2.7% |
| Doctors | 5,557 | 10.8% |
| Dentists | 1,041 | 8.6% |
| Editors, writers | 872 | 5.0% |
| Rabbis | 434 | — |
| University teachers | 192 | 2.6% |
| Secondary school teachers | 317 | 0.8% |
| Elementary school teachers | 1,323 | 0.5% |
| Private teachers | 461 | 4.3% |

This high percentage of Jewish professionals in the Weimar Republic formed the basis for the outstanding scientific and cultural accomplishments of the Jews in Germany. At the same time, the Jewish intelligentsia were the favorite target of the predominately antisemitic educated classes, which saw in the Jewish professionals above all unpleasant competitors and destroyers of the German spirit. Not by chance, the professionals belonged to those occupational groups that were the first to be persecuted by the National Socialist dictatorship and to be banned from practice.

Employment of Jewish women lay below that of the general female population in Imperial Germany, yet another factor against the integration of the Jewish minority into the bourgeoisie. Until the middle of the nineteenth century most Jewish women were still working in the family business, mainly as saleswomen or bookkeepers. But after the social advancement of the Jews, in keeping with the middle-class outlook, work by a wife or daughter was regarded as degrading, and if it occurred at all it was concealed. Accordingly, in 1907 31 percent of all women but only 18 percent of Jewish women were gainfully employed. Of the latter, half worked in the family business or were East European workers. Many Jewish women were tailors and seamstresses in the ready-made clothing trade, small-shop owners, or employed saleswomen. Among the first women students, 11 percent were Jewish; thus, Jewish women students were more greatly overrepresented than were Jewish students overall. In the Weimar Republic the proportion of gainfully employed Jewish women rose above 27 percent, while employment of the general female population stood at 34 percent. This increase was brought about not only by premarital work by women, which was growing more prevalent; just as much it was the result of the economic crisis of the Jewish middle class.

Just as the occupational pattern of the Jews differed from that of the general population, their social stratification also departed from the norm. The nineteenth century had permitted the Jews in Germany an unparalleled social rise from an existence near the bottom of society into the bourgeoisie. If until mid-century this process took place but slowly, also as a result of the economic crises, with the success of the industrial revolution it accelerated rapidly in the 1850s and 1860s. After the crisis of the years of rapid industrial expansion had been overcome, in the 1890s at least two-thirds of all German Jews belonged to the middle class, as the preserved tax records show us. What makes this truly special is that this upward social mobility occurred mainly within the traditional Jewish occupations, that is, predominately in commerce. The path led upward from peddler and occasional dealer to middle-class merchant and further to factory owner, wholesaler, or banker. In contrast, the numbers of the Jewish social lower class, including day laborers and household help, were decimated, a process that was presumably aided above all by emigration overseas. To be sure, after 1880, when the immigration of East European Jews began, this number grew again.

Despite having become part of the bourgeoisie, within the Jewish minority in Imperial Germany there were clear class barriers, described by Hermann Makower (14) and Conrad Rosenstein (16). At the top of Jewish society there was a group of business magnates and multimillionaires, such as Albert Ballin, Gerson Bleichröder, Max Warburg, and Carl Fürstenberg. Part of this Jewish financial aristocracy favored the style of life of the Junkers and on average was politically more conservative and open to conversion than were the rest of the Jews. Within the Jewish bourgeoisie prosperous entrepreneurs, merchants, and persons of private means, as well as physicians and lawyers, formed the upper stratum that was found in the community governing boards and that played the leading role in the Jewish organizations. After these Jewish dignitaries came the members of the broad middle class, the many shopkeepers and independent traders with good income. The petty bourgeoisie consisted in part of traders and artisans of modest means, in part of employed salespeople, traveling salesmen, public employees, and school teachers. Finally, the Jewish lower class was made up primarily of day laborers, the most modest retailers, who were without capital, and factory workers.

In the Weimar Republic, inflation, the world economic crisis, and unemployment also severely worsened the situation of the Jews. Above all, inflation struck the many businessmen among the Jews, who were living in the age of capital interest, as well as the little self-employed people and those in the independent professions. Pauperization was clearly reflected in the rising welfare expenses of the Jewish communities. In 1931 almost a quarter of the Berlin Jewish population was supported by the community, and in the same year over 14,000 Jews inquired at the Jewish employment exchange about vacant positions. Not least, the share of East European Jews among the Jewish population, having risen to one-fifth, contributed to the clear decline of the social level of the Jewish minority after 1918. Also the pattern of general economic developments caused the Jews to lose the financial advantage that they had possessed in the nineteenth century thanks to their early knowledge of the capitalistic economy. The increase of combines and trusts, the growth of cooperatives and the state economic sector had a negative effect on Jewish entrepreneurs. Because of centuries-old tradition and justified fear of antisemitism they were for the most part unwilling to relinquish their independence by joining large bureaucratic hierarchies in subordinate positions.

## Internal Jewish Life

Before emancipation the Jewish community embraced the social and political life of its members, as well as their religious and cultural life. Economic relations alone linked the Jews with their environment. This changed in the second half of the eighteenth century, when interest in the surrounding culture first awakened among a small group of Jews. The European Enlightenment, with its new conception of religion and new humanitarian view, made possible an encounter between Jewish and Christian intellectuals. In scholarly circles and salons individual Jews and Christians began to discuss scientific and literary subjects. There arose a distinct Jewish enlightenment movement, which was centered in Berlin and about the person of Moses Mendelssohn. The chief aims of the Jewish enlighteners were, above all, the purification of the Hebrew language, the introduction of standard German as the everyday speech of the Jews, and the expansion of Jewish education through secular knowledge. In Berlin, Dessau, Wolfenbüttel, Breslau, Frankfurt am Main, and other communities, progressive Jewish schools were founded after 1778, which no longer placed the main stress of instruction on religion, but on general education. Education became a fundamental concept for nineteenth-century German Jewry. Education was to facilitate acculturation, show that emancipation had been merited, and also lead to the social recognition of the Jews among the Germans.

In his life and thought Moses Mendelssohn combined traditional Judaism with the European culture of his age. He lived in strictly orthodox fashion even though his understanding of Judaism as a religion of reason with revealed law had been influenced by the Enlightenment. His disciples already took the next step and began to doubt the continued validity of Jewish religious law. Some of them regarded the laws only as a historical protective fence for the preservation of the true core of Jewish teaching. Therewith the door was opened to a Jewish reform movement. It began cautiously, with local reforms of the prayer service, and was continued at the conferences of the reform rabbis, who removed Hebrew prayers and references to the Messiah from worship. This dissolution of traditional Judaism inevitably led to the reduction of Judaism to a religion. Judaism ceased comprehensively shaping the lives of its followers, and became a creed. The Ghetto Jew became the German Citizen of Jewish Faith.

Religious reform took place simultaneously with the process of emancipation, and there were strong mutual influences between the two developments. The German states did not shy from intruding directly into the religious affairs of the Jews. Thus, in 1823 the Prussian state prohibited all religious reform, while, on the other hand, Baden and

Württemberg introduced the hierarchical consistory organization, which was entirely alien to Judaism, by law. The consistories then undertook centrally directed reforms. In Stuttgart, in fact, a public servant headed the consistory of the "Israelite Church Authority."

For many Jews the first half of the nineteenth century was a time of great religious insecurity. The so-called educated Jews, those Jews who participated in public cultural life, often more or less gave up strict adherence to religious law or even became religiously indifferent. In the first half of the century almost 6,000 Jews in Prussia were baptized, but this was still less than 1 percent of the Jewish population. At least until the mid-1800s the majority of Jews in the countryside of Posen and in southern Germany continued to live in orthodox fashion and to preserve the traditional form of Jewish life.

At mid-century, in many communities rabbis who still held office had only Talmudic training and barely any modern education. Especially in the cities they grew increasingly out of touch with their acculturated congregants. Around 1815, in addition to their Talmud studies, future rabbis began university study, in part voluntarily, in part because they were compelled by state laws. This two-track, contradictory form of training was ended only in 1854 through the founding of the first rabbinical seminary in Breslau, which Moritz Güdemann describes in his memoir (13).

As elected officials of the Jewish communities, from which they received their salaries, the rabbis had a hard time of it, since their communities were religiously divided almost everywhere. In the nineteenth and twentieth centuries most of the larger communities were split between liberals and orthodox, but in Imperial Germany the liberals already constituted the great majority, and in the Weimar Republic only 10 percent of the Jews still adhered to orthodoxy. Nonetheless, both groups together made up the *Einheitsgemeinden* (united communities) that were typical for Germany, even if in each one the individual synagogues were either liberal or orthodox. The leading theologians were Abraham Geiger (1810–1874) on the liberal side, and Samson Raphael Hirsch (1808–1888), the founder of modern orthodoxy. Geiger taught that the Jewish tradition was subject to historical change, and thus he created the possibility for reform. Favoring a decidedly universal perspective, he eliminated entirely the national elements from Judaism. Because of such views, even as rabbi of the Breslau community he was not permitted to teach at the rabbinical seminary there, which advocated a conservative direction. He therefore created a liberal seat of learning in Berlin in 1872, the Hochschule für die Wissenschaft des Judentums (Institute for the Scientific Study of Judaism). In addition to the various forms of liberal Judaism there was also the small radical reform movement, which was centered in the Genossenschaft für Reform im Judentum (Society for Reform in Judaism), founded in Berlin in 1844. It undertook extensive innovations, including the introduction of Sunday worship.

In its attitudes toward its surroundings, orthodoxy did not remain what it had been in the eighteenth century. It now strived to combine full adherence to religious law with normal, everyday life and modern culture. Samson Raphael Hirsch firmly opposed liberal Judaism and propagated the establishment of separate orthodox communities, for which the Prussian parliament created the legal requirement in 1876. Thereupon, the ultra-orthodox seceded from the united community and founded its own communities with synagogues and its own educational system. Esriel Hildesheimer, the rabbi of the Berlin secessionist community, Adass Yisroel, established an orthodox rabbinical seminary there, which his granddaughter Henriette Hirsh (17) lovingly describes in her childhood recollections. Samuel Spiro (20), on the other hand, provides a critical depiction of the Talmud school of the Frankfurt secessionist orthodox community. However, the majority of the orthodox remained within the united communities, which in the larger towns appointed a liberal and an orthodox rabbi wherever possible. In the country, where tradition and social conformity were stronger, orthodoxy was maintained into the twentieth century. In the towns, with their educated Jewish middle class, it quickly lost influence, in part, too, because that middle class viewed orthodoxy as an obstacle on the path to social integration. Very soon the level of Jewish knowledge dropped steeply, and, as expressed in the memoir of Clara Geissmar (15), religious uncertainty grew. Emil Schorsch (36) describes impressively how estrangement from Judaism became a major problem for many communities.

Memoirs provide a good source for the study of religious practice in everyday life. The religious questions most often treated by the authors concern the Jewish holidays and the observance of the dietary and Sabbath laws. Even in the case of those who later turned away from Judaism, the descriptions of family celebrations and of the Sabbath have a strong positive emotional coloring. The holidays form part of their deepest childhood memories, and the remembrance of them helps to preserve religiosity. On the other hand, the question of faithfulness to the laws is often portrayed as a source of conflict within the family, whether between generations or between husband and wife. The grandparents, the parents, or the wife are observant, while the sons and grandsons, or also the husband, only partially observe the laws, and each makes his own choices. Here differences specific to sex can be observed: as keepers of domestic ritual practice, women remain faithful to tradition longer. While at home the mother often continues to maintain a kosher household, the husband opens the store on the Sabbath, sons write at school on Saturday, students at the university no longer eat kosher; adaptation to social norms is widespread. Participation in worship was reduced for many to the High Holidays, and children often received inadequate religious instruction, or none at all. When personal religiosity diminished, and the community could no longer create social bonds, while the desire for pompous self-display grew, there resulted such opera-like prayer services amid uninspiring splendor as described in the case of Berlin by Conrad Rosenstein (16).

Religious indifference had many forms and stages. The Christmas tree, as part of contemporary German culture, was adopted by many families, and this can be seen as a symbol of their extreme readiness to fit in. In the presence of their employees, middle-class families avoided all Jewish expressions, indeed anything Jewish at all. This denial of Jewishness, which could intensify to the point of self-hate, showed how far the crisis of Jewish identity had advanced. Paul Mühsam (27) hated the Hebrew and Yiddish expressions that his parents still used, and he despised the "repulsive carryings-on" of the East European Jews in the synagogue of Zittau. In some families it became customary to have the children baptized right after birth. For obvious reasons there is little mention of conversions in the memoirs, but Leopold Freund (6) and Clara Geissmar (15) make clear that conversions resulted much more from social than religious motives. For it was, after all, the pressure of antisemitism which most strongly prompted conversion. On the other hand, many religiously indifferent Jews, such as Walther Rathenau, rejected conversion as opportunistic and remained Jews in the formal sense. As among the Christian educated middle class, education often assumed the place of religion, becoming a kind of religion itself.

The immigration of East European Jews added still another form to the broad spectrum of Jewish religiosity. In the main the immigrants came from orthodox or hassidic families, even if some of them had meanwhile turned to socialism. Many East European Jews, hailing from the same region, gathered in small prayer houses, which were located in the East European Jewish neighborhoods of Berlin and other cities. In his remembrances Emil Schorsch (36) provides an impressive description of these prayer houses, which were characterized by warmth and social intimacy. The immigrants, on the other hand, were unable to accustom themselves to the German form of orthodoxy. The East European Jews were legally foreigners, but they were members of the Jewish united communities. Many Jewish communities tried to deny the aliens the right of vote within them. But this succeeded only in Saxony, where the East European Jews were in the majority and precisely for that reason did not receive the vote. Other communities retained the census vote, whereby the poorer East European Jews were automatically disadvantaged. It was typical that social rather than religious differences provided the actual cause for conflict between German Jews and East European Jews.

Even after emancipation, the Jewish community remained more than just a purely religious institution. In fulfillment of Jewish law, it continued to assume educational and social tasks, but also served as the place for debate of Jewish questions. Whereas in the nineteenth century these questions primarily concerned religious conflicts, later clashes with East European Jews and Zionists came to the fore. In the Berlin community, during the Weimar period there were heated campaigns during the elections for the representative body, especially when in 1926 for the first time a coalition of Zionists, orthodox, and East European Jews, a Jewish national grouping, had won the election and now determined community policies. The great majority of German Jews rejected Zionism at this time and saw in it a threat to their identity as assimilated German citizens. Many East European Jews, on the other hand, who came from the Jewish national cultures of Poland and Russia, were adherents of Zionism.

The German Zionists, united since 1897 in the Zionistische Vereinigung für Deutschland (Zionist Organization of Germany), had first concentrated on developing their doctrine and building their organization, and they had also supported the work of building a Jewish Palestine. Only a small number of Jews adopted the idea of the Jewish national community and rejected assimilation. The majority remained anti-Zionist and wanted to create a unity of Germanness and Judaism. When the Balfour Declaration of 1917 granted the Jews the right to a national homeland in Palestine, the Zionist movement gained influence and exerted a stronger attraction on young people in particular. Some of them went to Palestine as pioneers. In the Weimar Republic the Zionist organization in Germany had about 10,000 active members and participated as the Jüdische Volkspartei (Jewish People's Party) in the elections for the representatives of the communities.

The Jewish communities were civic bodies and assessed all members a community tax according to their income. All Jews living in the local area belonged to the community so long as they had not withdrawn from it. The communities were governed by their elected representatives and the board of directors. The mode of election varied widely; the census vote existed in part into the Weimar period; and women were not entitled to vote. In 1933 there were 1,611 Jewish communities in the German Reich, of which most were rural communities with greatly reduced membership.

The city communities, on the other hand, increased their numbers so greatly through urbanization that in the Weimar period the Berlin community required 1,500 officials in order to perform its tasks. The community was responsible not only for rabbis, synagogues, and cemeteries, but also for social work and for the Jewish schools, hospitals, and old-age homes. It maintained libraries and community newspapers, and administered endowment and retirement funds. The memoirs of Alexander Szanto (38) provide a look into the self-governance of the Berlin community during this time. The large communities soon had to support the dwindling small communities, since the latter had ever less means at their disposal with which to maintain religious life. Not least for this reason there were mergings of communities on a statewide basis. The Preussische Landesverband jüdischer Gemeinden (Prussian State Union of Jewish Communities), founded in 1922, incorporated two-thirds of all German Jews and had over seven hundred member communities. But before 1933 there existed no umbrella organization of all Jews in the German Reich.

In addition to the communities and unions of communities there was a large number of other Jewish organizations, which operated nationally. The most significant was the Centralverein deutscher Staatsbürger jüdischen Glaubens (Central Association of German Citizens of Jewish Faith), which spoke for the majority of German Jews. When the antisemitic parties gained their biggest election successes in 1893, Jewish notables founded the Centralverein (CV) as a defense organization. At first it dedicated itself exclusively to combating antisemitism, but more and more it became an organization that also worked internally to strengthen Jewish self-awareness and to maintain Judaism. In so doing, it stressed the union of Germanness and Jewishness, and it was not lacking in nationalistic sentiments. The CV developed a clear opposition to the Zionists, especially since both organizations were building at about the same time. To be sure, the Zionistische Vereinigung (Zionist Union) remained much smaller in number than the CV, but thanks to its radical character it exercised a strong attraction on the youth and permeated the lives of its members in an entirely different manner than did the CV, which did not intend to impart any new ideas. The turn to Zionism almost had the nature of a conversion, whereas in some circles membership in the CV became a matter of course. To become a Zionist, on the other hand, meant that one would come into conflict with one's family and the entire Jewish environment. When the First World War broke out, the members of both organizations rallied enthusiastically to the flag. In this instance, too, a "truce," called for by the Kaiser, was in effect between the parties. For many Zionists and also for some of the other Jewish soldiers, the encounter on the eastern front with the living national culture of the Jews of Poland and Russia became an experience with lasting effects.

Only a few of the other large Jewish organizations can be mentioned here. The Jüdische Frauenbund (Jewish Women's Federation), founded in 1904 by Bertha Pappenheim, defined itself as part of the middle-class German women's movement, but at the same time promoted a consciously Jewish religious view among its members, who numbered as many as 50,000. It created educational and welfare institutions for women, advocated professional training for them, fought against white slavery, and demanded the vote for women in the Jewish communities. Ottilie Schönewald (37), who served until 1938 as the last president of the Frauenbund, was one of the few women in the Weimar period to occupy an office and to be elected to the governing body of a Jewish organization.

Social work was performed by over 3,000 local welfare agencies, which joined together in 1917 in Berlin to form the Zentralwohlfahrtsstelle (Central Welfare Agency) in order to coordinate their work. Here, too, Jewish women played a major role as volunteers and later as professional social workers. The Hilfsverein der deutschen Juden (Aid Society of German Jews), which was created in 1901, organized aid to Jews in other countries, particularly in eastern Europe and Palestine. During the First World War the Secretary General of the Hilfsverein, Bernhard Kahn (31), built up a broadly based relief organization for the East European Jews in the areas occupied by Germany. After the war Jewish veterans joined together in the Reichsbund jüdischer Frontsoldaten (Reich Federation of Jewish Combat Soldiers), a patriotic veterans' organization that defended the honor of Jewish soldiers against antisemitic attacks.

Beyond these, there were also numerous Jewish youth groups, which adopted in part the ideas of the youth movement, and in part tended more to foster Zionist ideas, or sought to combine both. In addition there were Jewish student groups, Jewish lodges, and cultural organizations such as the Verband der Vereine für jüdische Geschichte und Literatur (Federation of Societies for Jewish History and Literature). The founding of these numerous organizations can primarily be attributed to the fact that because of strong antisemitism Jews were often not welcome as members in the general German organizations. Many of the Jewish organizations published their own newspapers and journals, so that well over a hundred Jewish periodicals appeared in the Weimar Republic.

In 1919 East European Jewish organizations joined together in a Verband der Ostjuden in Deutschland (Federation of East European Jews in Germany). Its responsibilities were to represent the interests of the East European Jews as foreigners, to fight antisemitism, which was aimed especially at East European Jews, and to provide self-help in the areas of work procurement, social work, and legal aid. The Verband, like most of its members, saw the Jews as a nation and supported the Zionist movement. As already described, the East European Jews, who in 1925 made up approximately one-fifth of the Jews in Germany, were socially and religiously clearly different from the German Jews. The latter felt themselves to be culturally superior to the immigrants and feared that their Jewishness, which was rendered most conspicuous by their dress and speech, could provide cause for antisemitic attacks on *all* Jews. For this reason, the German Jews endeavored to solve the problems of the needy immigrants through welfare work, but, unless they were Zionists, the German Jews rarely accepted them as possible friends or marriage partners. The East European Jews were often left entirely to themselves, in their own neighborhoods, workers' clubs, and small prayer houses. But also among them—especially among the intellectuals, students, and those with greater means, as well as among the members of the second generation—there was readiness to acculturate. In Berlin, East European Jewish artists and scholars carried on a cultural life of their own, and in the Weimar period they made the city a center of Hebrew and Yiddish literature. The life histories of Joseph Lange (18) and Kurt Katsch (19) are examples of a successful integration of East European Jews, but they are probably more the exception than the rule, particularly since many of the East European Jews were only in transit to western Europe and overseas, while others returned to eastern Europe.

The Jewish communities and organizations were directed by men only, and even after 1919 women remained the rare exception on the boards. In contrast, women traditionally played a great part in the welfare work of the Jewish communities. The wife had a strong position in the family, although as a Jewish and middle-class family its structure was doubtless patriarchal. Nonetheless, within the family the Jewish wife traditionally was better positioned in relation to her husband than was her Christian counterpart. For Judaism was handed down by both the male and the female through religious roles that, to be sure, differed, but influenced one another. While the husband was bound to study the Torah and devoted himself to community tasks, it was the wife's responsibility to keep a Jewish home. She saw to the observance of the dietary laws, prepared the Sabbath and the holidays, and adhered to the requirements of Jewish sexual ethics. In addition to the woman's religious duties in the home and family, until the middle of the nineteenth century she also had economic responsibilities. Since the men were traders and thus mostly gone during the week, the women often ran the business in town, sold and received wares, and kept the books. Until the First World War the Jewish family was almost exclusively dependent on traditional matchmaking. Relatives, friends, or professional marriage brokers recommended the partners to each other and checked to see whether they were compatible in terms of family circumstances, lineage, and means. For marriage was, above all, the union of two families, as was also deemed natural, for example, among the peasantry, the aristocracy, and most of the burghers of the nineteenth century.

Social advancement limited the Jewish wife to the family, since her former work in the business was viewed by the bourgeoisie as a form of social discrimination. At the same time, as a mother she now had fewer children to care for and was assisted by household help. She devoted the free time thus gained to musical and literary interests, cultivated social acquaintanceships, and promoted the education of her children. In many Jewish families the wives took the leading role in cultural matters, while the husbands mainly devoted themselves to the business. Attendance at cultural events such as theater performances, concerts, and lectures was so much a matter of course in Jewish families that Jews made up a considerable part of the audience in all German cities. Just as families had once stressed Talmud study, they now placed extraordinary emphasis on the education of their children. For this reason, Jewish children were greatly overrepresented in the secondary schools. In 1906 in Berlin they made up a quarter of all pupils at classical Gymnasiums and even a third of all pupils at the girls high schools. Even rural Jews did all they could to enable their children to attend secondary schools.

## Jews and Their Environment

The relationship between Jews and the larger society cannot be described in simple terms. It appears in one light from the Jewish perspective, and in another from that of the Jews' fellow citizens, and in an entirely different light to today's observer, who can never ignore the terrible end of this relationship. For today's reader many of the autobiographical accounts from the era before 1933 will appear to be documents of an "imagined security," as one author terms it in retrospect. But are they really? Had the Jews in Germany, after their emancipation, developed the art of only partially registering Jew-hatred? Or were there areas that were free of such hatred? It is difficult to answer this question with any accuracy, since the relationship between Jews and non-Jews not only differed from one place to the next and among various strata of society, but was also conditioned by the political and economic developments at any given time. In rural areas, where the Jewish and the Christian populations were religiously more conservative, both groups lived in social separation, but they still kept up neighborly ties. The relationship was much different than that in the cities, where it was more a matter of individual acquaintanceships between members of the same social stratum. Here it sometimes happened that Jews—above all, members of the upper class, academics, or artists—socialized only with Christians. On the other hand, there is much biographical evidence from the life of the Jewish bourgeoisie to show that its members associated predominately with one another and remained separated from their Christian counterparts as though by a glass wall. Such conditions could also be observed in the middle-class Jewish neighborhoods of Berlin-West. In his work every Jew associated with non-Jews; in private life association with fellow believers was the rule.

The character and quality of Christian-Jewish social relations were more important than their extent. But one must differentiate between personal friendships based on individual choice and socially unavoidable relations such as those with neighbors, school-mates, and professional colleagues. In these relations, it was less the individual Jew than the Christian majority who set the tone, and it was often hostile. If one reads the memoirs with this in mind, amazingly little hatred becomes visible before 1918. To be sure, the authors report local excesses against Jews, professional obstacles, or conflicts at school, but they place greater stress on the harmonious relations between Jews and their environment that existed at the very same time. And it should not be forgotten that Jews had learned to avoid open conflicts through preventive attitudes. How else is it to be explained that Jews always preferred independent professions to being employed by another? Positive Christian-Jewish social relations are often depicted in a way that makes them appear as the exception, for example the respect of the peasants for the hop-farming of Eduard Silbermann (5), or the praise by the village pastor for baker Kirschner's pious way of life (7).

The effects of antisemitism on the life of the Jews as a group were considerable. In the first half of the nineteenth century and in the 1848 revolution, physical excesses were perpetrated against Jews on several occasions. Above all, a tense and threatening situation arose in the countryside when impoverished peasants, who had accepted credit and pawned their fields, became financially dependent on Jewish traders. The economic rise of the Jews at the same time that many peasants were being reduced to poverty through agrarian crises and agrarian reform was socially highly explosive. In the towns, it was in particular pauperized craftsmen and small storekeepers fearful of competition who supported economic antisemitism.

Following an epoch of political liberalism and prosperity, when the first serious economic crisis of Imperial Germany occurred there arose an antisemitism of unprecedented effectiveness. It was not limited to single groups or parties, but rather it permeated broad segments of the middle class, as an integrative element of a nationalistic ideology. The bearers of antisemitism were mostly middle-class and agrarian groups, as well as the universities and the educated bourgeoisie, while the working class was largely immunized against the new ideology by social democracy. The full development of the capitalistic economic system brought with it radical economic and social changes, whose negative consequences were blamed first and foremost on the Jews. The antisemitic position was antiliberal; it was also anticapitalistic, but for the most part only when Jews were involved. The rapid spread of antisemitism was furthered by the economic crises that occurred periodically between 1873 and 1894, by the generally antimodern mentality of the bourgeoisie, and by the weakening of political liberalism. The state and society in Imperial Germany assumed a stance toward minorities that was marked by aggression and notions of them as an enemy. Hatred for "enemies of the Reich," such as Poles, Catholics, and Social Democrats, was an essential component of internal politics. In such a social climate the Jews, who had largely retained their identity, although in altered form, were especially threatened, since they no were longer active on the edge of society, but instead more at its center, at least economically and culturally.

Jews most often experienced antisemitism as individual discrimination in their private daily associations. No Jew could escape this omnipresent expression of enmity toward him. Mainly, he already encountered it as a child and had to expect it at any time. It is not by chance that the experiences with antisemites described in the memoirs took place in the three institutions of socialization: the school, the university, and the army. These institutions almost never permitted Jews to attain positions of leadership, and thereby they created a climate of discrimination that encouraged antisemitic behavior by pupils, students, and soldiers toward Jews in their ranks. Almost all Jewish young people were exposed to negative experiences that could influence their psychic, social, and political behavior as adults. Walther Rathenau wrote: "In the youth of every German Jew there is a painful moment that he remembers all his life: when for the first time he becomes fully aware that he came into the world as a second-class citizen, and that no amount of ability and no personal merit can free him from this situation." Antisemitic experiences in early childhood, as Paul Mühsam (27) describes them, were traumatic and led to the permanent loss of innocence in association with schoolmates, and to a lasting depreciation of one's feeling of personal worth.

At the latest, when the young Jew had finished school he found himself doubly confronted with antisemitism: in his choice of profession and in fulfilling military service. In the early days of Imperial Germany aristocrats made up over half of the officers corps, and before ordinary citizens were accepted into it they were checked to be sure that they came from "better circles" and had a reliable conservative outlook. Jews had no chance, and larger numbers of them were promoted to officer rank only during the First World War. Of approximately 100,000 Jewish combatants about 2,000 became officers.

That this did not mark the end of anti-Jewish attitudes in the army was shown in the fall of 1916, when the Minister of War ordered a count of all Jews at the front. This was occasioned by the charge of shirking and was experienced by Jewish soldiers as a renewed form of severe discrimination.

Antisemitism became even more evident at the universities than in the schools and the army, and it was practiced by professors as well as students. The fraternities and corps, which characterized student life, either did not accept Jews at all or accepted them only if they adapted to the point of self-denial. Philipp Löwenfeld (25) tells of students who changed their names and avoided their relatives in order to be admitted to a Christian student association. The Deutsche Burschentag (Congress of German Fraternities) voted in 1896 no longer to accept Jews into the fraternities. The Verein deutscher Studenten (Union of German Students), which was founded in 1880, when signatures were gathered for the antisemitic petition, was aggressively antisemitic. Half of the students in Berlin signed this petition, which demanded that the Reichstag (Parliament) repeal the emancipation of the Jews. As a result of their social isolation, in 1886 the Jewish students in Breslau founded the Viadrina, the first Jewish fraternity, which was soon followed by others. Its special significance lay in the fact that it was at the same time the first Jewish organization that actively opposed antisemitism and, in so doing, pledged its allegiance not only to Germanness, but also to Judaism. At first many Jews rejected such an exclusively Jewish and, in addition, activist organization, since it appeared to evidence that the social integration of Jewish citizens had failed. In 1896 the Jewish fraternities combined to form the Kartell-Convent (KC; Challenge Assembly) and retained the practice of dueling, whereby they sought to combat anti-semitic insults. As of 1895 Zionist fraternities were also formed and joined together in the Kartell jüdischer Verbindungen (Alliance of Jewish Fraternities). Later many leading Zionists came out of their ranks.

The majority of German Jews took longer than the students before they were ready for an organized, i.e., political, response to antisemitism. Would not the founding of a body for the defense of Jewish rights declare that the Jews were more than just a religious group? Thus, for twenty years they only reacted to rising antisemitism individually and privately. Some went so far as to conceal their Jewish identity as much as possible. Faced with antisemitism, many others took the step of conversion. But most remained silent, assuming that in a cultured land like Germany antisemitism could only be a passing phenomenon.

In the parliamentary elections of 1893 the antisemitic parties gained sixteen seats in the Reichstag. This was their greatest election success ever. While the election campaign was still going on, a society to combat antisemitism was founded, the previously mentioned Centralverein deutscher Staatsbürger jüdischen Glaubens. From a union that was supported only hesitantly by many, the CV grew to become the largest Jewish organization before 1933, with a broad network of local groups. The CV fought an-tisemitism with informational brochures, with initiatives against antisemitic candidates in elections, and through its legal defense division, which represented hundreds of plaintiffs each year. In keeping with these tasks, more than one-third of CV functionaries were lawyers.

The military defeat at the end of the First World War, the fall of the monarchy, the revolution, the political and economic instability of the postwar years, and, finally, inflation caused antisemitism to emerge with an aggressiveness unknown until that time. As Henry Buxbaum (32) relates, it could easily become life-threatening to Jews. The largest antisemitic organization, the Deutsch Völkische Schutz- und Trutzbund (German National Defensive and Offensive Alliance), created in 1919, had about 200,000 members. Among the parties the Deutschnationale Volkspartei (German National People's Party) and the Nationalsozialisten (National Socialists) had anchored antisemitism firmly in their party platforms from the start. But its effects extended far into the middle-class centrist parties. The antisemites constantly slandered the Jewish Germans, calling them shirkers in the war, war profiteers, inciters to revolution, traitors to Germany, and the rulers of the press and cultural life. A main target was the East European Jew, at whom racism and xenophobia were most openly directed. Bavaria even attempted to expel all East European Jews, a move that Philipp Löwenfeld (25) opposed as a lawyer. During a phase of relative economic and political stabilization between 1924 and 1928, antisemitism receded somewhat, but then, after the international economic recession began, it again grew in influence with the electoral success of the National Socialists. Even before 1933, the NSDAP propagated the boycott of Jewish stores, and at most German universities the antisemitic NS-Studentenbund (National Socialist Student Alliance) won the majority of students over to its side.

How did the Jewish population react individually and as a group to the rise of antisemitism? Many members of the older generation, molded by Imperial Germany, and the middle generation, who had fought in the First World War with great patriotism, tended to view antisemitism as a passing concomitant effect of the economic and political crises. However, this does not mean that the majority underestimated antisemitism in its political significance and remained passive. Rather, one can observe a clear reaction of the Jews as a social group, a reaction that extended from its voting pattern, to its increasing involvement in leftist parties, to systematic opposition to antisemitism by the CV and the Reichsbund jüdischer Frontsoldaten. The CV pursued a rational program of education and refuted antisemitic propaganda point by point, an undertaking that from the start could have only a very slight possibility of success. Among the numerous publications of the CV were an anti-Nazi handbook, a white book on National Socialist terror, and a guide to opposing antisemitic arguments. In addition, the CV ran a regular news service, in 1932 alone achieved two hundred sentences on the ground of incitement to boycott, and repeatedly succeeded in having the antisemitic, rabble-rousing newspaper *Der Stürmer* confiscated. In the last elections of the Republic the CV supported non-antisemitic parties with funds and campaign materials. But all of these efforts by the Jewish minority of less than 1 percent of the population were doomed to fail so long as the majority of Germans were not determined to rescue the Republic.

The political isolation of the Jews, who were without allies, reached its highpoint in 1933. In the nineteenth century the Jews had seen their political home in liberalism, but with the weakening of liberalism in Imperial Germany and its disappearance in the Republic, they lost this support, which, moreover, had always been dubious on the part of the liberals.

The emancipation of the Jews had taken place in the period of developing national feeling and the struggle for a German national state. Between 1815 and 1848 the Jews began to integrate politically and to view themselves as Germans. Most politically active Jews, like Gabriel Riesser, saw the question of Jewish emancipation only as a subquestion of the emancipation of the bourgeoisie as it strived for a state governed by a national constitution. In so doing, they allied themselves entirely with liberalism, believing in a natural community of Jews and liberals. They documented this in the Revolution of 1848 by their strong participation as representatives, members of political clubs, fighters on the barricades, and journalists. Five unbaptized Jews were elected to the National Assembly, and Gabriel Riesser was its vice-president. But the anti-Jewish riots during the Revolution contributed to the disappointment of Jewish hopes, and many, like Hirsch Oppenheimer (4), advocated a channeling of revolutionary energies, or they sought refuge in the existing government as a source of order.

After the failed revolution liberalism took a new direction. The majority of liberals allowed Bismarck's foreign policy success to convince them that national unity was of greater priority than the realization of a liberal, constitutionally governed state and accepted the creation of the Reich as an accomplishment of the Prussian authoritarian state. The German Jews welcomed the founding of the Reich with great hopes and along with the rest of the bourgeoisie voted for the Nationalliberale (National Liberals) and the liberal-left Fortschrittspartei (Progressive Party). But when the Nationalliberale oriented themselves to the right and went over to a policy of protective tariffs after Bismarck's swing to the conservatives, the representatives of commerce and the banks, who advocated free trade, and with them the leading Jewish politicians, Eduard Lasker and Ludwig Bamberger, left the party in disappointment. They formed the left-liberal party Freisinn (Liberal Party), which was favored by the majority of Jewish voters. As the sole bourgeois party, Freisinn was ready to advocate full, constitutionally guaranteed rights for Jews, and not to cooperate with antisemites. For this reason, it was attacked by antisemites as the "Jews' defense troops," and it rapidly lost many voters.

Because of their class affiliation, typical Jewish voters (after 1918 also women voters) decidedly kept their distance from the Social Democrats and, along with rest of the bourgeoisie, saw in them the party of subversion. However, socialism as an idea and the uncompromising stance of the Social Democrats toward antisemitism exercised an increasing attraction on individual Jewish intellectuals, as the example of Phillip Löwenfeld (25) shows. Among Jewish intellectuals, salaried employees, and petty traders before 1918, the Social Democratic Party gained the support of approximately 15 percent of all Jews entitled to vote.

The same political changes that altered the voting patterns of Jewish voters also led to changes in the pattern of party membership of the Jewish Reichstag representatives. Before 1878 there were sixteen unconverted Jews serving as representatives in the Reichstag: seven National Liberals, six left-liberals, and five Social Democrats. Between 1893 and 1918, Freisinn lost more and more voters and the National Liberals stopped nominating Jews, leaving only two Jewish representatives of Freisinn in the Reichstag, as compared with fifteen Jewish Social Democrats. In contrast, Jewish liberals were still more strongly represented in the city councils. The number of Jewish city councilors and city aldermen in Imperial Germany was high, about 1,400. For many Jews local political office served as a compensation for the public activity in the civil service of Imperial Germany that was denied them.

In the Weimar Republic Jews did gain access to state and government offices, but their political situation rapidly worsened. A number of Jewish socialists and communists played a visible role in the November Revolution, the soviet governments, and the Bavarian soviet government, something that the rightist parties seized on as an opportunity to brand Jews as traitors and the authors of the revolution. Since Jews were now also attaining positions of political leadership, the antisemites used this to defame the hated new state as the "Jew Republic." This did not remain mere propaganda. The murder of foreign minister Walther Rathenau in 1922 showed that in this atmosphere of civil war Jewish politicians were always at risk.

After the war the left-liberals came together in the Deutsche Demokratische Partei (DDP; German Democratic Party), among whose founders were such well-known Jews as Albert Einstein, newspaper publisher Rudolf Mosse, and constitutional lawyer Hugo Preuss, who designed the Weimar constitution and was therefore a main target of the antisemites. According to estimates at the time, 60 percent of all voting Jews voted for the DDP, and it was accordingly defamed as the "Jew Party." As the party lost votes it leaned farther to the right and in 1930 joined with the racist Jungdeutsche Orden (Young German Order). That put an end to the liberal center, and in its majority the German middle class had aligned itself with rightist parties. Of necessity the Jewish voters then oriented themselves more strongly to the left. It has been estimated that before 1930 as many as one-fourth of the Jews voted for the Social Democrats, but that later probably more than half of the Jewish voters looked to the SPD (Social Democratic Party of Germany) for support against National Socialism. As theoreticians, functionaries, and editors, Jewish intellectuals played an important role in the SPD, and to the end they were also represented in the Reichstag by men of Jewish origin. After the murder of Rosa Luxemburg Jews continued to occupy influential positions in the Communist Party leadership, until the Stalinist campaigns against intellectuals led to their exclusion. In the last phase of the Republic young Jews such as Wolfgang Roth (34) cast their lot in growing numbers with the Communist Party, so that the Zionists had to warn against "red assimilation." According to the account of Gerhard Bry (41), Jews participated in the attempt by the group Neu Beginnen (Fresh Start) to organize a united antifascist front of various leftist groups before 1933.

In summary, it should be stressed that in 1933 the Jews in Germany composed a predominately middle-class minority, which was most heterogeneous in its world outlook and religious views, and had no overarching representative organization. Socially and politically they were dangerously isolated; economically they exhibited the crisis symptoms of the middle class. The greatest asset of this minority was its cultural accomplishments, based on an extraordinarily high level of cultivation. Contrary to the expectations of their emancipators, most of the Jews in Germany had preserved their Jewish identity, which after the decline of religiosity was also maintained through secondary forms of expression, above all in the further prevalence of the principle of in-group marriage.

## Persecution and Self-Help after 1933

National Socialist policies on the Jews will not be portrayed here, but rather life under the conditions created by these policies. The autobiographies make evident what National Socialism meant for the everyday life of the Jews, how intensifying persecution destroyed their means of existence, shattered their relations with the world about them, and negated their advanced cultural integration. At the same time, they document the will of the Jews to help themselves; and they provide insight into their religious and cultural life in the time of persecution. And, finally, the memoirs convey the trials of mass emigration and the horror of deportation.

"As Jews we are faced with the fact that a power hostile to us has assumed rule in Germany," the *Jüdische Rundschau* could still write on 31 January 1933. With the designation of Hitler as Chancellor of the Reich racial antisemitism became part of government policy, and once all principles of law and order were abolished, it attained possibilities of expression that had been unimaginable until that time. It was difficult for Jews who had grown to maturity in the traditions of the authoritarian state and the educated middle class to comprehend this changed situation. After more than one hundred years of acculturation and two generations after legal emancipation had been concluded, the Jews were so German that any attempt to disfranchise them as "aliens" appeared to them to be as improbable as it was unfounded. It was impossible for most adult German Jews to discard their German identity simply because the National Socialists dictated it.

The National Socialist threat could be more clearly recognized by Jewish socialists and communists, who, as leftists like Philipp Löwenfeld (25) and Wolfgang Roth (34), were among the first to be persecuted and forced to flee Germany. After the Reichstag elections of 5 March 1933, a wave of antisemitic laws and acts of terror began. They reached their zenith on 1 April 1933, when the party and the SA organized a boycott of Jewish businesses, which was declared a retaliatory measure for the alleged "horror stories" of the Jews abroad against National Socialist Germany. The day of the boycott, on which the SA stood guard in front of all Jewish businesses, appears in many memoirs as an incisive experience. It deeply impressed on those affected by it their lack of rights, their helplessness, and their social isolation. The first of April had little significance in regard to the economy and foreign affairs; rather, its meaning lay in the fact that the Jews were openly stigmatized as the first step toward their racial segregation, their expulsion from the social body. The boycott sought to force a public antisemitic consensus. But there were still individual Germans who did not allow themselves to be pressured into antisemitism and, as Marta Appel reports (39), demonstratively bought in Jewish stores.

The April boycott was followed by decrees to dismiss Jewish officials, judges, lawyers, and physicians. Jewish artists as well as most of the Jewish employees in non-Jewish firms were also dismissed. Exempted from professional exclusion were wage earners who had begun working before 1914 and combat soldiers, so that a large percentage of those with a university education were able to lull themselves with a false feeling of security, whereas many of those affected—to their later good fortune—soon emigrated. The antisemitic wave of spring 1933 occasioned about 25,000 Jews, many

East European Jews among them, to flee Germany or to emigrate. In June 1933, 14 percent of all Jews in Germany were unemployed, and among workers and employees the number reached 31 percent. But almost half of all Jews were self-employed persons, who in the trade and industrial branches were not directly affected by professional exclusion. In many cases, however, their business profits were now reduced by the continued boycott.

Material want and physical distress grew. And the recognition also grew among German Jews that now, abandoned by the society around them, they had to bridge their internal differences and seek support and help among themselves. But many of them believed that the "bad dream" would not last; they could not grasp that in a cultured land such as Germany they should have been deprived of almost all rights overnight.

In April 1933 the Zentralausschuss für Hilfe und Aufbau (Central Committee for Aid and Reconstruction) was formed as a self-assistance organization. It was the first organization that was created jointly, in reaction to the persecution, by representatives of Jewish groups with varying orientations. The Zentralausschuss was a precursor of the Reichsvertretung der deutschen Juden (Reich Representation of German Jews), which was founded in September 1933 and which, in 1935, after the Nuremberg Laws, was forced to be renamed the Reichsvertretung der Juden in Deutschland (Reich Representation of the Jews in Germany). This first umbrella organization directed the Jewish self-assistance activities in the years from 1933 to 1939. Among its responsibilities were economic assistance, schooling, emigration aid, and welfare work. It also represented all German Jews with regard to the government. This was an extremely difficult task, since the members of the executive, who were constantly subject to the supervision and arbitrariness of the Gestapo, had to try to protect all Jews as far as possible, without becoming hostages and being arrested themselves.

In the Reichsvertretung the Jewish communities and state associations worked together, just as did the CV, the Zionistische Vereinigung, the Reichsbund jüdischer Frontsoldaten, and the Jüdische Frauenbund. In an atmosphere of complete legal insecurity the Reichsvertretung sought successfully to organize solidarity and aid among Jews. Its president was Berlin rabbi Leo Baeck, whose personal qualities as a spiritual leader gained him recognition from all Jewish groups. Given the common threat, the internal conflicts among the Jewish factions abated. The Reichsvertretung expressed the will of the Jews to self-assertion, but it did not offer resistance in the political sense. As a small, mainly middle-class minority, overaged, politically fragmented, and without allies, the German Jews lacked all of the prerequisities for collective resistance. There was, of course, political resistance by individual Jews. Over a thousand of them worked illegally as part of the organized left, primarily in the SPD and the KPD (Communist Party of Germany). The Reichsvertretung was considerably more conservative in its assessment of the situation. First of all, it expected the rule of law to be reestablished and advised only those young people to emigrate who had no career possibilities. It advised older people to persevere within the country.

The so-called Nuremberg Laws of 15 September 1935 decidedly intensified the situation. As a consistent realization of racial doctrine, they definitively made the rights of the individual dependent on his or her "race," which was determined by the state.

One now differentiated between "citizens of the Reich" with political rights, and mere nationals. Jews could only be nationals, and thereby Jewish emancipation was nullified. The Gesetz zum Schutz des deutschen Blutes und der deutschen Ehre (Law for the Protection of German Blood and German Honor) forbade marriage between Jews and non-Jews and made extramarital sexual relations between them punishable by law. The Nuremberg Laws defined a Jew as someone with either three or four grandparents of the Jewish faith: the racial definition of Jewishness was founded on the religious affiliation of one's forbears. Also considered Jews were those who, as "mischlings," had only two Jewish grandparents but who professed the Jewish religion or were married to a Jew. These laws greatly aggravated segregation, the more so since all association between Jews and non-Jews of the opposite sex was now criminalized and thus highly dangerous. Thousands of charges of "racial disgrace" resulted.

The exclusion of the Jews from gainful activity made itself felt more and more and soon affected the economy also. At the start of 1938 over half of all businesses directed by Jews were already either liquidated or forcibly "aryanized," i.e., sold to non-Jews, almost always far below their value. Of the fifty thousand Jewish businesses that had existed in 1933, by the middle of 1938 only about 20 percent still had Jewish owners. The businesses that remained turned small profits—except for those that sold goods with which the emigrants supplied themselves. Many Jews became dependent on welfare, which they received in only slight amounts from the state. In the winter of 1937–38, the Jewish Winter Aid, one of the welfare institutions that the Jews had created as part of their self-assistance program, had to support 20 percent of all Jews. The budget of the Reichsvertretung had long since been too small, and monies from the American Jewish Joint Distribution Committee helped to cover the costs. The Wirtschaftshilfe (Economic Assistance Office) of the Reichsvertretung, described by Alexander Szanto (38), tried to provide individual Jews with the resources for new undertakings on the smallest scale, so that they would not lose all means of earning a living.

An important and costly department of the Reichsvertretung was its educational work. Marta Appel (39) shows in her recollections how severely Jewish children suffered at the public schools from isolation and racism. They therefore left them in growing numbers. In 1936 the Reichsvertretung was already maintaining 160 often newly created schools. They employed 1,200 teachers, who also developed new curricula and instructional materials with Jewish content. Great efforts were made to give the young the kind of schooling and vocational training that would open up a future for them abroad. By 1937 possibilities for university study had disappeared entirely, and apprenticeships were hardly to be had, so that collective training centers had to be set up for Jewish youth. These centers also enabled the professional "retooling" of young adults, who wished to qualify for emigration with the help of a new vocation. Alexander Szanto (38) and Ernst Loewenberg (40) offer insight into the organization and problems of these training centers in the large communities of Berlin and Hamburg. At the beginning of 1938 there were ninety-four collective training centers for farming and crafts, home economics and nursing, and 23,000 young persons had already completed vocational training at them.

The Zionist organizations played a significant role in the training and vocational retracking. The quickly growing influence of Zionism after 1933 especially evidenced itself among young people, who streamed to the Zionist youth groups and Hechalutz, the pioneer organization, in great numbers. There they found a new prospect for the future. The task of Hechalutz was preparation *(hachshara)* for immigration to Palestine. In the over eighty Hachshara centers, some of which were located in other countries, 17,000 young German Jews were able to train and afterward immigrate to Palestine under the limited quota for workers. The young people mainly received agricultural instruction, learned Hebrew, and practiced communal living.

Another component of Jewish self-assistance activity was the Kulturbund deutscher Juden (Cultural Union of German Jews), created in 1933, which had as many as 70,000 members and maintained several dramatic ensembles and an opera, as well as orchestras and choirs. It provided cultural events with Jewish artists for an exclusively Jewish audience and was strictly supervised by the Reich Ministry of Propaganda, whose censorship compelled it increasingly to perform only Jewish authors and composers. The memoir of Kurt Baumann (42), one of the founders, describes the work of the Kulturbund, which existed until 1941. Still other cultural institutions were the Jewish *Lehrhäuser* (houses of learning), centers for adult education and rediscovery of Jewish tradition. Martin Buber and Ernst Simon were the decisive forces in this movement. The Jewish press, which had developed extraordinarily in Germany, was under strict supervision, so that critical articles had to be disguised, if they were able to appear at all. In 1934 the number of Jewish newspapers and journals came to about 120; in 1938 there were still 65. The book production of Jewish publishers also remained extensive. Schocken Verlag (Schocken Press) was the most active and, among other things, published the classics of Jewish literature in the popular Schocken Bücherei (Schocken Library).

The rediscovery of Jewish culture was most often combined with the turn to Zionism. The rapid growth of the Zionist movement after 1933 no doubt was a reaction to persecution and disfranchisement. Zionist teachings made it possible to bear discrimination and segregation more easily, for it explained these as a typical element of Diaspora history and opposed them with the idea of Jewish nationhood and the goal of founding a state. In this way Zionism made it easier for its followers to separate themselves socially and culturally from Germany, and along with a new identity it gave them a new outlook on life. This is portrayed with great force by Edwin Landau (33). The National Socialists recognized the Zionists because they viewed themselves as part of the Jewish, and not the German, people and furthered the desired emigration. The CV, on the other hand, could be active only in limited ways after 1933, since its insistence on Germanness was viewed by the National Socialists as a provocation, and the Gestapo kept watch on its committees.

The complete social isolation of the Jews and the boycott of Jewish businesses were more pronounced in rural areas than in the cities. For this reason, thousands of Jews fled the villages and small towns to the anonymity of the cities, where they were not so directly exposed to social discrimination and the arbitrariness of the local party and SA leaders. Internal emigration and emigration abroad began to basically change the age structure and social profile of the Jewish communities.

Seen in the long term, emigration under duress—flight from Germany—was the prime reaction of the Jewish population to their peril. Emigration was an act of self-assertion, but not an act of resistance, since it was entirely in accordance with the National Socialist policy of expelling the Jews, practiced until 1941. The memoirs show that a variety of factors determined the point in time at which the decision to emigrate was taken. Among them were not only personal jeopardy, vocation, and resources, but also age, connections abroad, and political assessment of the situation. The older, more successful, and better off one was, the more one had to lose and, generally speaking, the later one decided to emigrate. Large numbers of youth were able to emigrate to Palestine or England on special children's rescue programs, whereas their parents reached other shores later, or not at all. Marta Appel (39) describes the dramatic parting of these parents from their children, which were often leave-takings forever. In the main, people over sixty emigrated only with other family members, or they waited until their children had gained a firm enough foothold abroad to send for them. Frequently it was then too late for them to leave. "Our children have turned into letters," those who had stayed behind often said, and this remark characterized the splitting up of families along generational lines.

For individual Jews emigration was a process that completely uprooted them socially, economically, and culturally and exposed them to the insecurity and poverty of exile. Once the decision to emigrate had been made, under the unbearable pressure of circumstances, the fight began for an entry permit, to take along money and valuables, and to secure one's immediate future abroad. German Jews tried to emigrate to almost every country on earth, but not one accepted them unconditionally, except for the port city of Shanghai. In most cases, the various countries required emigrants to have capital assets, training in certain underrepresented professions or, as did the United States, to have someone in the country who would assume full responsibility for the emigrant's support. Every country limited its receptiveness, so that starting in 1938 hundreds of thousands who wanted to flee found no land that would accept them.

There exist no exact statistics either for the total number of emigrants or for their distribution among the individual host countries. According to qualified estimates about 280,000 German Jews succeeded in emigrating, something that would better be described as fleeing the country, if such flight had not required months of bureaucratic preliminaries. The chief host countries were the United States (130,000), Palestine (55,000), and England (40,000). Of those who fled to France, Holland, and Belgium, most were later deported during the war to the death camps, unless they had already succeeded in moving on. An odyssey through several countries was the fate of many emigrants. Outside Europe, Argentina and Brazil each accepted over 10,000 German Jews, South Africa 5,000, and the classical countries of immigration, Canada and Australia, only about 2,000 each. The Hilfsverein der deutschen Juden constantly tried to find new possibilities for immigration, counseled the emigrants on possible destinations, and procured means of transportation and financial assistance. But despite its close cooperation with Jewish aid organizations abroad it was unable to increase the number of visas. It became clear that the Jews were not only powerless in regard to their persecutors, they were also helpless to affect their rejection as refugees.

Immigration to Palestine was the only kind to be centrally organized, and it was done by the Palästina-Amt (Palestine Office) in Berlin. This office distributed the immigration certificates that it received monthly in limited numbers from the British Mandatory government. There were three kinds: certificates for workers, which were received by those who completed Hachshara; certificates for "capitalists," i.e., for persons with assets of at least 1,000 English pounds; and, finally, certificates for students with guaranteed support. A good third of the German-Jewish immigrants were "capitalists," many of them non-Zionists; another third were agricultural settlers and workers. As a special group of immigrants, 5,300 young people reached Palestine through the so-called Jugend-Alija (youth aliyah). This organization to save children, which had been founded in Berlin in 1932, brought young people, unaccompanied by their parents, into the land to make possible their training and their absorption in kibbutzim. Thanks to a transfer agreement, Palestine immigrants had the best chances of taking capital with them to their new homeland. The transfer loss until 1936 amounted to only 15 percent, and by the beginning of the war had risen to 70 percent. For all other countries, in 1934 the loss was already 60 percent, and, finally, in 1939 it was 96 percent, not counting the high tax for fleeing the Reich, which everyone had to pay.

Emigration meant the complete and almost always final break with German society. But Jews who did not emigrate were already outcasts from society. Their recollections show how the racist policies of disfranchisement and terror altered the social relations between Jews and gentiles step by step to the point of total segregation. Many tell of friends and acquaintances who withdrew from them after 1933 and in the best of instances communicated to them in advance that they were compelled to do so for the sake of their positions. Many Jews began to keep their distance from non-Jews early so as to spare themselves disappointment and discrimination, or in order not to endanger their friends. Thus, for example, Ernst Löwenberg (40) warned his former pupils against speaking to him on the street. This forced avoidance of association led to social alienation and finally to total isolation. It was this turning away of the majority from the minority, this silent antisemitism, that made the crimes that came later possible.

Although the integration of the Jewish population into the society as a whole had never been complete, one must finally ask what reality it had possessed at all before 1933 if it could be undone to such an extent within six years. The party and the government used the antisemitism existing in the population in order to completely exclude Jews from society through terror, propaganda, and deprivation of rights, and there were no protests against it. It was this background that made possible the Pogrom of 9/10 November 1938, which confirmed and even intensified the isolation of the Jews.

As of fall 1937, the situation of the Jews worsened ever more quickly. The pressure to "aryanize" businesses became inescapable. In April 1938 the Jews had to register their assets. In July 1938 almost all Jewish doctors who were still active lost their practices, as did the lawyers that September. Finally, on 28 October 1938 the Reich government deported at least 15,000 Jews with Polish passports across the Reich frontier to Poland. Among them was a couple named Grynszpan, who since 1914 had been keeping a tailor shop in Hannover. Their seventeen-year-old son was living in Paris, and after he received news of the deportation he shot the embassy secretary, vom Rath.

The National Socialist authorities used the murder as an opportunity for the great Pogrom of 9/10 November 1938, an operation planned for the entire Reich. It was carried out by the party, the SA, and the SS. The population looked on. In the end, 91 Jews had been murdered and almost 30,000 arrested, more than 1,000 synagogues were set ablaze or demolished, and 7,500 Jewish-owned businesses were devastated. Those arrested were imprisoned for several months in the concentration camps of Buchenwald, Sachsenhausen, and Dachau, where hundreds died of mistreatment.

In the memoirs the November pogrom, cynically played down in the vernacular as "Kristallnacht," is seen as the beginning of the policy of annihilation. For Jews the pogrom was an experience of helplessness, immediate mortal danger, and the complete deprivation of rights. The massive rush for the inadequate numbers of visas and immigration certificates was the reaction that the National Socialists had wanted.

Terror and imprisonment were followed by a tide of new anti-Jewish decrees, which brought about the exclusion of the Jews from economic life and their total financial plunder. Jewish children were forbidden to attend public schools, with a single exception Jewish newspapers were forbidden, and all Jewish organizations were declared to be dissolved. As the recollections of Alfred Schwerin (44) show, under the most severe conditions and in constant negotiations with the Gestapo the communities nonetheless commenced their efforts to free the prisoners, accelerate emigration, and support many of their members in distress.

The Reichsvertretung der Juden in Deutschland ceased to exist and was replaced by the Reichsvereinigung der Juden in Deutschland, which was forcibly created in February 1939. Its staff was identical to that of the earlier Reichsvertretung, but its structure was fundamentally different. Every Jew, in the sense of the Nuremberg Laws, was necessarily a member, i.e., membership was a matter of "race," not religion, so that now Christians of Jewish descent also had to belong to it. The Reichsvereinigung was under the direct jurisdiction of the Gestapo and therewith, as of the end of 1939, the Jewish Department of the Reichssicherheitshauptamt (Reich Main Security Office) under Adolf Eichmann. This direct dependency set limits on the scope of its activities whenever it sought to represent the interests of the Jews in this helpless situation—even though it was compelled to follow the orders of the Gestapo. There was no longer a single area of Jewish life that was not supervised or directed by the National Socialist power system; even worship took place under watch.

In the short time between the November pogrom and the start of the Second World War about 80,000 Jews managed to leave Germany. Great Britain was the only land to ease its immigration restrictions because of the emergency, and it accepted 8,000 children, who immigrated without their parents. After the war broke out, the possibilities for emigration shrank rapidly. Up to 1941 about 8,000 Jews were able to flee to Shanghai. Michael Meyer (45) was one of those who still illegally got to Palestine in 1939–40, while Elisabeth Freund (46) left Berlin on the last emigration train in October 1941, in order to sail from Portugal to Cuba. Then emigration was forbidden, and the deportations began.

Once the war started, the lives of the Jews were further restricted. They had to turn in their radios and telephones; were subject to nightly curfews; were concentrated in special "Jew Houses"; were permitted to shop only at designated hours; received smaller food rations; and, finally, were no longer allowed to use public transportation. At the same time, as Elisabeth Freund (46) reports, more and more of them were used as forced laborers in defense factories. The consequence of these measures was that Jews were living as prisoners in a ghetto, without having been formally imprisoned.

Emigration left behind in Germany a Jewish remnant of 163,000 persons that in October 1941 amounted to only 30 percent of the Jews who had been living in Germany in January 1933. In addition to those who had emigrated, more than 70,000 had died since 1933, without this loss being balanced through births among the overaged population. Of those who remained behind in 1941 over two-thirds were older than forty-five, and there were 20 percent more women than men.

The Jewish population of Baden and Saar-Palatinate had already been deported overnight to southern France in October 1940. Approximately 7,000 persons were living in Gurs and other camps in the most primitive conditions, but some, like Miriam Gerber (47), were able to escape the later deportation to death camps. The Reichsvereinigung had protested in vain to Adolf Eichmann against the deportation to France. Thereupon, it set a day of fasting and remembrance for all of its staff and secretly informed the foreign press. A member of its executive board paid for this with death in a concentration camp.

Marking the victims prepared their mass deportation from the Reich. As of 19 September 1941 all Jews of six years and over had to wear the Yellow Star. On 18 October 1941 the first Jews were deported from Berlin. The mass deportations did not end until February 1943 with the arrest in the factories of the last Jewish forced laborers. Since the summer of 1941 most of the transports had been going directly to Auschwitz as "east transports," or as "old people's transports" to Theresienstadt. In all, about 134,000 German Jews were deported, of whom very few survived.

The Jews in Germany were now living on borrowed time. Fear of being summoned for the next transport filled every remaining moment. Given this desperate situation those affected had only two possibilities: illegality or suicide. Illegality meant going into hiding or escape to another country, mainly Switzerland, under the most difficult circumstances, and it was possible only for those who were younger and robust. Probably as many as 10,000 Jews lived illegally, and of them less than a third survived. The accounts of Camilla Neumann (49) and Hermann Pineas (50) provide an idea of the enormous difficulties of an illegal life, with its constant worry about papers, shelter, and food, and the complete dependence on numerous helpers. For the elderly there remained only suicide, as a last act of self-determination. The recollections of Käte Mugdan's death (48) show what great human strength and dignity could be expressed through this decision. Approximately 3,000 to 4,000 mostly elderly persons took their own lives immediately before deportation.

In the summer of 1943, after the mass deportations, excepting those who were living in mixed marriages, Germany was considered "judenfrei" ("free of Jews"). At this same time, in the interest of the German war economy a completely opposite development began. Because of the acute lack of armament workers, in 1943–44 over 100,000 Jews from Poland, Hungary, and other European countries were brought to Germany as slave laborers for German industry in such concentration camps as Buchenwald, Ravensbrück, and Bergen-Belsen. In reality, then, the German Reich was never without Jewish population. For the few Jews of Germany living in "freedom" there was an administrative center in the Jewish Hospital of Berlin in the years from 1943 to 1945. The hospital stayed open the entire time until 1945, as did the Jewish cemetery in Berlin-Weissensee. It housed a surveillance office of the Gestapo for the remaining Jews, and a prison for those caught living illegally. The recollections of statistician Bruno Blau (51), who was a patient at the hospital until 1945, contain a unique report on the events in this vast complex of buildings. According to his testimony, 800 Jews remained alive there and witnessed the liberation of Berlin with him.

Very few Jews had survived in Germany. Many had succeeded in escaping in time to other countries. Over a third of Germany's Jews had been murdered. The continuity of German-Jewish culture was destroyed. Whether it can ever again be renewed must remain an open question.

# *The Age of Emancipation, 1780–1871*

# 1 Itzig Behrend

❧ BORN IN 1766 IN GROVE (HESSE-KASSEL); DIED THERE IN 1845.

Our family chronicle. Recorded by our dear departed grandfather Itzig Behrend in Judeo-German; translated into German in June 1893 by Dr. Magnus Cohn (Hannover). Copied by Dr. Hermann Behrend of Bückeburg, the son of Gotthelf Behrend, partly from a copy by Herr Hermann Berg of Warburg, partly from a printed chronicle of Prof. Abraham Berliner. New York, 1950, 44 pages.[1]

*Itzig Behrend spent his whole life in Grove (near Rodenberg), where there was only a rural community with few Jewish families. He owned a house with barn and stall, and dealt mainly in grain, cattle, hides, wool, provisions, and yard goods. The modest fortune he earned from this allowed him, in 1817, to buy the house of the burgomaster. He had three of his sons learn a craft. Besides births, weddings, deaths, storms, and inflation, the chronicle, which begins much like an annal, also records in increasing measure the political events of the times. In the following selection, these receive special attention. Behrend reports, among other things, on the French invasion, the founding of the kingdom of Westphalia (1807–1813), the emancipation of the Jews there, and the creation of the Jewish Consistory.*

This is the story of Jitzchak (Itzig), the son of Jakauf, known as Jakob.

Jakob was a son of Bär, Bär a son of Jakob. I, Itzig, am the third son of my father Jakob of Rodenberg. I was born in Grove, in house no. 65. I still recall my great-grandfather Jakob, who lived to the age of one hundred. His son was named Bär. Bär married a woman named Chaja from Hildesheim and fathered four daughters and two sons, of whom my father was the oldest. [. . .]

Our wedding took place on Sunday and Monday, the first days of the lunar month Ijar 1793.[2] On Wednesday, Sidra . . . (February 11, 1796), with God's help we moved into house no. 88 in Grove. And Jitzchak took Rivka into his mother Sarah's tent.[3]

On May 13, 1800, Jewish male subjects from the age of 15 to 40 were summoned to Gudensberg by Landgrave Wilhelm IX[4] for military conscription or exemption. And so it was. But the *parnassim* of the communities made an arrangement at high cost, of which our portion, paid here to the local tax authorities, amounted to 100 talers.[5] Since the Landgrave was away on a trip and came back on *Schwuaus*[6] and wanted to leave again in a few days, the *raw* (rabbi) instructed the *parnassim* to go to him in Weissenstein on *Jontew*[7] (since this was permitted by the Law), and there, with a great deal of money, they averted the *gesere* (evil decree). [. . .]

On May 9, 1803, all of us *Schutzjuden* (Protected Jews) here and in Nenndorf were summoned at the behest of the local merchants and the towns of Witteln and Aplern. That is, the merchants had petitioned the court to the effect that we should not engage in commerce, sell from door to door, or employ many servants (clerks). We then presented a document of protest in Rinteln by way of Fürstenau, which cost us 13 talers and 21 groschen. Feibisch O.N., Meyer and his brother Gumpel, I, Itzig, and my brother Aron contributed to this sum. Thereafter, we heard no more of the matter. May God continue to grant peace to us and all Israel. [. . .]

On May 15, 1803, all of us Jews gave a ball with music at the rathskeller, since on that day our Landgrave had been named a Prince Elector. In addition, on that morning seven psalms, selected by his honor Rabbi Löb Berliner of Kassel, were sung in the *schul* (synagogue). And on the same day, the Jews of Kassel,[8] [. . .] about which we received a printed book. The ball cost us, that is, my father, Itzig, Aron, and Abraham, 15 talers. Since that time, the *Leibzoll*[9] has been abolished in all of Hesse. [. . .]

In June 1803, the French, under a commander named Mertier, marched into the kingdom of Hannover, which they wanted to occupy, since England had not kept to the peace treaty.[10] Hannover's troops wanted to resist, but they thought twice about it and drew back *b'schaulem* [peacefully]. The French marched in undisturbed. Some of their patrol and volunteer corps plundered and set fires, but the ones who were caught were severely punished and shot. At that time, we had many of our friends' valuables in our house. They feared that they would lose everything. Those were our friends from Nienburg, Stolzenau, Ohes, and Baschehusen (Barsinghausen).

In the month of Elul [August/September] most of the French left the Hannover Principality and passed through Hesse to Bavaria. The ones who remained stocked up provisions for a year in Hameln.

At that time, I, my brother Feibisch, and the merchant Scher bought from the French a lot of new and used iron, such as wheels, winches, chains, and blacksmith's gear—one batch for 3,000 talers—all of which the French had taken from the armory in Hannover. A good part of this was sold by us for 1,400 talers, and a part for me and Feibisch for 400 talers, and in February 1806 part was sold here at an auction for 600 talers. At that time there were still goods on hand with a net worth of about 400 talers, of which some 110 talers counted toward expenses.

From December to February there were many Prussians, Russians, English, and Swedes in the territory of Hannover, but they all went home without having achieved anything. [. . .]

At Rosch Haschana 1805 I turned 39 years old in good health, and never in my life had the grain prices been higher than in that year: barley cost 1 taler and 6 groschen, rye 1 taler 24 groschen, oats 24 groschen, beans 1 taler 15 groschen. [. . .]

In January 1806 the French emperor named the king of Prussia administrator of the Hannover Principality. In return, the king ceded Ansbach, Bayreuth, and Wesel, along with Kleve, to the Emperor Napoleon.[11] But as the latter wanted all of Prussia as far as the Weser, he brought a large army to Prussia and invaded the province of the Prince Elector of Hannover, as well as Hesse and Brunswick, took away their arms and seized the land, and both rich and poor had to supply whatever provisions he needed. The emperor's brother, who was the king of Holland, marched through with great numbers of troops and there was much plundering. From here the Dutch army marched to Magdeburg and Berlin, where Bonaparte had set up his headquarters, then to Pomerania and Poland, and overran Prussia entirely. This fall, until today, the 25th of December, there has been no frost, but rather almost summer weather.

This year, 1806, at Michaelmas, rye cost 2 talers and 9 groschen, wheat 2 talers 12 groschen, barley 1 taler 6 groschen, and oats 30 groschen, and prices fell so low by December that wheat cost 1 taler 24 groschen, oats 15 groschen, barley 24 to 30 groschen, and rye 1 taler 18 groschen. In May, rye and beans cost 1 taler. [. . .]

In January 1808 the Emperor Bonaparte installed his brother Hieronymus [Jerome] as king of Westphalia,[12] on condition that he [Napoleon] would keep half of the principalities in the kingdom. It [the kingdom of Westphalia] includes the principality of Minden, Ravensberg, Osnabrück, Paderborn, Hildesheim, Kassel, Göttingen, the Harz, Eichsfeld, Goslar, Halberstadt, and Magdeburg, along with their estates. When the king assumed rule, a deputation of *parnassim* went to Kassel to pay lavish tribute to him, each according to his means. He issued all kinds of new decrees, some of which freed the Jews from their chains and declared them citizens equal to the *gojim*. Everyone can live and trade and practice a craft as he wishes.

On the 1st of March, the king was paid homage by all.

After January 27, 1808, by royal decree the Jews will cease paying greater fees than the Christians. We used to have to pay money for our protection, but now no more. Instead, each of us will take out a patent for whatever trade he wishes to ply.

A tavern costs 1 taler a year, timber trade 2 talers, a yard goods business 4 talers, a butcher shop 3 talers, a grain business 5 talers, a wholesale wine business 4 talers. In the past, we had to pay one heller more excise on a quarter (liquid measure) than the *goj*; we also had to give the tongue of a slaughtered animal to the rabbi; and for every slaughtered head of cattle we had to pay, besides the meat heller, 1 taler to the tax authorities. And there is no longer a poll tax. [. . .]

On August 6 [1808] the king of Westphalia came to Nenndorf with an entourage of various gentlemen and ladies, 60 persons and some 300 soldiers, both Foot Guards and Horse Guards. The soldiers were quartered in Gross-Nenndorf, Klein-Nenndorf, and Gross-Rodenberg. All of us local *Jehudim* [Jews], along with Feibisch Nenndorf, supplied them with meat, bread, straw, and fodder, as well as spices and poultry. The latter was ordered and certified by a supervisor named Messier and paid for by a quartermaster, nota bene with a nice deduction. The knowing person will catch on.

When the king arrived, sixteen maidens from the town in white dresses with green trimming, presented him with a poem on a taffeta or velvet pillow, and in return he gave each of them a pair of gold earrings and a necklace, which were bought in Nenndorf from Aron Escamp of Hamburg.

Moreover, the king was kind to everyone. Best of all, he decked out from head to toe three gentile *chasanim* and *kalles* (grooms and brides) in festive clothes, and besides that he gave each couple 300 talers in cash as a dowry. They had to marry during his stay here, on a Sunday. On that occasion, there was a great ball, open to everyone, with grand fireworks, festive lights, pole-climbing, races, cannon salutes, and a lottery with all kinds of *s'chaures* (goods), part of which we supplied. The brides and grooms received wares from me and Gumpel that were worth about 300 talers. [. . .]

In August 1808 the emperor Napoleon took a big army to Spain and conquered all of it. He deposed the king and set up his brother Joseph as king.

In May 1809 Napoleon marched with an army to Austria and conquered it.

In September 1809 the two signed a peace treaty. Napoleon now demanded the Austrian emperor's daughter as his wife, and this was granted him. [. . .]

From 1809 to 1811 there was no trade in produce, and at that time I, Aron, and Leib had 2,400 talers worth in store, and we could not sell anything. In September 1811, the merchant Helmke from Hannover turned up unexpectedly and bought everything from us: rye at 28½ groschen, barley at 25½ groschen, wheat at 1.10 in hard coin, with free delivery to Hannover. The loss on that was 300 talers.

The Lord gave, and the Lord hath taken away; blessed be the name of the Lord, from now until all eternity! Amen – Selah. [13] [. . .]

The year 1810 was a quiet time with no business, and for this reason I was often at home and dependent on what little business I did there. In order to earn something in some other way, I obtained the office of tax collector for the community of Grove, at Mühlenstrasse and Rodenberger Tor. My fee for the monthly collection was 37 groschen and for additional collection I got 2–3 groschen per head. [. . .]

In January 1812 many French and Dutch marched through here once more on the way to Danzig. Their passage lasted until the end of March. Every day during that time we had to billet all kinds of people speaking every possible language: Swiss, Croats, Dutch, French, Italians, Germans.

In January 1813 this army returned from Russia, like sheep without a shepherd, *mechulle mit die Pulle* [broke and drunk].

In July 1813 the president of the Jewish Consistory, Israel Jacobson, [14] came to Nenndorf with a coach, riding horses, and servants. One Schabbes he attended the *schul* of my brother Feibisch. He himself functioned as *chasen* there and he also chanted the Torah portion for the week, and then he delivered an edifying sermon. The next Schabbes he wanted to attend the *schul* in Rodenberg, but he was hindered by bad weather. Then he came here on the Thursday before his departure, gave a lovely sermon in *schul*, and said a prayer of thanksgiving because God had restored his health in Nenndorf.

We, my brothers Feibisch and Aron and I, Itzig, sent him, as the president of the Israelite Consistory, a German letter, in which we expressed our respect for him, and our teacher, Herr Sussman Cohn, sent him one in Hebrew. The testimonial was presented to him on a green and gold embroidered pillow by three young girls dressed in white, my daughter Marianne, my niece Pesche (Betti), the daughter of my brother Feibisch, and my niece Caroline, the daughter of my brother Aron. Caroline gave a fitting speech. Also present was my nephew Behrend, Aron's son, who had just become Bar Mizwa, and who recited his *drosche*. [15] Our president was deeply touched by all this. Soon thereafter, all four children received presents from him. Behrend got a silver medallion, Caroline a pretty sewing-cushion, Marianne a string of yellow beads, and Betti the same. For the rest, he behaved in a friendly and kind way to rich and poor. He gave the poor handsome presents of money. His stay in Nenndorf had much pleased him and on the day of his departure he regaled many of the spa guests, also inviting several local personages. Zahn supplied the food, and there was no lack of wine and music. It cost him over 100 talers. During his stay at the spa he took his meals *(koscher)* from Gottschalk.

In May 1813 many French troops marched through, with 20,000 wagons loaded with fodder, grain, and bread, and with many oxen and cows. The train was on its way to Magdeburg. War had broken out again between the Russians and the French. Prussia and Austria had allied themselves with the former. In July there were many battles, and they cost both sides many lives.

In October Cossacks marched to Kassel and they drove out the king of Westphalia and the whole Westphalian Corps. Two weeks later Hieronymus returned to Kassel. Many of the town's citizens were severely punished because they had not helped the king. Scarcely had he established himself again in Kassel when he was once more driven out by the Swedes, Prussians, and Russians.

The Prussian commanding general was Blücher, while Janetschek commanded the Russians. It was under their leadership that Kassel was taken. Then they marched to Hameln and Prussian Minden, in the direction of Holland. At the end of October the kingdom of Hannover was also restored to its earlier standing under von Bremer and von Decken. The Prince Elector of Hesse also returned to Kassel, and there was great joy and celebration. We Jews, too, said the *Hanaussen Teschuo* prayer,[16] with music, after the weekly portion of *Tauldaus* in the synagogue.[17] On the next day, Sunday, the Christians celebrated the day of his return. The National Guard marched with a band to the church. That evening, there was festive lighting and a ball. [. . .]

After the king of Westphalia, Hieronymus, who had reigned from 1807 to 1813, had been driven out by the allies and our Prince Elector had returned to his land, the former local collectors had many unpleasant quarrels with their communities over the war contributions, which, as the communities now charged, they had supposedly imposed too heavily and kept for themselves. Thank God, the accusation did not affect me. No one even said anything to me in this regard. *Haudu laschem ki tauw* (Thank the Eternal One, for He is good . . .).[18]

On December 16, 1813, a proclamation by the Prince Elector appeared in which he summoned his subjects to volunteer for army service, since he had to muster 24,000 men. Many did volunteer, since they thought that they could be forced to serve. It was also rumored that all those from 18 to 50 would be called up. From Rodenberg the following reported voluntarily to the Rifle Corps: my son Bernhard, the sons of Head Forester Kleinstöber, Pastor Kinder, Bailiff Deichmann, and several others. They were taken by Kilian to Rinteln, and the trip cost nothing. My son Bernhard received from me 30 talers in cash, a gun (13 talers), a game bag (5 talers), a wallet (1 taler), and in addition he got a cloth overcoat and trousers, 3 shirts, 3 pairs of stockings, and a silver pocket watch as a present from his Aunt Jette.

From Trier we received news, and again from the fortress of Cheonsville, which was besieged by the Hessians, saying that they had to battle stoutly against the French.

On August 14, 1814, my son Bernhard came home on leave from the garrison of Treysa, near Ziegenhain, but on the 22nd of August he had to leave again, along with the other riflemen and militiamen. For the trip, 2 louis d'or, and from his Uncle Feibisch he received a ducat engraved with the Ten Commandments and other beautiful sayings. On the 27th I got a letter from him from Bettenhausen, near Kassel, where he had his quarters, which were afterward again in Treysa, and on the 15th of November he came home on leave. At the end of December, with intervention by the burgomaster, I petitioned the Prince Elector directly for his discharge, which cost 31 groschen.

On January 3, 1815, his discharge was indeed sent to me by the War Minister, at a cost of 2 talers. Thereupon my son sent his army coats to his captain in Ziegenhain. At the beginning of March his captain wrote to him saying that he would have to come once more in the matter of his discharge, in order to settle accounts. This trip cost 12 talers.

From the time Bernhard was apprenticed to the Head Forester until the present his army service has cost me 120 talers, not counting clothing and pocket money.

On February 11, 1815, he went to Hamburg to look for a position there. He took along a new bag with Sunday and weekday gear, a silver watch, and 8 louis d'or in cash. After he had been there for two weeks he found work with Haymann Engel, who owns a wholesale business for English textiles. His pay for the first year is 90 talers with room and board, and he is content with it. In January 1816 his master raised his salary to 150 talers, and finally to 200 talers. In 1817 he went to work for another merchant, by the name of A. E. Cohn, and there he got 300 talers. In 1819 he returned home, brought approx. 400 talers with him, along with a full set of clothing, and a watch that strikes the hour, worth 12 louis d'or. [. . .]

On March 14, 1815, and by the Jewish calendar on the 2nd of Adar [scheni], my esteemed father, after a short illness, passed away peacefully in his 83rd year as a result of infirmity.

Present at his deathbed were my brothers Feibisch and Aron, the cantor Bornheim, and I, as well as all of the members of the local congregation. He had invited all of them for a leave-taking and had a *Mischebeirach*[19] said for them. He begged all present for forgiveness, in the event that he had ever injured them, pledged 2½ talers to the poor fund and bequeathed whatever was left of his estate in cash to the poor. On the 3rd of the month of Adar [scheni], that is the 15th of March 1815, his honorable burial took place. Bornheim said a memorial speech for him in the house where he died and the teacher Sussmann said one at his grave. In 1816, on the 3rd of Adar [scheni],[20] his gravestone was erected in the presence of the entire congregation. On this occasion Rabbi Sussmann gave a memorial speech.

My dear departed father was a most honest and upright man. As a member of the congregation he bore the same burdens as the rich, far beyond his financial circum-stances. He was, however, not rich in earthly goods, but rather he was rich because he was content with what had been granted him. When we, his children, often pointed out to him that his charitable deeds exceeded his monetary means, he soothed us, saying that it is good to surpass oneself in this respect. "You will get it all back. The Lord will fight for you, and you shall hold your peace. You will advance in the world and it will be your lot to dwell in honor in our congregation, which will increase." — God fulfilled these words. Most of his children had two houses, except for his son David, who because of the war had to leave his residence of that time and move to Hameln. He also lived to see us all led to the *chuppe*.[21]

In the month of Ijar [April/May] 1815, the Jewish community in Rodenberg bought the Holzmann house on Hinterstrasse for 800 talers cash. It was intended as a dwelling for the teacher and his wife. Our prime goal, however, is to build a synagogue behind the house in the garden. For our present *schul* is now too small for us. While we used to number 4–6 families, we are now 14. Local members and some good friends from other places have donated some 300 talers for construction. The former president of the Jewish Consistory in Kassel sent 50 talers, and I gave 52 talers as well as the ashlars for the east wall of the new synagogue. Our teacher, Rabbi Sussmann, lives in the house and pays 28 talers rent.

In the month of Ijar [April/May] 1816, we requested an estimate of costs for the planned construction of a solid building of 38 square feet [*sic*] from the following craftsmen: mason Wilkening, who asked 900 talers for masonry, carpenter Meyer (400 talers), joiner Pfingsten (1,100 talers), locksmith [Hintze] (150 talers). Since this estimate of costs was too high for us, we contracted with carpenter Steege in Maltringhausen for 630 talers and with mason Völker in Nenndorf for 450 talers. Thereupon, our local carpenter Meyer came to us and claimed to have a firmer right to the work. We then compromised with him at 650 talers for the carpentry, and with mason Wilkening at 600 talers, with joiner Pfingsten at 730 talers, joiner Bake at 10 talers for some odds and ends, locksmith Hintze at 60 talers, with Hohmeyer for a plank on Tegtmeyer's side at 20 talers, and at 80 talers for painting. The total was 2,182 talers.

The synagogue was consecrated on Thursday, the 19th of Elul 1819[22] in the following way: at five o'clock in the morning we all gathered in the old *Schul,* said the psalms of the day, then prayers, followed by the reading of the *Parsche,*[23] after which Gumpel Levy gave a farewell speech. Then Rabbi Sussmann also gave a speech fitting to the occasion. Rabbi Leib Pollak had come too, with his son and three musicians, and they enhanced the ceremony with song and music. Then the *Sefer-Toras* [Torah scrolls] were taken from the ark and the married men made seven rounds of the *almemar* [lectern] with them. And then we marched in procession to the new synagogue. The oldest congregants walked up front with the Torah scrolls, the *Hanaussen-Teschuo*[24] was carried by two boys, who were preceded by two torchbearers. Then came the musicians, and behind them men, women, and children. When they arrived at the building, Rabbi Leib Pollak gave a speech, and then they entered the synagogue through a portal of honor. Here, too, seven rounds were made with the Torah scrolls, which were then placed in the ark. Then Rabbi Sussmann and the schoolboys recited a psalm. Rabbi Sussmann gave still another speech. Then Rabbi Pollak and his son sang some psalms, accompanied by the musicians. My brother Feibisch then recited the blessing *Schehechijonu*[25] and the entire congregation called out a loud Amen!

Many people had come from the neighboring towns to attend the ceremony, and many Christians turned up also. Officials and clerics, even the police were there. The celebration came off beautifully and was praised by all. Forty poor Christians received presents of 6 groschen in cash and 6 pounds of bread. Gottschalk had cooked for the out-of-town visitors and found ready takers. A dance until midnight in the rathskeller concluded the beautiful celebration. [. . .]

In May 1819 my son Philipp was apprenticed to the dyer Kessler. He must learn from him for three years, and it costs 100 talers. I also must pay the fees for his registration, and I paid, too, for my son's room and board. From January 1820 until

February 14, Kessler was closed down because of the heavy frost. During that time he learned print-cutting from Voges in Lauenau, and that cost only 18 talers. He took his meals at Jakob's, who asked nothing, but he made up for it at a later time. On May 22, 1820, he was registered at the dyers guild in Oldendorf. That cost 3 talers 24 groschen. On February 18, 1821, at that same place he received his apprenticeship certificate and his journeyman's papers. That cost 5 talers. In 1822 he took to the road and found work in Lübbecke. Soon after that he came down with typhus, was cared for at Rabbi Schimon's, where he lay sick until *Erew* Rosch Haschana,[26] at which time he returned home by cart. His treatment cost almost 70 talers. [ . . . ]

In May 1823, my son Philipp again went journeying. He worked in Berlin and Hamburg, then went up the Rhine and to Lorraine, where he worked for a Jewish master craftsman. Then he traveled to Paris. There he found work in a calico factory and was paid ½ taler a week. Then he went to Lyon, where he worked until December 1825. Learning his profession, with various expenses such as travel money etc., cost about 375 talers. [. . .]

At Michaelmas 1826, I bought the Pomy house for 700 talers in gold in the name of my son Philipp. With sundry costs, that came to 1,815 talers. In 1827 we began building the dye-works. With equipment, that cost 1,400 talers.

In 1828 Philipp started operating his dye-works. May God bestow His blessing on it. First build a house and then take a wife, is the counsel given by one of our sages. And Philipp followed this counsel. [. . .] In June 1825 my son Abraham was apprenticed for two years to a tinsmith in Lübbecke named Ladorf, whom he paid 35 talers. He roomed and boarded at my son-in-law Ennoch's, for which I paid 50 talers. He finished his apprenticeship in January 1827, but had to stay at home because of conscription. Only at the end of December did he receive his passport and journeyman's log. He then went to Hameln, where he found work. At noon, he ate at the home of my brother David. His other meals he took at the master craftsman's. He paid for his board from his earnings, each week 18 groschen. On April 30, 1829, he again took to the road. May God protect him on his journey. [. . .]

As mentioned above, my son Abraham went journeying again in April 1829. He worked in several large German cities, then he made his way to Italy and found work in Milan, Florence, and Venice. He returned home in 1832 to ply his trade as a master craftsman, for which permission was granted him.

In July 1824, the Wenzel house in Rodenberg was bought for Abraham. The price was 1,105 talers. However, the burghers kept him from moving in. He lodged a complaint with the administration in Rinteln, but was turned down. He then turned to the administration in Kassel, which granted him permission. When my son Abraham wanted to move in, superintendent Bär and locksmith Neuhauser came and protested. Then a rescript arrived from Minister Hasenpflug, who said that Abraham should not move in until he had investigated the matter. Abraham now appealed to the various authorities, but they all refused him. The burghers had actually sent the butcher Pomy to Kassel, in my view not in vain. The burghers of Rodenberg had gotten together his travel costs, and among the signatories one could read the names of the pious Jews Gumpel and Calmann Levy, each with a contribution of 24 groschen. Thus they fulfilled the great *mizwa:* "Love they neighbor as thyself," but at the same time they honored the prohibition: "Thou shalt not follow a multitude to do evil."[27]

Since my son had been caused so many difficulties in moving into the Wenzel house, he bought the house of the nailsmith Hattendorf for 800 talers, had it torn down and built anew. When they were in the midst of tearing it down, Burgomaster Biesterfeld went with some consorts to the authorities and hoped in this way to prevent Abraham from building. They said that the Jew did not want to pay the regular community taxes. He was right to refuse because they also contained the taxes for church, school, and clergy, and since the emancipation the Jews were not obliged to pay them. Bailiff Deichmann told them that they should buy the house back from Behrend, and if he did not want to pay the community taxes he owed they should sue him. If they had no other wishes, they should just go home. That is what they did, and surely with sad hearts. But they were not to be discouraged and again sent a deputation to the authorities. Among them was the shoemaker Netscher, who offered to buy the house and then rent it to Christians. The bailiff dared them to try that. Thus their efforts were in vain. On the next day we engaged the help of Biesterfeld and consorts in tearing down the house, and they cooperated. After the house was built and consecrated with prayer, my son moved in. He could echo the words of the psalmist: "God, Thou were my help and hath humbled mine enemies."

In the month of Marcheshvan [October/November] 1838, Abraham married Friederike, a daughter of Mathias in Gehrden. The wedding was celebrated in my house, and 50 relatives and friends were invited. The costs came to about 50 talers, of which Mathias bore half.

October 12, 1829. My son Israel also devoted himself to a craft. He was apprenticed to a master turner in Allendorf. Because of a leg ailment he returned home. When he was well again, in January 1831 he went back to the turner. But the latter fell sick and died. I now engaged another master craftsman in Nienburg, from whom he learned the trade, and in 1832 he because a journneyman. He took to the road and worked in Holstein, Mecklenburg, the Rhine region, Munich, and Vienna. In April 1837, he came back in order to establish himself. He immediately received a patent and got much work. He had his shop at Philipp's and took room and board at his brother Bernhard's.

On September 6, 1838, my son Israel moved into his new home, the house that Abraham had once bought. Times had changed and he could move in with no trouble. Meanwhile, he had become engaged to Hendel, the daughter of my brother Abraham in Hanover. The wedding took place in Grove on May 22, 1839.

1. A partial printing (pp. 1–28) of this manuscript was published by Professor Abraham Berliner in the translation of M. Cohn in *Jahrbuch für jüdische Geschichte und Literatur*, Vol. 12 (Berlin, 1909) pp. 109–134. This unscholarly printing contains many insertions by the translator, which have been omitted in the present printing, except for a few word explanations (which are included in parentheses). — Since the chronicle was clearly not written as events unfolded, but often only subsequent to several years of events, the chronological sequence frequently became confused. For the sake of readability this was corrected by some changes in order. — A partial English translation of Itzig Behrend's memoirs, presumably rendered from the Yiddish original, appeared in *Midstream*, 33, No. 8 (October 1987), 25–30. The translator was W. Bonwitt.

2. 13 and 14 April 1793.

3. Genesis 24:67

4. Both in print and in the manuscript it mistakenly says Wilhelm II. Wilhelm IX reigned from 1785 to 1803 as Landgrave of Hesse-Kassel. With the acquisition of the Electoral Privilege in 1803, he became Prince Elector Wilhem I, was deposed from 1806 to 1813, and then reigned once again as Prince Elector from 1813 to 1821.

5. On 11 October 1781 the so-called Edict of Tolerance of Emperor Joseph II was also adopted in Hesse-Kassel, whereby mandatory military service for Jews was introduced.

6. *Schawuot;* Shavuot; see the Glossary.

7. Holiday; according to the Law, traveling and driving are not permitted on holidays. But in emergencies a rabbi can provide dispensation from this prohibition.

8. Part of the sentence is missing.

9. A special poll tax that Jews had to pay on their own person at every city gate. In Prussia it was done away with already in 1787, in Hesse-Kassel in 1803, through the intercession of the Court Factor, Wolf Breidenbach.

10. Peace of Amiens of 27 March 1802 between England and France.

11. Treaty of Schönbrunn, 12 December 1805.

12. The founding of the kingdom of Westphalia and the investiture of King Jerome came about through the constitution of 15 November 1807, which granted the subjects of all faiths equal rights and therewith declared the full emancipation of the Jews.

13. Job 1:21.

14. By a royal decree of 31 March 1808, the Consistory constitution for the Jewish communities was introduced in the kingdom of Westphalia. The Braunschweig Privy Councilor and banker Israel Jacobson, as president of the Consistory, directed the communities in a strictly authoritarian manner and introduced numerous reforms.

15. A discourse that draws upon rabbinic literature in order to interpret the Torah portion for the week. When a boy becomes Bar Mitzvah (see Glossary), he gives such a commentary during the ceremony.

16. Traditional prayer for the ruler, which is contained in the prayer book.

17. Genesis 25:19–28:9.

18. Psalm 136:1.

19. A blessing.

20. 3 March 1816.

21. That is, to marry under the wedding canopy.

22. 9 September 1819.

23. . . . followed the reading of the Torah portion . . .

24. What is probably meant here is a framed text on the reader's desk, which is carried into the new synagogue (cf. footnote 16).

25. A prayer of thanksgiving at the start of the holidays or upon new events, such as the consecration of the synagogue.

26. The eve of the Jewish New Year festival. Jewish holidays always begin at sundown on the previous day.

27. An ironic citation of Leviticus 19:18 and Exodus 23:2.

# 2  *Ascher Lehmann*

 BORN IN 1769 IN ZECKENDORF (UPPER FRANCONIA); DIED IN 1858 IN VERDEN (HANNOVER).

Ascher Lehmann (Lämmle ben Aron Weldtsberg), Diary. Edited, with a foreword, by Max Lehmann, and with a family tree. Gerwisch, near Magdeburg, 1936, 72 pages. Private printing. Written 1845–1850.

*This "diary" is an autobiography of Ascher Lehmann, who mainly describes his life as a peddler of wares of every kind during the Napoleonic era. Born near Bamberg, Lehmann left his home in 1786 and went off to Prague to study Talmud. The completely destitute* bocher *sustained himself through numerous odd jobs, finally gave up his studies, and became assistant to a Prague leather merchant until 1789, when, fearing conscription, he returned home, where he vainly tried his hand at peddling. Thereupon, he decided to emigrate to the kingdom of Hannover, where in the years 1795–1815 he did good business with the troops of the English and French armies that were marching through, and with their military depots. Having become a Protected Jew of Hannover in the year 1804, he became a citizen of the kingdom · of Westphalia in 1810, in Verden. But in 1815 he once again had to become a Protected Jew of the king of Hannover, who had returned, and to accept a new restriction on the freedom of trade.*

Since until my sixteenth year I had always received instruction in Jewish subjects and was a good pupil, I was supposed to go to Prague in order to continue Jewish study and become a *raw* [rabbi]. In 1786, after Sukkos, I left home for Prague. Since my parents (of blessed memory) had provided their three daughters with a dowry and, due to many lawsuits and illnesses, their capital had also dwindled greatly, they could give me but little travel money. From the place of my birth to Prague it is only thirty-six miles.* I thought that I could complete my journey in twelve days and so I was satisfied with the 5 guldens that they had given me. With a knapsack on my back, I traveled seven hours to Bayreuth, where I arrived in the evening. I ran into the local *chasen,* and he asked me where I came from and where I was going. At the same time, he asked me whether I, as a *bocher* would perhaps like to have a *blett.*[1]

"If you don't have a lot of money with you," he said, "you will be glad that you can get a *blett.* It is fourteen miles from here to Eger on the Bohemian border. You won't find a town there with any Jews. You will have to use up money enough."

I accepted the first *blett,* and it turned out as the good man had said. One has to spend money not only for food, but in every town and borough I had to pay 10, 12, and even 18 kreutzers as poll tax.[2] On top of that, I had to stay in poor inns and I got the scabies. I realized why my beloved parents had given me only 5 guldens: they were counting on adequate support from my dear brother, who at the time was earning a lot of money in Prague, and some *bachurim* from Prague had told and assured us that in Bohemia one could live so cheaply that one could get by for a whole week on a single gulden. And that is how it was. A roll or bread with butter costing one kreutzer, which here was three pfennigs, I could scarcely consume all at once.

But I had reckoned without my host. After a difficult journey, I arrived at the first Bohemian border town, Eger, which is a mighty citadel. I had entered a big building an hour earlier; from afar I saw men walking about. They asked me for my passport and I showed it to them. Then they took me into a large hall. There were several men there in different clothes and uniforms. They took my knapsack from my back, opened

---

*A mile = 4.5 English miles.

it, and searched me down to my undershirt. Since they found no contraband and also no new clothes, I was allowed to go on. I arrived in Eger on Friday afternoon. I stopped at a common inn and asked the innkeeper if there were Jews living in that place.

"Yes," he said, "only five, but all are wealthy people. They also have a cantor here."

I asked where the *schul* was, and I went to the *schul,* where there were yet other *orchim.*[3] After *schul* a nicely dressed man spoke to me asking whether I would like to accompany him. I went along and came to a house that was like a palace. In the hall there was a big store with many lights, where a nice looking young man was standing. I became frightened because I thought I was at the home of a progressive, who surely was *trefe.* But it wasn't that way. He had a lease for manufacturing tobacco products. In all of Austria, in every town and hamlet, only one person was permitted to sell tobacco, and it was a government order to keep the store open on Schabbes and *jontew,* for which purpose he had a gentile clerk; all the rabbis allowed it because it was an order of the Emperor himself. And he had a table the likes of which I've never seen again in all my days: a long dining room, in front of every person two large silver candelabra, each with eight branches, for every person two silver plates, for soup and roast, everything made of silver, several forks and spoons. It was the same with the food; there were all kinds of dishes, and on Schabbes afternoon, too, there were double portions of *kugel* made with *lokschen,*[4] and with the very best fruit, fruit of every kind. I looked around more than I ate. His wife was bedecked with jewels, as were his daughters. His workers as well as the private teacher, the salesman, and the clerk were all dressed expensively. For years I could not get it out of my mind.

Then I went to Pilsen, where the Christmas fair was taking place. In front of a house I read that there was a Jewish eating place therein. I went in and saw a beautiful woman, who was busy making fancy cakes. I asked for something cheap to eat. The woman ordered her maid to bring me a plate of vegetables. While I was eating she asked me the usual questions. I told her of my troubles. She said: "You have another 14 miles to Prague. If you ask me, you should stay with me for two weeks. I have many customers who have their food brought to their homes, and I need help. You will get your fill of good food here and on top of it people will tip you."

No one was happier than I! Especially since there was someone from Prague there who told me that no one in Prague takes a *bocherchen* into his house before Passover. If I got there earlier, I would have to spend money to eat and drink at inns. He also told me that two days before the end of the fair there would be a market here for *bachurim, meschoresim,*[5] and maids. I could then hire myself out to a *jischubmann*[6] as a *bocher* for his small children.

The man in the eating house was a musician, played at *chasnes,* and was a glazier by trade. The couple had five children, the oldest of whom was 10. They said: "We will keep you until after Passover. Then you can come home with us. It's only two hours from Pilsen." They lived in K. Within an hour's distance there were three *jeschubim,*[7] who had a *schul,* a *chasen,* and a *schochet,* and every *jischubmann* had his own *bocher* for his children, but they did not want to pay me. I thought that if at the *bocher* market I could not get a better deal, then—thank goodness—I had at least a place to stay during that hard winter, and I thanked the dear Lord upon lying down and rising up.

The fair was over. I took the meals and bills to the customers. They paid for the meals and gave me a decent tip. Afterwards, I counted it up and I had, in cash, 15 Kaiserguldens or 10 talers. No one was richer than I! I went to the square on Sunday, after the end of the wholesale fair. Sure enough, there I saw about twenty girls who wanted to be servants, thirty men who wanted to hire themselves out as *meschores,* but only a few *bocher.* Men came with their wives to hire a maid or a *meschores.* The maid was asked where she came from, whether she could cook, churn butter, and milk. The *meschoresim* were asked whether they could speak the Bohemian dialect and whether they understood Kashubian, for there the border to Germany was out and out Bohemian. Hardly anyone was able to understand a word these downright Bohemian burghers and peasants said.

There were few *bocher* but also few takers. Then there came a stocky man wearing a fur cap and a caftan, with a cane in his hand, and asked me whether I would perhaps accept a position as a *bocher* and instruct four children, the oldest of whom was a boy. I said: "Yes, but only until after Pesach." "Good. How much do you want?" I asked him how much he would give. Five guldens, was his answer. "Not more?" "No," he said. "*Masel, broche,* and *scholaum,*[8] I accept," I said.

Then I had to pay him a pledge to assure him that I really would go to his home, because, as he said, he had some business on the way. There was a wagon there at his inn, where I was to go right away. I introduced myself to the carter who was supposed to take me early the next morning, free of charge, to the place where he lived. I was still too inexperienced and thus I had not asked the man where he came from and how far it was still from Pilsen. I went to my eating-house family, which was alarmed that I had hired myself out. They asked me to whom and where to. I didn't know any of that.

The husband himself went with me to the inn to look up our man in order to ask him where I was going. But neither he nor the carter was at home.

I said goodbye very early in the morning. The good woman packed me white and black bread with roast meat and a quarter of a roast goose. Since I showed up at the carter's punctually that morning, the first thing I asked him was where he was from. The peasant was a real Bohemian, did not understand me, nor I him. He called and gestured for me to climb on. It was an empty wagon, like a hay wagon or a wood wagon, no seat or anything else on which to sit. I took my knapsack and sat down on it and stuck my feet through the rungs, and so we went, at a trot, without stopping, for eight hours.

At four in the evening I arrived at a wretched house that had to be supported so that it wouldn't collapse. The peasant stopped and gave me a sign to get down. Then a big pretty Jewish woman came out with five children. The woman rejoiced that she had gotten a *bocher* for her children. I got off the wagon to go into the little house, but I could not stand on my feet because they were almost frozen. The good woman and her eleven-year-old son led me into the little living room and took off my shoes, for boots at that time were not yet fashionable in that region; they also wanted to take off my stockings, but I wouldn't stand for it because I didn't want them to see my bad legs. Then, supported by the two, I had to go out the back door and walk around in the snow. Eternal praise and thanks to the Lord, my legs healed!

In the evening the woman prepared a meal, a browned gruel, which tasted very good to me. At nine in the evening I had to climb a ladder with the two oldest sons. We got to the attic and lay down on a bed prepared for us. Since the blanket was too narrow for three persons, the son took some sheepskins that were lying around there and we covered ourselves warmly. Breakfast the next morning was a milk soup with bread and butter. They even had a milk cow tied in back by the entrance hall, and also a calf for rearing, which was already quite big.

I now began my instruction. The woman gave me a square board on which an alphabet was pasted. There was the eleven-year-old son, who already began to read the *Aleph Bet*[9] quite fluently. The second son, nine years old, didn't know much yet. The seven-year-old daughter hardly recognized an Aleph. I said to the woman that the oldest son should start learning the *tefillah*.[10] Oh, was she ever happy!

*[By a trick Lehmann escapes this miserable position after a week and stays in another Bohemian village for two weeks as the helper of a Jewish butcher.]*

Then I wrote to my dear departed brother that I was coming to Prague at Pesach and that he should take care of my lodgings, and that I was coming in order to continue my Jewish studies. I also wrote to my parents, blessed be their memory. Two weeks later I received a letter from my brother in Prague, along with a package. It contained two slaughtering knives and a whetstone. He wrote that he could not support me, that I should learn *schechita*[11] with the *chasen* in K., which he would pay for. As a tutor and *schochet* one could certainly earn something.

I began learning and was supposed to take *kabbolo*[12] from the local rabbi shortly before Pesach. I had finished learning and the *chasen* went with me to a *dajan,* that is, an assessor of the rabbi who bestows the *kabbolo,* and he gave me a sermon and warned me that one could easily lose one's soul practicing *schechita.*

This alarmed me so much that I sent the knives and the whetstone to the *chasen* and resolved never to become a *schochet,* which later I often regretted. For when in 1795 I came to Verden and carried on my own business until 1806, at which time I married, I lived on coffee and fried potatoes. Sometimes on Fridays I cooked myself some fish and frequently thought that if I had received *kabbolo* I could slaughter a sheep and fry myself the liver. That is why it is good if a young man learns everything that he has a chance to, even if he does not intend to make use of it.

A week after Pesach I traveled to Prague, which was 15 miles away. I stayed on the highway, where every evening I had to lodge in a town or village where there were no Jews, and I had to draw on my money, so that I brought barely 5 guldens with me to Prague.

On Wednesday evening I arrived tired in the Prague Jewish Quarter and took a bed at a Jewish inn. The man asked me all kinds of questions. I said that I had a brother there who worked in the office of a rich man named Moses Zeckendorfer.

"Oh," cried the innkeeper, "I know him quite well. He is a noted, clever, handsome man. He is with Reb Guttenplan, who owns three factories. Your brother gets a good salary, he will support you well."

Thursday morning, I went to look up my brother, and since I kept asking street boys, the greatest riffraff of Prague, they constantly sent me in the wrong direction. Finally, there was a man good enough to show me the house, which I had probably passed twenty times, for the Jewish Quarter is as big as Verden, except that there are many more streets and nine big, massive prayer houses and probably fifty small ones. I entered the house and asked for the office scribe Moses Zeckendorfer. I found him sitting at his desk with other scribes. He did not know me anymore. Finally, he said: "What do you want here?" "I'm supposed to continue my Talmud studies. Our good, pious parents want that." He: "I can't support you. I will give you ten ducats. Go back home and help our parents in the business."

My feet were covered with blisters and I was supposed to journey back again. I cried bitterly and was stupid enough not to accept the ten ducats he offered me. I went from him empty-handed and didn't say anything to my innkeeper.

On Friday the innkeeper said to me: "Listen, little *bocher,* go to the main street. There are probably a hundred wooden stands there. In one of the stalls you will find an official, and he will give you a *blett.* Otherwise, it might cost you too much until after Schabbes."

I listened to the man and went to the stall and received a *Schabbesblett.* When, after asking many times, I found the dwelling, I gave my *blett* to a man who looked like a servant. He told me to wait a little. Then, a handsome man came and gave me a gulden, with the following words: "Go to the eating house. Have a meal. I am not taking in a stranger for meals today because this evening I am going with my wife to the theater."

I was satisfied with that, went to my lodgings and asked how much it would cost for that evening and the next afternoon. "Eight groschen," was the answer.

After the meal on Schabbes, I went to look around. On the main street, where I had gotten my *blett* at a stall, there were perhaps one hundred such stalls, but all were closed. This street is almost one and a quarter hours long* and eight times as wide as our street. As I stood there lost in thought and contemplated my present situation, a *bocher* came along who was some two years older than I. For one recognizes the *bocherim* by the long hair on their neck.

He gave me his hand and said: "*Gut Schabbes,* my friend. I suppose you are a stranger and probably an *Aschkenas* (that is, a German)."

I told him my birthplace. "Oh, welcome, fellow countryman," he cried, "I am from Baiersdorf, four hours away from Zeckendorf."

When he saw my predicament he said: "We'll soon find a way out of this."

"See the stalls? Tomorrow there will be men here who will take *bocherim* into their home. For every householder in Prague has committed himself to take an *unterbocher,* that is, someone who has not yet finished his Talmud studies. But whoever has studied for several years and is declared finished receives a tutor's position in the house of rich Jews, or he goes back home. Depending on how much such a tutor knows, he receives yearly as much as fifty to one hundred talers and is fed splendidly. But he must tutor the *unterbocher* without pay if the latter is poor, and instruct the children of the house."

*Approximately 4 miles.

On Sunday, my compatriot picked me up at my Jewish inn and we went to the stall where one is told where there is an opening for an *unterbocher*. The woman in this stall checked in a book and said:

"Day before yesterday, such a position became open, one of the best. There the *bocher* have it good, plenty to eat and to drink and also a good bed. The reference will cost you one gulden."

I gave her a pawn, my silver kneebuckles, with the provision that if I were accepted she would get her gulden. She wrote on a piece of paper: Reb Henoch Singer on Zigeunerstrasse. It was easy to find because he was the lead singer with the best *chasen* and had one of the biggest and best boardinghouses. I was received in a very friendly manner, and the woman had not lied. The food was good and plentiful. At noon and in the evening there were no less than thirty to forty people at the table, and there was an abundance of the best food. But I had to work as a waiter, bring the food to the table, clear it off, and sharpen knives. Yes, I even had to help the girls make the beds, since every morning some fifteen to twenty had to be made.

I did it with pleasure, for I had it good. The master of the house and the mistress were very kind to me. But what was my sorrow? There was no *oberbocher* there, since their children were all grown up. Thus, I couldn't learn anything. I asked to be allowed to go to the Jewish *collegium* in the mornings, at least to hear the rabbis, among others, the head of the *jeschiwe*. I was permitted to do that. But what good was listening if at home I had no books?

*[He then serves three months in the home of a banker, where he is poorly treated, and finally he finds a good position with a Prague leather merchant.]*

So I went to the leather merchant and was introduced to his wife. For the master was studying Talmud with two *oberbocher* from five in the morning until late in the evening. He was an extraordinarily pious man, and a millionaire to boot. He had two sons, who were already in his business. But his wife was the head. Further, there was a pretty eighteen-year-old daughter, along with several servants and two *oberbocher,* who studied only with the master and his sons.

I was hired and had it so good that I could regard the year and a half I spent there as the happiest time before my marriage. For my young age and with my weakly body I had taken upon myself too difficult a job. Daily, with the exception of Schabbes and Sunday, we had to store five hundred to a thousand pieces of cowhides and calf- and sheepskins. It was such a harsh winter that we wrapped our feet with a sheepskin, and frozen blisters hung from our fingers because of the wet skins. We thrashed our hands against our arms till the blisters were gone. The work was very hard. Our supplier brought many skins daily, more skins than we could manage.

The worst time for me was from the first to the tenth of January. Since the slaughterers were all doing piecework, each one received advance payment, and since my master trusted me more than all the other servants, I had to take the slaughterers' advance payment to their homes and had to drag bags with five hundred to a thousand talers in convention coins, count them out, and get receipts daily.

But no matter how hard the work, it did not irk me, since I had it quite good. I was liked by my master and mistress and the children as if I were a member of the family. I had to go for walks with the beautiful daughter of the house on my arm, also to the theater, and always I had to go along when she went shopping. I could eat and drink as well as my master, and at times even better; for the cook also liked me, since I sometimes helped her with her work.

Thus I could earn money. We were paid twenty guldens every half year. In addition, the horns were removed from the big oxhides, and the tails were cut off; the heads of the cowhides and the feet of the sheepskins were also cut off. The drivers wanted to make things easier on themselves in this way, and the tanners who brought the leather didn't ask questions. Every three months we sold twenty ducats worth of horns, calf heads, and sheep feet. We divided the money among ourselves, so that I had many pieces of clothing, and after other expenses I still had thirty ducats left.

Then, Emperor Joseph II summoned all the Jews and said that his mother, Maria Theresa, had restricted the Jews very much. He was going to grant them the same status as every other people. They could live where they wanted, could marry whenever they wanted, and do business where they wished; but they had to become soldiers.[13] He was about to start a war with the Turks.

There was an uproar among the Jews. They began crying and wailing. In the big new prayer houses they said *tillim*,[14] they fasted, and held vigil until midnight. Yes, the rich Jews bought officer commissions for their sons; one day a soldier, the next day a noncommissioned officer, on the third day an officer.

Now the Emperor called on capable men to set up regular schools. All Jewish children were to learn several languages, writing, and arithmetic. My brother volunteered, was examined and received a position in Lemberg and got a yearly salary of four hundred ducats. Then he sent for me and asked if I could make use of his old clothes. I thanked him, wished him a happy journey, and left him.

In the meanwhile, the newspaper said that the Jews had to become Austrian soldiers. Then my parents, blessed be their memory, wrote to me that I ought to come home without delay, although as a foreigner I was free. I had a passport, for which I could have gotten a hundred ducats because no citizen could get a passport at any price. And whoever ran away without a passport was regarded as a deserter. And still they ran away by the hundreds.

On the orders of my dear parents, then, I had to go home and leave my good position. Several of my compatriots showed up at my departure, and we left Prague in the month of *Rausch Chaudesch Ijar* 1789[15] with saddened hearts, especially I because I had one of the best masters and mistresses and had taken in 30 ducats within one and a half years. For a *meschores* to save such a sum was a rare thing in those days. In the fall of the same year, in Braunhausen, at the home of my wife's grandfather (of blessed memory), I received two and one-half talers salary for half a year, and had to drag fifty to eighty pounds for miles and miles, had to fetch calves from several miles away, in the process of which I tore my nice good clothing.

As I've said above, we, the four of us, left Prague, and in thinking of my parents and brothers and sisters, whom I had not seen for three and a half years, I forgot Prague entirely. We marched six miles every day. It didn't occur to us to ask about Jews or to request *bletts*. We all had money, one more than the other. But were we ever surprised that in towns and hamlets the body tax had been abolished. Whereas on the journey from Eger to Prague we had to pay at least five guldens, now we could spend them on food. The following Friday I arrived home and my dear departed parents and the entire community rejoiced with me.

But what to do now? My father, of blessed memory, probably still had goods that were worth several hundred guldens. Peddling was not restricted in those days. I went to Fürth and Nuremberg, bought still more marketable wares for the money that I had brought along, and went peddling. But when I came to the acquaintances of my father and offered my wares, with one voice the Catholic peasants, their wives and daughters said: "Oh, you pretty fellow, what a pity that you will go to hell and purgatory. Get yourself baptized!"

I packed up my wares and left their house. That is how it went in many houses and villages on the way. Boys who were herding cows or pigs called out to me: "Jew, *mach Mores!*"[16] If I didn't immediately take off my hat, they threw stones at me.

I came home, cried, and said: "I can't stand this treatment. I will not go to the country again to these *reschoim*."[17] But they really weren't Jew-haters.

Thus, I went to another area, where there were more Lutherans. There, however, I couldn't sell a thing. One found villages with some forty to eighty peasants who didn't have a penny's worth of goods bought from a merchant in their houses. They wore nothing but what they had made themselves of wool or linen. Among a hundred women or girls one cannot even find an ell of silk ribbon. The ones who are well-off wear gold or silver braids on their caps, and the poor wear no caps at all but rather a white linen scarf on their braided hair. Thus I roamed about until Schawvaus without being able to earn a single taler.

*[In 1795 Lehmann decides to go to the Kingdom of Hannover, and first he stays with his relatives in Bruchhausen.]*

I hired myself out to my wife's grandfather until *Rausch Chaudesch Ijar* for a salary of two and a half talers. I had to buy calves sight unseen, had to carry fifty to eighty pounds of meat miles and miles to the inns, and I wore my good clothes to a frazzle. I hired myself out in Hoya to Reb Leb Spanier for a salary of seven and a half talers. I went peddling with wares and got half the profit. But I also had to see to the slaughtering, in order to deliver the necessary kosher meat to the households. Since I had no customers I had to sell the *trefene* meat[18] cheaply, so that I lost money and three years later had barely ten talers left. With this money I went to Büchen, did business for myself, and spent one taler a week for room and board. I got thirty talers worth of wares on credit, slaughtered sheep and calves, and between *Rausch Chaudesch Ijar* and *Rausch Chaudesch Cheschwan*[19] 1795 I earned some one hundred talers. But it was such a severe winter that by Pesach 1796 I had spent all my cash except one-third of a taler.

Then the English commissaries set up big stores of oatmeal, hay, and straw in Rethen, Neinburg, Hoya, and here in Verden. Everyone rushed to buy. I also hurried there and bought very profitably. But I could not sell it to anyone because those who had agreed to deliver did not buy from everyone, so that they alone would profit. I went to Rethen. The following major suppliers were there: Reb Nathan, David Michel, Salomon Heilbronn from Hannover, and Mendel from Göttingen. They had four hundred to five hundred talers in cash. There were, however, so many sub-suppliers that there was no longer anything left for me. I begged our all-bountiful Creator for help. He heard my plea, blessed be His Holy Name forever and in all eternity. Reb Herz in Rethen, of blessed memory, found me a job with a supplier. I had to watch the day laborers, who were packing oats into sacks of one hundred pounds each, while they were weighing them; on each sack I had to mark a G. R. with my brush, and then I had to deliver them to the storehouses of English and French emigrants in exchange for a voucher or a receipt. For that I received a pistole a week. At the beginning I ate at the home of Selig or at Schragenheim's parents and spent a taler a week for my daily meals. Soon thereafter Reb Herz Rethen gave me free board with good food. By the end of August I had three hundred talers left.

Where to now, I asked myself. Then eight regiments of French hussars and eight regiments of English cavalry decamped on the heath near Scharnhorst. I went there. Since an English supplier, who bought all his supplies from the peasants himself, did not need a sub-supplier, I did business with the soldiers. I bought and sold watches and pipe bowls, and I also got myself new wares such as silk scarves and handkerchiefs, stockings, etc., and I ate my meals for board money in Bücken at the home of Reb Löw, of blessed memory.

In the fall, these troops went away, and I didn't know what to do. For whenever I wanted to do business, I was told that I was not a Protected Jew and also not a *meschores*.

I decided to go back to my home, but it was difficult to get a passport. Finally, I got one and I traveled from there to Kassel. Then I heard that the French were in Bamberg and that they were taking all young people into the army. I deliberated back and forth, but my money had dwindled to about ten talers and I had only an old English watch left that was worth five talers. Once again the question was, where to. I absolutely did not want to hire myself out as a *meschores* for calves. Then our almighty Creator gave me the idea to come here to Verden, and I came.

When I arrived here, the soldiers captured in France also arrived, and each one received one hundred to two hundred talers in back-pay. Thus everyone had his pocket full of money and bought whatever he saw, especially pocket watches. I sold my watch for ten talers and right then and there could have gotten rid of another hundred. But where to get some? With my ten talers I hurried to Bremen. I ran about looking, but found no watch dealers. Luckily, I came upon an old watchmaker who had twelve old watches, all of which I bought from him, and for my twenty talers accepted four bad ones. I had scarcely arrived here when I sold them all at a good profit. At night, I hurried to Bremen, in the morning I arrived with six watches, and toward evening they were all sold. I rushed back to Bremen and bought some more. As soon as I showed my face again, thirty soldiers came, and all wanted to have watches. Whatever I asked for, I got. Within two weeks I went twelve times to Bremen, where I was able to get only some fifty watches. But the soldiers' money was soon gone, and then it was all over with the watch trade. Then I went to the auction and bought old clothes and bedding, and I did a good business.

Verden was full of jewels, pearls, gold, and silver. I bought everything at a good profit until 1803. By the third of June, when the French came into the land, I probably owned between a thousand and fifteen hundred talers. That is when business with watches really started. I traveled to Hamburg and got to know a watch dealer who sent me several dozen weekly by mail.

An entire regiment of the Eighth Infantry, with a division and regiment general, stayed here in Verden. In one year I sold six hundred talers worth of watches, and also was cheated out of several watches.

*[In 1810 he becomes a citizen of Verden, which at that time belonged to France.]*

But with God's help I did good business with all sorts of wares. Those were the days when one could buy much leather, a dicker[20] for about twenty-four or twenty-seven talers and get forty in return. Here, I bought fourteen hundred sheepskins from local butchers and got back sixty-six percent of it in leather from the tanner Schwaner in Hoya.

I bought gold and silver objects; among other things I bought a big chest from a French division general, six ells long and five wide, filled with clothes of velvet and satin, and tablecloths, which I sent to Hamburg, where I sold them for the printed calico that they manufactured there. There was a general's uniform with golden fittings, epaulets weighing a pound. I gave him eighty talers for it and got twice as much in return.

Only textiles were not to be had. English wares were taken away and some burned. German goods could not cross the border. From France came corduroy and cottons. One ell of corduroy cost one and a quarter talers, and the English kind, a thirty-seventh of cotton, half a taler. But it wasn't even worth sixty pfennigs. Coffee cost one and a half talers, sugar one taler. But despite all those prices one was satisfied.

Since I had to billet soldiers in my cramped quarters, I rented myself a big house. I didn't have to pay rent, but I did have to take in billetees and pay the usual taxes and duties. That cost me a lot. I had to fix up my living quarters, all the time billet six to ten men, give them food and drink, and a good bed without charge. And we were glad if they placed real Frenchmen with us. For if they were treated well and in a friendly manner, they were satisfied with a decent meal. But Italians, Alsatians, and Hollanders couldn't get enough to eat. Also, the Frenchman was the most honest soldier of all, the Hollanders the worst, but the Cossacks as well as the other Russians are even worse.

Now comes the worst period that can possibly happen in a person's life. On the first day of Pesach in 1813 the French general, Prince von Reuss, came from Bremen with two thousand eight hundred men, and attacked some three hundred Cossacks who had been roaming about between here and Bremen. The French pursued the Cossacks, who drew back to Rotenburg. They marched in here at noon and all looked as black as Moors, for each had shot off sixty cartridges at the Cossacks, hitting only one. These two thousand eight hundred men made camp on the courtyard of the cathedral, and most households had to send food there for eighteen men. We did also, and it was Pesach. Right away I bought ten pounds of meat, a bread, and new spoons, knives, and forks. Our Schabbes-woman had to cook in her house and take the food there, and Jewish Alsatian soldiers came and ate *mazzelockschen*[21] at our table.

Toward evening the rumor spread that the general had heard that last Wednesday our municipal council had been ordered by the Russians to remove the French Eagle and put up 'George Rex' instead. Therefore that evening they were going to loot and set fire to Verden. My dear wife was still in childbed with Hannchen. Just imagine how worried we were. I ran to the house in which Dr. K. was living at that time and where the Prince had his lodgings, in order to find out something. Unfortunately, it was more than a rumor.

The doctor's wife ran to the kitchen and screamed at the top of her voice. I ran after her and asked why she was screaming like that. "Ah," she said, "the French claim that 'George Rex' has been affixed and the eagle removed. So first they are going to plunder and then destroy everything."

I forgot that when the French marched in, a Cossack stabbed a soldier in the neck, below his chin, and the soldier ran into the house and wanted someone to help him stop the bleeding. I called the surgeon N., who bandaged him. Now I couldn't get rid of him again, and I put him into the billeted bed. Toward evening it was announced that there would be a heavy penalty for any citizen hiding a soldier. Since I had heard from the doctor's wife what was going to happen, I had reason to speak to the Prince himself. I knocked on his door and without waiting for an answer I stood before him, where he was sitting with many staff officers. Very politely, he asked what I wanted. Given his politeness, I recovered and said:

"Your Grace issued the order not to hide any of your people. I have a wounded soldier lying in bed whom I can't get rid of."

"Good," he said, "if we remain here, you will get a voucher. If we march on, he will be picked up. What is your house number?" he asked. "114," I said. The adjutant had to write it down. I fell on my knees before him.

"What is the meaning of this?"

"Your Highness, I am pleading for the city. Your landlady is in despair. She just said that your men are going to plunder and set fire to the city."

"Yes," he said, "you Verden rabble have so quickly forgotten our great Emperor and are turning to the King of England. Now let him come and help you!"

I said very boldly: "Only God in heaven can help."

Then it occurred to me that it was the second night of *Lel Schimurim*,[22] and I took courage anew and said:

"Your Most Serene Prince, master and governor, you have the power in your hands; you can make thousands unhappy in a few hours, and neither you nor your corps will gain anything by it. What is the peaceful citizen to do? Drive off the accursed Russians? Our Emperor has taken our weapons. A year ago everyone had to deliver his weapons on penalty of death. After all, we were French already in 1803, and since then we've had the Eighth Infantry Regiment here and got along in brotherly fashion. Tell us what we are supposed to do. If tomorrow the Prussians come and day after tomorrow the Austrians! Whatever they order must be obeyed."

He said: "Have you been sent by the townspeople?"

I said: "Not at all. But think of the women and children! Also, my wife is at present in childbed, and I have another five little children. Where are we to go?"

They began to laugh and showed me the door. I ran by way of the Sandberg and wanted to take a few day laborers into my house in order to defend myself, but no one wanted to leave his home. I came home and didn't say a word about it to my wife. [. . .]

Because no goods were allowed to be brought into the land, not even from Hannover, since it was Westphalian and here it was French, I earned money and more money. The products, too, cost little. The best calfskin cost a good nine groschen, an oxhide or cowhide one and a half talers. There were also gold, silver, jewels, and pearls, and I earned a lot on them.

Then a French general named Biron came with his wife and seven children. He was a real savage. He chased the finest people from their homes and used them as lodgings. Once I met him on the embankment when he was coming from drill, and I lifted my hat and asked him if he might not have something to sell. He said that I should come to him the next morning at nine o'clock. I went to the house on Paradeplatz, where some of his servants were lodging, and asked them whether their master was a good person to do business with. They laughed and said that in Vienna some Jews wanted to buy something from him and he chased them from his room with a dog whip. I lost my desire to go to him, but I drank a schnapps and regained my courage. The clock struck nine and I stood before this barbarian. "Ha," he said in French, "he wants to buy something!" Immediately, he stood up from his chair and fetched a general's uniform with two epaulets, each weighing a pound, a big hat with broad braids, a saber case with braids, three or four sword belts with much silver, gilded buckles that I thought were of brass, and only much later, when I wanted to sell them as brass to the local beltmaker and had them cut off, did I see that it was the finest fourteen-part Parisian silver, weighing over two pounds.

I asked him how much he wanted. Five louis d'ors, he said. I took my purse and gave him five louis d'ors. He thought that I would perhaps offer him less for it, and then he would have beaten me and driven me out of the room. He was quite flabbergasted. I took my things, which were worth over a hundred talers, and bid him goodbye. He called after me that I should return in one and a half hours.

I went to him full of fear. He led me into a hall, and there was his very pretty wife. There stood a leather-covered trunk, seven feet long and four feet wide. He unlocked it and said I should take a good look and tell him how much I would give him for it, and he went to his room. The woman spoke too much in French. I didn't understand a tenth of what she said. She claimed that these things were extremely valuable. She said that they had cost six to eight thousand francs. There were velvet and silk dresses, wide satin wraps with silver clasps and coronets, bed sheets of fine Brabantine linen, each length ten quarters wide, and twelve complete sets of dinnerware, all of fine quality. I packed everything back into the trunk and asked him how much it would cost. He said that he didn't know the value, I should make an offer. I was afraid to offer too little. If I did, I'd get a beating with his dog whip, as his servants had prophesied; if I offered too much, I would suffer losses.

I got up my courage. Since his wife would also not state a price, I said: "General, sir, I will offer you an amount that will make it difficult for me to turn a profit. I will give you eighty louis d'ors for it."

His wife screamed: "It is worth over two hundred!" He, however, made a sign to his wife, silently took the key and said: "Bring the money and then my people will take the big chest to your home." That took a huge load from my heart. I did indeed receive the chest with its beautiful contents, on which, with God's help, I earned over five hundred talers.

Not long thereafter, on October 18, 1813, the Battle of Leipzig took place and the French lost. Little by little, they were driven to Paris. Napoleon was banished to the Island of Elba. There was peace then. In June 1815 [1814?] we celebrated the peace festivities. I heard that every householder had a sign made in front of his windows because the city was going to be illuminated. On the top of a big wooden panel I had a painter paint seven lean cows grazing on a heath, and below seven fat cows grazing in the grass, and had him inscribe above it: "Past and Future." It was the most beautiful sign, lit on both sides by tin lamps filled with tallow, so that the entire city gathered in front of it and admired it.

Then there came cavalry sections of many regiments of the English Legion for the purpose of recruitment. From Gottschalk Schwabe, who at that time was living in Bremen, I took over the supply of oats, hay, straw, bread, meat, brandy, and wood. I could have grown rich from that if Schragenheim had become my partner. But he wanted to have two-thirds profit, and I was to get only a third. Since supplying, which lasted three years, was assigned anew every three months, he constantly lowered the prices on me, whereby he himself suffered losses, since the deliveries amounted to almost one hundred thousand talers.

Then, in 1815, Napoleon once again returned to Paris. The entire military had to go once more to Brabant, where on June 18, 1815, the final battle was fought at Waterloo. Napoleon fled onto an English ship that took him to St. Helena, from whence he did not return. With that there was peace in the whole world.

In 1815, the provisional government granted us state protection and the license to deal in all kinds of articles, for which we had to pay a tax to the merchants. The letters of safe conduct were valid for three years. During this time, the merchants kept after the magistrate to withdraw the textile business from us. In 1818, the last day of Pesach, we were called to city hall and ordered to bring along our licenses. We received a new one that excluded textiles and everything made of wool, even woolen socks, caps, or vests.

I was not satisfied with that. I protested against it, petitioned the bailiwick, which sent me to the ministry, and every document from Dr. Münchmeyer here, Dr. Freudenthal in Stade, Dr. Gumprecht in Hannover, cost five to six talers and so many trips that they amounted to five hundred talers. I could get nowhere, even though I had the best recommendations. The local magistrate was not favorably inclined toward me. I had a stock of woolen goods, including fabric, worth two thousand five hundred talers, owed Böse in Hannover eight hundred talers, several hundred in Brandenburg, and also to Ernst Bros. in Braunschweig for frieze and cotton, and was not permitted to sell a pfennig's worth. I was in despair. My wife embraced me, cried, and comforted me with the words: "Trust in God. He will help." He did help, praised be His Holy Name, forever and in eternity. I arranged with the town steward Vocke to make it known that starting with the 17th of July there would be an auction of textiles that would be sold to the highest bidder. Trustworthy buyers would receive credit until Martinmas. Then, from Monday until Thursday, he sold sixteen hundred talers worth at great profit. The sale would have been continued after a few days if the merchants of Verden and Hoya together had not effected an order from the bailiff that the steward not be permitted to go on selling. My other textiles and cottons they took to city hall and sold at a public sale, a tout prix.

In the third year, I became tired of petitioning, and my consultant, Councilor Z. in Hannover, a good man, had pity on me and said: "You are wasting so much money on petitions and journeys. If you were now to receive permission to sell freely all other woolen wares except cloth, you should be quite satisfied." I told him that I would think about it. I went home and told it to my wife. She was satisfied with it. I, being a humanitarian, was always well-disposed toward my *chawerim*,[23] although toward me they were deceitful and false, as even today, as I am writing this, they are still all hostile toward me. On August 4, 1825, I said sincerely and honestly to Jakob Seligmann, Samuel Schragenheim, and Meier Joseph Herzberg that I already had a hundred talers in costs. If each of them gave me fifty talers, I would see to it that they could sell their wares freely. They were very pleased, shook my hand in agreement, and after four weeks we had our license in hand. I asked each for the promised fifty talers, and received not a pfennig. Schragenheim was to blame because he said that I had petitioned for myself and they had just slid in along with me. He wouldn't give me anything and so the other two also gave me nothing. I didn't want to go to court.

Thus, we all did business with woolen wares but not with cloth. But trade became worse and worse, since the peasant doesn't go where he can't get cloth, coffee, sugar, tallow, and cart grease. The peasants owed me several hundred talers in debts when I began to sue them. What did they do? They said that once, in the years from 1822 to 1826, when I was forbidden to sell cloth, they had bought it from me for clothes. Charges were brought against me and I was sentenced to pay five hundred talers penalty and eighty-five talers expenses. Now I was really in a fix. However, our All-Bountiful Creator saved me, blessed be His Holy Name.

*[Unfortunately, Lehmann does not say how he was saved.]*

1. *Blett* = "Billet," i.e., a ticket for free meals and bed at the place of a member of the Jewish community.

2. Special tax for Jews, which was abolished in Austria in 1781.

3. Guests (Hebrew), Jews from other parts.

4. "Kugel" is the traditional Jewish side-dish on the Sabbath; it is baked in fat in a round pan. "Lockschen" are noodles.

5. Farmhands, servants.

6. Country Jew.

7. Villages.

8. Happiness, blessings, and peace.

9. Hebrew alphabet.

10. Prayer book; i.e., the son was supposed to be prepared for his Bar Mitzva.

11. Slaughtering in accordance with ritual prescriptions.

12. License for ritual slaughtering, which is issued by the rabbi.

13. The Austrian Edict of Toleration of 1781 designated, among other things, the introduction of military duty for Jews starting in 1781.

14. Psalms.

15. New moon festival of the month Iyar (April/May).

16. Traditional call of the enemies of the Jews, who thus forced the Jews to take off their hats in greeting if they did not wish to be exposed to further molestation.

17. Enemies of the Jews (literally "villains").

18. Since certain parts, for example, the hind part, of animals slaughtered even in the kosher manner are regarded as trefe, Jewish butchers sell these inexpensively to Christian customers.

19. That is, in the spring-summer season.

20. Early German measure for skins: a dicker consists of ten pieces.

21. The Schabbes-woman is a Christian maid who takes care of the housework that is forbidden to Jews on the sabbath, e.g., heating. Here she is charged with the feeding of Christian soldiers, who are allowed to eat bread on Passover, while the Jewish soldiers receive Matzokugel at Lehmann's.

22. "Nights of Vigil"; at Pesach. According to Exodus 12:42, God protects his people, especially on the two nights of the Seder.

23. Comrades, colleagues.

# 3 *Isaac Thannhäuser*

BORN IN 1774 IN ALTENSTADT (BAVARIAN SWABIA).

A short biography of Isaac Thannhäuser, religion teacher in Fellheim, from his earliest youth to his old age. Prepared by him. 21 pages. (Originally in Hebrew characters, but written in German.)

*In this incomplete memoir, which only covers the period to 1802, the future teacher Isaac Thannhäuser reports on his wretched life as a peddler in the small states of East Swabia. He was born in Altenstadt, an estate of Prince Schwarzenberg in the vicinity of Ulm. Although gifted for Jewish study, after his father's death (when the boy was only thirteen), he had to hire himself out as a porter and peddler's helper. During his joyless youth he never advanced beyond an often illegal, door-to-door peddling. The "coalition wars"—the wars of the European allies against revolutionary and Napoleonic France starting in 1792—and their troop movements provided him with the only opportunities for some occasional trade. After his reluctantly concluded marriage, he settled in Fellheim in the vicinity of Memmingen, but continued his itinerant trade until poor health moved him to take on the job of teacher in Fellheim. His memoirs, written mostly in a tone of lament, are one of the few sources that provide direct insight into the hard daily life of the Jewish underclass.*

The place of my birth is Altenstadt. I was born on the 11th of Tamuz 5534 [June 20, 1774]. I was the only son of good parents and had four sisters. My father, a man of reason, gave me a sound education. He had me learn what could be learned in those gloomy times, had me instructed by two rabbis. With the first, I studied all of the practical subjects and later I studied *Gemara* (Talmud) with him. With the second, I first studied Raschi's commentaries on the Torah and later the remaining twenty-four books with Raschi.[1]

I was also sent to the German school. I had to cross the borough to Illereichen daily and there learn reading, writing, and arithmetic from the schoolmaster, who was himself very limited.

My parents, who dedicated me to Torah study, expected that I would have a brilliant future, because I truly did have the bent and gift for such study. And my career did proceed quite smoothly, without hindrances or unusual occurrences, until my twelfth year. And thus my parents believed that their wish to send me elsewhere to study the Law had more or less been fulfilled, when suddenly fate upset their plans and destroyed all of their hopes, and mine, in one stroke.

At the start of my eleventh year, my father began to be sickly. At first they thought his ailment was minor, but gradually it became more and more worrisome. No costs were spared, doctors were consulted, but unfortunately it was all in vain. I had not yet reached my thirteenth year, and my father was no more. With his death—as will be seen further on—the whole plan for my Torah studies ended.

My father had a brother by the name of Rabbi Hirsch, who lived in Ichenhausen. He made him my guardian, and since as a businessman he could not always be in loco, an overseer named Berli was also chosen. He was the brother-in-law of my father and my uncle, and he alone was the cause of my adverse fate.

After my father's death they did permit me to study until my Bar Mizwa, but the plan to have me study further was immediately dropped. The pretext for this was that such study costs a great deal and it could mean sacrificing my inheritance (of which I was unfortunately deprived by said Berli).

At the beginning, the estate of my father was not inconsiderable. A month after his death, my oldest sister received her portion. She got as a dowry 600 florins, as did each of my other sisters, and my mother, who passed away three and a half years after my father, was left an equal portion.

According to the law of our Torah, I, as the only son, was to receive two portions. That would amount to 1,200 florins, and from the estate of my mother I was due at least another 100 florins and the dwelling. Especially the two scats in the synagogue were mine, as well as the *seforim* (books).[2]

After I had completed my thirteenth year, it was decided that I could no longer board at my mother's because she now had to live from the money she had inherited. So I was given over to the already mentioned Berli. This Berli, a man without means, who was able to nourish himself only by constant bankruptcy, owed my father money, how much I didn't know. This debt was canceled, since for two years I lived in his house as shoeshiner, stable boy, hunting dog, and nursery maid. In the process, I was so filled with fear that I was more afraid of my guardian than of death itself.

My uncle in Ichenhausen was, to be sure, an honest and upright man, but it was his flaw to place too much faith in Berli and to trust him more than he deserved. Whatever he said had to happen, since he was able to disguise his dishonest intentions in such a way that one never found him out. And it also mattered a good deal that Berli's wife was my uncle's own sister. So they had to close an eye to his doings.

Since the future also had to be provided for—someday I should be able to earn my own keep—they harnessed me to the peddler's trade, as a young foal is harnessed to a cart. But I was not made for that.

An old but also good man (the father of Bernhard Levi) took me into his business. They bought me buttons, eye glasses, big and small mirrors, and other notions of that sort. With them I was to learn how to peddle. But the first time I set out with these new goods I broke one of the biggest mirrors. I did not know how to handle it properly. This was an omen that I would never like peddling. It stirred nothing but aversion in me.

Finally, they placed me as a porter with a man who took long trips. He carried on his business in the area of Lake Constance. I traveled with him for four weeks on a single trip, but could no longer go back home, because this man, with whom I was traveling, was, to be sure, not unjust, but his means were limited and as a result he was very frugal. The meals I got from him on the road were very slight and coarse, and I was not used to that. When I finally returned home, with great toil and completely exhausted, my mother, who was still alive at the time, began to cry and was horrified at my pale face and miserable appearance.

I finally accustomed myself a bit more to this abuse, went with the man on trips and envied the ones who were able to carry a heavy load, since I believed that my sole fortune lay therein. For then no one would be able to reproach me any longer with being useless in life. That is how greatly and deeply an underage boy with no parents can be humiliated by unscrupulous people with hearts of stone. I, the son of a noble-minded father, who had been taught only beautiful, lofty thoughts, was forced to lend myself to the most ignoble business.

About a year after my father's death, my second sister also married and settled in Ichenhausen. And also my third sister matured and became a lovely, refined, and very virtuous girl, who after my mother's death was taken into Berli's home as a servant.

My otherwise good, pious, and worthy sister was, so to speak, the sole, innocent cause of all my misery. For Bernhard Levi (that is what I will call him from now on) had a brother, and he courted my sister. But where was he to settle? He had no home of his own, and according to the laws decreed at that time by Schwarzenberg, the prince under whose protection we were then living, no one was permitted to marry who did not own a home. For that reason, homes were very expensive, sometimes selling for 1,200 to 1,300 or 1,400 florins. This far surpassed the means of my future brother-in-law. Some way had to be found to send me from my hometown. The plan was hatched. When my uncle came from Ichenhausen, they went to the higher court in Illereichen and pointed out that I was still very young and without ado wanted to turn my house over to my sister. They even took me, an underage boy, to the court. The judges were biased in favor of my brother-in-law. The report was sent to Prince Schwarzenberg in Vienna. Not long afterward, permission was issued to grant my brother-in-law special status, and the marriage procedures began.

Now their prime thought was to send me from my hometown. I had to hike to my uncle in Ichenhausen, where I would most likely also have to pay board. For my capital could not have simply disappeared.

I spent one and a half years in that house. With good intention and to spare others, I will skip over this period in silence. Only because it is absolutely necessary for the narration of my later life will I mention the fact that in this home I learned what it means to be nothing but a slave. One word from my uncle or from his wife and out of fright and fear I would have run through hell. It is most likely that if I had been forced to pass another half-year with this stingy woman, I would have been worn down by sorrow, hunger, chills, fever, and excess burdens. [. . .]

My uncle hired me out as a servant for very little pay to a man named Eli Hirsch. He was a good man, but his means were very limited. I felt as though I had been delivered from hell and transported to paradise, for now no caustic and offensive words were aimed at me, and I ate normal food. When my uncle arranged my pay and working conditions on my behalf, he even said to him: "I know that you are partial to learning scriptures. So this boy is all the more suited since he also has a gift for Torah study."

He [Hirsch] was a very religious and God-fearing man. He studied diligently, but his knowledge was meager. When he saw that I was far beyond him his joy was boundless. Every morning when I was at home I had to study Torah with him. On the Sabbath, when he was not sleeping I was busy studying with him. When he now saw that I had acquired no little Jewish learning, he felt guilty for having me with him as a miserable peddler of no means at all. Once he asked me why I did not pursue my Torah studies further and if I were not inclined toward it. And when I answered that I would like to but that my uncle did not allow it, he said: "Just wait! I will see to it that your uncle is persuaded. It would be irresponsible to neglect such natural talent."

With that, he went to my uncle, and took along some distinguished men who were convinced of my desire to study. They described all kinds of possibilities to him, for they would have claimed it as their merit if they had been behind a young person's Torah education. And happy I would have been if they had prevailed with their plan. But my uncle remained pitiless: "I don't want to squander what little money the boy has in such a way. Torah study costs a great deal. He should, and will, become a businessman." And that is where matters remained. I was a wandering peddler. Every week I went with my bundle on my back to Dornstadt, Tomerdingen, and Westerstetten. These places lie two and three hours south of Ulm on Stuttgart Road. They belonged to the Elchlingen monastery, and my employer had permission to send a helper there with goods. He himself did, in fact, have his business acquaintances in this domain, but only on this side of the Danube, in Klein-Pohlheim and Gross-Pohlheim, in Neringen, Laibenstraus, Dihlfingen, and Elchlingen.

I staggered on in this most degrading condition for two years, and saw nothing ahead that could have been useful or advantageous for my future. Instead, I remained a wretched pack-bearer and hawker to peasants.

*[Thannhäuser's next employer is Bernhard Levi in Illereichen.]*

My uncle Isak Seligmann, who likewise was a poor man, lived in Altenstadt. He took merchandise from Bernhard Levi on credit and went on little trips with it. I had to go along, carrying heavy burdens after him and staying always in off-limits areas, where mostly I had to sit in the public houses and wait for him to return. I myself could undertake nothing at all. Because of the strict prohibition, one did not dare, for one would have risked losing the goods one had along. Oh, how often in such tedious hours did I regret leaving Ichenhausen. But now there was nothing I could do.

Finally, the two of them, Bernhard Levi and Isak Seligmann, parted ways. The latter could not keep up payment and always owed the former a balance. But how could it be otherwise? His goods were priced too high, since Levi himself had to accept everything at the highest price. So his profit was small, his costs high, and Seligmann had to stay in arrears. Business with Seligmann was stopped. Since at that time the Frankfurt fair still was not covered, Bernhard Levi gave me a batch of high-priced old-fashioned goods that had gone out of style. I was supposed to sell them for cash, and only cash, in order to start up a new fraudulent business in Frankfurt. I was left to myself, and could travel to wherever I wished, but nowhere could I show myself openly with my goods. I made trips, visited the fair in Munich, too, took in a little money, and for that they showed satisfaction with me. But only in order to ensnare me still more.

Around the year 1793, Bernhard Levi traveled in the fall to the fair in Frankfurt am Main, secured credit there, and brought home goods, but everything one-third more expensive than normal. For such buyers must always take what others do not want, and at a tremendous price.

Now the period of my adverse fate really began. I was given a load of goods that I had to send by transport or take along with extra help to get it from place to place. This occasioned high costs. There could be no thought of profit since other dealers sold the goods at less than what I had paid for them. I was always hearing: "Just take in cash, even if there is no profit." Naturally, a large loss resulted that way. If, for example, I journeyed to the fair in Munich, no matter how much I skimped I still had 50 florins in expenses, since in those days the Bavarian customs added such high costs to the goods. There was no profit to be made from my wares. When I returned home from a trip they took the money I had earned and said nothing. But even this silence displeased me since I expected nothing good from it. I often lamented my circumstances to Bernhard, but I was always fed with hopes of a better future.

*[Feeling cheated by Bernhard Levi, in 1793 Thannhäuser starts a business of his own.]*

Now it was a question of what I should do, and the answer was that I should go into business for myself. From my capital I was given 100 florins, not all of it in ready cash but about 30 florins in liquid or half-forfeited debts that my deceased father was to have collected. I was left to stagger on in the wide world. Nowhere did I have a secure, legal abode. I had to buy on credit; for 70 florins one can buy a small stock of goods with which one can travel. When I was at home, I had to spend 26 crowns daily on weekdays for board, on holidays 36 crowns, however. I was heavily burdened, but still I would have scraped through if, for the first time, the French had not then entered the country. But even three months before their arrival anyone without acquaintances in the vicinity could earn nothing, since rumors of the Condé Corps were spreading frightfully and oppressively.[3]

Here is the story:

When the revolution in Paris had reached its height, that is, when they guillotined King Louis XVI—a prince from the royal house of Bourbon, Prince Condé, set out across the Rhine with a large army. He joined with the Austrians and with the army of the Reich (at that time, every Reichsgraf and every monastery had to supply a number of soldiers to the contingent in order to form a special army), and camped for a long time on the bank of the Rhine. Finally, the French were victorious; they beat back all three armies, that is, the Austrians, the Condé Corps, and the army of the Reich. Then it was rumored that the Condé Corps was destroying everything wherever it went, that they were robbing, burning down whatever and murdering whoever fell into their hands. It was said for a while that home reserves would be mustered and would put up a fight against them. So many tales were being told about them that everyone was scared.

Finally, one day in July, at two in the morning, a messenger from Balzheim came over to the high bailiff's office in Illereichen with the news that one had to join the home reserves immediately. He said that the Condé Corps had set out and was plundering, murdering, robbing, ravishing, and laying waste everywhere. The march was hastily arranged and at one o'clock High Bailiff Kolb and Revenue Director Dirner came riding up with a few hundred men from the town. Then we heard: "Jews, allons! You've got to come too!" Most of the single men did go along. With pitchforks, shovels, hoes, pikes, and whatever else one could get one's hands on in a hurry. And so we reached the linden tree on the road near Jedesheim. Then a rider came up from behind us and called out "Halt!" We halted, the rider came closer, and finally he said: "Go back, go back! It's all called off."

We went home as happily as if we had conquered whole countries. The peculiar thing about this was that on just that day the same terror spread throughout the length and breadth of the country. Everyone set out and was on the march for an hour, without knowing where they were to go. And they were all immediately called back again. It was a mystery.

Two weeks later the news came from the Rhine that the French had crossed over and attacked the three armies. They all took flight and the Condé Corps really did enter our country, but they harmed no one. That was when the army of the Reich was completely disbanded. It was surrounded by the Imperial troops and the Condé Corps. Their weapons were taken from them and they were sent home like beggar boys. What great honor!

I had already been living for four to five months without having earned a heller. Thus, of the 100 florins I had received, which now were worth only 80, nothing remained. I complained to my uncle. Finally, they again gave me 150 florins, but that was all that I got from my inheritance, aside from my books, my seats in the synagogue, and my house, which, as it turned out, they took from me for a third of its worth.

I was now thrown back on myself. I had no one in whom I could confide. My sister, though she was a capable woman, could not help me since her own financial means were very middling. I wandered about aimlessly, without purpose and abandoned by all. Oh, how often did I cry the most bitter tears when I witnessed how members of other families conversed with each other and deeply sympathized with one another in joy and sorrow, how they helped and supported one another, while everyone treated me so indifferently, so insensitively, without feeling.

A few years passed in this way. I often thought that it would be best if I sought a wife so that I could have a friend to whom I could tell my concerns. But how could I support her? Nowhere did I have a lead that even in the toilsome peddling business could help me find a region where I could ply my trade without great hardships. When I set out on the road, tears were often my companion. Oh, how often did I wonder what would become of me. What a bright future I had envisaged in my childhood, and what a sad life I must now lead! Oh, my good parents! You, who were kind to all. Oh, father! You, who supported the poor, consoled the widows, assisted the orphans—if you knew how others are treating me your spirit would rebel!

However, religion was again and again my consolation. I took refuge in God. I asked Him to show me a way that would provide me with a secure existence. And yet I was always diligent in my peddler's trade, fended for myself fairly well, and built up sales regions for myself in Grönenbach and its surroundings. Although I didn't have permission from the higher authorities, I was well acquainted with the lower officials, had the best of friendships among the burghers of Grönenbach, and now believed that I had come a step closer to my goal.

This, partly agreeable, time may have lasted about a year without any particular occurrences or adverse run-ins. In some months I saved a bit, and in others I lost what I had saved. Finally, fate played a trick on me, and this was the reason—as will be seen further on—that I left my hometown and settled in Fellheim.

At that time, Grönenbach belonged to the Kempten abbey, where there dwelled an ecclesiastical prince and twelve capitularies. To the townlet of Grönenbach there belonged a few other little towns that together formed a provost's district. One of the capitularies, the uncle of a deceased Baroness von Reichlin née von Welteki, was transferred to Grönenbach Castle as provost. And she recommended Gerstle as Court Jew. Suddenly that was the end of my circle of acquaintances there. All the burghers of Grönenbach were eager to get to know the Court Jew. The word was spread that cheap goods were to be had; wherever I went, it was said that I had commerce with the Court Jew. That gave me all the more reason to fear the police. I wandered about the area of Grönenbach, but with a frightened heart and without any business. So I was back at the beginning again and didn't know what to do.

I sometimes thought of taking on children for instruction, since I was capable enough at that time of being an excellent teacher, but in those days one was ashamed to be called *bocher* or *rebbe* (a married teacher) and, to my great disadvantage, the prevailing arrogance held me back.

Finally, a marriage plan grew out of the doings in Grönenbach. A local by the name of Gerschon bar Salomon came to my uncle Isak Seligmann and said: "Your nephew Isaac ought to marry Gerschon's daughter. After all, Grönenbach is his district."

This struck my uncle as a good idea, since he thought he would reap a nice reward from my brother-in-law David if he helped to remove me from Illereichen. He took this plan to my brother-in-law and my sister. Whom could it please more than them? They immediately began presenting the matter to me in a most attractive and advantageous light, first through my uncle Isak Seligmann, then through said Gerschon, and finally through my sister herself. First of all, they said, Gerschon is a very secure man (materially); second, Grönenbach will remain your district; third, Gerschon is an upright man with many friends; every Sunday he is sought out by many merchants; he'll give you a share (in his frauds!); fourth, his daughter is able and honest, she served long in other homes (how I came to view this, I'll be kind enough to pass over in silence); fifth, you'll get a nice little house, a wooden cabin, and besides that 200 florins in cash. Your brother-in-law will help you outfit your house. The whole thing will cost you little.

As a young man still unfamiliar with tricks and subtle ruses, who believed that all people were of noble mind, as I was toward all others, I found nothing more impossible than for someone to mislead his own brother for selfish reasons; I, who was accustomed only to obeying others' commands, accepted this plan, promising that I would carefully look into it.

First, I went to my cousin Rebecka Bacher, who had been married for about a year. The young, inexperienced woman advised me not to pass up the match, and she praised Gerschon highly (perhaps because she was inexperienced, perhaps in order to have a blood relative nearby). I had a look at the little house and found that it was not much to my liking. I struck up a conversation with my prospective bride but found her to lack Delilah's powers of persuasion. But since one does not need women as Privy Councilors, I would have paid less mind to this and it would have frightened me off less than the miserable, shabby little house.

So I was hesitant about a match of this sort and really began to waver. Besides that, there lived in Altenstadt a most worthy man named Moses Hirber, who had a beautiful girl named Beila. I liked her and her father would have deemed himself lucky to have me as a son-in-law. He did business in Oberbalzheim and Unterbalzheim. He would have assigned me a district and given me shares, and I had already decided to go ahead with this match.

But when my brother-in-law and sister found this out, the storm broke loose. They saw so many disadvantages in the union that anyone would have been scared off. "You want to marry a girl like her, a girl with swollen feet?" said my sister. If I hadn't been so gullible and trusted my sister so much, I should have asked her: "Have you already inspected her feet?" But I was too much of a fool, with too much regard for family, and I started to grow disinclined.

But to ensure that in the end I might not decide on this match despite all, my brother-in-law summoned my sister from Ichenhausen. They won her over (how, I don't know), and she used all of her persuasive powers, brought her decisions to bear as those of the eldest sister, and she either convinced me or so benumbed me that I agreed to the match in Fellheim.

My uncle came to Altenstadt in November 5538 (1797). From there, he, my brother-in-law David, and I went to Fellheim and paid the *knes*.[4] For my part, I promised to pay 600 florins in cash and goods. My father-in-law gave me half of the little house that I now own, and the other half was rented. In the eight years that the house was rented he took in 200 florins, and that, along with a wooden hut, is what he gave me as my marriage portion. But I didn't own a stick of furniture, nor did I have much in the way of linens. Since my father-in-law had been (untruthfully) described to me as a caring parent, I entrusted him with acquiring all that I needed on credit, both utensils and beds. The bill ran high. I would have paid less and gotten better wares if I had bought from strangers. In short, he didn't pass up his chance.

A great deal of my money was used up. Everything hit me, and according to my guardians I owned only my own house, my Torah scroll, my books, and my seats in the synagogue. I demanded my father's account book and, in general, a complete reckoning. But they granted me nothing. At that time, I was still too inexperienced and too timid to complain. But that wasn't all. Out of excessive brotherly love and bad calculation—to my shame, I must admit it—I let my relatives in Ichenhausen and Altenstadt have my house for 400 florins, although at that time it would have been worth at least 1,000 florins. On top of that, I had already given my sister books for 20 florins. I still had 400 florins. I sold a few stands for 100 florins, and perhaps I owned about another 50 florins in other possessions. But by the time I was married, at least 400 florins of that were spent. Counting the 200 florins I received as a dowry, I had something more than 300 florins left, and from that I was supposed to live.

But before I continue my story I must add here that during the year when I was engaged I had nothing but troubles. I had no liking for Fellheim, nor for my father-in-law, nor for my betrothed. If my conscience had not told me that one must not shame a Jewish daughter, and if also I didn't have to keep in mind the district of Grönenbach, without which I wouldn't have known where to turn, and if I would not have had to pay a *knes* of 200 florins to dissolve the engagement, I certainly would have called it off.

My trip to Fellheim made me so happy that I would have been just as glad if someone had shot me. But time and habit make everything bearable, and so it was with me too. My wedding took place in November 5559 (1798). Lots of people came, from Illereichen, Ichenhausen, Binswangen, and Schöpfheim. They were all cheery, all in a good mood. Only I was not.

I would have gladly changed places with a galley slave. I liked neither Fellheim, nor its inhabitants, nor their customs (at that time, state laws hadn't yet been introduced). Perhaps I disliked all that because I was loath to leave my hometown, or because the people there really did practice many abuses that others elsewhere took no note of, or maybe because my parents-in-law were most vulgar and repulsive people.

As far as my young marriage is concerned, at the beginning I did everything merely out of duty. There was no thought of true, tender love. Oh, how sad it is for a young man to be married and neither love nor be loved in return. What negative effects such a life must have on one's health. But was anything else possible?

It had been purported to me that my wife could read the Hebrew prayers and, in general, read well; also, that she could write a bit. But, oh, how lacking I found her to be! They told me what a good housekeeper she was. Oh, how poorly she kept house! They told me that she was sensible. But, oh, how dumb she was! They told me that she was kind and gentle. But, oh, how stubborn, and, upset over trifles! She could (and still can) start the worst squabble and then sulk for three, four, five, or six days, and even longer. If she then starts talking again, new disputes spring up. To be sure, I had recognized many of these flaws already during the engagement, and that's why I was so hesitant to marry; but I blamed much of it on her shyness. I was, however, mistaken.

Right after my marriage, my father-in-law and brother-in-law Raphael repeatedly reproached me for the expenses my many wedding guests had caused them. In keeping with the marriage contract I had paid 33 florins as a contribution and, for the rest, they had to feed everyone. My wife began to pay a bit more heed to my wishes, and I began to find her whims more bearable. Gradually I was becoming used to them. And besides, she was pregnant. Little by little, love began to nestle in my heart, and I also gladly granted her, too, a cozy corner therein. Thus a year passed quite tolerably, even if now and then there were many unpleasantries.

As for my business, at that time the Austrians were once more fighting the French on the shore of the Rhine; there were large supplies transactions; many companies were formed; rich and poor earned lots of money. On the advice of my brother-in-law David, who lived in Altenstadt, I also tried to get a business partner, but I was new in these parts and therefore wanted to turn to my father-in-law. But he was a stupid, headstrong person, who preferred to concern himself with the deals of his boss, Gerstle, and who seemed to gain greater pleasure and advantage from buying stolen goods than he did from any other commerce. He wanted no part of it. I had no other choice but to work alone. I bought spelt, something that I could get in my district. But that was not the right region for selling much of this product. Nevertheless, every week I managed to earn 12, 15, and up to 20 florins. But, in the process, I had more unpleasant experiences and bad luck than anyone ever.

Here is a short description of how much nastiness I experienced within a single week: One Monday or Tuesday, when I was on the way to Grönenbach, I met in Memmingen a man from Ottobeuren who offered me hay—which at that time was much in demand. I bought twenty hundredweight from him, contracted in writing for him to bring it to Memmingen by nine o'clock on Thursday morning, gave him a laubtaler[5] as a pledge, and sold the hay straight off to Leyser Wolf (may he rest in peace), and would have profitted 12 to 15 florins from the deal. Then I went to Grönenbach and bought some spelt there and in the area. On Thursday morning I went to Memmingen for the hay, which already hurt me because I could have bought still more spelt. The weather was bad. I waited in Memmingen until ten o'clock, but no hay arrived. I walked toward Calves Gate to see whether anything was on the way. Finally, the man from whom I had bought the hay came running up and said that it was forbidden to sell hay in the Ottobeuren domain, and he returned my taler. I could not call the man to account; all I could do was go to Leyser Wolf and tell him that I was getting no hay. I had to deem it an act of kindness that he let me off. I went back to Grönenbach, got wet through and through since it was pouring rain, bought a bit more spelt, and had all I had bought transported to Zell because I had already engaged a carter there who was to drive the spelt to Memmingen. But when I arrived in Zell my carter said that he couldn't haul anything to Memmingen since he had to transport something for Samuel ben Mose Bachrach. I looked for another carter but couldn't get one, and I had promised to deliver by Friday. Finally, Betsch, the *goi* with whom I was sharing a room, said that he would drive me if I gave him a laubtaler. I had no other choice, gave him a laubtaler, and he drove me to Memmingen. When I reached the gate, the keeper stopped me and said: "This isn't the gate for Jews. You'll have to go through the Ulm Gate." At that time, Memmingen was still a Free Imperial City, every Jew had to pay a poll tax of 10 crowns daily, and Jews were allowed to enter only through Ulm Gate. I don't know what had gotten into the fellow, since otherwise he always let me through. "My wagon has gone ahead," I said; "I've got a delivery of Imperial grain here," and I wanted to run off. At that, he took hold of me, and a miserable sentry from the sentry booth jumped to his side and tried to hit me with his (probably unloaded) musket, which I easily pushed aside. I had to retreat, but by no means was I allowed to enter. I quickly ran to Lindau Gate, entered unchallenged, and looked for my wagon. The carter asked me complainingly where I had been so long, and said that the farmer for whom he worked had ordered him to return soon. I had my spelt brought into the granary so that it could be delivered to Hirsch Löwenstein from Altenstadt. In the middle of weighing he tried to cause me trouble, and I put a halt to the weighing. At last, Raphael Landauer from Hürben arrived. He was happy to take the last of my spelt, and I can claim that despite all my troubles I earned 22 florins on my goods.

Meanwhile, the time of my wife's delivery was nearing. The fall Holy Days were approaching, too; I had only a few weeks in which to do business. I came home on Friday, Sunday was *Erew* Rosch Haschana,[6] and that evening my wife gave birth to my first son, Moses. The birth was painful, to be sure, but—thank God—both were and remained healthy. Only my savings suffered terribly. Backward Jewish customs cost an awful lot of money.[7] The *socher,*[8] the Jewish cook, the *bris milo,* the *pidion-haben,*[9] the Holy Days, the wasteful nurse. These things were already emptying my purse.

After the Holy Days I went out into the district. There was no longer much demand for spelt, but my modest door-to-door trade went fairly well until Purim drew near. Then one heard once again that the French had crossed the Rhine, and that gave rise to new lament. Business slowed down. Toward Schawuos they really did come. There was one scare after another. However, since they marched straight on toward Vienna, there was no danger—but also little to be earned. This took place around the year 1800.

Meanwhile, my capital was shrinking. In the spring of 1801 the French returned. One could earn something by buying their booty, but—fool that I was—I allowed myself to be frightened off when the two *parnassim,* Leyser Wolf and Moschele, told me no, and that really hurt me. Finally, when I saw that no one paid them any mind, I wanted to go through with it, but by then there was nothing left. [. . .]

In earlier times, I tried to find work with suppliers as a manager and received many promises from various people, but there were always all kinds of pretexts for shattering my hopes. I now reconciled myself to peddling and put all my energies into providing for my wife and children. But I constantly ran into adversity. I went out into the provinces with my brother-in-law Raphael. Fate was always kind to him, but it seemed to hate me. If ever a transaction turned up that yielded a profit, it happened always when I was not in the district.

Here is an example: In the desolate place of Ruckbols, a quarter-hour from Grönenbach, there lived a farmer who owed me 17 florins, but I was unable to get anything
from him. So I bought a cow from him in place of payment, gave half of it to David
bar Israel, and on Sunday morning we set out together to fetch the cow. It was nearly
winter and in the forenoon the ground had frozen. When we reached Waringen with
the cow after midday, I said to David: "Let's keep to the road and not take the footpath
with a cow as old as this." David said: "No, this way we'll save a quarter-hour." I
was used to giving in, and did so this time too. We walked down the footpath with
our old cow. And what happened? The weather became mild, and the ice melted. In
many spots the marsh on which we were walking was covered with water. There was
a beam stretching across, but it was too narrow for a cow. We had to lead my old cow
through the water and, God help us, it got stuck. There I stood and didn't know which
way to turn and what to do. Finally, we decided that David should hurry to Dickenreis,
which lay about a quarter-hour ahead. After a long while, David finally returned with
a peasant and a horse, and the peasant helped us pull the cow out of the swamp. I
paid the peasant, plodded on with the cow, and reached Memmingen at nightfall. I
had to leave the cow overnight with the "sconcemaster" at Kempten Gate. But I went
home. David began haggling with me, and I had to set his share of the cow at 12
florins because I was unable to turn the deal alone. We fetched the cow on Monday,
slaughtered it, and it was made kosher.


*[End of the fragment]*


1. Salomon ben Isaak Raschi (1040–1105) is the most important Jewish Bible and Talmud
commentator. His works were also used in the instruction of children. (Translators' note: There
is no English equivalent that would adequately render the multiple nuances of the German verb
*lernen* in its Jewish cultural-religious context. We have translated it variously as "to study Torah,"
"to study the Law," "to study scriptures," or, where the meaning is clear, simply as "to study.")
2. Seats in the synagogue were sold in order to finance its building. Thus, they could be
bequeathed and resold.
3. This was the émigré corps of Prince Louis Josephe de Condé (1736–1818), who left
France in 1789 and on the Rhine assembled a corps of émigrés that fought on the Austrian and
Russian side against the French Republic until 1801.
4. A penalty, the amount of which was set down in the engagement contract, in the event
that the engagement was dissolved. In addition, the contract always stipulated exactly the amount
of the dowry.
5. Designation for the French ecu d'argent of the eighteenth century; it was very current
in Germany.
6. The New Year festival began on Sunday evening.
7. In the manner of the Jewish Enlighteners, Thannhäuser describes certain Jewish customs—in this instance, that relating to the birth of the first son—as "backward."
8. Merchant (Yiddish).
9. The symbolic redemption of the oldest son, who is regarded as a firstborn, dedicated
to God. The ceremony follows thirty days after the birth. *Bris milo* (circumcision); see Glossary.

# 4 *Hirsch Oppenheimer*

BORN IN 1805 IN GRONAU (HANNOVER); DIED IN 1883 IN HANNOVER.

Louis Oppenheimer, Biography of our Departed Father Hirsch Oppenheimer.
Hannover, 1922, 8 pages.

*Oppenheimer's son Louis (born in 1854) describes the rise of his father from a poor
country Jew to a banker. Hirsch Oppenheimer started out in Gronau as a retailer
and then began trading in secondhand goods and farm goods. Around 1840 he was
commissioned by the Hannover government with the local representation of two state
enterprises, a foundry and an ironworks. He laid the foundation for his fortune after
the Hamburg fire of 1842 by buying up great quantities of molten metal. Soon he
was active in the area around Gronau as an insurance agent and provincial banker.
In 1848 he served the government by using his prominence to check the revolutionary
unrest in Gronau. Religiously orthodox, he fulfilled the office of Mohel throughout his
life. In 1867, he moved as a banker to Hannover, where once again he assumed
various honorary posts in the Jewish community.*

Our grandfather, Israel Oppenheimer, lived in Gronau on Leine—starting
when, I don't know—and was married to Zipora, née Samson. He died in January 1813
as a result of an accident while crossing the frozen Leine, which was covered by snow,
and he lies buried in Rössing. He left behind six children. [. . .] According to a record
at my disposal, dated June 25, 1813 in the county court in Gronau, which at that time
belonged to the Kingdom of Westphalia under Jerome Napoleon, our grandmother
assumed guardianship with the assistance of a coguardian, Michael Freudental of Bod-
enfelde, and a friend of the family, Municipal Councilor Tenne of Gronau. At this time,
the aforementioned prince issued the order that all Jews in his domain should take
German names in place of their previous ones, which were modeled after their fathers'
names, such as Jacobsohn, Isaaksohn, etc. Thus our grandfather named himself Oppenheimer, while his two brothers called themselves Rothschild and Sternberg.

A few years later, my grandmother married her second husband, Mendel Elb, and
shortly after this marriage our departed father was sent to *cheder*[1] in Wunstdorf, where
he lived as a boarder until his Bar Mizwa. He was supposed to celebrate this religious
rite at home. According to his own tales, which he told us often enough, he received
from his stepfather as a present *one taler,* and with this money he was to establish his
business and livelihood.

And so on Sunday morning he went on foot to Hannover and with his fortune of
one taler he bought himself some small wares with which he then did business in the
area of Gronau, where he knew every one and every one knew him, and in a few days
he had earned with his taler one taler or more.

In this way, and since on his journeys he had no expenses—he was willingly and
gladly received for the night by his customers and acquaintances—he kept increasing
his working capital and soon was able to buy bigger and better wares and thus earn
more. But despite all the hardships he had to endure while earning his living, he used

every free minute to improve his education and, by his conduct, to gain the respect and affection of all of his acquaintances, friends, and customers, so that soon he was able to establish closer ties with the most respected circles and authorities in Gronau and, when his fortune had increased sufficiently, to open a store for the public in his hometown.

In 1829 he was sworn in as a citizen of the city of Gronau, a position which at that time greatly honored him as a Jew and for which he had to pay a fee of 3 talers and some 20 groschen.

In 1833, he became engaged to Johanne, née Enoch, born on March 26, 1811 in Celle, and on October 20, 1833 his future wife and any children they might have were also granted citizenship. In the following year, 1834, our father married and received a dowry of 300 louis d'ors and a trousseau of 100 louis d'ors, which for conditions in those days was quite a lot. His father-in-law, Wolf Samuel Enoch, had a candle and soap factory in the same town. His wife's maiden name was Herz.

With our mother a more joyful, better, and happier life began for him, and the business also improved visibly. In addition to his small mercantile undertakings, he began buying and selling metals, bones, glass, and pig's hair, and later also grain and wool, and in all these dealings my mother helped him devotedly.

His thoroughly upright behavior in every respect soon gained him the affection of the authorities, and very often he was consulted by them in important deliberations. When the royal government of Hannover (King Ernst August) started the two mining and ironworks, Georg-Marienhütte and Eisenwerk Carlshütte, father was entrusted by the then county bailiff von Bothmer with the representation of both companies in Gronau, which gained him an entirely new type of customer. The former company made iron of all kinds for locksmiths and smithies, the latter iron stoves and articles of cast iron. Thus his position in the locality was strengthened anew, so that soon the entire area of Gronau regarded him as a savings bank and advisor and followed his recommendations in every way.

While, despite all, father's business still had to be called small, in 1842 an event took place that was to increase his fortune considerably, but which also testified to a spirit of enterprise and energy on a grand scale. In those days there were already newspapers, and in one such he had read that in Hamburg an entire section of the city had been destroyed, that big storehouses with metals of all kinds had burnt out, and that the latter supposedly were towering above the ruins in the form of a large metal mass. Without hesitation he tried to borrow the liquid capital of the authorities in Gronau, and he rode to Hamburg, where he had a brother-in-law, Samuel Enoch, in order personally to learn the facts concerning these metals. Uncle Samuel advised him against such an undertaking, since even the Hamburg wholesalers did not dare to purchase, but he looked at the things and, as there was no competition, bought the entire mass for a very low price.

Then he borrowed huge ship's cranes in Hamburg, had them erected over the mass, hired many workers and had ditches dug crisscross below the mass, and had fires made in them through which the metals slowly melted apart. The iron chunks fell aside, while the lead, copper, tin, and zinc were collected in the ditches.

Meanwhile, he himself rode to the directors of the Georg-Marienhütte and the ironworks Carlshütte, sold them all of the iron, on his way back stopped in Gronau, had all the available wagons drive to Hamburg, had them loaded there, and had some drive to Osnabrück and others directly to Delligsen to deliver the iron. At the same time, he also sold the remaining metal to Hamburg firms, and with that he laid the foundation for his considerable fortune. A fews years later, he made a similar business deal when he purchased a Danish warship stranded near Geestemünde, which he, together with a firm in Bremen, salvaged with the help of divers.

Later he also became the representative of the Aachen and Munich fire insurance and the Aachen hail insurance companies, which brought him as clients all of the big landowners and the peasant population of the environs of Gronau, and these, too, soon listened to him and followed his advice without question.

The best proof of the confidence from which he benefited came in the year of the 1848 Revolution. As the insurrection expanded throughout our fatherland, the Revolution also broke out in the kingdom of Hannover and especially in the bailiwick of Hildesheim, and soon it spread to Gronau. The authorities and the municipal council gathered in the school located on the market square in order to discuss the necessary steps against the rebellious citizens who were making a racket on the large square, but could not arrive at any results. Then father offered to negotiate all alone with the crowd and to quiet it down. The authorities considered this risk too dangerous and did not want to endanger his life, but they allowed themselves to be influenced by his self-assured manner, and thus he went alone to the crowd and said to them, according to his own story: "Citizens, friends! You are making such a racket here and you want a revolution!" General agreement! "You probably don't even know what that means, but you do know that I have your well-being at heart, and I therefore advise you to disperse and go home, and remain calm. If you wish to change the existing ordinances, elect a commission, which should come to me tomorrow and with which I will go to the mayor. I promise you that everything possible will be done. But if you don't do that and you cause unrest and the like, then you ought to know that everything will be ruined, and I too, and therewith naturally you will be also, since your money is in my keeping. So, once more: do what I advise." Again, great approval and the cry "Long live Hirsch Oppenheimer!" And after that the whole revolution ended.

On the next morning the elected commission did appear and demanded that the workers of the neighboring village, Barfeld, who had been granted the right to fell trees in the Gronau forest not be allowed to do that in the future and that this work be consigned to local workers, and a few more such trifles. Naturally, all that was granted, the revolution in Gronau taken care of, and a new page was written into the history of our father's honor. [. . .]

In 1865 our parents decided to move their residence and business to Hannover. I have in my possession a certificate of the municipal council of Gronau about it, which I want to reproduce literally as a remembrance and as a model for members of the family:

"We certify herewith upon the request of Herr Banker Oppenheimer that during his residence of many years and his long conduct of business he has behaved in every respect in such a manner that he must be regarded among the best citizens of this city, as concerns both his honesty in the most diverse business enterprises and the treatment of the people with whom he has had business dealings. The result of Herr Banker Hirsch Oppenheimer's diligence is that his family is among the wealthiest of this city and, judging by all circumstances, it is to be assumed that he has acquired a considerable fortune.

"We issue this certificate with the additional comment that we are reluctant to see Herr Banker Hirsch Oppenheimer and his family depart from our midst, in which he associated with the most respectable families. Gronau, April 23, 1865. The Municipal Council."

At that time, however, the plan to leave Gronau was postponed and, for the time being, was dropped, due to the war with Prussia, which broke out in 1866 and was lost. But the plan was carried out in 1868. Israel and William, however, still remained in Gronau with the business until the year 1872/73. But then they opened a bank below the old firm in Hannover, in which, from 1873 until 1878, I was also active.

Father had scarcely taken root in Hannover when there, too, he was entrusted with honorary offices and carried these out in his usual sure and selfless manner, so that he was soon just as honored and beloved in Hannover as he had been in his native town.

1. Literally "room"; Hebrew designation for a one-room Jewish elementary school attended by boys until the age of thirteen.

# 5   *Eduard Silbermann*

BORN IN 1851 IN KOLMSDORF (UPPER FRANCONIA).

Eduard Silbermann, Memoirs, 1871–1917. Munich, 1916, 252 pages.

*As son of a trained clothmaker, who had a dry-goods business in the country, Eduard Silbermann grew up near Bamberg in the Franconian village of Bischberg, where one fifth of the population was Jewish. His well-to-do family was also engaged in some farming and hops-growing. Silbermann depicts the course of the Jewish year in the orthodox community, and the neighborly relations between Jewish and Christian inhabitants of the village. When the Jews of Bavaria finally received the right of free movement in 1861, the family moved to Bamberg, where Silbermann had a brilliant career as a Gymnasium pupil and at his graduation in 1871 received the gold prize medal of the Minister of Culture. Later he studied law and in 1879 became the first Jewish prosecuting attorney in Germany. He held office as president of the Senate of the Higher Regional Court in Munich.*

About a year and a half after my birth, in October 1852, my parents moved to the village of Bischberg, which was about an hour and a half from Kolmsdorf and an hour from Bamberg. Here my father's clothmaking trade gradually turned into a dry-goods business. Since the population of the village and its environs consisted predominantly of farmers and peasants, who had little time to do their shopping on weekdays, the store business was carried on mainly on Sundays and Christian holidays. On Sabbaths and Jewish holidays my father always closed the store.

Of course, my father did not spend the weekdays idly. He looked up his customers in the surrounding villages, took orders for goods, and also brought merchandise to their homes. In present-day legal terminology, such business activity would be designated as "door-to-door sales" or "traveling sales trade." However, this manner of commerce was in no way degrading in those days, when despite the 1848 Revolution the energies of the Jewish population were still repressed in every way. All of our coreligionists who did not succeed in establishing legal residence in a larger city and who lived in the country, perforce or by choice, were dependent on retail trade and peddling if they were to sustain themselves at all.

Besides my father's business, farming also brought in something, and even if it was not much, at least it was enough to supply a large part of our required minimum of grain, potatoes, and fruit. He also owned a small hop field. This was one of his favorite spots. It was also extremely profitable. I know that it was sold by my father in the fifties for 70 gulden (120 marks). The yield in hops was, on the average, 50 kilograms, that is, one centner a year. Depending on the price of hops, which fluctuated in different years between 5 and 500 marks per centner, the profit was a more or a less satisfactory one. On the average, one could count on a profit of 50 to 60 marks a year. I still remember that in 1860 or 1861 my father earned the sum of 100 crowns for one centner of hops reaped from this field (1 crown is 2 guldens or 42 kreutzers, or 4.62 marks), thus *462 marks.*

My father did most of the farming himself. He worked hard with hoe and spade. Even today I see in my mind's eye how my father, returning tired from his business errands and after a small refreshment, went to the field with a hoe on his shoulder, often accompanied by one or several of the boys. We made ourselves useful by pulling out weeds and such. "Hard at work, Herr Silbermann," greeted the neighbors, who regarded the Jew with a certain respect.

Participating in the field work at harvest time was something we especially welcomed. To be sure, gathering ears of grain behind the women reapers during the heat of summer was in itself no great pleasure, but the prospect of being allowed to partake of the afternoon repast and to drink beer with the women reapers did offer a small compensation for the effort, especially in light of our rather modest demands.

Proudly we brothers sat on the returning ox-carts, stared at by our Jewish comrades, who hurled at us the title "peasant boys," which they regarded as a derogatory term, while we felt that it honored us. Once an old Israelite called after me: "The *scheketz* (Christian boy), he's not even wearing a cap!" Orthodox Jews always had their heads covered. [. . .]

In Bischberg there had long existed a Jewish community, which basically shared the fate of the other Jews in the Princely Bishopric of Bamberg. On the whole, the Jews were not subjected to such severe oppression in the territories under ecclesiastical jurisdiction as in the secular ones, even if in the former they were not always bedded on roses. In the Princely Bishopric of Bamberg, for the most part they were also treated with leniency.

In 1803 the Princely Bishopric and its some 1,500 Jewish families were annexed to the crown of Bavaria. The Jews gradually became citizens, even if second-class ones. The Edict on the Jews of June 10, 1813, which in part is still valid today [1916], was definitive in regard to their legal position.[1] To characterize the preconstitutional law, I am including verbatim a few of its provisions:

2. Entry in the Jewish registry, to be drawn up by our police authorities, is required in order to enjoy the rights and privileges granted in this edict.

11. All immigration and domicile [of foreign Jews] in the Kingdom is absolutely forbidden.

12. The number of Jewish families in those places where they do exist at present may not, as a rule, be increased; rather, it shall be gradually decreased if it is too high.

Basically, then, the edict aims at the gradual elimination of the Jewish population as such. On the other hand, it cannot be ignored that the edict also contains provisions favorable to the development of the Jewish population. To be mentioned here are: the obligation to assume family names; prohibition of huckstering and peddlery; permission to engage in farming, trades, operation of factories, and proper business (with certain limitations, of course); dissolution of the "Jewish organizations" and the assignment of the Jewish population to political communities; protection of freedom of conscience; and creation of legal bases for religious institutions.

Since neither the existing general laws nor even less the Edict on the Jews granted the free development of economic and other strengths and talents, there gradually began an emigration of Jews from Bavaria, whose destination was mainly North America. There are probably few Jewish families in Bavaria from which no member emigrated. Our extended and immediate family, too, provided a fairly large number of emigrants. These emigrants, in many instances, gained great wealth, reputation, and honor abroad. For them, it was fortunate that in place of the old fatherland, which treated them as second- and third-class citizens, they acquired a fatherland that saw in them the free human being.

Still, the emigrants did not forget their old fatherland; they maintained their connections with it, visited it, and donated money to it. In the World War their sympathy is on the side of Germany.

After these not entirely superfluous digressions, I will return to the Jewish population of our village. In the 1850s, Bischberg had quite a large Jewish population: among a total population of some 700 to 800 souls there were approximately 35 to 40 Jewish families with at least 150 souls. The Christian population made its living primarily from farming, while the Jewish family heads were partly engaged in business of every kind, and partly practiced trades. Farming, even if only as a secondary undertaking, was pursued by a few.

During my youth there were four Jewish butchers, a shoemaker, a tailor, a glazier, and a soap-boiler in Bischberg. The Jewish population had not attained great riches, but there existed among them a kind of prosperity. To be sure, in those days people with assets of some 30,000 guldens (about 50,000 marks) were already considered wealthy. I know of perhaps three such families from my youth. Two of them happened to have the name Goldmann.

At the beginning, my parents did not yet belong to this class of *kozinim* (the rich). Gradually, however, by the end of the fifties, they did become prosperous, yet—since in their behavior they avoided any display of wealth—they were not regarded officially by the Jewish population as belonging among the *kozinim*.

On the whole, the Jewish population lived in peace with the Christians. Above all, the Jews were not bothered or molested in their ritual practices and customs. At the time of the yearly church fair, the Christian families sent "fritters and fair bread" to Jewish homes, while we reciprocated at Passover by sending matzos, which were much-liked by the Christian population. In many Christian homes the superstition prevailed that the possession of a little piece of matzo protected them from lightning. As is well known, a piece of *afikomen*[2] is kept the entire year in orthodox Jewish homes. Perhaps this is the source of the superstition.

I still remember very clearly how on the evening of "Kol Nidre" the small synagogue was filled with Christian onlookers, who wanted to watch the Jews in *tallis* and burial shroud celebrating the "long day."[3]

Among the Christian population there were also at least five or six families that had converted to Christianity perhaps at the beginning of the last century, for example the families Kohn, Haupt, Zimmermann, and Christenmeyer. In all of them there still lived the memory of their origin. One, whose grandfather had been baptized, spoke the Jewish jargon—which in those days one could still often hear in the country—better than many real Jews. He often said to us Silbermann boys on the evening before the fast: "Boys, do you already have apples, grapes, and such for *Schechejune* (the blessing at the beginning of a year)? Come and get them at our place." I often heard an elderly woman from one of these families call out: *"Juched schemoh"* ("Blessed be His name," an exclamation similar to "Jesus, Mary, and Joseph" among the Christian population). One felt little or nothing of the often customary malice of renegades toward their former coreligionists. Many descendants of these families are now employed as workers and day laborers by Jewish businessmen in Bamberg. None of them achieved anything special.

Conversions to Christianity did not occur in Bischberg during my youth. The worst swearword in Jewish circles was *"meschummed."*[4] I remember that we children applied this designation to a Jewish boy—his father was a well-established master shoemaker—at times of disagreement. His godfather, a certain Moritz Hirsch of Bamberg, had been baptized in the fifties, a rare occurrence in Bamberg, too. Moritz—that was the boy's name—became so infuriated over this insult (he could not deny the fact of his godfather's baptism) that he was about to become violent, but we thwarted him by taking flight.

Naturally, any special socializing in such a small place was out of the question. Still, to the extent that it occurred, the Jews did not shut themselves off from the Christian population. Closer relations existed, of course, among the Jewish families. The Sabbaths and holidays—all of which were still strictly observed—brought the Jewish inhabitants together, not only in the synagogue but also in many instances in the individual families. Every family event brought them together, one event the children, another the adults. Especially for us children, for instance, the *"Holekrasch"* was a day of celebration. Some three to four weeks after the birth of a child, the Jewish children gathered in the home of the newborn. They placed themselves around the cradle and cried: "Holekrasch, Holekrasch, what will the baby be named?" The father or the mother of the child would then announce the name. Thereupon the children would lift up the cradle again and cry: "X shall be its name!"

With that the act of giving a name was completed. The attraction for us children was the distribution afterward of salted chickpeas, fruit, gingerbread, and such things that followed thereupon. On the origin of the term "Holekrasch" there exist the most varied interpretations. The designation could be distorted Hebrew, German, or French.[5] We children were not yet concerned about those kinds of etymological investigations, for us Holekrasch was always great fun. If the newborn child was a boy, then the Jewish women got together several days before the *bris milo* (circumcision) for the *Jidd'sche katz* (Jewish candle) at the home of the woman in childbed. While enjoying coffee and cake, they made the wax candle needed during the circumcision.

Thus, the *mizwo* (fulfillment of a religious law) at the same time provided the occasion for a kind of "coffee clatch." Bar Mitzvas, engagements, and weddings were occasions for visits and joyous gatherings. Death, too, brought the Jewish population together. The seven-day-long mourning period (*Schiwe*) was still strictly observed. Since the mourners were prevented from preparing food, their other coreligionists took this task upon themselves. Everyone sent food and treats according to their abilities, so that the mourners often were not able to exhaust the abundance of supplies.

Purim was a merry time. We children went from Jewish home to home in our masks. The disguise as a rule had to do with the story of Esther. Most of the time a short festival play was put on. Here, too, the main thing was receiving presents—fruit, cake, etc.—and money, too, was not spurned. Sometimes during the distribution of the latter there arose serious disagreements that ended in a genuine brawl. But very soon reconciliation took place.

One important holiday for us children was *Erew* Pessach (the day before Passover). After morning services, the children in the Jewish homes picked up the *gebaddelte chumez* (the leavened goods gathered the evening before).[6] The *chumez* was then burned sometime between nine and ten o'clock in the "Nickel," a wide ditch between two field paths near the village. Our teacher, Fränkel, who recited the blessing over the removal of the leavened goods, appeared regularly at the ceremony. We jumped over the fire and sometimes went home with singed pants. The consequences from this did not worry us.

The noon meal was meager, since one was not allowed to eat *chumez* any more and matzos could not yet be eaten. That much the more plentiful was the evening meal during the Seder. My father held the Seder in the prescribed manner, without, however, adding any special explanations. Today, as embarrassing as it may be, I must confess that on the evening of the Seder I was more concerned about the size of the matzo balls than the plight of our fathers in the land of Egypt. That during the entire holiday period we got matzo soup instead of our morning coffee gave us special pleasure.

The High Holidays Rosch Haschana and Jom Kippur were celebrated solemnly and very strictly in the village and especially at our home. On the day before Rosch Haschana we had to fast for half a day, on Rosch Haschana until after the shofar was blown, and on Jom Kippur before Bar Mitzwa until the removal of the Torah.[7]

On the two days of New Year, as on the Day of Atonement, the men wore their burial shrouds; the women were all dressed in white. Some could not castigate themselves enough; a very old man, nearly ninety years old, for example, *stood* the entire day of Jom Kippur, without sitting down. Of course, a spiritual change may not always have occurred as a result.

We did not have a Sukka. Instead, a communal tabernacle, which everyone could use, was erected in the "Jews' Yard." My parents did not make use of it. They probably did not want other people minding their business.

Another important day was the Simchas Tora festival, on which we boys marched about in the synagogue with little flags and which was especially good and plentiful. On the evening before there was regularly a Simchas Tora ball.

Chanukka was not celebrated very festively in our home. We boys lit lights, but only *one* each day—in order to save costs. Each one of us also received a kreutzer as *Chanukkageld,* which, however, we could not spend but had to save. In this way each one of us laid the foundation for a small savings fund. It was augmented by presents given on visits from relatives, by presents from customers (tips), birthday presents, etc. Later the gifts flowed somewhat more abundantly. Thus it happened that when I entered the university in 1872 I had savings of some 400 to 500 marks. [. . .]

Although during the time described here one could not speak of actual antisemitism, as it developed in the eighties, and although there was the best understanding between the Jewish and the Christian populations, nevertheless we Jewish children did have to suffer teasing and scolding by Christian children from time to time. The expression *"Judenstinker"* was used not at all infrequently on these occasions. While most of the other Jewish children did not react to it, I never put up with anything. At the very least, I shouted after the name-caller, using an analogous and equally fragrant word combined with "Christian."

In Bischberg there was a German grade school in which, at the time I entered it, boys and girls were taught together. A short time thereafter a separation of the sexes took place. In addition, there was the Jewish religion school. Instruction at grade school took place between 8:00 and 11:00 in the morning and from 12:00 to 3:00 in the afternoon. Sundays and Wednesday and Saturday afternoons were free. In the summer there was instruction only in the morning. There were two-week vacations at grain and potato harvest time.

Instruction in the Jewish school was given daily with the exception of the Sabbath and the holidays and vacation, from 10:00 to 12:00 in the mornings and from 2:00 to 4:00 in the afternoons. The conflict between the time of instruction at the German grade school and at the Jewish school was eliminated by having the Jewish pupils dismissed from classes in the grade school at 10:00 and 2:00. Then, between 10:00 and 11:00 and 2:00 and 3:00, instruction in the Christian religion and the Bible was given at the German school. For lunch, of course, there remained only a brief span of time, gained by our Jewish teacher dismissing us some 20 minutes before 12:00. We raced home, where the frugal meal was already on the table. Like our fathers during the exodus from Egypt, we tossed the food "with girded loins and staff in hand" into our mouth and set out at a trot again to the German school. As compensation, the evening meal, which was taken at 6:00, was more abundant. This was our main meal anyway, since father was often absent at noon on business.

While at noon we did not get meat, except, of course, on the Sabbath and holidays, it did constitute a part of our evening meal. Of course, even in the evening we children did not get very big portions of meat. For us the saying held true: "You can't become full on meat." Nevertheless, we always ate our fill. Even if we preferred the better things, we were also satisfied with the others.

A frugality instilled from youth on pervaded the whole household. My mother was a housewife such as one scarcely ever finds nowadays, constantly active in the business and filling in for my absent father to boot. When I read the "Praise of the Woman of Valor" in the Proverbs of Solomon[8] (the Friday evening liturgy), I always think of my blessed mother. And yet despite her constant troubles and labor she was always of a cheerful disposition and could tell us children wonderful stories. "She opened her mouth in wisdom and the teaching of gentleness was on her lips."[9] This sentence is inscribed on her gravestone. [. . .]

The Jewish teacher Fränkel—he is still alive today at an old age (eighty-five years) here in Munich—was about thirty years old and full of enthusiasm when I entered school. He did not belong to the strict branch of orthodoxy. Upon his initiative, many an innovation in regard to ritual was introduced in the synagogue. While before his time the order of prayer was entirely traditional, he succeeded in having the Blessing for the King (which still today is said in Hebrew in the Kanal-Synagogue in Munich) recited in German. A great many of the *piutim* (poetic pieces which were inserted in the usual liturgy during special Sabbaths and holidays) were eliminated and thus the service was shortened. He also introduced a boy's choir. He insisted on order and good behavior during the services. Frequently he gave sermon-like speeches. Actual sermons were rare, since the community of Bischberg did not have its own rabbi and the district rabbi, residing in Burgebrach, appeared very rarely for a guest sermon.

Teacher Fränkel took great pains to impart to us basic knowledge in religion, biblical history, and the Hebrew language, which to some extent was taught grammatically. To be sure, a great many of the pupils, boys and girls, were unable to follow at all. On the other hand, my brother and I acquired a rather good knowledge of these subjects. If I consider that at the age of eleven I had already reached the point where I could translate the Prophets and other writings—not to mention the Pentateuch—and that I understood all the prayers of the daily and Sabbath services, and also a large part of the holiday service prayers and the Haggada too, I can confidently maintain that my subsequent religious instruction at the Gymnasium in Bamberg did not produce any special broadening or deepening of my knowledge of religion and the Hebrew language.

Since in my later life I never completely broke with the traditions of my youth, even if at times there were periods of laxness, and I continued to be interested in Jewish writings, my knowledge of these subjects has remained with me to this day.

Whenever I lead the Seder at the home of Frau Counsellor of Justice Feust, as I have been doing regularly since the death of our cousin Julius Feust in 1906, I am able to present the recitation with complete comprehension, so that each time this wins me the appropriate praise. On the High Holidays, in the Kanal-Synagogue I can follow the services, which proceed completely in accordance with the old rite, without becoming bored as do many others. Indeed, precisely *this* service, which brings back to memory my early youth, has a special appeal for me, while many of those attending the Kanal-Synagogue cannot understand why *I* attend this synagogue. Here, I have often felt the solemnity of the Sabbath and the feast days that was not present at home. And when on Jom Kippur I spent my time here, uninterrupted from early morning until the end of *Neile*,[10] I often said to myself that this day was a truly festive day (not only a fast day) for me. [. . .]

In this regard, I also want to mention that the foundation for my knowledge of the Catholic religion was laid in the German grade school. Often instruction in the Catholic religion was given even at a time when Jewish pupils were present. My good memory retained the material taught at such times. The Lord's Prayer and the Credo became almost more familiar to me than the Thirteen Articles of Faith set down by Maimonides.[11] The text was mostly about biblical material of the New Testament. Once I felt quite uneasy when the lesson concerned the "prophecy of Christ about the destruction of Jerusalem" and the end of the world. The prophesied appearance of "the sign of the Son of Man and the falling of the stars from the heaven" frightened me most. My mother, whom I questioned at home, said to me that "we do not believe in these things, what is not in the Torah is not true," and that I need not be afraid. I was reassured by this authoritative explanation. [. . .]

On the Sabbath and the holidays, ritual also affected pleasure, since one was not allowed to write, tear, break, pick, and the like. Part of the morning was taken up by attendance at services, which we boys regularly participated in, as we also participated to some extent in a kind of "choral singing." Teacher Fränkel insisted that we cultivate a correct pronunciation of Hebrew, just as he succeeded in banishing jargon in school.

We also took part in the services the evening before. After the services the wonderful Friday evening awaited us. The magic of this evening has often been described. None of the descriptions approaches reality. Whoever experiences this magic personally will never forget the impression. When in later years I, as a bachelor, saw the Sabbath lamp glowing from a window in a far-away city on Friday evening, I was overcome by a sort of homesickness for peace and Sabbath tranquility. I have never again attained the height of belief and pleasure on which I stood as a child on the Sabbath and holiday eves. All surrogates fail their purpose. Bring back the Friday evening and you will save Judaism!

The evening was spent exclusively within the family. Father and mother still in the vigor of youth and we children around the table, with sparkling eyes and happy hearts! After the customary dinner, to which we children did ample justice, our father told us of his experiences of the week, our mother of her hometown, Lichtenfels; at other times we played "lottery," "bell and hammer," and similar games. Sometimes there was reading aloud. Spellbound we listened to the novels of Louise Mühlbach: "Emperor . . . and His Times," "Maria Theresa and Her Times,"[12] and the various other historical novels. That was my first source of knowledge of more recent history. I was especially interested in the Napoleonic era. My mother always had a predilection for Napoleon. She may have inherited it from her father, who according to her account tugged at his skullcap every time he pronounced the name "Napoleon," in order to give expression to his admiration, for Napoleon had been a great *"Ohew Israel"* (friend of the Jews). [. . .]

The people's revolution of 1848 did not bring the German people freedom, or emancipation to their Jewish compatriots. Apart from a few greater or lesser concessions, things essentially remained as they had been, especially in regard to legislation on Jews.

For the Jewish student of law who did not intend to open the way to a career with baptismal water, only the prospect of attaining the status of advocate—which was bestowed through a royal appointment—became an incentive. Helped by such an appointment, many an old legal trainee or aspirant belonging to the Mosaic religion was able to enter the promised and longed-for land of the legal profession, among them also my great-uncle Dr. Karl Feust in Furth. There was nothing else one could become.

The efforts of the Bavarian government to bring the Jews into the crafts were in the main unsuccessful. Centuries-old customs and character traits were not easily eliminated by a legislative act. Besides, a craft alone, though it was solidly grounded, yielded little gain, especially in the country; and the Jewish population, consistent with its entire historical development, was dependent on material possession. It was this, after all—if not primarily, then at least in good part—that had rescued them throughout all persecution and abuse. That is why they took up trades that were more related to business and from which the transition to business or industrial enterprise was easier. Thus the clothmakers later became dry-goods dealers and fabricants, the tailors became clothing manufacturers, the shoemakers became dealers in footwear, etc.

The greater endeavor was to get to bigger towns, away from the village, where conditions of livelihood were difficult. However, since the system of registration under the Edict on the Jews was still legally in force, relatively few succeeded in achieving the goal. A person had to wait for the death of another or for a stroke of luck in order to become registered. In this way, several Jewish families from Bischberg moved to Bamberg or even Nuremberg between 1848 and 1862. The Bamberg families Kronacher and Morgenroth originated in the Bischberg of this time. My parents did not attain this desired goal until legislation opened the way. In Section 15 of the Parliamentary Decree of November 10, 1861, it was declared that: "The restrictions existing in accordance with Sections 12, 13, and 18, Paragraph 1 of the Edict of June 10, 1813 concerning the circumstances of members of the Jewish faith, as regards their rights of residence and exercise of trade and the provinces this side of the Rhine, are abolished." To be sure, that did not create freedom of movement, but it did at least bestow equality of status with the Christian population in essential points.

At this point I must make a brief digression. My father was a conservative person, consistent with his half-peasant origin—firmly rooted, an opponent of innovations and experiments. Ceaseless work and frugality were for him the only way to attain something. He was not very bent on prestige, and his kind of work seemed to satisfy him. Modern social and financial ambition, which had stricken many Jewish circles, was completely foreign to him.

My dear departed mother, on the other hand, had a more progressive bent, just as she very much also represented the family's intellectual side. Her grandfather, on her mother's side, was a respected rabbi (Feust in Bamberg). Among her maternal relatives there were scholars from all fields. Her oldest brother was battalion doctor in the royal army and had gone to Greece with King Otto. Her brothers were highly educated business people. Although she herself had been brought up simply, she was not unversed in literature. She knew the German classical writers in part; she read Shakespeare, Walter Scott, and Balzac with relish. It is from her that I heard about Kotzebue for the first time. She kept herself informed with respect to belles-lettres as much as possible and to the end of her life she was an avid reader of the *Frankfurter Zeitung,* and all that in addition to her many activities in the business and in the household. A woman the like of which nowadays is becoming more and more rare. It was she who constantly prodded my father on.

Kolmsdorf, a little village of a few hundred inhabitants, was for her a kind of exile after she had been used to town life in Lichtenfels, a well-known, small commercial town in Upper Franconia. Her socializing was restricted to the Jewish women of Walsdorf, petty people living in modest circumstances and, as far as education was concerned, far below her. In Walsdorf was the synagogue, where people met on the Sabbath and the holidays and gathered socially otherwise.

The men, who were hardly educated, lived only for their business, constantly talked only about it, and were, moreover, given to coarse manners and bad habits. Even fights among themselves and with Christian inhabitants were not all that rare. Who can hold it against her if she strove to get away from such a place?

Thus, after the futile attempt to move directly to Bamberg, she managed to improve her situation by moving to Bischberg. She insisted that we boys get a higher education than is offered by grade school. After my three brothers completed grade school, as was usual at that time, about three years after Bar Mitzva, they attended the commerce school in Bamberg for two or three years, and while doing so they returned to Bischberg every evening. Around 1858, after his theoretical training, my brother Simon was sent to Aschaffenburg as an apprentice in a store that sold dry goods.

After the law of 1861 had cleared the way, my mother did not cease urging my somewhat skeptical father to move his domicile to Bamberg. I can still remember today how my father pointed out that city life was too expensive and that if he became *"mechulle"* (insolvent) it would be my mother's fault. My mother, however, did not allow herself to lose sight of her goal, and so my father decided to submit a petition for legal residence in Bamberg. There were no difficulties getting legal residence since my parent's situation with regard to sustenance was a secure one. They already had a fortune that for the conditions of the day was not entirely insignificant. On Jom Kippur of the year 1862, my father was delivered the permission for legal residence. Great amazement and great excitement in the Jewish community! That was the beginning of the decline of the community! The exodus continued, and after some twenty years the community, which had lost part of its members through death, had dwindled to a few members: some widows and not very well-to-do small-business people, who led a wretched cultural life. So that at least on the highest holidays (Rosch Haschana and Jom Kippur) it would have a *minjan,* the once flourishing community had to be content with *orchim,* (poor guests), who in part showed up voluntarily and in part were commandeered from Bamberg. Later, the few remaining ones also vanished. Today there is only a single small family in the community, with whose departure or extinction the Jewish population of Bischberg will have disappeared. A typical example of the uprooting of Jewish rural communities to the city.

It took a few months to make preparations for the move. On December 22, 1862, we moved to our newly acquired house at Austrasse No. 522, which bordered directly on Grünen Markt. We were in a new situation. City life and its demands made themselves felt, no matter how much my parents, especially my father, tried to stave off too great a change. Above all, the business was expanded. My brother Simon returned from Aschaffenburg and put to use the experiences he had acquired in a city firm. For all that, the business remained geared to the rural customers, the average city customers, and the factory workers. The old rural clientele still had to be visited by my father, even if less often. But the business was primarily a store business. My parents did not yet have outside employees. For the time being, my brothers Simon and Salomon were sufficient help, since my mother, too, was often active in the store. At times and on days when things were especially busy, we other children were also recruited. Quite often, when I came home from school during the fair or on a weekly market day, I had to go to the store at once, if not to wait on the customers then at least to mind it. With envy, I sometimes watched my schoolmates setting out to the "Plärrer" to visit show booths while I was occupied in the store.

Farming was of course out of the question after my father sold his land in Bischberg, including our house, which bore the number 46. A kind of connection with this house still exists today inasmuch as the balance of 1,000 marks of the purchase money mortgage is still in the books. A third of it belongs to me.

We were allowed to, or rather had to, devote ourselves to such other household tasks as might turn up. Many a time, even when I attended middle school, I carried wood, chopped into small pieces, from the street into the house, or a loaf of bread to the baker in the bakeshop. Once when I was doing the latter I met up with our headmaster; since I couldn't remove my cap I was in an embarrassing position. The loaf of bread that I was carrying on my head prevented me from even nodding. Well, the matter ended in a satisfactory way. The headmaster didn't even see me. Nevertheless, I took advantage of this incident, whenever possible, to "shirk" this honorable office, which, moreover, brought no gain. On the other hand, the task of collecting installment payments on Sundays from some of the customers who bought on credit and lived mostly on the "mountains" remained my exclusive right until my Gymnasium days neared their end. Even in my later years I often dreamt that I was on this business errand, without, of course, knowing the individual residences any more, and I was always glad when I woke up.

Also in outward appearance—especially in the case of us children—we had to submit to a change in Bamberg. Matters of toilet were not really taken so seriously out in the country. Now and then one even ran around on the street like other boys, without anything on one's head or feet, like a "schechezle,"[13] as old Frummel used to say. Still, we did not live a life of great luxury. And since, to begin with, my father also had to bear his customers in mind, and since these were not the best tailors, not to speak of clothing manufacturers, our suits were also not first-rate, even if, compared to earlier times, one could not fail to recognize an improvement. [. . .]

In those days the Jewish population of Bamberg consisted of 500–600 souls; part were old-established families, part were newcomers. Among the former were primarily the so-called *gewirim* (that is, wealthy people), mostly hop dealers.

I recall that for a long time, on visiting days, that is, Saturdays (back then, the majority of Jewish businesses were closed on Saturdays), many Jewish women, even from the ranks of the "prominent," came by to visit (whereas the men generally did not make visits).

Since, however, it soon became evident that we led a life that differed to some extent from the ways of the Jewish population, and that with regard to dress we were closer to the Christian population, it was assumed that we lived in modest circumstances, and since in Bamberg, too, "genteel" and "prominent" were mere synonyms for "rich," the relations of the "prominent" with us cooled off. We were regarded as peasant Jews.

The Christian neighbors, however, were more than satisfied with our conduct. A big merchant living across from us, Lamprecht, a man of the old stamp, who had ample opportunity to observe our doings at closest quarters, said to me once: "You are Christian Jews. Hats off." Of course, in the eyes of the Jewish population this was no praise. The "taint" was somewhat lessened in the course of time, but it was never completely removed. And even when my parents had attained greater prosperity and in reality were worthy of being counted among the "prominent," they were not quite regarded with due esteem. There were times in life when we were made to feel it.

"Socializing" in the real sense with the Christian population did not take place, apart from chance meetings in public places and the like. A pronounced antisemitism did not exist in those days, and on the whole the population was tolerant. Since my parents expected nothing but additional financial burdens from associating with the "prominent" and, as already mentioned, the "prominent" were not keen on associating with them, and since, in turn, another part of the Jewish population was really below us, there remained only a few families that were suitable for us to associate with. Thus it came about that our social life was a narrowly defined and insignificant one. My parents, who were intensely occupied the entire day in the business and otherwise, found pleasure in relaxing in the evening among their own and in occupying themselves in other useful ways.

Now and then we went to the theater, which at that time had its own management. Whether it was run especially well is another matter. At any rate, I very much enjoyed attending the theater. For each one of us it was a holiday when he was allowed to go to the theater. I still remember well how my dear departed brother Salomon once saw *Undine* in the theater, in which play, if I'm not mistaken, there appeared the "Kalos tinthe chomokrene" (the source bubbling with lovely joys). He was carried away with delight and made our mouths water for this treat.

On Sabbath afternoons during the summer, starting at about four o'clock, a large part of the Jewish population gathered at the beer gardens. Food was unpacked, and then we helped ourselves to the leftovers from the noon meal, fried goose skin and corned beef, tongue, and other things. At worst, we made do with cheese and bread and butter. A large mug of beer (somewhat more than a liter) still cost 5 kreuzers and 15 pfennigs. Even in those days, the Hain and Michelsberg were also popular recreation spots. Less often did one climb up to the Altenburg. One did not go on outings on Jewish holidays. On the Christian ones, there was, as a rule, no time for that. With regard to the latter, they were not considered any differently than they had been earlier. In the family itself, only the Jewish holidays were viewed as holidays.

At the beginning, at least, the store was strictly closed on the Sabbath, even if my brother Simon, who was working in a store in Aschaffenburg which was open on this day and on the holidays—except New Year and Jom Kippur—gradually introduced a more lax observance, which my brother Salomon then also took up. Even if publicly the store had to remain closed, they did not fail to serve the customers who had a pressing need on such days, and later also those who simply came.

In the afternoons, they, too, stayed away from the business and devoted themselves to amusement and reading. In the country, it was not regarded as odd that on Sundays the Jewish population wore their workday clothes since Jews had their "Schabbes" on Saturday. In the city, it was different: here the Jewish population, at least the better ones, dressed better or truly festively also on Christian holidays. [. . .]

The question of a choice of occupation now became urgent.

In light of my successes in the Gymnasium, on the one hand, and, on the other hand, due to the fact that since 1870 my brother Philipp was also working in my father's store, so that there did not exist the need for my help, everyone was agreed that I should pursue an academic career, that is, a profession with an academic preparation. The study of medicine did not appeal to me, especially since my uncle, Dr. Philipp Zenner, had often warned me against this profession; he spoke of much toil and small financial success. Of course, his own life story may have exerted the greatest influence in this matter. Nevertheless, I also did not feel an inner inclination for the profession.

For my part, I did now and then think of studying classical languages and literatures. But in those days the prospects for a government position as a teacher at a secondary school were still very slim; even today, when the law of July 3, 1869[14] on the Equality of the Confessions will soon be a half-century old, the prospects are not especially splendid. In addition, my parents wanted to hear nothing about a profession whose future was uncertain. Thus, there remained practically only the study of law.

My parents, and especially my father, had visions of the future "lawyer." My father had a kind of respect for this profession. He himself had all kinds of legal experiences due to the lawsuits that were carried on through the years, and he liked to speak of legal matters. Among his customers and acquaintances, he had a great reputation as an "expert in legal questions." Often, the farmers asked my father, "who was smarter than any lawyer," for advice on legal and also on financial matters. At any rate, my father's counsel was *cheaper* than that of the lawyers.

With pride my father looked upon the future lawyer. I would have been the first in the Silbermann family to attain this honor. On my mother's side there were more lawyers and jurists. My great-uncle, Dr. Karl Feust,[15] for example, was a lawyer. His son Philipp was at that time a legal clerk, and a short time later he became a lawyer. Herzfelder, a son of Dorothee Herzfelder, a daughter of Reitzle Feust, was a legal clerk, and in the 1870s he also became a lawyer, in Augsburg. I have already mentioned the legal clerk Epstein. At a later time there were also Julius Feust and a grandson of Dorothee Herzfelder, Karl Würzburger, the former in Munich, the latter in Bayreuth.

I, for one, had neither a special inclination for law nor a dislike of it. If I wanted to take up an academic profession at all—and that I did want—then, the way things stood, there remained only jurisprudence.

I did not consider civil service. In those days, Jews had not yet attained appointment. Not until 1874 was the first Jewish judge appointed in Bavaria. This was the brother-in-law of our cousin Dr. Philipp Feust, Max Berlin in Nuremberg, who retired several years ago as Counsellor of a Higher Regional Court. In the year 1876, my cousin Adolf Epstein followed him as assistant judge at the municipal court in Munich I. With the intention of becoming a lawyer, I decided to study law.

1. Through the abolition of the article concerning the registry in 1861 and the Law on the Emancipation of the Jews in 1867, the emancipation of the Jews of Bavaria was finally achieved by 1871. The articles in the law of 1813 on the Jewish religious community, however, remained in effect until the end of the Empire.

2. A little piece of matzo, which according to an old custom is taken by the children during the seder meal and saved until the next year as a good-luck piece.

3. The "long day" is the Day of Atonement, Yom Kippur, on which one fasts until sundown. The holiday begins on the preceding evening with the chanting of "Kol Nidre" ("All Vows"). In addition to the prayer shawl (tallis), the men wear the white *kittel,* which is later used as their burial shroud.

4. Baptized Jew, renegade.

5. Some scholars trace Holekrasch back to "Hollekreis," the circle of the legendary and fairytale figure Frau Holle.

6. During the Passover holiday, one is permitted to eat only unleavened bread (matzo); therefore, on the preceding evening a ceremonial search for leavened goods takes place in a thoroughly cleaned house, in the process of which each time a little piece must be "found" for burning.

7. That is, children who have not yet been Bar Mitzva; before the age of thirteen they had to fast on Yom Kippur only from the evening into the next morning. This was not a religious duty but rather a pedagogical measure in preparation for the day's fast for those who were of age in the religious sense.

8. Proverbs 31:10–31.

9. Proverbs 31:26.

10. *Neile* = to close (Hebrew); the final portion of the Yom Kippur service, about the closing of the gates of heaven before judgment is passed.

11. The Jewish religious philosopher Maimonides (1135–1204) set forth the basic principles of Judaism in thirteen doctrines.

12. Louise Mühlbach, pseudonym for Klara Mundt (1814–1873), wrote several dozen historical novels, among them *Kaiser Leopold II und seine Zeit,* 3 vols., 1860, and *Maria Theresia und der Pandurenoberst Trenck,* 4 vols., 1861, which are probably the works referred to here.

13. A small Christian boy.

14. Passed by the North German Parliament; introduced in Bavaria through the Imperial Law of April 22, 1871.

15. Karl Feust (1798–1872) was a son of the Bamberg Chief State Rabbi. He attained his doctorate in law in 1822 in Würzburg, was secretary of the Jewish community of Fürth starting in 1831, and was admitted to the practice of law only after the legislation of 1848. Feust was among the first Jewish law students and jurists in Germany.

# 6 *Leopold Freund*

BORN IN 1808 IN BADEWITZ (UPPER SILESIA).

Leopold Freund, A Biography. Breslau 1867 (printed in the publishing house of the author), 44 pages.

*After the death of his father, Leopold Freund had to leave the Gymnasium in Leobschütz penniless and, following his brother, he set off on foot to the Jewish mission house of Count Recke-Volmerstein in Düsseltal near Düsseldorf. His hope for permission to train as a surgeon was not fulfilled, and he left the institution disappointed and unbaptized. In Berlin, in 1828, he began his apprenticeship as a typesetter, and in 1831 he became typesetter with Brockhaus in Leipzig. In 1834 he started his own job press in Breslau, which, after difficult early years, he was able to expand into a thriving publishing house and newspaper press. Starting in 1842, he printed the* Handelsblatt *and the* Breslauer Morgenzeitung. *By accepting advertising, he was able to increase the circulation of the liberal* Morgenzeitung *to 15,000 copies in spite of numerous censorship controversies and press lawsuits. Freund typifies the educated and politically involved printer.*

## I.

I was born in Badewitz, in the district of Leobschütz in the year 1808, on the evening before the Chanukka festival (December 14). My father was the son of a pious Jewish businessman, and before he was granted citizenship he had the name Falk Badewitz. In 1812, when the state granted the rights of citizenship to the Jews on the condition that they assume first and last names, my father took the name Valentin Freund. My mother's maiden name was Friederike Plessner. They are buried next to one another in the Jewish cemetery in Kosel.

I spent the first three years of my life in my native village, until my parents moved to the district seat, Leobschütz, where my father began immediately to found a Jewish community. He brought several close and distant relatives to Leobschütz, provided for the religious needs and education of my five siblings, my brothers Bernhard, Heimann, Salomon, and Joseph, as well as my sister Ernestine. In my sixth year, in 1814, my father engaged as my tutor the teacher Wiener, who later was the butcher and cantor of the community of Leobschütz. In 1817 my father sent me to my grandparents Plessner in Kosel, where the Jewish teacher at that time, Ring, enjoyed the reputation of a fine pedagogue. I stayed in the school of Herr Ring until 1819. From there I went to my oldest brother, Bernhard, in Ratibor, and attended the recently founded Gymnasium, where I was accepted in the fifth grade. Here, too, I was not to stay long. After only half a year I was taken away by my parents and sent to the Gymnasium in Leobschütz, where I remained almost seven years, until July 15, 1827. I left while in the twelfth grade; a few weeks later I would have been moved up to grade thirteen. I have retained my partiality for this Gymnasium, and, besides several presents for the school library, I have made a bequest for two Jewish pupils of the Gymnasium.

My father, who had in the meanwhile moved to Kosel and there lost his entire fortune, died in 1826, on the 1st of November, and my mother, who kept up the business with my brother Salomon, was not able to go on giving me the little bit that I had received for my studies during my father's lifetime. Even while my father was alive, I had already been dependent for years on my own efforts and the support of my distant relatives in Leobschütz. This state of affairs became unbearable to me after my father's death, and, poor and abandoned as I was, I wanted to go to Breslau or Berlin, either to continue studying or to learn something else.

At that time, my brother Joseph was in Düsseltal near Düsseldorf at the institute of Count Recke-Volmerstein,[1] where he was learning to become a joiner and had converted from Judaism to Christianity. This example was tempting. Joseph's few letters from there to our mother were enticing, and I thought that if there were nothing for me in Breslau or Berlin, at worst I would go to Düsseltal, perhaps to attend the academy in Düsseldorf, or find a place somewhere else. But how different things turned out to be there!

With a few items of clothing, some linen, and about 6 to 7 talers in cash, I took to the road on the 25th of July and, to start with, I went into the unknown to Breslau. Here, besides my cousin Eduard Plessner, who at that time was learning the mason's trade, I found no one to look after me. He himself was partly dependent on the help of strangers. Thus, because my stay in Breslau was too expensive for me, I decided to go as far as Neumarkt; from there I was going to write to Joseph, asking whether I would be received in Düsseltal and, if so, whether he could send me money for the journey. I put up at an inn outside the town, slept on straw for half a sovereign, and lived there for about 5 sovereigns a day. I waited a week for an answer from Joseph. I waited another long, anxious week, but no letter arrived. My brother, you see, had in the meantime left there. I had no choice but to take to the road again and go to Berlin. I journeyed on foot for ten days and finally on a hot day in August I arrived in Berlin.

With my knapsack on my back I came to Unter den Linden, still without purpose and destination, when a young man addressed me and asked: "Most likely you are Leopold from Leobschütz?" Through a lucky coincidence, my brother Joseph, who had left the institute in Düsseltal as a journeyman joiner, had found me. He led me to his living quarters, and took me to some compatriots and distant relatives, in particular to my father's former bookkeeper, Herr Josefson, whose wife, née Loewenberger from Brieg, received me very cordially.

Without help and all alone in the world, however, I did not want to give up my plan of going to Düsseltal. I couldn't think of anything else; what was I to do in the big, unfamiliar city? I believed that in order to become someone I had to convert. For this purpose, my brother introduced me to the professor of law Bethmann-Hollweg,[2] the future Minister of Education. The latter invited me for the evening to his prayer hour and asked me to come the next day. I appeared at the designated time. "Young man," he addressed me, "what you need to do is go to Düsseltal, become a true human being, and save your soul. Go in the name of Jesus Christ. Here is a directive for our cashier; he will provide you with the means so that you can make the journey on foot to Düsseldorf. You will be traveling with two other future proselytes; and now see to it that you make us and all good Christians happy."

With a heavy heart I went to the cashier of the Society, the paperhanger Wohlgemuth, at Scharrenstrasse No. 11. There I got several unctuous speeches, some little treatises, instructions for the trip and the route of the journey, along with money, and was assigned to my traveling companions. The next morning the three of us traveled by country coach to Brandenburg and continued from there on foot. My traveling companions were Sittenfeld, at present the owner of a printing press in Berlin, born in the kingdom of Poland and brought up in Brieg, and a man from Posen, a young, strong person by the name of Buchwald, like myself without any support. We quickly became friends; after all, we were youths, I not quite eighteen, my two companions in misfortune almost the same age.

From Brandenburg we journeyed on foot through Magdeburg, Halberstadt, Hildesheim, Minden, Herford, Bielefeld, Soest, Unna, Hagen, and Elberfeld to Düsseltal. I parted from my travel companions in Unna because I didn't want to put up with the dictatorial ways of our fellow traveler Sittenfeld. After a fifteen-day journey I knocked on the gate of the former monastery Düsseltal, which Count Recke had converted into an institution for the salvation of neglected boys and girls of the Rhineland and Westphalia and for the "conversion of young Israelites to Christianity." The next morning I was summoned to the Count, who was reading my letters and who asked me whether I was inclined to convert to Christianity and what I wanted to become. After I had given the Count an affirmative answer to his first question and answered the second by saying that I would like to attend the recently founded academy in Düsseldorf or at least be trained in Bonn as a surgeon of the first class, he destroyed my plans with the question: "Do you have the means to attend the academy in Düsseldorf or the university, in order to become either one or the other?" When I replied negatively to this question, the Count said: "Then choose one of the professions available in the institution, either joiner, locksmith, tailor, shoemaker, or the like." I shuddered. Had I had gotten as far as the last grade in a Gymnasium for this? But what was I, a poor forsaken creature, to do? I chose joinery.

Although the treatment by the foremen in the workshops was humane, I cried from pain when on the first evening I lay down on my hard bed. I thought of the plans of my youth; and now, on top of the denial of my religious feelings, the prospect of becoming a simple joiner after three long years!

I decided during the almost sleepless night to take a look at everything here first and to act according to what I experienced. The house warden Bormann, a Pietist in the true sense of the word—outwardly pious, humble, and seemingly flawless—encouraged me to convert, and so, on command, I went to prayers morning and night, but was inwardly happy when I heard there was no rush with baptism.

In the meanwhile, Sittenfeld and Buchwald had also arrived. The former also chose joinery and the latter tailoring for his vocation. I soon became weary of the monotonous monastic-militaristic life in the institution, the more so since I had to struggle with the dry teachings during religious instruction. The frequent rolling of the eyes of the institution's Pastor Schmidt disgusted me, and I went to the carpenter's bench only very reluctantly. But for the time being things had to stay the way they were; I planed, roughed, mortised, and starved. For the food in the institution was, you see, more like prison food.

Thus week after week passed; for reading we got treatises upon treatises, which by no means made me like Christianity but instead, due to its mystical content and unconditional submission to the crassest belief, alienated me more and more from Christianity. To be sure, I still went to the devotional hours and Sunday sermons, but all this increased my longing to get away from Düsseltal and to remain true to the faith of my fathers.

One day Sittenfeld had journeyed over to Elberfeld, I don't know for what reason, and had told me that the highest seat of the Society for the Advancement of Christianity among Jews[3] was there. Thereupon I thought up a plan. No one could keep me in Düsseltal. Thus, away from this institution for conversion! But I was without means, without a single penny! I now began to save some of the few pennies that I received at the institution, wrote letters home for some fellows at the institution until late in the evening, made overtime to earn a few additional pennies, and one day I asked the Count for a day's leave to go to Elberfeld. In Elberfeld, I was directed to the merchant Herr Schniewindt. I trustingly told him my situation, that I couldn't stay in Düsseltal any longer and would rather go back to Berlin in order to receive training there more appropriate to my education. "What do you want to become?" the friendly old gentleman asked me, bearing true Christianity in his heart. "I want to study surgery; if that cannot be done, I want to learn some sort of skill, for example that of a typesetter or some such, for which the Greek and Latin I have learned could be useful." Thereupon Herr Schniewindt sent me to the merchant Herr Müller, the treasurer of the Society, and after a night spent anxiously awake and crying, the next noon I received the longed-for travel money of 10 talers for Berlin, with the directive that the Count would be informed about this and I would be released from the institution. I flew more than I walked from Elberfeld to Düsseldorf, thanking God for his mercy, and late in the evening I reached the institution, very tired from the four-and-a-half-mile walk.

Next morning I was ordered to the Count, who had already been instructed about everything from Elberfeld. The Count, a kindhearted, pious, gentle man, a paragon of Christianity in all his actions and utterances, urged me to remain true to my resolution to become a good human being, and assured me of his good will and help also with my plans for Berlin.

In the first days of January 1828, on a bright, beautiful day, I left the institution, envied by Sittenfeld, Buchwald, and many others. I had told Sittenfeld of my plan to learn typesetting in Berlin, and that moved him to devote himself later to this skill at the printing press for religious pamphlets in Elberfeld. When I said farewell to Inspector Bormann, I was allowed to keep the army gear I had received at the institution, a gray, ordinary cloth jacket, the same kind of pants and vest, and the main thing for the 70-mile journey on foot, two pairs of good leather shoes. I strapped on my knapsack, which weighed 50 pounds, and free as a bird in the sky I left through the eternally closed gate of the institution. I went to Düsseldorf in double-time, still afraid that there might be a counterorder. In Düsseldorf, with the Count's permit in my hand, I had my passport as a Gymnasium pupil endorsed with a visa to Berlin by way of Frankfurt am Main, and, on the same day, I went up the Rhine to Cologne. Being so near to the

Rhine, I wanted, curious as I was, to make the Rhine journey, even if it meant sacrificing money and my feet. Thus, in a few days I reached Frankfurt, by way of Koblenz and Mainz.

In Frankfurt, as I discovered there by chance, there exists a Jewish society for the support of educated or learned Jewish travelers. I turned to this society, and my fortune of some 12 talers, which I had in Düsseltal, was increased by a subsidy of 5 talers.

Economizing most prudently, I now traveled from Frankfurt by way of Kassel, Nordhausen, Stolberg, Harzgerode, and Bernburg to Magdeburg, towards Berlin. I had chosen this longer way deliberately, because I knew that my second brother, Heimann, was working as a Jewish teacher in Bernburg. He had left home in 1818; in the years 1812–1815, he had been a volunteer rifleman in Lützow's troops, and there, like so many others, had become completely useless for society. After he had ruined the business that my father had established for him in Leobschütz, he was barely making a living as a teacher, and was leading a restless life. In Bernburg I found him again. I will never forget the scene when we recognized each other. After a sojourn of several days, I took to the road and headed toward my future destiny. During my journey on foot to and from Düsseltal, which amounted to nearly 170 miles, I gathered much practical knowledge, my self-confidence grew, and I learned perseverance and thriftiness; for I saw how little other, less fortunate ones who traveled with me needed for living.

## II.

On a cloudy day in the very mild winter of 1828, at the end of January, I arrived in Berlin for the second time, in order—this time bearing in mind my goal in life—to make something of myself, cost what it may. With God in my heart, I resolved to pray and to work, but to amount to something, even if I had to go hungry.

I went to the former landlady of my brother Joseph, to Frau Kuhfahl, rooming house proprietress at Mittelstrasse No. 36, and to my true friend Josefson, who at that time was living on Mühlendamm. I told him trustingly of my situation, that under no circumstances did I want to become a Christian, that I wanted to study as a Jew, and, if that wasn't possible, to learn a trade or skill. After Herr Josefson convinced me that one could not study without having the means, he suggested that I choose some sort of trade. I decided in favor of my old plan to learn typesetting, and immediately Herr Josefson took me to the benefactor of the Israelite Society for the Advancement and Acquisition of Trades Among Israelites, Herr Ullmann. This old and benevolent gentleman, known to all Berliners in those days, took me to Herr Leopold Krause, at Adlerstrasse No. 6, now the address of Privy Councilor C. R. Littfass, and after brief transactions, at the end of January 1828 I was a well-established apprentice typesetter at Herr Krause's under the supervision of foreman Hardt, with a weekly allowance of one taler for board. I kept my lodgings at Frau Kuhfahl's for 10 sovereigns per week and I had to live all of seven days on 20 sovereigns. Often for days I ate army bread, which I bought from soldiers, and potato soup. Herr Ullmann told me that after having had many bad experiences the Society could help me only if after some time they became convinced that I was worthy and really wanted to learn something. In spite of my hunger and other distress, I remained true to my intentions, and after three months the Society began to help me: I received paid meals, that is, a lunch every week, at President Jacobson's,[4] and from six other benefactors—the names of the honorable men are Joachimsthal, Veit, the editor Josef Lehmann, Lawyer Löwenberger (now Chief Tribunal Counselor in Berlin), Ludwig Lesser (pseudonym Lieber), and the businessman Schayer—grants of ten sovereigns to one taler each month. Shortly thereafter, Herr Josefson again found me board twice a week with the jeweler Riess on Spandauer Strasse—blessed be his memory—and finally also board at Herr Adolph Schayer's. Thus, four times a week I had at least a warm lunch, and at Herr Riess's and President Jacobson's more than enough. I received boots and some items of clothing from the Society.

I pursued my trade cheerfully and with such zeal that after only a year of apprenticeship I could be called upon for a difficult setting, and after a year and a half of apprenticeship I received one and a third talers for board and at night I got to typeset the *Kurier,* a small daily feuilleton paper of four octavo pages printed by Saphir.[5] In those days theater reviews were still so much in demand by a public of eager readers that they were written directly after the performance ended, typeset at night, corrected and printed early next morning at four o'clock, and at seven o'clock they were ready for distribution. The present generation knows little or nothing about Saphir, but every encyclopedia will supply information about this Jewish humoristic writer. He soon got to know me and discovered in me an educated typesetter. He, too, made me quite a few presents, for he had a good heart, but a heart that frequently ran away with his reason. Often, when he was too lazy, he gave me his season ticket to the theater, and I myself wrote the review, which I later typeset and corrected. Here I must not forget a friend of Saphir, his assistant editor Eduard Oettinger, who also did many nice and kind things for me and looked after me wherever he could.

At that time I also turned to a friend of Saphir, Doctor Herlossohn in Leipzig, and under the pseudonym "Leopold Klarissa" sent him contributions from Berlin for his belletristic journal *Komet.* The elder of the two Borcherts is probably the only one alive in Breslau who had read my contributions of those days and even today he still teases me with the name Klarissa. [. . .]

Through our printing shop, which did all the work of the Royal Theaters, I had become well acquainted with theater life and later attained the undeserved honor of becoming leader of a claque that I organized for the brother of the music director Meyerbeer, the rich banker Beer, in the interests of his lover, the solo dancer Mies St.-Romain, who at that time was the chief rival of Fanny Elsler. Mostly, they were only students from various colleges of the university, who were well instructed by me, and frequently by means of thundering applause, which we cleverly used, we outmatched the greater number of Elsler fans from the Garde du Corps, and other officers.

I also made good progress in my craft, and after I had apprenticed diligently and ably for almost four years, but after a very conspicuous scene with my somewhat grim foreman Hardt, and not having been done justice by my supervisor, I left him at the beginning of September 1831, without his permission. A year earlier I had been levied and trained for the 20th Militia Regiment as a militia recruit.

*[Freund describes his later activity as a newspaper publisher in Breslau.]*

The former editor of the *Danziger Dampfboot,* Dr. J. Lasker, was employed at the theater here as dramatic adviser. The theater directors Nimbs, Reimann, and Kiessling were unable to realize the aims of the enterprise and separated in the year 1852; as a result, Lasker too, became untenable. Reimann asked me whether I would be inclined to engage Lasker as editor of my *Anzeiger.* I accepted the proposal, and Lasker turned the paper, which till then carried only police and local news and especially much fiction and poetry, into a paper in which the latter were only secondary, while the main stress was on short political articles of liberal persuasion.

On Tuesday, March 29, 1853, I added to the already familiar title the heading *Kleine Morgenzeitung,* a name that even today is still popularly used to designate my newspaper, although it disappeared from the title eight years ago.

Lasker's editorship was quite outstanding as far as the belles-lettres part was concerned, but his oscillating political opinion was not very, or not at all, satisfactory. A short time after he joined me, Police Councilor Werner, who had founded the *Anzeiger* with me, received an order from his department to leave the editorship because, according to the laws enacted in the meanwhile, no civil servant was to function as an editor. The direct reports of the police news were witheld from him, and thus he no longer could do anything for the paper. [. . .]

The circulation of the *Anzeiger* under Lasker, as well as the number of advertisements, just would not increase. I realized that a paper without advertisements, no matter how well edited, could never become popular. But how to achieve that? At that time there was a *Tagesanzeiger* posted on street corners, published by Ed. Gross, who was doing a respectable business with advertising. I therefore decided to publish the same in conjunction with my newspaper, and in such a manner that whoever advertised in the *Kleine Morgenzeitung* would have the advertisement placed in the street poster free of charge. I worked out the plan for this in Karlsbad, returned to Breslau on August 30, 1855, and on the 1st of September of the same year the first issue of the *Strassenanzeiger* appeared according to the above-mentioned arrangement. This undertaking, although not approved of by Lasker, was a success. On the 1st of September, there was still, as usual, one quarter to one-half page of advertisements in the paper. Eight weeks later there were two pages, and so it went on and on with increasing success. The circulation increased no less, and at the end of 1859 I already figured on an edition of over 5,000, which in Breslau was an incredible success.

1. In 1811, Adalbert Graf von der Recke-Volmerstein (1791–1878) took over the former Trappist monastery Düsseltal and there maintained, besides a home for young people at risk, a Pietist center of education for Jewish apprentices willing to be baptized.

2. Moritz August von Bethmann-Hollweg (1795–1877) was a professor of law in Berlin starting in 1823 and belonged to the Pietistic conservative circle of friends of Friedrich Wilhelm IV. He founded the German Protestant Convention and from 1858 to 1862 he functioned as the Prussian Minister of Culture, Education, and Church Affairs.

3. Founded in Berlin in 1822.

4. Israel Jacobson (1768–1828) was court agent in Braunschweig and President of the Jewish Consistory in the kingdom of Westphalia. Starting in 1815, he continued his efforts on behalf of Jewish reform in Berlin, where, in 1823, however, the government had his synagogue closed.

5. Moritz Saphir (1795–1858) was a well-known Austrian satirist and critic, who, after temporary sojourns in Berlin and Munich, published the paper *Der Humorist* in Vienna, starting in 1837. He was baptized in 1832.

# 7  *Ahron ben Moscheh Kirschner*

 BORN IN 1827 IN BEUTHEN (UPPER SILESIA).

Emanuel Kirschner, Reminiscences from My Life, Aspirations, and Work. Wörishofen, 1933; supplemented by his son, New York, 1947, 251 pages.

*The following excerpt from the memoirs of the Munich cantor and professor Emanuel Kirschner (1857–1938) depicts his childhood experiences as the son of a poor baker in Upper Silesia. Ahron ben Moscheh Kirschner, the father of this musically talented son, learned the baker's trade and, first in Rokittnitz and then in Karf near Beuthen, ran a store, which primarily served the Polish population of Upper Silesia. In 1868 he moved with his wife and ten children to Beuthen. His small bakery shop not only was at the same time the living room and bedroom of the family but also had to accommodate the piano of the son Emanuel, who was training to be a cantor. The relationship of the family, which led an orthodox life, to the clergymen and the population is presented positively.*

My father, Ahron ben Moscheh Kirschner, was born of my grandmother Liesel, née Dresdner, in Beuthen, Upper Silesia, on March 2, 1827. After he had quit primary school and learned the baker's trade, he left home and traversed Germany as a begging or working journeyman up to Danzig, from whence he wanted to emigrate to Turkey. Difficulties with his passport, however, not only prevented this plan from being carried out but also prompted the authorities to deport my father back home. Here he worked in his learned occupation until his twenty-sixth year, at which time he found the opportunity to take over a grocery in Rokittnitz, a village located two hours away from Beuthen.

At that time, in 1853, Rokittnitz was still an unattractive village with a Polish-speaking population numbering some few hundred souls, the male part of which consisted mostly of miners. Their cultural level certainly left a great deal to be desired, but they were harmless and good-natured—though only when they were sober.

When payday came, however, the money, hard-earned in the dark, wet womb of the earth, in the ore and coal mines, jingled in their pockets. As a rule, their first visit was to the inn, where they drank liquor often to the point of unconsciousness. The drunkenness of those who came staggering home often found an outlet in the abuse of wife and children. But still, between my father and the Catholic population there developed such a close relationship, based on trust, that in our day, with its religious and political instigations, it seems like a fairy tale from olden times. Father was able to gain such trust only through strictly straightforward business conduct and through unselfish advice in bad and good days, and as a human being who was always ready to help. [. . .]

German was spoken only in my parents' home and in a second Jewish family of the village, that of the tavernkeeper Grätzer, but the language used to speak with the population was Polish, which in the end we commanded better than German. The sounds of Hebrew, too, thrust themselves upon my ears, thanks to my father, who was fond of singing and who with the power of his deep bass cultivated not only the German and Polish folksong but above all the melodies of the synagogue. Also, every morning father or mother recited to us children the first portion of *"Schema Jisrael"*[1] which we had to repeat. [. . .]

A forest extending several kilometers was intersected by a highway that connected Rokittnitz with the nearest village, Miechowitz. Several Jewish families lived there, who, especially on the holidays, formed a *minjan* and at whose religious events my father led the prayers as *baal-tefilla*.[2] To make it possible to get from one place to another on the Sabbath and holidays, however, an *eruw*[3] had to be placed at approximately half the distance. My father fulfilled this duty by placing a meal upon a tree branch on the eve of the holiday, on *erew jontew*. But often this *eruw* had already disappeared on the next day, thanks to the forest animals, who relished the discovered feed. [. . .]

In contrast to all other holidays, on Jom Kippur my parents had to sleep over in Miechowitz. We children were in safekeeping with Sophie, of course, but house and home had to remain without a master on this night. Now, to keep away pilfering elements, my father came up with the lucky idea of setting the fox to keep the geese. He summoned the rascal Pieczek, who was as familiar as he was notorious, and asked whether he could entrust him with guarding the house, whereupon Pieczek proudly replied: "Panockzu (Sir), where *I* guard no thief will dare touch even the smallest thing." This man had character, kept his word, and as often as he may have taken over the watchman's duties, never did he pinch our property, nor were others allowed to do it. I am convinced that even without this protection we would have been faithfully guarded by the entire peasant population; for all too often my parents had the opportunity to relieve need, to help raise the impoverished up again.

It was not a rarity that peasants who had gone downhill through mismanagement proposed to my father that they give him their lands in exchange for his commitment of provisions for life. By accepting this proposal, my father could have become the biggest landowner of the village. He preferred, however, to go on living in modest economic conditions, to gain and keep the trust of the local population through honesty in his business activities, and not to amass riches in that manner.

*[In 1865 the parents move to Karf near Beuthen for the sake of a better education for the children.]*

The two-and-a-half-year stay in Karf brought us children, who daily had to trot to Beuthen to school, as a rule by Shanks's mare, many a more or less agreeable change. In the summer, when the weather was nice, it was a pleasure to walk to the town with bare feet, between rippling grainfields and past the Theresia pit. In contrast to the peace-loving village youth of Rokittnitz, some of the fellows working in the Theresia pit distinguished themselves by extraordinary roughness. On our way home we were, luckily not often, attacked by such bandits with the words: "Jew, give us something or we will kill you like a frog!" Lacking money, we redeemed ourselves with steel nib, penholder, or slate pencil, and, in double-time, we were allowed to hurry on home, where lunch and dinner, combined into one abundant meal, awaited us. [. . .]

The war against Austria destroyed my parents' means of existence in Karf. Many of my father's debtors, who had gone off to war, could no longer meet their financial obligations after their return home. Thus the reserves, the capital acquired in Rokittnitz through diligence and economy, vanished like snow in the sun. The trade connections that my father had with customers in Beuthen prompted him to give up the bakery and our living quarters after the collapse of his business and to set about rebuilding his existence in Beuthen.

In 1868, after a two-and-a-half-year stay in Karf, our move to Beuthen took place. There, my parents lived with ten children, a maid, and a baker's apprentice in a dwelling that consisted of a baked goods shop, combined kitchen and living room, a windowless, dark storeroom, and a bakery. This dwelling formed the back building situated on Kirchgasse, whose front house extending to the Ring was used for business and residential purposes by the owner of the entire property, the merchant C. S. Guttmann. The baked goods shop, behind whose counter, ornamented with fake coins, my mother sold crisp rolls and fresh-smelling loaves of bread from the very early morning on, served also as bedroom for my parents, as well as dining room for the entire family. There also was a daily guest for lunch, either a pupil from another town who attended school in Beuthen, or a stranger, alias *schnorrer,* passing through.

Often venerable old men with long beards, who had come from nearby Poland, entered our store and took from the pockets of their caftan a salted herring, which, with fresh bread and onions, made up their sumptuous noon meal. As businessmen—they were mostly flour dealers—they probably could have afforded a more bountiful meal with meat dishes, but the *schechita*[4] in Beuthen did not seem reliable enough for their overly pious orientation. Opposite our dwelling on a vacant square, dairymen from Peiskretscham brought their milk to market. In the winter months, when the half-frozen dairymen, driving their wagons, arrived in the town at five o'clock in the morning, they directed their steps first towards our store, in order to warm their nearly stiff limbs by an iron stove that radiated sweltering heat. For us children, who slept in the kitchen-living room and were fit for work, that was the signal to leave our not too cozy beds. After all, for lack of space four of us had to sleep in the only bed, while on the floor next to it every evening a place to sleep was readied for the rest of the siblings.

For the children helping in the store, and I was among them, the day's work began with the morning prayer, which our mother urged us to do with gentle words, our father, however, with zealous severity. Many a time he converted Solomon's wisdom, "He that loveth his child, chasteneth him," into painful practice. After eating breakfast, two or three of us were loaded down with one-handled baskets, to deliver breakfast rolls to numerous customers. [. . .]

Each Thursday night, leading into Friday, our mother, who now rests in *Gan Eden,*[5] helped braid the *berches*[6] and sprinkle them with poppy seed. After they had risen, father shoved them into the oven and kept a close eye on them so that they would turn out well and serve as a tasty adornment of the Sabbath table of many Jewish families.

When this work-filled night had passed, Friday morning demanded no less energy and prudence of my mother. No sooner had she served the customers than the local beggars appeared in masses to receive their weekly donation, and she had to give instructions and make preparations for the worthy reception of the holy Sabbath.

In the afternoon, the board floor was cleansed with broom and scrubbing brush of the dirt that had accumulated amply in the course of the week, and it was scrubbed until it had regained its natural white appearance, heightened even more by a layer of whitish yellow sand that was strewn over it. The store seemed transformed when mother, in her festive Sabbath dress, lit the Sabbath candles on the table covered with dazzling white linen, while father and we welcomed the Sabbath solemnly in the House of Worship.

Having returned home, with a hearty "Gut Schabbes" father and his entourage entered the cozy room sparkling in the glitter of the lights. After father finished blessing us, going back and forth, he welcomed the *malache haschores,*[7] and after that he enthusiastically struck up the song of the *esches chajel,*[8] with its many links to our dear mother, who was gently smiling to herself and finally was allowed to enjoy her well-earned Sabbath rest. During the quite abundant meal, father intoned *semiros,*[9] which were less familiar to us. But shortly before *benschen,* our clear, high-pitched voices united with father's mighty bass in *semiros* that resounded far off and that often aroused the attention of interested passers-by. Among these was the village priest, who had to go past our house on his way to church.

In this connection, I remember the following very typical incident. Some silver spoons were stolen from my parents. In spite of persistent inquiries, the thief was not discovered. In some way, unknown to me, the priest found out about this misdeed and mentioned it from the pulpit during the Sunday church service, more or less in the following words: "When, on my way to church, I pass the house of the Jewish baker Kirschner, sometimes Hebrew song from the mouths of the parents and the children reaches my ear. By that alone I recognize that in that house the family leads a pious life, pleasing to God, which we Christians, too, must treat with respect. Whoever misappropriates the possessions of such a man is committing a mortal sin. As I have recently learned, such a sin has been committed against this man. If the wrongdoer is among you, then he can undo this mortal sin and atone only by the immediate return of the stolen possessions to their owner." On the following day, our silver spoons were back again.

In this regard, I remember another episode in which the priest also played an important role. Like lightning, it illuminates the complete contrast between then and now, between the once peaceful relationship among the different religious communities and the presently widespread, systematic incitement of the German people, promoted from above with the goal of making difficult, indeed destroying, through defamation and the deprivation of civil rights, the possibility of existence for German Jews in what until now was their fatherland.

The teachers of the Jewish school did not, as a rule, overburden the schoolchildren in their care with too much book knowledge. But once a year there took place the public school examination, for which we were properly drilled weeks in advance. The dreaded examination day had finally arrived, and we, dressed and washed spic-and-span, waited intently for what was to come. Then the door of the classroom opens and, accompanied by the teacher and the community board member Reb Mosche Guttmann, in comes a giant of a man, dressed in clerical garment, who musters us pupils with a benevolent expression and a penetrating look. This was the priest Schafrannek, a staunch 1848 democrat, who asked Dr. Ginsberg to give him a Pentateuch and to our boundless surprise began to read Hebrew sentences from it, which we had to translate. After the examination, whose results seemed to have satisfied him, he urged us with warm words to cling faithfully to our belief, not only spiritually, to acquire the content of the Holy Scripture, but also in the outside world, in trade and commerce, to make the fulfillment of God's word the principle of all that we do.

How vastly does the pure humanity of this Christian priest distinguish itself from the world view of racial madness and brutal hatred of the Jews which at present is causing such horrible things.

1. "Hear, Oh Israel" (Hebrew), main prayer of the Jews, after Deuteronomy 6:4–9.
2. Prayer leader (Hebrew).
3. Orthodox Jews are forbidden to go further than one kilometer from their home on the Sabbath or a holiday. However, where travel is necessary for religious reasons, a second place of dwelling is symbolically established on the day before by putting down a plate of food on the way, in order thus to avoid violating the law.
4. Slaughtering (Hebrew) in accordance with religious prescription.
5. Garden of Eden, Paradise (Hebrew).
6. Braided white bread eaten on the Sabbath.
7. "Serving angels"; referred to in the song of this name sung to welcome the Sabbath.
8. Song in praise of the virtues of the wife, after Proverbs 31:10–31.
9. Sabbath songs (Hebrew).

# 8  *Philipp Tuchmann*

 BORN IN 1810 IN ÜHLFELD (FRANCONIA); DIED IN 1883 IN DESSAU.

Moritz and Franz Tuchmann, Chronicle of the Tuchmann Family of the Older Branch. 1895 and 1910, 85 pages.[1]

*Franz Tuchmann tells of his father, Philipp Tuchmann, who grew up in Ühlfeld as the son of the hop grower and hop dealer Marx Tuchmann. The three sons and five sons-in-law of Marx Tuchmann all devoted themselves to the hop business, which, with the rise of larger breweries and the opening of the hop fair, experienced a boom. Philipp Tuchmann first learned the tanner's trade, since in Bavaria Jewish craftsmen had priority in obtaining the right of residence. He spent his journeyman years in Prussia and Poland. In 1838 he passed the examination for the master craftsman certificate, but then became a traveling salesman in his father's hop business. When encountering difficulties, he decided in the 1840s to "emigrate" to Dessau. There he traded very successfully in hops and coal, which he obtained from Bohemia by ship. In 1856 he expanded the business with a timber enterprise and established a sawmill.*

At the beginning of the nineteenth century, the Jews in Bavaria were ordered by the authorities to assume a German name, since until then they had used only a Jewish forename.[2] Until that time my grandfather bore the name Mordechai. When he was then asked by the judge of the provincial court in Neustadt on Aisch which German name he wanted to take, he was very much intent on getting as short a name as possible, and inasmuch as he was dealing in hops he suggested the name Hopf, which was, however, refused him because shortly before another person, Loeb Hopf, later the son-in-law of my grandparents, had already assumed this name. Since, in addition to hops, my grandfather also dealt in hop cloth, a kind of canvas made of flax, hemp, and jute, which is used for packaging hops, he hit upon the idea of taking the name Tuchmann.

As far as I can remember, my grandfather Marx Tuchmann was a very enlightened man and was held in high esteem, not only in Ühlfeld but also in the environs, because of his upright, strictly honest, unselfish character. He detested all money transactions and especially any dealings that could somehow be offensive, and from far and wide people came to him not only to get his advice but also to associate with him.

My grandmother Marie Tuchmann, née Engelmann, from Floss, whom I still remember clearly, was a very domestic, economic, and thrifty woman, whose entire fulfillment was in knowing that her husband and her children were doing well. She had little taste for pleasure, but that much the more for domesticity and business, so that she herself did a small trade in the house with paints, glue, etc., and was always happy that she earned something with it daily. It was also mainly she who got my grandfather to sell hops, in addition to his farming and hop growing, and who later steered not only my father but also her other two sons and all five sons-in-law to the hop business.

My grandfather was engaged in agriculture and devoted himself mainly to hop farming, but he was also not adverse to the propensity to build, and he not only erected a big house with rear buildings for himself, but also brought about the construction of the magnificent synagogue in Ühlfeld, under his direction. As already mentioned, upon the initiative of my grandmother he also turned to the hop business by purchasing the hops grown in and around Ühlfeld and bringing them with his own horse-drawn wagon to Hersbruck, Happurg, etc., where at that time Bohemian hop dealers always stayed to buy hops. [. . .]

My father enjoyed rather good schooling in Ühlfeld, since his parents saw to it that their children were given a proper education. Because at the beginning of the nineteenth century there was legislation[3] in Bavaria that greatly oppressed the Jews, and since in accordance therewith Jews were not allowed to become businessmen or merchants, and, furthermore, were forced to learn a trade, my father decided to become a tanner, and he was apprenticed to Master Tanner Nickel in Neuhof near Markt Erlbach. This four-year apprenticeship was not exactly a part of my father's most pleasant memories, for, on the one hand, the occupation brought with it the unpleasant work with skins, water, and acids, and on the other hand, my father, as a result of his religious upbringing, was forced to cook for himself in those four years; and since the strenuous apprenticeship did not always allow him enough time to prepare meals, he could not supply his body with the strength he needed by eating properly and enough.

After concluding his apprenticeship in 1827, he set out journeying on October 11, 1827. During this time, too, he had enough perseverance to maintain his religious eating habits. In 1834 my father became a master craftsman. So many difficulties were caused him by the guild, however, that he lost his desire to practice the craft, and upon grandmother's encouragement he turned to the hop business. It was very useful to him that his father, Marx Tuchmann, was engaged in hop growing and the hop trade himself, and therefore it was easy for him to familiarize himself thoroughly with this pursuit in his father's business. Even while journeying, he was very interested in breweries, since his father, after all, had a hop business. He got to know brewers here and there and very soon sensed that in the cities of Central and North Germany there was, without any doubt, appreciation for Bavarian hops. He made his first trips as a hop dealer on foot, from place to place, and attained quite decent results for those times (1831–1838). I would like to mention especially that in the Duchy of Altenburg, where he had worked as a tanner's apprentice for some time and had made many acquaintances, he also did good business as a hop dealer and there acquired the customers he had later, when he set himself up on his own. For in Altenburg there existed a communal brewery, a brewery in which most of the householders were entitled to brew beer at their own expense. My father then sold the needed hops to practically every one of these people entitled to brew, and even if the quantities to be supplied to each were not exactly big, still, taken all together, approx. 40–50 centners were sold per year.

Solomon Tuchmann, the older brother of my father, who covered the Rhineland and Westphalia, did a very similar business. The profit from all these sales, however, still went to my grandfather, in whose business the two sons were still active at that time. Only after my Uncle Solomon, as well as my father, had married did both together run their own hop business for some years, and in doing so made considerable headway.

In the early forties, my father was already able to maintain a small one-horse chaise and a coachman. Since there were still no railroads and only very bad coach connections, he was thus able to undertake his ever-increasing business trips at his convenience, and in so doing it now happened quite frequently that he stayed on the road three to four weeks.

To the extent that there did not exist many big breweries, as is the case now, but that brewing was done mostly only on manors or in the cities in the so-called communal breweries, business in those days was quite difficult. Since at that time only weiss, malt, and bitter beers were brewed, the so-called top-fermented beers, the consumption of hops per individual customer amounted to one to ten centners a year, and thus at the beginning my father had a turnover of 400 to 500 centners yearly. In the bigger cities such as Berlin, Magdeburg, Leipzig, and Stettin, which my father also visited on his business trips, the demand was greater, but here one had to reckon with the competition. Also, in those days my father could not expand his business that much since the purchase of hops from the growers mostly took place in exchange for cash, and means were not yet sufficient for bigger purchases. I still remember having heard from him quite often that when his cash was insufficient he bought hops from intermediary dealers for which he didn't have to pay until St. James' Day (July 25th). These purchases, of course, turned out to be more expensive than from the grower, and thus a part of the profit was lost at the start.

Through his incessant activity, my father gained more and more customers, and thus he was forced to get credit from so-called moneylenders (like Meyer Kohn in Markt

Erlbach and Frauenfeld in Büchenbach) and on this credit to borrow money at a not exactly low rate of interest. Such money on credit was gladly granted him, as he was known as an industrious, diligent, and decent man. Also the fine, pleasing characteristics that my father possessed contributed no little in making him much-liked by everyone. Anton and Joseph Kohn, of the above-mentioned business in Markt Erlbach, which they continued later in Nuremberg under the name of Meyer Kohn, told me in the 1870s with great pleasure how welcome a guest my father always was at the home of their parents.

The business grew more and more, but as much as father enjoyed it, his work was made very difficult for him since, due to the political troubles starting in the mid-forties under King Ludwig I and Minister Abel, oppressive conditions were brought about for the Bavarian Jews. Thus, for example, the authorities were instructed to see to it strictly that all those who were not practicing the trade they had learned take it up again, above all, however, that all Jews who had gone over to business give up the same and return to their trade. Because of these ordinances, the judge of the regional court of Neustadt on Aisch, who was already inclined by nature to chicanery, had free rein for his despotism, all the more since he always found protection from above and was deemed to be right in all matters. For this reason, a complaint about him was completely hopeless from the start. We also had to suffer harassment from the gendarmery; for example, it was forbidden to treat the hops with sulfur, since the authorities not only saw in this procedure a deception but they also regarded it as a fire hazard, since the devices for it were very primitive in those days. Thus, it often happened that gendarmery and commissions suddenly appeared in Ühlfeld and conducted house searches for sulfurized hops, and as soon as they found such, or perhaps even surprised people in the process of sulfurization, they immediately confiscated all the supplies and either threw them into the water, had them buried, or destroyed them in some other way. The result of this was that many people could scarcely get ahead, became completely impoverished, and were greatly embittered toward the state and the authorities.

To all these harassments by the authorities was added the envy of the local population, for after some other Jewish families had observed how my father had gradually advanced, they took him as a model, likewise turned to the hop business, and gradually also became successful. This, however, awakened the envy of the non-Jews, and thus a hatred of Jews came into being that equaled the antisemitism of today.

Even if my father was harassed most sorely by the judge of the regional court and the gendarmery, it probably would not have been out of the question to reduce this chicanery if he had done as others and met the officials halfway with gentle words and with cash. However, since he had an upright, honest character and was also somewhat inclined to be hot-blooded, he didn't want to hear of it. He decided it was better to leave his fatherland, Bavaria, in order, on the one hand, to avoid these constant irritations and malice, but, on the other hand, also to give his children a better education than was possible in Ühlfeld, which was cut off from any railway connection and had no prospect of ever getting one. On April 28, 1847, he emigrated with his family to Dessau, a city he had visited often on his journeys.

It was a great undertaking for my father to leave his place of birth, his fatherland, to which all his memories were bound, his parents, his siblings, and the friends of his youth, in order to move with a big family to a distant, unknown place. He hoped, however, that in Dessau he had made a good choice, because this city lay right in the center of his clientele, because at that time it had the best schools of Germany, and because the authorities and citizens of Dessau were already completely enlightened and the Jews there enjoyed the same esteem as everyone else.

The move with a wife, five small children, and a maid was no small matter in those days if one considers that the highways were still quite poor and the railroads in their first stage still left a great deal to be desired. The journey went first from Ühlfeld to Bamberg in four hours by horse-drawn vehicle, and from Bamberg to Hof by train. There we stayed overnight and on the next day continued by rail to Plauen, from where once again a horse-drawn vehicle had to be used to reach Reichenbach. From Reichenbach we went by train to Leipzig, Halle, Köthen, and Dessau, where we arrived at eleven o'clock at night and were awaited and received with open arms by my father's acquaintances. They saw us to our house, Franzstrasse No. 6, which was bought from Wolf Jacoby and which we still own today.

In comparison to Ühlfeld, Dessau was a rather big town, in which the court and the government were located. The inhabitants received us in a friendly way, so that soon we settled and found ourselves in a much better situation than that in Ühlfeld. Because we immediately had our own house, my parents had it easier with getting settled. My father was able not only to attend to his business with more calm, but also, since my mother was not yet familiar with North German conditions, to help preside over family life when he returned from his business trips, usually at the latest every Friday. With great pleasure, my mother was bent on providing her husband and her children with a pleasant home, appropriate to our circumstances. Also, this devoted woman was always concerned about the education of her children. Through constant great economy, achieved by spending only little for her housekeeping, and also by looking after the business in an extraordinary manner, the financial circumstances of my dear departed parents were quite good and improved from year to year.

Since the main business did not keep him busy the whole year through, my father got the idea of occupying himself additionally with the sale of fuels (peat, coal, etc.). To this end, he had big boatloads of Bohemian coal, which he bought up personally in Bohemia, shipped down the Elbe to Dessau, and earned some money with that, too. However, the growing competition in these commodities caused him to give up this business after a few years and to devote his entire energies to such products as were used by the breweries in those days, namely, pitch, honey, syrup, drying racks, etc. When my father was on his trips, my mother, who was also very active in the business, took care of shipping the articles and also tended to the correspondence, so that my father could always be calm and without worry on his business trips. Through this great industry and economy my parents advanced more and more, so that they were in the agreeable position of being able to tear down the rear part of their property and erect new buildings there, thanks to which fairly large stock rooms and storage spaces were created, which were most necessary since the old ones no longer sufficed for the increased business activity. The new rooms gained by the construction were also very welcome to my parents, since the family had grown in the meanwhile and needed more space. In 1855, the neighboring property, Franzstrasse No. 5, was also bought, not too expensively, from the pensioner Hirschberg, and thus the living rooms and attics could be expanded even more.

My parents were very much concerned about giving their children as good an education as possible. They sent their sons to commercial school, their daughters to the so-called Braun's Girls Academy, both at that time among the best educational institutions in Germany—and they also did not neglect having them instructed privately in addition, so that, well-prepared, August (in 1855), Franz (in 1856), and Louis (in 1858) could be apprenticed to businessmen in Magdeburg. In those days, that did mean something, since the yearly expenses for upkeep and apprenticeship amounted to 300 talers. But by no means did my parents shrink from these expenses, since they realized quite well that thorough training was absolutely necessary for a businessman.

In 1856 my parents were anxious to create a livelihood for their sons, since not all could engage in their parent's business. At that time my father became acquainted with a master builder, Karl Krause, in Dessau, who proposed the idea of entering into a partnership and together building a sawmill and operating a lumber business. This idea became reality, the sawmill was built, and soon the business was making great progress. After four years of joint activity, Krause, who had a frivolous character, withdrew, and my father took over the business by himself. [. . .]

Even if my departed parents came to Dessau with a fortune of approx. 200,000 marks, which in those days could almost be called rich, significant amounts of money were still withdrawn from the hop business, because on the one hand the hop business demanded quite large investments at that time, and on the other hand there were the dowries of the two daughters. And therefore Franz and Louis, who had to work mainly in this enterprise, had it quite hard, especially since Bavarian beer brewing began to flourish and foreign countries were building big establishments for this purpose and enlisted the financial aid of the hop dealers.

1. Inserted in English in the autobiography of H. Metzger (LBI Archives). The German original was made available by F. C. Tuchmann in New York.
2. Bavarian Edict on the Jews of 1813, Section 4.
3. Bavarian Edict on the Jews of 1813, Section 13. According to this law, only one son in each family received the right of residence. Beyond that, only those were admitted who could show that they were engaged in manufacturing, trade, or farming.

# 9 *Martin Lövinson*

BORN IN 1859 IN BERLIN; DIED IN 1930 IN BERLIN.

Martin Lövinson, Story of my Life, Part I: The Golden Days of Youth. Berlin 1924, 128 pages.

*In these recollections of his youth, Counselor of Justice Martin Lövinson tells about his father, the son of a Danzig businessman, who rose to become a well-to-do furniture manufacturer in Berlin. There, in 1858 Siegfried Lövinson founded a factory for carved oak furniture, in which he employed journeyman joiners and unskilled workers; and he also had work done in the penal institutions in Spandau. The rising firm exhibited in the first World Fairs in London and Paris. In 1865 the family moved to Charlottenburg, at that time still an independent royal seat, where they set up an orthodox synagogue in their home. Having attained the position of well-to-do bourgeoisie, the family enthusiastically welcomed the founding of the Reich and the complete legal emancipation of the Jews. During the period of rapid industrial expansion in Germany after 1871, S. Lövinson acquired numerous properties in Berlin; in the early eighties, however, he was compelled to file for bankruptcy of his firm.*

The 22nd of August 1857 has always been celebrated as the official engagement day [of my parents]. The wedding came exactly a year later. In the interim, the bridegroom founded his own business. On her deathbed, his mother urged him, her youngest son, my father, Siegfried, who was not yet 30 years old but had advanced well in his business career, to have at heart the interests of his older brother Louis, who in spite of unusual ability had not been able to achieve a regular middle-class existence, in contrast to the oldest son, Moritz, who, at the time when she was closing her eyes, was already a respected physician at a young age. Louis, who had learned the craft of bookbinding after a rather adventurous journeyman's life, had become a political agitator during the turmoil of 1848. As late as June 15, 1848, he had organized the storming of the armory—an undertaking that according to all reports was quite rash—and to the deep sorrow of his mother he had ended up in jail for a lengthy time. Now, Siegfried was supposed to win him back to middle-class life. In accord with the promise he made to his dying mother, and to the surprise of his employer, Hermann Gerson, he gave up his promising position in the latter's business and, under the name Lövinson Brothers, opened a factory for carved oak furniture—at first on cramped business premises on Brüderstrasse. Since the business took an encouraging upswing, soon the transfer into larger rooms proved to be desirable, and thus when my parents married [in 1858] the headquarters of my father's business activity was on the second floor of house No. 8 on Unter den Linden, where he remained until the middle of the seventies. Later the business became a partnership limited by shares, and finally a corporation; but in the storms of the great commercial crisis that followed the feverish profit making of the boom years around 1880, it was ruined. My father and his brother Louis were the directors until the end. They and a number of relatives and friends suffered great losses during the collapse. [. . .]

My father's ever-sincere care for released convicts can be explained by the above-mentioned fate of his brother Louis. It is a sign of the many likable characteristics that I always admired in him that when a prisoner being released was recommended to him by the director of Spandau, where part of the carvings were produced, he placed him in his factory without hesitation, even in a position of trust. His chief bookkeeper, old Habekost, the office helper of many years' standing Marschner, the coachman Taubenheim, and also the stainer Printz, whose job was to keep the furniture in our private residence in order, were said to be this kind of protégé.[. . .]

My parents kept a strictly ritual Jewish household. Even if my father kept his business open on the Sabbath and did not avoid traveling, as long as I can remember he always said the prescribed prayers in the morning. It was only later that I noticed that he did not put on the *tefillin* (phylacteries). But he did wear the *arba kanfot* (small prayer shawl) beneath his undershirt, on his bare body.[1] That there was cooking at our home on the Sabbath and the High Holy Days I heard explained to grandmother Hirschberg as a measure undertaken in consideration of the small children. She herself, however, observed the old ritual laws in this regard. Every Friday we took her *schalent*[2] to the matzo oven on Heidereutergasse, opposite the old, so-called Great Synagogue, and picked it up again at noon on Saturday after the end of the main service, nicely baked and still warm. Even our freethinking Grandfather Lövinson did not refuse our dear grandmother's occasional invitation to the tasty meal. I did see him, too, in the synagogue on the High Holidays, when, even at a young age, I was brought along by my parents. Otherwise, however, he had completely freed himself from the old tradition.

The present-day system of renting seats did not yet exist at that time; whoever did not own a seat, took any empty place at the service without trouble, particularly since entry into the House of God was not restricted in any way but rather was encouraged. Thus, as soon as I could walk I was very often taken along to the Old Synagogue, to which my grandmother went regularly, my mother as often as taking care of the little ones permitted, and the men of the family on the main holy days. Even today the organ is still banned from this old House of God. But the festive singing of the choir, of the celebrated cantor Lichtenstein, and of the congregation, as well as the sermons of the very popular, warmhearted rabbi, Dr. Sachs, made an indelible impression on my young spirit, even if I understood neither the German nor the Hebrew recitation; I cannot imagine my life without them. The wish to understand these beautiful customs, which elevated one above everyday life, awakened within me very early (and that was surely my father's pedagogic aim). Of the welfare institutions of the Jewish community, on the other hand, at that time I only got to know the old-age home on Grosse Hamburgerstrasse. There, from time to time, bringing small gifts we visited an old miss, Emma Sachs, who must have been somehow related to grandmother and who, as I seem to vaguely remember, spent her last days and years there with an even older sister. So our parents placed value on awakening in us love for our ancestral religion and the thought that religion is lived and experienced, and not invented or contrived. [. . .]

The year 1864 brought the German-Danish War, the victorious end of which we were privileged to experience from the window of our business, Unter den Linden, when as spectators we watched the festive entrance of the troops. Our father was filled with lofty patriotic enthusiasm by the splendid course the war had taken after so many years of peace. His enthusiasm manifested itself in the fact that he acquired the wood of seized enemy artillery mounts from the army administration and in his factory had all kinds of keepsakes carved from it, which were sold for the benefit of the war victims. Ashtrays, cigar cutters, and similar little things can still be found in the possession of family members.

The business had taken a real upturn at this time. Our house was frequented by well-known architects, such as Oppler, the designer of the synagogues in Breslau and

Hannover. Employing Gothic motifs, he had designed a little table with two small benches, which was intended for the children's room and served all of us children as our first desk. [. . .]

The literary needs of the family were served by the *Vossische Zeitung,* which was still coming out as a small-town weekly, and by the big illustrated magazines *Gartenlaube* and *Über Land und Meer.* But we probably did no more than look at the pictures, since we were still too small to stay up when mother read aloud every night. I know for sure, however, that it was still on Bellevuestrasse that we became acquainted with our later favorite Wilhelm Busch, whose *Münchener Bilderbogen* was a preferred birthday wish of ours.

I have probably told everything that I remember from my first six years, during which I did not leave my hometown, since the custom of summer trips was still restricted to the more prosperous circles, while we regarded ourselves as belonging to the middle class. At most, there was perhaps sometimes an "excursion to the country," the goal of which, however, was always grandfather's estate in Treptow. As far as I know, the annual factory outing was always to Pichelsberge. The workmen and clerks set out early in the morning in charabancs, and in the afternoon the bosses and their families followed after them in their landaus. [. . .]

The High Jewish Holidays always brought about an enormous change in our daily schedule. I have mentioned the installation of the house synagogue, which our father had set up mainly to make it possible for our mother, who at that time would not have used a vehicle on the holidays at any price, to attend the services. The example for the children, who by all means were to be familiarized with a strictly religious life, was no doubt decisive in this undertaking. Of course, quite early there arose within us questions as to whether it was entirely consistent that our father unhesitatingly used the streetcar on the Sabbath and High Holidays, that we did write in school on the Sabbath, indeed, that we were allowed to participate in the Christian religious instruction until the first year of secondary school. But for all of these inconsistencies we were given an explanation in accordance with the prevailing enlightened views, especially, for example, that the fulfillment of civic duties had to go hand in hand with the recognition of complete equality of civil rights. Whoever was now admitted to the public schools, as we were, had to comply with the general school regulations; whoever opened a business in the German homeland also had to keep it open to customers on the generally accepted workdays and close it on the public day of rest.

Above all, however, it was pointed out that the many Christian laborers and employees were entitled to demand consideration of their religious feelings as well as their financial interests in all these matters. The concept of tolerance, which was to become a guiding principle throughout our lives, was thus placed at the center of our civic and religious philosophy of life. Just as we, as a religious minority, had to take the interests of the state into account, in the private sphere we also had to exercise absolute respect for the reverence with which our fellow citizens of another faith were attached to their religion and its particular customs. I can only say that in those days, before the invention of social and racial antisemitism, the views of our Christian environment completely coincided with our own.

Thus, the others welcomed it almost with appreciation that we Jews, too, were to have a regular prayer service, and the few coreligionists living there did not mind at all that our father relieved them not only of the troubles but also completely of the costs of this institution. [. . .]By affixing a curtain, a wardrobe was transformed into the holy ark, and it happened that in the possession of the families there were two Torah scrolls, which were willingly made available for the good cause. As cantors, two dignified old men were found, Herr Ebenstein and Herr Cohn; the former had previously been teacher, cantor, and *schochet* in Neuruppin and now lived in retirement in Berlin, while the other tried to make a modest living with a small business. Since they could not travel by any vehicle on holidays and, in addition, their duties kept them busy from morning until night, they came out to us early on the evening before the holidays and received board from our mother.

To her sorrow, however, she could not offer them lodgings, because every room in the big house was occupied by other guests. First of all, of course, Grandmother Hirschberg was at our place, then there regularly appeared Grandfather Lövinson, who otherwise was such a freethinking man, and finally an old brother of Grandmother Hirschberg, called Uncle Schlaume. He had been a townsman who cultivated some land while living in a small town of the Mark or in Pomerania—I think it was in Berlinchen— and at that time he must have already been close to eighty years old. He did not have a wife or children, and, on the small pension that had remained him after the sale of his property, he lived in Berlinchen with decent Jewish people on Stralauerstrasse, or earlier still on Königsgraben, where we seldom visited him, except for his birthday or in case of sickness. On the holidays, however, he was our honored guest. For he had played a role in world history. He was among the few Jewish volunteers who had set out from his Pomeranian homeland in 1813–1815 and had marched with the allies against Napoleon all the way to Paris. We squeezed him dry of war stories, and we regretted only that he had not been with our idol Theodor Körner in the same troop of Lützow's volunteer corps but instead had served modestly as an infantryman with the no less courageous militia. The other old people teased him a great deal about his war stories. They said the bullets had probably passed through his throat piece by piece, and had in mind the so-called Polish Kugel,* a favorite dish that was in high regard among the older generation as a side dish with *schalet*. Things became especially interesting when once the old father of our poetically inclined Uncle Hermann Hersch turned up for the holidays from his Rhenish home of Jüchen. The latter had participated in the Wars of Liberation on the French side, and the agile and probably better educated Rhinelander certainly knew how to tell stories better than the slow and somewhat tight-lipped Pomeranian. It was old Hersch, whose German and Hebrew script was like a copperplate, who put the beautiful caption below the picture that hangs in my workroom and shows the stately house in Charlottenburg of which I am telling here. It is a maxim from the *Sayings of the Fathers* and it reads: "Do not heed the container but only what is inside it."

Today, one can hardly imagine how my mother, besides keeping up the household, also managed, with complete attentiveness, to receive our many guests. For the ones

*The German word *Kugel* means bullet.

mentioned until now did not make up the entire flock. During the wars, the Jewish soldiers from the hospitals in Charlottenburg also came regularly. But that was still not all. Word soon got around about the beautiful prayer service, and whoever showed up for it and didn't have a place to stay or to take holiday meals, without much ado became a guest of our parents. Thus the large garden room, in which we dined at such times, was just as full of guests as in the days during the entry of the army in 1866. Of the acquaintanceships made at this time I will mention only two. Once, during his walks, Grandfather Lövinson discovered among the diggers who at that time were making a broad highway from the narrow pass at Spandau Hill a hardworking young man whom he recognized as a Jew and to whom he spoke thereof during a break. He turned out to be a bookbinder from Russia and was named Hermann Presakowicz, or perhaps Polakewicz. Like many Jews and Christians, he had fled from his inhospitable homeland to escape the unbearably long and hard military service, and had found work in his profession only temporarily. In order not to become a burden to the charity of his coreligionists, without hesitation he seized the first opportunity to work that came his way. Now, however, he received help, not only for the holidays, on which he naturally was a guest like all others at our table, but also in the long run. At first father took him into his factory as an unskilled worker. Later, when we had moved back to Berlin, he also did many repairs at our home. In a house that belonged to my father, he found rather primitive lodgings, which were all the cheaper for that, and soon, with my father's support, he was able to acquire his own tools and he became an independent master craftsman in his own trade. [. . .]

The story of the Charlottenburg years so far has shown that our household had assumed the character of a quite well-to-do, even if not luxurious, middle-class home. Our father acquired the means for that from his visibly thriving business. The abolition of compulsory guild membership in its final ramifications had made it possible to adapt oneself freely in business matters to the desires of the public; thus, for example, besides furniture the factory also produced clocks and musical instruments, ivory carvings, and similar things. Our keen interest was aroused for a long time by an example of such small works of art, a little wooden egg in which a tiny chess set was enclosed, and by similar devices that gentlemen carried around with them as containers for the popular Bullrich digestant salts. With such novelties the firm made its first appearance at the Leipzig fair, and later at the world and national industrial exhibitions that were coming into being in that decade. Thus, the name of the firm can be found among the exhibitors in London in 1863, and especially, moreover, at the great World Fair of 1867 in Paris. On such occasions my father spent weeks, if not months, abroad and made valuable contacts in foreign countries. There was even a branch established in London, which was managed by Julius Jacobi, a Danzig compatriot of my paternal family. At the Paris fair the firm was represented by young Siechen, the future head of the brewery of this same name, which was very famous in his day and probably still is. Many a friendly relationship resulted from the exhibitors working together during the preparations for such an undertaking and during its implementation. At such times, the men were together a lot, in foreign places and on the road, and their association often continued when they were back home.

Of course, even at that time my father was not spared serious difficulties. I will mention only the three wars, with the unavoidable interruptions of credit and sales, as well as a devastating fire, which, if I am not mistaken, in the night of the New Year (1868–69) reduced the factory to ashes. Also, after the war, in 1870, there was a big strike by the workers in that whole line of business, which despite the owners' principles, known to be favorable to the workers and democratic, also spread to our factory. With his unusual flexibility, father was able to surmount all these grave misfortunes. When the sale of furniture faltered during the wars in 1866 and 1870, and at the same time cholera, with all its threat, came to Berlin and spread horror in the city, which was still without sewers, he invented a disinfectant, which, as I recall, consisted of peat litter and ferrous sulfate and was to be poured into the commodes that were in use in almost all living quarters. The components arrived by waterway, since the rear of the factory, where they were blended, bordered on the Spree. The disinfectant was sold in big paper bags, which bore the label "Antimiasmaticum." A large advertising company saw to the recommendation of this very timely remedy, which must have been quite practical, and delivery to the consumers was carried out by the factory workers, who were not sufficiently occupied with their actual tasks, by means of a few charabancs that father had gotten hold of for this purpose in Charlottenburg and whose owners, in such bad times for business, were glad to have found profitable earnings, during the week, too. [. . .]

And so my story has reached the year 1871, my twelfth year, and now I must part from these most beautiful years in my memory. A fateful hour has arrived, not only for our small family circle but for political and social conditions throughout the fatherland. The victorious war ended in the glorious Peace of Frankfurt and the founding of the new German Reich. On the 15th and 16th of June the proud troops had marched into the new imperial city, and it made an indelible impression on me that once again I was able to observe the magnificent spectacle from the window of my father's business. The day before, we had watched the decoration of the triumphal route, which was done by the artists in a way never imagined possible. The route went from Kreuzberg by way of Belle-Alliance-Strasse and Königgrätzer Strasse, past Potsdam Gate, through Brandenburg Gate to Unter den Linden, which marked the highpoint of the decorations, and to the Lustgarten. The unveiling of the monument for Friedrich Wilhelm II, which had just been completed there, was the final act. I don't remember what the monuments, made of light materials and set up temporarily along the main points of this triumphal route, represented. They must have been embodiments of the victory, of the German and the more narrowly defined Prussian fatherland.

What made this unforgettable occasion superb was the elated mood, which no one could resist. Even if the captured guns that lined the entire route reminded one that the road to the unification of the fatherland had led through three bloody wars, the joy over the end of this time of great violence was still stronger than the pride in the victory gained. The entire world expected, above all, the end of the hard internal struggles among the parties and among the separate German lands and, as a result of peace, an upswing in trade and industry, from which, in turn, art and science would receive the best incentives. The likable figure of the over-seventy-year-old first emperor of the

Hohenzollern dynasty, who, for his part, was so modest, seemed to secure the monarchic system for all time to come. The strong opposition that Bismarck had brought upon himself by his political conduct subsided, not only in the face of his successes but also because of the greatness that he showed when, disavowing his earlier Junker ideals, he had not hesitated to pay the price for the unification of Germany by granting the new Reich a seemingly democratic-parliamentary constitution.

Old republicans joined in the jubilation, and Uncle Moritz recast an old 1848 freedom song into a German song of unity. It begins with the words:

> Forward! Forward! Germany's sons,
> With courage forward to the fight,
> Let no one ever dare to mock
> Our freedom and our rights.

Wilhelm Taubert, the well-known composer, did not pass up the chance to set it to music. Let me add the second stanza here. It goes something like this:

> For life's greatest goods,
> For the German fatherland,
> We stand as guardians and protectors
> With head, and heart, and hand.

The song, of which thousands of copies were sold at the beginning of the war for the benefit of the wounded, has impressed itself on my mind, as has the "Watch on the Rhine," which so accurately depicts the attitude of an entire people, although I do not mean to compare the two songs in their poetic power.

We Jews were also especially affected by the change in the internal situation. Due to the law of 1869 on the equality of religions in all of Germany, the barriers that had been erected before the Jews by the laws prohibiting their admission to office had now fallen. One did not expect that society and the practice of the authorities would maintain these barriers for a long time to come, and would erect new ones. There had been Jewish officers in the war of 1866; in the French war, numerous Jews achieved a similar recognition of their devotion to duty and their courage. Two cousins of my mother, Moritz and Albert Marcuse, sons of the oldest brother of my grandmother, returned from the field with the Iron Cross, the former as a captain in the medical corps, the latter as a lieutenant. Now there were Jewish judges and civil servants, whereas formerly even an appointment as a lawyer had scarcely been attainable for a Jewish civil servant even after years of unpaid civil service. Thus, in our circles, too, the joy and hope were almost beyond description. Not that every Jew now longed for a government position, but the fact that the feeling of a basic disfranchisement, of helotry, seemed to have been taken from us lifted our spirits and spurred us on to accomplishments in the service of our fatherland, from that time on also in the areas of peaceful development.

---

1. *Arba kanfot* is a garment worn under their clothing by orthodox Jews. It has four knotted cords *(tsitsit)* at its corners, as prescribed in Deuteronomy 22:12.

2. *Schalent (schalet, cholent):* a Sabbath dish, which must be prepared on the day before since cooking, as a form of work, is forbidden on the Sabbath.

118

# 10 *Faibel Siegel*

BORN IN 1807 IN WALLDORF (NEAR MEININGEN); DIED IN 1887 IN
MEININGEN.

Moritz Siegel, My Family History. Meiningen, 1900–1917, 298 pages.

*Moritz Siegel (born in 1842) describes the Jewish community in the village of
Walldorf (Sachsen-Meiningen), in which at the turn of the century the 567 Jewish
inhabitants constituted more than a third of the village's population. The religious
reform movement, cultural assimilation, and economic progress found quick acceptance
in this rural community. The Siegel family belonged to the leading families of the
village, valued highly the education of its children, and socialized regularly with
Christians. Faibel Siegel, the author's father, worked his way up from being a
textile dealer to being the owner of the wholesale weaving mill of Siegel, Elsbach &
Co., which employed hundreds of Thuringian home-weavers, imported yarns from
England, and exported them primarily to South Germany. When the Jews in
Sachsen-Meiningen were finally also granted freedom of movement in 1868, Siegel
transferred his wholesale business to the capital, Meiningen.*

In Walldorf three families of feudal nobility shared the power. The families
von Diemar, von Bibra (formerly von Wolfskehl), and von Marschallk exercised their
commercial and judicial hegemony, each within its own precisely demarcated domain.
Jurisdiction over every villager lay solely in the hands of his estate lord. The latter could
even decide over life and death when, after 1686, Duke Bernhard I of Meiningen sold
his episcopal jurisdiction and tithes rights for 3,000 talers to the Walldorf liege lords.
This diversity of jurisdiction among the three noble families, whose relations were not
always amiable, caused a variety of unwholesome acts, feuds, and spiteful incidents
among the Christian as well as the Jewish villagers. Even for the Jewish population,
which at that time still consisted of a small number of families, there were different
houses of prayer, indeed even different bakeries for the *Mazzot* that were required for
Passover—so that no member of one patrimonial domain needed to have anything to
do with another.

The subjects of the von Bibras and the von Marschallks associated with one another
in a manner that was at least still bearable. Most of the trouble came from the von
Diemar circle, since this feudal house itself was not very peace-loving. It was not until
1789, after the Bibra and Marschallk Protected Jews had already established common
religious institutions, that one of my forebears, my great-grandfather Abraham Hol-
länder, succeeded in bringing the three communities under a single jurisdiction and also
gained the assent of the three noble lords. [. . .]

It is not surprising, given such fragmentation as prevailed at that time in the
Walldorf community, that one encountered much quarreling and discord, especially
since in the course of the years the Jewish community, which consisted of nine families,
had experienced an often unpleasant expansion through new arrivals. Every new soul
who was granted protection was a fresh source of income from protection taxes for the

nobles, whose financial situation was not very favorable and whose estates were run down through mismanagement.

That among the new settlers there were some not very laudable additions to the population was small wonder. After all, during or after the Seven Years War the nobles had taken in a great number of Wallachian and Galician Jews who were roving about in the wake of the troops and toward whom the earlier residents maintained an attitude of rejection even into the time of my youth. They steered clear of everything associated with them, which they disparagingly designated as "Wallachian Trash." [. . .]

When the German people arose to battle the French usurper, some vestiges of the feudal era, such as the hegemony of the nobles within their feudal estates, also vanished. They simply became estate owners who no longer had a say in the administration of justice. That was the end of their outrages. The three-headed hydra of unrest in Walldorf had breathed its last. In 1808 Walldorf reverted to the Ducal House of Meiningen, under which conditions developed more securely and better than earlier. [. . .] It was beneficial for the Jewish inhabitants that under the new regime they were granted entry to the trades, indeed that such entry was strongly promoted.

My grandfather ran a textile business with the help of my father, his second son. The third son learned the bleacher's trade; after his apprenticeship he became a journeyman, spent a time away from home, and the later elevation of the business to factory production could be ascribed entirely to the new order of things. [. . .] Especially at the insistence of my very intelligent grandmother, my grandparents decided that the youngest son was to learn the weaver's trade. That he did and, in keeping with craft practice, my uncle was apprenticed in Meiningen to a master weaver named Triebel, whom I knew when he was already an old man. Then my uncle went off for several years as a journeyman. According to the evidence of his journeyman's papers, he worked, among other places, in Frankfurt am Main for the father of the world-renowned politician and democrat Leopold Sonnemann,[1] who founded the *Frankfurter Zeitung,* and for a period in Höchberg in the vicinity of Würzburg, where the family lived at that time. Once back home, my uncle completed the Master Craftsman test, worked alone for a short time, then with the help of a few journeymen, and when this did not suffice to fill the orders that were coming in, he allotted outside work to other master weavers, who welcomed this regular employment in a time that offered little opportunity for income. My father, who occupied himself with selling the wares they produced to merchants and dealers, at first took short trips into the environs, but then journeyed farther and farther, until the original handicraft production gradually grew into a factory production with a few hundred workers employed in home industry. Thus, in the towns and villages of the state as well as in the nearby Rhön region an imposing number of weavers were working for the business.

But things did not proceed that smoothly. For when other master weavers saw how the new business prospered and especially how it expanded more and more thanks to my father's adroit commercial management, clannish pettiness and envy came into play, and it was said: "He has no right to that; only a competent weaver, belonging to a guild, has the right to sell such textiles." And upon his denunciation by these envious people my father was henceforth prohibited from marketing. If his business, which had just started to thrive, was not to close down, my father had no other choice than to apply himself likewise to the weaver's trade, if only as a matter of form. Already twenty-six years old at that time, he had himself registered as an apprentice with Master Lehmuth, a weaver friend in Herpf, and after a time he qualified as a journeyman. At the same time, he quietly tended to the business at home, even though he was constantly threatened with intervention by the envious master weavers with their small enterprises.

And sure enough, when he produced the piece of handicraft that qualified him as a journeyman (it was not his own work at all, but that of Master Lehmuth), they also demanded that he adhere to the prescribed three-year journeyman period that was required in those days for qualification as a master craftsman. But in this instance, too, a solution was found. The acts of spitefulness that were committed against my father because of his success had gained him much sympathy. The people with whom he came into contact had learned to appreciate and respect him for his judicious nature and his open, honest character. Once, on one of his business trips to Gotha, he visited his close acquaintance, the highly regarded merchant Arnoldi,[2] the founder of the big Gotha Fire Insurance Company, and complained to him of his aggravations and asked him if he might not wish to help. Arnoldi was disgusted by the bullying of my father and immediately assured him of his support. He summoned a master from the local weavers guild, described the matter to him, and asked him to register his young friend as a journeyman and to have him recognized as one for the period of the journeyman years, naturally with immediate leave for as long a time as my father wished. That is how it was done, and while my father's journeyman papers were in distant parts, he conducted his own, growing business at home.

But this ficticious journey lasted only a very short time. The then high bailiff (the designation for today's district president) in Meiningen, Baron von Bibra, who was favorably disposed toward my father and sought to safeguard the interests of the district by protecting an industrialist who provided many poor people with a living, personally advised my father to petition him for dispensation from the remainder of the journeyman years. It was indeed granted, to the vexation of his opponents and despite their protest. The sample of work required for qualification as a master craftsman was then also produced as a matter of form, that is, my father added a few rows to a piece of goods that was already on the loom, whereupon the head masters of the guild, who were well inclined toward him and informed about the purpose of the examination, issued him the master craftsman diploma, which I still possess, as well as a certificate, dated 1837, exempting him from the craftsman's journey. Now my father was able to devote himself to the business undisturbed. [. . .]

The Jewish community [Walldorf] reached its peak in the year 1837 when, among 1,580 inhabitants, it counted 567 souls. Then many emigrated to America, so that in 1855 only 493 Jews were still living there. After freedom of movement was enacted in 1866, their number diminished rapidly. By 1900 only 85 Jews were still living in Walldorf, while the population numbered 1,537.

If formerly there was a great number of poor Jews in the community who, especially at the time of the holidays, received charitable gifts of money, flour, and the like, this situation gradually changed for the better. Thanks to the emigration of many to North America and the greater freedom of movement granted the Jews in trade and vocation, their circumstances improved markedly so that by the end of the sixties there were almost no recipients of charity at all among them. Anyone who witnessed the last traces of the earlier period of isolation, anyone who knew the last representatives of those old days, must admit that he had witnessed a transformation that the new generation cannot even imagine. [. . .] Among the Jews of my childhood there were some odd characters, who in their appearance and in their patriarchal, old-fashioned habits stood out in the new era like memorials to days long past; they found it hard to adjust to the changes. As is easily understandable, in the transitional period from old to new observance with regard to religion there were also two clearly separate groups within the community. The more liberal group predominated; it claimed most of the better families, who also stuck closely together and by virtue of their better position in life as well as their higher degree of education exerted the strongest influence and determined the direction of the community.

In the years of my youth, these two factions also went their own ways socially, so that on the holidays, for example the Festival of Weeks or the Festival of Booths, the celebrations were held separately. In our social circle there prevailed a highly proper tone, within the boundaries of the most refined customs and manners, and to be included in our circle was regarded as a privilege. Already at that time we celebrated our balls with a gay dinner and lively conversation, with speeches and wine, and although our menus did not conform to the prescripts of ritual law, this was no cause for us to enjoy ourselves less. The dietary laws were not strictly observed by the younger generation, most of whom had seen the world and thereby departed from the old customs. I remember quite well, already as a seven- or eight-year-old boy, seeing young grown-ups from my family circle or other circles smoking their cigars on Saturday and eating at the inns. This was at the end of the 1840s. To be sure, the fact that many young people had received their training in the outside world contributed to this; the growing association with non-Jews and attendance at secondary schools also bore part of the blame; and, in addition, liberal thinking in Christian circles at that time carried over to the Jewish population. What had once been regarded as inadmissible, that is, writing on Saturday, was permitted by Rabbi Hofmann,[3] and was also not objected to by his successors, so that gradually one old custom after the other crumbled away and this produced new circumstances.

Thus, Walldorf soon gained the reputation for being very liberal among communities that were more hesitant in their reforms. After their oppressive abnormal position had been changed and they received more rights affording them greater equality to the other citizens (even though full emancipation came about only in 1856, or rather 1868,[4] and even then was freighted with heavy citizen taxes), the Walldorf Jews felt the need for education. This is evidenced by the fact that within the community there existed alongside the community-supported school, itself under the direction of Josef Sachs, a second, private school with two teachers, directed by Selkan Gutmann, and that in addition to it a small number of families, including ours, employed a private teacher in order to permit their children the best possible instruction. As a result, during my entire schooling I was taught only with the children of a few families that were linked in closer friendship. There were but 15–18 of us pupils, and we are indebted to our capable teachers for setting learning goals that went beyond those at other schools, including even the town schools. I recall that together with a few more gifted pupils of the upper age groups I had instruction in botany, zoology, mineralogy, algebra, and history, subjects that were not normally taught at elementary schools.

These circumstances differed greatly from the earlier ones during my father's youth, when school attendance was not compulsory and—as I heard from the experiences of old people—the teachers, who themselves had not received halfway adequate training, were also often dubious persons incapable of imparting to the children any knowledge worth mentioning. In those days the greatest importance was attached almost entirely to learning Hebrew, and even this mostly in a very inadequate way. Whatever my father had learned in this regard for the needs of his extensive business dealings (and he was able to express himself deftly in written German) he had acquired mostly on his own, but—to be sure—it did not go beyond what was necessary. He often lamented that in his youth there had been so little opportunity for education; with his native intelligence he would have surely gained much from it. This feeling that his learning was insufficient was the main reason why he strove so eagerly to give us children the best possible schooling. For all his thriftiness, for all his simplicity and his modesty in regard to himself, and for all his endeavor to raise us, his children, to be that way too, there was one area in which no sacrifice was too great, in which he was prepared, gladly and generously, to spare no costs: when it came to furthering us through instruction, or when we requested books from him for our improvement; in short, whenever it was a matter of having us children learn something. And for that, as well as for his model of strict righteousness, we owe him eternally a special debt of thanks. This is something that I have always felt from the very bottom of my heart. [. . .]

There was no lack of social activity in my parents' hometown. From among the better Jewish families, together with a number of Christian townspeople, such as pastors, teachers, and a few farmers, in the 1840s a social organization, "Casino," was formed, which not only aimed at providing pleasure but rather sought to serve the general desire for culture and education by founding a library. Nor were the requisite forces of mind and spirit in short supply. Christian and Jewish clergy, teachers and burghers got along splendidly with one another, and since at that time among the Jews, too, a number of people had acquired some solid skills—there were even good musicians and singers among them—there was no lack of refined, uplifting pleasures. As a child I was often taken along to such evening entertainments. At that time, until the end of the sixties, Walldorf was a much-visited and also commercially significant town. But after the restrictions on freedom of movement were lifted and all German citizens received equality before the law, many people, and particularly the better families, moved to nearby Meiningen,⁵ still others to more distant towns.

There were always many visitors in my father's house. Because of the business, many people came and went. Especially on delivery days, when hundreds of weavers brought their finished wares, it was sometimes too lively. It became necessary to cut back, and this was achieved by taking on a factor in Kaltersondheim on Rhön. In those days the weavers produced lots of ticking, material for feather-bed covers, and lining fustian, especially the latter, which sold well into the seventies but then was superseded by more elegant articles. We had sizing machines and drying machines with boilers in use in our home and later also in Meiningen.

The importance of the business, which from 1863 to 1867 my father headed jointly with Siegmund Elsbach (who later moved to Berlin) in order to eliminate competition between their two enterprises, is mentioned in Humann's *Geschichte der Juden im Herzogtum Meiningen,* where it is referred to as the largest weaving mill in Thuringia.[6] Already in the thirties, my father went on business trips that took him mainly to Bavaria, Baden, and Württemberg. To sell wholesale, he then visited the once very important fairs in Frankfurt, Würzburg, and Bamberg—for a short time with wares, but later only with samples; then, in the circle of his acquaintances, he had to relate his journeys, which were much admired in those days. Thanks to his gift for exact observation and his superior talent for telling stories, he was always able to find topics that he thought were worth narrating. In the thirties, he once also brought the first matches home with him from a trip. [. . .]

In the first years of his business, my father traveled by foot from Walldorf to Schweinfurt, and probably from there also to Würzburg, just as he also covered the stretch to Frankfurt am Main several times in the same way. Later, when his circumstances allowed it, he used the mailcoach. Starting in 1858, we had a train connection to Lichtenfels, later also to Schweinfurt. Formerly, carters from the Schweinfurt region came to us once every week and transported the bales to South Germany, to which the major traffic extended. The yarns that were needed for production were imported mainly from England, from Liverpool and Manchester, and the correspondence in English that arrived from certain firms often caused problems, for which reason, in addition to instruction in French, I had to take lessons in English, to acquire at least what was essential in this language. When, years later, I had attained this goal, the import of English yarns proved no longer to be necessary, since in the interim spinning mills in Germany had developed rapidly and well and were able to meet the demand within the country.

1. Leopold Sonnemann (1831–1909) was born in Höchberg, in the vicinity of Würzburg, as the son of a master weaver. His father later became a manufacturer in Offenbach and Frankfurt am Main.

2. Ernst Wilhelm Arnoldi (1778–1841), manufacturer in Gotha, founded the Gotha Fire Insurance Company in 1821 and in 1829 the Life Insurance Bank.

3. After study at the Talmud school in Fürth and at Marburg University, Josef Hofmann (1806–1845) became rabbi in 1838 in his native town of Walldorf. He represented the liberal tradition and authored the State Synagogue Regulations for Sachsen-Meiningen of 1844.

4. The law of May 22, 1856 prescribed numerous special regulations for Jews that were revoked in the duchy of Sachsen-Meiningen by the law of February 25, 1868.

5. The Jews were expelled from Meiningen in 1819, and not until the ducal law of February 25, 1868 was it possible for them to move to the capital without restriction. In 1898 there were already 490 Jews living there.

6. Arnim Humann, *Geschichte der Juden im Herzogtum Sachsen-Meiningen-Hildburghausen* (Hildburghausen, 1898), *Schriften des Vereins für Sachsen Meiningsche Geschichte und Landeskunde,* Heft 30, p. 109: "In the industrial field, the large fustian weaving mill of Siegel, Elsbach & Co. in Walldorf made significant contributions. Until the seventh decade of our century, it was, along with the Suhl weaving mill, the most important in Thuringia."

# 11 *Itzig Hamburger*

BORN IN 1811 IN SCHMIEGEL (POSEN).

Hermann Hamburger, Memoirs 1837–1920. Breslau, 1920, 47 pages.

*Hermann Hamburger (born in 1837) relates the life of his father, Itzig Hamburger, who joined the paternal wholesale business at age thirteen. Itzig accompanied his father, a wholesaler in dry goods, on his regular buying trips to the trade exhibits in Frankfurt an der Oder and Leipzig, as well as on his sales trips to the fairs in the region. Thus there emerges a vivid picture of the everyday trials of merchant life in this period and of the important role of the Jewish merchants in the provinces of Posen and Silesia. At the age of 19, Itzig Hamburger established himself independently as a dealer in cloth, leather, and rags. His success permitted him to move to Breslau in 1857, where he started a new company, and later he founded a branch in the city of Posen. He expanded his business by manufacturing linen, and placed direct orders with the weavers, dyers, and printers.*

In those days, life in Schmiegel provided many pleasures and much stimulation for the mind. The little town is not far from the German border. Most of the inhabitants are German and at that time a large number of respected and educated men and women belonging to old, esteemed families lived there. They owned capital and old family property. They had houses in town, fields and vineyards in the surroundings, and for the most part formed the so-called patrician class of the town. They were free of the usual patrician snobbery and maintained good relationships with the other burghers, including the Jewish burghers. My parents also lived very comfortably, happily, and peacefully there. They lived in the same place as their parents, were surrounded by a large family circle, and in the town itself enjoyed the highest respect of both Christians and Jews. At the end, my father was head of the town council, my father-in-law was at the time alderman and the mayor's right hand, and several other members of the family belonged to the town council.

Social differences between Christians and Jews did not exist in those days. My father was on friendly terms with the pastor and the district medical officer, the latter of whom came from an old, established town family and received the rare privilege of being allowed to reside not in the district seat but rather in his native town, which belonged to the district. He was a very capable, experienced doctor, who was much in demand in the town and its environs, a man of high general education as well as humane and tolerant character, as was the pastor, too. The latter prepared me in Latin for the Gymnasium. He was a very jovial, merry gentleman, quite corpulent, and he could hold his liquor. He could down quite a bit without succumbing. On Saturdays and Sundays, the two days of rest, people generally gathered in goodly number for a morning pint at the King of Prussia Inn. The burghers of the different faiths socialized there in the nicest harmony, and often there were heated arguments between those of different political persuasions, but rarely between religious persuasions. My mother associated in as friendly a way with the Jewish ladies of the town as she did with the Christian, and she was invited to coffee hours and tea parties just like anyone else. There was also a citizens' common recreational club in town, in which there was not a trace of exclusivity.

In those days it was not like today; those were the first stages of the constitutional state. With few exceptions, the entire citizenry of the land was liberal. In the province of Posen, the Jews were allied with the Germans against the Poles. Economic interests were still not as prominent a part of the political struggle as they are today. The party struggle was more concerned with political freedom and equality of the various classes and religions. To lend their endeavors practical significance, the liberals placed special value on religious tolerance toward those of other faith, and for decades the good mutual relations remained undisturbed—until later they gradually dissolved as a result of the sad effects of antisemitism. [. . .]

My parents left the town of Schmiegel after my grandparents had died, to move to Breslau. They did this not because they no longer felt at home in Schmiegel but because my father no longer had a field of activity there (for reasons of health he had long since had to give up his trips to the fairs). Another reason was that our parents wanted to provide us with a better education in the city. Also, my father had already set up a larger and more appealing area of work for himself in Breslau. Together with his nephew Josef Hamburger from Posen, he had founded the firm of J. Z. Hamburger & Co. in the late 1840s in Breslau. Thanks to the leadership of his very intelligent and capable nephew, a most circumspect and cautious merchant, it had developed well. Thus my father did not have to start anew in Breslau, but rather he became immediately active as a qualified partner in the management of an enterprise that was already in full swing.

In other respects, too, my parents were no longer strangers in Breslau. They found a large circle of relatives and friends there, and thus, aside from some unavoidable incidents, their life in the city turned out to be a series of pleasant and happy years. While their dear young daughters were still living at home and later, when almost all of us children were living in Breslau after we married, our parental home was the focal point of the family and guests were never lacking. It was always full of cheer and lively cultural activity. Well-educated men and women gathered in our home, which was always open and hospitable, and this lovely, happy family life without a doubt contributed much to lengthening my parents' days and enabling them to attain an unusually advanced age, and to the very last hour of their lives it preserved for them the awareness of their good fortune. For us children this knowledge will remain one of the most beautiful features of our lives.

Today, when we observe the stores of the big cities with their vast departments and goods, the shining displays in their show windows, the splendidly outfitted offices with their luxurious appointments, we forget entirely from what small beginnings some of them emerged. The firm bearing my father's name, which was founded in 1830 and in the course of time attained wealth and great respect in the business world, also arose from very modest origins. At the start, it was part of my grandfather's business. In those days there were no specialty shops as we know them today, offering their customers but a few articles, these, however, in the greatest variety and most tasteful selection. One carried more or less every kind of article that could possibly be sold, and in one and the same store could be found coffee and sugar alongside spirits, shoes, books, toys, fancy goods, and fabrics, and every sort of odds and ends imaginable. To be sure, every article was available only in very limited selection and in small quantities. People simply bought only regular wares for everyday life, and few luxury articles; and it was not one's own taste that decided but rather what the merchant happened to have in stock. The customers were the middle classes and the poorer city-dwellers and the peasants from the country. The well-to-do and rich burghers and the nobility of the region bought in the few big stores of the city, or they ordered what they needed from the larger district or provincial capitals.

My grandfather had a wholesale dry-goods and piece-goods business. The piece goods were of varying provenance. He usually bought his merchandise at the Frankfurt and Leipzig trade exhibitions, where the manufacturers from the Rhineland and Westphalia, Saxony and Silesia flocked together and offered their products in large depots. Customarily, one remained there for a week and more; one allowed oneself lots of time and without any haste and with great care and consideration bought what one would probably need until the next exhibition. But one had to put in quite ample supplies, since the forwarding of goods from where they were manufactured to replace those that were not in stock or sold was expensive. Also, because of the great distances and inadequate means of transport they remained en route for a long and very indefinite time, so that one could never tell whether they would arrive on time. If an article was sold out one had to pass up replacing and selling it again until the next fair. My grandfather had the clever practice of selling his goods slowly just after the fair and waiting until the others had greatly reduced or completely sold out their stores; then he had no competition and could dispose of his wares at better prices. But he was also better able to do this than the others, whose limited means did not permit them to wait long. As already mentioned, the sale of goods took place mainly at the fairs.

My father was taken out of school when he was thirteen, and at even this young age he had to help in the business and participate at the visits to the fairs. He soon showed that he was very clever and able, and wherever it was necessary he lent a capable hand. He married at the age of seventeen, and in January 1830 my grandfather set him up independently by assigning him some articles from his own business, the so-called Silesian articles, to sell for himself. On January 1, 1830, at the age of eighteen years and two months, my father opened his own business under the firm of his name, J. Z. Hamburger. My grandfather outfitted the business premises for him in the neighboring house, which [. . .] was built for my great-grandfather, Meier Hamburger.

The business premises, or the store, as it was called back then, was about 4 to 5 meters long and 2 or 2 1/2 meters wide, not particularly spacious by today's standards. It was also not exactly suited for an especially rapid expansion of the business, but at that time one did not have great hopes for quick progress and increase of trade. Circumstances changed only little and over longer periods; chance changes in fortune and economic conditions did not occur; the population also remained the same; and one's estate increased only by virtue of what one earned and saved through hard work and a frugal way of life. My father took up his residence in the same house. It consisted of a living room, which faced the courtyard, and a narrow, bright alcove that was used as a bedroom, and a very dark kitchen. There was also a room up front, which, however, was almost always kept locked and opened only on holidays, when we were expecting guests. In this modest dwelling my parents' first four children were born, and all of them had to find room in it. But finally these quarters became too cramped, and also the store no longer sufficed. Another story was added to the house and all of the front ground-floor rooms of the house were used for business purposes. In this way, the store doubled its size. This did not happen until 1846, after the birth of my sister Rosa.

My father received a further article of trade from his parents-in-law, our grand-parents Löwenthal. It was a leather pattern for shoemakers. This article was sold only in the town, and its purchasers were the many shoemakers living in Schmiegel. They were not always the best payers, and thus there was always much fuss and trouble. Later my father added to his trade with other merchandise a rag business, and finally also the selling of indigo. He conducted the rag business in the following way: At that time it was customary for the so-called rag collectors to go from house to house in town and in the surrounding villages with pushcarts pulled by a dog and to collect rags and other discards that had gathered in the course of time and that people were glad to be rid of. They announced their presence mostly by sounding a bell or by certain cries, and both rich and poor came from all sides carrying their accumulated stocks. The rag collectors brought them into town in their pushcarts to the rag dealers and sold them for a small sum. The discards were then separated from the rubbish by the women sorters in the so-called rag rooms and were then sorted into wool, linen, and cloth remains, and the like, and sold to the paper mills. It was a dirty, bad-smelling, but not unrewarding business, and my father gave it up, together with the leather business, only later when he moved his residence from Schmiegel to Breslau. In those days people called my father's business "The Store of the Three L's" (Leinwand – Leder – Lumpen).* The rag business was taken over by my father's brother, Salomon Hamburger, and successfully carried on until he moved to Posen in 1860. My parent's nephew, who for many years managed the Schmiegel firm of Marcus Landsberg, took it over from him and managed it until his death in 1893.

As I have mentioned several times, the sale of my father's and grandfather's wares was carried out mainly at fairs in the form of wholesale trade. The customers lived mostly within a small radius of 70–80 kilometers from Schmiegel, and selling took place at the fairs in the towns that lay within this radius. The trip to these fairs entailed great hardships and privation. At that time there were no railways in the province of Posen. The roads were good, but not all towns were connected by roads, and thus one was mainly dependent on the old, poor, unpaved thoroughfares, which the heavily laden wagons could hardly traverse when the snow was melting in the spring and fall, or after heavy downpours. The fair visitors came from an area that extended from the trade center of Schmiegel toward the north, east, and west. The south is the German side of the area and was not frequented, since it was oriented more toward Breslau and the merchants had their suppliers there. The fairs took place from Monday through Thursday; the rest of the week remained free. Back then, trade lay entirely in the hands of the Jewish merchants, and so the authorities could not avoid taking the Jewish holidays and days of rest into consideration when scheduling the fairs.

*That is: "linen, leather, rags."

Packing and loading the merchandise into big freight wagons usually began on Saturday evening, and it was done in the following way: In the rear space of the wagon open goods such as calicoes, cheesecloth, fustian, etc. were skillfully stored, in such a way that they could serve the travelers as a bed. In the middle and in the front space of the wagon the filled boxes and bales were stowed and fastened to the wagon with thick ropes and chains. Spread over everything was a cover of coarse linen drawn across hoops, which was supposed to serve as protection against rain, snow, and cold but was most insufficient and in the summer even bothersome, since it held back the air. One set out toward midnight and, if the fairs were farther away, usually did not arrive at one's destination until the evening of the next day. The wagon drove up to the fair booth, which was built of wood. But only the empty board walls stood there; the shelves, ladders, and racks for accommodating the goods were brought along. One had to nail them together and set them up oneself for placing the merchandise. After this job, which demanded little time, was done, the goods were unloaded and a bed for the night was prepared in the fair booth from merchandise that suited the purpose, in the same way as had been done on the wagon. To be sure, the bed was not very comfortable, but one was tired from the trip and the work one had done, and that produced sound sleep. Provisions also had to be brought along; for in the small towns with their few visitors from the outside one found agreeable fare as rarely as one did a lodging at the inns. Satisfactory meals were made more difficult still by the ritual dietary rules. Bread, butter, coffee, cheese, and herring were about the only permissible food. In some few towns rooms were rented, and one always looked forward to these choice fairs, since there one was not as exposed to the effects of wind and weather as in the fair booths.

Early in the morning the goods were unloaded and set up on the shelves. The day's business took place in a simple manner—to be sure, not without much haggling and bargaining, as was the custom in those days. It was liveliest in the early morning. That is when the customers chose the merchandise that they tried to sell during the day to the peasants, men and women who streamed into the town in droves to bring their farm products to market. This manner of retail business between buyer and seller was as interesting as it was peculiar. The sellers were mainly Jewish traders, and the buying public consisted of Polish peasant women who had no knowledge of the quality of the goods or of their actual value. From the start, they approached every purchase with the prejudice that they were being cheated and thus had to bargain down the proposed price as much as possible. As a result, the seller was forced to push up the price of his goods as much as he could, and the difference between the quotation of the seller and the low offer of the buyer was sometimes so great that one could not imagine at all how one would be able to achieve agreement between these risky extremes. No transaction, not even the smallest, could be carried out without loud screaming and shouting. And with curses and imprecations and after long haggling one finally arrived at the desired goal. The same wild scenes were repeated when the goods were being measured and cut, and so these transactions offered, in part, a very lively and emotional but also frightening picture of the business between traders and consumers in the Polish towns and villages of that day and, in part, also of the present. In the course of the day, business at my father's and grandfather's wholesale trades, along with that of some competitors, slackened off. Now and then a dealer fetched himself an additional piece of goods as a supplement or substitute for a pattern or article that had sold out. In the evening, before sunset, the money for the sold goods was collected. From the profits that their sales at the fair brought them, the customers paid for the goods that they had bought or still owed money on from earlier. This collection business was not without risk; for the marketplace was streaming with homeward-bound noisy and mostly drunken Polish peasants who, if they were not held in check by the police, tended all too easily to physical violence and thievery.

But there were menaces enough on these trips to the fairs, aside from the trials of the day and the journeys by night, the effects of the weather, and of the poor roads and thoroughfares; most specially in the fall and spring there were also many other difficulties and dangers. How often, when the wagon was stuck in mud and snow, did one have get down from it in order to move it from the spot by pushing it! (In the years 1859–1864, I myself still endured these joys and pleasures.) In bad weather one often had to fetch a team of horses from the next village if, despite all effort, our horses were unable to budge the wagon, and often one had to hold out for hours in wind and rain until the team, which was not always to be had so quickly, finally arrived. Usually, the loaded wagons of my father and grandfather drove together, and if danger threatened they drove in such a way that one could help the other with a team. In my experience, it once happened that in the dark of night the heavily laden wagon, which the sleeping carter had driven into the ditch, fell over and its occupants barely escaped with their lives. One also was not spared holdups by robbers, and thievery. Late at night it was all too easy to slit open the linen cover on the lightly guarded wagon and remove a few pieces of loosely stacked merchandise. To be sure, such a maneuver was rendered difficult by the fact that a few persons had bedded down for the night on top of the pile and would awaken immediately if criminal hands were to carry on their mischief beneath them.

From time to time, some quite comical scenes took place. A tailor from Schmiegel, who was very slight of figure and afflicted with a humpback, was once taken along to the fair in the winter as a passenger or helper. To protect himself from the cold, he wrapped himself in a big coarse linen blanket, so that he assumed entirely the form of a bale of goods, and he lay down to rest on the pile of merchandise at the rear of the wagon. During the night, thieves cut open the linen cover and to their great joy a large bale fell forthwith into their hands. The rogues, overjoyed at their fine booty, immediately opened the bale to share their catch, and to their amazement there emerged our hump-backed little tailor—who was happy to get away with no more than a good beating.

The year of the 1848 revolution was especially hazardous for visitors to the fairs. The cannon roar of the battles during this Polish rebellion under Mieroslawsky,[1] from March until May of 1848, often resounded into the midst of the fair's bustle. When they fought the battle of Miloslaw, in which the Prussian troops under General Blumen were defeated by the greater power of their enemy, our fair salesmen were at the fair in Schroda. They clearly heard the cannon roar and the battle, which was only a few miles distant, and they could thank their lucky star that they got away safe and sound. My father often told of the violent storms of that agitated time, of the fears and distress to which he and his companions were exposed, but which they always luckily escaped. For the unarmed Polish peasants, whose hearts were naturally on the side of the rebels, also cast threatening glances at the property of the Germans and were waiting only for a signal to attack and rob. At that time payment was almost always in silver coin and small coin, and once it happened that the bottom of the wooden chest that was filled with moneybags came loose and fell to the ground in broad daylight amidst a stirred-up crowd. But as good luck had it, nothing was lost.

Often one encountered trains of armed rebels on the open highway; they were armed mainly with long scythes, consisting of a long handle with a scythe blade that was fastened to the handle vertically and not at an angle like the scythes that were used for farming. In addition, the scythe was outfitted at the top with a barbed hook. Because of this weapon people commonly called the Polish rebels the Grim Reapers. Meeting up with them was certainly very dangerous, and it was always most fortunate if you got away in one piece.

But even if the Polish peasant is coarse and heavily given to drink, he nonetheless is good-natured by character and disinclined to any sort of cruelty, and thus he can be quickly satisfied with a drink and a good gratuity. In the time of the Polish revolution, robbery and murder, outrages and atrocities, such as are unavoidable in times of war, were only seldom committed in the province of Posen. The leaders, Polish nobles of mostly refined and aristocratic origin, maintained good discipline among their men. Thus, despite all the dangers to which we were exposed during the short Polish rebellion in 1848, we and ours always got away safely and without real harm. The few pleasures that these trips offered we enjoyed in the early morning hours of beautiful summer and fall days when, walking alongside the wagon, we passed through the green forests, breathing in the fresh morning air, admiring the magnificent sunrise and the broad view across fragrant meadows and undulating grain fields to the border of the horizon, which in this rather unattractive Polish flatland was not hemmed in by mountains and hills.

Before father founded his business, and for a long time afterward, the transports that served the firm were still far from perfect. Our means did not yet suffice to buy expensive horses. The horses had to be strong and big-boned in order to pull the heavy freight wagon, but aside from that they could have all sorts of deficiencies and blemishes if these brought down their buying price without detracting from their work capacity. Thus, older horses were often acquired that were otherwise healthy but had been retired because of external defects. It also occurred sometimes that one of the horses was half or entirely blind. For the eye is the least important attribute of a good draft horse. The teams always consisted of three horses, and thus the middle one, which was led along by the two side horses, could be completely or partly blind without harming the whole conveyance. The matter became a subject of jokes and local witticisms, and it was claimed that Hamburger's horses needed only two eyes among them, the right horse a right eye, the left horse a left eye, and the middle horse could be blind in both, and that was really all that a good freight wagon needed. Later, things gradually became better. With increasing prosperity, better horses were bought that were good enough to be harnessed even to the Britschka (Polish), the so-called charabanc of those days. Only the richest Christian burghers of the town and the nobility of the surrounding area owned coaches and equipages back then. Although my grandfather's financial situation would have allowed him to own an equipage, he did not; for his modesty, and his fear as a Jew of appearing to show off, most likely kept him from doing as the others did. In later years, the freight wagon was allowed to travel alone, under the supervision of the carter and the fair helper, and one journeyed in a comfortable touring carriage, with which one reached one's destination in a shorter time and more pleasantly.

I have described here more or less how Jewish business was conducted well into the middle of the previous century, and yet the wholesale dealers were the privileged aristocrats of the fair trade. How much more difficult was it for the smaller and poorer Jewish traders, the retail traders, who brought their goods to market in little rented carts, who put up their wares for sale partly in booths, partly spread out on the ground, and for the peddlers, who had to carry their bundles themselves, on their backs, from village to village. How many dangers and troubles, unpleasantries and hardships, how much hunger and thirst they had to endure; and how often did they have to go without sleep and spend nights on the thoroughfare. And on top of that there was the hate and contempt, scorn and derision and mistreatment to which people could still subject them with impunity in those days. To bear all this requires more courage than one is generally inclined to credit Jews with. Whoever says that the Jew is cowardly either does not know or does not want to know how capable the Jew is of devotion and sacrifice in bearing tribulation and toil. Back then his whole life was a schooling in struggle and danger, in constant resistance against people and the forces of nature. Day in and day out he had to attain anew the basis of his existence. The Jews have always proved themselves to be courageous in war, too, and have stood their ground amidst the hail of bullets. Many distinguished themselves and won medals of victory. But the greater courage was shown by those who daily braved the dangers of their life's pursuit, who without fear or hesitation again and again took up the battle for their existence and that of their wives and children, even though thousands succumbed in the struggle.

The trips to the fairs were continued until 1864, when the business was moved from Schmiegel to Posen. My father had to give it up in the early fifties, since the difficulties and exertion and irregular manner of life had damaged his health, and the doctors earnestly forbade him to go on. Earlier, toward the end of the forties, together with his nephew Josef Hamburger, the son of his oldest brother Baruch, he had founded a business in Breslau that bore the name J. Z. Hamburger & Co. and at first was managed solely by said Josef Hamburger. Later his brother, Meyer Hamburger, joined the business. Until the death of my grandparents, my father and mother maintained residence in Schmiegel. Only in 1857 did they move their domicile to Breslau.

The business in Schmiegel remained and was conducted in the same way as earlier on my father's account by his tried and trusted coworkers of many years standing, Marcus Landsberg and Maier Miadowski. The leather and rag business had been dropped, and the indigo business was continued as a sideline. We supplied the indigo to the dyers who worked for us in Schmiegel and the area, and also sold some of it to them for their own use. In the fall of 1859, Miadowski withdrew from our company to establish himself independently in his hometown of Bojanowo, and I took his place in the business. In 1864 the business was moved to Posen. The strenuous trips to the fairs really had become burdensome for us. Thanks to improved transportation, the city of Posen had meanwhile developed into the center of business in the province. At the fairs our trade extended only to a small sector of the province, but in Posen the arteries from all parts of the province converged. Thus, Zacharias Hamburger & Sons decided first to transfer their business to Posen, and we soon followed. The company in Posen was entirely under my management. In Schmiegel, in the meanwhile Marcus Landsberg had married Rosalie Hoppenheim, the daughter of my mother's late, oldest sister, and had taken over my grandparents' dry-goods business as well as my father's, and also the rag trade that my father had carried on until that time. He managed these businesses successfully until his death in 1893. I directed the business in Posen until 1869. The business in Schmiegel and later in Posen had collaborated very closely with the Breslau firm of J. Z. Hamburger & Co. It ordered some of its merchandise from there, and some was procured through them as intermediary. When my father decided to transfer his business from Schmiegel to Posen, my father's Breslau associate, his nephew Josef Hamburger, opposed the move most energetically because he feared that this could harm the Breslau company. As a result of the ensuing disagreements the two split and the firm of J. Z. Hamburger & Co. was liquidated.

My father opened his new business under the old company name at 20 Carlstrasse, in the building that belonged to the goldsmith Gumpert, who was still alive at that time, and whose firm still owns the same building today. My brother Heinrich had completed his apprenticeship in the dry-goods business of Gerstenberg & Glücksmann and had received his further training in a large Berlin store. My brother Albert had just completed his training. After the split both immediately joined my father's new business as coworkers. From the start, the business grew very nicely. A few years earlier, my father had acquired the house at 1 Graupenstrasse, and when the business required greater space as a result of its expansion, at the end of the sixties he moved it into his own building. Meanwhile, the enterprise in Posen had also developed quite well and had expanded considerably. It served a clientele in towns that on the one side were situated as close to Breslau as to Posen, and on the other side there were customers in places that lay closer to Posen, but they could be reached just as well from Breslau as from Posen. Thus it was quite possible to combine the business of the Breslau store with that of the Posen branch and to direct both from Breslau, thereby reducing operating costs. For that reason, the Posen branch was closed in 1869, and Breslau remained as the company's sole store. Together with my brother Heinrich, my father took me into the store as a partner. Shortly before that, my brother Albert had gone to Landshut, where he opened a linen mill as a partner of Adolf Fränkel, who earlier had married my parents' niece and foster child, Jenny.

Just selling, as my father had done on such a small scale in Schmiegel, from the very start did not satisfy his constantly striving spirit. It had always been his nature to probe through reflection the causes and origin of all things. For a long time his mind was occupied with finding out how the wares that he sold were produced, and it was his intention and endeavor as far as possible to produce his wares himself. His business trips frequently took him to Breslau and the factory towns of Silesia. He learned about manufacturing, the weaving mills there, the dye-houses, printeries, and finishing shops. His clear mind, his quick grasp of things, and his sense for the practical helped him to do this. He quickly acquired a good knowledge of this field, and he began training able workers for himself in Schmiegel. In those days and in part still today, all sorts of trades, including the weaver's trade—in a very primitive manner, to be sure—were pursued there. The weavers processed coarse fabrics that had been spun by the peasants of the area on simple old distaffs, in part from flax that they had grown themselves. They wove these fabrics for a meager weaver's wage, mainly on order from the peasants for use in their homes. My father soon provided them with more abundant and better-paying work and introduced the so-called fast-shooter, which considerably reduced the weavers' working time and brought them better earnings. However, lack of intelligence and resistance to innovations greatly impeded the introduction of improvements among the local weaver population, and the weavers wanted to have no part of new articles.

For that reason, my father welcomed it when the government permitted him to employ a fairly large number of inmates at the Rawitsch prison as weavers. Most of them were not originally weavers and first had to be trained at it. My father engaged a master weaver, and after some problems were overcome the work proceeded smoothly. The then prison director Müller was a refined, amiable, educated man, whom I still vaguely recall from his visits to my father in Schmiegel, which took place quite often. He was well disposed toward my father and tried to promote my father's plans as much as possible. It was especially interesting for us children that prison inmates had to work for us. When I was but a boy my father once even took me along on one of his trips to Rawitsch, and even today I still remember the shudder that I felt when I was told that the poor prisoners worked for us and sometimes were even physically punished and locked up if out of malice or carelessness they produced poor goods. In Rawitsch my father was able to expand his field of enterprise considerably. He had various cotton and half-linen articles made there, mainly unbleached and striped muslin and, in larger volume, especially a coarse-thread muslin for dyeing purposes, which for many years we regularly delivered in larger quantities to a dyer in Grätz named Gumpert. This man was a giant in figure, brawny and tall, but at the same time one of the most good-natured and amiable people. He was attached to my father in true friendship, often came to our home, and of course was always afforded the best hospitality. My mother also liked him much. Until his death he remained one of our most faithful customers.

Even back then my father had also taken charge of the finishing business, as well as the dyeing and printing of unbleached calico and muslin. He employed the dyers and printers of the city and its surroundings, and also to a great extent establishments in Reichenbach (Silesia) and the area. Gray and black lining materials could only be produced in Langenbielau in those days, and our business connection with Christian Dierig had already started at that time and by today no doubt has existed for more than sixty years.

1. Ludwig von Mieroslawsky (1814–1878), Polish revolutionary, was arrested in 1847 in the province of Posen for planning a Polish uprising. He was sentenced in Berlin, but freed in 1848. He then led the armed uprising in Posen in 1848, which was finally crushed by the Prussian army after it had first suffered a defeat at Miloslaw.

# 12 *Moritz Güdemann*

 BORN IN 1835 IN HILDESHEIM; DIED IN 1918 IN BADEN NEAR VIENNA.

Moritz Güdemann, From My Life. Written in Vienna, 1899–1918. 298 pages.

*Güdemann was the son of a slaughterer in Hildesheim and attended the episcopal Gymnasium in his hometown. In 1854 he began his studies at the rabbinical seminary in Breslau, the first academic institution for the training of rabbis in Germany, established in that same year. After studying eight years at the university and the seminary, he received his first position as rabbi in Magdeburg in 1862. In 1866 he became rabbi in Vienna, where in 1891 he was promoted to chief rabbi. Conservative in religious matters and anti-Prussian politically, Güdemann, in addition to his work as a rabbi, was also active as a scholar. He published several papers on Jewish history, and the anti-Zionist work* Nationaljudentum *(1897).*

I must have been very young when I began to read German and Hebrew, for I cannot remember this beginning. But I do remember that I copied the German and Hebrew letters—I was scarcely more than five years old at the time—and that when guests came I had to give proof of this skill, of which my father was very proud. Already at that age the idea of becoming a rabbi was instilled in me, so that I named this profession when I was asked as a child what I wanted to become. The rabbi, or, by title, actually *Landrabbiner,* was the most respected man among the Jews of the city and the province. At least for my father there was no one greater, no one more honorable. This attitude of my father was transmitted to me when I was still a child, and so it was natural that I chose the profession of rabbi as my vocation, or that I was influenced to choose it, and thus my training was aimed at this profession.

When I was eight years old, I was sent to the episcopal Gymnasium Josephinum, or purely and simply Josephinum, as this institution was called, to the *Quinta,* the lowest class, in which I had to stay three years. This was the prescribed period of time. [. . .] I cannot complain about my teachers at the Gymnasium; I even retain genuine gratitude toward some of them. And yet today, at a very advanced age and with considered opinion, I can maintain that some of the teachers were mistaken in their evaluation of their pupils, because they did not consider their personalities. Almost all the teachers were clergymen, and, due to their celibacy and childlessness, in the course of time they may have lost true understanding for young people. With my schoolmates I had the best relationship. The fact that I was a Jew, and the only one in the Gymnasium, never brought insults or other unpleasant incidents upon me, either from the teachers or from my schoolmates. Indeed, they showed regard for my faith and religious attitude. Naturally, I did not write on the Sabbath and on the Jewish holidays. If a teacher inadvertently assigned an "Extemporale"—a written test—on one of these days, my Catholic schoolmates usually reminded the teacher that I could not write on that day, whereupon another day was designated. On the other hand, I did participate in some of the customs and practices that were incumbent on my schoolmates as Catholics. During singing class I sang the litany and other religious songs with them, and neither

I nor the teachers and pupils were offended by that. I even sang a solo part, in a motet by Mozart—only during singing lessons, of course, not in church. [. . .]

Once, I also listened to a long series of sermons that were delivered by the famous Jesuits Roth and Klinkowström[1] in the cathedral. I don't recall that there were incitements against Jews in them. Of course, the Jews in Hildesheim were not wealthy, but they all lived in good circumstances, took pains to lead an upright life, valued their religion, and cultivated pleasant, often friendly and close relations with their Christian fellow citizens. There was no question of any civil and political emancipation of the Jews in the kingdom of Hannover in those days. They received no distinctions and no government positions, but Hildesheim did have a Jewish lawyer and Jewish physicians, much respected among the Christians and also much consulted by them. However, my mother did often tell me that when she was a child no Jew was allowed to appear on the street on Corpus Christi Day and that sometimes they shouted "Hat off, Jew!" at the Jews; but during my childhood, I never experienced discrimination or derision because of my religion. In 1848, the legal status of the Jews became equal to that of the other citizens.[2] [. . .]

In the summer of 1853, it happened that the news of the establishment of a Jewish theological seminary in Breslau reached Hildesheim. This occurred in a roundabout way. One day, appeals were circulated among the Jews of Hildesheim in which the forthcoming establishment of that seminary was described as a great danger for Jewry. The appeals had originated with Rabbi Samson Raphael Hirsch[3] in Frankfurt am Main and had been sent everywhere. The occasion for the outcry was probably the possible appointment of H. Graetz[4] at the planned seminary. Graetz had once lived at Hirsch's in Oldenburg and had shown the latter great respect, but then had split with him and his religious views. Through these appeals I found out for the first time about the intended establishment of said seminary.

On one of my frequent visits to my sister and brother-in-law in Hannover, I also looked up Dr. Wiener and spoke with him about the new institution. Dr. Wiener taught at the Teachers College in Hannover and had acquired a good name through several works in the field of Jewish history. Wiener then informed me thoroughly about the seminary but also about what I would have to do if I wanted to remain true to my intention to become a rabbi. Above all, he made it clear to me that my studies would remain without foundation if I were not completely at home in the Talmud. Only through this portal would I be able to enter the essence of Judaism and the history of the Jews, and become familiar with both. It was a very urgent warning that Wiener addressed to me, and I must gratefully give this man the credit for showing me the way to my future. The impression with which I parted from Wiener was by no means pleasant. I felt like someone who is starving and who has just been served an unwelcome dish, but I said to myself, it has to be! The thought of choosing another profession did not occur to me: the profession of rabbi was very clearly intended for me from childhood on, and also the choice of this profession seemed to me an obligation of honor towards my late father, so that I did not even think of another profession. Thus, I left Hannover and secretly vowed to devote myself completely to the study of the Talmud. And this I did.

As soon as I had arrived at home, I borrowed from Rabbi Landsberg the treatise *Baba mezia*[5] and immersed myself in it so deeply that I hardly set apart one or two hours a day for rest and exercise. Just as those endeavors that one finds difficult also attract one, I was drawn for the same reason to Talmud study. The more effort I put into it, the more I took pleasure in the problems that it presents and in the attempted solutions, which I wrote down on small pieces of paper and slipped between the pages. Later, Landsberg showed me these notes, which he had carefully saved. Also the lessons that he now gave me were more animated, livelier, and more successful. I then wrote to the future director of the seminary, chief rabbi Dr. Z. Frankel[6] in Dresden, and asked to be admitted. A very polite response, which made me very happy, contained the approval of my application. Studying eagerly, especially the Talmud, I awaited the coming of August, when the seminary was to be opened. [. . .]

On Thursday, August 10, 1854, on a warm summer morning, the seminary was opened with a simple ceremony.[7] Of the faculty there were present the director Dr. Zacharias Frankel, Dr. H. Graetz, Dr. Jacob Bernays, and Dr. B. Zuckermann, and also the curators Milch, Prinz, and Dr. Lewy. The number of pupils amounted to ten or twelve. The ceremony took place in the big hall on the third floor, which is also used as a prayer room. Afterwards, we went to the garden, which was well-kept and spacious and, like the house, made a very pleasing impression. Then we pupils went to the promenade. Here I had a very discouraging conversation with a colleague named Landsberg, who was quite advanced in years. He came from the province of Posen and had already acquired much rabbinical knowledge, and when I told him that I was still weak in that area he said that I would do better to abandon my intention to become a rabbi, because whoever is not proficient in the Talmud in his youth would not get very far in it. But another, already elderly man, Meier Lewy, who himself was a good Talmudist and who, although he did not attend the seminary, associated with us, calmed and encouraged me.

Labor omnia vincit improbus. I, too, learned the truth of that. I threw myself with all earnestness into these studies, applying myself to them until deep into the night and early morning. In this I benefited from the help of a young man who had just come to Breslau from Hungary to pursue a secular education. He was Benjamin Szold, who later died in Baltimore after many years of service as a very respected rabbi. He had a fine head, surveyed and understood at a glance the elucidations of the Talmud commentators, which filled entire folios, and was able to retell their content with unusual clarity. That way, I was introduced to the sharp-witted debates and soon became one of the most ardent discussants in our director's course. Once I went so far that the director reprimanded me in an insulting manner. I stayed away from the class, but the director soon sent for me and placated me—that is how unassuming and loving this man was toward his pupils, whom he, childless himself, used to call his children. No less profoundly stimulating than the director was also Professor H. Graetz, who lectured on Jewish history, as well as grammar and exegesis. Jacob Bernays, who died in Bonn as head librarian, stirred our interest from another perspective. He lectured on the *Kusari*,[8] but he also established a link with classical studies by having us read Phocylides or Latin literature on biblical themes. [. . .]

Among the teachers, including also the mathematician Dr. Zuckermann, there prevailed at that time a marked enthusiasm for the task they had taken upon themselves. This same enthusiasm was also transmitted to us pupils, among whom there were several who, as Prussians, Hannoverians, natives of Baden, etc., had enjoyed a thorough Gymnasium education. This was less the case with the pupils who came from the province of Posen and from Austria. The director entrusted me with the task of teaching them the basics of Latin and Greek, which not only flattered me but also earned me money. Then, when in the second year of the seminary Dr. M. Joel[9] arrived, my teaching stopped. [. . .]

I and my colleagues fared less well at the university than at the seminary. Here, we lacked all guidance in the prescribed course of studies. Thus, on my own I chose Arabic and Syriac, and then also Persian. I did not get very far in any of these fields, however. Arabic was not well staffed in Breslau in those days; Syriac was given by the outstanding expert on this language, Bernstein, who, however, was already very old and whose course we mostly attended in his apartment. Persian fascinated me, and Stangler, who taught this language, was also a stimulating teacher. But there was no connection between this literature and my rabbinical studies; at most, I was able to explain one or the other word in the Talmud through my Persian. Very stimulating and fascinating were the philosophical lectures of Braniss,[10] a baptized Jew from Kempen who enjoyed a great reputation but who was already very old. I heard his famous scholarly talk against the well-known leader of the reactionaries in Prussia, Stahl, whose name had previously been Schlesinger and who as a baptized Jew became a pillar of Christian Pietism.[11] Braniss versus Stahl—one baptized Jew against another! The magazine *Kladderadatsch* described said talk as a "Stahlstich,"* and there was much talk about it at the time in Breslau. It would have been better if at the university I had continued my classical studies, in which I was well versed from the Gymnasium. I became more and more remote from them, while I never became quite comfortable with my Semitic studies. For my doctoral thesis I used a Persian manuscript. For a long time now, I myself have no longer been able to read my own dissertation.

Seven years were prescribed for studies at the seminary, a long time when you have it before you. When soon after my arrival the professor of geology, Römer, who came from Hildesheim and to whom I was referred, asked me about the length of my studies and I told him, he called out surprised, "Seven years!" and threw up his hands. Now, more than seven times seven years have passed, and by the grace of God I have lived to see the fiftieth anniversary of the Breslau seminary. But during those seven years, many students became untrue to the seminary and the profession of rabbi. The long period was good in that one had the opportunity for self-examination. Many students then became capable men in other fields. My more immediate colleagues were Rahmer, who died as a rabbi in Magdeburg, Bamberger, who died while holding this position in Königsberg, and Seligsohn, who died in 1858 while still a student at the seminary. [. . .] In 1856 the four of us moved to the seminary, where we got two attic rooms as living quarters. In the winter masses of snow lay before our beds when we awakened

---

*A pun on the name Stahl, which means "steel." A *Stahlstich* is a steel engraving, but here it implies a dig against Stahl (*"sticheln"* = "to make digs at").

in the morning, for there were no stoves up there. The beds, too, were primitive and did not provide any warmth. The wife of the house servant cooked our breakfast coffee, and since a few blobs of fat from the milk usually gathered on the surface, a special arrangement was agreed upon according to which each of us was allowed to serve himself first and capture these blobs of fat. In the winter we used a heated room, situated on the first floor, for studying. Here, in the evening, when we had come from the university, we used to take our very frugal supper, a piece of bread with cheap-grade butter, and a Stettin apple, which we usually bought on the Ring on the way home from the university. We studied until late into the night. At midnight, coffee was made. For this purpose we took turns at climbing onto a chair and holding the tin can over the gas flame until the coffee was done. We probably never went up to our attic room, in which we were greeted by freezing cold, before 1:00 or 1:30. This way of life differed so greatly from the normal one to which I was accustomed from childhood on that it did not remain without consequences. I got an intestinal catarrh, and now our common study room became my sickroom. There I lay for days and weeks, lonely and deserted, except that now and then one of my colleagues or Herr or Frau Spiegel visited me briefly. I regained my strength slowly, but in addition to my physical state there was also the depressing awareness that I was destitute and was facing an uncertain future. [. . .]

In the same year, 1858, I also took my doctoral examination, in which Persian was my major subject and Professor Stenzler the chief examiner. Today I hardly know anything of this language, for my later studies took another direction. Also in the same year, on the High Holidays I delivered a sermon for the first time in a congregation, in Brieg. I received much acclamation. I had given my maiden speech several months earlier at the seminary. I must have possessed some talent for declamation, for at the Gymnasium, too, I was always chosen to speak in public, but each time I ran the risk of faltering from fear. One can imagine how my heart pounded when I stepped to the pulpit of the seminary for the first time. But it turned out quite differently, for scarcely had I spoken the first word when my fear disappeared, and afterward everyone praised my relaxed bearing and good delivery.

In the following two years, I was called to Berlin to preach on the High Holidays in the additional synagogues set up by the governing body. At that time, I got to know the famous homilist Dr. Michael Sachs,[12] who received me in a very friendly manner, invited me to his table, and on my departure supplied me with cigars. In 1854, when I moved to Breslau, I had heard him preach and at that time did not think that I would come close to him in this area. But I did. [. . .]

Then came preparations for the important event of graduating the first rabbis from the seminary. This completely absorbed me. Frankel had set no great store on the doctoral examination at the university; he did not want us to acquire this title, and was right, for the theologians of the other faiths did not bear it either. But the young people, including me, were not to be stopped. At graduation I was supposed to give the ceremonial address, which I prepared with great care and which Bernays checked. He made some criticisms that bespoke a fine feeling for language. For example, I had used the words "effectiveness in office," which he had me replace with the more correct "activity of office," but on the whole he seemed to like the speech even if he did not say so. It is printed in the *Monatsschrift*[13] of 1862, as is the entire report on the festivities. The ceremony took place on the 3rd of April, with an introductory speech by the director. There were three of us: Rahmer, who died as rabbi in Magdeburg, Perles, who died holding this position in Munich, and I.

After the festivities, there was a meal at the director's place, at which all the teachers and a few guests were present, among others also Joseph Lehmann from Glogau, the founder of the *Magazin für die Literatur des Auslands,* who in those days had brought Frankel to Breslau and had presented a scholarship to the seminary. He was a famous man, a friend of many great literary figures, among them Heinrich Heine, and a loyal Jew. In an after-dinner speech he remarked how important the seminary and the present ceremony were, because they had restored to the profession of rabbi its historical significance. In Berlin, he had been the "cadet" of the governing body of the Jewish community, which was headed by Gumpertz. When the latter was asked by minister Eichhorn what the rabbi actually represents, he supposedly answered: "Whatever a rabbi can do, every one of us can do." The result of this odd depiction of the rabbi's position was that rabbis were completely ignored in the Prussian "Jews Law" of 1847 and that, in a special law, civil marriage was introduced for Jews. In fact, in Prussia rabbis did not—and even today still do not—have the same status as Christian church officials: the latter, and, of course, even more so the clergy, are exempt from local taxes, whereas the rabbis are not. I mention this only in connection with Lehmann's speech. There were also other after-dinner speeches, and the festivities came off very nicely.

Meanwhile, the rabbi's position in Magdeburg had been advertised, since the previous holder of this office, Dr. Ludwig Philippson,[14] the founder of the *Zeitung des Judentums,* translator of the Hebrew Bible into German, and author of other writings, intended to retire. I submitted my application and was invited to give a trial sermon at Passover, 1862. The cousin of my father, who had already received me very cordially when I moved to Breslau in 1854—she had married for the second time and was now called Frau Fanny Hirsch—had probably helped to bring the invitation about. [. . .] Not long after my departure, I was chosen for the position. The notification by telegram and then the written appointment made my mother and my siblings very happy and caused a great sensation in Breslau, where I was well-known. The salary that was promised me was low—800 talers. With that I was supposed to cover all my needs. But the sum seemed like a fortune to me, and it was also no small thing to become the successor of a man well-known in wide circles. I was to assume my new office in August, and that meant to prepare for the real world. [. . .]

In Magdeburg there had previously existed a large Jewish community, whose distinguished religious scholars are mentioned in the responsa collections of the Middle Ages as "the wise men of Maideborch"—this being the older name of the city. But the community had been expelled in 1492. The Spanish example had found adherents.[15] The present community is relatively new and is in part composed of Alsatians who had reached the Elbe with Napoleon's campaign as sutlers and purveyors, but also as combatants. [. . .] Also, many Jews from the Anhalt region settled in Magdeburg. The community was not wealthy, but, on the whole, was well-to-do and had in its midst very educated families. The House of Worship at that time was big, but plain and lacking in good taste. The Torah scrolls, too, were without adornment. When I complained about this at a meeting of the governing body, one of the gentlemen said that the Torah did not need any adornment. "That is correct," I replied, "but you can say the same thing about your wife, and still you will adorn her." I undertook a collection and brought the first traditional silver ornament for the Torah scroll to Magdeburg.

The relationship among the members of the community was a loving one. The few poor people were supported generously. Annually, there was a brotherhood banquet of the *"chewra kadischa,"*[16] and on this occasion the poor or the destitute sat among the most respectable persons. [. . .]

The only person [in Magdeburg] with whom I could talk about Jewish literature and learning was the very knowledgeable cantor Nathanson, an outstanding, well-read man, to whom I owe many an idea. I think of him in friendship and love. Philippson, too, valued him. Otherwise, there was no one in the community who knew Hebrew properly. Dr. Carl Siegfried, who was a teacher at the Dom Gymnasium there, asked to learn it from me and visited me for that purpose. I read different writings with him, among others *Meor Einajim* by Asariah dei Rossi.[17] Siegfried was soon called to Schulpforta and then to Jena, where he died several years ago as professor and Privy Church Councilor after years of a lingering illness. I never saw him again, but we corresponded and remained close friends. During his illness, upon his suggestion I revised for him the article "Jews," which he had written for the Brockhaus encyclopedia.

I also got many an idea from the book dealer Fischl in Halberstadt. I was able to buy only few books, but he lent me many for my perusal. In this way I enriched my knowledge of Jewish literature and discovered the pleasure of scholarly work. I also undertook historical studies and published a short history of the Jews in Magdeburg. Another work dealt with the rabbinate in the Middle Ages, which my teacher Graetz judged very favorably. Both papers appeared in Frankel's monthly.[18] When in the course of time my younger colleagues in smaller communities made apologies for their scholarly inactivity by saying that they were without stimulation and without a larger collection of books, I had to tell myself that in Magdeburg I was also lacking in both but that I still persistently tried my hand in this area, and this was of great significance for my later career.

1. Max von Klinkowström (1819–1896), a Jesuit from Vienna, was well-known as a preacher. Starting in 1849 he was active as a lay missionary, among other places also in Westphalia and Hannover.

2. Protected Jews existed in the kingdom of Hannover until the Jews Law of 1842. Through the law of September 5, 1848, the Jews then received full political and civil rights.

3. Samson Raphael Hirsch (1808–1888), leader of Neo-Orthodoxy, was rabbi in Oldenburg from 1830 to 1841 and as of 1851 rabbi of the Israelitische Religionsgesellschaft in Frankfurt am Main, the first separatist orthodox community.

4. Heinrich Graetz (1817–1891), Jewish historian, was the author of the eleven-volume *Geschichte der Juden von den ältesten Zeiten bis auf die Gegenwart (History of the Jews)*. In 1854 Graetz became Lecturer for Jewish History at the rabbinical seminary, and in 1869 also honorary professor at the university.

5. Tractate in the Talmud that primarily treats questions of rights and property.

6. Zacharias Frankel (1801–1875) became chief rabbi in Dresden in 1836, and as an adherent of a moderate reform he was in charge of the newly founded rabbinical seminary in Breslau, starting in 1854.

7. Güdemann then refers to his description of the opening of the seminary, which first appeared in print in 1904 in the October issue of the magazine *Ost und West* and was reprinted in *Das Breslauer Seminar, Jüdisch-Theologisches Seminar (Fränkelscher Stiftung) in Breslau, 1854–1938, Gedächtnisschrift,* Guido Kisch, ed., Tübingen, 1963, pp. 297–301.

8. A polemical work in dialogue form by Judah Halevi from the twelfth century, directed against Aristotelian philosophy. Jacob Bernays (1822–1881) was an important classical scholar, who qualified in 1848 as a university lecturer in Bonn, where he returned in 1866 as associate professor and director of the university library.

9. Manuel Joel (1826–1890) became lecturer for classical philology, philosophy of religion, and homiletics at the seminary, as well as rabbi in Breslau in 1864.

10. Christian Julius Braniss (1792–1873) taught philosophy in Breslau from 1826 on and was influenced above all by Hegel and Schleiermacher.

11. After an orthodox upbringing, Friedrich Julius Stahl (1802–1861) converted in 1819 to Lutheranism, became the leading conservative political theoretician of Prussia, and as a proponent of a Christian theory of the state opposed the emancipation of the Jews.

12. Michael Sachs (1808–1864); in Berlin since 1844, he was one of the leading Neo-Orthodox rabbis and became especially popular through his sermons.

13. *Monatsschrift für Geschichte und Wissenschaft des Judentums,* Vol. 11, 1862, pp. 166–173.

14. Ludwig Philippson (1811–1889), rabbi and author; in 1837 he founded the *Allgemeine Wochenzeitung des Judentums* (1837–1932), which he edited until his death. Starting in 1833 he was rabbi in Magdeburg, but had to give up this position for reasons of health. From 1862 to 1889 he lived in Bonn.

15. The great expulsion of the Jews from Spain also took place in 1492.

16. Holy Brotherhood (Hebrew). This organization existed in every community for the care of the sick and for burials.

17. Asariah dei Rossi (1511–1578), the greatest Jewish scholar of the Italian Renaissance. In his work *Meor Einajim* ("Light to the Eyes"), he was the first Jewish historian to use non-Jewish sources.

18. Güdemann published twenty-nine papers in the *Monatsschrift für Geschichte und Wissenschaft des Judentums,* edited by Zacharias Frankel; the ones mentioned are in volumes 13 and 14, 1864–1865.

# 13 *Moses Seligmann*

BORN IN 1809 IN LANDAU (PALATINE BAVARIA); DIED IN 1887 IN LANDAU.

Caesar Seligmann, My Life: Recollections of a Grandfather. 161 pages. Written in Frankfurt, 1934; London, 1941.[1]

*Caesar Seligmann was born in 1860 in Landau and died in 1950 in London. A leading personality among the liberal rabbis of Germany, he recalls here the life of his father, Moses Seligmann. The scion of an old rabbinic family, Moses Seligmann dedicated himself for many years to Talmud study, attended the yeshiva in Frankfurt am Main, and only later turned to general studies at the Gymnasium and university. In 1836 he qualified as a rabbi, but because of voting irregularities he was not named to the office of rabbi in Landau, for which he had hoped. Thereupon he became a dealer in secondhand books and lived for a time in Paris. Finally, in 1862, he obtained a position as lecturer at the Protestant Teacher's Training College in Kaiserslautern, where Jews, too, were educated.—In the*

*recollections of his childhood, Caesar Seligmann depicts the state of the Jewish
community in Kaiserslautern and his impressions of the Franco-Prussian War.*

My father, who was born on February 25, 1809 in Landau, was four years
older than Aunt Lenchen and three years younger than Aunt Malchen. The first years
of his childhood were passed when Landau was still French, and Papa never forgot that.
In that Landau of his childhood years, and also of my own, the relations between Jews
and Christians were so good-neighborly and natural that there were no barriers between
them. Landau was an urban place, in contrast to Palatine Westrich. It was a real enclave
within the old Palatinate, which, until the time of the French Revolution, was split into
so many small parts that in the eighteenth century it had no less than thirty-seven
different ruling houses. Among the Jews, who numbered about fifty families at the
beginning of the nineteenth century, there was an extraordinarily active, spiritual life.
Jewish tradition and Jewish knowledge had a venerable history in the community.

From childhood my father was destined to become a rabbi. Starting in his earliest
years, he studied the Talmud, at first with the Landau rabbi, Herz Kann. When he
was sixteen his father sent him to the most famous *yeshiva* of that time in southwest
Germany, in Frankfurt am Main, where Rabbi Salomon Trier taught.

My father's dearest friend at the Frankfurt *yeshiva* was Isaak Kauffmann, from
Buchsweiler in Alsace, who later dealt in secondhand books and published the Rödelheim
prayerbooks. Together, they had many a delightful experience, which testifies to the
fact that in his youth my father was not as earnest as he was in later life. The two
shared the same room. Next to them, separated by a thin wall, some *yeshiva bachurim*
[Talmud students] practiced blowing the shofar whole nights through before the start
of the month of Elul, and interrupted their sleep. They hit upon a brilliant idea to
secure their peace. It was a true student prank. They waited for an evening hour when
the nocturnal trumpeters were not at home, went into the neighboring room, found the
shofar, and stuffed thin paper into both its openings until it was firmly lodged there
and the shofar no longer emitted a sound. At night they listened eagerly from their
beds and heard the poor *bachurim* blowing again and again with all of their might and
not knowing by what devil the holy instrument was possessed. The result was that my
father and his friend could sleep undisturbed. Even in his old age, when my father told
me this story in a jovial mood, the tears ran down his cheeks for laughter. He held two
fingers to his mouth as one does in blowing the shofar, puffed out his cheeks, and
imitated the comical tone that emerged from the hoarse shofar.

The well-known French essayist Alexandre Weill, likewise a friend from my father's
youth, relates most delightfully and vividly in his autobiography, *Ma Jeunesse,* what
went on in the *yeshiva* of Rabbi Salomon Trier. "After we had drunk coffee, we joined
Rabbi Trier. Hardly half an hour passed and we were engaged in an intellectual bout,
a battle in which assertion and answer, argument, yells, and roars surged back and forth.
Questions and answers crossed, flew, bounced back, until the ear-splitting shouts were
suddenly cut off by a deathly silence. Everyone ruminated over the question that had
been put to them, searched for a compromise that would solve the contradiction, or for
a new explanation for an inexplicable text. A passerby, who had heard us, would have

surely taken us for raving madmen. The rabbi usually allowed us to sink into a labyrinth of contradictions and to the very last kept his solution from us—until he then revealed it with a smile of contentment on his lips. Often his solution was received with endless hurrahs and foot-stamping. On the other hand, when his answers did not satisfy us, and our objections rained down on him heavily from right and left, he gave way to feelings of indignation and at times to a fit of anger. At such moments he was wont to lift his small desk and set it down with a thud, so that a cloud of dust whirled up, enveloped us, and cut off our talk. Then it was our turn to smile. But it was not a smile of satisfaction but rather of disapproval. We wanted to hear reasons, and not the din of a desk." [. . .]

I will now return to my father's student days in Frankfurt. He studied at the Frankfurt *yeshiva* for six or seven years. Devoted entirely to Talmud study at the beginning, he later occupied himself, as did most Talmud scholars in those days, with profane disciplines. He was compelled to do this particularly by the examination in Gymnasium and university subjects required as of 1828 by the Bavarian government of candidates for the rabbinate. He prepared himself privately for the Frankfurt Gymnasium, whose three upper classes he completed from 1831 to 1834. He was especially attracted to classical philology, to which he was motivated by his inborn gift for language.

His Hebraic knowledge was unusually great. When he instructed me in *Chumesch* [Torah] with Raschi commentary, he never had a book before him. He knew the entire *Chumesch* by heart. He had mastered all of Talmud and rabbinic literature, as well as the Zohar[2] and Modern Hebrew. Thanks to his philological talent, he was expert in Hebrew and Chaldean grammar, whereas he felt less attracted by so-called belletristic writing or by philosophy. When my father departed from Frankfurt, Rabbi Trier issued him a sterling authorization for the rabbinate, something that in those days was called *morenu,* and today mostly *hatoros horoo.*

Since the diploma from a Bavarian Gymnasium was required for a position in Bavaria, my father registered as an extraneus for the secondary school examination at the lyceum in Speyer, and passed the examination on August 30, 1834. But a few minutes after the start of the questions, the royal test commissioner, Professor Dr. Fr. Thiersch, declared: "Ex ungue leonem" ("You can tell the lion by its paws").

Thereupon, my father registered at the University of Heidelberg. After two semesters, he went for the spring semester to the University of Munich, where he studied for three semesters, passed the humanities examination in the fall of 1835 and the Bavarian rabbinical examination in May 1836, and received, in addition to his *hatoros horoo* from Rabbi Salomon Trier, still another from Rabbi Hirsch Aub in Munich.

Thus, my father had every prospect of being elected rabbi in his home community of Landau, where his family was highly respected and he himself was known and honored as a *lamdan* [scholar] since his youth, and where in 1836 the position of rabbi was just being vacated. He was twenty-seven years old at the time, and a fine future, free of worry, was opening its gates before him. But things were to turn out other than he had expected.

*[Because of irregularities in the election, Seligmann did not receive the position.]*

Given the superabundance of Bavarian candidates for rabbinic posts, most of them emigrated to North America; and since my father had no prospect of getting a position as rabbi in Bavaria (at that time there was still no united Germany), he followed the example of many others and in 1846 emigrated to Paris. He worked there in the library, wrote a doctoral dissertation, and tried to found a kind of Philanthropin[3] like the one that had come into being in Frankfurt. His plan failed because of lack of interest on the part of the Parisian Jews. For two years my father remained in Paris with both his sisters, who had emigrated there with him. At the urging of his sisters, who were unable to acclimatize in Paris, but above all because of the political upheaval of 1848, the three returned to Landau. Following his favorite inclination, my father set up a training institute in Landau, which sent forth highly cultivated men, bound in deep love to Judaism. But from the beginning, enrollment was so weak that the training institute could maintain itself only until the middle fifties. Thus, at the age of forty-five my father stood *vis-à-vis du rien.*

During this difficult time, he decided to establish the above-mentioned secondhand bookstore, which also entailed the selling of prayer books, *machsorim,*[4] Bibles, and ritual objects for the publisher I. Kauffmann in Frankfurt. In 1858, his forty-ninth year, my father's financial situation, secured after the founding of his bookstore, finally permitted him to marry. Later I will tell of my mother, Leonore née Neugass of Mannheim, and of her forebears.

In the long run, practicing commerce could not satisfy my father's mind, which was directed toward scholarly and pedagogical activity. Then my father's life took a fortunate turn, the result of a significant address that he delivered in 1861 at a meeting of the governing bodies of the Palatine Jewish communities, and of a simultaneous initiative of the Palatine district government. It involved setting up a division for training Jewish teachers, which was to be linked with the Protestant college in Kaiserslautern. The educational level of Jewish teachers in both general and Jewish subjects was extremely poor at that time. Thanks especially to the ardent support of the head of the Department of Education, Government Councilor Jordan, who held my father in the highest esteem and maintained friendly relations with him, my father's plan, promoted with great energy, met with the most positive assistance on the part of the district government. The latter fervently supported the plan at the Bavarian Ministry, which at that time was especially concerned with drawing Jews into public life and educating them. At the same time, my father was recommended as a lecturer at the college. In keeping with my father's proposals, in the future no candidate for a teaching position was to be admitted to the teacher's examination who had not received training at the college. The Jewish students were to receive their prerequisite training in a preparatory school before they were admitted to the college, and they were to be put on equal footing in every respect with the Protestant students. Just like the pupils, their teacher was to be accepted as an equal member of the faculty at the college.

The proposal of the Palatine district government, that is, my father's proposal, was approved in full by the Ministry, and in 1862 my father was employed by the state as a lecturer at the college (with the title of professor). He received an annual salary of 600 guilders, and in addition the corresponding income for religious instruction at the

Gymnasium, the *Realschule,** and the girl's high school, as well as for pastoral duties and conducting worship at the jail and penitentiary. Altogether, this came to approximately 900 guilders or 1,360 marks, of which, however, thanks to my father's very simple demands and great thrift, we consumed 900 marks yearly at the most. The rest was put aside as a dowry for my sister and as savings for us children.

Thus, my father had attained his goals (though, to be sure, only in his fifty-third year), and there began for him a twenty-two year period of intensive, highly rewarding, and richly blessed activity. [. . .]


I have retained but few memories from the grey monotony of my schooldays. Mainly, they are linked with a great expectation or disappointment, with a joy or sorrow of my sensitive soul.

The Teacher's Training College was an excellent school. One learned everything effortlessly there. Since I was the sole Jewish pupil in this Protestant school, I attended Protestant religious instruction as an outsider, so to speak, which I felt myself to be and was so regarded by the teachers and my schoolmates. In this way, at an early age I became thoroughly familiar with the Christian catechism, the New Testament, and the main facts of church history, and I often raised my hand when the others had no answer. But always with the awareness that I really was not part of that.

Those days were the most tranquil time in the life of the German Jews since the Emancipation.

The following event, which took place at the beginning of the 1870s, is interesting and characteristic of the attitude of the Christians toward the Jews at that time. When there was a vote in all Bavarian towns on the introduction of the communal schools (this is what they called the nondenominational schools in Bavaria because they were not established by the state but by the communities), and in the "den of democrats," Kaiserslautern, the referendum turned out in favor of the communal schools, there was a meeting of the town council, to which the Catholic and Protestant clergymen and my father, as representative of the Jewish faith, were invited. To honor the new communal school a big school celebration was to be held during which the grade-school children, following an old custom from the thirteenth century, were to make a round through the forests that surrounded the town. At the discussion concerning the organization of this procession, the question arose as to which faith should walk at its head. The Protestant minister thought that the Protestants had this right since they were the majority religion. But the Catholic priest claimed priority for the Catholics as the older faith. Thereupon, the Protestant minister, who was as humorous as he was amiable, answered: "Fine, I accept the argument of antiquity, but then the Jews take precedence." And thus it was decided. Unfortunately, the procession did not take place, because there was a cloudburst that day.

The vote on introducing the communal school took place in the large hall of the Fruchthalle, the most beautiful edifice in Kaiserslautern, modeled in Early Renaissance style after the Strozzi Palace in Florence. My father took me along to the vote. He said

*A middle school (fifth through tenth grade); also *Realgymnasium,* i.e., a Gymnasium that stresses modern languages (rather than Latin and Greek), mathematics, and the natural sciences.

to me on the way: "You do not know what a difficult step I am taking. I am to vote for the abolition of the Jewish school, and yet I know that this is a misfortune for Judaism; a boon for the Jews, but a misfortune for Judaism. You are unable to understand this now, but perhaps someday you will remember what I am saying." I have never forgotten these words. When I asked my father how he was going to vote then, he answered: "Against my own heart, for the communal school. As a Jewish teacher at a Protestant college, I have to."

In my last school year, the Franco-Prussian War of 1870–71 broke out. As a ten-year-old boy I experienced this in all of its breathtaking emotion, its tensions and enthusiasm, its earnestness and exultation. Kaiserslautern was the headquarters of Prince Friedrich Karl of Prussia. Everyone called him the Red Prince. In the very first days after war was declared Kaiserslautern was packed full with billeted soldiers. Very early one morning we were awakened by many-voiced shouts: "The huhlans (uhlans) are coming." We dressed quickly and ran to the nearby main road, which had been built by Napoleon I from Paris to Mainz and which outside the town of Kaiserslautern was called Kaiserstrasse. From early morning until late at night endless lines of uhlans, cuirassiers, and hussars with their colorful uniforms and handsome steeds filed past us, a brilliant, unforgettable sight. Without stopping in our town they rode on to Saarbrücken and Metz, where they battled to bloody victories near Mars-la-Tour and Gravelotte.

At every time and place during those July and August days the "Watch on the Rhine" was sung, whistled, drummed, and played with utter enthusiasm.

At the beginning of August, we traveled to Landau, as we always did during vacation. It was not so simple. Because of the cattle epidemic, there stood disinfection cabins smelling of chloroform at all the train stations. One had to spend a long time in them. Then there were endless waits because of the troop and prisoner transports. I was at the train station in Landau when the first transports with wounded men arrived there after the Battle of Weissenburg. I will never forget the dreadful sight. Poorly bandaged men with bloody red dressings, the feared, half-black Turcos, terribly mutilated, groaning with pain, all crammed together in cattle cars! I was dying of pity, and all of us who had come to the station passed the charitable gifts that we had brought with us to the wounded Frenchmen, for which they were touchingly grateful. All hate for the French, which had been planted in us through stories and songs, dissolved in the face of this human misery.

We were back in Kaiserslautern when the news arrived of the Battle of Sedan and the capture of over one hundred thousand Frenchmen together with the Emperor Napoleon. The town was illuminated, people believed that therewith the war had ended. And they jocosely commented on the internment of the French emperor in Wilhelmshöhe Castle with the pun "Napoleon's fall is Wilhelm's rise."* When the French occupiers withdrew from the Pontifical State and the Pope protested in vain against the occupation of Rome, a humorous riddle passed from mouth to mouth: "Who are the three sickest men in the war?" The rather disreputable answer, which we boys enjoyed immensely,

---

*Wilhelmshöhe, the name of the castle, translates literally as William's Heights.

was: "King Wilhelm, because he must constantly eat; Napoleon, because he had to vomit; and the Pope, because he sits on the commode and can do nothing."*

On the 18th of January, the day of the imperial coronation in Versailles and the renewal of the German Reich, there gleamed opposite the once magnificent Barbarossa Castle a banner depicting the old, legendary emperor and the old ravens flying off.

Then the day finally came (to be sure, more than a half year later) when peace was concluded and the troops marched home. I experienced that myself. We boys went far, far into the distant, western forests to meet the returning soldiers. We bound oak wreaths to place about the helmets of the officers and common soldiers and to hang across their chests.

My easily enthused heart swelled with tremendous patriotism in those days, as it did until the First World War. And for that reason, when my father yet again let forth the often-heard, ominous exclamation "For shame, Aschkenas [Germany]!", which fell upon my enthusiasm like a cold shower, I dared to counter shyly: "Why do you always say that?" Whereupon my father answered fiercely: "In their eyes you will always remain the Jew. I do not wish it on you, but I fear that you will see for yourself someday that in Germany *rischus* (hostility toward Jews) is ineradicable." [. . .]

In the college school and also later at the Gymnasium, I had only Christian friends. A truly sincere friendship bound me to some of them. My father, too, had only Christian acquaintanceships. Above all, that was because the Jews of Kaiserslautern, unlike those in Landau, had no actual communal life. Most of them had come from the little forest village of Westrich or from the small towns that lay far from the traveled highways. They possessed neither Jewish nor general knowledge. Very few families presented a laudable exception. There were almost no old-established families. Whereas an official census from the year 1833 showed that Landau, along with Grünstadt, was the largest Jewish community in the Palatinate with a count of 1,116 old-established Jewish inhabitants, the Jews in Kaiserslautern numbered only 251 souls. By 1880 this number grew to 716. Until the Franco-Prussian War the economic situation of the Jews in Kaiserslautern was bad, and this caused the neglect of spiritual and religious interests.

1. A slightly shortened and revised version appeared under the title *Caesar Seligmann (1860–1950): Erinnerungen,* Erwin Seligmann, ed. (Frankfurt: 1985). The present text reproduces sections of the original in the archive of the LBI. It appears with the kind permission of E. Seligmann.

2. The major work of Jewish mysticism, the cabala. It originated at the end of the thirteenth century in Castille.

3. Jewish high school in Frankfurt.

4. Festival prayer book.

*The "disreputable" answer derives from a triple pun: German *"einnehmen"* means both "to conquer" and "to eat"; *"sich übergeben"* means "to surrender," but also "to vomit"; and in the above context, *"auf dem Stuhl sitzen"* means "to sit on the Holy See" or "to sit on the commode."

## 14  *Hermann Makower*

BORN IN 1830 IN SANTOMYSL (POSEN); DIED IN 1897 IN BERLIN.

Hermann Makower, Memories of my Youth. 17 pages.[1]

*The Berlin Legal Counsel Hermann Makower depicts his and his father's childhood. The latter came from Mackow in Russia, journeyed westward as a* **bocher,** *secretly learned German, and while working as a private tutor was inspired to acquire a humanistic self-education. After his marriage, he lived in the home of his father-in-law, a legal adviser in Santomysl (Posen). He started a small business, but was unsuccessful at it. He dedicated himself primarily to reading and was a religious liberal. He placed the highest value on the education of his son Hermann, whom he sent to the French Gymnasium in Berlin. Hermann's school days were marked by great privation, but he became an excellent pupil. He struck up a friendship with the son of the head of the Jewish community, Meyer, at that time the richest Jew in Berlin, and soon gained insight into the most varied social conditions.*

In Santomysl there lived a man who had gained a reputation in the province of Posen as a legal adviser and honest person. During the French occupation he had received the right to appear before the small claims court; and when Posen was again under Prussian administration the courts granted him the right to prepare written documents for the claimants. It actually happened that in order to settle an inheritance claim this man once journeyed from Santomysl—just imagine!—to Elberfeld, and thus he was regarded in his little town as a Ulysses or a Franklin.

Someone, I don't know who, told my father that this learned and pious man had two daughters to marry off, the second of whom was reputed to be even more beautiful than the first, but that both were very pleasant ladies, the elder of a milder temperament and a more confiding and, at the same time, aristocratic character than the younger. That man, whose name I don't know, advised my father to make the acquaintance of the elder one and court her. He said that my father could visit the man's home unknown and, as a journeying *bocher,* get to know the young ladies without inhibition. My father agreed and set out on the journey. He arrived in Schroda, a mile from Santomysl, and looked for a vehicle that could take him to his goal. At a rest station he did indeed meet a man from Santomysl, who, however, did not want to drive back. My father used the conversation with him to ask what sort of reputation the legal adviser in question enjoyed. "The worst," the gentleman replied, "he takes on everything; my case he lost." My father's conversation partner pointed out to him that there was a carter from Santomysl in town who would be driving back. My father sought him out and rode with him to Santomysl. With my own eyes I once saw that noble carter and his pitiful horse and wagon. An enemy of all luxury when it came to leather harnesses, he drove a somewhat emaciated horse with reins that were scarcely thicker than the thongs on his whip. One can imagine what a soft, comfortable seat for pleasant talk the straw sack was on which the carter and my father sat. Once more, my father used the opportunity to inquire about the reputation of the legal adviser whom he intended to visit. "The best," answered the carter, "there's not a more capable thinker and more honest, pious man in the whole province. People flock to him from far and wide to get his counsel and support. He wins them all. He won my case, too."

Thus, my father turned up in Santomysl well-informed, got out at the carter's home, and went with seeming innocence to the house of my grandfather to pay his respects. He had to wait in the big antechamber since my grandfather had someone consulting him in the rear living room, where there stood on a shelf, most authoritatively and neatly ordered, *Das Königlich Preussische Landrecht* and Kamptz's and Raabe's *Annalen*. The two daughters of the house went in and out of the antechamber, tended to this and that, once even cast a glance at what was "evidently" a *bocher,* who, however, showed surprisingly little resemblance to his fellow Jews. My grandmother, on the other hand, was pluckier, asked the gentleman his name and about the intent of his visit and where he came from, so that she could announce him. But my father skillfully evaded her questions. After this inquisition, my grandmother disappeared—later I will tell why. Finally, my grandfather's conference was over. He opened the curtained glass-paneled door into the front room, discharged his client, and with a motion of his hand bid my father to enter his room. This came to pass and my father found himself opposite the legal adviser who had won and lost cases, and the Prussian Common Law and Kamptz and Raabe were the sole witnesses to a conversation whose content I cannot reveal since those witnesses have remained mute.

And my grandmother? The bustling woman had noticed that something was in the making. The object of her questioning had not told his name but had evaded answering. He could not have dropped from the sky; so she found out with what carter he had come, and the carter was asked in detail whence the gentleman he had transported had come and whether the gentleman wanted to visit my grandfather, or whether his trip had another purpose, and so on.

After her inquiries had borne results, my grandmother speedily baked two cakes, two large cake pans full! I do descend from a clever grandmother, don't I?

Of the later period I know only that my parents lived in a small room in the home of my grandparents and ate with them. This little room, which one reached by way of a perilous staircase, had space only for my parents' beds, a chest of drawers, a table and a chair, as well as the cradle of my older sister Hannchen. There was no more space in this attic room with its one window, and when I first saw the light of day in just that place, out of pure physical necessity the need made itself felt to find other lodgings.

My father had to think about a living. To be sure, he had received a generous dowry of about two hundred talers, and my grandfather, who knew nothing about business, initiated my father, who never had any talent for commerce, into the secrets of merchandise exchange and monetary intercourse, all according to philosophical principles and the wise teachings of "our masters." This bore sumptuous fruits, at least in part. My father bought two hundred talers worth of leather and paid cash; thus, to the joy of his family, he bought cheaply. To that point it truly was a good thing. Then he sold his merchandise at a higher price and calculated the profit. This, too, would have certainly been good had not the buyer made off with the wares, never to be seen again. Despite all the philosophizing, my mother's dowry had vanished into thin air; the poor legal adviser could not replenish it, and my father consoled himself with the thought that it was not necessary to wallow in riches. My father—God bless his soul!—retained this commercial talent until the end of his life.

Later, after I had gone to Berlin, he set up a little shop, as that gave him the occasion to travel to the fair in Frankfurt an der Oder and to visit me at the same time. His principle was to immediately pay cash and never to take anything on credit, since later he might not be able to fulfill his obligations. I inherited from him this horror of owing anyone anything, and that was quite good since later he afforded me, and was able to afford me, only little cover funds. But for a merchant who owned almost nothing the principle of not taking credit, while certainly very sound, was not very promising. If he brought back lovely textiles from the fair, he rejoiced over the artistry of the fabrics, the beauty of the designs, and the colors; but if a peasant woman came to buy, then he either advised her against the purchase because the material was perhaps not colorfast after all, or not pure linen, or not durable, or too costly for her, or—in the event that my father was reading Lessing at that moment—he referred the peasant woman to my mother so that he could go on reading undisturbed. Thus it is clear that through my lineage I was predestined for commercial law.

My father bothered little about his business and did not grieve over its meager profits. He always taught me that it was not important to earn a great deal, but rather to spend little. For then one didn't require much. Out of conviction, he lived like a Diogenes and never allowed himself any luxury. On the other hand, he read avidly. I recall particularly that he read Mendelssohn, Lessing, and the Encyclopedists. His favorite poet was Schiller, whose onomatopoeic genius he admired. At a very early time, I learned poems from him and had to declaim them while standing on a table, in order to learn how to stand firmly and freely. In the same manner, I also had to recite some hymns in the Hebrew language—with the most correct pronunciation and stress, after the meaning of every word and inflection had been explained to me. Perhaps my predilection for etymology can be ascribed to that. He absolutely insisted that I speak German as purely as possible. He detested nothing more than the jargon that one heard all around. My grandfather, too, spoke a beautiful German. In addition to my education and his readings, including Prussian Common Law, which he had learned to comprehend and interpret from my grandfather, he occupied himself with the founding of a congregation school, and he appointed a qualified teacher for it, who privately tutored me and my older sister—in French, too.

The position he assumed in regard to religion is peculiar and, in view of the orthodoxy that prevailed around us, noteworthy. My grandfather was orthodox, but not fanatical. He observed the ceremonial laws strictly, even conducted a prayer service in his home every Friday evening. My father, on the other hand, was liberal, as is understandable given the main thrust of his reading. Every Saturday he went to synagogue for an hour, and on holidays for several hours. He would place me on his seat and have me translate some especially poetic or stylistically beautiful prayers, particularly the psalms, from the prayer book that lay before him on the desk. Whenever all around us prayers were being recited with inordinate haste and with yells (because there is a spot in the Bible that says: "and they cried out to the Eternal One"), he said to me: "You must understand and think about what you are saying. Let them babble!" At home he observed the dietary laws, but without attributing any kind of significance to them. On the many fast days that were customary at that time he had us eat in the rear room in order not to cause annoyance to his fellow believers. At the same time, he taught us that one must always eat moderately, seldom more than necessary, and on certain days less than necessary. My mother did what he thought only with hesitation, and on the Day of Atonement not at all.

My father's social circle was very limited. The Jews who lived in town had for the most part a quite low level of culture and their strict orthodoxy made association with them difficult for a freethinker. On the other hand, my father did get together with a liberal church superintendent and, after an orthodox Protestant had replaced him, with a convivial and pleasant Catholic deacon. We children also did not associate much with the town children, especially not with the boys; particularly because of their ugly manner of speech, father did not deem it advisable. But once he said to me that two brothers about whom he had heard praiseworthy things were coming to visit an uncle, and he recommended that I get to know them. I did and, being about eight years old at that time, saw them often. We played the following game: We were allowed to say only one-syllable Hebrew words. Whoever was addressed had to answer with a word that had the same first letter with which the word said to him had ended. The trick was to force one's opponent to begin every answer with the same letter. Whoever ran out of words lost. One of these brothers, whom I lost sight of for many years, was the later well-known Member of Parliament Lasker.[2] While we were both working in Berlin as assessors, he once looked me up to renew our acquaintanceship. He told me that when I went to Berlin (at age nine) he still lived for a time in Santomysl and from then on had always been interested in me and my progress at the Gymnasium. I had remained in his memory especially because of my good looks; my upright, elastic gait, my smooth hair that hung to my shoulders, my careful way of dressing, and the purity of my speech had caused him to view me as something different from the other boys in town. One sees from this that Lasker, who had not been endowed by nature with much of an appearance, paid attention to these externals.

Aside from Lasker, probably only my dear mother believed that I was really a beautiful child. From my childhood years I recall only that at the age of four I must have had a nice handwriting, since at that time it was shown around in town as a model; but I also recall that when I entered the Gymnasium in my ninth year I caused my writing teacher to despair. He found that my handwriting was too bold. This had come about because for a long time I had helped my grandfather by copying his memoranda or their enclosures. I recall further that my father once took me along when he had to go to the court in the nearby district seat. The room, in which several judges were sitting, the mass of books, and the speeches of the involved parties and the lawyers made a powerful impression on me, since—thanks to the copying I had done—I already knew something about legal contests and their procedures.

When in my ninth year the director examined me for acceptance at the Gymnasium, he asked me somewhat casually at the end what I wanted to become, and was visibly astonished when I answered without hesitation: a lawyer. He laughed heartily about this child just out of diapers who had already planned his future life.

But I must tell how it came about that I was sent, of all places, to Berlin. In those days, it was a six-day journey with the mailcoach from Santomysl to Berlin, and since the mailcoach was too expensive, it took somewhat longer with a transporter (carter). Because of its distance, Berlin was still basically beyond all consideration for the people in my native region. At first they deliberated sending me to the Gymnasium in Meseritz or Trzemeszno (I no longer know which), as they had one or two other boys. Furthermore, there was concern that people in Berlin were not pious and that I would soon liberate myself from the old customs. This last consideration made no impression on my father. And the question of whether I should remain in the province or go to Berlin was decided by my father's thesis: "Civilization comes from the West; one must go toward it."

For a man who in his whole life went only a few miles past his town, who knew how slight the means were that he could provide, and who was beset by anxious people who told him to keep the child in his proximity, this decision was something remarkable. He was aware that this could be risking my downfall. But he resolved to send me. A brother of my mother was studying theology in Berlin. He had agreed to take me in with him. We passed through Posen and found lodging for the night at an acquaintance's, where I slept—or was supposed to sleep—on a sofa. In the morning they found me sleeping a healthy, refreshing child's sleep on the floor. I had not awakened when I rolled down. My father introduced me to a Dr. Samter (later a town councilor in Posen) and asked him at which Gymnasium he should enroll me. The gentleman named the various Gymnasiums and their special features. As soon as he named the French Gymnasium and described its teaching methods, my father was resolved to take me there. He said that he could not see why one should learn the ancient languages thoroughly and the living languages, French and English, but poorly. A person who wanted to make his way in life would have to master the living languages. (Just think that my father held this view already forty years ago!) So I arrived in Berlin and on the next day I was presented to the principal. My mother had decked me out splendidly, according to her own best judgment, exactly like the Polish estate owners did when they sent their children to school: a single-breasted blue jacket with a stand-up collar, trimmed in front with braids (like the hussar uniforms), braided buttons, two cords that ran from the chest across the shoulders and joined in back, at their end a silver tassel; further, a four-cornered cap and a knapsack for my schoolbooks, newly made in Santomysl and as heavy as a soldier's field pack. It must be confessed that in Berlin this costume was somewhat conspicuous for a schoolboy, but I felt very good in it. Anyone who sets out to conquer the world has to be a splendid fellow.

My examination by the principal turned out tolerably well, but I faltered in arithmetic. Why did he have to ask me what half of 97 is? To have to divide two uneven numbers by two was really an indecent demand.

The principal told my father that—particularly in French—I was actually ready for the second class. But I was deficient in arithmetic, and for that reason he wondered whether he should place me in the second or first class. He was very astonished when my father answered: "Then I have a request: Place him in the first class. Let him rise through the ranks. Maybe that way he will make it through the Gymnasium."

And so it happened, and since chance willed it that on graduation from the Gymnasium I was Primus omnium, I fulfilled my father's hope entirely.

My father's concern over leaving me so alone in the big city with a poor student, my uncle, who could seldom be at home, moved him to look for some further connection for me. A contact was found. A learned and rather well-situated old gentleman, a relative of my grandmother, was cantor in the Berlin congregation. My father looked him up and asked him to permit me to pay him a visit now and then. The gentleman granted this, but said to my father: "Do you know what you are doing, Herr Makower? You are bringing the boy to Berlin, having him learn something here, and then . . . then he's going to look down on you." "Let it happen," my father replied, "as long as his accomplishment someday gives him the right to do it!" Is this not a generous and unselfish thought?

I need not say that the older I became the more I honored and admired my father for having become what he was in the circumstances in which he lived.

My life in Berlin during my youth was a rather sad one. I needed love, and was alone. No female being, neither my mother nor my sister nor anyone else, lent me support. I also lacked male company. The uncle with whom I was living was rarely at home, and thus I was entirely on my own. But I was also lacking what was most basic. I learned early that one could go to school without having eaten anything. A little piece of dry bread was at times all I wanted—and did not have. I learned then how little a person can live on, and for that reason, later, when I was faring better, I never really indulged in culinary pleasures. But early on I also experienced something else, which was more bitter still.

Whenever tuition had to be paid, whenever new schoolbooks, notebooks, newspapers, maps, or other such things had to be bought, there was no money available. My uncle simply did not have it, and one had to wait for some favorable occasion for procuring what I needed. The teachers pressed me and were angry that I was not bringing the books and other things. I could not bring myself constantly to admit my poverty: I also did not wish to experience the pity of my fellow pupils. I was often reprimanded by the teachers for my forgetfulness or negligence, reprimands that were justified from the standpoint of the teachers but that hit me unjustly. Naturally, a notebook that I had patched together from the blank pages of letters did not look acceptable; naturally, the blue cover of a notebook for good copies was not clean if I had made it for myself from the paper in which they wrapped sugar cubes in those days. I learned back then to suffer unjustly and at the same time to acknowledge that the person who was inflicting the suffering believed himself from his standpoint to be just—without entirely recognizing the other's situation. I had such dear teachers that they probably would have supported me instead of censuring me if they had known my situation. The result of these experiences was that all my life I have judged the actions of others considerately, fearing that I did not have a proper overview of the other person's situation after all.

When I was about ten years old, they started doing gymnastics again at the Berlin Gymnasiums. Participation was not mandatory, but voluntary. Basically, in those days one still saw a disguised revolutionary in every gymnast. From the start I took part in the gymnastics energetically. I emerged from my cramped little room and was among other children. The whole thing was fatiguing. To dash in the hot sun from the Gymnasium to Hasenheide, which at that time lay a quarter-mile beyond the town wall and, since the spot had just been laid out, was without shade, and then to go back into town and sit down at my homework by the light of a candle stump and after a skimpy supper, was rather trying. Still, I was never absent.

Gradually, I began to know some of my fellow pupils and I became acquainted with the greater comfort in which they lived. Never in such instances did I feel a trace of envy or ill-will; I was happy that others had it better. Once, when I was at the home of the son of the humorist Kossack, who was well-known at that time but now is probably forgotten, I was especially impressed when I saw in the hall that stood at the son's disposal complete suits of armor and found sabers with which, in our children's games, we fought the most violent but, luckily, bloodless battles. When, in 1881, a celebration in honor of the king was to take place in the synagogue and they looked for boys who wanted to sing, I volunteered and at the celebration stood next to a boy who told me that the day before he had been accepted at the French Gymnasium. This boy, with whom I remained in touch throughout my life and with whom I took almost every examination on the same day, from the second class to the assessor's examination, is now the Honorary Counselor Meyer in Berlin. His father was a somewhat odd man, an aristocrat, tight-laced, at home an absolute, patriarchal ruler, strict and firm, and intolerant of other views. His "written" permission was required for me to be allowed to visit his children, so anxiously did he seek to ward off all harmful influence from alien elements. The family was respected and widely known; everything possible was done for the children's education, but a quickening breath of freedom and gaiety were lacking. This pedantry extended to the private tutor, a medical student, and although the social niceties were strictly adhered to, there was a certain coldness in the home, and the spirit remained unfulfilled. Given the effusiveness of my inner being, my striving for depth, and my dedication to ideals, this sober school of proper bearing and aristocratic behavior had a wholesome influence. I owe much to that home, not merely in regard to the external support I found for my daily needs but also because I was introduced into a family that practiced an ordered, strict upbringing.

To be sure, I never warmed up to them. In yet another way, my visits to that home were significant for me. For the first time I found myself in the company of rich people, while I myself was as poor as a beggar when I first came into contact with that family, and was just as poor when I left them many years later after having been private tutor to the children of the oldest daughter. Although I saw that wealth eliminates many troubles that confront the poor and provides much help that the poor lack, I also saw that it does not affect people's happiness in life. The rich have other worries than the needy and suffer more than these do from imagined problems, which hurt just as much as the ones with a real basis. For that reason, I never felt the wish to be rich. Rather, my wishes did not go beyond wanting to possess as much as necessary in order to be as independent as possible.

I observed how many people, who by no means had bad inclinations, were forced by necessity to stoop to deeds and actions that they would not have committed of their own accord, or to behavior of which I disapproved. For example: not voicing their views when they should have, or using expressions of flattery that were not meant sincerely, or excusing when serious reproach—no matter what the consequences—would have been called for, and so forth.

I also observed something else in the course of the years. When I got to know that family, it was regarded as the best family not only among the Jews of the town, but also beyond it. Although in my own life I got to know only two or three generations,

I witnessed how other families rose in society while that family's distinction faded. As years passed, it was no more highly regarded than others, and many strokes of misfortune that struck the family—through no fault of its own—robbed it of its particular splendor. Although I never concerned myself with the wealth of the family members, I do believe that the third generation will be counted among the well-to-do but not among the rich. I observed that in the normal course of events, in about three generations the position and wealth of families change, so that in a hundred years what once was at the bottom is at the top, and the other way around, that especially wealth does not, as a rule, remain in the same family for an inordinate time, and this observation influenced my views of social problems.

Finally a word about the religious convictions that I discovered in that home! As is clear from the above description of the old head of the family, he set the prevailing tone. He regarded himself as a pious man in the orthodox sense, strictly observed the dietary laws, the holidays, and the like. But I have never had any real understanding for his kind of piety; to me it appeared entirely arbitrary. In Santomysl I had gotten to know what orthodoxy is, and the old fellow did not come close to practicing all that I had seen there. He set his own limits, and he was no doubt entitled to do that; only he could not demand that others also stop at these limits. Being young, as I was, I loved the either-or principle and said to myself: If the gentleman wants to be orthodox, then he must be completely orthodox; at least I claimed the right for myself to set my own limits and to find salvation after my own fashion. I made no bones in that family about my views, but it never led to a conflict.

1. The manuscript was kindly placed at our disposal by Dr. K. J. Ball-Kaduri. The German spelling of Santomysl is Santomischel.

2. Eduard Lasker (1829–1884), the leading National Liberal, was born in Jarotschin (Posen), studied law, and in the years 1856–1870 was assessor at the Berlin Civic Court.

# 15  *Clara Geissmar, née Regensburger*

 BORN IN 1844 IN EPPINGEN; DIED IN 1911 IN MANNHEIM.

Clara Geissmar, Remembrances. Mannheim, 1913, 255 pages. Private printing.

*Clara Geissmar depicts here the orthodox milieu of her childhood, from which she later became entirely estranged. At the time of her birth, her father, who had already retired from his business, was living in modest prosperity. Friendly relations between Jews and Christians were a matter of course in Eppingen. Clara attended the public school and received additional instruction from the pastor. At age eighteen, she married the Jewish lawyer Josef Geissmar and the married couple lived in Konstanz—as the sole Jewish family. With new social obligations and in a cultural environment molded by Protestantism, Clara was seized by deep religious uncertainty and she took refuge in a kind of religion of literature and the arts.*

Even on weekdays at the noon meal, the ritual washing of one's hands before eating and the blessing over bread and salt were a religious practice. The Hebrew prayer at the end of the meal was recited aloud by father and quietly by the family. After the evening meal, my brother Moses usually came by with his wife, Sara. The evident delight of such evenings, the fulfillment of the religious prescriptions, the feeling of warm familial fellowship—this daughter-in-law was dear to my mother's heart—all of that lent these evenings a consecration, or rather an atmosphere that combined outward contentment and a satisfied spirit that in later years no sensual or spiritual pleasure provided me.

At a time when the innovation of freshly brewed coffee had not yet been introduced, my mother suffered greatly from the warmed-up sabbath breakfast. Her needs were so few and modest. But she had an absolute aversion to two things: warmed-up coffee and inferior fruit. To drink rewarmed coffee on Saturday morning, that was still tolerable, but to do it again in the afternoon was almost impossible. However, a schoolfriend of hers, who lived only two houses to the left of us, had married the assistant administrator of our little town. Every Saturday, my mother regularly had herself invited for afternoon coffee there, and regularly at four o'clock the servant girl from Schmidts' came and, opening the door, called out: "Frau Regensburger, coffee is served." [. . .]

But once these pleasant Saturday afternoons were interrupted. My mother was an avid newspaper reader, and at that time there were ugly persecutions of Jews under the slogan "Hep, hep!"[1] In my hometown one did not feel them; the various religions coexisted peacefully. But my mother took the ill tidings much to heart, and her lively imagination may have further inflated those matters that the newspaper writers usually describe vividly enough. As it was, her gentle spirit was easily oppressed. One evening, while my parents were sitting at their dinner, a stone came flying through the window-pane, without injuring anyone, however. My mother became extremely agitated. That someone dared to do such a thing to her husband's home—she always thought far too little of herself—filled her with indignation and bitterness. She refused to have the shattered pane replaced. She wanted everyone to see what had been done to our house, and they would all have to be ashamed. And with that, she grew very melancholy. When the Schmidts' servant girl brought the usual message, my mother sought an excuse and sat at home with her gloomy ponderings. Again a week passed and mother was still bitter and oppressed and did not respond to the four-o'clock summons. Then Herr Bailiff Schmidt himself came to check on things. He told my mother that until then he had considered her to be a reasonable woman; but he had been mistaken: she was not one. To risk a friendship of many years because of what some gutter-snipe or some other crude person had done was a most foolish way to act. If she did not go with him right away, he would never return and he would forbid his wife all association with her. This uncompromising manner had its effect, and after a while my mother's head and heart were back in their right place. She again went regularly to Saturday coffee. [. . .]

When I recall the Friday evenings in my parent's home, I have a warm feeling in my heart even today. The preparations were as careful as they are nowadays when one hosts an evening party. The freshly cleaned rooms, the cozy warmth in the winter, the seven-armed brass lamp with its seven little flames whose wicks were braided from cotton wool in the morning. The home-baked potato breads, called *barches,* the green-grain soup, the goose giblets in the winter and the fish in the summer, the latter prepared in a manner that was said to have been customary when the Jews were in Babylonian captivity. Then a dessert, likewise of a special Jewish kind. For Saturday afternoon two closed iron pots were already brought to the baker on Friday. One contained the "settled soup," which was usually a mixture of barley, peas, a chunk of beef, a piece of pickled and smoked breast, which simmered together in the baker's oven to become a tasty dish that was both soup and meat in a single course. The other pot contained the *schalet* or the *kugel* (which latter dish is a kind of English kidney pudding), both of them delicious items, but only for strong stomachs—for which reason during the summer, when one feels better with lighter fare, apple and cherry tortes took their place. I accompanied our servant girl when she took and fetched these Saturday dishes. [. . .]

When father came home from synagogue, we met him at the living room door in order to have him bless us. First mother, then the children. He placed his hands on our heads and in Hebrew words he quietly said the blessing that has become common to all: "May the Lord bless you and keep you." Before the beginning of the meal, ritual washing of the hands with a short blessing; the hand-washing took place at a corner cupboard that was almost as high as the room and above and below contained compartments for household purposes. In the middle was attached a so-called pouring cask, a brass container with faucets that provided the water for the prescribed washing of the hands. Behind a narrow little door of this corner cupboard was the cloth for drying our hands. Before the meal father said the blessing over the bread, cut off a little piece for each of us, which he dipped in salt and then passed around. Then the evening meal began.

It was a very special treat for us children when a child of the Israelite community received its name. All the children of the community were invited, that is, it was taken for granted that all would come, that as soon as it became known that somewhere a "Hollekrasch"—as they called this ceremony—was taking place, all the children of the community would go there. They stood in a circle around the cradle of the four-week-old child, and the strongest boys of the congregation raised the cradle high and called out in their loudest voice: "Hollekrasch, what shall the child be named?" Thereupon the congregation answered with the child's name, as it had been told to them by its parents. The raising of the cradle and the answer of the children were repeated three times; then the ceremony was over. Now came the reward. Usually three baskets were standing ready, one with sweets, the second with nuts, and the third with fruit. Some children brought little bags along in which to store their present. In wealthy homes there was more, in poor homes less.

The circumcision day of the boys was a festivity for which cakes were baked and there were various sweets, and a banquet was held to which the out-of-town relatives came. We children got the best of everything. Best of all was the Pessach meal (Easter [*sic*] meal).[2] One sat in a circle about the round table; in the middle of the table there was a hill of matzohs, each of which was covered with an embroidered little cloth. Finally, there was the loveliest of the cloths, on which stood the house's most beautiful silver objects, little pierced-work baskets, cups, etc. They contained the symbols of the Easter meal: some grated horseradish (what it was supposed to mean, I no longer know),[3] then grated apples, made brown with sugar and cinnamon; this mixture was intended to represent the mortar that the Children of Israel used for the structures that they had to build for their tormentors in Egypt. In a little basket there was a roast bone, which was supposed to represent the Easter lamb that was once roasted in Jerusalem. One was not permitted to taste it; on the other hand, one could eat the bitter herbs, the horseradish, the mortar with matzoh when certain passages of the Haggada were read aloud. The Haggada is a small ancient Hebrew book with many woodcuts that contains the history of the exodus of the Children of Israel.[4] The father of the house recites the text aloud, the others follow and sometimes answer in chorus. As soon as I could read (I learned to read Hebrew almost as early as German), I read aloud the passage that falls to the youngest child of the family and consists entirely of Hebrew questions about the significance of the day. The master of the house answers, that is, he continues the narrative that he had already begun earlier. After its conclusion, when the prophet Elijah is called upon to appear and I as a child opened the door for him, our cat always leapt into the room. Then came the washing of the hands, but on this day the water was handed around in a massive silver basin, first to my father, for whom a splendidly embroidered blue silk pillow, which was used only at Easter, was placed in the sofa corner, then to my mother, and so on. Then came the well-earned supper. Reciting the "Haggada" always lasted two hours. After the meal, we again took up the "Haggada," and the story of the "Kid" was recited.[5] [. . .]

The booth was set up at our home and at our relatives' exactly as it is prescribed in one of the Five Books of Moses, in the decree for the Feast of Booths.[6] In every pious Jewish home there had to be a room somewhere from which one could see the open sky through the roof beams. This room served as the booth. A sort of trapdoor or some other kind of contrivance made of boards let down onto the beams protected the room from rain. Aside from the green branches on the walls, the decorations of a booth consisted of fruits of all kinds, whatever the season had ripened. Apples, grapes, nuts, corn, grain stalks, in between long cutout chains of gold and silver paper, and if it was to be really splendid, lanterns, of the kind that one lights during the so-called Italian Nights.

On Christmas Eve, which brought me nothing—since my parents considered a Christmas tree in a Jewish home to be absurd and Jews who gave Christmas presents simply ridiculous—I was quite envious and sometimes could not hold back my tears when I saw the poorest of the neighboring homes beaming in the glow of the candles. But during the Feast of Booths I had something the Christian children did not have. Whoever I liked was allowed to sit in our booth.

Then came Chanukka and later Purim, days of pure rejoicing. The Chanukka festival is a celebration of victory. On this day a Maccabean triumphed with his stalwarts over the Syrians and saved the tribe of Judah from destruction. There were special vessels (ours were of silver), with seven divisions, each of which was for a wick and oil.[7] For seven days each male family member lit one of these oil lights, that is, on the first day one, on the second day two, on the third three, until on the seventh day all seven were burning. In homes where there were many male members there was a radiant illumination on the inside window sills, where the Chanukka lamps were usually placed.

On each of the seven evenings after the lighting, the Chaldean[8] victory song was sung, and I sang along proudly and happily. For almost forty years I have not taken part in this festival, but the five stanzas and their special melody are both present in my mind; I could still sing them by heart. In honor of this glorious time, needlework was set aside in the evening, and there were social card games.

The happiest holiday was the Purim festival. It was a day of joy. The villain Haman, an antisemite, wanted to wipe out the Jews. King Ahasveros, however, who had married the Jewess Esther, had Haman hung on the very gallows that he had erected for the Jew Mordechai—after Haman had been humiliated by having to lead Mordechai through the city on a splendidly bridled horse and to call out: "Here is the man whom the King wishes to honor." The Jews celebrated a joyous holiday and sent one another presents. In those days, this sending of presents, in the form of tortes and sponge cakes, still took place throughout the Jewish community. The poor made use of the occasion and produced baked goods and brought them to the rich, for which they then received a gift of money. In the evening, we put on costumes, and once we even performed a funny skit. If I couldn't think of anything else, I put on boy's clothes and had a moustache painted on me with charcoal, and I went to my relatives and came home with lots of cookies. [. . .]

Our [cook] Jette was clear-headed, liked to read, and often did it at a time when she should have been concentrating on the cooking. Once I had to memorize a ballad by Schiller. It was one that she liked, and she decided to learn it too, and took the volume of Schiller into the kitchen. When my mother went into the kitchen shortly before the meal to test the dishes, as was her custom, our Jette quickly hid the book in the empty soup tureen. On that day we got our soup served up with Schiller's poems.

Among classical works my mother prized *Hermann und Dorothea* more than any. In her opinion, it was a second Bible. She enjoyed reading Walter Scott and, most of all, Dickens and Heine. Walter Scott's first novels appeared when she, still an adolescent, had already lost her mother. From her eleventh year on she had no school instruction because she was needed in the household. Reading these excellent books brought her pleasure, elation, and knowledge. But she had to do it furtively; such a need was considered something eccentric, impeding practical work. [. . .]

While the novels of Dickens lay about freely at our house, the various Heine volumes—along with Dickens he was mother's favorite author—were locked away so that I would not read them. That only led me to be even more intent on reading Heine, and thanks to my mother's absentmindedness I very often found occasion to do it. If I know a large part of the poems by heart, it goes back to my reading at that time. I wrote verses myself, mostly when I was hurt and wanted to anger someone. [. . .]

I have now written about many persons who were close to me during my childhood and schooldays, but I have hardly named all of the dear people who contributed to preserving everything so warmly in my memory. There were our milk suppliers, the Gebharts, a respected farmer family, from whom our servant girl fetched the milk each evening, when I frequently accompanied her. Over the many years, there formed a kind of friendship with them. Our immediate neighbors, the bookbinder Kepner, the post-master Wittmer, the soap-boiler Zutafern, the beer brewer Schäfer, the baker Riegler, Glöckler, and their families, all of them frugal, diligent, upright people, with whom we had an ever-constant, warm relationship based on years of habit and mutual respect. While I was jumping about and playing with the other children after supper in the summer, my mother sat on a stool in front of the house. Then, little by little, the neighbors came by and sat down on our three stone steps. When I had played until I was tired, I sat down at my mother's feet and listened. They conversed on every possible domestic topic, but they also complained and wailed much about the weather. It was never right. Except for hoeing, my mother took care of our large garden by herself. The neighboring women, too, worked lots in their gardens during the summer. One usually hired day laborers only for the fields, if one was not up to it oneself. [. . .]

I had passed my early childhood in a pious home and had experienced the joys and sorrows, the privations, and the inner satisfaction that Judaism provides its adherents. [. . .] One belonged to a totality, whose blessings were sensed only by those who through steady observance—which meant steady privation—lived up to all of the laws and prescriptions with which Judaism surrounded itself as with a fence.

The new environment into which Josef introduced me removed me once and for all from this world. So much that was good and beautiful descended upon me in my new world that it almost exceeded my power to absorb it spiritually. There were hours in which I felt empty and unfulfilled. There was a corner of my soul that neither my husband's love nor the most beautiful passages of Shakespeare and Goethe were able to fill. I missed belonging to a religion. Once I went to church to observe the Protestant service. When the service was introduced "in the name of the Father, the Son, and the Holy Ghost," words that one had to interpret in order to arrive at some meaning, the Hebrew words occurred to me that introduce Jewish prayers: "Hear, oh Israel, the Eternal, your God, is one, a single, eternal Being." When at the end the congregation was dismissed with the words "May the Lord bless you and keep you," I thought of my father, who, when I went to meet him at the door on his return from prayers on Friday evening, laid his hands on my head and in the original Hebrew said the words that the Protestant clergyman bestowed upon his congregants on their way home. I did not go to a Protestant church again.

At that time, my brother Leopold presented me with two volumes of historical and political essays by Treitschke. Today, I can hardly recapture the enchantment to which I succumbed on reading these essays. What was most on the mind of the young National Liberal movement, the subjects to which the men's conversations constantly returned, was expressed here in beautiful form by an ardently progressive soul. Never had I been so enthusiastic about an author. While young fellows and girls of my age had their Schiller phase, I felt nothing of the kind. I had my Treitschke phase. His language alone intoxicated me. My unsatisfied religious need was fulfilled by the firm belief in a moral world order that runs like a red thread through everything that Treitschke discusses. When the year 1866 later proved that he was right in saying that "the brutality of the petty German provinces can be overcome only by another kind of brutality, through the brutality of the Prussian sabres," he appeared to me to be a prophet. No Jew and no Catholic can write that way, I told myself. Only a Protestant can achieve something like that.

When we were alone, we spoke much about the religious education of our children. We agreed that our life in the Judaism of our childhood had left something within us, an extract upon which we could draw for the rest of our lives. We also agreed that children could encounter the essence of religion only through its external forms. Josef desired that we introduce these external forms into our home. As he never bothered with the practical details in any real matters, it was hard to figure out what these individual forms were to be. Above all, Friday evening and the Sabbath were to be celebrated. But if Saturday is not also celebrated by other friends and acquaintances, and especially if the children see their father carrying on his weekday activities on Saturday and that he has his holiday on Sunday like everyone else all around us, then Saturday can hardly be maintained as a day of rest.

The outward forms of Judaism, this wall with which it surrounded its God, can only stand when the many Asiatic stones and pebbles from which it is formed hold together. If one removes a single stone, the whole wall shakes and finally collapses. Only Orthodox Judaism is stable. Every reform means collapse. Nothing could be done.

Now I wanted the children to be raised as Protestants. Frau von Rechthaler, with her zeal for the liberal Protestant cause, told me what her friend Zittel in Heidelberg had once said: "All of the churches are educational institutions; Protestantism is the best." Josef wanted to know nothing of it. If only because of his father there could be no thought of it. The children were still so small that the question was not critical. That one visit to church still made itself felt within me; it would not have been easy for me to send my children to the Protestant church. But since that time, because of its effect, I was won over by Protestantism, despite all of the negative sides, which in later life did not remain hidden from me. I was not interested in Christ. Not even if regarded as a human did this noble, majestic figure attract me. His lack of human weaknesses repelled me. We come to love personalities who are far superior to us only through their weaknesses, and these were nowhere to be seen. The only thing in the New Testament that gladdened and enriched me were two pronouncements: "And though you have all but have not charity, etc." And "You shall know them by their fruits." I believed to see the fruits of Protestantism, palpably, in the national and national-economic sense. I believed in what it was destined to be, perhaps in accordance with its nature, and I found that in this sense Lessing, Schiller, and Goethe had also been good Protestants. [. . .]

I discussed my religious problems with my Protestant friends, who would have been happy if we were to have had our two children baptized. A tender soul once had tearful eyes at the thought of how our little Leopold would someday fare in the world, at all that he would have to suffer if he were to grow up a Jew. Whenever we talked about it, Josef said again and again that, as best as possible, the children simply were to be given a Jewish religious upbringing. Both of us felt the same aversion to modern Judaism, with its abundance of stringency and its lack of depth, and which maintains itself only through negation. But Josef was unable to help me in my distress; more than once he was quite impatient at my abnormally one-sided stress on the religious question. Protestantism, whose merits he did not fail to appreciate, was in his eyes certainly a good school for humane upbringing, but he said that it had destroyed so much that was vital to our life that he found it unacceptable. My father-in-law, to whom in my distress I had explained my reasons for baptizing the children, wrote me an incensed letter that upset me completely. Karoline found that earlier she had liked me much more. My brother Leopold pointed out to me that in order for a person to live successfully for himself and others he has to do justice to a whole series of claims. If he devotes himself to a single one of these claims at the expense of all the others, that can bring about his ruin and the ruin of those close to him. "The deepest abyss is within ourselves."


1. The Hep-Hep storms of 1819, which passed through all of Germany, also led to physical violence against Jews in Baden. Their causes have been sought primarily in the economic distress of the petty bourgeoisie.

2. The quite inaccurate use of Easter *(Ostern)* for the Jewish Passover (Pessach) festival persisted in German long after it had become obsolete in English. The author employs it throughout this passage.

3. The pungent, bitter horseradish is meant to recall the bitter suffering of the Jews in Egypt.

4. The Passover Haggada contains the prescribed texts for the family ceremony of the Seder meal. The modern version stems for the most part from the tenth and eleventh centuries.

5. The Song of the Kid concludes the Passover Haggada and in its folksong character probably originated in the fifteenth century.

6. Leviticus 23:42–43.

7. The Chanukka festival, which celebrates the resanctification of the temple after the Maccabean Wars, lasts for eight, rather than seven, days. Thus, the Chanukka menorah has eight lights, plus one that is used to kindle the others.

8. Likewise an error of the author: the Chanukka song has a Hebrew text.

*Imperial Germany, 1871–1918*

# 16 *Conrad Rosenstein*

 BORN IN 1910 IN BERLIN; DIED IN 1978 IN ISRAEL.

Conrad Rosenstein, The Well, A Family Chronicle. Israel, 1958. Manuscript, 64 pages.

*The father of the author went from the province of Posen to Berlin, where he ran a modest wholesale business for barber's supplies. During the week he visited customers, while his wife managed the correspondence. In addition to his parents' work, Conrad Rosenstein describes the life of the Jewish community in the synagogue on Fasanenstrasse—not without critical reservations. He became Bar Mitzvah under the tutelage of Rabbi Leo Baeck. Rosenstein depicts the style of life of the "better" Jewish families from the circle of his relatives and acquaintances with irony. Later, Conrad Rosenstein studied dentistry, was expelled from the University of Freiburg in 1933, and received his degree in Bern. Until his emigration to Palestine, he was a dentist at the Jewish Polyclinic in Berlin.*

My mother's work was varied. Along with her obligations as a housewife, she took care of all sorts of office chores for my father, who was usually on the road five days a week in order to visit his customers in strictly demarcated areas. His itinerary was determined by my brother, who outdid all of his schoolmates and most of his teachers, too, in his knowledge of transportation schedules and cities and towns in the German Reich. He drew complete maps for my father and provided everything with the necessary notations so that my father could depend entirely on his weekly plan. The correspondence was watched over by my mother. She preferred this kind of office work to sitting at "the cash register" in the retail shop. She regarded that as somewhat degrading. In the first years of her marriage, when my father still owned his shoe stores, she had to submit to her fate. Even in later years she viewed this as a distressing period. Father had taken over these shops from his younger brother, who himself lacked a skillful touch at the business and at bottom was quite happy that he could "unload" it onto my father. No doubt this act was not entirely fair. This period gave rise to a certain latent aversion on the part of my mother toward father's family. It lessened only in the course of years and finally even changed into sincere liking. But at that time she felt cheated. She demanded independence from the family and autonomy in her work. For that reason, she was quite content when my father decided to give up retail selling and to "travel" in the provinces. The vocation of the Jewish traveling salesman was customary. Somehow it belonged to the category of human activities that are "inbred in Jews." In any event, that is what simple folk maintained, and in the end the Jews themselves believed it. Half-truths, if they are constantly hawked, become accepted as truths.

My father traveled loaded down with heavy sample-bags, and by no means were errand boys always there to lend a hand. If in the propaganda clichés of the antisemites it was often maintained that Jews avoided physical labor, one can say very objectively of my father that he, at any rate, earned his bread by the sweat of his brow. The stereotype later lost its meaning for me completely when I got to know the Jewish farmer in Palestine, who, generally speaking, and certainly as far as climate is concerned, labors under much more difficult conditions than the German peasant.

When my father returned from his "tour," he immediately went to the center of town to buy merchandise. His own stocks always remained small, since his working capital was limited. On the other hand, he was intent on supplying his customers as quickly as possible—"promptly," as business German puts it—in order not to allow the suspicion to surface that his small wholesale trade in barber's supplies was inferior to larger enterprises, or that in comparison with them it was not efficient. In the mind of the little Christian merchant it was hard to forgive the Jew if he remained the small-time man that he was. One secretly expected him to be a "big businessman." For this reason, Mama preferred to write in letters to customers: "As Herr Rosenstein of our firm informed us . . . ," and never "my husband." People would have immediately suspected that wife and husband were the firm's sole personnel. "Herr Rosenstein of our firm . . . " left the little man some room for imagination. If one day such a customer came to the city and looked up his supplier of many years, he was taken aback that in reality things were so simple and limited. Papa and Mama then felt shame at their insignificance in commercial life. Nevertheless, the little people remained loyal to my father; they even called him a "white Jew"—which was intended to be a compliment of sorts. At the start of Hitler's rule, they usually let my father enter through a "back door." They received him after business hours; they awaited him in their private quarters in order not to lose the connection with a man whom they wished well and of whose honesty they were convinced. To be sure, that was only a temporary solution, which, as the regime increasingly consolidated, became ever more risky for "Jew servants."

When father returned from purchasing, the office work—the packing of packages—began immediately. Mostly I was the one who rushed on Sunday evening, loaded with packages of every size, to the one open postal window of the train station to ship off the "first batch." All this writing, reckoning, and packing kept my parents on the go until the late evening hours. But when Monday came, my father was already traveling, loaded down, but never glum, never weary of his trials, but rather quietly resigned to his obligations, like a faithful horse that never thinks of straying from its path. This exceptional probity, which does not allow an "evil thought" to arise, was striking. The asceticism of his way of life, which was not at all perceived as a burden, was probably also something traditional, a kind of rabbinic concept of "living within the Law." Not that my father would have reflected on it, for reflection was far removed from his modest manner of thought. This asceticism was a conditioned way of being that, strange as it may sound, had been adopted, experienced, acquired as a synthesis of Jewish-Prussian values.

Besides these activities in the business, my mother had her own, specific domain. In our childhood years, my own and my brother's, she diligently gave piano lessons. During the First World War, when my father was called up for army duty, the store was sold out helter-skelter and at a loss. (At that time my father had switched to a very thriving enterprise for infirmary uniforms, and numerous seamstresses brought giant bundles every day.) So my mother supported us with her piano lessons, which she gave to sons of the respectable middle class, spoiled daughters, and yawning damsels. Her adaptability was astonishing, her inner alertness, the adjustment to every situation, something that was in keeping with her generation. The hectic conditions of the time demanded from the little man, especially if he was a Jew, the ability to adapt if he did not want to go under. That was something unknown to the prior generation.

Since our mother was often busy outside the home during our early childhood, we were left with a servant girl. She told us scary stories or allowed us to roam about in the park. She sat on a bench with a lover and flirted, until the evening bugle-call summoned the soldiers back to the barracks. Frightened and as though benumbed, she searched for the children who had been left to her care. — For many years, my mother also sang in the choir of the Fasanenstrasse Synagogue, until that infamous "Kristall-nacht," when this synagogue in the west of Berlin went up in flames and the communal life of the Jews in Germany ceased to be.

The Fasanenstrasse Synagogue played a decisive role in the Jewish life of the Reich's capital. It was, so to speak, the symbol for "how far" one could go in the Jewish emancipation in Germany. At times people talked even more about the "Jewish Reform Congregation" than about this synagogue.[1] Still, the Reform Congregation was not a symbol, nor was it "typical," but rather it was a gross exaggeration, inasmuch as it consciously abandoned Jewish tradition in order to follow the style of the church. It substituted Sunday for the Sabbath, and the sacred language of Hebrew was abolished totally. The style of worship thoroughly emulated the Christian prayer service. This was not the case at all in the Fasanenstrasse Synagogue. Here the tradition that had been created a generation earlier was preserved: modern form, to be certain, but still with the old content.

At the beginning of the century, at fantastic cost, a splendid, cold colossus of a building was erected, with adjoining buildings, a lecture hall, a library, and the well-known "nuptials hall," which was decorated with Cadinen tiles from the private man-ufactory of the German Kaiser. His Majesty had also put in an appearance after the consecration of the House of God, and the Kaiser joked a bit about the wealth of his Jewish subjects.

For decades Chief Cantor Magnus Davidsohn functioned there, a former opera singer of imposing appearance, somewhat stiff, with the airs of a heroic tenor, blond, and solemnly presumptuous: a cross between Joshua ben Nun[2] and Parsifal. He always entered the chancel, his stage, only after the organ prelude. A radiant gold door opened. With the hymnal, alias *siddur,* in his arm, a star-shaped priest's cap on his head, the folded prayer mantle draped across his shoulder like a shawl, he strode in his robe to the dais, head held high: every inch the star. At the *kiddush* on Shabbat[3] he used to raise the silver goblet aloft: it was a kind of Grail scene. But it cannot be denied that his emotive recitation was impressive. At times he also interrupted his singing in order to declaim, sonorously and pratingly. Perhaps without knowing it, he was imitating the great reciter Ludwig Wüllner. Davidsohn had a very metallic-sounding tenor-baritone voice, neglected the soft tones, and loved powerful delivery. But he commanded broad musical abilities, so that he was able to appear successfully in public concerts. For the rest, he was in truth deeply devoted to his vocation in the synagogue, even if there was quite a bit of charlatanry in his "priestly" manner.

For many years, Rabbi Dr. Juda Bergmann preached in this synagogue. As a person he was very attractive, a broadly educated man, but largely "corrupted" by the liberal style. People claimed that he had copied his manner of speech and gestures from his father-in-law, Rabbi Dr. Rosenzweig[4] of the Great Synagogue. He loved the gently lyrical style of the Christian preachers. Not seldom did I use my gift for satire in order to imitate this rabbi. I usually reaped rich applause from my audience. I entertained rooms full of company with it. It was really discouraging to see how this highly cultivated man condescended—I was almost about to say "lowered himself"—to squeeze a few sentimental tears from the parvenus of Kurfürstendamm. Dr. Bergmann was a Zionist. Even before the German Republic collapsed, he emigrated to Eretz Israel with his large family.[5] It was all the more remarkable that for decades his congregants had detected nothing of his longing for Zion. As a rabbi, one could withhold something like that from one's "devout listeners."

In personal association, Dr. Bergmann was one of the most dignified, helpful, kind, and estimable personalities during my childhood. I never saw him except in his frock coat. To see him once in a bathing suit at the Baltic resort of Kolberg was such an indescribably comic situation that even today I recall it with laughter. He was eating a blueberry tart, which Frau Rabbi had baked for the whole Bergmann clan, and the blue juice was running into his goatee when, standing on the beach, he caught sight of me. He asked me at that time what profession I wanted to take up someday. "Journalism," I answered. "Oh," he said, "that's fine for times when you have absolutely nothing else to do." But since the occasion could not pass without a moral maxim, he then added: "Our profession does not form us, we form our profession. What we bring to it determines its worth." [. . .]

The highpoints of synagogue life were the regular sermons of Dr. Leo Baeck, the great teacher, religious philosopher, and leader of German Jewry.[6] Unfortunately, Leo Baeck's organ of speech was not very pleasant. His voice sounded tortured, squeezed, sometimes plain whiny. But the construction of his sermons had an almost classic beauty and was exemplary. The wealth of insight, of spirituality far surpassed everything that liberal sermonizing otherwise had to offer. Although attending synagogue did not exactly interest me, as a student I still went to the synagogue almost regularly, at any rate during my student days in Berlin, whenever Dr. Leo Baeck was scheduled to preach.

He also presided over my Bar Mitzvah. I know that I went with my father when he paid his respects to him before this important day. Dr. Baeck inquired in much detail about the little town from which my father came. I have also not forgotten the content of the confirmation speech. Even today, I vividly recall this event. Dr. Baeck spoke about "holy joy." He proceeded from the fact that the consecrated boy is called up "to the Law," is a "Bar Mitzvah," which, as the others see it, undoubtedly signifies a restriction of his freedom. For while the world generally regards "living within the Law" as a necessity, it is not exactly seen as a "delight." He said that it was the singular quality of Judaism to have accepted the Law and, with inner joy, to take pride in it. For only the Law gives the human being his true human freedom; within it he elevates himself above the common creature. But this joy is not "unrestrained mirth"; rather it is lofty, holy joy, which he prayed that heaven send me, the "Bar Mitzvah," at that hour.

It was also fortunate that on this festive occasion I read from Mishpatim,[7] a Torah portion that deals with obligations toward the poor, a social law, recited in a pleasant singsong, which Chief Cantor Davidsohn had taught me. People congratulated me generally, since I had a highly appealing boy's voice and also was able to "strike a good pose." Mama said that I was now a grownup, which was perhaps due to the unbecoming hat that I had gotten as a gift on that day.

Dr. Baeck presented me, as was customary, with a German-Hebrew prayer book, whose pathetic, hollow devotional style made quite a few concessions to the church worship service. Here Judaism was already divested of its deep content. It was constantly glancing outside, worried about what our Christian fellow citizens might think. The force of Judaism no longer lay within the Jew himself, and so he became a kind of dummy of his own person. One awaited legitimation from the world outside. Achad Haam[8] once formulated it in this way: The Western Jew lost his inner freedom in order to attain an external freedom; the East European Jew possesses no external freedom, but still possesses himself. When this "Yid," unsightly and unclean, exulted or sobbed under the cover of his *tallis,* he still knew that he was a descendent of Abraham, Isaac, and Jacob. In him there was the joyous cry of the *chassidim* and the fervor of the *tsadikim,* the mysticism of the *Zohar* and the wisdom of the *Gemara*— the sum total of an entire history.[9] The history of the *German* Jew, on the other hand, told of the princes of Mark Brandenburg, of the Prince Elector and the Prussian kings, the Kaisers and the Republic. That was "his" history. This statement contains as much truth as it does deception. We had heard about our own Judaism only from adaptations for young people; the text, the *Tanach,*[10] was basically alien to us. In Dr. Bergmann's religious instruction this original source was as good as unknown, to say nothing of religion classes at school. Thus, my *nigun*[11] was but a little prayer shawl that I had learned to carry on my shoulder from Chief Cantor Magnus Davidsohn. Thus, my grandmother said, very much to the point; "He has the *nigun.* Too bad that he is lacking the Hebrew words."

To the extent that the liberal community considered its situation, it felt this discrepancy quite clearly. I even believe that the people in the Reform Congregation sensed the same thing when on Sunday the Jewish clergyman delivered them a lecture on Rembrandt and the Old Testament. Any self-criticism would have had a devastating effect.

They tried to cover up the spiritual problems with liturgical music. The esthetically objectionable quavering, sobbing, whispering, the unhesitating cries, these stylistic elements of the *nigun,* delivered by often naturally talented persons of the first rank: all that was rejected and replaced by the romantic cantilenas of Lewandowski. But there were also Birnbaum and Friedmann, and among the younger ones Kornitzer, Nadel, and Bloch, an entire repertory of refined synagogue music, which a more cultivated audience very gladly accepted.[12] At the Fasanenstrasse Synagogue there was the excellent blind organist Altmann, and above all Theodor Schönberger, my uncle. As a child, I liked to accompany my mother to the choir loft of the synagogue in order to sit on the steps that led up to the organ. Master Altmann explained to me the construction of the three manuals, the pedalboard, and the levers, and with his fingers he skimmed over the Braille score. Then he caused the mighty instrument to rumble so that I shuddered. In Theodor Schönberger the synagogue possessed an exceptional, artistically earnest personality. The choir could compete with the best church choirs in Berlin. Synagogue concerts, with Magnus Davidsohn as the performing cantor, accompanied by choir and organ, were a musical event of which the Berlin community could be proud. To belong to this choir of the best professional singers was a privilege in which my mother took no little pride—entirely aside from the fact that the modest monthly salary also helped her to balance the budget.

The special festive events of the Fasanenstrasse Synagogue, free performances that we children liked to goggle at, were the wedding ceremonies of the prosperous Jewish circles from Kurfürstendamm. Gleaming lacquered coaches pulled up, drawn by dapple-gray horses; a footman in braid-trimmed uniform jumped down from the box, doffed his top hat, and opened the door. Inside, the coaches were lined with white silk, and the bridal couple strode over spread rugs into the wedding hall. A press on the button by the "castellan," bustling Herr Kaatz, and the organ thundered. Wide doors were opened. Temple attendants, rather corpulent gentlemen already grown grey in their official devotedness, carried burning candles. The rabbi and cantor appeared in full array. They followed the potbellied *"schamoschim."*[13] Then came the flower-strewing children, the sweetest little baskets in their hands, a rococo idyll. Naturally, everyone's attention was focused on the bride and bridegroom. The veil-bearers and relatives followed them; elegant and festively bloated, they ambled slowly through the gigantic building. Choir singing resounded and hired opera members sent harp and cello tones down from the ramp of the choir loft, while the entire gathering assembled picturesquely around the wedding canopy. Then the ceremonial speeches of the rabbis began, stereotypical, set addresses, empty and solemn. They applied to everyone; all that was ever needed was to insert the new names. Yet, the pomp and ceremony brought tears to the eyes of the guests. No sooner had the coaches arrived than a crowd of gapers streamed into the synagogue, a mostly Christian audience that especially enjoyed Jewish weddings and was downright blissful, overwhelmed—rather like when Richard Tauber sang—when the wedded couple, parents, and parents-in-law fell into one another's arms, hugged and kissed: a love-demonstration of Jewish intimacy, more tender and emotional than in the Kaiser Wilhelm Memorial Church. "In this respect," said the good people, "the Jews outshine us."

Thus, my mother's domain was varied enough. And in later years there were also very nice family events, when every Tuesday evening we had "chamber music." My mother sat at the piano, a family friend, a Prussian Gymnasium teacher, played violin, and a Hungarian chemist, a business friend of my father's, played cello. They played nothing but Haydn, Mozart, and Beethoven. As far as I can recall, their performance had an amateur quality, but still it was held together musically and in a charming way through the discreet directives of my mother, who took her role seriously and accomplished it in the best possible fashion.[. . .]

The epoch that started with the First World War, when the European avalanche began, had achieved its gnawing, exhausting effects. It was pure folly to be living in Berlin. For there could be no doubt that my parents' life would have proceeded much more peacefully if in the early years of their marriage they had not been so set on spending their lives in the capital. For the members of a minority, however, it is always easier, emotionally more beneficial, to live wherever there are as many people of one's own kind as possible. In Berlin one was less exposed to the growing antisemitism than in small towns. One had one's own honeycomb of autonomy. Basically, it was not a matter of interest if some gentleman or other, wearing a top hat and with a prayer book in hand—not even wrapped in newspaper—went to the synagogue for holiday worship. The neighbors barely took note of it when the shipment of matzo boxes arrived. One lived, after all, in a large apartment house, and the others minded their own business.

My father's youngest sister lived in a small town in Pomerania, owned a house, a garden, and property. But the mimicry that was necessary for Jews went so far that, in order to prove her patriotic sentiments, she had even hung a picture of Field-Marshal von Hindenburg in her stable. By no means did she dare miss the marksmen's festival, and to belong to the voluntary fire brigade was a national duty. If all around them people shouted ''hurra'' once, then the few Jews shouted ''Hurra, hurra, hurra!'' The triple shout gave them away as Jews. In return, they were granted the privilege of entering—on tiptoe—into business relationships with the big landowners east of the Elbe and with other landed proprietors. There they were addressed by their first name, as a sign of special favor, and were then permitted to make themselves scarce again.

In Berlin one had it better. The Jewish community was large and influential, thanks to Jewish capital. Taken with a a grain of salt, one could say that the Jews were Germany's best taxpayers. Their exceptional intelligence had the effect of ''cranking up'' business life. They stimulated artistic endeavor and the press. The Jews contributed decisively to the remarkable development of Berlin in the twenties. In those days—to be sure, for eight or nine years only—Berlin became the center of Europe. So it seemed enticing to live in Berlin, above all if one was a Jew. [. . .]

Café Leu on Oranienburger Strasse, immediately next to the administration building of the Jewish community, was, so to speak, the foyer of the Jewish ''parliament.'' The community administration did, in fact, have a broad field of work. It maintained special funds for the poor and the sick, for Jews in transit, and for widows and orphans. It paid salaries and pensions to its officials and employees. It had its own tax division. The community owned a Jewish museum, which was excellently directed; also, old-age homes, hospitals, synagogues, schools, training institutes, libraries, and legal aid offices. It owned cemeteries and lots, administered inheritances, and supplied guardians. It gave scholarships to pupils, students, and academicians. A community newspaper reported on all activities and events in Germany and, above all, in the Reich capital. The officers of the community carried on all sorts of negotiations with the state treasury and the Prussian Ministry of Culture. They were elected democratically, by free, secret ballot. For decades, the majority was German-Liberal, as defined by the Centralverein Deutscher Staatsbürger Jüdischen Glaubens.[14]

The directors, officers, and personnel of the community administration gathered at Café Leu. There, as it were, one could hear the heartbeat of Berlin Jewry. At times Dr. Weisse turned up, the dignified pulpit-orator of the Great Synagogue, a kind of bishop of Mosaic origin. The talmudist Albert Katz philosophized there, and was led by the nose by Fabius Schach.[15] The Zionists fought their battles against the members of the Centralverein there. The Orthodox intrigued against the Liberals, the Liberals scrapped with the Orthodox. There the Western Jews rejected any association with the East European Jews, and the East European Jews provoked their western brethren from across the table. Collections for charity began there. As though from a telegraph operator, one learned there of antisemitic excesses. Sammy Gronemann[16] caricatured the entire "tempest in a teapot" with caustic derision and a loving heart. Cantors, who loitered around out of boredom, played skat there for hours at a time, and reported on the first-, second-, and third-class burial services at the big Jewish cemetery in Weissensee, and on the ostentatious mausoleums of the upper crust and the look-alike graves of the poor. In this coffee house, many "Jewish jokes" originated, which then were circulated, and there Fabius Schach gathered rich material for his commentaries; there he found an inexhaustible source of Jewish folk culture. [. . .]

I had already become acquainted with aristocratic homes when I was halfway through the Gymnasium. Papa had cousins with villas, people who lingered at their pond with a fishing rod and who reported on their world tours as we sat stiffly around the coffee table. I also had schoolmates from wealthy homes. Nevertheless, they liked very much to visit me, participated with the greatest pleasure in our raffles, and were very happy when they won crayons or an alarm whistle. (Papa had bought everything wholesale.) The boys kissed my mother's hand. We young fellows were already reading the exciting dramas of the hero Theodor Körner. We scraped out a "bourrée" or a "saraband" for one another on the violin. We outdid ourselves with Handel's Largo. Mama accompanied us.

At their homes music was played only in the music salon, and reading was done in the Biedermeier room. Delicacies were served us in the children's room. The Bar Mitzva celebrations turned into banquets in high-society style. Entire libraries were piled up as gifts. Cameras, opera glasses, bicycles, stationery cases, watches, and tiepins were "presented." It rankled me that my mother had bought nothing more than a thin volume by Fontane for me to take along as a little gift! One felt like a beggar in the presence of such abundance. Limousines rolled up in the quiet streets, and young maidservants in black and white helped the ladies out of their fur coats. Some of them were deeply décolleté, and they were fragrant with a variety of choice perfumes.

At the table, silver platters were handed around, on which poulardes rested in asparagus and salads. Cornucopia, such as I had never seen, had been sent by the Koschel Company. Flowers poured out of them in rare splendor, and cool dewdrops still clung to the blossoms. At every setting there were place cards. I, too, had my "couvert," and the menu was given in French, a French for which my school knowledge was simply inadequate. There were words that I had never heard. I was as careful as the devil not to use the wrong silverware; I was outright afraid that I might disfigure the fish with the meat fork, that the sherbet spoon might be left over and give me away if I used the dessert spoon instead. Believe me that I felt quite ill at ease, that I constantly feared that I would commit a faux pas and possibly stain the damask tablecloth! It would have been a disaster! I would have been disgraced; but what am I saying: unmasked! But the gentlemen in evening dress did not even take note of me. They were toasting the ladies. But a humpbacked, very kind little grandmother, from whom all the family wealth derived, bent down to us and asked whether we were happy.

For my return home after midnight—I was very tired—they put me in a hired taxi. For the first time in my life I gave tips, and I felt very embarrassed in doing it. I somehow had the feeling that it was not proper. But it probably would have been improper not to give any.

1. The Berlin Reform Congregation, founded in 1845, broke most radically with traditional Judaism. The Fasanenstrasse Synagogue favored the Liberal orientation in Judaism.
2. Joshua, the successor to Moses as leader of the People of Israel.
3. The chanted Sabbath blessing over the wine during worship on Friday evening.
4. Adolf Rosenzweig (1850–1918), rabbi in Berlin beginning in 1887, was a Liberal and published numerous works on Jewish history.
5. Juda Bergmann (1874–1956), rabbi in Berlin beginning in 1908; he emigrated to Palestine in 1933.
6. Leo Baeck was born in Lissa in 1873 and died in London in 1956. He became rabbi in Berlin in 1912, and in 1933 president of the Reichsvertretung der Deutschen Juden.
7. Exodus 21:1–24:18.
8. Pseudonym for Ascher Ginzburg (1856–1927). Achad Haam was one of the most important representatives of cultural Zionism.
9. *Chassidim* are the adherents of *chassidism,* the popular mystical movement that arose within Polish Jewry in the eighteenth century. Ecstatic reverence for the perfectly pious ones, the *zadikim,* is a special part of it. — The *Zohar* is the major work of older Jewish mysticism, which first arose in Spain at the end of the thirteenth century. — The *Mishna* (see Glossary) and the *Gemara* together constitute the Talmud.
10. Bible; this word, which is used colloquially, stems from a Hebrew abbreviation of the books of the Bible.
11. Melody, synagogue song.
12. Louis Lewandowski (1821–1894), choir director in Berlin, and Eduard Birnbaum (1855–1920) were the leading composers of this music. The others are Aron Friedmann (1855–1936), cantor in Berlin; Leon Kornitzer (1875–1947), cantor in Hamburg; Arno Nadel (1878–1943), choir director in Berlin; Ernst Bloch (1880–1959), Swiss composer.
13. Synagogue attendant.
14. The Centralverein was founded in 1893 as an organization to combat antisemitism and was the largest Jewish association. Its members defined themselves as Germans of the Jewish faith and for the most part favored left-liberal parties.
15. Albert Katz (1858–1923) and Fabius Schach (1868–1930) were both Zionists of East European origin and worked as journalists. For a time, Katz edited the *Allgemeine Zeitung des Judentums.* Schach later became an anti-Zionist.
16. For Sammy Gronemann, see his memoir, no. 28.

# 17 *Henriette Hirsch, née Hildesheimer*

BORN IN BERLIN IN 1884; DIED IN TEL AVIV IN 1970.

Henriette Hirsch, "Memories of My Youth." Manuscript dated October 1953, Ramat Gan (Israel), 85 pages.

*The author, who was born in the building of the Berlin Orthodox Rabbinical Seminary, creates in her childhood recollections the picture of one of the leading*

*orthodox families in Germany. In the foreground stands the dominant personality of*
*her grandfather Esriel Hildesheimer (1820–1899), who founded the Seminary in*
*1873 and was rabbi of the Berlin secessionist congregation. Henriette's father,*
*Hirsch, taught history at the Seminary, became very active as a publicist and in*
*social work, and dedicated himself, among other things, to charitable work in behalf*
*of the East European Jews and to raising funds for the Seminary. The twelve-member*
*family, whose home was known for its hospitality, was supported by their Hirsch*
*relatives in Halberstadt, the owners of the well-known metals firm. After the death*
*of her grandfather and father, the author trained to become a teacher and in 1807*
*she married the doctor Remy Hirsch.*

When one went through the wooden door into the building, a little wooden
staircase led upstairs into the rooms of the Rabbinical Seminary, whose founder and
director was our grandfather. Opposite this wooden staircase, that is, left of the entrance,
wooden steps also led up into our private dwelling. First, about ten or twelve steps up,
came our grandfather's apartment; we lived on the third floor. Only our common dining
room and living room were downstairs. Father's study and our bedrooms were upstairs.
Both floors were connected by a winding internal staircase. It was a wonderful playground
for us children. Nothing was more pleasurable than to run up and down the round
winding staircase.

Grandfather's study dominated the second floor. It was taken up by a large desk,
giant bookcases, and his countless books. As far as I can recall, he had only Hebrew
books. I never saw him reading any other kind, although profane literature was by no
means foreign to him. I remember how he sat at his big desk or his work table, always
occupied with enormous tomes of the Talmud, *Gemara,* or with other study of Hebrew
literature. The room was furnished very simply, as was his small bedroom, which adjoined
the study and which he shared with his son, later Rabbi Meier Hildesheimer, who was
still unmarried at that time. [. . .]

Someone was once supposed to have said that Number 12a Gipsstrasse was not
situated in Berlin at all, but that the house stood somewhere in the wide world, beyond
all bad influences and wicked people. And so it seemed to me, also!

Even though it was by no means a luxurious house, it is still self-evident that a
house with so many people, so many rooms, and so many different individual claims
demanded a great deal of work, and it was part of our mother's ever-calm nature to
have brought an atmosphere of peace into this busy milieu. First of all, there was concern
for my grandfather. As far as I am able to recall him, I see him in my mind's eye as
an elderly, venerable, quiet, and always friendly man, who walked somewhat bent. He
had an unusual career. He had been born to a family of scholars of very modest origin,
in Halberstadt. He studied at various *yeshivot* to become a rabbi, and then went as a
rabbi to Eisenstadt in Hungary. He was already highly acknowledged and respected
there. He lived with his family in the ghetto, but he had many connections to the
outside world. From there he received an appointment in Berlin [in 1869], where he
became the rabbi of an orthodox secessionist congregation and at the same time the
founder and director of the Rabbinical Seminary. In Halberstadt, through his zeal,
diligence, intelligence, and ability, he had attracted the attention of the very prosperous

local family Hirsch. This was a very wealthy, respected business family with several brothers, whose wish it was to find for their sister "Jettchen" a man whom, by virtue of his unusual intelligence, scholarship, and knowledge, especially in the field of Torah, they would deem worthy of marrying their beloved sister. They knew the budding Rabbi Hildesheimer and his family from Halberstadt, and they chose him. They married—and through this union my future parents became cousins, for my mother was a young daughter of one of these Hirsch brothers from Halberstadt.[1]

At first my grandparents lived in Eisenstadt. Both grandparents had strong cultural interests. They attended plays and concerts, and saw to it that their children not only became familiar with Jewish learning, but that they also received a secular education. My grandfather had studied mathematics and philosophy at the University of Berlin and expected of his children and his students that along with their Torah studies they occupy themselves with other branches of knowledge as much as they were able. Already at that time, my grandfather espoused the view that a true scholar needed not one-sided knowledge, but rather knowledge that was as broad as possible. Since his scholarship and learning were soon well-known in the orthodox circles of Western Europe, he was appointed to the aforementioned position in Berlin. So my grandparents moved with their large troop of children to Berlin. They had six sons and four daughters. They moved into the house at 12a Gipsstrasse. Very soon the synagogue was consecrated and the Seminary was opened. As far as I know, it was the first Rabbinical Seminary of this kind, in which the rabbinical candidates could be enrolled at the same time in profane disciplines at the university.[2] Neither as the rabbi of this new separatist congregation, Adass Jisroel,[3] nor as director of the Rabbinical Seminary did my grandfather ever receive a salary. He regarded his work as a contribution to the dissemination, deepening, and understanding of orthodox Judaism, and in this view he was understood and supported completely by his wife and her family. Without this understanding and same outlook on the part of the Hirsch family, it would have been virtually impossible to lead such a life.

The Hirsch family was very affluent. At that time, German industry experienced a great upswing, and the firm of Aron Hirsch & Son fared accordingly. Thus, money was regularly sent from Halberstadt to support the family of Rabbi Hildesheimer. I recall that there was always money that had been sent from Halberstadt lying in the drawer of my grandfather's desk. When it was used up, more came. And everyone who needed something took money from this seemingly bottomless drawer. Whether there was any sort of check, I don't know. But I do not think that there was. What an ideal situation!

To lighten the burdens of the large household with its many children, one child or another was sent to relatives in other towns, very often to Halberstadt. My father was one of them. And so the two cousins, my father and mother, met and came to love one another. I assume that a very close friendship already existed between them in their young years, for our mother often said that father had done her school lessons and written her school compositions for her. Since he then went to Halberstadt very often, very soon there developed the great love that united my parents all their lives and that in its harmony and closeness was a shining model for us in our earliest youth. My father told us how he translated the *"Pirke Avot"*[4] for mother from Hebrew into

German and, what was much more prosaic, how he cracked, shelled, and mailed her a bagful of fresh nuts because he knew that she enjoyed eating them. [. . .]

In addition to grandfather, at the beginning there lived in our house his two unmarried sons (Gustav and Meier) and an unmarried daughter (Jennie), who later married and settled in Nuremberg. Then there were my parents, at first with three, then four, five, and six children. It seemed that the house was able to expand. Naturally, there was a lot of household help. First of all, there was a cook, an orthodox woman, on whom one could depend one hundred percent for *kashrus*. Then there was a house-maid, Anna, whose task it was to keep the apartment clean and tidy. She worked for us for many years. In my grandfather's last years, during which his mental powers greatly diminished, she was more or less entrusted with tending to him, and she gained a sympathetic understanding of his habits and mentality that was truly touching. She was not Jewish, but was so familiar with Jewish custom that more than many another she often intuited grandfather's habits more than she knew them as fact. Thus, for example, in one of the last years of his life, when he was no longer entirely able to speak, he once displayed a visible unrest. He walked nervously back and forth, and no one knew what he wanted. Suddenly Anna said to him: "Herr Rabbi, no doubt you want to say *levone mekadish*," that is, the blessing for the full moon, which he used to recite every month.[5] "Yes, yes," he said with great relief, went down into the courtyard and said the blessing. Another time, she had laid out a different suit for my grandfather. He came out of his room greatly agitated and did not want to put it on. At that, Anna said to him: "You can go ahead and put it on, Herr Rabbi, it is no longer new. You already wore it on *Rosh Chodesh*."[6] It was my grandfather's habit on this special day alone to wear something new for the first time. I relate these details only to show what deep understanding even the non-Jewish help had in those days for us, our home, and our customs.

To characterize my grandfather, I would now like to mention a few small details that were typical for his most simple way of life. To the extent that his private studies allowed, he took trips rather frequently, in order to collect money—of course, for charitable purposes—from rich Jews who lived in other places. Even if the trip was long and tedious, he traveled third-class. In his day, German trains had three classes. The cars in the first class were reserved solely for the upper crust. Most of the better-situated middle class traveled in second class, which was outfitted with upholstered, comfortable seats. My grandfather traveled only in third class. He sat there reading or resting a bit on the hard, bare seat, usually riding back and forth on the same day in order to work for charitable purposes. In Berlin itself he took only the omnibus. There were also horse-trams, but they were more expensive, and even in the omnibus he climbed the steep, winding steps up to the top deck because there the ride cost only five pfennigs, in contrast to ten pfennigs down below in the tram. The manner of his correspondence was also very indicative. He wrote in a very clear hand, but with tiny letters. To save paper, whenever it was at all possible he wrote the answer to a letter that he had received between the individual lines of that same letter. These were signs of his boundless frugality and modesty. His great kindness and humaneness were documented in his every deed. As a benefactor, he was known far beyond the borders of Germany. Once a letter arrived with the address: "To the Chief Rabbi of Germany." It was delivered to him, although there could be no thought of such a position. His congregation was rather small, much smaller, at any rate, than Berlin's Jewish community. Nevertheless, his authority was widely acknowledged.

We children have the warmest memory of his hearty, always cheerful personality. Whenever one of us was sick and had to lie in bed, he came up the winding staircase to us every day and sat down at our bed, even if it was only for a few minutes, for he was always very busy and a certain number of people made claims on his time. "But," he said when he sat down next to us, "one may not disturb a sick person." And so he sat with us for a few minutes to gladden us with some cheerful words. It is understandable that such a serene, cheerful, whole personality was not without influence on our development, since we lived our entire youth in his sight and in complete togetherness with him, and all the more so since his kindness and humanity were passed on entirely to our father. My father had boundless respect for his own father, and he constantly instilled us with it also. At the noonday meal we were not permitted to sit down until grandfather was seated, and my father stood up from his chair whenever grandfather entered the room. [. . .]

The visitors who came to see my father had mostly some kind of concern about which they wanted to get my father's counsel. Many came who worked together with him in charitable institutions. There was hardly a Jewish organization, hardly an institution to whose board of directors he did not belong. There was the Hilfsverein der Deutschen Juden, the organization Esra, the Verein für jüdische Geschichte und Literatur, and whatever they were all called. My father worked and sacrificed himself for all of them in like manner.[7]

He worked most intensely after the terrible pogroms in Russia. Throngs of helpless, completely ruined Jews came to Germany without any means. They could not remain there. My father immediately formed a committee that provided monetary support to enable these poor, persecuted people to go on living. In Ruheleben, near Berlin, an assembly point or transit station was set up, at which the piteous refugees were gathered. They were supported there for a few days with food and lodging, before they were sent on to America. Often refugees came to us who had nothing in hand except a note that said: "Hildesheimer, Berlin." *That,* they knew, was an anchor. It made the most awful impression on us children, who experienced all of that, when one day a boy of about ten, completely distraught, came to us with his aunt. He had witnessed the murder of his parents! The terrible shock had robbed him of his speech. My father provided for him, found him proper lodgings and treatment, so that over the years he regained the power of speech. [. . .]

My father's involvement in welfare activities claimed a large share of his working hours. I often ask myself where he found the time for all the countless things that came along. He was a lecturer in Jewish history and the geography of Palestine at grandfather's Rabbinical Seminary. He was so well-versed in the geography of Palestine that he often argued about this or that route with experts who had traveled through the land. Most of the time, he knew better. It was his deepest wish once in his life to be able to travel to Palestine. Unfortunately, he was never there. He often expressed his wish to settle at the foot of Mount Carmel. As I later heard, someone was said to have asked him to assume a teaching post in Beirut. My mother persuaded him not to do it. She feared that the Middle Eastern climate, which at that time was still very notorious, would be harmful to his and our health. How often did we later discuss how differently our fate would have turned out if we had emigrated from Germany back then. But one cannot argue using "ifs." We remained in Berlin and father founded the paper *Die jüdische Presse,* a weekly, for which he sacrificed very much work, time, and effort, without success in regard to influencing the general public or in gaining the earnings that he had expected. It was an enormous load of work, which he had taken upon himself in addition to his many other obligations. Above all, he lacked intelligent and interested coworkers of his own caliber, which meant that the entire burden and responsibility lay on him alone. Every morning he went to the Café Bauer at the corner of Friedrichstrasse and Unter den Linden and sat there surrounded by a huge mountain of all of the newspapers that appeared in Germany, to copy or cut out everything that could interest his circle of readers. Everyone there knew him. He was often the center of a large group, for everyone knew that he could be found around noon at his regular table on the second floor right. How often was he sought out there by this or that person, pestered, disturbed, distracted from his work, which was so important to him. It was not easy to fill a weekly on one's own with interesting and varied items. How often did he come to our breakfast table on Thursday mornings, joking, and ask with a laugh, but definitely with a serious undertone: "Do you perhaps have an editorial for me?" Every article had to be written, every proof had to be read. How often were we sent in the afternoon to the printing shop of Herr Itzkowsky, a few houses down on Gipsstrasse, to deliver or fetch proofs for father.

My father had studied history at the university. He had a tremendous, universal knowledge, and he possessed an unusually good memory. That he was a man of very special gifts can be seen in the fact that he was the favorite student of Professor Mommsen. Mommsen's expectations for my father's future had been boundless, and he had hoped that father would qualify as a professor at Berlin University. But my father's sense of duty led him on other paths. He regarded it as his obligation not to satisfy his personal ambition but to live and work for the good of his Jewish people. And to that he devoted his entire capacity for work. Mommsen could not understand it. My father often said that whenever he saw Mommsen on the street he quickly went around the corner so that he would not be called to account by him. A small bust of Mommsen always stood on father's desk.

Aside from the regular obligations that made their claims on my father, every now and then there were special occasions to which he devoted his energies totally. There were the terrible ritual murder trials, at which, courageously and outspokenly, he testified in defense of many an unjustly accused person. I recall the dreadful trial in Xanten.[8] A family named Levy was accused. After their clearly just acquittal father had them move to Berlin, set up a new shop for them, and helped them build their lives anew. — Then there came the hearings in the Reichstag on the prohibition of ritual slaughter.[9] I recall how he gathered countless opinions from experts in order to prepare enough material to counter the prohibition. — Then there were the antisemitic maneuvers of an Ahlwardt or Stoecker, which he opposed through the spoken and written word, courageously and without regard for hostility against his person.[10]

I often wonder where he found the time to accomplish so much. His day, too, had only twenty-four hours. He granted himself very little sleep. As soon as he awoke in the early morning, he got up. On his table there stood a little coffee machine, which was heated with a petroleum wick and which mother had already prepared the evening before. He immediately made himself a cup of good, strong coffee, and then sat down at his desk and began working.

He also visited rich people, to collect money from them for charitable purposes or for maintaining the Rabbinical Seminary. The Seminary was supported through donations and collections. As far as I know, the students never paid tuition. Often he traveled to other cities in Germany for the same purposes, after my grandfather had grown too old to carry out this obligation. In general, it must be said that father was in every respect the heir and successor to our grandfather. He was his heir in the spiritual, human, and moral sense. Of the six brothers he was by far the most distinguished, and already at that time he was recognized and honored by the entire immediate and more distant family as its head. His advice, his judgment were authoritative, and in many a family dispute his opinion was regarded as definitive. He was an outstanding, brilliant speaker. When he spoke at a public gathering, the audience was swept away by the persuasiveness of his speeches, and thanks to this eloquence many "givers" gave more to charity or for father's wards than they would have had it not been for this superb gift of speech and persuasion. The kindheartedness that he expressed, his captivating, amiable ways, and his partly humorous, partly serious manner of expression played a decisive role in all of this. [. . .]

Both of my parents tried hard to make grandfather's difficult old age easier for him. They both endeavored to maintain the character of Number 12a Gipsstrasse that grandfather had given it by virtue of his great personality. The last years of his life greatly weakened his intellectual powers, and his physical strength also abandoned him. He died in the winter of 1899. All of Jewry mourned him deeply. A great man, a great Torah scholar had passed away! Day and night the Torah was studied at his deathbed.[11] His many students regarded it as an honor to sit there and pray. In one of the final hours before the burial, father went to his bier with us six brothers and sisters. He drew us close to him and said a few words to us about grandfather. At the end, he said: "My beloved children, never forget as long as you live what kind of grandfather you had." For me these words and the situation have remained unforgettable.

I think back, full of thanks and respect, to these sage words, which father spoke to us in that impressive hour. How wise it was of him, how farsighted to use precisely these words. He did not urge us, for example, to be as pious as grandfather had been, nor did he have us promise to keep the commandments as he had kept them. Nothing of the kind! That would have been an obligation that he did not want to place on us. He just simply spoke the words: "Do not forget what kind of grandfather you had." I believe that all of us have kept this promise to him. The ethic of our grandfather's outlook on life was transmitted to us. Ethically and morally, we have continued his life; we have never forgotten him. His personality has been preserved in us, and still today, after so many decades, I recall full of love and gratefulness all of the happy hours that we owed to his loving-kindness.

His burial was an overwhelming event. The streets through which the funeral procession passed were closed off by the police. Hundreds and hundreds of people followed the hearse on foot, and a seemingly endless procession of mourners walked behind, from the house of mourning to Weissensee. They were men only. In accordance with a wish of our grandfather, no women were to go to the cemetery, not even his daughter. During *schiwe* [the period of ritual mourning] we had no end of visitors, of course. One spoke only of grandfather and the great works that he had accomplished for Judaism.

1. In 1863, the metals firm of Aron Hirsch acquired the brass works in Eberswalde near Berlin from the Prussian state and expanded it into a large concern. The director of the enterprise was Gustav Hirsch (died in 1898), who built a synagogue on the factory site and, as a member of the board of directors, generously supported the Berlin orthodox Rabbinical Seminary. In 1880–81, the Seminary had twenty-one students, who came predominantly from Eastern Europe.
2. This is an error. The students of the religiously conservative Rabbinical Seminary in Breslau, founded in 1854, were enrolled at both the Seminary and the University of Breslau.
3. The orthodox Berlin congregation Adass Jisroel was founded in 1869 after the death of the last orthodox community rabbi and was led by Esriel Hildesheimer until 1899. After the enactment of the 1876 Prussian law on leaving religious communities, Adass Jisroel established itself in 1885 as a separate secessionist congregation (orthodox secessionist congregation).
4. "Sayings of the Fathers," a Mishnah tractate of the Talmud.
5. Rather, the author means the blessing on the new moon.
6. The Day of the New Moon, a semiholiday and the first day of each month in the Jewish calendar.
7. The Aid Society, founded in 1901, supported Jews in Eastern Europe and Palestine (compare the memoir of Bernhard Kahn, no. 31). The organization Esra, founded in 1883, promoted agriculture among Jews in Palestine and Syria. The Society for Jewish History and Literature was founded in 1892 in Berlin and later had over 200 local branches.
8. At the ritual murder trial in Xanten in 1891 the slaughterer Buschhoff was charged with, and acquitted of, murder. The author has apparently confused him with the slaughterer Levy, who was charged with ritual murder in Konitz in 1901.
9. The charge that ritual slaughter was animal torture was a favorite theme of antisemites. They petitioned unsuccessfully in the Reichstag in 1887, 1889, and 1901 for the prohibition of ritual slaughter.
10. Hermann Ahlwardt (1846–1914), a radical antisemite in Leipzig, was a member of the Reichstag and was sentenced to prison for libelous attacks on the Jewish weapons manufacturer Löwe. As the Berlin Court Chaplain, Adolf Stoecker (1835–1909), likewise a member of the Reichstag, founded the Christlich-Soziale Arbeiterpartei and became the leading antisemitic agitator in Berlin.
11. Like praying, Torah study at a deathbed is a customary religious practice in traditional Judaism.

# 18  *Joseph Lange*

BORN IN 1855 IN KOSMINEK (RUSSIAN POLAND); DIED IN 1935 IN BERLIN.

Joseph Lange, My Life. Handwritten manuscript, 124 pages, dated Berlin, 1934/35.

*Joseph Lange was the son of a Polish glazier. He attended the Talmud School in Kalisch, became a teacher at seventeen, and in 1876 fled from conscription into the tsar's army across the nearby frontier to Ostrowo (province of Posen). Soon he moved on to Berlin, where he scraped along as a glazier and temporary helper. By arrangement, in 1878 he married into an orthodox family that financed his training as cantor. As one of the numerous East European Jewish cantors in Germany, he served at first in Lippehne (Neumark), where he became naturalized in 1883. He was cantor in Garz (Pomerania) in the years 1885–1905, and in Kulmsee (West Prussia) from 1906 until 1921, when Kulmsee became Polish and his three sons established a store for him in Berlin. — In the following version the linguistic peculiarities have been retained.*

There came to Ostrowo a relative, a Herr Berke from Kosminek. He was a tailor and soon he found a permanent position. We saw one another often and were as thick as thieves. Since he, too, didn't like it much in Ostrowo we soon decided to go to Berlin. And then, out of the blue, the news came that Berlin had been struck by a great hailstorm and glaziers were much in demand there. This news was quite welcome to me, and soon we had readied ourselves for the journey to Berlin. A Frau Salzmann, who had a sister living in Berlin, gave us her address and recommended us very warmly.

Yes, traveling—but a trip to Berlin also costs money and we, unfortunately, were deep in *dalles*.[1] I had to find a way out and God soon helped us: I sold my winter coat and a pair of very good pants, and with this money we both went to Berlin by train. Can anyone possibly imagine what two young people coming to such a metropolis from a tiny place, from Kosminek, said? No, no, no one could! But I was happy to see Berlin, and my friend Berke, too; I still remember it as if it were today.

Well now, thank God we had an address of a Frau Krause, née Salzmann, who lived on Kleine Alexanderstrasse, at number 27, and at whose place we were to take lodgings. We couldn't go by taxi, because we didn't have money and because in those days no such "miracle carriage" existed. What did we do? We picked up our feet and our suitcases and went off. We didn't know whether we were coming or going, until we arrived at Kleine Alexanderstrasse—but we did arrive. Luckily Frau Krause was at home. She lived there in a basement, and when we handed over her sister's letter she finally let us enter and said: "If the two of you agree to sleep together back there, in that small room"—it was only a tiny dark hole—"and pay ten marks a month, without coffee, then you can stay at my place." Overjoyed, we laid down our bundles. Unfortunately, we had had only very little to eat that entire day. Tired and starving, and with completely empty pockets, that's how two nice fellows came to Berlin.

My friend Berke took me to a Herr Pulvermacher, who also happened to be a glazier and came from Poland, from a small town near Kalisch. He lived on Landsbergerstrasse in a rear building, five or even six floors up. The kitchen, bedroom, dining room, and so on were all in one, and he was blessed with a large family. Herr Pulvermacher could not have had much joy from his grand visitors, for he himself was not a rich man. He could scarcely make a living—and on top of it, five little children—and from us he soon heard that we brought nothing but empty pockets and therefore intended to touch him for money! After we poured out our sorrows and begged and pleaded, the good man gave us all of 50 pfennigs, which he only lent us. And with these 50 pfennings we went to a beer cellar, bought half a bread, butter for 10 pfennigs, and a whole bottle of weiss beer, and it tasted better to us than the best roast goose.

After we had eaten our fill, we went to look at the Imperial Palace at Unter den Linden. We thought the place where Kaiser Wilhelm lived had to be something wonderful! But on the outside we saw a completely black, smoke-stained house so that we said: "Someone like Kaiser Wilhelm couldn't possibly live in such an old house." From there we then went back to Pulvermacher on Landsbergerstrasse. We wanted him to advise us what the two of us should do. He said: "You, my dear Herr Lange, are a glazier, but you are an unlucky fellow because you missed out on something and came to Berlin too late. Had you come two or three weeks earlier I could have given you a lot to do and you would have earned good money. Still, I don't want to turn you away completely. Come to me tomorrow morning and we'll see if there is anything to be earned, that is to say, whether we'll find some glazing work for you."

My friend Berke also went looking and got work at an acquaintance's. I went with Herr Pulvermacher from street to street and from house to house. And after we had carefully inspected the windows from top to bottom, and panes happened to be smashed after a hailstorm, we politely inquired whether we could replace or repair that pane or panes. Thus we went day after day, and I was fed up to the teeth with this running around. In the end I had worn out more boot soles and had starved more than I had earned in the process, and I was now forced to look for a job elsewhere.

On Königstrasse, I found work, that is to say, employment, with a Herr Gelhar, who was a master glazier, but it did not last long, for scarcely had I been one or two days with him when he threw me out with the worst abusive language, calling after me: "You're no glazier! You know what you are? A bungler. You don't have an inkling about glasswork. Get out of my house!"

My friend Berke left Berlin secretly—or, better said, skipped town—and now I was all alone! What happened to me can scarcely be described. I lived on dry bread and water almost the entire week, and only seldom was I able to afford some sausage scraps for 10 or 20 pfennigs. I became so desperate that I wanted to return to my home.

One nice day when I was walking down a street in despair, I met a young man who was walking around with a glazier's box and whom I addressed as a colleague. He, too, was from Poland and soon we became friends. I poured out my troubles and told him what miserable luck I was having and how my master had let me go. When I finished with my story he said to me: "You're a *schaute,*[2] why do you need a master? Do what I did. Buy yourself a little glazier's box and go from house to house. Then, in the yard, you yell out: 'Panes or glass work done here!' " No sooner said than done! Soon I went to a joiner, had such a box made, and from then on I was a self-employed master glazier!

At first things were all right, that is to say, I earned enough for food. But this, too, didn't last very long. I was not up to the occupation and that's why I was short of money. Everyone can no doubt imagine vividly that my life was not exactly a bed of roses and that I was very sorry that I had come to Germany and was to live my young life with *tsores*[3] and in suffering. Only *betochon,* my great trust in God that no human being perishes who hopes and trusts in Him, saved me. And I said to myself: "Things won't always be so sad and bad for me!"

And it's true; there did come completely different times—but unfortunately not any better. At the same time that I was in great need, I was acquainted with a certain Israel Nenadel and his family. He lived in Berlin, at 1 Walnertheaterstrasse. They were from Warsaw, and Nenadel was a saddler, who worked for a firm making only leather bags and the like. One day there came to these people, to this family, a young man, also from Warsaw, who had fled on account of the army and who took lodgings at Herr Nenadel's. This young man, too, did not have an occupation, however, and didn't know what he should do, that is to say, what he should try. Then Herr Israel Nenadel got an idea that perhaps would have been good if we had been real businessmen and had been born in Germany, and also had had the right *mesumin*.[4] Of all three things not one applied: We had no training in business, nor were we German, and *mesumin*— the others had it but not we. And what was to become of us, or better, what did Herr Nenadel tell us to do now? As I've said, Herr Nenadel was a master saddler. He made only leather bags for a big firm. Now Herr Israel Nenadel made us the following proposition: "I will make leather bags for you, which you will buy from me for cash. With these wares you will travel to fairs, and you will see that you'll make a good and profitable business with them." The plan sounded quite marvelous and very nice, and since my friend could scarcely speak German, he was almost forced to take me as principal or copartner. But he asked from me a certain amount of money as deposit, which unfortunately I did not have. Soon the dear Lord helped. By pawning my last good suit and selling my diamond, I made a deposit. The business was soon opened and in the trade register the firm was entered as "Dalles, Dalfen and Co."*

The first trip we took to a fair was to Strausberg, near Berlin. There we sold just enough to barely cover our costs. For the second fair we went to Pritzwalk. Pritzwalk is in the Brandenburg Marches and in those days still did not have any rail connection. So we had to take the trip from a station before or after Pritzwalk by stagecoach, that is to say, by carriage. This journey to Pritzwalk is, or was, for me a disastrous one, or better said, almost my ruin. We departed for Pritzwalk around seven or eight o'clock in the evening from the Lehrter Station, but since Pritzwalk had no rail connection we had to get off, and arrived at a village about twelve o'clock at night. Before we had thought about it, the stage coach and the omnibus were gone, and there was no doubt that we were now in a bad way. We looked at one another like two monkeys. What now, spake Zeus! We went to the village and looked for a peasant who would take us to Pritzwalk. No peasant wanted to talk to us and they chased us away with their mean dogs. Finally one was going to take us, but for the trip to Pritzwalk he wanted 24 or 25 marks, which neither of us had. We decided to leg our way along.

Today I have to laugh about it—in those days I wasn't able to laugh—when I tell you, my dear ones, that in wind and rain, without eating or drinking anything, we arrived safely in Pritzwalk around one or two o'clock. The big fair was over, it had come to an end. Tired and starving like a dog and without a penny in our pockets, we were forced to make some money. We sold—that is to say, we gave away for practically

*Yiddish: "Poverty, Poor Devil and Co."

nothing—several items so that we could return safely to Berlin. Squeezed together like herrings in a barrel, ten or twelve of us left for the railway station in a wagon, and finally, early, we all arrived in Berlin. Each of us took his bundle and went home—I to 27 Kleine Alexanderstrasse, and my *chaver*[5] to 1 Walnertheaterstrasse. When we had to part, he said: "When you have rested, come to my place and we will settle accounts." I could vividly imagine already how that would turn out for me, and I was not mistaken. With this in mind, I went to bed as soon as I was in my "digs" and slept as soundly as a rat until the next morning. I got up and, without eating anything, went to my friend's. Scarcely had I entered when he broke up the *chavruse*[6] and our friendship, and added: "The business is either too big or too small for two people. We didn't earn anything, thus there is nothing left of your deposit. Here is a mark, buy yourself an estate for it or whatever."

Who can possibly feel the way I did? And if until then my life had not exactly been a bed of roses, now I was completely finished and was justified in asking: "*Meajin jawo esri*—from whence cometh my help?"[7] I answered this question to myself by saying: "Help comes from Him who created heaven and earth," and although it came only slowly, it did come. A beautiful maxim says: "Whoever trusts in God, has built a sturdy home."

It was shortly before New Year, Rosh Hashana, and this time of the New Year was to be a happy one for me, and was to bring me something good. I looked for a position as a cantor's assistant, but that, too, unfortunately did not work out, for I was, after all, unknown in Berlin. But at Yom Kippur I did succeed in getting a position outside of Berlin, in Beelitz, to lead the prayers for *Schachris*.[8] Since there were no rail connections to Beelitz at that time, one had to first go to Potsdam and from Potsdam to Beelitz by coach. From Berlin to Beelitz there were fellow travelers who had been asked by the congregation in Beelitz to come for the *minyan*. Having arrived in Beelitz I went to the cantor there. He was an old, very dignified gentleman who greeted me in a very friendly manner, calling me a "colleague," and soon undertook to examine me. After I had sung a few things for him, he said: "You seem to be quite a fine Polish *chasen*. You have a wonderful voice and, as you probably know, you are supposed to exercise the function of a *Schachris-Mincho*."[9]

It was a coincidence, or rather perhaps fate, that I had gotten to Beelitz and there, at Cantor Brill's home, got to know Herr Simon Presch, who later became my brother-in-law. It was also an unusual coincidence that Herr Presch had been discharged from his military service in Treuenbrietzen and had been asked by Cantor Brill to stay with him as his guest. I must admit that when Herr Brill was introduced to me I scarcely spoke two words with him. Soon I was asked to eat at a Herr Marcus's place, and when the beautiful *achile*[10] was over I went to the temple. This temple was an old building. In the middle of the temple there was an *almemar*,[11] as used to be the custom, and one could see from that that earlier the Jewish community had been larger than it was now. Herr Cantor Brill directed me to a seat next to Herr Presch, and now I must frankly say that I did not find him to be a pleasant neighbor, because he wanted only to talk with me and pray hardly at all. I, on the other hand, rebuffed, that is to say, refused any conversation. Whether I had led the prayers for the first time well or poorly I don't know, and it is not for me to judge. But I certainly can say that in Beelitz I led the prayers the way I had seen and learned at home and the way I felt like doing it then. The Almighty, who knows and judges the thoughts of every human being, has judged me too, but He has also heard my prayer!

The holy day passed and with a happy heart everyone went home unburdened of sin. After the meal Herr Marcus went to his moneybox and paid me my salary—21 marks in gold and three marks extra, a larger sum than I had ever known! I also visited my colleague and then went to bed. Early in the morning, between seven and eight, a bus went from Beelitz to Potsdam. When we arrived everything was already occupied; only two very bad seats, all the way up front by the coachman, were left for two people, and I and Herr Pesch took these two seats. The coach barely started to move when the conversation began. Said Herr Presch: "Had a good fast, did you?"[12] "I thank you for your kind inquiry." "Why were you so proud yesterday? You didn't speak a single word with me." "Oh no, sir, you seem to be mistaken: far be it from me to show pride, but to chat with you, for that I was too serious, and the day yesterday was too holy. Now, if it suits you and you find it agreeable we can both have a nice conversation." One word followed another. I gained confidence in the young man, whom I was seeing for the first time, and began to unload my whole case and life's story like goods at a fair. Herr Presch listened to my presentation very attentively. He was very moved and tried to console me by making a brief comment: "What, you want to get married? You really don't have to worry about that. Just listen to what I'm about to tell you: I have a sister who lives with my mother. My father in Meseritz has been dead now for three years. My two brothers, who live in Liebenau near Schwiebus and together have a business there, would like to marry off my sister, and I think you would be the right husband for my sister. I am now going to Potsdam, will visit my old boss, Herr Rothe, will then go to Meseritz to my mother and sister, and then to my brothers. I will discuss everything with them and if my brothers agree to that and take the first step, then we will see what can be done with you." In the meanwhile we had arrived in Potsdam. Now Herr Presch asked for my address, also gave me his, and we parted. "Auf Wiedersehen."

> *[In 1878 Lange marries Malchen Presch, and her family enables him to train as cantor and teacher.]*

I applied in Lippehne, Neumark, was invited to go there, and after I was tested I was chosen unanimously at a salary of 450 marks a year and was engaged as teacher and cantor. On July 1, 1880, I moved to Lippehne. The congregation sent a big wagon with a big draft horse. The carter's name was Schulz, and soon the furniture was loaded onto the wagon. My brothers-in-law Nathan and Philipp came and accompanied us for a short stretch of road and pressed three marks into my hand. We got onto the wagon and slowly started off. The trip went like this: Meseritz, Schwerin, Landsberg, up hill and down dale to Lippehne.[13] It was not a short trip; it took 26 to 27 hours. In the afternoon, towards four o'clock, we arrived safely in Lippehne and were cordially welcomed by the first chairman, Herr Rosenberg. Soon coffee and cake were sent by a family and we were happy and so content as if I had won in the lottery.

After I had been in Lippehne for a short time the burgomaster there sent for me and kindly invited me to come to him. Scarcely had I entered when he opened the files that were lying there and said: "You are employed here by the congregation as a synagogue official. Do you know that the law says that every Jewish official must be a German citizen?" This was a terrible blow, because I knew that the matter was not an easy one for me. On the spot I asked the kind gentleman in what way I could attain German citizenship. "Well, you must have the following documents for it: first, a birth certificate, second, certificates of good conduct from the places where you stayed here in Germany, and third, your Russian discharge. If you have these papers, send them all with a request to the government in Frankfurt an der Oder and ask for citizenship." I was able to get all this easily, but as my now-departed father wrote to me, in no way could I get the discharge. So I asked that the burgomaster give me some time for this, or that he simply leave me in peace.

One day the following happened. One can, and certainly must, regard and describe this event as a miracle. One Sunday, it was April 23, 1882, I happened to be walking back and forth in a garden. This garden was by a big lake, separated from it only by a fence. Suddenly cries for help resounded: "Help, help! A child has fallen from a bridge into the water!" Quickly I jumped over the fence, hurried to the bridge, took off my coat, and dived into the water, and thus, endangering my own life, I safely rescued the child. Many, many people, who had gathered by then, were standing on the bridge with long poles, but no one dared risk his own life to save another human being. They did try to do it with the poles, but they were hardly long enough and, besides, the child was near death and was no longer able to take hold of a pole. I jumped from the bridge, swam several meters, grabbed the little one by his clothes, and handed him over to the people. All too quickly the news spread in Lippehne and I was scarcely at home, in order to take off my clothes, when my place was full of people who congratulated me heartily on this deed.

On the next day I was called to the police, the facts were recorded, and I was recommended for a medal for having saved a life. Unfortunately, the government turned this down on the grounds that I couldn't get it because I was not a German! Now the matter was to go first to the Russian tsar and emperor in order to obtain his "approval," which would have caused a lot of trouble and expense, and thereupon I gratefully declined. Because I had forgone a monetary reward I was honored by the authorities in Frankfurt an der Oder only with a commendation, which had the following text:

> "The cantor and teacher Joseph Lange from Lippehne, in that same place, on the 23rd of April of this year saved the six-year-old boy Franz Phienow, son of the worker Phienow, from death by drowning. He is herewith publicly commended for the sacrifice and decisiveness that this deed entailed.
>
> The District President
> Signed, von Stabosch

The above copy is sent to you for your kind information, with the note that the publication of the laudation has taken place in the official gazette of the royal government in Frankfurt an der Oder and will also be published in the local gazette. Lippehne, October 21, 1883.

The Police Administration<br>Signed, Arndt

After a short interval, I thought very seriously whether this was not a favorable moment for me to contact the authorities about my citizenship. So I went to the burgomaster to hear what he would say. Although the burgomaster was kind and friendly, he could only tell me that I had to have the Russian discharge and that without it nothing could be achieved with the authorities. The clerk, a Herr Parmann, who knew all my files and was on friendly terms with me, looked at me for a while, and when the burgomaster turned his back to us, he said to me: "Why don't you come and see me?" That was what I needed. In the afternoon I was at Herr Parmann's place. I didn't have to tell him much, and he gave me the following advice: "You see, my dear Lange, you won't be able to do much with our burgomaster. We must now find another angle. Make a request to the President. I will show you what to write." Immediately I sat down, picked up the pen and wrote the request in which I said: "I am enclosing all my documents, such as birth certificate and certificates of good conduct, and so on, but the certificate from Russia I can unfortunately not get because every matter in Russia must be paid for exorbitantly, and since I receive only a very small salary from my congregation I am not in the position to pay this great sum by myself." — It was hardly three or four weeks before I was called to the police and Herr Parmann handed me the document and cordially congratulated me as a German citizen. Who can possibly imagine my joy! No one was happier than I!

1. Poverty.
2. Fool.
3. Sorrow, worry.
4. Money.
5. Comrade.
6. Partnership.
7. Psalm 121:1.
8. Morning prayer.
9. (Prayer leader at the) morning prayer and afternoon prayer.
10. Meal.
11. An elevated lectern for reading the Torah, which since the nineteenth century no longer stands in the middle but rather at the front wall of the synagogue.
12. On Yom Kippur one fasts for twenty-four hours, from sundown to sundown.
13. The distance traveled from Schwiebus to Lippehne, via Meseritz (Posen), amounts to about 100 kilometers. Lippehne is situated in the northern Brandenburg Marches, on the border of Pommerania, and in the 1880s had sixty Jewish inhabitants.

188

## 19 *Kurt Katsch*

BORN IN 1893 IN GRODNO (RUSSIAN POLAND); DIED IN 1958 IN LOS
ANGELES.

Kurt Katsch, From Ghetto to Ghetto. Undated manuscript, 198 pages. Written
in Berlin in 1934 with Rudolf Frank and Kurt Landsberger.[1]

*The actor Kurt Katsch (originally Issar Katz; in the United States, Katch) came
from a poor East European Jewish family. His father was an itinerant preacher; his
mother became insane. The family fled from pogroms from Grodno to Austria, where
for a time Kurt Katsch attended the Gymnasium in Lemberg. He then became a
traveling wine salesman in Germany and subsequently led an unsettled, vagrant life
until 1916, when he found a benefactress who made it possible for him to receive
training at the Max Reinhardt School in Berlin. During the Weimar period he
played main roles on the leading German-language stages. In 1933/1934 he
appeared in the theater of the Jüdischer Kulturbund in Berlin and then went to the
Yiddish theater in Warsaw as its director. In 1938 Katsch emigrated to Hollywood,
where he became a film actor.*

I read one day [in Vienna]: "Traveling wine salesman wanted for Germany.
Inquiries at Herr Federbusch, 24 Kleine Schiffgasse." Germany? The word sounded
enticing to my ears. That was, after all, the land from which our language came, the
land whose rising power we admired from afar.

Immediately I set out on my way. When I got to see the manager, he said: "My
son-in-law is in Magdeburg. He represents a big wine firm there. Write a job application
immediately to Herr Schindler in Magdeburg." I sat down and wrote a letter, in which
I described my irrepressible enthusiasm for work in the most glowing colors. As evidence
for my physical strength I enclosed a photograph on which I could be seen in sports
dress, my bared arms raised, my biceps flexed, every inch the athlete. I had never learned
to write a job application, and yet without knowing it I had hit upon the right thing.
After just a few days Herr Federbusch asked me to come to him and told me that his
son-in-law was very enthusiastic about my letter. To be sure, he said, I would not have
to push barrels as, judging by my photo, I seemed to assume, but there was a lot of
work there. Thereupon he gave me a suitcase, put five crowns into my hand, bought
me a ticket to Magdeburg, and thus I traveled across the border.

Off to Germany, Germany!

In the evening, at ten o'clock, I arrived in Magdeburg and went straight to Herr
F. Schindler, to present myself. He looked me over and was satisfied with my appearance.
"Now go to the railway station, to the hotel Weisser Bär," he said to me, "and take
a room there. Here is a price list, memorize it exactly, so that you can tell the difference
between the wines. Here is an order book, in it you will write the orders and give a
copy of it to the customer, so that you have something to show. Have yourself awakened
tomorrow morning at seven o'clock and then go to Schönebeck. When you call on
customers, say: 'I represent the Rüdesheim winery on the Rhine.'"

"On the Rhine?"

"Of course on the Rhine, not from Magdeburg! But don't interrupt me. You just say: 'I represent the Rüdesheim winery on the Rhine and would like to take the liberty of making you an offer.' "

"I have to write that down."

I pulled out my note pad and in the meanwhile he continued with his speech: "On each order you will get twenty percent commission. If you sell a hundred marks' worth, you will have earned twenty marks." That I understood without writing it down. He concluded with the words: "Here are ten marks; that's for your expenses for the day. In the evening you will come back with the last train and tell me how much you've sold."

I did as he told me, took a room in the hotel, had myself awakened at seven in the morning, went to Schönebeck and called at the very first house on Bahnhofstrasse. When the owner of the apartment opened the door for me I began saying in a halting German mixed with Yiddish: "I represent the Rüdesheim winery on the Rhine . . . " At that point I got stuck and leafed through my notebook for the end of the sentence. When I had finished stammering it and looked up, I found the door closed. Nobody was there.

Thus I ran from early morning till late in the evening, but no one considered buying anything from me. It was as if all the people of Schönebeck had sworn off drinking. Completely crushed, I went back. I had to think of how my mother had stood behind the store counter and waited for customers. Is selling that difficult? If I go back to Magdeburg now and tell Herr Schindler my experiences of the day, he'll surely throw me out, and that will be it for me.

Timidly I knocked on his door. The boss opens and looks at me expectantly. I was on the verge of tears as I told him how I ran up and down stairs from early morning till late in the evening. I had even skipped lunch in order not to lose any time. Schindler laughed his head off; to me it sounded like cruel mockery. Then he said: "Listen, Kitty, if you stay so keen, you will become my best salesman."

"You think so?" I asked doubtingly. I still thought that it was mockery. But he was serious. F. Schindler was one of the best judges of people I have ever met.

"Certainly. You have the talent for it. You just have to try it once more. Go back to Schönebeck tomorrow morning at seven o'clock."

Horrified I cried out: "For God's sake, anywhere but Schönebeck! Every child there knows me already!"

"That's just why you will go to Schönebeck," he said with unshakeable calm, and gave me another ten marks. And again I went to Schönebeck, without any idea of where I should turn.

Until five o'clock in the afternoon I ran around, completely in vain. Then I got hold of a baker and a tinsmith, one of whom bought six and the other eight bottles of wine from me. At least that was two orders for 72 marks. When I returned to Herr F. Schindler, he looked at my order book, was satisfied and said: "From today on you are a great traveling salesman. Get on the train again tomorrow and go back to Schönebeck."

I was flabbergasted. "How come Schönebeck again? Are there no other places in Germany except Schönebeck?"

"Certainly, Kitty, but you haven't yet been to the fashionable part of town. That's where the rich live. By now you have the skill you need to talk to the better customers. You'll see, you will have success there."

So I went to Schönebeck for the third time. Everyone knew me already. Even the policeman at the market square smiled at me from under his bushy mustache. When I returned to Magdeburg on that evening I had 300 marks' worth of orders in my pocket. My boss embraced me and called me a "whiz."

What helped me on all of these calls was the art of persuasion that I had inherited from my father. Hadn't he, too, made his fortune with a single sermon? To be sure, my German was still very miserable, and I had the greatest trouble learning this language without some sort of instruction. But whatever I said sounded so convincing that the people had to listen to me whether they wanted to or not.

The beginning of my speech was always as Herr F. Schindler had instructed me: "I represent the Rüdesheim winery on the Rhine and would like to take the liberty of making you an offer." Only now, just to make sure, I would stick my foot in the door so that it not be slammed shut again and that I be heard out.

Usually the customer then said: "Thank you, we don't need anything." I replied: "Yes, I know that. That's exactly why I'm here. I have a Spanish wine; it's real medicine for your little ones. Every morning and evening a little glass full; I've seen frail children gain two pounds a week using it." Then, if a child appeared, I pulled out a bag of candy, and in the end the children held on to my coattails and cried when I wanted to leave.

It became unplesant only when from time to time I was welcomed by a big barking dog. I was very afraid of these yelpers. But here, too, I was resourceful. I bought myself a terrier bitch and called on my customers with her. Then, whenever such a mad cur shot out of the open crack of the door, the dog's rage melted like butter in the sun at the sight of my Frieda (that was the name of my terrier lady). The old yelper transformed into a young lover, and I could finish making my offer.

When my boss saw that I had such success he sent me throughout all of Germany, and so I crossed the land from east to west and from south to north. Whenever I arrived in a city I would present myself as a foreign soccer player and visit my fellow club members there. The next day I would go to the parents of the players and sell them my wines.

I was especially successful once in Pomerania, and this province was regarded as particularly difficult. Even on my way there I sold the wine by crates and barrels. First to the conductor and then, when the train stopped, I got onto the locomotive and dealt with the engineer and the stoker with such success that the latter bought 50 bottles of Mosel wine from me, and the former a whole barrel of brandy flip. It was at that time, in Köslin, that I sold the most expensive wine in my life: six bottles at 40 marks each.

The trip continued to Stolp. There I went to the villa of a wine grower, who received me in a big vestibule. Everywhere there were swords and armor. He obviously was fond of war. The man received me with the respect due an expert and colleague. When I began my sales pitch, he interrupted me: "Now I will first show you *my* wine." He rang, a servant came and brought an open bottle. The bottle lay in a padded little basket like a child in its cradle. I had never seen anything like that before. "Well, go ahead and try it!" And he looked expectantly into my eyes.

Cold shudders went up and down my spine. I had never in my life sampled wine. I knew only that it was an involved procedure, almost a science, and one could easily reveal one's ignorance in the process. But now I had to do something. Fear fired my imagination. I raised the glass, held it to the light, took a little sip, spat it out onto my hand, rubbed the drop on my palm in all directions, then, bending down to the light I looked closely at my palm, sniffed, and finally said: "The wine is not bad, but watery."

"Since . . . when . . . does . . . one . . . sample . . . wine . . . like . . . that?" And the wine magnate from Stolp cast a threatening glance at the swords and armor.

"Don't you know? It's the latest method," and while saying that I looked into his eyes, amazed at such ignorance. The man was so dumbfounded that he did not dare make a peep and actually bought a barrel of wine from me. Still, I was happy when my Frieda and I were outside again.

With some of the big money that I earned this way, I had bought myself elegant clothes. In addition, just like my boss, I wore silk stockings and patent leather shoes, and, on my hand, a diamond ring. Herr Schindler, for his part, was already sending me people whom I was supposed to train. Here, too, I did exactly what my boss did. When an older traveling salesman presented himself to me, I taught him the reliable speech: "I represent the Rüdesheim winery on the Rhine and would like to take the liberty of making you an offer." Then I pressed ten marks into his hand and sent him to a place in the vicinity. The next evening he came back, gasping from exertion and sadly informed me that he hadn't sold a bottle. I laughed my head off: "Young man, if you stay so keen you will become my best salesman."

Again I gave him ten marks, and again he returned without an order. I even tried for the third time. When, however, he again returned without having accomplished anything, I threw him out, saying furiously: "You are the greatest disappointment of my life." The poor man had to go back home on foot. Obviously I was not as good a judge of people as my boss.

> *[Out of weariness Katsch gives up his activities as salesman. At the outbreak of war in* 1914 *he is living in Berlin with a dancer, who had taken him into her care after he had attempted suicide.]*

In the morning the desk clerk of the hotel in which we were living came and said that I had to report immediately at the police precinct, since I was a foreigner. Without a collar and without breakfast I went to the precinct. Several other people were also there. After a while a police car pulled up, the so-called paddy wagon, which we were supposed to get into. An official observed ironically that the gentlemen from police headquarters wished to meet us personally. I protested. A well-dressed gentleman, who had also been waiting with me, objected vigorously to this treatment. Thus the two of us were allowed to take a taxi. With this car we drove to police headquarters and went into a room in which forty to fifty people were sitting.

"Do you have documents with you?" I was asked.

I had only a certificate from the Gymnasium in Lemberg, which I presented. I was then led out, and I asked the man who was accompanying me whether I would be locked up. He said no. Suddenly he opened a door, quickly pushed me in, and closed the door behind me. I wanted to open it again immediately, but I noticed that it had no handle. At the top of the door there was a small hole to look through, but only from the outside. Opposite it there was a barred window, rather high on the wall. Then there was a bed, which was fixed to the wall, a small stool, a small chamber pot, and on the wall, the rules. I was in jail. No amount of banging or shouting helped.

They left me without food until six o'clock the next morning. Then I had to clean the cell, got black coffee and a piece of dry bread. Then, down into the yard for a walk. In the courtyard I saw hundreds of foreigners who were in the same situation as I was. Englishmen, Frenchmen, Poles, yes, even a negro. There I found out that for fear of espionage all foreigners who did not have sufficient identification were being locked up.

I said to the person who was quietly telling me this that I had a girlfriend staying at a hotel. He advised me to write her a postcard right away. I did that, went back to the cell and there got potato soup with a little piece of meat. Luckily, the bed was let down and I could stretch out on it. Since I was still not entirely well and much weakened by these upsetting experiences, I didn't find it so bad at all to be lying on a bed, alone, in the quiet of the prison.

On the next day, the same story. I had to go to the yard again, but soon I had enough of the monotonous, tedious marching in a circle and went back to my room. That was lucky for me. For at this moment coming down the stairs was a captain whom I had met at the Mascotte. He was with the headquarters and on duty. I rushed up to him. But he didn't seem to know me any more. He stood there with an official expression, listened to what I was telling him, and replied briefly and in a military tone that I should wait to see what would happen with me. With that, he disappeared.

But a few hours later I was released. So he had recognized me, after all, only he was too smart to show it. I now ran on foot like one possessed, from Alexanderplatz to my hotel on Albrechtstrasse. There I found my dancer, lying in bed in tears. My card lay beside her, the letters completely smudged by tears. In front of her was her breakfast, and I couldn't help pouncing upon the rolls, that's how hungry I was.

But what to do now? Neither of us had any money. Immediately I telegraphed Herr Schindler in Magdeburg but got no answer. Then I found out that on Potsdamer Strasse there was a relief committee for Russians who as a result of the war had not been able to leave. There I received 100 marks. With this money I went to my previous boss in Magdeburg. Parting from the dancer was difficult for me.

In Magdeburg I rented myself a very simple garret in the home of a poor woman, and right away paid the 15 marks that it cost monthly. Now I had my peace. Upstairs, when I looked down from the skylight, I heard soldiers marching by on the street and singing. I was seized by the enthusiasm for war that was all around me. I wanted to march with them, to fight! The stories of my grandfather, who had also been a soldier and whom I resembled in so many ways, came to mind. I was also strong enough. So I hurried to the headquarters and signed up as a volunteer. After a lengthy wait I was informed that as a foreigner I could not serve in the Prussian army. But they told me to register with the Polish Legion; it was fighting on the side of Germany and Austria for the liberation of its country from Russian rule. Immediately I submitted an application there, but after a week I received notification that they had more than enough people; I was to report once again later.

Now I had to look for a position in order to make a living. First I went to Herr Schindler. But he pressed three marks into my hand as if I were a beggar. At first I didn't want to take them but to punch him in the face instead, but then I did take them after all.

On the next day I met an acquaintance, likewise a former traveling wine salesman, who was in the same miserable situation as I. We made plans together in order to stay afloat. We remembered a nephew of Schindler's, who was also a traveling wine salesman and earning so much money that he could easily give us some of it. We looked him up and told him of our need. But he said with no feeling at all: "Who cares about that?" Furious over this rejection, we decided to go to him once more and, if he again acted so hardheartedly, to teach him a lesson. When we arrived on the next day he was eating a dish full of whipped cream. Smacking his lips, he refused our plea for help. Then my friend took the dish and slapped all of the cream into his face. That was sweet revenge.

Finally I did find a job. I sold chocolate and tea cubes for packages to the front for a Berlin merchant, and soon orders were pouring in. But for the time being the merchant withheld my commission, and when I wanted to demand it from him one day, he had disappeared with the money.

Now began a bitter time of hunger. At night I often sneaked into my landlady's kitchen, took some bread and soaked it in water; that was my only meal. Finally I went to the Magdeburg soccer club and there found a Prussian officer who took pity on me. He gave me army bread and canned goods. That saved me from the worst hunger.

Finally, with the help of an acquaintance I found a position at the office of the Magdeburg streetcar company. There I received 90 marks a month, which after my period of going hungry seemed to me a splendid salary.

At noon I ate very cheaply at the city mission. The woman in charge was an intelligent, friendly lady who often talked with me. One day I met a countryman there, a Russian whom I called Sasha. He was a wealthy fellow, a kind of perpetual student who received a generous allowance from his parents, who were living in Montreaux. His ideal was to be a gentleman. In his jacket pocket he constantly carried printed instructions listing everything that a true gentleman must possess. Whenever he had bought one of these things, a cigarette box or a certain perfume, he crossed out the corresponding entry on his list. Thus it didn't take very long before he attained his goal. I regarded it as my duty to emulate him as well as possible and to the degree that he aided me in this with his greater financial means.

Every morning and evening we had to report at the police precinct. This took place in the following way. We stuck our heads in the door and called out "Morning," whereupon we received a loud "morning" in return.

For eight months I alternated between work and pleasure. Then an employee in our office took his life and I was designated to take his place. Well now, even in those days I had one quality typical of actors, that of being terribly superstitious. Sitting as

I was at the desk of the person who had hanged himself, I wasn't able to work at all. I constantly saw the man hanging from the rope and I had the feeling that the dead person wouldn't give me any peace until he saw me hanging, too. I asked to be assigned to another desk. I was told, however, that I should be happy to have such a job, and if it didn't suit me, I could leave. So I left the place and went home.

At four o'clock I went back once more in order to collect from the cashier the money I had earned until then. When I came out onto the street again I saw a policeman waiting for me. I immediately ran back up the stairs and tried to speak with the boss. But he refused to see me. I found out only that in accordance with regulations he had reported me to the police as unemployed. That was the reason why the policeman was waiting for me.

Now I was arrested and taken to the citadel. There they had an underground camp with several hundred people, a very seedy lot. I firmly refused to accept that; finally, since I was already being treated as an enemy alien, I employed a ruse of war and declared that I was a Russian officer and demanded treatment in keeping with my rank. That helped. After several hours the notification arrived: incarceration in keeping with rank. So once more I was sitting in a cell. There I discovered a bell and all night long I rang it out of rage, until the jailer was going to put me in chains. Then I finally stopped.

On Sunday morning a police assistant came and asked me why I had left the streetcar company. I told him the story of the suicide, and that I had no more ardent desire than to find a job again. Thereupon the police assistant called out: "March, go home, but be sure to report tomorrow morning by twelve o'clock that you have a job!" No one could run faster than I did from the prison. When I appeared at the city mission for lunch, the woman in charge greeted me full of joy. Here I discovered that it was she who had used her influence in my behalf.

But where was I now to get a job quickly? Then I heard of a Herr Schmidt who had a cork factory. On the next day I went to him and asked him to employ me without pay. He answered: "Fine," but I would also have to work, have to sort cork.

Beaming, I went to the precinct at twelve o'clock and said I had found a position. So everything was fine. On that day I really did sort cork from morning till evening. On the next day I only stayed two hours, and on the third only one hour. A few days later things had reached the point where I merely entered the factory and greeted the boss with the words: "Good morning, Herr Schmidt, how are you?" Then I went off with my friend Sasha. Soon we were known all over town. We were called the loafers of Magdeburg.

*[Katsch finds an educated benefactor in a woman he refers to as "Ladylove." She enables him to take acting lessons at the Max Reinhardt School in Berlin in 1916.]*

I still recall as if it were today how I arrived at the Potsdam station. I no longer felt like a poor outcast but rather looked forward to an enticing future. And I had a person to whom I meant something, I had a "ladylove," and for me that was like a home, a new, good, friendly home. I would soon also feel at home there, in the big city. Right in front of the station I ran up to the first policeman I saw and asked him: "Where should I live here?" He really meant well by me and after brief consideration he sent me to a pension on Leipziger Strasse. A long, healthy sleep took all the tiredness of travel from my bones.

Before eight o'clock in the morning I was already on Schumannstrasse and went, for the first time, through entrance gate number 13. There on the left, the yellow building, that was the theater; that is where the school of acting was. But everything was still closed. Instruction did not begin until ten o'clock; before then no teacher was there either. Another two hours separated me from my goal. I did not leave. I walked nervously and expectantly back and forth in the courtyard, in which so many great and famous actors had stood.

At exactly ten o'clock I was announced to the director of the school, Max Reinhardt's old comrade-in-arms Berthold Held. He received me with the words: "Well, we'll soon see what you can do." Again I had to wait outside for a while; then he finally called me in. He was no longer alone now. At his side sat a blond woman with an open face and kind expression. She had a monocle in her eye and was smoking a cigar. She was Lucie Höflich, the great artist, the wonderful human being. At the very first glance I felt that this woman was something special. I stared at her. In her eyes lay my fate.

"What do you want to recite to us? What have you learned," Held asked.

"I know a good poem in Polish."

"But as a German actor you can't recite something Polish!"

Then Lucie Höflich said, "Come on, let him, let him speak the way he's accustomed to." The bright resonance of her voice and the natural authority that spoke from her words touched me wondrously. Without a trace of anxiety I said my Polish poem. I spoke it with my whole soul, completely under the spell of the great personality sitting there before me. During my rather long recitation I did not take my eyes off her for a second. I was as if hypnotized.

Again I was sent out. When I was called back once more Frau Höflich had disappeared. In a more friendly manner than before Held addressed me: "Well now . . . you are quite a talented fellow. Frau Höflich liked you especially well. We will admit you to the school. Well then, a cordial welcome!" I scarcely dared to breathe. Then he continued: "First you have to learn some techniques, then you can go straight into the second course. I'm sure you want to start learning parts soon!"

Did I ever!

Probably every acting student, especially if he has the luck to attend the Reinhardt School, declares his time in school as the most beautiful of his life. And that it certainly was. The students took part in the great task that was being accomplished in the two buildings at that time. They were the rising generation. Some of the much-admired stars had also started in such a modest way, and the greater and more accomplished they were, the friendlier they were in their relations with us beginners.

We were allowed to attend every performance, every dress rehearsal. We filled the spacious rooms from the backstage to the cellar of the D-T—the very cozy theater restaurant—with laughter and enthusiasm, pleasure in our work and the spirit of our youth.

I was twenty-three years old at that time. My best friend was Erich Riewe, who had gotten to the acting school by pure coincidence. He had accompanied a friend to the qualifying examination and then, on a sudden impulse, declared that he, too, wanted to recite something. His friend was turned down, Erich was admitted.

The star of the school was Gerda Müller, a marvelous, intelligent girl of immense vitality and unusual artistic maturity. It was rumored that she had been on the stage earlier, that she had played big roles and only then had she applied for admission at the school. I don't know if this legend is based on truth. If that is the case then it definitely speaks for Gerda Müller's artistic insight.

For the students and the teachers I was the "talented foreigner." Especially Professor Ferdinand Gregory, the most learned among German actors, showed much interest in me. He concerned himself thoroughly with my training and even gave me private lessons without taking money for them. He sharpened my sense for artistic responsibility and, again and again, like Lepanto, the diction teacher at the school, he told me kindly and consistently to perfect my extremely faulty pronunciation.

For us East European Jews pure German is an especially difficult matter. I know East European Jews who even after thirty or forty years still do not speak German without an accent. That, then, was hard work. But I didn't give up. Even today, before every role, indeed, even before every performance, I still do the pronunciation exercises that Lepanto and Gregory taught me in those days. I can remember, for instance, that the word "Mond" presented me with insurmountable difficulties. Back home one pronounced "Mond" with a short "o". For months I practiced it. Wherever I went or was, from the time I got up to the time I went to bed, on the street and at the café, constantly: "Mooond, Mooond, Moooooond!"

I was especially happy when Lucie Höflich, whom I adored fervently, gave me a few lessons. I studied the role of Franz Moor with her. I also remember Eduard von Winterstein with special gratitude. He was an acting teacher of high caliber, full of imagination and temperament. He knew every play by heart, not only the male, but also the female parts.

Julius Bab[2] lectured to us about literary trends, with special attention to German literature. His favorites were Hebbel and Anzengruber. I followed his expositions with great interest.

Thanks to "ladylove's" insightful preparation in Magdeburg, I was not a stranger to the themes that were treated. I was familiar with Hebbel, Rilke, Dehmel. I was already able to contribute, and I was no longer a "barbarian," although there was still much of the "barbarian" about me. Already in Magdeburg I had tried to acquire finer manners. Everywhere I happened to be, I observed how people ate and drank, dressed and moved, and I tried to become like them. At the movies, too, I studied West European civilization. For me these film actors were purely and simply gods, higher beings who walked on clouds. Wanda Treumann and Viggo Larsen, stars of silent film, became my teachers in manners. Never in real life had I seen any of the film actors whom I knew from the screen.

One morning I was standing by the doorman's lodge in the vestibule of the Deutsches Theater when I heard Herr Zimmermann, the venerable, long-bearded door-

man, greet a small elegant gentleman with the words: "Good morning, Herr Lubitsch."
The name shot through me like a stroke of lightning—Lubitsch![3]

"Are you the Lubitsch from 'The Pride of the Firm'?"

"Yes."

I was transported. He was delighted by my childish enthusiasm and we became friends. I got to know his whole circle, in which I felt good, and I think he also liked me.

At that time Reinhardt[4] was staging Georg Büchner's immensely exciting drama *Dantons Tod* for the first time. The entire acting school was involved in the street and court scenes. I played a woman of the masses, a shrew with a drum. This was not a usual walk-on, it was an unwritten part, a figure from the imagination of master Reinhardt. There I could at least give vent to some of my pent energy. And that I did. Years later my excellent colleague Johannes Riemann told me that Max Reinhardt said at that time: "You'll see, we will hear of this fellow yet. But don't tell him anything. Otherwise he will give me no peace!" I was even drawn in this "role," for it was a striking character. I was proud of it, prouder than of many a bigger role that I later played in different circumstances.

1. First printed in 1934 in the entertainment supplement of the *Jüdische Bibliothek*. A selection from a part of the memoirs not printed here appeared in the *Frankfurter Allgemeine Zeitung* on July 24, 1969, under the title "As Nathan and Othello."

2. Julius Bab (1880–1955), Jewish theater critic, director, and dramatic adviser, who published numerous writings on the theater and literature.

3. Ernst Lubitsch (b. 1892 in Berlin; d. 1947 in Hollywood), actor and film director; moved to the United States in 1922.

4. Max Reinhardt (b. 1873 in Baden bei Wien; d. 1943 in New York), directed the Deutsche Theater in Berlin starting in 1906. Because he was a Jew, this most famous director of his day had to leave Germany in 1933.

# 20 *Samuel Spiro*

BORN IN 1885 IN SCHENKLENGSFELD (HESSE-NASSAU PROVINCE); DIED IN ISRAEL IN 1960.

Samuel Spiro, Recollections of My Youth in Hessian Jewish Communities. Undated manuscript, 45 pages. Written in Israel in 1948.

*Spiro's memoirs describe his youth until 1904. The grandfather and father of the author were teachers at the state Jewish elementary school in Schenklengsfeld, near Hersfeld. In this Hessian village community of about fifty Jewish families, most of the Jews were cattle dealers and peddlers with a good income. Spiro depicts the traditional Jewish life in the village as well as the economic role of the Jews. He was most intensely exposed to antisemitism during his time in the Gymnasium in Hersfeld. In 1899 Spiro's father transferred as a teacher to Fulda, where the orthodox rabbi kept an authoritarian rule. Destined by his father to study Talmud, after two months the Gymnasium graduate quit the yeshiva of Rabbi Breuer in Frankfurt am Main and studied medicine. In 1938, Spiro was able to emigrate to Palestine, where he became a physician for the Youth Aliya movement.*

I have decided to record these recollections because life in the Jewish communities of Hesse differed greatly from the life of Jews in other German communities, in regard to their composition, their level of education, their customs and occupations, as well as their outlook on life, and it seems worthwhile to me to preserve this in memory. Also, I would like my children to know in what circles and under what external and internal conditions I lived my youth.

I was born in 1885 in the village of Schenklengsfeld in the Hersfeld District, the rabbinical district of Fulda, Kassel County, Hesse-Nassau Province, in the kingdom of Prussia. Until 1866 this county belonged to the Electorate of Hesse, which was annexed by Prussia after its victorious war against Austria and its German allies. In 1914 there was still in Hesse-Nassau a Hessian Rights Party, which did not recognize this annexation and even nominated its own candidates for the German Reichstag. In the end, however, it could attract only 400 votes, proof that the population had completely accepted being joined to Prussia. Especially among the Hessian Jews, whose number was quite considerable and who were joined together in numerous larger and smaller communities, there was no opposition whatever to Prussia. Great hopes were placed in the Prussian Crown Prince, who was also Crown Prince of the German Reich and who had repeatedly expressed himself unequivocally in favor of equal rights for Jews and against antisemitism, which he called the disgrace of the century.

More than any others, the Jews of Hesse, which was the bastion of antisemitism in Germany, looked up to this prince with deep trust. But in 1888, only three months after he took power, he succumbed to a pernicious disease, and many Jewish hopes were buried with him. His successor, the woeful Kaiser Wilhelm II, showed little liking for his Jewish subjects.

My grandfather, who was born in 1817 in Fulda as the son of a merchant, became a teacher in 1840 at the Electoral-Hessian Jewish elementary school in Schenklengsfeld, and in 1866 he was named a civil servant by the Prussian government. Hesse was one of the few Prussian provinces in which there were *state* Jewish elementary schools based on old edicts. My grandfather was a very learned man, in both profane and Talmudic subjects. He was far better educated than the average teacher of that day. In his youth, he had attended the famous yeshiva of Rabbi Seckel Wormser in Gelnhausen for several years, and he was one of the few men permitted to bear the title of *"Morenu Raw"* without being a rabbi.[1] He had also learned French and English. I recall that in the last years of his life—he died in 1892—when he was pensioned for reasons of poor health, he instructed his grandchildren in English. We children had little liking for this instruction, for my grandfather was an unusually strict man. In the community his authority was undisputed. People spoke of him with great respect, at times also with fear. The simple village Jews, who sustained themselves through cattle dealing and peddling, had tremendous respect for erudition, although they themselves were uneducated. This respect expressed itself in the pride with which they sent their children to the Gymnasium in the neighboring district town of Hersfeld, the director of which, by the way, was the famous Duden, the author of the German dictionary that was acknowledged all over the world as the standard work. In religious questions there could be no opposition to the decisions of the "old teacher," as my grandfather was called in contrast to my father, his successor. But his advice was also solicited in other community questions and in many private affairs. I was seven years old when my grandfather died, but even now, fifty-six years later, I can still see the immense crowd of people who had rushed to the burial procession from all of the villages in the vicinity, among them many non-Jews, who, like the Jews, paid great respect to the "old teacher."

As my grandfather's successor in office, my father had soon gained the same position in the community as my grandfather. Although the majority of the community's members, with whom he had grown up, addressed him with the familiar form "Du," he was able to keep some distance between them and himself, and this nipped in the bud any attempt at crass intimacy. No one dared call him by his first name; even his former schoolmates, who were of the same age and whom he naturally called by their first names, called him "Spiro." But that did not harm his good relations with them. He equalled his father in knowledge. He was a *Talmid-Chacham,*[2] had mastered French and English, and even after he had passed his fiftieth year he learned Latin. He perhaps even surpassed his father in talent. He was an excellent speaker and a feared debater. In my judgment, this gift was not always beneficial, for he was only too well aware of his intellectual and rhetorical superiority and often applied them in behaving dictatorially. Nonetheless, he was popular in the Jewish community, where his knowledge and his helpfulness, which knew no limits with regard to community members, were valued. There was a common saying in the community: "Without Spiro no one can marry, no one can be sick, or die." But he was also highly regarded among the non-Jews. Before patriotic festivities, such as the Kaiser's birthday or the celebration of the victory at Sedan, the officers of the patriotic organizations, peasants, or master craftsmen would come to him to have him write their speeches. He probably wrote hundreds of petitions to the authorities, for Jews as well as for non-Jews. Both the Jewish and the gentile teachers of the district were bound to him in friendship.

Thus, there were great regrets when he was transferred in 1899 to teach at the newly founded Jewish elementary school in Fulda. A friend from his youth in Schenklengsfeld said to him at that time, in Hessian-Jewish dialect: "If you'd of died, we'd of cheered ourselves and said: that's my *Hashomayim,*[3] but that you're leaving us alive, that we don't understand." I am sure that he sometimes wished he were back in his old community. When he was transferred to Fulda, his life suffered a break that never fully healed.

At that time—in the eighties and nineties of the last century—the Jewish community of Schenklengsfeld was one of the largest and most prosperous in the rabbinical district of Fulda. It numbered about fifty families, whose heads were almost all cattle dealers and peddlers. The majority belonged to the so-called middle class, but there were also some rich families and only very few really poor ones.

Schenklengsfeld was a farming village of about 1,200 souls, and the Jews made up about twenty percent of the population. Relations between Christians and Jews were friendly until the middle of the nineties, at which time the antisemitic movement in

Hesse gained strong impetus, and an antisemitic representative for this electoral district was even sent to the Reichstag. The election meetings were often stormy. There were also rows between Jews and gentiles, but after the elections there was peace again in the village, even if relations were more tense than before. My father, who attended the election meetings along with the other Jews, always carried a knotty walking stick.

There were special reasons for the fact that antisemitism was able to achieve such great success particularly in Hesse. Thanks to cattle dealing, which was the main source of sustenance for the Jews in every Hessian village, the relations between Jews and peasants were very close. The Christian peasants, who often lived in difficult economic circumstances, turned to their Jewish business friends for credit, and received it in return for repayment with interest and pawning their estates. If the peasants fell into arrears with their payments, the Jews had the estates parceled and sold them, often at high profit, to other, prosperous peasants. The Jews who pursued this somewhat offensive business were called "estate butchers." They were not many in number, but they contributed significantly to the fact that the seed of antisemitism in Hesse fell upon especially fertile ground. As always in the history of the Jewish people, the entirety was held responsible for the faults of a few. These "estate butchers" were not held in high regard among the Jews either, but they had influence in the community through the wealth that they had acquired by their underhanded dealings. My father fought against these methods, which in effect dispossessed the impoverished peasants, but his efforts failed because of the greed of the "estate butchers." However, the majority of Hessian Jews earned their livelihood honestly, and their relations with the peasants were trusting. The large estates had their so-called Court Jews, with whom they concluded all of their cattle transactions. The attempt to oust these Court Jews was considered highly dishonorable and led to deadly hostility between the concerned parties.

Cattle dealing had assumed extraordinary proportions. At the cattle markets in Hersfeld and Fulda, hundreds of Jews and peasants from the immediate and more distant environs came together, and there one could observe the cleverness of the Jewish cattle dealers and the slyness and tenacity of the peasants. Curses that were not meant seriously, oaths that were never kept, flew back and forth. After long, futile haggling they parted, swearing that they would never again have business dealings with one another, only to take up negotiations again after a few steps, and to conclude them. Once I heard a cattle dealer swear: "I'll kick the bucket right here, and better that my rear end should go *kappore* before I deal with you again."[4] With these words he left his customer standing there, only to return immediately and begin bargaining with him again. Another popular oath was: "I'd first go blind here," whereby they pointed to their chest. Or: "I'd first not go in health to *kever Yisroel*."[5] An oath that was employed with special frequency was *"maneschome,"* a corrupted form of "meine *neschome*" (in German, "upon my soul"). The word *"osser"* served to reinforce a negation.[6]

I was once witness to a comical scene in the train, where two cattle dealers, while conversing, had missed the station at Fulda, where there was a cattle market, and had gone on in the direction of Hersfeld. When he noticed his error, the one called out: "I'll jump *maneshome* out the train," while the other one, who was no less excited, yelled: "You *won't osser* jump out the train." These shouts were repeated a few times without anything happening. At the next station they quietly got off.

I especially enjoyed watching the goings-on at the cattle market, and I skipped many a school hour in order to witness these interesting transactions. I gained more insight into the life of the folk by doing that than through long treatises. The language of these Hessian Jews was a strange mixture of corrupt German and just as corrupt scraps of Hebrew, but it bore no similarity to Yiddish.[7] For non-Jews and also for Jews from other regions it was an almost incomprehensible language. [. . .]

The Jews found foreign words rough going. Their meaning was either turned around completely or distorted. Thus, "Spediteur" became "Spenditar," "Diskretion" became "Kredition," and "publik" even became "Republik." A popular saying was: "I've simulated (thought) about it." With the peasants, these cattle dealers and peddlers spoke peasant's dialect, in which they were completely fluent.

The cattle dealers were on the road almost the entire week and did not return home until Thursday afternoon or Friday morning—often with cattle that they had bought. Since most of these Jews were orthodox and ate only strictly kosher food, they had to take upon themselves great deprivations in eating, for there were no kosher meals to be had in the peasant villages. It is almost impossible to imagine the spartan life of these dealers. All week long they lived from bread, sausage that they took along with them, black coffee (they did not drink milk while away), and fruit. Each one of them had his *tefilin* with him, of course, and the peasants were used to seeing their Jewish business friends put on their *tefilin* in their homes. I am sure that not a single cattle dealer of that generation ever shaved.[8] On Friday, the beard was clipped with a scissors or removed with foul-smelling sulfur barium.

An hour before the beginning of Shabbat, the men strolled through the village streets in their Shabbat suits, and a good while before the start of worship people gathered in the courtyard of the synagogue, where the events of the day were discussed and the experiences of the past week related. During prayers there was true reverence. The service was solemn and dignified and strictly traditional. [. . .] The stern head of the community board, called the Parnas, allowed no conversations, and chatterers were frequently hit with a fine, which he was permitted to impose up to a certain amount. That took place with the words: "You are fined a pound of wax." The fine was reckoned on the price of wax.

The offices of the board in the village communities were not bestowed according to wealth but according to merit. The heads were not elected, but rather they were named by the Office of the Israelite Community Heads, of which there were four in Hesse. The Office of the Israelite Community Heads was an institution recognized by the state, and was presided over by the provincial rabbi. He had great legal authority, and, especially if the rabbi was an energetic man, this could lead to a dictatorship over the community, as it did in the rabbinical district of Fulda.

I have retained especially vivid memories of the night of the Shavuot festival and the night before *Hoshana Rabba*.[9] On these nights, the whole community came together to "learn," each in his own *chevre*.[10] The "learning" took place in private homes. The tables were festively set and covered with all sorts of fruits and baked goods. At midnight there was coffee and cake. My father had to visit each *chevre* for a while, and I was permitted to accompany him. Those were wonderful nights for me, less because of the "learning" than because of the sweets that I could eat. Every family in whose home the learning took place sought to offer its best in the way of food and drink, and on the next day their hospitality was compared in the synagogue courtyard. I also much enjoyed "*kapores Schlagen*," for while the chickens were being swung about, in my mind I already saw them boiled and fried.[11]

Basically, the community was one large family. Family celebrations were celebrations for the entire congregation. If someone died, every home mourned. On the day of burial every tradesman returned home to take part in the *levaya*.[12] During *shiva* every woman who visited brought cake or poultry to the mourners' home. During *shiva* for my father's mother we children stood before the house almost the whole day, and whenever we saw a visitor approaching we dashed excitedly into the room and said, "Mama, another woman is coming with a basket."

For the most part, the members of the community were "*Amrazzim*," uneducated people, who could recite the Hebrew prayers more or less correctly, to be sure, but did not understand their content. But this did not diminish their reverence. We members of the younger generation, who were learning Hebrew grammar at school, particularly enjoyed spotting the mistakes that the elders made when they got to lead prayers on the day of *Jahrzeit*.[13] Only a very small number of the community had the ambition to understand something of the prayers that they recited. In Schenklengsfeld, on Friday evening and at noon on Shabbat some ten men assembled in our house, where my father studied *Kitsur* and *Mishnayot* with them.[14] We children called them the "learners." They pursued this studying with great zeal, and it was touching to observe how these workworn, tired men clung to everything father said, in order to hear words of Torah from him.

Even as a little boy, I had to take part in these learning sessions. Unfortunately, it was my father's ambition to make a great Talmud scholar of me. So I was forced to learn to read Hebrew at the age of four; at the age of five I learned to translate *Chumosh*,[15] and at six a portion of *Mishnayot*. By forcing me in this way, my father achieved the opposite of what he intended. Learning Hebrew became torture for me, and when, after I finished the Gymnasium, my father sent me to Breuer's *Yeshiva* in Frankfurt against my will, the upshot was that after only two months in that stifling atmosphere I ran off, and for the next thirty years—recalling the torments of my youth—I could not bring myself even to take a peek into a Hebrew book. [. . .]

In Schenklengsfeld the Jews made up twenty percent of the total population, but their political influence was greater than their number would have warranted. In those days, there existed in Prussia the so-called three-class voting right, which afforded the propertied classes special rights at elections. Each of the three classes was to elect the same number of delegates, and since the majority of Jews were more prosperous than the peasants, they belonged to the first two classes. In Schenklengsfeld, a single voter voted in the first class, and he was a rich Jew. His one vote had the same weight as the total ballots of the third-class voters, who constituted the bulk of the population. A large percentage of the Jews voted in the second class. Thus it came about that there were seven Jews among the twelve representatives in the village council of Schenklengs-feld. Even if the Jews did not misuse their majority in the village council, it was still an unhealthy condition to have twenty percent of the inhabitants form the majority in this council, a condition that contributed to strengthening antisemitism. Circumstances were similar in numerous other Hessian villages with a Jewish population. It might be mentioned here as a curiosity that in Rhina, a village in the Fulda rabbinical district, there were more Jewish inhabitants than Christian. Despite that, they had a gentile burgomaster, elected by the Jews. Even if a Jew had been elected burgomaster, never would he have been confirmed by the Prussian government. Rhina had only one Jewish vice-burgomaster.

The rich Jews had the understandable wish to provide their children with advanced schooling, and so some children were sent to the Gymnasium in the neighboring district town of Hersfeld. I was one of them, a "wunderkind." At that time there was no train line between our village and Hersfeld. The distance was fourteen kilometers, and to get there one had to ride one and a half to two hours in a horse cart. At times I even covered the distance on foot. I myself was prepared in Schenklengsfeld for the third year of the Gymnasium.

For me this preparation entailed much suffering. My father had seen to it that there was always a Jewish doctor in Schenklengsfeld, who tended the sick in the entire area. Mainly, they were very young doctors who had just completed their university courses and were gaining practical experience in Schenklengsfeld. One of these doctors declared himself willing to instruct me in Latin. When his work as doctor kept him especially busy, instruction took place at irregular intervals. When he was less busy, he gave me a lesson each day. But the lack of people to treat embittered his nature, and I was the lightning rod for his bitterness. If I made a mistake, I had to lay myself across a chair, and then this pedagogue of the rod beat my behind with a leather strap that had a knot at its end. On such days I always regretted deeply that there were not more sick people in the region who needed medical help. Due to fear of my father, I dared not say anything about these whippings at home, for I would have had to admit that I had not known something, and then I would have possibly gotten another "educational bonus." But once, on a Shabbat, when I came home crying and rubbing my aching behind after such a pounding, and it was found that my rear was covered completely with weals, this "Oneg Shabbat"¹⁶ was too much even for my father, and he forbade any further instruction. I then took Latin lessons from the local Protestant pastor, who was regarded as an antisemite. He always behaved properly toward me.

Once the pastor allowed his true thoughts to show. During the elections to the Prussian State Parliament, whose representatives were elected through open ballot by so-called delegates, the candidate who was not an antisemite defeated the antisemitic candidate by a majority of one vote. My father was one of the delegates, and his vote had been more or less decisive in the election. He had to go to the district town of Hersfeld to cast his ballot as a delegate, and, for this reason, he had to cancel lessons at school for the day. The pastor, who was clearly unhappy with the result of the election, told me in a very upset tone, in his capacity as state-appointed school inspector, to demand of my father that he not cancel lessons without prior permission from him, the school inspector. Thereupon, my father gave me the unpleasant task of returning to the pastor and telling him that he, my father, refused to accept such messages through me, and that he requested Herr School Inspector to bring them to his attention officially in writing. And since I feared my father more than the pastor, I had to carry out this assignment for better or worse. This little episode testifies to my father's sense of independence even toward superiors.

The instruction that I received from the pastor in Latin and from my father in other subjects was successful. I passed the entrance test for the third year, and—as seldom happened—even my father was satisfied with me on that day. For me this day signified a new, important period of my young life. It meant that I would leave my parents' home at the age of eleven and a half and enter a Christian school.

At that time, Hersfeld was a bastion of antisemitism. It was a typical petit bourgeois town, where it was part of good form to be antisemitic. At the Gymnasium, too, one felt this antisemitic atmosphere at every step, less among the teachers, who generally treated Jewish pupils without prejudice, than among the pupils, who behaved coarsely and coldly toward their Jewish classmates. The principal of the Gymnasium, the famous Duden, a highly learned man, was widely regarded as an antisemite, but he was not active politically. He behaved correctly toward the Jewish pupils.

In Hersfeld there existed a Jewish community that was constantly growing, thanks to the influx from the surrounding villages. That was when the flight of the Hessian Jews from the countryside began, and many rural communities that had once thrived, and still did in my youth, gradually dissolved through the drive toward the towns.

In Hersfeld I lived in the house of an uncle (the husband of my mother's sister), who, like many members of my family, was a teacher and taught at the Jewish elementary school. He was blessed with a flock of children, and all seven of them were excellent pupils. My uncle himself was an unusually refined, gracious, lovable man, who was highly respected in his community. He was one of the few truly pious people I met in my life, a person who practiced what he preached. Thanks to his model, the Hersfeld community, in which there had originally been many non-observant members, later became one of the most religious in the district. Twice during my three-year stay in his home, the otherwise kind man boxed my ears, once because I had given my aunt, his wife, an impertinent answer, and the second time because I had neglected to put on *tefilin*. That morning I had hiked fourteen kilometers from Schenklengsfeld to Hersfeld and did not have the time to put on *tefilin* before school began. But I can swear that it was the only time during that period in my life when I did not fulfill this commandment.

In 1896, a new, very beautiful synagogue was built in Hersfeld. My father, who besides his other abilities could also claim musical talent, had composed a Hallelujah, which was sung at the consecration of the synagogue and thereafter was a permanent part of the liturgical melodies of the Hersfeld community, sung with great enthusiasm by the entire congregation on Shabbat and holidays. As the son of the composer of this joyous hymn I was well liked by the members of the community.

The social stratification of the Jews was somewhat different in Hersfeld than in the villages. There were a number of cattle dealers there too, as well as some "estate butchers," but by then many merchants also lived there, whose level of education, though, with few exceptions, was no higher than that of the cattle dealers. Almost all of the children of these Jews were already attending the Gymnasium, with greater or lesser success. There were six Jews in my class at that time. Only two of them had been promoted to the class at the start of the school year, however, whereas the other four were "Old Boys," that is, repeating the class. Except for me, not one of them completed the Gymnasium; they did not even get as far as the middle school examination, but, nevertheless, all of them became good merchants. [. . .]

Although my uncle was strictly orthodox, we had to attend the Gymnasium on Shabbat. Since there was no "*eruv*" in Hersfeld, one could carry nothing there on Shabbat.[17] One's handkerchief was sewn to one's jacket pocket. I had to take the books that I needed for classes to the caretaker of the Gymnasium on Friday and fetch them from him again on Sunday. I did it unwillingly, since I was ridiculed for it by my schoolmates, including the Jewish ones. Naturally, the Jewish pupils did not write on Shabbat. Only a single teacher took offense at that; all of the others respected our religious sentiments. In my youth I fulfilled all of the religious commandments conscientiously. My religious fervor increased especially before tests and whenever report cards were handed out, and at such times I was very generous with my promises to God to fulfill his commandments.

Among my schoolmates there was a Christian boy of Danish background. His father had fought on the Danish side in the war of 1864 between Prussia and Denmark, and since he lived in a region that was ceded to Prussia, he entered the Prussian state service after peace was concluded. This boy, who was one of the best pupils in the class and also very strong physically, was free of any antisemitic feelings and came fighting to the aid of any Jewish classmate who was being molested by antisemitic pupils. And such beatings of the few Jewish boys by their combined Christian schoolmates was a daily matter. One was laid over a so-called toll bar that was held in place by a few fellows, and then every pupil had the privilege of giving one a smack on the behind, and since there were about twenty-eight Christian pupils in the class, in the course of a month these smacks added up to a rather considerable sum. But if the muscular Dane Olaf Olerog was around, even the toughest customers watched their step.

There were no social contacts at all in Hersfeld between Christians and Jews. The two faiths were completely separated, and even later I never experienced in Germany such an absolutely antisemitic atmosphere as in Hersfeld. [. . .]

In 1899 my father was transferred to the newly founded Jewish elementary school in Fulda. For him that meant both an advancement and a step down. It was an advancement inasmuch as he was sent to a town with better educational opportunities for us children, who were now able to live at home again, and also inasmuch as he could now associate with cultivated people and put his intellectual abilities to better use. Since in the village my mother had to live under very primitive conditions, the move made her life easier. It was a step down because the unrestricted high-handedness that he had enjoyed in the village was now all over with. He was no longer the focal point of the whole community, but rather one official among many, who had superiors above them. He, who for decades had been used to giving orders, now suddenly had to take orders. In addition, the stifling atmosphere of religious fanaticism that predominated in Fulda under the rule of a zealous rabbi was alien to his nature. This rabbi made truly dictatorial use of the great power that he possessed by virtue of the Hessian Ordinance on the Jews.

The Jewish community, which at that time consisted of 175 families, was composed of a small number of old-established families, who in part had lived in Fulda for centuries—among them also the Spiro family—and who proudly called themselves "Old Fuldans," and of a large number of Jews who had moved there from the surrounding villages. The basic religious outlook of the community was strictly orthodox. Sad to say, there was much religious hypocrisy in the community, especially in the circles that were close to the rabbi and outdid themselves in subservience to him. The members of the Governing Board of the Israelites and the community directors, whom he selected, were not always the most noble of the nation. The rabbi was not a good judge of people.

Among the independent-thinking men of the community there was great ill-will toward the rabbi and his circle, but as long as the rabbi was alive it was never possible to create an organized opposition. Anyone who dared to desecrate the Shabbat by keeping the store open or through other work was pilloried from the pulpit. He persecuted the Zionist movement with special hatred. A branch of *Misrachi,*[18] which had been formed in Fulda, was dissolved upon the rabbi's order. The religious education of the youth was a mockery of every pedagogical principle. The secondary school pupils were forced to attend synagogue every morning. Whoever came late or not at all received penalty points. Attendance at synagogue was checked by pupils whom the rabbi deemed worthy and who were thereby encouraged to practice a repulsive system of denunciation. I myself witnessed a scene in the synagogue that is probably unique in its kind: The rabbi, wearing *tallit* and *tefilin,* chased a sixteen-year-old Gymnasium junior, who had left the synagogue before the service had ended, into the synagogue courtyard, boxed his ears, and forced him to return to the synagogue. And no one dared to rebel against such acts. This did not remain without consequences, though. A great many of the pupils who were taught under this regime turned away permanently from orthodoxy once they had escaped the rabbi's dictatorship. In fairness, it must be admitted that, at any rate, this rabbi was a personality who also demanded of himself what he required of others.

The rabbi was especially feared by the teachers of his district. Every Thursday the teachers met in Hersfeld or Fulda to study Talmud, and the rabbi led the "learning." Woe to the teachers who did not turn up at these sessions. They were regarded as being religiously unreliable. Whoever did not know the rabbi cannot appreciate what that meant. To be sure, the teachers did not come unwillingly to these study sessions, for this offered a good opportunity to go shopping in the town. Those teachers who were at the same time *shochtim,* something that was common among village teachers, had particular reason to fear this stern man. From time to time they were tested by the rabbi in regard to their competency. They had to "produce a knife," and pity the poor person in whose knife the rabbi found a nick *(Pegima)* that had escaped the *shochet.* Then the rabbi himself made tiny nicks in the knife, which the *shochet* had to discover. I still see before me the fear-filled faces of these teachers and *shochtim,* who after an unsatisfactory result turned to my father seeking advice and help. For the teachers in the small village communities *shechita* was an important source of income, which dried up if the "Fulda *Raw*" "wrote off" the teacher as *shochtim.*[19] It was one of the rabbi's particular practices to *search* for lacks and deficiencies in the religious domain. He once discovered that a *mohel,* who had been discharging his duties for over twenty years, had made mistakes in carrying out circumcision. The rabbi was overcome by great agitation, and he ordered that all of the children and young men who had been divested of their foreskin by this same *mohel* had to appear before a strictly orthodox physician in Fulda to have their *kashrus* examined. A big operation to identify all of these children and young fellows began, and in fact there were children, partly already of school age, in whose cases it was possible to ascertain defects. All of these children were circumcised a second time at the command of the rabbi-dictator. I myself belonged to the clientele of this *mohel*. When the misfortune was discovered, I was already a student, and when I came home during the university vacation my father informed me that I would have to have the *kashrus* of my circumcision examined by the aforementioned orthodox physician. But on that occasion I even resisted the demand of my strict father, arguing, for one, that under no circumstances would I consider a second circumcision and, also, that I was perfectly satisfied with the result of the first. Soon the word got around in Fulda that the son of the teacher Spiro had refused the examination, and there was occasion for indignation, or amusement, depending on the religious views of the community members. But holding my head high, I proudly braved the dirty looks of the orthodox. [. . .]

It was all the easier for our rabbi to give free vent to his feelings as an atmosphere of religious fanaticism was prevalent in arch-Catholic Fulda. Eighty percent of the pupils and teachers at the Gymnasium were Catholic, and they were subject to the strict supervision of the Catholic clergy, who with an iron hand obliged the pupils to be "pious." So in these circles the rabbi, too, found full understanding for his educational methods. [. . .]

Of thirty-three pupils in the senior class, there were twenty-eight Catholics, four Jews, and one Protestant. It was typical for the spirit of the school that of the twenty-eight Catholics eighteen became priests.

The Catholic principal of our Gynnasium, a deeply religious man, had the best of relationships with the Jewish pupils. Never would he have tolerated an offense to their religious feelings, and, with the exception of a single Protestant teacher, not one of the teachers dared to say anything that was antisemitic or hostile to religion. And this antisemitic teacher, too, was stopped in his game by the director.

Relations between the rabbi and the Catholic clergy, especially the bishop, were excellent. During the ritual murder trial against the slaughterer Buschhoff in Xanten in the Rhine province (at the end of the nineteenth century in the "Kulturland" of Germany!), our rabbi convinced the bishop of Fulda, the later Cardinal Kopp, to take a public stand against the old wives' tale of ritual murder.[20] His declaration at that time caused a tremendous stir in the whole Catholic world. Also when the prohibition of ritual slaughter was being debated in the German Reichstag, the rabbi, aided by the Catholic representative from Fulda, successfully influenced the Catholic Centrist Party, one of the largest in the Reichstag, to reject the resolution to outlaw ritual slaughter.[21] That must be acknowledged as one of his positive activities. On the other hand, for years he waged a bitter fight against the Association of Jewish Teachers Organizations, which was influenced by the liberals, as well as against the German Organization of Rabbis, and through his unbridled extremism he caused much harm. But in his battle against Zionism and his hatred for it, including religious Zionism, he far surpassed the liberal rabbis. [. . .]

The social strata of the Jewish population of Fulda were entirely different from those in neighboring Hersfeld. In Fulda there already existed a so-called upper class of university graduates, educated merchants, some industrialists, bankers, and some officials. Then there was the class of the old-established families, who by virtue of their Fulda roots thought that they were better than their brethren who had moved from the villages. The latter formed the third social layer, and it was almost impossible for them to be accepted into so-called high society.

After our move to Fulda, my father joined the Jewish social club, Casino. In those days it was considered an honor to be accepted into it. The vote was secret, and I witnessed the tragedy of many a one who did not carry the vote and for whom rejection was tantamount to social ostracism. And yet those rejected were often more honorable than the ones who had refused them. Later the prestige of Casino sank considerably when a *Bne Briss* lodge, to be accepted in which was the greatest ambition of the community members, was created in Fulda. When I came to Fulda for a few days from Berlin, the first thing my acquaintances who belonged to the lodge asked me was: "Are you a member of the lodge?" And when I said no, I felt their respect for me sink. As beneficial as the activity of the lodge was in big cities, in small towns membership in it led in like measure to a social conceit that was surely not the intent of the founders of the lodge. Certainly, there were in the small towns, too, freethinking men of high intellect who smiled knowingly at the self-important affectations of the lodge members, but the bulk of the community members, who did not belong to the lodge, looked with envy upon the "Chosen" who were deemed worthy of membership, while the "Chosen Ones" basked in the brilliance of their Chosenness.

This is not to deny that through lectures in the lodges interest was awakened for intellectual and spiritual questions, but in the small towns most members regarded these lecture evenings primarily as social events. Even among many of the secessionist orthodox,[22] the craving to belong was greater than their so strongly pronounced urge to cut themselves off, and against the will of the young rabbi, the intellectually unimpressive son of the "Old *Raw*," they joined the lodge.

A local *Misrachi* group could no longer be founded in Fulda; the influence of the young rabbi sufficed for at least that much. On the other hand, the old rabbi had been unable to prevent the founding of a local Zionist group open to all, whose members were in the main non-orthodox, even if this local branch slept a deep slumber. Gradually, the religious liberals, too, gained a greater say in Fulda, for over the years their number had sharply risen. The young rabbi, who tried at first to follow in his father's footsteps, was really not the one to oppose the changed spirit of the times over the long run, and so he finally had to allow a representative of the liberals entrance into the community board. The rabbi did not have to regret consenting: this opposition member gradually became completely "loyal to the government" and watched closely that the strictly orthodox line of the community was adhered to. [. . .]

In the spring of 1904 I finished the Gymnasium in Fulda and the question of my choice of profession had to be discussed. Despite his very worldly attitudes, my father had not yet given up the hope of making a great *raw* of me, whereas my mother, who knew me better, expressed the view that I was not suited to be a rabbi. A provisional decision was reached to the effect that, for the start, I would attend the Breuer *yeshiva* in Frankfurt am Main and that the decision on my choice of profession would be reached during my studies there. As it soon turned out, this was an unfortunate decision.

With heavy heart, I set out on my journey to Frankfurt in April 1904, to enter the *yeshiva* as a *"bocher."* I reported to the almighty rabbi of the secessionist congregation and director of the *yeshiva,* Dr. Breuer, a son-in-law of Samson Raphael Hirsch,[23] as the youngest *bachur* of the *yeshiva.* I stood throughout my audience with His Highness, and was little encouraged by it. It immediately became clear to me that my sojourn in this world of zealots would not be a long one. Almost all of the *yeshiva bachurim* were young men without means from Hungary and Galicia. There were only two German Jews among the pupils: besides me, a son of the highly esteemed banker Samuel Strauss of Karlsruhe, who was well-known among the orthodox for his piety and charity. Since I knew far less than the other *bachurim,* some of whom were already true *lamdanim,*[24] I was assigned a "driller," a so-called *"chaserbocher,"* who tried hard to fill in the large gaps in my knowledge. [. . .]

I had opportunity to acquaint myself with the religious arrogance and personal conceit of the leaders of the Frankfurt orthodox secessionists. They were orthodox, but not pious. Piety requires compassion, and they did not show a trace of compassion. In this respect, they had a good model in their lord and master, Rabbi Breuer. His hatred for everything and everyone not associated with secessionist orthodoxy was boundless. His hatred was especially great for the likewise orthodox rabbi of the large Jewish community in Frankfurt, the outstanding, scholarly, and tolerant Dr. Horovitz, who enjoyed the greatest respect in wide circles of German Jewry.[25] His name dared not be mentioned in Breuer's presence. How far the hatred for the more liberal tendencies of the Frankfurt community went is best illustrated by the fact that Breuer's successor refused to attend the burial of Rabbi Horovitz. This was a position for which even some of his own followers reproached him. No doubt Breuer was an eminent Talmud scholar, but his erudition was combined with such inflexibility and lack of understanding for the young generation that these approached the master only with fear and trembling, to the extent that the word "approach" can even be applied in regard to this man.

One day, one of Breuer's sons took me to task, saying that it had been reported to the *Rebbe* that I was attending the theater and the opera. He added these words: "That is something we do not like." I could not deny the fact, but I also could not promise that I would forgo this pleasure. My situation in these surroundings became ever more intolerable and my antipathy toward this form of orthodoxy ever stronger. To whom could I turn to free myself from this predicament? At best, to my mother, who would have understood me but whose influence in such matters was slight. Finally, I decided to act on my own. I took heart and went to the *Rebbe,* to inform him that, realizing that I was not cut out for *yeshiva* study, I had decided to leave the *yeshiva.* I listened with complete composure to the scolding of the rabbi that I was lazy and unwilling to learn, since I knew after all that this would be my last meeting with him and that my career as a *yeshiva bachur* would be ended that same day. This decision marked the beginning of my inner independence from my father, who until then had determined how my life would be shaped, without regard for my wishes and inclinations. It also marked the end of my occupation with the Talmud and any other Hebrew literature. If earlier, thanks to the pressure that had been placed on me to devote myself to the holy books, I had dedicated myself to their study with a certain distaste, now enough was enough, and neither my father nor others were able to combat this distaste. This hurtful experience, which I had suffered in my youth, continued to affect me for thirty years, and only in *Eretz Israel* did I succeed in conquering my revulsion for Hebrew and in reawakening the love for Hebrew that I had felt in my *early* childhood.

1. The title *Morenu Raw* (Hebrew for Our Teacher, the Rabbi) may be used only by someone who was trained and authorized to be a rabbi. Not everyone who bears this title functions as a rabbi.

2. A Talmudic scholar.

3. "It comes from heaven."

4. " . . . and I'd rather break my rear end before I . . . "

5. "I would rather pass up the pleasure of being buried Jewish."

6. "forbidden."

7. This is a false philological claim. Rather, it is a matter of Hessian and West Yiddish linguistic forms.

8. In accordance with the biblical commandment in Leviticus 19:27, orthodox Jews reject shaving with a razor.

9. The seventh day of Sukkoth. For "Shavuot" see the Glossary.

10. Each one studies the Talmud in his own "group."

11. The author describes the folk custom of *Kapores schlagen,* which is widely practiced among traditional Jews on the day before Yom Kippur. In this act of expiation, the man takes a rooster, the woman a chicken, swings it over his or her head, and says penitential prayers, in which the animal is designated as an expiatory sacrifice. Then one slaughters the animal and gives it, or its equivalent in money, to the poor.

12. Burial.

13. *"Jahrzeit"* means the yearly commemoration of the death of one's parents or other close relatives. The Kaddish prayer is said for the deceased person and a Jahrzeit candle is lit. The mourner can also be assigned the function of chanting the prayers in the synagogue.

14. *"Kitsur"* refers to the *Kitsur Schulchan Aruch,* written by Salomon Ganzfried in 1864. This work summarizes the most important commandments and prescriptions of Judaism in their ritual meaning for the life of the orthodox. *Mishnayot* are sections of the Mishna in the Talmud (see the Glossary).

15. *"Chumosh"* is the five books of Moses.

16. "Joy of Sabbath."

17. An *"eruv"* is a "Sabbath border." In orthodox Judaism carrying something on the Sabbath is forbidden as a form of work. Walled cities are regarded as extensions of personal living space, in which carrying is permitted. If the city wall is removed, a symbolic sabbath border, generally a chain, must take its place to permit carrying.

18. Misrachi Zionists are an organization of national-religious Zionists, which was founded in Vilna in 1902. It sought to achieve the Basel Program on the basis of the Torah.

19. This means that he was declared religiously unfit to serve as a ritual slaughterer.

20. In 1891, antisemites accused the ritual slaughterer Buschhoff in Xanten of the ritual murder of a boy who had been found dead. They forced two sensational trials, which ended in acquittal. The later cardinal Georg von Kopp (1837–1914) was bishop of Fulda until 1887, but at the time of the ritual murder trial in Xanten he was already the prince-bishop of Breslau.

21. In 1899, antisemitic representatives in the Reichstag unsuccessfully introduced a bill to ban ritual slaughter as a form of cruelty to animals. Along with experts, it was especially the Centrists who decisively opposed the bill.

22. Beginning in 1876 it was possible in Prussia to withdraw from the Jewish united community without converting. A radical group among the orthodox took advantage of this and

founded separate "secessionist congregations," whereas the majority of the orthodox remained in the united congregations.

23. Samson Raphael Hirsch (1808–1888), the founder of Neo-Orthodoxy, was from 1851 rabbi of the orthodox Israelitische Religionsgesellschaft in Frankfurt am Main. As the author of the withdrawal law of 1876, he created the first secessionist congregation in Frankfurt. His son-in-law, Salomon Breuer (1848–1926), became his successor and in 1890 founded the ultra-orthodox yeshiva and the Verband der Orthodoxen Rabbiner Deutschlands.

24. Scholars.

25. Marcus Horovitz (1844–1910) became the rabbi of the Frankfurt Jewish community in 1878. As a leader of German Jewry, he founded the Allgemeine Rabbinerverband in Deutschland and the Verband Traditionell-gesetzestreuer Rabbiner. Since Horovitz died during Breuer's lifetime, the remark concerning participation at the burial is unclear.

# 21 *Johanna Harris, née Brandes*

 BORN IN 1879 IN OBERAULA (PROVINCE OF HESSE-NASSAU); DIED IN 1964 IN BOSTON.

Johanna Harris-Brandes, My Happy Childhood in the Village: Experiences from the Years 1880–1890. Undated manuscript, 96 pages. Written in the United States.

*With narrative talent the author describes the milieu of her childhood in the Hessian village of Oberaula, in the district of Ziegenhain. Among the one thousand or more inhabitants there were twenty-five Jewish families, who made their living mainly by cattle trade. Johanna's father was the teacher of the state Jewish primary school, conducted the services in the synagogue, and did the kosher slaughtering. In spite of the antisemitism, which was felt everywhere, the Jewish and the Christian teachers of the village were close friends. After all, they shared the bleak and financially sorry situation of belonging to the same professional group. The recollections illustrate the life of simple village Jews, the difficult position of the Jewish teacher as the head of the community, and the rural forms of antisemitism in Hesse.*

Our father was certainly not a brilliant teacher, and certainly no pedagogue. In a city school the children would have laughed in his face, but here this was unthinkable. The children regarded him as something ordained by God and accepted him as such. The children also felt that he was kind to them all, and especially to each one individually. He looked at them with love and kindness when they had learned well, and with concern and distress when they did not succeed. This odd, old teacher had himself remained a child at heart, and the great purity of his heart and his strict morality were of the kind that one encounters only in people who have little contact with the outside world.

As much as possible the teacher protected the children from their own ignorant parents, who were often crude. He did not tolerate their being exploited at home to the limits of their strength, or their being senselessly punished. He can tell by looking at them when things are not right at home. He goes to the parents, listens to them tell why they are dissatisfied with the children, speaks kindly to them, and in the end laughs with them and says: "Have patience, the children are well-behaved and good, tidy and diligent; I won't have you say anything against my schoolchildren. One day you will see how later in life the boy or the girl will stand the test. You will get joy from them yet. Were you angels as children? They have to vent their energies, and just think how hard the children have it, especially when, being poor as we all are, at the age of fourteen they must leave home and face hardship. For God's sake, let the children have a little joy at home, let them frolic." And because the teacher was strict and honest, the parents believed him and knew that the children were in good hands. Even if they didn't like him as a human being, they held him in high esteem as a teacher.

Our father was an autocrat, an absolute ruler. The children of the community were his unlimited domain. If somewhere in his realm a child is born, after school he puts on his little black coat, brushes his shoes to a polish, combs his white hair and his long white beard, and goes to the house where another child has been born to his care. He regards himself as the keeper of order; he attends to things, checks to see whether the woman is doing all right, whether she has everything she needs, in short, whether everything is as it should be. Then, with great satisfaction, he examines the child and ascertains that it is not deformed. Woe, if that were not the case! The child must also be entered into his synagogue register, for in those days births and deaths of Jews were not yet recorded at the registry office, but rather in the synagogue register. Now our father once again feels himself to be the advocate of the newborn. The child's father would give it God-knows-what-kind of old-fashioned, horrible name. He would call it Itzig, Schmuel, Voel, or Hirsch; a girl perhaps even Reis or Mahd. "Nothing doing," my father calls out firmly, "such a name would only bring the child ridicule; it would be mocked and derided because of it. The child shall be registered not as Reis but as Röschen, not as Mahd but as Meta, not as Itzig but as Isidor," etc.

If somewhere a child had become ill, then, too, the teacher put on his boots, went there, and had a look; and if the child turned out to be seriously ill, he kept vigil at the sickbed with the parents and another member of the community. And if one was actually dying, he was called in the dark of night, if he hadn't already been sitting at the bedside from the evening before, and he stayed there until the painful end was over.

At the home of a dying adult the entire community gathers to say the prayers for the dying with him, and afterwards to lift him off the bed and place him upon straw. Only two people remain there to keep vigil. The next day the women gather and together sew the burial shroud. The men make the coffin, and thus burial in accordance with Jewish custom costs little or nothing, so that the mourners are not distracted from their sorrow by money worries.

The death of children especially affects my father, for something is taken from his realm. Just as, according to his words, "no leaf falls from a tree without God's will," that is how unequivocally he thinks about his authority over the handful of people that make up his community.

Once a small, two-year-old child had become so gravely ill that my father decided it would be better for the child if it died, died quickly, rather than endure the agonies of brain fever. On a regular weekday, at twelve o'clock, he sent word to all men of the community that they should immediately appear at the synagogue. It did not take long; not one was missing. "Let us pray that the child die quickly," my father said curtly, as was his way. Without hesitation the entire community did so. Even death could not oppose my father's strict command, and the poor, tortured child died on the same day.

*[The Jewish school is located next to the house of the pastor, who is also the school inspector.]*

The new, young pastor, full of energy, took his office and the school seriously. The difference in the accomplishments of the Christian school as compared to those of the better Jewish school gave him much to think about. Why shouldn't one be able to merge the good school with the inferior one and assign three teachers to the Christian school, which was very big anyway. The old Jewish teacher was employed by the state and really achieved a great deal. The village school would definitely improve. Then, after some time he could be replaced by a Christian teacher, and the Jewish children could get their little bit of religious instruction from anyone. That seemed so good to him that he thought it would be generally accepted.

"Impossible," cried my father when the pastor tried to make this plan palatable to him. "While the peasant children lack all incentive from their parents for learning, the Jewish child enters school full of desire to learn and with a thirst for knowledge, and it is urged at home to learn. An additional factor is that the Christian population, because of the antisemitic Sunday paper and all kinds of other influences, is secretly hostile to its Jewish fellow citizens, and this is passed on to the children. Because of envy and ill-will, there would arise a hostile atmosphere, unwholesome for all of the children, which would be detrimental to any school and teacher."

"Let's try a little experiment," said the pastor, "let's begin by sending the Jewish girls to the knitting school, which is conducted by the local midwife, and I am sure that the children will get along. For the boys I have already arranged for the compulsory gym classes (earlier gym classes were not obligatory), and a friend of mine, a gym teacher, will come here and teach them."

"Herr Pastor," my father cried out delighted, "how nice that we have got such a progressively-minded man as school inspector. Only I think," he continued, "that the prerequisites for common education would first have to be set through example by the leading segment of the population." "How am I to understand that?" asked the pastor, somewhat irritated. "Let us take, for instance, the young Jewish doctor who did his studies not in taverns but over serious books, a very brilliant, well-educated man. Herr Pastor, you, too, are his neighbor, aren't you? Have you, or the district judge, or the postmaster, or the chief forester ever exchanged a word with this man?" "How could I?" the pastor cried. "As a Jew the man stands outside of society, he is not one of our notables. As little as I can associate with the gendarme, much less so can I with a Jew. Incidentally, you mentioned the district judge. Well, he associates as little with the pastor as I associate with the teacher." Father replied: "Excuse me, Herr Pastor, I must go to services. I shall see to it that the girls be sent to the knitting school and the boys to gym lessons. Good day, Herr Pastor."

To start with, Jenny and I were sent to the knitting school. Freshly bathed, neatly combed, dressed in our Sabbath print dresses, the two of us, feeling festive and proud, went to the large Christian school. We curtsied before midwife Borneller and gave her our hand very timidly, for she was a person commanding respect and, for us children, surrounded by a mysterious charm. She looked very clean and distinguished in her attractive peasant costume; she had a rosy face, friendly but serious blue eyes, and neatly parted white hair. She took us by the hand and led us to a school bench very close to her; she smiled at us encouragingly and checked our knitting materials. But we felt shy and insecure among some fifty girls between six and fourteen, all of whom sat there armed with knitting needles. Not a word was spoken, there was deathly silence, one heard only the knitting needles. Little by little we breathed somewhat more freely in that big schoolroom, in which no Jewish child had ever sat before. When we had recovered a little, the knitting, too, became easier; our hands did not tremble any more. Then, through the silence, which was interrupted only by the clattering of the needles, there suddenly resounded a very loud voice, shouting: "Borneller, somethin' stinks, somethin' stinks." Borneller pretended not to hear anything. Then the entire bunch of girls screamed together: "Borneller, the Jews done it, the Jews done it." Neither we nor any other Jewish girl ever went to the knitting school again. [. . .]

Beautiful are the long Friday evenings in winter. But if the evenings are beautiful and long, the days are that much the shorter and busier. Steadily and quickly, we have to break twigs for making fire, because, you see, one is not allowed to do that on the Sabbath. We have to carry the wood behind the stove, clean ten pairs of shoes. The older brothers and sisters must lug plenty of water, scrub the whole house and all the rooms. Mother must cook for two days, one of us must help her with it, another one quickly do the errands. Finally, at four o'clock everything is ready. Then we run to the brook, get washed, no matter how cold it is; our hair is combed, and we all put on our Sabbath clothes. "I hope you didn't forget to make the raisin wine, cool it, and place it beside the delicious homemade *barches,* which is lying under the little cover, so that father can say the blessing over it."

Mother lights the candles, covers her eyes, blesses the candles, and thanks God, who has given us the Sabbath. Then mother sits down in the chair, in which no one else is allowed to sit. She lifts her dress and timidly shows us her swollen legs. Oh how glad she is that once again a working week is over. Then, one by one we go up to mother's chair, bend down, place our head on her lap, and are blessed by her. She speaks the blessing softly, and her hands rest on our heads. Paula quickly places a few blooming flowers on the table, which is covered with a white cloth, and she draws the white curtains. So, now father and our brothers can return from the synagogue. Ah, here they are already. Quickly we look out the window at the people returning home from the synagogue, to see if perhaps there is not a stranger among them, maybe a traveler or a former pupil of my father's here for a visit, or even a beggar; at any rate, something new in our little world. To have a beggar as a guest, who would not like that? One questions them for news about the outside world. But today we have no luck.

Father comes upstairs, casts a stern, searching glance around him to see if all is in order. We go up to him, he blesses us and then speaks the prescribed blessing over the wine and the bread, sings a song in praise of the Sabbath, drinks of the delicious raisin wine, which certainly doesn't make anyone tipsy, and already the wonderful, steaming soup is on the table. Father, pleased, pats mother's back and praises her and says: "As smooth as oil. One could bring a dead man back to life with it." Then there are sweet-and-sour white beans and a piece of meat. "Everything is wonderful," praises father, but mother scolds him because he is gulping down his food too quickly after she spent the whole day cooking it. Then we sing the well-known *"Schir-Hamaalaus,"*[1] and then we pray. My mother, in the meanwhile, inspects with pleasure all the clean, freshly washed children's faces and smiles contentedly. Tears of joy, real, fat, big tears roll down her face. This is mother's troop review. She is the general here, a proud victor. Gloriously she fought the battles of labor, mended baskets full of linen, made all the clothes for the children, fed them with scant means, raised all eight of them, and, something she always mentions with emphasis, "brought all twelve of them into the world, healthy, with straight limbs." She can be content, and she is.

The table is cleared silently, the morris board is fetched. Some play morris with father; he checks to see who pays attention and who does not. He lets the younger children win once in a while, which makes them very proud. Some play lotto. The big children read. This evening mother reads without knitting. Father likes to tell us little stories about horrible ghosts. He makes our flesh creep and afterwards he checks to see whether we are afraid, something he sternly forbids.

*[In the evening the Christian teacher, who is a friend, often comes secretly to visit, which the pastor must not find out.]*

A long shadow of a man stoops in the doorway, so that he does not bump his head, enters, silently gives my parents his hand, and silently sits down on the sofa, the same spot that he has occupied at the same hour for many years now. After a half-hour, when he has recovered from his silence, he gets ready for the conversation. It's the same words; the theme has not varied in all these years. Each one of us knows what he is now going to say. Finally, he forces it out. In a sepulchral voice, which comes from deep down in his chest, he says: "What did you have to pay to smithy Hannes's Liesbeth for butter this week?" "Sixty pfennigs a pound," my mother answers briefly, without interrupting her reading. For half an hour he digests what he heard. My father, his long pipe in his hand, walks around the room probably some twenty times, all the while deep in conversation with himself. He talks vehemently with his hands, now and then he shakes his head, in addition he envelops himself in thick clouds of smoke, gesticulates excitedly, and finally, exhausted and sighing, he sits down beside Gutfreund on the sofa. Now and then Gutfreund shakes his head. Suddenly something occurs to Gutfreund. For a few minutes he grunts in preparation, clears his throat some twenty times, and then it comes out: "What did you pay this week for the eggs?" Interrupted in the middle of her reading, mother first looks at her knitting, then at Gutfreund, sighs, and says: "The butter man pays only two pfennigs apiece, but Trine wants two and a half for them." Terrible sounds of horror, a deep uneasy grunting in place of words come from his corner.

After ten minutes he has again recovered and says: "Well, yes, Trine, she knows what price to ask, that's why she is so fat and her boys are so dumb." Again after a quarter of an hour, an endlessly long grunting and clearing of his throat announce a new tide of words. He looks at my father, who is waiting patiently, and then it comes forth: "Tell me, Moses, have you already read this week's *Preussische Lehrerzeitung* that I sent you?" All this was said very softly and cautiously. Moses, my father, however, could not help being an incorrigibly excitable little man, and without any transition he hurled these words into the face of the bewildered man: "Have you read what Bismarck has again cooked up against us teachers? The additional pay has been denied." At that, Gutfreund, in sudden panic, leaps up, grabs father by the collar, and says quietly: "For God's sake, why are you screaming so, Moses? Such talk will cost you your neck. Don't walls have ears?" While saying this he points with his hands towards the parsonage. Excited, my father jumps to the window, draws the curtains closed, looks up to see if the windows are shut tightly, jumps again to the end of the sofa where Gutfreund is sitting in the farthest corner of the room, quite a distance from the window, takes Gutfreund by his chin and says to him excitedly but quietly: "Listen, I'm telling you, the Social Democrats are right, but one just can't say it. That fellow Bismarck ought to be given the ax!" Gutfreund would never have said a word in reply to something like that, but to someone in the know a very contented smile, long, deep grunting, a clearing of his throat, and peculiar sounds coming from deep within his scrawny chest betray his approval.

"Bebel once again gave such a fine speech," the voice of my mother can be heard. "Did you read in the *Kasseler Tageblatt und Anzeiger* what Paul Singer and Karl Liebknecht said about the Civil Service Pay for Teachers Act?" A long deep grunting substitutes for an answer.

"Yes, yes," my father cries excitedly, "our *Preussische Lehrerzeitung* doesn't print things like that. But I'm telling you, Gutfreund, even if I live to be eighty I will fight until the last day of my life to see that we Jewish teachers get paid for our services as cantor in the synagogue, and you Christians for your services as cantor in the church." Again a long satisfied grunting at the end of the sofa. "Here I get up twice every week at five o'clock and have to lead the prayers for a solid hour in the ice-cold synagogue, because they have to leave so early for the cattle market, and the whole year I don't get a single penny for my services," my father shouts excitedly and, pointing with his index finger toward the parsonage, he continues: "That one over there takes the easy way out, no church begins before ten o'clock in the morning, and he gets paid nicely for it and has his big, fine house, his wonderful garden, and who knows how much in donations."

"Well, I've been playing the organ for twenty-five years now and take care of the second church all by myself," Gutfreund says quietly, all the while shaking his head, "and did I even get a penny for it?"

"Really," my father mocks now, "don't you get those good plums that grow on the graves next to the church?"

"You can have them if your mouth waters for them," Gutfreund grumbles fiercely. "And something else I wanted to say: That one over there is envious of you, scolds his peasants from the pulpit, telling them that they ought to take it as an example that your Jews show up punctually and in full numbers in the synagogue, long before daybreak and again in the evening, not to mention Schabbes and the holidays. Listen, Moses, you really ought to pay something for that," says Gutfreund, and happy about his joke, turns up his narrow lips in a thin smile from one ear to the other.

"If you are out to annoy me, I'll kick you down the stairs, you old blabber," says Papa laughing.

"At your place I always open up so, talk so much. I've become very tired. Good night to all. Don't send me the newspaper so late."

"Give your wife our kind regards," father calls out to him softly on the stairway, and he is gone. On the street, however, he does not belch and grunt. That could betray him, for in the winter he must take the village street. In the summer, on the other hand, he has it good; he can reach us by the narrow little lane along the brook, around the back through the rear door, to pick up father for a walk in the woods. After he has gone, mother smiles indulgently about him and shakes her head, but father jumps to his defense, places himself in front of mother, and cries: "Do you remember how I looked for a wife for him?" "Well," father continues, "it wasn't easy." In his recollections, he is still full of enthusiasm.

"I have to tell you, his sister cheated him out of his patrimony because he was allowed to become a teacher. At that time I told him: 'Listen,' I said, 'you've got to marry a rich woman so that you yet acquire something for yourself. A teacher ought to be a wealthy man. It's the only way that you can command the respect of your peasants.' 'Listen, Moses, never in my life will I be able to manage that, to look for a wife, and a rich one, to boot, no, only you can get an idea like that.' 'Gutfreund,' I answered him, 'leave it to me.' "

In remembering, father begins to feel good and fiery and courageous in his mind and heart. "Of course I didn't take him along anywhere. I looked at the girls and questioned their fathers. A few times things had almost reached the point where the rich peasant wanted to put one over on me, but I told him: 'No, the girl is not educated enough, I don't find her beautiful enough for my best friend.' Finally, then, through a newspaper advertisement I found his present one—tall, strong, and healthy as she is, she had worked in Kassel as a cook, had saved a little. Such a girl, after all, has breeding and polish, and can cook." "But," my mother now says contemplatively, "she hardly utters a word." "That's exactly why she is well suited to him," father says cheerfully, for he has to praise his accomplishment. "I'd like to be a little mouse and listen when the two of them are alone together," mother laughs. "What do you mean," father cries angrily. "Of course, he can't compare himself with me, but they did manage to have three children. One of them died. Well, that could happen to anyone, especially since he is somewhat consumptive. Oh no, I won't have anything said against him, he is my friend, my only friend.—Good night, my little madam. It is my pleasure to go to bed, and I think you, too, have read enough. You don't have to read the whole newspaper. You don't have to devour it completely. Good night, then, my sweet, cool, white rose. Ha, you can be glad you have a fire-spewing, boiling volcano for a husband," and with a loving glance at his wife who keeps on knitting and reading, the old teacher warbles cheerfully: "You are my rest, you are my peace, sent me by the Lord above," and betakes himself to the icy regions of his bedroom.

Except for Gutfreund, my father had no other friend in the village and did not associate with anyone. His Jews are much too uneducated for him. Cattle trade does not contribute to refinement. It is not a nice business; one can feel very sorry for them. When you hear how neighbor Justus negotiates over his oxen, your hair stands on end. Justus has raised the oxen from their birth. According to his own words, he loves them like his own children. Indeed, one day he said to my mother: "I would rather see my Mariechen carried from the farm to the cemetery than my oxen." Mariechen was a somewhat backward, weakly little thing, who couldn't work much. His oxen, however, *they* could work, *they* helped to cultivate the hilly, rocky field. After all, the farmer judges the creature by the work it gets done.

He had to sell them, his strong oxen. They, the hardworking ones, had to be slaughtered so that the abominable townspeople, who were too lazy, too weak for field work, could enjoy their meat. He couldn't vent his rage on the city people, but he could on the miserable Jew who bought his oxen and led them away. Oh, Justus needed the money to buy a good many things, especially his beloved liquor, which the damned innkeeper—"worse than a Jew"—didn't let him have without cash. And the worst thing of all was that on the strength of this deal he had already been borrowing money from the Jew throughout the summer, so that he didn't even get that much from it any more. Probably close to ten times he chased the Jew from his farm with the nastiest terms of abuse, which can't be repeated here. He got up his courage and rage with drink whenever he saw the Jew coming, in order to be able to curse and insult him even more crudely. He knew, after all, that the Jew would come back. The Jew-trader knew his real feelings; he wasn't squeamish and he came again and again, until Justus urgently needed the rest of the money, and until he could take the oxen along.

And just as with Justus, that is the way it was with most of the peasants. The field was barren and rocky, the harvest often not adequate to feed the big family; cash was needed for things that the peasant could not produce, like sugar, rice, fabric for the Sunday suit, shoes, and above all for the liquor, which the peasant, working hard as he did, didn't want to be without. He borrows the money from the Jew. Of course he deals with him, even gets some cash from doing it. But he has many debts, church taxes, school taxes, and whatever he still has to pay to brother and sister after taking over the little farm. So he is inevitably tied to the Jew.

Extensive cattle breeding was impossible. The cattle could not always be sent to pasture, because in the winter they couldn't be outside in the ice and snow; not even the sheep—they, too, had to winter in the barn. Throughout the short summer the cattle, oxen as well as cows, had to pull the plow, bring home the wagons, in short, they helped cultivate the field. If cows work hard, they produce little milk, and it is used up by the big family of the peasant, which rarely eats meat.

The peasant puts the blame for all his worries, all his bad misfortune on the Jew. And when finally the long awaited Sunday arrives and he would like to forget his troubles for a short while amidst the pious singing in church, he once again hears how the Jews crucified his Savior and Redeemer. The pastor, who does not know what he should keep telling the stupid peasants, depicts this crucifixion in as hair-raising and bloodthirsty a way as possible, as if it had happened only yesterday. The peasant thinks: "That's how I, too, am crucified every day," and his aversion swells to hatred. Not the lean earth, not the hard drinking, not the big family, no, the Jew is to blame for everything.

Whether the Jew frequently put one over on the drunken peasant or not, who can tell. Wherever there are people on this earth, there are always two kinds, honest and dishonest, good and bad. There is no such thing as only good ones or only bad ones. And then the peasant, who knew no way out of his need, often preferred the Jew who lent him money to the cassock of the pastor in the pulpit, to whom he could not go to borrow, or to the miserable do-nothing, the teacher. For such people he had to pay out money, for a teacher who kept the children in the useless school when he badly needed them for work in the field.

My father, however, hated those Jews of whom it was said that they had cheated this or that peasant out of everything he owned, hated them with such burning hatred that words failed him. And where did he show them his hatred, his disgust, his contempt? After all, he never got together with them, except in the House of Worship. Here, then, when they stand there, their prayer shawls wrapped tightly around them, huddled in deep prayer, when they fervently kiss the Holy Scripture, my father looks at them with a frightening look and says to them in a low voice: "Usurer, hypocrite, corrupter."

Indeed, he even forgot himself to the extent that he spat in front of them in the House of God. He did not sit down among them when he did not have to stand in front of the altar, but rather apart, among his school children. The old teacher was an upright man, but not very wise in the ways of the world. The devil would have been let loose, and above all my father would not have been able to keep his office, for the ones whom he insulted thus were the few wealthy and powerful ones in the community and had a lot of say. My mother, however, with a calm look and clever words, with hands that spoke soothingly, set things in order again. She hid behind the door when, after such scenes, the men were leaving the synagogue; then, of all times, she had to catch a hen in the yard, or she took the twig broom in her hand and had to quickly sweep it. She intercepted the men in question. Whatever was said then wasn't much, but it was like oil on the excited tide and calmed the embittered men.

Alas, there still were many in the community who had no goodwill toward my father. All these men who the whole week long ran from village to village with a herring and a piece of black bread in their pocket, a heavy bundle on their back, strenuously driving the cattle before them, and who at home also cultivated their meadows and fields, all those who, dirty and tired, worked themselves to death all week long, they were to be dictated to by this teacher, this do-nothing, as to what they should and should not do! On top of that he wanted to get paid for it. He didn't want to take gifts. "Zdoko," charity, that is, as the Holy Scripture commands it; fine, they would practice that. But he wanted to be paid for it, to be paid for leading the prayers. He did not want to accept alms, whereas he should have done it out of piety. No, this teacher ought to be thrown out. But he was employed by the state, they were powerless. Also, each one of them—touch wood—had eight or nine, or even ten children. The children learned well from him, and so one had to bottle up one's rage and say nothing. This dogged conflict lasted for thirty-five years.

When father celebrated his fiftieth anniversary at the job, the community gave him as a present two silver fruit bowls, or better, centerpieces for a table, which one was supposed to fill with fruit. Father had not even known that something like that existed. No one in the community had known it, but someone in town had talked them into it, telling them that this was something "very fine," and, after all, he always wanted to be so refined. In order not to tax the wallets of the different members of the community too heavily with this purchase, they had had the ancient, tall oak trees in the Jewish cemetery chopped down and had sold them. When the old teacher heard that because of these silly, useless centerpieces they had had the old, venerable oaks cut down, under which he wanted to rest from his life's hardships, indeed, under which he had ordered that he be buried, the hoary man raged like wild: "I'll throw their gifts in their faces, along with the decoration of the fourth class" (which was to be presented to him in public by the district administrator). "Let Kaiser Wilhelm add his errand boy's medal to his other riches, I don't want it, I refuse to accept it," shouted my father, red as a beet from anger. My mother certainly had a difficult task getting him to the point of accepting these things in silence. During the ceremony itself, when the district admin-istrator, the district school inspector, and the rabbi of the province delivered their addresses to him, there hovered above the entire gathering something like an uneasy oppressiveness, like a storm cloud, for the one so greatly honored stepped from one foot to the other, looked at no one, acted as if he were bored, and as if the entire festivity bored him. He looked only at Gutfreund, who stood in a corner, his hand pressed desperately over his lean chin and thin mouth, as if he wanted to say, as he often did: "Listen, Moses, your talk will cost you your neck yet." His eyes did not leave his friend. The district administrator, who noticed the tortured expression of the man being honored, wanted to add something especially nice, something personal. He spoke of the numerous grandchildren of the old teacher. But precisely this was a sore point. Certainly he had a few grandchildren, whom, however, he had never seen and never wanted to see. His sons had married Christians. His daughters had not been able to marry because he could not give them a dowry. Angrily, my father made a fist, his eyes spoke: "Be quiet! I don't want to hear another word!"

1. An introduction to the prayers sung after the meal.

# 22  *Max Daniel*

BORN IN 1891 IN BUBLITZ (FARTHER POMERANIA); DIED IN 1963 IN SAN FRANCISCO.

Max Daniel, The Story of My Family. Manuscript dated San Francisco, 1963, 15 pages.

*Max Daniel was born in the small Pomeranian district town of Bublitz, where his father Sally [Sol] was a wholesale merchant in wool, leather, and iron. He reports about the activities of his father as chairman of the Jewish community and about the consequences for Bublitz of the charge of ritual murder in Konitz. In 1901 the family moved to Stargard, in 1905 to the capital of the province, Stettin, and later to Berlin. In Stettin, the port of departure for emigrants, his father founded a welfare organization for Jews in transit from Russia. Max Daniel studied pharmacy, became a pharmacist, emigrated during the Nazi period to the United States, and, until 1963, had his own pharmacy in San Francisco.*

On the whole, the Jews did well in Bublitz, also in regard to their economic existence. It didn't make a difference where one made one's purchases, people were friendly and comradely to one another, and I know that genuine friendships between Jews and Christians had existed for generations.

After grandfather's death my father was elected first chairman of the Jewish community. The Jewish community had a *Chewra Kadischa*.[1] Mostly, a meeting was held once a year, and in some years there was a dinner at a Jewish restaurant. Generally the community kept kosher. The butchers had their cattle slaughtered according to Jewish rites by the synagogue official, and they greatly appreciated the higher price for the kosher meat. The peasants brought their goods to the weekly market in the town and preferred the Jewish customers, since they received better prices from them for special, less common wares.

I know that in the town of 5,000 inhabitants there was *one* real antisemite, who was generally referred to as Rosche Hahn, as distinguished from the other Hahn families. In 1898 the Konitz ritual murder affair brought unrest, and in Neustettin the synagogue was burned down by antisemitic arsonists.[2] The culprits were never found. In our town, too, one side of our cemetery's wooden fence was set on fire. The fire was discovered right away, and more serious damage was prevented. Schoolchildren sang the song:

> Isn't it awful
> What happened in Konitz:
> The pack of Jews slaughtered
> The Gymnasium pupil Winter.

When this reached the ears of the superintendent of the Lutheran church, he immediately took action. He assembled the whole school and announced that any child heard singing these verses would have to go to school an additional year as punishment.

At exactly the worst time there was once again a fair in Bublitz. Among the exhibitors in the marketplace, not far from our house, there was a Jewish merchant with gingerbread. It was in the afternoon hours, when the country folk had already drunk a good deal, that suddenly we saw a huge crowd around the booth. A peasant lout was shouting: "That's the Konitz murderer." The people roared in response and were about to assault the poor exhibitor. Then my father ran out of the store, picked up a gnarled stick, grabbed the troublemaker by the scruff of his neck, threw him to the ground, and beat him until the stick broke into pieces. The beaten man couldn't move for the pain; later, people helped him to get up. No one in the crowd stirred, they drew back frightened and quickly disappeared.

After my father had finished the job, he brought the rescued merchant and his wares to the safety of our house. As he was entering the house, he saw the policeman standing idly by the town hall on the opposite side of the street. Braun was not exactly popular among the Jews. My father then left fly at him, calling out loudly across the square, asking whether that is the way he conceived of his job, or whether he was supposed to help someone in need. Braun was probably afraid to hear even more from my father and retreated into the town hall. This decisive behavior also made a deep impression on the Christian citizens, who later came to us in swarms to thank Sally Daniel.

I can say with justified pride that my father was the friend of the whole town. What he said, counted. All matters pertaining to . . . organizations were deliberated under his chairmanship, and he also belonged to all of them. He was active in many posts in the municipal administration. The burgomaster often came to our place to consult with him. He belonged to the group of auditors in the municipal savings bank, and he was the head of the building commission. Whether it was the gymnastics club or the citizens' aid society or the choral society, he always set the trend. Whenever these clubs had their gatherings or dances, he and my mother were always present. In addition, he was a good dancer and led the contredanse and the polonaise. In the country, it was the same. He was always invited to weddings with my mother. Even if they didn't have the time to attend, they still gave presents. He did not participate in parades of the rifleman's guild and the veteran's associations; my grandfather had done that in his day. [. . .]

In the summer of 1897 there was a song festival, to which the choral societies from the other towns in Farther Pomerania came. In front of our house a platform was set up and decorated with much greenery. Then, when the parade of the societies marched with a band through the town, it stopped by our house and my father delivered his address from there. In the evening there was also dancing in all the halls of the town. A commemorative newspaper appeared, published by the Bublitz district paper, to which my father contributed many poems. Thus there was always something going on in this small town, and because of that life never became boring. The Jews took an active interest in all these pleasures.

Religious life also was greatly cultivated by the Jews and offered much stimulation. People went to the synagogue regularly. On the festival of *Simchas Torah* the young people were invited for a shower of sweets in the afternoon, after the decoration of the Torah. Before the evening services we boys placed nuts under the folding seats, and when the old gentlemen sat down, there was a cracking sound, which was great fun for us. If we could, we tried it again. On this evening we were easily forgiven, for, after all, it was the joyful festival of the Torah. On the holiday of Schawues my mother had magnificent crowns of flowers, which she had gotten from the gardener, placed on the Torah scrolls. These decorated Torah scrolls were a wonderful sight.

In October of 1905 we moved to Stettin. There a delightful time began for all of us. The schools were excellent and we felt happy there. Stettin was a very liberal city, friendly to the Jews. The department stores all belonged to Jews; the Jews also dominated in other branches of business. Class prejudice no longer existed here, except among Jewish academicians, who fancied themselves superior and thought they lived accordingly. I attended the Realgymnasium, simply called the Friedrich-Wilhelm school. There I spent my most beautiful school years.

There was a lively spirit in the Jewish community, inspired especially by the outstanding rabbi, Dr. Heinemann Vogelstein.[3] Lectures were presented regularly in the Literary Society. The evenings were well attended, and I didn't skip a single one. Also, in 1905 the Jewish Gymnastics Club was founded, which had a Zionist ideal as its basis. At the beginning there were many people who did not want that. But in a relatively short time the membership of this club increased considerably. [. . .]

Soon after our arrival, the Jewish community of Stettin entrusted my father with an office that he held for all the years that we lived there. (Already during his days in Stargard he was asked by the chairman to share with him the burdens of the congregation.) He was charged with the supervision of the *Chewra Kadischa,* as well as with marking the place during the Torah readings and looking after the itinerant beggars. The latter liked to come to him, since they knew that he also gave them much from his own pocket and on every Sabbath brought poor people home from the synagogue for a meal.

It was 1905. The Russo-Japanese war brought to the port of Stettin many Jews from Poland and Russia. There were pogroms there, and whoever could fled from those countries.[4] My father then created a refugee organization. It was thanks to his effort that everything went off peacefully in our city. A house was rented as quarters. My father immediately turned to the Hilfsverein der Deutschen Juden and to the Alliance Israélite Universelle to get subsidies for his plan.[5] The means were very modest, but I am sure that he contributed personally. A Jewish mailman with his family was placed in this house to manage it. The house, in the old part of Stettin, had four floors. On the first floor lived the mailman, and that is also where the common kitchen was. On the upper floors were the lodgings. Now, this shelter had to be protected against any kind of abuse by the transients, and also the meals had to be cooked. That is where Frau Vogelstein, the rabbi's wife, helped. My father had also gotten my mother very much interested in it, and thus there were seven ladies, each of whom offered to work there one day a week, from morning until evening. An exact account of the guests, which could be examined by the police at any time, was kept. Every day refugees came, rarely with some money, mostly without any.

The means that were available sufficed at most for rent and board, but not for the further journey. Once again, an idea of my father's helped: Travelers were to earn the travel money themselves. He saw to their employment in Jewish businesses. The money that each person earned was handed over to the committee and saved until there was enough—also to meet the requirements for Canada. The shipping company of Consul Kunstmann[6] and also the Stettin Steamship Company permitted passengers to be taken along without payment—not in all cases, but as far as possible. Furthermore, when the money was exhausted a collection was taken up among the members of the Jewish community. This service, performed by both my parents with much love, made them very happy. The greatest number of émigrés came in the years 1905–1910. It was a beneficent activity that was carried out there, and everyone could be helped. Anyone could help himself through the work that was arranged for him, and thus he did not have the depressing feeling of helplessness.

The itinerant beggars in Poland also knew that my father gave freely. One day a servant in the office found a printed book about many German cities, with a list of whom to look up and how to behave in each instance. Of my father one could read: "Is at home at two o'clock and is charitable." Of another gentleman, also a member of the committee, it said that one should talk to him only about Torah.

 

1. The *Chewra Kadischa* ("Holy Society") is a society for the care of the sick and burial of the dead, which traditionally exists in every Jewish community.

2. The ritual murder incident in Konitz (West Prussia) did not begin until 1900, when antisemites accused Jews of the murder of a Gymnasium pupil. During the subsequent trials, pogroms took place in 1901 in Konitz and in cities in Pomerania, in the course of which the synagogue in Konitz was destroyed. The synagogue of Neustettin, on the other hand, had already gone up in flames in 1881, when the first antisemitic riots occurred in Pomerania.

3. Heinemann Vogelstein (1841–1911) was rabbi in Stettin from 1880 on. He became the founder and president of the Vereinigung liberaler Rabbiner as well as recognized leader of the religious-liberal trend in German Judaism.

4. Beginning in 1881, violent pogroms repeatedly took place in Russia, which caused more than one million Jews to emigrate. In 1905, the year of the first Russian Revolution, the October pogroms claimed over 800 victims.

5. The Alliance Israélite Universelle, founded in 1860 in Paris, like the Hilfsverein der Deutschen Juden, founded in Berlin in 1901, rendered help to the East European Jewish emigrants. The Hilfsverein ran the Zentralbüro für jüdische Auswanderungsangelegenheiten (Central Office for Jewish Emigration Matters), created in 1904. On the Hilfsverein, see the memoirs of Bernhard Kahn (31) and the Introduction.

6. Wilhelm Kunstmann (1844–1934) founded in Stettin and Swinemünde the largest private shipping company belonging to a Jewish shipowner.

# 23  *Edmond Uhry*

BORN IN 1874 IN INGWILLER (INGWEILER, ALSACE); DIED IN 1954 IN NEW YORK.

Edmond Uhry, Galleries of Memory. Manuscript dated 1946, New York.

*Edmond Uhry grew up in the small Alsatian town of Ingwiller (pop. 2,250). His father owned a general store, but also dealt in cattle and grain, and ran a little hotel with restaurant. The author describes life in Ingwiller, including Jewish orthodox life there, in detail, and stresses the dislike of the inhabitants for the North German officials who were installed after the annexation. Uhry attended the Gymnasium in Bouxwiller and emigrated at the age of sixteen to America, where two of his brothers received him. In New York he worked his way up to the status of a medium-level businessman and became a board member of the Free Synagogue of Rabbi Stephen S. Wise. The following excerpt describes his emigration in 1891.*

*[The following material has been taken from the original manuscript written in English.]*

I was not quite ten years old when my oldest brother, Emile, left for America in March 1884. The German laws with reference to emigration affecting males specified that a request for exclusion from the German Union had to be filed before the age of seventeen. This was called securing an *Entlassungs-Urkunde*. When granted, departure had to be made within six months from the date of issue, otherwise permission would be revoked and the person's name retained on the list of eligibility for military service at age twenty.

There was some slip-up in Emile's case. Two days before Pesach, it was discovered that the time of grace would expire on the first day of Pesach. No preparations for travel equipment and steamship accommodation had been made. It was decided that he must leave home before sunrise the next morning, which was Erev Pesach.

A good friend assisted in this, taking him not to the railroad station nearest our town, but to one farther away, from where he could not be so easily traced. He went to Romanswiller to our aunt, and there, after the holiday, our parents met him with his bag and baggage. He then went on to France and embarked from Le Havre to the United States.

The authorities were very prompt in checking up on his time of departure and destination, but all went smoothly. [. . .]

I vividly recall the gloom at the Seder table with the empty chair of the first-born, and also the feeling of responsibility I shared through the importance of secrecy in this matter.

Parents of this era wonder how those of that day could bring themselves to send to the four corners of the earth their teen-age boys. Each mile of distance equaled ten of today. Ocean travel was slow and dangerous and the expectation of a Wiedersehen more remote than now. And yet nearly every family in our town sent boys out into the world. Greater opportunity and more freedom in new lands were inducements, but taken less into account in making the decision than was the fact of compulsory military service.

Three years of this was looked upon with great dread. We lived in frontier country in an atmosphere charged with Prussian militarism. We were a people resentful of the injustices of the Bismarckian system and continually fearful of the recurrence of war. Escape from this by their sons took the sting out of the pain of parting, and there was in some cases the hope for an eventual permanent family reunion on the ground staked out by their pioneering sons.

The United States and a few of the South American countries held the greatest attraction for them. Wherever one from a town would settle, others from the same district would join him. New Orleans was the first point of destination for most of the early émigrés from our section. Some of our family came there in pre–Civil War days. The French atmosphere of Louisiana appealed to them. I was thrilled to find in the Building of Inventions and Patents at the Century of Progress Fair in 1939 the facsimile of a steam engine patented in 1852 by Uhry, resident of Louisiana. Cincinnati also became a point of vantage and long preceded New York as a place of settlement. Through business and marriage the émigrés spread out through the South.

My brother Moise came to New York in 1886. I still can feel the state of anxiety that hung over the family during the ten days of his crossing. About that time there had been a fatal accident on the Atlantic. Mother prayed throughout the days and nights. When a cable announced his safe arrival in New York, I galloped through the streets to broadcast the good tidings. [. . .]

The realization that the time for a decision as to my vocation was at hand weighed heavily on the minds of my parents. Advice was sought from many sources. Military service and war clouds became important factors, but by October [1890] my departure for the United States became the definite solution. [. . .]

Several matters, trivial from our present-day viewpoint, but of importance in that day, caused a delay of several months in my departure. First, there was the crossing of the Atlantic in winter; next the assembling of a suitable wardrobe; and lastly my absence from the festivities in connection with the dedication of the remodeled synagogue. The ready-to-wear age was far off. It took several trips to Strasbourg and Saverne to get things together. When Mr. and Mrs. Simson of New York visited relatives in our town, they suggested that I join them on their boat, the Umbria, in late November. This was October, and their kind offer was declined for the reason that my underwear had not yet been bought. The fact that I never had worn underwear gave this matter additional build-up for comedy. It had to be Dr. Jaeger's sanitary wear, manufactured in Stuttgart, twenty-eight suits, in assorted sizes. Mr. Simson, who became my first employer in New York, often referred to this when he charged me with the speedy execution of a special order.

The importance of the synagogue dedication was chiefly due to pressure from without. From the time I was fifteen, and in the absence of better, I was lionized as a leader in the junior social set from three to ten years above my age. I brought in new songs, kissing games, directed Kasperle Theatres (Punch and Judy shows), and wrote rotten rhymes for special occasions, an incurable disease recurring in these days. Common sense, and some pressure from my brothers from this side [United States], overcame these deterring considerations, and a second-class passage was bought on the steamship La Bourgogne, sailing from Le Havre on January 10, 1891.

There were farewell trips to relatives, packing and repacking of trunk and valises. Repacking became necessary by the continuous influx of "just a little trifle" that each of about fifteen or twenty families wanted me to take along for relatives dispersed throughout the United States. These "trifles" ranged from a ten-pound box of green mustard through bottles of brandy, handkerchiefs, stockings, chocolates, to pastries, mostly molasses cakes (syrup-kuchen), unobtainable in the American "wilderness." Some of these suppliers stayed around to see that their packages were safely placed in the trunk and kept repeating their instructions about prompt deliveries. I had secret plans as to the disposal of some of those containing chocolates and pastries, but several days of mal de mer disturbed them.

After my trunk was locked and bound, one of the mixers of the sticky cakes brought a salad bowl filled with more of her specialty and insisted that container and all be stuck in somewhere. I was home alone at that time, and her insistence led to a heated argument between us, resulting in the loss of my voice for several days, and the permanent loss of a tenor in the making.

The day of parting, Wednesday, January 7, 1891, came all too soon. The weather was cold and dreary, the countryside bleak, the heart heavy. But the adventure before me and the youthful curiosity were sustaining. [. . .] I was on my way to the Promised Land, to a new life.

My father accompanied me to Saverne. A fifteen-year-old boy from Bouxwiller joined me there. We arrived in Paris on Thursday morning, where Mr. and Mrs. Issac Levy, friends of friends of my folks, met me. I was their house guest until Friday night, when they took me to the Gare St. Lazare for the boat-train leaving at midnight.

It was a frightening experience for me to find myself overnight transplanted from our city of 2,200 to this ocean of humanity and into this cyclone of motion. Mr. Levy took me to his store on the Boulevard Montmartre, and when he thought I was sufficiently acclimated to the panorama of traffic, recommended a walk along the Boulevards. Crossing a street felt like being caught in the rushing current that drove the wheels of the flour mills at home, into which nobody ever ventured. In my bewilderment, hopping from one miracle and show window to another, I would lose my sense of direction. My impression of courtesies from passersby and the readiness of the gendarmes who lent me their protecting hands like personal escorts will never vanish from my memory. I was happy when night came and when my hosts suggested that I retire early since they had to return to their place of business.

I had never seen or used gas or electric light. My brother, who had lived in Colmar, where there was gas illumination, had warned me against the dangers of blowing out the light or not completely shutting off the gas, or worst of all of finding a jet that turned all the way around. This latter was a rare occurrence but I managed to meet it there. Light on again, off again, until my last match was used. Exhausted, I fell into the arms of Morpheus with the light on. I awoke with a start in the dark room. My host on his return home had quietly turned off the gas while I slept soundly. Sure that the gas was escaping when I awoke, I sat by the open window through this cold January night.

My mother had instructed me to buy a bonbonniere for my hostess at Paris. Instead I purchased two pounds of Felix Potin cooking-chocolate. When the time for presentation came, I was bashful and weakened, and my over-supply of the sweet was swelled by this undelivered gift. My traveling companion and I finished it en route to Le Havre, and thus had the second all-night chocolate-spree of our trip. [. . .]

We sat up from Paris to Le Havre from midnight to seven A.M. in a third-class compartment with Italian immigrant families, howling babies, cursing fathers, weary mothers.

On arrival at Le Havre the steerage passengers were served an onion soup breakfast on the dock. As second-class passenger, I was entitled to a breakfast in the dining salon that did much to compensate me for the heartaches and anxieties of the past days. [. . .]

Thus endeth the story of my life as a European from my birth in April 1874 to my departure from Le Havre on January 10, 1891.

# 24 *Isidor Hirschfeld*

BORN IN 1868 IN KASPARUS (WEST PRUSSIA); DIED IN 1937 IN HAMBURG.

Isidor Hirschfeld, Diary. Undated manuscript, 75 pages. Written in Hamburg in 1921.

*Isidor Hirschfeld's mother ran a country pub in West Prussia; his father went peddling with horse and wagon. At the age of fourteen Isidor was apprenticed to a Jewish textile business in Preussisch-Stargard; at the age of eighteen he went to Berlin. In 1893, together with his brother Joseph he established the Bros. Hirschfeld ladies' wear company in Hamburg, which by 1912 did 2.4 million marks' worth of business yearly and had over five hundred employees in sales and production. The company opened branches in Bremen, Lübeck, Leipzig, and Chemnitz. With naive pride the author tells of his rapid social ascent until the World War.*

Our parent's house, newly built in 1875, was awfully big, not only for *my* thinking in those days but also according to the opinion of the people living in the area. It had four rooms on the first floor, a large room where guests ate and drank, and, adjacent to it, the storehouse, which was divided by a goods counter; next to it was a better room, which was in fact the bedroom, living room, and dining room, but it was also used for the "better" guests. Then there was the grand room, where the most distinguished guests were entertained, like head foresters, chief forestry superintendents, and others; and the fourth room was the family room, where the children slept, girls, boys, by twos or also by threes (the third one was laid at the foot of the bed). I slept with Emil in the guest room on a specially built table that could be converted into a bed in the evening. We went to sleep although the guests were still conversing noisily, with much spitting, and drinking hard liquor.

This liquor, corn whiskey, which father distilled himself, was called "Bumchen," and a "Bumchen" cost five pfennigs. There were people who drank a great amount of "Bumchen" and then, when drunk, started a quarrel. Often fights started, too. Then mother intervened with her energetic voice. Sometimes it also happened that she slapped such an adolescent. At any rate, the guests had respect for my mother. Of course, there was a lot of talk about politics and the restoration of Poland. In the evening, some even brought along the Posen "Polish News" to the tavern, and often at the end they sang the old song "Poland is not lost yet . . . "

Today, when the restoration of the Polish state has become a reality, I have to think of Windthorst's[1] words: "A legitimate will, enegetically asserted, will become reality."

Weddings, too, were celebrated in the tavern, and then there was much lively dancing. The sale of beer was the main business on these occasions, for once the people were in a whirl and drank a beer for 10 pfennigs after every dance, they did not notice that in the meanwhile it was being mixed with water; then a barrel of beer brought in perhaps three marks more.

Timber deals were concluded at our place, and that brought good business. On the other hand, people from the Berlin government came, forestry commissioners and chief forestry superintendents, who, because of the good and inexpensive meals, had reserved lunch or even a room. Lunch cost 2 marks, a room for the night 50 pfennigs; it was, so to speak, first-rate. Father was also a Royal Prussian Forestry Accountant for 15 marks per month. He probably wasn't able to do the bookkeeping for that; my sister Emma took care of it.

In 1912, when I visited Kasparus with Frieda, I was very disappointed by our house, which had once seemed so "big." Now I found the house small. I found the rooms so small and especially with such low ceilings that I bent down instinctively in order not to bump my head against them. But I found many beautiful memories of home and parents. I rode out to our land, and to our beautiful big meadow by the water, met many friends, especially my friend Peter Koclawski, who had become the village magistrate but had left his job on account of the school strike. He had seventeen children and was doing fairly well. I drank a bottle of wine with him and we talked about our youth. He, too, had been a forest worker. I also saw my wet-nurse again, the old Manuczewski, who was seventy and who had been a servant in my parents' house when I was born. I asked her in the presence of Frieda if she still remembered the little boy who was born at the time when she served at Frau Hirschfeld's. "Oh," she said, "his name was Isidorek." I told her that I was this Isidorek, gave her presents, and she couldn't get over it and kept crying out in Polish: "Boże, Boże, God oh God." I could not converse with her since now I can speak only fractured Polish, but I could see how happy she was, and afterwards she brought us a basket of eggs. To the church in Kasparus I donated 1,000 marks.

There were twelve of us children at home. Father's sister, Aunt Ida, also lived with us. In short, it was a big household. Mother was unusually efficient; she always managed to do her work. Of course, she got up as early as five o'clock in the morning. That is when the first customers came for their brandy. Mother took care of the children, the household, and the animals, and also of the guests and the store. Father was mostly on the road. And everything got done! In the evening she still mended and knitted and darned—how mother managed all that is still a mystery to me today. We never had a doctor; with so many children everything was treated with home remedies. [. . .]

Until about 1875 we still had an observant home. Mother came from an orthodox family, father was more liberal. On Saturday no business was transacted; the customers had to plan accordingly. The restaurant business was, however, open; that was an official regulation. But nothing was sold in the store. During the Easter holidays the business was completely closed, or rather, as the Jewish Easter prayer book prescribes, it was entrusted for a period of eight days to a third person so that our Easter cakes (matzos) did not come into contact with bread.[2] Also on the High Holy Days in the fall the business was closed and our parents went with us boys for services to Schliewitz, so that we would get to know the customs and prayers. We associated with the neighboring Jewish families, and this happened on occasions of joy and of sorrow. If there was a *bris* somewhere, one went there so that ten Jewish men *(minyan)* were present, and in cases of death one naturally showed the greatest sympathy and was ready to help.

*[In 1882 Isidor Hirschfeld becomes an apprentice in nearby Preussisch-Stargard.]*

My three years went by very quickly. Soon I was relieved from the dry-goods stockroom. I was sent up front as a temporary helper to the aprons, pants, and dress-cloth stockrooms, and finally to the linen stockroom. For the latter only meticulous people, who packed neatly, were taken, because all white fabrics were wrapped there in paper. I still remember Fränkel's tablecloths with their measurements of 200 by 280 centimeters.

It was the second year of my apprenticeship. The shop clerks told me that I was efficient, that I was doing the job of a clerk. Trousseaus, to which the boss tended, were the most important item in the business. The clerk lent a hand with the wares. At this I held my own. I was a great help to my boss. I didn't wait for the boss to ask for the wares. I figured it out myself and handed my boss the items that sold well. That was appreciated, and I was in my boss's favor. He had faith in me. If something important had to be taken care of, then I had to do it; if large sums had to be taken to the post office, something that otherwise only the bookkeeper did, I was now the one to do it. Sums of up to 30,000 talers were entrusted to me. If I received instructions to do something, I did it quickly and didn't make any private visits. The other workers were furious about it. They said I wanted only to gain the favor of the boss and the clerks. I didn't pay any attention to the fools. The bosses and clerks always gave me credit for that. I also did jobs on my own and did not wait until the task was assigned to me. I simply found work myself. In general, I was ever eager to seize the initiative, and it was always the right thing.

Once, however, I had to take serious reproaches, and my boss's liking for me threatened to disappear. Father had debts on goods for 400 to 500 marks with my boss and didn't dare to borrow new credit. Our rival firm, H. M. Wolfheim, offered him credit and father made purchases there for about 400 marks. My boss discovered that and seriously reproached me, since he was of the opinion that I had taken my father there. It was due to the fact that father was short of money.

My three years of apprenticeship were coming to an end, and I was summoned to the boss. He asked me if I wanted to stay. I said yes, but mentioned that I could not work for a small salary (the qualified workers received 15 marks per month and free board and lodgings). He proposed 15 marks per month, and after four months 35 marks per month, which I happily accepted. That I could report to my parents, and it should prove to them that I was capable. [ . . .]

Our way of doing business was outdated; there were no fixed prices. We had to name a price, and the customer made an offer. For that reason, every transaction was difficult. Although one learns a lot from it, we already saw then that our way of transacting business needed reforms. Thus clerks were engaged who were supposed to introduce innovations in order to improve business. We got a clerk whose name was Lindenstrauss. He was a so-called "grabber," who conducted business in the following way: On a ticket he wrote "Reserved for Lubkowski, 27½ talers," and attached this ticket to a suit. If a customer came who was inclined to buy, he waited on him; he talked with him about military matters and farming, and finally said: "Friend, how much money do you have in your pocket?" If the answer was "30 talers," then he said: "Listen, I have a first-class suit. To be sure, it is reserved for my friend Lubkowski. I'll be more generous with you. Here, you can have it, as you see, for 27½ talers." The deal was made. I write this only as a description of what is meant by a so-called efficient "grabber" of a salesman. In those days there was no such thing as posted prices, clear to everyone, but instead every deal involved haggling. Our boss, however, didn't like this "grabbing" business. Lindenstrauss was dismissed. He went to Berlin and got a job at the Golden 110.

We also had a wholesale business. Merchants—mostly Jews—from the neighboring villages were our loyal customers. The institution of the traveling salesman, however, spread, and the wholesale dealers from Berlin sent them to the small villages. We lost these customers, since people preferred to buy from traveling salesmen.

In the fall of 1884 I got a letter from Joseph saying that he had received the "order" from Uncle Meyer to write to me that I should come to Berlin. Berlin, then! The dream of every clerk from the province! To be sure, there was not yet a position. But Uncle would find one. Some said I was being "hoodwinked" to Berlin, but I jumped at the opportunity.

*[Isidor Hirschfeld works for Sielmann and Rosenberg in Berlin; in 1889 he becomes their branch manager in Hamburg, where in the fall of 1893 he opens his own ready-made clothes shop with his brother Joseph.]*

In December we could already tell ourselves that our existence was no longer in danger. We felt that in Hamburg our way was acceptable. We wrote our parents, who then promised to visit us at Christmas time. We prepared everything to make our parents' stay in Hamburg pleasant. First we planned the presents. Then it occurred to us that for years father had wanted a fur cape. Mother wanted a cycling cape (the fashion of the day). For mother we got a cycling cape lined with squirrel fur from Tiedemann and Co.; for father we bought pelts and had a fur made for him. Both together cost us 600 marks. Then it was arranged that Joseph would pick them up in Berlin and come here with them by express train, which at that time had just been introduced. And that is what happened; our parents traveled fourth-class to Berlin, and second-class in the express train from Berlin to Hamburg. I picked them up at the railway station with a hack that had a good horse, since father loved good horses.

The train arrived at eleven o'clock in the evening; the cab stopped on the corner of Admiralitätstrasse. I quickly ran ahead and illuminated the store, the shopwindows, and the street with arc lamps, and then our parents were allowed to come with Joseph. When they entered the store, Joseph hung the coat around mother's shoulders and I put the fur on my father. That is how we received our parents and ushered them into our happiness, our business.

Our dear parents were speechless. Pale, perplexed faces. They couldn't absorb the impression. We had trouble making it all seem normal to them. We said: "That's the way it is in big cities, either it works or it doesn't." In short, we had to speak frivolously, since we saw that our parents were unable to get over this grandeur. They, however, said: "But boys, 8,500 marks' rent, it's not possible that you can survive paying that!"

Then we went out, had a kosher meal, and took our parents to the hotel. But they were incapable of saying a word.

On the next day, the first day of Christmas, our store was open. We sat father and mother down behind the cash register. Business was lively, and our dear parents saw how the money flowed into the register. Only then did they look pleased and only then did their tongues loosen. Mother said: "God gives you everything." I noticed that our parents, because of everything we had offered them on their arrival, were, in the true meaning of the word, speechless. That is the impression they had gotten of our business and the expensive gifts. Yet the size of the entire shop with its two windows was only 150 square meters.

Our parents left extremely happy. On the 31st of December we took inventory and balanced the books. As bookkeeper we had taken our friend Max Josephsohn, who is now procurator at the consumers cooperative. For if we should go bankrupt, the books had to be in order; then at least one wouldn't have to go to prison. We were very afraid of bankruptcy.

Josephsohn had a job and could come only in the evening at eight o'clock. That was fine with us; we sent the employees away in order to take care of the matter ourselves. We told him the stock and at ten o'clock the books were balanced. Josephsohn said: "Gentlemen, your books are done. In the three months of your company's existence you have a profit of 9,500 marks!" We were paralyzed and cried out: "Josephsohn, you're lying, it's not true, you're pulling our leg. We'll give you a hiding." "No, no, look, such and such is your balance." But we could not imagine that in three months one could earn this sum; in the first year all we wanted to do was come out even. We checked once more and our joy was boundless when it turned out to be true. We set to work in the year 1894 with a new spirit.

The spring season of 1894 took the desired course, so that we decided to go to a health resort. One had to "be seen." Perhaps a girl with money would fall in love with us. Joseph went to Westerland-Sylt, and I went to Helgoland for a week. In those days a person who could afford a trip to a health resort was considered rich. On the whole, people did not travel; employees did not go on vacation trips.

We got to know people, and that was useful for our business. The year 1894 brought a gain of 40,000 marks, so that we could settle everything in cash right away, and the doors of suppliers everywhere were open to us. At the end of 1894 we could regard our existence as secure. We felt accordingly and could think about marrying.

Our friend Liebner then wrote to us for information about a family Heckscher, in regard to a possible marriage. We were able to give him positive information. He became engaged and the wedding was supposed to take place in the spring. We were invited. I declined because of the expenses, but Joseph insisted on it and ordered tails for both of us. Then he also bought two golden watches, and upon Joseph's instructions Fräulein Lerche bought two diamond studs. The clothing was new from head to toe, and after we had shown ourselves to our employees we went to the wedding as two gallants. We made an impression as new eligible bachelors in Hamburg.

At the wedding party Joseph got Fräulein Falk from Hannover as his dinner partner. He had seen her repeatedly the previous summer in Sylt. At the wedding party she sang the song "Conductor, dear conductor," and Joseph told me afterward that he liked his dinner partner very much. On the next day I made inquiries of the relatives living there. We met next evening at a restaurant. I noticed that they first wanted to inform themselves about us. Ferdinand Rose inspected our books. Joseph then went to Hannover to get to know her better. He promised me it would be only a matter of getting to know her better; as yet, an engagement did not come into question. The train arrived in Hannover at 11:30. At 12:00 I was informed by telephone of the engagement. The wedding was to be a few months later. The dowry amounted to 25,000 marks. The closer the date of the wedding came, the less certain did the 25,000 marks seem to the Falks. They asked for a marriage contract by which the sum would be guaranteed. To be sure, we regarded this as a vote of no confidence, but we agreed. The marriage was very happy. They had two children, Hans and Werner Hirschfeld. But after only one year of marriage it turned out that Joseph was doomed to die.

*[Joseph dies, but two other brothers join the business.]*

In the year 1896 we rented the front premises for 10,000 marks and renovated the place ourselves. At that time I had in mind two entrances to the store; for in those days a store with two entrances and five shopwindows was something spectacular. The renovation cost 12,000 marks; we had to do it at our own expense.

At the end of 1900, then, there were three of us in the business. From then on, our firm began to grow. This was in part because the commodity of ready-made clothes was expanding. Blouses and skirts, which until then were unknown in the manufacture of ready-made clothes, could now be stocked for sale.

During a stay in Marienbad I also went over to Karlsbad. There I saw a display construction in a mahogany frame. I decided to build something like that at our place, too. The two entrances were removed; a wide entrance with two doors was installed, and all of the display windows and the doors were done in the finest mahogany, which was extremely imposing. In addition, I built an extension in the courtyard. Mirrors were put up on the back wall, and if one looked into the business from the outside, the mirrors created the effect of an enormously long store. The second floor, too, was joined to it by a broad flight of steps, so that from then on we had a very big store.

At the time of Joseph's death (1899) my fortune consisted of 43,000 marks. For a fairly large business that was, of course, quite little. In addition, I had considerable expenditures because I was supporting the entire family according to my circumstances, so that the accumulation of capital increased relatively little. We three brothers worked hard in the store, day and night. There was a harmony that could hardly be any better. Our dwelling on the fifth floor of the business building was most simple. In a small room two slept in one bed because there was no room there for three beds. But then I mostly took my brothers out to eat. Tobacco they got free. They could also take a trip to the seashore at the expense of the business. Almost daily reports were sent off to our parents. The work that we did was actually not for my business but for our parents, for they were at the center of everything. [. . .]

In 1908 we once again undertook an expansion by adapting the entire building to our goals. Further expansions followed in 1910. The present arrangement of our store was undertaken in 1913, when we established a milliner's shop, and besides ready-made clothes began to carry finery. Our business reached its peak in the years 1910–1912! At that time our turnover had increased to 2,400,000 marks. [. . .] Then came the war in 1914, which decreased sales greatly. In spite of that, the number of our employees had risen to 500–600 persons. Our company set the trend in Germany; in Berlin we were considered the biggest buyers.

1. Ludwig Windthorst (1812–1891); leader of the Catholic Center Party and opponent of Bismarck in the Kulturkampf.
2. This explanation is not entirely correct. By Easter the Passover holidays are meant. During this time, according to Jewish law one is not permitted to have leavened bread or other leavened products, since in commemoration of the hurried exodus from Egypt only unleavened foods may be eaten. Store and tavern must therefore be rented for the duration of Passover to a non-Jew.

# 25 *Philipp Löwenfeld*

 BORN IN 1887 IN MUNICH; DIED IN 1963 IN NEW YORK.

Philipp Löwenfeld, Memoirs. Undated manuscript, 953 pages. Written in New York sometime between 1940 and 1945.

*The Social Democratic lawyer Philipp Löwenfeld undertakes in these recollections to point out the roots of German fascism in the Wilhelmian Reich. Having grown up in Munich as the son of a lawyer and honorary professor with social-political interests, Löwenfeld, under the influence of Lujo Brentano, developed early a critical attitude toward Wilhelmian society. He studied law, attained his doctorate in the field of social law, and in 1912 joined the Social Democratic Party and belonged to its right wing. During the Weimar Republic he was a well-known political lawyer and journalist. In 1933 he was forced to flee to Switzerland, and later he emigrated to New York. Although his memoirs are interesting above all as a history of the SDP, our selection focuses primarily on Jewish themes, such as assimilation, mixed marriage, antisemitism in the army and among students, and the SDP and the Jews.*

Once, I was also taken along to a spa, to Marienbad. On that occasion, my grandparents went along, too. In those days, Marienbad was a place where people came together from all over the world. Before we set out, I was outfitted with my first pair of long white pants and white shoes, of which I was tremendously proud. The international character of Marienbad, with its bathing and promenading, was completely amazing and unprecedented for me. But there for the first time I also learned the difference between Western Jews and East European Jews, all from different countries.

At that time, there was also a large number of Jewish families in Munich who had immigrated from Eastern Europe. The old-established Jewish families had, on the average, less association with them than with the old-established non-Jewish population. In part, this was due to the fact that the East European families tended to belong to the orthodox congregations and thus, for the most part, also went to synagogues other than those attended by the old-established Jews, and for that reason they did not know one another particularly well. But externally, in their dress and customs, for instance, the East European Jews differed as little from the rest of the population as did the old-established Jews, and thus there was nothing peculiar about them for us children. In Marienbad this was different. There, for example, the rich Polish and Galician Jews exhibited a material opulence that was completely new to us. On the other hand, the orthodox appeared on the scene in their historic garb, with their long coats and beards and sidelocks. One noticed this especially in the case of stately young men with enormous brown and red beards. On this occasion I experienced for the first time the feeling of strangeness that can occur among Jews. Of course, at that time I did not yet suspect that for others such external details could cause feelings of disdain and hostility. For me their whole appearance and in part also their animated gesticulations simply seemed comical, especially when one encountered a procession of such long coats in the middle of the forest or on the promenade.

We took our meals in the "liberal-kosher" restaurant called "New York," which had once borne the name "Baruch." The strictly orthodox restaurant was named "Löwenthal." Only with difficulty could my grandfather be convinced that he could eat in the "New York" without sinning against his religion. He didn't really quite trust the rabbinic supervision under which the restaurant claimed to run. His suspicion that there was something funny about the "New York" was nurtured by the fact that they sometimes served roast venison. Since, as is well known, a pious Jew may eat only ritually slaughtered meat, he resisted the explanation that these deer were in keeping with the religious requirements, since he knew that, as a rule, deer were shot. It required skillful persuasion on the part of my parents to convince him that the roast venison in the "New York" came from captured and ritually slaughtered deer. Again and again he asked my father whether we were not duping him in a sinful way. I think that this is why the food in the "New York" never tasted quite right to him. [. . .]

As children we could hardly understand why the Jewish families associated more with one another than with Christian families, since it was, after all, only a matter of difference in religion. Even more, it was completely unclear to us why some people imagined that they were more refined if they socialized with Christians than if they were in the company of members of their own religion. As we gradually became aware, besides the factor of religion the social position of the parents played the main role in this. This became quite apparent, for example, when we boys were sent to our first dancing class. The sons of the "refined" Jewish families, the ones with money or titles—for instance, the children of councilors of commerce, counselors of justice, and senior medical officers—were invited to the "Christian" dancing class. The children of "ordinary" merchants, on the other hand, were excluded from the "Christian" dancing class. This was very disturbing for me because my two best friends were children of "ordinary" Jewish merchants, and I would have much preferred to be with them. When I told this to my father and mother, both of them said that this matter had nothing to do with religion, that I should not be foolish, and that I should attend the "better" dancing class. The instinctive feeling of the liberal Jews of that time, which was often somehow confusing for us children, did not express itself only in that form. My mother, and many other Jewish men and women, also found a child to be prettier if it "did not look Jewish." My mother prided herself on the fact that—in her opinion—this held true for her children.

But the same Jewish circles were deeply indignant if a Jew was not loyal to the Jewish community, especially if he had himself baptized. My father used to express this by saying that "one does not abandon a besieged fortress." Thus, for many of the Jews of this generation it was much more a question of character than of awareness to stick to one's Jewish guns. For reasons of character they condemned the people who wanted "to make things easy" for themselves or their children by converting. They were most suspicious, too, of all of those people who, because they did not adhere to the teaching of monotheism, officially withdrew from the Jewish community, became dissidents, and did not join a Christian church. In such cases one generally said that this was only a preliminary to conversion, that it was a matter of "renegades," in any event. That is what we learned from our parents and religion teachers in like measure.

The inner contradiction of these tenets was, to be sure, often painfully realized by us children, although not by our parents. Why should it be a question of character to remain within a group if it was more refined to associate with the others? And why, conversely, should the others be better than us if, in our opinion, we had a true religion, and, according to our religion teachers, the only true one? It was not clear to us, of course, that the retreat into the religious community represented a more or less conscious attempt by the Jews to pretend to themselves, through assimilatory gestures, that their recently attained emancipation was the expression of genuine equality.

During our education, we were completely shielded at school and at home from the knowledge that there existed a Zionist ideology and a genuine Jewish national consciousness. I believe that I was at least eighteen years old when I learned something about these things, about the teachings of Herzl and his spiritual successors. And I learned even this only in connection with stupid jokes, such as: "A Zionist is a Jew who wants to send a second Jew to Palestine on the money of a third Jew." For that reason, it made a deep impression on me in my boyhood—I must have been about twelve years old at the time—when I heard a discussion between my father and a Jewish professor, who was a friend of his, and I heard this colleague tell my father that he was feeling more Jewish every year. I heard my father oppose him with arguments such as: "To be a Jew is a condition, and not a merit or a taint; one should neither pride oneself on it nor be ashamed of it." His friend insisted that this was an inadequate position, and, pressured by him, my father began to retreat a bit and to concede to him that he really felt exactly the same way. But almost no one was ready to admit that in those days. Most people clung to the doctrine that Judaism was simply a particular religion of German citizens who had the same rights as all others.

*[In 1905 Löwenfeld is graduated from the Gymnasium.]*

It was originally the wish of my parents that I serve in the field artillery, of which there were three regiments in Munich. They learned after inquiry that the First and Seventh Field Artillery Regiments were, in principle, antisemitic, which means that they generally did not accept Jewish one-year volunteers, and in no case did they promote them to reserve officers. For some rich Jews, this was precisely the reason they tried to have their sons serve their one year of duty in these regiments. Even in the military domain some wealthy Jews imagined that they were more "refined" if their sons were tolerated in an environment that was free of Jews. The Third Field Artillery Regiment accepted Jewish one-year volunteers and normally allowed them to advance to the rank of noncommissioned officer. It also admitted them to the course for reserve officers. When a Jewish one-year volunteer was "fit" to become a reserve officer, as a rule he was not promoted to this rank within the regiment, but rather in the First Service Corps Battalion, which was garrisoned in Munich. Thus, everyone knew the joke about the order of the day that prescribed participation by the reserve officers corps in the army worship service on the birthday of Prince Regent Luitpold as follows: "The esteemed Catholics are to go to the cathedral, the esteemed Protestants to Saint Marcus Church, and the gentleman from the Service Corps to the synagogue."

My parents did not define the concept of civic pride according to the motto of many rich people, which was: "They don't want me, so I'll push myself on them." Thus, I was to serve my volunteer year with the Third Artillery Regiment. But before I could report to them, I suffered an accident that in the doctor's judgment would have ruled out riding for many months, whereas marching and running were not forbidden. For this reason it was decided to place me with the infantry. The First and Second Infantry Regiments, which not only accepted Jewish one-year volunteers but also took small percentages of them into their reserve officer corps, had already closed their registration lists by that time. There remained only the possibility of putting me in the king's own infantry regiment, the Bavarian Regiment of the Guards. To be sure, it did not refuse Jewish one-year volunteers, but there was the ill rumor that it neither admitted them to the courses for reserve officers, nor accepted them as reserve officers. That was all the same to me, since I had no ambition ever to become an officer. Rather, like my parents, I viewed the proper performance of military service as the fulfillment of a legal duty, the necessity of which I did not deny, but which I also did not feel to be more than a necessity. At any rate, in this way I came to be the sole Jewish one-year volunteer of my age-group in the regiment. [. . .]

When I joined the Royal Bavarian King's Own Infantry Regiment in Munich as a one-year volunteer on the first of October, after having finished the Gymnasium that July, my "superior," who was to provide my "military training," was the cadet Baron von P. He had always been one of the worst pupils in our class, and Dr. von Arnold had always emphatically pointed out his questionable capabilities. Now, suddenly, he was supposed to be qualified not only to teach me how to walk and stand, but also to impart to me the essential concepts of discipline, order, and patriotic spirit. I was supposed to stand at attention before him and, with my hands against my trouser seams, answer to his commands with "Jawohl, Herr Cadet!"

I could not believe that my classmate, who probably would not have been graduated if he had not copied terribly from his Jewish fellow pupils, was suddenly to be my commander. So I took heart and wanted to see what he would do if I approached him in a comradely way. When he ran into me in the barrack-yard, I said, without even an attempt at standing at attention "Good morning, P.," as we pupils had done among one another for nine years. But he was a fine one for that. He made a furious racket, shouted with rage in a voice that could be heard from afar, and threatened to have me locked up if I should again have the cheek to infringe the discipline that I was bound to show him, or to address him, let alone to use the familiar form of address as I had tried to do, or not to salute him properly.

This attitude, which was as stupid as it was roguish, made a deep impression on me. I told myself that something must surely be amiss in a state that permitted such injustices, nay, even prescribed them. It was on the basis of this experience that I first began to concern myself with the questions of class formation, social power, caste privileges, and similar problems. Despite the social outlook and profession of my father, I had been raised until that time as an average middle-class boy, and the method of school instruction, too, had hardly familiarized us pupils with sociological problems.

*[Löwenfeld studies law in Munich and, in addition, political economy with Lujo Brentano.]*

The student fraternities were without exception antisemitic. Not that they cultivated, say, a political antisemitism, let alone a mob antisemitism, such as Hitler, Streicher, and their cronies introduced in Germany, but rather it was a social antisemitism of the kind that a sector of so-called "good" society traditionally practices in America. Just as their homes and social events are closed to Jews, just as no Jew finds employment in their businesses, and just as these social groups spend their vacations at spots that are "restricted" to exclude Jews, so it was, too, with the "spirit" of the German student fraternities. The fact that certain of these fraternities, but by no means the most prestigious, as a rare exception admitted a rich Jew did not change the picture at all, but rather confirmed it. As a rule, precisely these rich Jews were people of the most inferior character. In their boundless obsession with complete assimilation and their mimicry, they not only went to the baptismal font, but they sought anxiously to conceal their Jewish origins. They changed their Jewish-sounding names in order to appear like autochthonous Christian members of society; they meekly avoided their Jewish relatives and their earlier Jewish friends, and were happy if a "Christian" who knew the truth assured them quietly, and more or less spitefully, that they did not look at all Jewish, that they were just like the "others." Today we know that in the end all of these people were caught in Hitler's machinery and that to be counted once more among the Jews was for them almost an even greater tragedy than the fact that they were deprived of their rights and drained dry, as Jews. Yet, there can be no doubt that one could see in their imposed identity as Jews a reckoning of fate that may certainly have been cruel in individual instances but in any case was still well-deserved. Although the ones who triggered this reckoning of fate were even more sordid specimens than the object of the reckoning, this does not at all change the fact that in itself there is something gratifying about the total futility of behavior that harms the community.

In regard to social antisemitism, the situation was hardly different in the student societies, gymnastic associations, Landsmannschaften,* and color-wearing student fraternities. Each of these groups, including the smallest, thought that it was something

---

*The word *Landsmannschaft* in this context denotes an association of persons from the same region or province.

"better" if it was free of Jews. If individual fraternities were somewhat more tolerant in this regard, matters became perceptibly worse among them, too, inasmuch as they presented it as a kind of favor on their part and a kind of privilege for the Jewish student if they made an exception and admitted him!

In his youth, my father had belonged to such a fraternity, which was called Adelphia and was later absorbed into another fraternity with the name Apollo. When I first enrolled at the university, there were, besides my father, a few other Jewish "philistines" in this fraternity, among them some Jewish higher-court judges and also the lawyer O., who was a Counselor of Justice and at that time head of the Jewish religious community in Munich. When I began my studies, I was also invited to join this fraternity. I wished neither to accept nor to reject the invitation until I had gotten an idea of the whole thing. So for several weeks I attended the events of the fraternity as a guest, and soon I was much repulsed by the backward and stupefying spirit that prevailed among the young people there. Boozing and more boozing, duels and other affairs that went with the fraternity code of conduct, card-playing at the coffeehouse, and conversations about their conquests of ever new girls, something that was of supreme interest to these adolescents recently turned loose on life. With the best of them, relatively speaking, one could still "talk shop" a bit. Although I was a beginning law student myself, I tutored a few real mental retards in the subjects that we took courses in together. The whole thing was so unpleasant and sobering for me that after some eight weeks of observation I declared that I could not join. I was especially glad that I had come to that decision when I learned not much later that the membership application of the son of Justice Counselor O. had been rejected. His father was a Jew, like mine. But he was "only" a well-regarded lawyer and a meritorious functionary of the Jewish community, and not a university professor. For the immature fellows who were empowered to accept or reject applicants, and for the Old Boys who secretly advised these promising youths, that apparently was decisive for the rejection.

But I also did not accept the invitations to join Jewish color-wearing fraternities, of which we had two in Munich. When I got some insight into their spirit and activities, I was quickly able to convince myself that they represented an exact, and for Jews an all the more ridiculous, copy of the drinking, dueling, and conduct-code customs of the "Christian" fraternities. But in the view of the latter, they were not qualified to give satisfaction; that is, in order to secure their German honor the "Christians" wanted only to bash one another's heads and chop up one another's faces. Thus the Jews were forced to make a virtue of necessity and secure and restore their German-Jewish honor by bashing Jewish heads and chopping up Jewish faces. As a rule, a member of Jewish "Licaria" could only smash a member of Jewish "Thuringia" in the mug, while a member of the genteel "Suevia" corps would not have dreamed of doing it. For him, in principle, only the skull of another corps student, and only if need be the face of a fraternity member or the cheek of a member of a color-wearing society, was "good" enough for this purpose.

It was especially the complete inner rejection of fraternities, which had resulted from my close observation of them, that made my participation in the Social Sciences Club, encouraged by Brentano, seem particularly desirable.[1] For me it was a real emotional relief when at my first meeting with the many excellent people who belonged to this club I already perceived the deep spiritual difference that existed between associations that in thought and feeling were basically rooted in an antiquated past, and groups that were defined by their respect for intellectual and scientific accomplishment, by a feeling of social responsibility, and the discussion of problems that are important for the present and the future.

My rejection of both Christian and Jewish fraternities also brought me close to the just arising "Independent Students" organization, which aimed to be the collective body of all students of both sexes who were not members of a student corps or dueling and color-wearing fraternities. Regularly enrolled students were organized into local Independent Students societies, such as the Independent Students Society Munich (in Munich). Whereas in the color-wearing and dueling fraternities former students, once they had completed their examinations, were called "Old Boys" and, not without good reason, "Philistines," in the Independent Students organization they were united in so-called provincial associations. In my native province, this was the Independent Students League of the Province of Bavaria, of which I was chairman for a longer period after I left the university. The idea for the Independent Students Association originated primarily in the same rejection of the antiquated student corps code of conduct that had so repulsed me. The Independent Students Association likewise completely rejected all racial and social discrimination and was open to every student of either sex who was prepared to join sincerely in its work. Naturally, this promptly earned the Independent Students Association the name of "Jews Clubs" from the dueling corps and fraternities. As far as the numerical composition of the organization was concerned, this was surely unfounded, since the majority of members were non-Jews. As regards the intellectual leadership, on the other hand, there can be no doubt that the cream of the young Jewish student population of the day played a significant, one can even say glorious, role therein. [. . .]

My increasing experience in the area of social science and social politics led me to ask myself even more urgently whether I was obligated by my convictions to take the appropriate step and join a political party. [. . .] The thought that a person should serve the community wherever he saw his personal ideas and convictions realized in comparatively greatest measure and where he could feel subjectively that he was on the right path spoke in favor of joining a political party. What prevented me longest from joining a party was the feeling that the political tie could perhaps force one to sacrifice one's better insights to the discipline of a party view, to defend something that one could not defend in good faith, and to attack something because it happened to be a practice of the party to do so.

My impressions of the German parties were anything but encouraging. From my individual perceptions I was able to determine that considerable ideological intimidation predominated among the members of the right-wing parties. In questions of customs policies and trade policies, and of agrarian and labor policies, the members of the right-wing parties, with few laudable exceptions, were sturdy proponents of pure power and money interests, which were often falsified in the basest way to appear as national interests. The middle-class centrist and leftist parties, which in membership were relatively weak and internally fragmented because they lacked slogans that could inspire the whole, often vacillated in their practical politics between a liberal and a reactionary attitude. But the position of the Social Democrats, who represented the extreme left in German politics of that era, also repelled me in many ways.

The party was still strongly influenced by such old radical slogans of revolutionary nature as had become classic, so to speak, in its developing years and were cultivated by its aged leaders, such as Bebel and Singer, and by younger, newly emerging theoreticians who represented a truly conservative revolutionism. Despite all of its radical gestures, in spirit the party had long since made its peace, or at least declared a truce, with the present order and did not seriously consider overthrowing the capitalistic system or the monarchistic state. Influenced by the rapidly growing union movement, which was not interested in creating a utopian state but rather in improving the situation of the working class in the present state, the so-called revisionist movement in the party did not see its goal in revolution but rather in evolution. It therefore showed great similarities to the position of Brentano, and under the influence of highly educated intellectual leaders such as Eduard Bernstein, Georg von Vollmar, Eduard David, Adolf Müller, and Max Schippel it had developed into an imposing factor in Social Democratic politics. But it found no way to assert itself over the Revolutionists through a majority. Revolutionism as such, however, had long since fizzled out and grown feeble. It was distinguished not by a productive spirit but rather by an orthodox and forced clinging to every facet of Marxist theory, including those that had to be considered as having been refuted by the course of history. [. . .]

This state of affairs deeply agonized me. I found that some of the theoretical principles of the party corresponded entirely to my own thought and feeling: its struggle for the liberation of the working class, for women's emancipation, for the elimination of class privilege and social arrogance. I also concurred warmly with a great part of the party's social criticism: its condemnation of the excesses of militarism, its criticism of the justice system, its positive accomplishments in questions of social policies, and many other of its activities. All the more was I repulsed by the mental drill by means of which the average party functionary was able immediately to explain everything and anything "scientifically" and "definitively." At that time there already prevailed in the party the truly bad habit of running down as "intellectual" every result of a thought process that was felt to be bothersome. By no means is the "egghead" purely a Nazi invention; rather, there were models for it in the Social Democratic movement. This was all the more painful since the historical brilliance and the dialectical training of the movement would have been entirely unthinkable without the work of the intellectuals Karl Marx and Friedrich Engels. In spite of this, for many years it was a favorite method among large sectors of the party to dismiss annoying opinions as the product of "intellectual" minds, which formulation was supposed to describe a certain decadence and a contrast to the sound thinking of the "simple" worker, which was allegedly native to the common people.

Finally, I could not ignore that despite all its assurances to the contrary the party had a lukewarm attitude toward the Jewish Problem. Among its spiritual fathers, Karl Marx and Ferdinand Lassalle had been Jews. Among the great party leaders who had attained real popularity was the Berlin Jew Paul Singer,[2] originally a rich manufacturer, who dedicated his life and fortune to the movement once he had recognized its validity. In those days, there were few Jews in the very strong Social Democratic Reichstag faction and in the German provincial diets, while the candidate lists of the party were, on the whole, kept free of Jews.

Among these Jews was the still young Social Democratic member of parliament from Mannheim, the lawyer Dr. Ludwig Frank,[3] who fell in battle as a volunteer in the very first days of the World War. He was one of the best minds among the Social Democratic revisionists, a great legal and political expert, a man of splendid appearance and rousing eloquence, whom many compared with Lassalle in the scope of his thought. On the occasion of a lecture that I gave in Mainz I met with him and we had a long talk. It turned out that he knew and valued my writings. He asked me straight away why I had not found my place within the movement. I answered by explaining all of the doubts that are described here. Thereupon, he said that all of my serious doubts were justified but that it was necessary that the positive workers make themselves available, otherwise there could be no improvement and everything would bog down even more. He, too, he said, had joined the party with deep pessimism, and yet he had succeeded in putting through much that was fresh against the opposition of the party orthodoxy. He said further that not everyone had to be a party agitator. But everyone should make a positive contribution. The very least was the necessity to acquire membership; and beyond that a functional participation was called for to prevent further weakening of the party system. With the objective weight of his arguments, with his heartwarming tone and his simple comradely nature, he convinced me that I would surely find the right place for myself in an organization that was striving after so much to which I, too, aspired.

Thus, at the beginning of 1912 I went to the office of the Social Democratic Party in Munich to register as a member. The party secretary, a man with a long, flowing white beard, who later became president of the Bavarian parliament during the period of revolution, received me properly but with great reserve. He assured me that he respected my father highly and had followed my efforts in behalf of Brentano with interest. All the same, for him I was perceptibly a young gentleman from a middle-class, professor's family, and members of this type were surely very rare in the local organization, which numbered several tens of thousands of comrades. Some of his reserve was probably also due to a certain shyness in personal relations, which I later had occasion to observe in him. After a conventional conversation of about ten minutes, we parted, but not before he had secured my promise to deliver some lectures on economics and social policy before the sections of the local organization. Until the beginning of the First World War, this was the only form in which the party made claim on my participation. At bottom, I was happy with this, since I did not have the feeling that I should involve myself any deeper in actual party-political activity. I shuddered especially at the thought that they could enlist me sometime for some sort of honorary office or political seat. [. . .]

I met my future wife after my university state examinations and doctoral examination, while I was doing practical social work. On separate evenings I taught civics twice weekly to workers and employees of all political orientations and parties at Schwanthaler School in Munich. In the next room, she taught handwriting to the same groups. At that time, she was a young student of German Studies, a pupil of the renowned Germanic philologist Hermann Paul. When we became betrothed after a brief acquaintanceship, we had to confess to one another that we most likely had to expect a good deal of resistance from both families. On my side there was nothing to fear from the acknowledged liberalism of my father. From my mother one could at most anticipate mixed feelings; for her father, who was still alive, was an orthodox Jew, who would in any case oppose the marriage of a Jew with a girl whom one would designate in today's Germany as a "pure Aryan."

My fiancée, on the other hand, came from a family in which a mixed marriage with a Jew was something unknown. To be sure, in school she had Jewish girlfriends to whom she was bound by genuine liking. But owing to tradition and home influences, the thought of marriage to a Jew had been, until very recently, something so completely alien that by her own admission she had said in company when discussing the problem of mixed marriage that one could just as soon marry a negro as a Jew. [. . .] For much of his life, the father of my fiancée respresented the interests of Friedrich Krupp of Essen at the Gruson Works. His views and attitudes were the mirror image of his position in life. He was a municipal representative of the German Nationals, very active in the Reserve Officers Club, and friends with all of right-wing society in Magdeburg. He was one of the cofounders of the "yellow unions," those alleged workers associations that passed themselves off as "conciliatory" in matters of economics and to which also the employers belonged, and whose true function was to supply the gangs of strike-breakers when the real unions went on strike.

Thus, it was to be expected that the announcement of our intention to marry would give us all sorts of hard family nuts to crack. Following our tactical plan, we first initiated my father. After he had convinced himself on the basis of personal impressions that my fiancée lived up to his spiritual-intellectual and ethical ideas, his attitude, as could be anticipated, was noble and chivalrous. My mother showed mild horror, but afterward acted in a familiar manner. Grandfather, from whom one could also no longer keep the engagement a secret, declared that he would jump out the window on the day that this wedding took place. The wedding took place, and he did not jump out the window. He overcame his negative feelings and not only behaved toward my wife in a formally correct way but also showed her his genuine liking.

When I entered the house of my future father-in-law to inform him of my intention to marry his daughter, the reception was icy cold. He obviously had already been gently alerted somehow by my wife's mother that the young Jewish lawyer who had announced his visit was "scheming" something. He received me sitting down, and had me remain standing. The following conversation evolved: "What can I do for you?" "I have come to tell you that your daughter Lotte and I intend to marry." "That is out of the question." "Then I can leave. I just wanted to do my moral duty and behave decently by informing you in person. As you know, as adults we do not require your approval in order to marry." Then, using the familiar form of address, he asked me to sit down. The ice was broken. With practical alacrity, he had convinced himself that it would be futile to continue with his tactics.

He then engaged me in a rambling conversation that went on for hours. Since the feeling of racial superiority was still unknown at that time, his shock that I was a Jew was somewhat neutralized by the fact that I was a professor's son, that in my career until then there was nothing bizarre, and my development to that point appeared to assure that I would soon attain full independence. That I was a pupil of Brentano caused some nose-wrinkling, for Lujo Brentano made the Magdeburg industrialists see red. When he got to the area of political views, I told him that I was familiar with his and respected his honest beliefs. I said that he should not ask me about mine, that they were irreconcilably different from his. I demanded from him in this regard nothing but respect for my own honest beliefs. He was decent enough not to try insisting in any way. Later, too, we never attempted to carry on political discussions or to influence one another politically in any way. He became the best, one can even say the most affectionate, father-in-law. [. . .]

I had to make the difficult decision of what personal position I would take if war were to break out. Thanks to my own army experiences and my entire personal and political development, I rejected—indeed, one can say that I hated—the military system. No matter what the risk, I would have happily joined any mass organization against war. I found the very thought that German militarism could be victorious in a war to be entirely disagreeable and repulsive. I told myself instinctively that the arrogance of the German military caste would know no limits. In the event of a German victory, one would have to fear in foreign policy a boundless excess of envy, hate, and greed, to which all efforts toward national integrity and the preservation of a reasonable balance of power among nations would succumb. It was clear to me that in domestic policy a German victory would lead to a complete domination by the military in the legal and social domains. In my mind's eye, I already saw how German civilians would have to step down from the sidewalk if they encountered Herr Lieutenant. I myself had participated long enough in senseless military drill to fear above all the terrible, stupefying effects of such a system. Although I had no more precise knowledge of the diplomatic connections, I felt intuitively that the coming war would not be a just German war of defense. For that, the conditioning of the masses, of which I became a reluctant witness, was geared far too much to clamor, racket, chauvinistic instincts, and personal and political calumny.

It was also evident to anyone whose thinking was halfway reasonable that a country as small as Serbia, and with its instruments of power, would not of its own accord attack a nation as large as Austria-Hungary was at that time, and, on the other hand, that Austria-Hungary, in view of the possible repercussions, would not have risked declaring war against Serbia without the open or secret backing of Germany. That is why I felt, without possessing any documentary evidence, that imperialistic Pan-Germanism believed that the time had come to test itself against so-called Pan-Slavism, as it was being nurtured by the tsarist imperialists. At that time, it still did not lie within the scope of my imagination that the German general staff would cynically breach every principle of international law and, violating the neutrality of Belgium, which was guaranteed by old treaties, would invade this land a few days later in order to gain strategic advantage over France, the ally of Russia, and that all of the preparations for this had already been made. For despite my total rejection of the political doctrines of the German general staff, I still had much too high an opinion of its ethical and intellectual qualities.

As a consequence of my views and my political education, my personal decision should have been directed at an unconditional rejection of the war aims that were being furthered. But I soon realized that the personal, political, economic, and social ruin that would have inevitably resulted from such a step would have been a useless sacrifice. Legally, it would have been a crime that would have deprived me of my civil rights and therewith of all political activity, even if it would not have caused my physical destruction. It might not have been necessary to shun consequences of this nature if the action had held out some prospect of moral or political success. But the moral effect of such a sacrifice was already ruled out in advance by the fact that, if war erupted, I had to reckon with a preventative censorship and all of the other instruments of military opinion-making. Thus, the prime prerequisite for a moral success, namely its exemplary character in a larger circle, would have been lacking. In view of the stance of the Social Democrats, one had to expect politically that the party would explain such a step as the private whim of a mentally more or less sound sectarian with no significant following. To my grief, I thus had to conclude that I would be selling myself much too cheaply to German militarism if I were to refuse to serve in the army.

It did not occur to me to join the masses of people who were reacting to their aversion to war, their fear of danger or of a responsible decision, in a "simple" way by fleeing to foreign lands. (In America there are many people living today as well-situated citizens who had made their decision on the basis of such considerations.) Germany was the country of my birth, whose citizen I was by right and duty, and with which for those reasons I myself had to deal critically. Without a doubt, this decision was also influenced by inherited and ingrained notions about the need for legality, perhaps even by that false devotion and loyalty that, in accordance with Kantian philosophy, one owes the ruler of the land even when he is destroying it. The doctrine that the German philosopher of law Kohler formulated by saying that every government was justified in and of itself as long as it existed and guided the state had struck much deeper roots in the education of the German and especially the German lawyer than the doctrine of the "eternal" rights, which, according to Schiller, the individual wrests for himself in his resistance against power, by "reaching into the stars." Particularly my father, who above all others exercised the deepest influence in my young years, was a firm supporter of purely lawful progress. I felt that a deliberate deviation from the path of legality would perforce result in a break not only with the state and society, but also with him. I was ever determined to risk my existence for my convictions, but never the relationship with my father, because I acknowledged in him that better self whose personal and ethical outlook one dared not ignore without compelling reasons.

Thus, I decided against my own conviction to report for military duty in the event of a war. At that time, I already had my reserve period behind me, and thus I was a noncommissioned officer in the Home Guard. Therefore, I did not expect to be called up immediately if war broke out. On the other hand, I no longer could choose where I was to report once I received my call-up papers. Thus, I decided not to wait for such a compulsory order; four days after the outbreak of war, I reported voluntarily to my home regiment, the Bavarian King's Own Infantry Regiment in Munich, and was accepted there.

1. The economist Lujo Brentano (1844–1931) was one of the cofounders in 1873 of the Verein für Sozialpolitik and awakened in many students the interest in social-political thought.

As a professor in Munich (retired in 1914), he established the adult education courses for workers to which Löwenfeld refers.

2. Paul Singer (1844–1911) became chairman of the Reichstag faction of the Social Democratic Party in 1885, and in 1890 the chairman of the party together with August Bebel. More than a million Berlin workers attended his burial in 1911.

3. Ludwig Frank (1874–1914) was the faction chairman of the Social Democrats in the Baden State Parliament, and in the years 1907–1914 he was a member of the Reichstag.—In the elections of 1903, 1907, and 1910, the percentage of Jewish Social Democratic Reichstag representatives, including dissidents and baptized Jews, was about 10 percent; thus, it was by no means slight.

# 26  *Philippine Landau, née Fulda*

BORN IN 1869 IN WORMS; DIED IN 1964 IN CALDWELL, NEW JERSEY.

Philippine Landau, Memories of My Childhood. Private printing. Dietenheim, 1956, 141 pages.

*The author describes her childhood in provincial Worms, where her parents had a thriving textile business. The store, in which her mother, too, was constantly present, represented the content and core of the family's life. In this business-oriented household, however, daughters and sons received very different chances for education. As far as religion was concerned, the family at first lived rather traditionally, but then it gave up the observance of religious law more and more, as far as this was possible in the Jewish community of Worms, which was very rich in tradition. — The author later married a doctor, lived in Berlin, and in 1938 emigrated first to Switzerland and then, in 1941, to New York.*

The street on which our house stood was the main street. It was the main artery of the small town, on which all business activity took place. Every house had one or several "shops," as the businesses were called, with the shop windows that went along with them; in these windows, called "oriels," the particular wares carried by the store were displayed. Our house, with its three floors and two large oriels, was one of the most stately. In its middle there was the entrance door to the shop. The shop was long, and I still see before me its divisions and the arrangement of goods. On both sides, the right and the left, there were counters on which the wares were laid out and shown. For lighting, there was a three-branched gas lamp above each counter, from which the bluish-greenish-purplish gas escaped with a loud hiss into three flaring lights. [. . .]

In the back of the store there were two more of these counters for other kinds of goods, which were kept there. All the way at the back, by a wide window through which the rear of the store received light from the so-called "glass house," there was also the "long bench," a simple, built-in, wide wooden bench on which the paper for wrapping the goods was kept. It was yellow, rough, and hard, so-called strawpaper, and, because of its stiffness, it was hardly suitable for wrapping. But it was cheap, and that was the main thing. At that time one was still far from providing oneself or one's customers a luxury that might have lured them into the store but which, in turn, would have paid off indirectly. In those days that was practiced only rarely, and in very simple form, and there was the inclination to accuse people who did it of unreliability and deception. They were probably forced to entice buyers for their inferior wares by such machinations and to deceive them about their inferior quality with such courtesies.

That, for example, was the viewpoint of my father, who preferred to think that people did know what they were doing when they came to him to buy good and durable wares, and that they could be thankful that someone sold them to them. It was also my father's practice to add the profit that he gained from his wares equally to every article, whether it was a piece of cheap nettle cloth or high-grade silk. Then, when, little by little, more modern-thinking and shrewd business people, speculating on the psyche of the buyer, almost gave away inferior merchandise as an extra or as bait, so to speak, in order to make an excessive profit on other items that were also purchased on the occasion, that was a world my father no longer understood, and he was certainly unable to adapt himself to it. Materially secure, thanks to what he had attained through many years of honest and respectable work, he preferred to withdraw completely from such a business world. During the closing sale that then took place in the store, he had the satisfaction of seeing how people really scrambled for his wares, knowing well that they were getting absolutely first-rate quality in exchange for their money.

The way in which the sale proceeded, even with such a rush of buyers, is inconceivable for a present-day business. After a sale was transacted and the merchandise was wrapped to be taken along, the salesman simply handed over the money he had received, and for which he had not made out a receipt, to my father or a member of the family, for we all helped on this special occasion. No one asked what had been sold, nor what quantities, and it would hardly have been possible to check, since the sale was taking place not only in the store on the first floor but also on two spacious floors above, called "storehouses." To set up a cash register at which someone would have entered the receipts was far fetched and unknown; cash registers appeared on the scene only decades later. But it worked. Even if, given the temptation that arose from this method, many a small sum may have gone into the wrong pocket, on the whole these tested employees, who had been with us for many years, were altogether trustworthy and one could depend on their honesty.

But back to the description of the downstairs of our house. Along the so-called "small office"—the entire little office was a tiny room—there ran a rather short hallway connecting the store with the fairly large room behind it, which was called the "big office" and was quite long and also divided in a very peculiar way. A wooden lattice separated the first part from the other, sizable part, which in turn was divided into special open booths. Here, one right next to the other, stood tall desks, desks at which one works standing, in front of which were placed especially high, sturdy chairs, on which sat, as they used to say in those days, the "young people" who kept the books. Two big double-desks stood facing each other, so that two people always sat writing opposite each other. There was no permanent bookkeeper. Instead, one or two especially qualified young people from among the employees were designated for that work. Occasionally, when business was heavy, they, like the others, had to help in the store and stockrooms, while, on the other hand, when business was slow, they were called upon to do the books. On the desks there lay big books, "the blotters," and the ledger, whose beautiful gray suede spine and flaming red label especially delighted my eyes, which were hungry for color in this extremely drab business atmosphere. Also, the fact that it was locked up ceremoniously in the big, heavy safe every evening endowed it with a special significance in my eyes.

Below the last of the double-desk pairs, which stood pushed close to the wall of the little office, almost in the dark, there were two drawers that had been assigned to my sister and me, and they were all the space that was granted us for our school things. In the corner of this section, on a wooden platform made for that purpose, there also stood rolls of oilcloth in every size. If one wanted to get to the drawers in back, one had to climb over this platform. For me, the oilcloth smell that prevailed there is inseparably bound to the memories of school and home in those days.

One can see that no one fussed much about us children, and we were far removed from those well-furnished children's rooms in which children did their schoolwork on special, anatomically-built chairs, undisturbed by noise and in the care of a protective and helpful governess. We were left to our own devices and were sometimes in a great quandary to find the quiet place we needed to do a written assignment. But that was entirely our business, and it did not trouble our parents at all. They had their own worries and thoughts, which revolved around the matters of the day. The children were not allowed to bother them or get in their way. I remember, for example, that one day, busy copying a composition, I was sitting at the table in the big office, which was also at the same time the room in which we stayed during the day, as well as our living and dining room. My father, assisted by one of the young people, was in the process of carefully wrapping and sealing a package to be sent off. Of course, that did not happen without turning and throwing the rather heavy thing, nor without enormous vibrations of the table, and when, after several slips of the pen while I was writing the clean copy, I dared to complain, I was not, as you might think, assigned another place, but instead, together with my work, I was energetically ordered out with words that were by no means gentle. Where and how I finished my work was up to me, no one racked his brain over it; one didn't give much thought to such little things—business came first. Because no one bothered much about us, we children, first of all, did not become spoiled or tempted to regard ourselves as being the most important people, and, second, we were forced to rely on ourselves in these matters and to bear responsibility.

Incidentally, my parents distinguished greatly in these matters between the boys and the girls. In the seventies and eighties of the last century in middle-class circles there still prevailed the view that schooling for girls was not to be taken so seriously. Certainly, they should acquire a foundation of knowledge, and if, of their own volition, they perfected themselves beyond that, then that was to be welcomed, for an intelligent woman was better than a stupid and uneducated one. But the decisive thing was that for the woman there was no graduation or important examination that would have either admitted her to, or excluded her from, a profession and a good career in the future, as was the case with the boys. Such a public role for girls was unthinkable and undesirable for these well-to-do middle-class circles of that time. Thus, whether they learned well or badly, they remained in school for the usual number of years. Later there followed, at most, further instruction in language and literature and a more or less dilettantish activity in the fine arts of music and painting, along with domestic training. Then came marriage, as the only intended, expected, and desired culmination. School and its accomplishments thus had nothing at all to do with a girl's later successes in life, which is the reason why parents showed only little interest in it.

It was different with the sons. It was important that they complete their work properly, so that they could move up to a higher grade at Easter promotion time and take the final examination at a time that was normal and thus not cause them to fall behind in comparison to others. That is why our parents had seen to it, even where purely external things were concerned, that the boys could do their assignments undisturbed by the business. They actually lived in a little house by themselves. This little house stood in the courtyard, opposite the office; originally it belonged to the neighboring house, and since my father was bothered by these all-too-close and inquisitive neighbors, when the chance presented itself he acquired the adjoining house, which he rented, after first separating for his purposes the little house, which stood in our yard. In this house, then, lived my brothers. It was a little house and was divided in the following way: On the first floor, completely at street level, was the kitchen, with an adjacent room, called the kitchen room, which served all kinds of purposes. On the only floor above, there were three rooms, to which a stairway led up from the courtyard. Two of these rooms belonged to my brothers as bedrooms and workrooms. The third and smallest room was occupied by the apprentices and the clerk, so that the house could be compared to an "enclave" reserved entirely for the male sex. [. . .]

My parents were not actually devout. Of the former piety, rites, and religious feeling in which their forefathers had been deeply rooted there had still remained individual traditional forms and customs, such as the observance of the High Holy Days with their various rules, fasting on the "long day" (Yom Kippur), and attendance at prayer services. But all that was now observed not so much from an inner need, but rather it was retained from custom and habit and, also, under the influence of the eyes of the small Jewish community, which would have regarded an abandonment of the show of external solidarity with Judaism by the descendants of such pious forebears as a sacrilege. Lacking were the prerequisites that allowed things to become truly alive and necessary: true belief and genuine piety. Fasting on certain days, the preparation of certain dishes, and attendance at the synagogue were things that had been customary for many years. Thus, they still survived externally, just as a structure from which almost all the supports have been removed in the end only barely holds together in its old form as long as no one touches it. A fresh wind, isolation from the old companions that used to surround it, knocks it over.

Thus, I recall very well the holiday of the "long day," Yom Kippur. In spite of the ambivalence and half-hearted way of doing things, which manifested itself in the fact that only some of the people at home observed the strict rules—my mother and we children never fasted—in spite of this arbitrary liberation, this emancipation, and the intrusion of other, more liberal views, on this day there still hovered over our home an aura of sacredness and deep solemnity, which no one could escape. On this holiest and highest holiday that Jews have, the pious beg forgiveness for all sins of which they were guilty in the past year, and castigate themselves before God, staying up and fasting.

For twenty-four hours, the whole night through, the pious remain together without interruption in the synagogue, in constant prayer and continuous worship. Most wear their white burial shrouds, which makes a sad impression and intensifies the solemnity of the holiday, with its special remembrance of the dead.

On the evening before Yom Kippur, before the family members go to the synagogue, a very ample and good meal is served to those who will be fasting. For they must fortify themselves for twenty-four hours, since not even a drop of water may pass their lips before the end of the next day. This meal, served at an unusual time, was already a great departure from the schedule of our domestic life, which was regulated by the clock. Both those who were fasting and those who were not went to the synagogue, and then after a while my mother and my brothers and sisters returned home to eat our customary meal at the customary time. We who did not fast adhered entirely to our normal eating habits, which at most were somewhat simplified and restricted, as a sign that by every right we actually should have been fasting. The next morning my mother again went to the synagogue with my father, but while he remained there till the end of worship, my mother returned for our somewhat abridged meals.

In between I visited her in the synagogue, and I have a very clear recollection of all the proceedings, as they appeared to me. In my best clothes and in the elated mood that children have when the regularity of everyday life is suspended, I would saunter through the Judengasse, which led directly to the synagogue. Long since, perhaps for half a century already, it had been divested of its real character. Only a few Jews were living there; only the most lowly and the poorest had remained, intermingled with wretched, lowly workmen and poor people of other faiths. The wealthy and well-to-do, all who could afford it, had escaped this dismal confinement in crowded conditions and had settled in a healthier and better environment, after the abolition of the strict regulations that had banished all Jews to this street, which, to be sure, they could leave during the day to pursue their jobs but in which they were locked up in the evening, like wild animals, behind a strong gate. Even on the street the uniqueness of the day was clearly felt. A constant coming and going of festively dressed men and women filled the street; some of them were on their way to the synagogue and some were coming from there, or simply taking a break from worship and spending some time in the open air. Acquaintances greeted one another and stopped to chat. The square in front of the synagogue was populated with all kinds of chatting and vividly gesticulating people—a bit of the Orient transplanted to the North.

Through this narrow street I went to the forecourt, to the entrance to the women's section of the synagogue.[1] Here, in this room with its heavy, old stone walls, dimly lit only when the entrance door opened and by a few clerestories on the sides, in the semidarkness of the hall was a confusion of people and voices—children who, like me, came to visit their parents or more or less seriously wanted to attend a small portion of the service, and women who wanted to interrupt the silence of the "long day" a bit with more worldly talk with neighbors and acquaintances who wanted to do the same. An assorted crowd, they all chattered and sat in the semidarkness of the vault. In the musty, close air one clearly distinguished the different odors of smelling salts and tonics of lemon and valerian, of which the women made use in the event that they suddenly felt weak, which, given the twenty-four-hour fast, happened frequently and often resulted in fainting and even more serious disorders. Probably no "long day" passed without unconscious women having to be carried from the House of Worship by men who quickly came running to help.

Then, when one had passed through this turbulent world, in which all the interests of the world outside were still palpable, and when the peculiarly heavy door of the synagogue had shut softly behind one, then one was immediately seized by the sacredness and solemnity of the place, and it filled the heart of the child, who had entered here still overcome by the light outside and the noises of everyday life. One was surrounded by another world, whose strangeness, whose detachment from everything that was common and usual, and whose sacredness at one and the same time enchanted, elated, and solemnly, almost painfully moved one. When the sounds of the organ resounded, the candles of the altar shone quivering through the twilight of the room, and the cantor's and the community's singsong chanting, which progressed in strange harmonies, reached my ear, I was in an enchanted, better world, full of holiness, in which only kindness, love, and noble thoughts had a place, and I felt strangely purified and lifted up into another, noble world. It was probably this pervading feeling of exaltation, which oddly enough was not linked to any concrete religious idea, that drew me to the synagogue, a feeling that even today still comes over me with the same indefinable quality when by chance I am to be present at a Jewish service. Is this perhaps the dormant memory of the feelings of departed generations?

In the dim room I looked for my mother's pew and, joyfully greeted and caressed by her and the neighbors, I was permitted to stand behind her and attend the services for a while. The women's section of the synagogue was separated from the men's part by a high, completely dividing grille. This separation, however, was only a symbolic one, and through the grille I saw praying men and boys, most wrapped in white burial shrouds, with the *tallis* that shimmered like silver around their shoulders. With violent movements, they rocked back and forth in prayer, or fervently beat their chest with their hands. At the same time, the ones who were praying said the prescribed prayers, loudly and rhythmically, half singing, half reciting, or they responded to the cantor's praying in the same manner. It was a strange feeling to see in this crowd of so oddly behaving and curiously dressed men one's own father, who now also suddenly looked entirely different and also seemed elevated into another sphere.

Once in a while my mother took me by the hand and went with me to a little, rather wild garden that adjoined the men's synagogue and that she called "Kaalsgarten." How it came to be called by this name and what it meant I don't know. At any rate, at that time I simply listened to its sound, thinking that it was Karlsgarten, which was quite plausible considering our soft South German pronunciation. This little garden lay somewhat raised between the prayer house on the one side and the ancient "Rashi Chapel," to which visitors made pilgrimages, and the *"mikva"* on the other side. It was, as I said, a ragged and untended little plot of ground. For me, who strangely enough, even as a small child, had an almost painful longing for nature, which I, growing up in narrow streets in a city of stone that could scarcely boast any green, could not satisfy anywhere, for me even this little spot of ground was a bit of paradise, and my happiness at being able to spend some time there was not the least of the sensations of these holidays.

I had already reached the age of understanding when I experienced the Yom Kippur on which my father, for the first time in his life, violated the commandment of fasting. As I have said, the forms of religious life in our house had become very lax in the course of years. Father was the only one in the family who, except for the "young people" of the business, still observed the prescribed commandments strictly, in part as an example to these "young people," most of whom came from religious families, in part, however, also out of superstition and fear that he would die that year if he did not fulfill the commandment of fasting. But the spread of liberal views on religion, and further the liquidation of the business, which also relieved him of the duty to set a good example to a number of young Jewish people in this domain, and not least the influence of mother, who with her easygoing nature found that one could also be religious selectively and comfortably, caused him to take this step, which was very drastic and momentous, as far as he was concerned. Thus, on this memorable day I witness lunch being served. Oddly enough, contrary to all custom, father is at home and not at the synagogue, as usual. He hesitates to sit down at the table, and I sense the importance of the moment and the tension as to what will happen next. My heart comprehends the difficult struggle that my father is fighting, but my mother urges him on and ridicules him. But only after she, laughing and joking all the while, has securely drawn the curtains and windowshades so that no eyes of the surrounding neighborhood can see the outrage, does he sit down to eat. After this decision, which was certainly very difficult for him, and after the belief that if he violated the prohibition he would bring severe punishment upon himself in the course of the next year had also proven to be false, my father, too, parted for good from the old strict customs, to which he had been bound, not by a true heartfelt need but rather only by fear, habit, and piety.

1. The famous synagogue of the old community in Worms was built in 1034 and in 1213 was expanded by the women's section. The ritual immersion bath (mikve) dates back to 1186, the study room (Rashi Chapel) to 1624. Salomon ben Isaac (1040–1105), the most important Jewish commentator on the Bible and the Talmud, studied and taught there. The synagogue was destroyed in 1938 and reconstructed in 1961.

# 27  *Paul Mühsam*

 BORN IN 1876 IN BRANDENBURG; DIED IN 1960 IN JERUSALEM.

Paul Mühsam, I Was Once a Human Being. Undated manuscript, 2,173 pages. Concluded in Jerusalem in 1956.

*Paul Mühsam grew up in Chemnitz and Zittau, where his parents owned a small shoestore. After his law studies and traineeship he settled in Görlitz as a lawyer. Dissatisfied with his profession, the sensitive and artistically inclined Mühsam devoted himself increasingly to literary creation. As a pacifist he was intensively involved in the German Peace Society and during the First World War he worked for the Red Cross in Berlin. After losing his law practice, he emigrated in 1933 to*

*Haifa, where he lived from a small mail-order stamp business and with the support of his children.—The following selection deals with problems of antisemitism and Jewish identity during his school years.*

Wherever the Jew went, he always encountered a certain mistrust at first, and had to fight for his place. He was by no means received with open arms. While a Christian pupil, just like every Christian citizen, in a certain way immediately belonged and, until proven otherwise, was considered decent, the Jew had to first legitimize himself and prove his decency. I was riled by the furtive whispering and giggling when some pupils from other classes saw me on the street; they were too cowardly for an open affront and therefore preferred to be able to turn the tables if necessary, so that in case of a reprimand they could feign innocence and allege that they had laughed about something entirely different, and thereby would have made me look even more ridiculous. One always had to consider, at the loss of one's naturalness, how one ought to behave, whether one should silently ignore a hurtful remark as too stupid or insignificant, or make an incident of it.

On Bismarck's eightieth birthday I was supposed to recite a poem I had written and that had been acknowledged as the best of all that had been turned in. On the way to the ceremony two pupils from another class passed me, of whom one whispered to the other that they did not exactly have to choose me, of all people, for that. The remark hurt me, yet it did not seem to me to be worth the effort of getting involved. But when a pupil in a lower class that I, as a senior, had to observe called out "Itzig" to me, I had him come forward and gave him a resounding slap. My father feared complications when I told about it at home, because he thought that the boy's father, a major of the Lithuanian Regiment, would not put up with it; but his offspring had probably very wisely concealed it from him. I, at any rate, had gained respect by getting tough.

Once, when I was crossing the street with several schoolmates, among them an aristocratic lazybones weighing a few tons, who had come into our class as a repeater and at first, like all new members of our group, had mockingly looked down on me, and a passing little pupil aimed an antisemitic remark at me, this von Trauwetter gave him such a dressing-down as I would have never managed. But it was humiliating to me, for he did not do it out of friendship but because I was in his company and he therefore considered himself personally offended, and I felt debased, like a Protected Jew. An anonymous postcard with antisemitic vilifications, addressed to me, also affected me painfully, no matter how gently my father pointed out to me that one is not spared such indignities in life.

I avoided talking about these things with my friend Bernhard; after all, only those who experience them can feel them. But once, deeply agitated, I poured my heart out to him, so that I almost would have cried right out on the street, so indignant was I about all these unfair accusations. He consoled me even though he was not quite able to empathize with me. It was not, however, just the scornful derision that so infuriated me because it offered no opportunity for objective discussion and could not be combated with rational arguments, but I also knew that narrow bounds were set to my future activities, while all doors were open to every non-Jew. In spite of the emancipation secured by law, a Jew at that time could become neither an officer nor a judge, nor any other kind of higher official, especially in Saxony, where the emancipation had gained acceptance only a few decades earlier.[1] And even though I was far from striving for such positions, the mere impossibility of attaining them was a heavy fetter on my sense of justice and self-esteem.

Besides, I had already learned by experience that social antisemitism is transmitted like an insidious disease from generation to generation. Which of my carefree childhood comrades knew what was going on in my soul while they were able to devote themselves to innocent pleasures? I was one of them, and yet this one thing, the fate of being a Jew, stood between us, something they did not know and would not have understood in all of its oppressiveness. After all, I felt it only with my heart, without comprehending it intellectually. If my acquaintanceships had been limited exclusively to my classmates, I would not have been affected by this miasma, which was not a product of the school but came only from the parents. But there were also numerous opportunities to associate with other pupils, not only in public, on the street, on the ice-rink, and during joint carousing, but also in school and its functions. At every patriotic commemoration we were all assembled in the auditorium. On Sedan Day the entire school marched as a body three quarters of an hour to Kaltenstein, where gymnastics were performed and a dance followed. And when this day of remembrance took place for the twenty-fifth time, after a solemn church worship service there was even a parade of all citizens and schools, in which we seniors were the standard-bearers. Bernhard in front with sash and sword, and my father, too, marched along among the veterans—the only time that I remember him putting on his medals. On Wednesday afternoons several classes always met for sports on the Weinau. On special occasions there were torchlight processions and ceremonial student drinking parties. And dancing classes, too, provided the chance to get together, not only with pupils from other classes and the Realgymnasium, but also with other social strata, with young ladies of society and their parents.

At that time the German Jews had been emancipated for decades, but the fact that neither then nor later, when the equality of rights was complete, were they generally regarded as full members of the community should have given every Jew food for thought. There were, however, only few who got to the bottom of this rather conspicuous fact and drew their conclusions from it. Most were dazzled by the radiance of European-Christian culture, whose brilliance, since the days of the ghetto, had more and more enthralled the spirits that had been freed from oppression and confinement. They remained in a state of ecstasy, so that, like people who had escaped from a prison, in the intoxication of attained freedom they thought only of ridding themselves as completely as possible of the slackening fetters of being a Jew and thoroughly assimilating to the Christian world around them, in the belief that in this way, be it with or without baptism, they would be able to escape their Jewish fate once and for all. This was a fundamental error, which would yet prove to be very disastrous. For within a Christian national totality, formed by a non-Jewish race, the Jew, for reasons of religion and origin, is a foreign element and does not cease to be regarded as such no matter how much he, having fully assimilated, believes himself to have been absorbed without distinction by the organism into which he intruded.

Certainly, it could be otherwise. Religion and race could completely recede as decisive factors in the life of a people and of nations in favor of humanity, which alone determines the value and essence of the person. It could and will perhaps someday be different, as has always been the case in smaller communities. But for the time being humanity has not yet come that far. For the present, religious madness and the brute instinct of races still play their calamitous role, with which no amount of talking will do away. There simply are things that cannot be justified from the lofty standpoint of noble humanity but that can be explained when one considers the circumstances.

In Saxony, the Jews acquired civil rights only relatively late, and that is why their percentage of the total population was, and still is, smaller than in other German states. Only two Jewish pupils were attending the Zittau Gymnasium when I entered it: Neubauer, the son of the preacher, who was four classes ahead of me, and, in my class, Salo Glaser. The latter was not much liked; he had characteristics that one tends to designate as "Jewish," but his way of being different derived only in part from his origin, and mainly from his personality. He was a romantic, idealistically inclined drea-mer. To be sure, no one took offense at that, but though by constitution he was good-natured and innocent, he became unpopular because he was forward, moody, and unsteady. That he was also a Jew was an additional incriminating factor. He stood somewhat outside the community, to belong to which completely was for me more an instinctive than a clearly felt need. It was not intentional when in one of the first classes, looking around because I had not yet been assigned a permanent seat, I sat down next to him. But when Senior Teacher Neumann remarked in a witty tone, "Naturally, the black-headed ones always stick together," I made up my mind to move away from him in order not to give cause again for a comment that was neither pleasant nor appropriate. But circumstances brought it about that later I got together with him rather frequently, since in Zittau there were only few Jewish families, and his parents, delighted to know of a comrade for their Salo, invited me quite often, and I complied with their request not unwillingly, not the least also because of his eccentric but beautiful and charming sister. Still, out of a feeling of community and because I really did not like him much, in class I was not much closer to him than were our other schoolmates. [. . .]

My parents always professed their Jewishness. Attempts to assimilate were far from their minds, if only because they had no ambition at all to play a role in public life. They were family people, who sought their happiness in the peace of their home and for whom loving care of me, shown by tireless sacrifice and selfless devotion, and the wish to smooth the way for me to a more carefree future and a better existence, constituted the substance and goal of their lives. My father came from a home in which Jewish tradition and piety were cultivated as a matter of course. But as much as he was attached to his inherited Judaism, in the grip of the liberal ideas of the day, he had given up all religious practice. He was pleased when he was elected as a representative of the Jewish community, and he regularly attended their meetings, but he never went to services. He had his belief and his inner piousness, and was much too enlightened to let himself be religiously edified by the preacher Neubauer, who, as it became known by chance, earlier, when he was still a "pants-selling youth,"[2] had lived with my father in the same quarters in Breslau, and whom my father rightfully regarded as a somewhat comical figure. But he demanded that on the High Holidays I attend the services, and for me that was torture and had less of an educational and uplifting effect than a deterrent one, not only at that time but for my entire life, so that if, despite all rejection of dogma and cult, I can still call myself a religiously motivated person, I became one not thanks to but in spite of those prayer services. Just as, in general, external influences are never able to form one's essential being, but rather always have a merely regulating effect, the human being, in the end, if he is able to develop unhindered, after all becomes only that which by his nature he was already meant to be from his most elemental beginnings.

The small Jewish community in Zittau did not have a synagogue but only a prayer hall in the form of a rented room in a house on a lively business street. Here, with the windows closed, the men sat crowded together, and behind them the women. We pupils were crowded somewhere against the wall, and there was such a lack of discipline, such a babble of voices, conversations, whispering, looking around, and letting oneself go, and the service was so far removed from any solemnity of atmosphere and ceremony that it could only be called an utter and complete chaos.[3] Already at that time I asked myself what all of these repulsive carryings-on had to do with God and religion, and if since my schooldays, except for special occasions, I have never again attended services, not even in synagogues in which worship was solemn and dignified, then this was not due to lack of faith, but, on the contrary, to a very profound faith. The Jew regards those persons as pious who at home and in the temple follow all the prescriptions of the law. But true religiosity does not consist in praying, nor in acts of worship, nor in dogmas, forms, and customs, and is not bound to specific places; but instead being religious means: by examining one's inner self to attain to the recognition of being one with God, and thereby to the feeling of the oneness of all things, and in the awareness of this highest responsibility to shape one's thinking, feeling, and way of life. And for me it is precisely this shaping and forming that is most important. But when once, in later years, in a circle of prominent Protestant theologians I held up kindness and love of mankind as the most essential factor in piousness, I was immediately rebutted: That is not religion, but ethics. Granted, "religion" does mean a bond and it regulates our relationship with God. But when the entire history of mankind teaches me that no positive religion has been able to place human beings in a relationship with God that makes them better and nobler and fills them with warm humanity, is it then not logical that I prefer an ethics that leads the soul upward, to a prescribed belief, which without any ennobling effect leaves the heart untouched and does not go beyond words? Ethics always proceeds from a religious foundation, from the recognition of divine omnipotence and the surrender to the will of God, but this is not to say that it must be validated by any positive religion. The religions, with their glorification of their founders, with their customs, magic formulas, and miracles, with their personification of God, and their concepts of sin and salvation, hell and heaven, and all the naïvete of their dogma, meant for simple souls, are transitory, historically conditioned phenomena in the history of mankind, born of the fear that is founded in the loneliness of the individual. [. . .]

I would probably have been more enriched by the Jewish spirit if my father, instead of urging me to attend those services, had imparted to me the knowledge of holiday customs and had observed the family celebrations, which at all times have contributed most to the bond among Jews through living tradition and reverent cultivation of the heritage of the past. For us, too, a holiday came but once a year, and business made it unavoidable that these were always the Christian holidays. Even on the High Jewish Holidays the store remained open. The only thing that reminded one of Jewish custom was the habit of commemorating the day of our grandparents' death by a night candle that floated on a layer of oil in a water glass placed on the sideboard.[4] My uncle Samuel always informed us on time on which day these anniversaries of death, regulated by the Jewish calendar, came. At Christmas no tree was set up, but we did exchange presents. The religious holidays, Shabbat, the Haggada, the tabernacle, etc. remained mere names for me, and I did know when Christmas was, but not Chanukah. To be sure, every Friday evening I saw my mother quietly praying to herself from her prayer book, conscientiously rising up at the prescribed places, but I myself did not have the urge to do the same.

No less than by the services, I was unpleasantly affected by my parents' habit of using in their daily informal conversation Jewish jargon, expressions borrowed in part from Yiddish, in part from Hebrew, pronounced in the Ashkenazic way.[5] The rich man was called a *kozen,* the poor man a *dalles,* the thief a *ganef,* the genteel person a *srore,* the stupid a *chammer,* the bridegroom was a *chosen,* the bride a *kalle,* the relatives were called *mishpoche,* a community *chavrusse;* instead of antisemitism one said *risches,* regrets were expressed by *nebbich,* ironic negation by *osser,* sympathy with *rachmones,* defiance with *dafke.* The lucky person had *massel,* the unlucky fellow *schlamassel, chochme* meant cleverness, *gewure* was pomposity, *simche* joy, *kauach* strength, *chuzpe* nerve, *ponim* face, *krire* cold, *chamime* warmth, *parnosse* profession, *meziehe* bargain, *tineff* bad goods, *bowel* old wares, *maure* fear, *charpe* humiliation, *sroche* stench, *menuche* rest. An honorable person was *bekowed,* a simple one *poschet,* a charming one *becheint,* a crazy one *meschugge.* There were surely far more than a hundred such words, with which the language was interspersed. Naturally they impressed themselves upon me, but out of deliberate opposition I never pronounced even one of them. [. . .]

If due to such rebellion I intentionally rejected the jargon expressions of my parents, this occurred in pursuance of an attempt at assimilation, which in other families had already been realized by the preceding generation. It was an expression of the wish to live in a community, which was possible only by getting rid of every trace of otherness. But this otherness was and is present, and the attempt was therefore doomed from the start. I was absorbed by the community, but not entirely. I believed myself to be like the others, but was rather often painfully reminded that this was an illusion. To draw conclusions from this, however, was not the trend of the times. I accepted the painfulness as something inevitable, without reflecting on the conflict of the soul brought about by it. [. . .]

I don't know what I would have given if it had been possible for me to belong to the school fraternity, in which all members and elder fraternity brothers were on familiar terms, and in which there reigned a spirit of unrestrained gaiety. Although Bernhard headed it, and although my classmates would have gladly accepted me, it remained an impossibility because of the opposition of the pupils of the upper classes and, above all, of the elder fraternity brothers, of whom several were not only antisemitic, but also considered it a meritorious activity to influence young people in this direction. And how easy it is to effect such an influence on young minds. It suffices to tell a few little jokes by which the Jew is made ridiculous, and already the poisonous seed is sown, which, when it sprouts, brings happiness to no one but distress to many, and, breeding hatred, drags down the soul. It was until then the most acute pain that I had experienced as a result of being a Jew, and which I silently bore within me for years without finding a compensation for it. Bernhard was prepared to give up the presidency, but I asked him to refrain from that. He would have harmed only himself, without doing me any good.

Certainly such symptoms could have been a warning sign to me that the road of integration into the Christian world is passable only for a stretch, but then ends before a closed door and does not lead into the open. Nevertheless, I lacked absolutely all of the inner and external qualifications for pursuing the path to the Jewish community. I knew nothing about Judaism. It offered me nothing whatever. For me it was only an empty shell, and I saw in it nothing but a burdensome fetter. The idea of baptism, however, which I frequently considered, I rejected for reasons of filial love and also because it would have taken place without an inner need, and it seemed to me to be cowardly, characterless, and contemptible to abandon the oppressed and join the side of the oppressors, embracing a religion for which, despite the most radiant genius from whom it took its name, almost 2000 years had not sufficed to fill its followers with a humanity that would have made such oppression impossible.

1. In the kingdom of Saxony the emancipation of the Jews did not take place until after the Revolution of 1848. As a result of its restrictive policies towards the Jews, Saxony, in 1871, had the smallest percentage of Jews in Germany, 0.13 percent (3,357 persons).

2. This expression comes from Heinrich von Treitschke's antisemitic writing "A Word about Our Jewry" (Berlin 1879/80): "Across our eastern border, year after year there makes its way from the inexhaustible Polish cradle a swarm of ambitious pants-selling youths, whose children and children's children will some day control the German stock exchanges and the newspapers."

3. In the community of Zittau, heavily populated by Eastern Jews, there evidently prevailed the traditional form of orthodox prayer, in which loud individual praying and reading from the Torah play a major role. Mühsam measures this by the modern form of the liberal service, which is influenced by Protestant ritual: There is a sermon, and value is placed on silence, discipline, solemnity, atmosphere, etc.

4. This is the memorial candle that is lit on the anniversary of the death of a close relative. As part of the commemoration one also recites the prayer for the dead (*Kaddish*) in the synagogue.

5. The German and East European Jews (the Ashkenazim) used the so-called Ashkenazic pronunciation of Hebrew, while the West European and Mediterranean Jews (Sephardim) use the Sephardic pronunciation, which is also the standard in present-day Israel.

# 28  *Sammy Gronemann*

 BORN IN 1875 IN STRASBURG (WEST PRUSSIA); DIED IN 1952 IN TEL AVIV.

Sammy Gronemann, Remembrances. Undated manuscript, 329 pages. Written in Palestine before 1947.[1]

*As son of the district rabbi of Hannover, Gronemann at first devoted himself to Talmud studies in Halberstadt and Berlin. Then, however, he switched to law and became a lawyer. After frequent confrontations with antisemitism, he joined the budding Zionist movement in 1898. He developed into one of the best-known speakers of the Zionistische Vereinigung für Deutschland and founded its regional chapter in Hannover. Starting in 1906 he practiced in Berlin and became a member of the governing body of the Zionistische Vereinigung as well as of the Zionist Aktionskommitee. During the First World War he took a special interest in the East European Jews, with whom he came into close contact as Yiddish interpreter at the headquarters of the Eastern Supreme Command. His recollections end with the year 1918. In the twenties Gronemann published several humorous novels, and after his emigration to Tel Aviv in 1936 he also wrote comedies.*

In May 1900 I participated in a Zionist conference for the first time, the delegates congress in Berlin. In those days this was still an event of modest proportions. It took place in the Cassel Hotel on Burgstrasse, and there I became acquainted with the leaders of German Zionism. Above all I got to know David Wolffsohn, Max Bodenheimer, and Adolf Friedemann.[2] Actually, I had met Wolffsohn much earlier, or, really, he had met me. It must have been around the year 1877 when he had taken me, a two-year-old baby, in his arms at a wedding in Prostken, East Prussia. Because of this, he used to call me his oldest acquaintance among the German Zionists.—I was struck by the organizational competence of Arthur Hantke,[3] and also of the young rabbi Wilhelm Levy, who was, incidentally, the founder of the Jewish gymnastics club Bar Kochba; further, I remember especially well Egon Rosenberg and Erich Rosenkranz. Of my old acquaintances I was especially pleased to see Lina Tauber and Jacob Wagner (who married soon thereafter—mainly, it was said, so that olive trees would be donated in congratulation). At that time it was decided to establish our own Zionist paper, and a small Jewish newspaper, published by the teacher Flanter, was acquired. This later became the *Jüdische Rundschau*. Heinrich Loewe, whom Lina Tauber supported warmly, was chosen as editor. [. . .]

From the start, I had had no illusions that work for the Zionist cause would be easy in Hannover. It was made especially difficult for me because I was the son of the rabbi. From some quarters the responsibility for my conduct was ascribed to my father, and there began an opposition against him that at times assumed highly unpleasant forms. My father, however, not only did not ask that I show some sort of consideration for his position, but he regarded it as his duty to step on the podium at almost every public Zionist gathering and give expression to his sympathy for the national movement. On the whole, however, it was asking much too much to expect that the good people of Hannover would completely change their attitude. They were brought up with thoroughly German views and felt that as a Jew one "had to more than fulfill one's duty" toward Germany, as it was stated later, during the war, in a declaration of the Centralverein. All they wished was to prove to the others that they differed from them only in religion and in nothing else. Instead of taking the view that belonging to the Jewish people in no way had to lessen the fulfillment of one's duties as a German citizen, they foolishly sought to deny the premise and maintained that they were full-blooded Teutons;

they denied all differences. They did not realize that precisely by this attitude they supplied the others with the best weapon against them. For in the end their argument meant nothing else but that if they were not Germans in the ethnic sense then the antisemitic position was justified. And every street urchin could tell by looking at their noses that they were not descendants of Hermann the German. Things went so far that they even tried to ignore that "enforced uniform" of which Heinrich Heine speaks—the nose. And the so-called tolerant circles, the liberals of, say, the stamp of a Rickert,[4] sang the same song.

And now a young person, scarcely fully fledged, came along and wanted to teach them that all these views, with which they had grown up and on which rested their entire position concerning all problems, were absurd. He demanded of those who fearfully attempted to hide their Jewishness and gave it asylum only in the synagogue, that they declare themselves openly as Jews and prove their solidarity with all Jews everywhere. That must have seemed unappealing and dangerous to them. In retrospect I must confess that I personally probably asked a bit too much of my good fellow citizens. It may be that I, who myself had only recently undergone that difficult spiritual operation through which the old inner prejudices were overcome, was now acting with special severity. [. . .]

In a relatively short time I succeeded in setting up a rather respectable organization in northwest Germany, and I was genuinely happy when at the Fifth Zionist Congress in 1901 Bodenheimer extolled this. It then became necessary for me to start traveling in order to hold lectures at rallies, only in larger towns, of course, and preferably where a local Zionist group did not yet exist. It was quite an interesting activity and not without incidents.

Things almost always happened the same way. It was a matter of finding someone who took the preparations upon himself, rented a hall, etc. The expenses were not great, since in general the speaker himself paid the costs of the journey and stay. Then one arrived, was received by the local representative, who immediately explained that there, in his town, the circumstances were especially difficult, that people did not want any part of Zionism there, and that especially the rabbi was a strict opponent, etc. But the meeting was overcrowded nonetheless. It was precisely the fierce agitation against Zionism that had made the people eager to see such a monster of a Zionist, and they expected at least an entertaining evening. Then one stepped to the podium in front of an ill-disposed audience and did one's bit. After my first experiences I took good care not to roll out all my artillery at the beginning, but rather I was content to develop logically the theory of Zionism and to prove the necessity and exclusiveness of the Zionist solution. Then, regularly, an opponent stepped forward, usually the local rabbi, who, after a few polite phrases with which he thanked me for the measured and clear presentation, condemned Zionism out and out. And only then, after this opposition speaker had drawn the sympathetic applause of his audience, came my actual rallying speech. Following the arguments of my opponent point by point it was easy to take him apart, to his great amazement and that of the audience, which, after the measured presentation, had scarcely expected anything like that. And then there was always great cheering and ovations by the surprised audience, which, of course, went home afterwards somewhat ashamed and contemplative. Thus interest was awakened and a discussion unfolded for weeks to come, and after the meeting a number of people did inevitably come forward, who then formed the foundation of the new group.

Following are a few examples of such discussions: Rabbi K. protested energetically against speaking of a Jewish nation. Certainly there had once been a Jewish nation, but as he and all his colleagues taught unanimously from every pulpit in Germany, it had fulfilled its mission, it was dead and could not be brought back to life again. To this gentleman I answered that his reasoning reminded me of the doctor who met an old patient and was most astonished that he was still alive. Upon the latter's declaration that he *was* still alive and felt very well, the doctor answered: "That's nonsense. As far as science is concerned, you are dead!" The other remarked, however, that, as a matter of fact, he was feeling very well. Thereupon the doctor replied with the greatest indignation: "Then you did not comply with my directions."—Rabbi V.: Zionism preaches national Judaism. He, however, acknowledges as Jews only such persons who somehow practice the Jewish religion. Whoever does not observe Jewish religious teachings to some degree is not a Jew. Thereupon I asked in all modesty: "Herr Rabbi, if there is someone living in your community who openly professes to be an atheist, subscribes to nothing Jewish except, at most, to the *Berliner Tageblatt,* and does not fast on the Day of Atonement, would you not bury this man in the Jewish cemetery? I am, as a matter of fact, convinced that you would bury him, of all people, with special pleasure." [. . .]

One must imagine with what enthusiasm we young Zionists were filled. Herzl was our idol. We admired his and his fellow combatants' courage. Borne by pure idealism, they had once again appealed to the Jewish people to exercise reflection and take up the struggle in spite of all the prejudices that confronted them. It was only then that we discovered that opponents of our idea did not shrink from expressing the worst suspicions against our idolatrously revered heroes, slinging mud at them and attributing the worst motives to them. They went so far as to suspect that our leaders were acting out of egoistic, even materialistic motives, that the establishment of the bank was nothing but an attempt to empty the pockets of poor naive Jews in order to enrich themselves. My personal indignation grew when of all things the orthodox publication *Der Israelit* in Mainz became the bearer of these aspersions. And at this time I received a request to give a propaganda lecture in Mainz. One can imagine with what joy I accepted this invitation. Boiling with rage, I went from Mannheim to Mainz. I came, I saw, I exploded. That was probably the biggest row that I ever provoked at a meeting. [. . .] Only gradually did I learn to tame the excessive temperament that I had exhibited in Mainz particularly. At many meetings, especially in Hannover, I often treated my opponents so mercilessly that it became difficult to find opponents who dared to step to the platform. That was, of course, very unfortunate, for it was the discussion that made the meetings attractive. But that surely was not what mattered most. Much worse, as I must confess today, was that my aggressiveness often truly exceeded the proper limits, ensuring me and the cause success, yet not in an entirely irreproachable way. [. . .]

The Fifth Congress (in December 1901) was drawing closer, the first I was to attend. I was downright feverish with anticipation. Today, perhaps, one can hardly imagine what an impression the first reports from the Congress made on us young German Jews. Again and again I read with the same enthusiasm the speeches by Herzl, Nordau, and the other protagonists, and also studied every one of the debates, including all of the speeches dealing with procedural rules. Those great programmatic speeches, however, had not only revealed a new world to me, but had opened hearts and evoked thoughts and feelings of whose existence the bearers themselves had no idea. It seemed to me almost inconceivable that I myself was now to be present at such a historic event as the opening of a Congress.

I went to Basel as a delegate of the Hannover group, accompanied by my co-delegates, Ivan Meyer and Jacob Schnelling. My first impression was occasioned by an encounter, insignificant in itself, at the railroad station in Frankfurt am Main. Through the crowd I saw several old bearded Jews walking along the train, dragging their suitcases with difficulty, and that pierced me to the quick. What are we, coming from comfortable circumstances and traveling to Switzerland as though on a pleasure trip, compared to those people who, perhaps at the greatest sacrifice, set out from their miserable Russian ghettos filled only by the one longing for their final deliverance. And when we arrived at dawn at the Basel railroad station, that impression intensified. But then, young, athletic-looking people, dressed in modern clothes, came running up with blue and white badges. We saw them greet the Jews from the East enthusiastically and, somewhat suspiciously eyed by them, take their suitcases and escort them.

Then, as we were driving toward our hotel, there was another impression. We went past the casino building, the headquarters of the Congress, and for the first time we saw the Jewish blue and white flag flying. And a big Hebrew and German poster announced to the whole world that we Jews, coming out of seclusion, had now entered the public arena. — I looked up to the balcony of the casino and remembered that episode from the Second Congress about which so much had been told, when on a Swiss national holiday the parade had passed there and the Swiss had cheered Dr. Herzl and his companions on the balcony—and for the first time in a thousand years the cry "Hail to the Jews" had resounded.

I not only felt feverish, I actually had a fever and was worried whether because of illness I would have to miss the opening of the Congress. But my condition improved quickly. I went to the congress office, received badges and materials, and began to look around. One impression followed upon the other. The milling crowd in the hallways and on the terrace of the casino café, on the Barfüsserplatz and in all the streets of Basel overwhelmed us, and we were happy, were delighted. But if we were so proud to see the Zionist emblems with the picture of Herzl in the shop windows, there was nonetheless manifest in our feeling of happiness something of the old ghetto mentality and the acquired feelings of inferiority. We still could not believe that we were permitted to declare ourselves a people and exhibit a flag. [. . .]

Finally, on the next morning the hour of the opening of the congress arrived. I sat humbly in one of the back rows and my heart leaped with joy when I looked at the overcrowded hall and the galleries. Indeed, this was truly the picture of a Jewish Parliament, not just a gathering like any other. Here one saw Jews from all parts of the world, representatives of all philosophies of life, who had united for a single purpose. All were filled with the same excitement that held me under its spell. Sheer delight and anticipation shone from everyone's eyes, as if in the next moment a miracle would occur and the prophet Elijah would enter and give the signal that had been awaited for millennia.

Three times the gavel resounded. Suddenly the lively humming that filled the hall grew silent. Everyone's eyes turned to the small door to the left at the back of the wide podium. It barely moved when a tremendous jubilation broke out. Everyone rose, banners were waved, everyone was wild with joy and enthusiasm. Herzl, followed by Nordau and the other members of the leadership, proceeded to the president's seat. It took a long time before the welcoming din subsided and Dr. Herzl could begin his speech.

*[In 1904 Gronemann goes to Berlin to take the second state examination.]*

Between the proletarian East of Berlin (Berlin E) and the aristocratic West (Berlin W) lies the Bellevue district (Berlin NW, in the Jewish vernacular called the "Nebbich-West"). Berlin E was the domain of the East European Jews, who, strangely enough, populated all streets bearing military names, as for example Artilleriestrasse, Grenadierstrasse, and Dragonerstrasse, while in the West, in Charlottenburg, Wilmersdorf, or the especially elegant Grunewald district, lived those who had "arrived." In Berlin, East European Jew and Western Jew were not so much geographic as temporal concepts. It happened quite often that Jews who had immigrated from the East at first took up quarters in the above-mentioned streets, then gradually attained prosperity, moved to the more elegant Bellevue district, the home of the better middle class, and then, rising on the social ladder, transferred their domicile to Charlottenburg and became Western Jews, who then often looked down on the immigrants of the East district with tremendous contempt. At a meeting of representatives of the Jewish community that occurred at a later time, Alfred Klee[5] once permitted himself the following jest when, as so frequently, the liberals were polemicizing against the elements coming from the East and supposedly provoking antisemitism. He asked: "I would like to ascertain which of the gentlemen of the Left actually arrived at the Anhalter station" (the station at which trains from the West arrived) "and which arrived at the Schlesischer station" (the East railway station in Berlin). Pointing with his index finger, he went from one to the next, and— lo and behold—without exception these gentlemen had themselves all immigrated from either Posen, Breslau, or Poland, or at least their forefathers were beyond doubt of East European origin.

It was in this Bellevue district that I spent the next months with my wife and sister, and the uneasy atmosphere of the impending big state examination scarcely cast a shadow on the very delightful student's life that we led at that time.

*[After passing the examination Gronemann establishes himself as a lawyer in Hamburg and intensively continues his Zionist work.]*

In the Ukraine there had begun an immense wave of emigration to America. The shipping agents of the large transoceanic lines had promoted it prodigiously, and masses of Jews and Ukrainians set out on their way. The groups were organized in Myslowitz and went by way of Ruhleben-Spandau to Rotterdam. Transit permission was granted only under the condition that the emigrants were to pass through Germany in sealed train cars, so that for days they were not permitted to leave the packed cars, not even to drink a cup of water at a pump. There was no possibility of getting fresh milk for the children or any kind of provisions at all. One can imagine what condition these people were in when they arrived in Rotterdam. By chance Änne [Berliner] had discovered such a group at the Hannover railway station. Resolutely, she had gone to the stationmaster and, against all the rules and the strict regulations of the railroad ministry, she had managed to have the keys to the cars handed over to her, and she provided the people with the opportunity to move about freely for at least a brief time and to supply themselves with provisions to some extent. Only Änne could accomplish something like that, such an incursion into Prussian bureaucracy. "I achieve everything with my eyes," she said, and her success proved it.

We now attacked the problem systematically. It turned out that such trainloads passed through Hannover three or sometimes four times a day, arriving regularly at 12:00 at night, 6:00 in the morning, and 4:00 in the afternoon. There were several hundred emigrants in each group. The night train and the early train each remained only twelve minutes in Hannover, where the cars were switched, while the afternoon transport remained in Hannover two hours, from 4:00 to 6:00. I then arranged the following: Each day I received a telegram, or even several, from the agent in Myslowitz, in which I was told how many men, women, and children to expect in every train. I organized a station service, at which I put to work all members of the local group, young and old. They had to do the shopping and store the goods in the buffet; then the appropriate station department took the goods to the right place. Whenever the trains arrived at night or in the early morning, we boarded them and quickly chose several trustworthy people, to whom we handed over the acquired things. A package was prepared for every single person, and there were also milk bottles for the children. This was taken care of during the switching of cars, and then, before departure, we got off. The people were tremendously surprised and very happy about the good fortune that came upon them seemingly from heaven. In the case of the afternoon train the procedure was different. Änne saw to it that a fourth-class waiting hall, in which a snack was prepared, was placed at our disposal, and next to every place there lay the appropriate package. One can imagine what kind of work this organizing demanded, and of course I had to set a good example and appear at the railroad station in the bitter cold of winter, at 5:30, and then, loaded down with milk cans, etc., climb up the stairs to get to the switching track.

Naturally, the whole thing required considerable funds, several thousand marks per month. But incredibly enough, that, too, did not present any difficulties, for when news of this undertaking spread, the money poured in from all sides, and here I must still express my belated appreciation to the Jews of Hannover, about whom I had many an unkind thing to say. The activity did not remain secret, of course, and it became a sort of attraction to watch such a supply operation, at least in the afternoon. And regularly onlookers gave contributions that at times were quite substantial. I remember a Christian gentleman slipping a hundred marks into my hand. The newspaper reporters had also soon discovered the event and expressed their opinion about this operation, actually in a very benevolent way. But for us this was not at all pleasant, for we were terrified of the interference of the ministry, whose regulations we were, after all, grossly violating. The Christian Travelers Aid Society also began to be interested in this matter and tried to organize a similar service for the Ukrainian emigrants. The attempt failed after a few days, however, and the ladies of the Aid Society hindered us more than they helped, so that without hesitation I also took over the provisioning of the Ukrainians.

Since I was still afraid that the sources of money would finally run dry, I turned to the Hilfsverein Deutscher Juden in Berlin. There, however, I found no approval at first. Instead, Dr. Paul Nathan and Bernhard Kahn[6] came posthaste to Hannover to implore us to discontinue the action. We could bring about the worst disaster, if, say, the emigrants brought in an epidemic, etc. Above all, however, the gentlemen could not accept that we were grossly violating the sacred commandments of the ministry. But we did not let ourselves be dissuaded, and I turned to the Deutsche Konferenz-gemeinschaft of the Alliance Israélite[7] (M. A. Klausner), giving them to understand that the Hilfsverein did not appreciate our drive. That was an opportunity for Herr Klausner to prove the generosity of the Alliance, and he immediately offered us a subvention. When I again reported this to the Hilfsverein—a special meeting took place in Berlin, to which I went with Änne's father—the competition of the Alliance naturally did not suit these gentlemen, and thus we got a subvention from them too, so that in the course of time we were able to give greatly needed help to some tens of thousands of emigrants. Later many moving letters of thanks came from America.

It was always very strange when we entered the cars. The unsuspecting people thought they were already in America or, at least, that they were to transfer to their ship. It always took minutes before the purpose of our visit was made clear to them. For me, the matter was of very special benefit: I could occupy my people in a useful way, their sense of solidarity grew, from their own experience they became acquainted with the misery of the masses in the East, and gradually they came to understand better the mentality of our East European brethren. At the same time, our achievements did impress the Jews of Hannover after all, and even if there were trends to inhibit or impede our activity, on the whole it was still the best propaganda that one could imagine, and we proved that we did not indulge only in notions of the future and in fantasies, but rather were ready for vigorous work. I believe that what we accomplished at that time was also a kind of *Hachschara*,[8] and many participants in that operation still remember with pleasure those months that brought us much work, but also great satisfaction.

1. The first part of these memoirs was published in Hebrew, with the title "Recollections of a Jecke" (Tel Aviv, 1947). An excerpt from the unprinted German original describing Gronemann's grandfather Karger appeared in *Jüdisches Leben in Deutschland: Selbstzeugnisse zur Sozialgeschichte 1780–1871*, ed. M. Richarz (Stuttgart: Deutsche Verlags-Anstalt, 1976), pp. 431ff. Gronemann also portrayed his experiences during the First World War in the autobiographical novel *Hawdoloh und Zapfenstreich* (Berlin, 1924).

2. Attorney Adolf Friedemann (1871–1933) was a coworker and the first biographer of Herzl, and in the years 1902–1920 a member of the Zionist Grosse Aktionskommitee.

3. Starting in 1905, attorney Arthur Hantke (1874–1955) directed the Zentralbüro der Zionistischen Vereinigung and was its president from 1910 to 1920.

4. Heinrich Rickert (1833–1902); member of the Reichstag 1874–1902. Originally a national liberal, starting in 1884 he became liberal. As of 1893 he was the leader of the Freisinnige Vereinigung.

5. Attorney Alfred Klee (1875–1943) performed leading functions in the Zionist organization, and in 1920 he was elected to the representative body of the Berlin Jewish community.

6. Paul Nathan (1857–1927) was president and Bernhard Kahn (1876–1955) was secretary general of the Hilfsverein der deutschen Juden, which was founded in 1901 and devoted itself to social work for East European and Palestinian Jews.

7. The Alliance Israélite Universelle was founded in 1860 in Paris as a Jewish world organization with branches in different countries. It worked for the defense of the rights of Jews throughout the world and performed extensive social and educational work. In aiding East European Jews and East European Jewish emigrants the Alliance and the Hilfsverein der deutschen Juden worked with and alongside one another.

8. Hebrew for "preparation"; in Zionism, preparation of the emigrants for life in Palestine through language courses and professional retraining for agriculture or the crafts.

# 29  *Charlotte Popper, née Lewinsky*

 BORN IN 1898 IN PREUSSISCH-STARGARD (WEST PRUSSIA).

Charlotte Popper, Remembrances of a Small Town. Undated manuscript, 8 pages. Written in Tel Aviv around 1955.

*Charlotte Popper grew up in Preussisch-Stargard, administrative district of Danzig, where her father ran a textile business. She depicts the Jewish community, split into three classes, and the dubious religious instruction that the pupils received. When the community hired a new rabbi, he not only introduced religious reforms but also influenced the youth toward Zionism. Thereupon the community council forbade him to perform any official functions.—The author later attended the Gymnasium in Danzig and studied mathematics in Königsberg, where she was active in a leading capacity in the Zionist Youth Organization. She became a teacher, and in 1923 she married in Hamburg. In 1936 she emigrated from there to Palestine.*

Until 1918 Preussisch-Stargard was a small town in West Prussia. In it there lived some hundred Jewish families. Jewish life was centered around the synagogue. The latter stood on a back street. From our kitchen window we could see it and watch when the candles were lit on Friday evening. Then my mother called out to father and my brothers: "It is time to go to the synagogue." After a while she reminded my brothers, who did not reach for their *siddur*[1] very eagerly, but instead usually put off their departure: "Rabinowitz is already rocking back and forth." Indeed, one could observe the cantor swaying to and fro at his lectern, and I was glad that one could not also hear his croaking voice.

The synagogue was surrounded by a very neatly kept courtyard. Considering the hedges by the fence and some humble flower beds in the front, some called it a "garden." The yard was big enough so that the young people could walk about during the *Yizkor* service[2] and exchange looks during this usually drawn-out break, and the girls could show off their new holiday clothes. The latter was also the motive for attendance at the synagogue by the rest of womankind, in addition to protracted chats undisturbed by any household duties. The ladies always came home from the holiday services in high spirits and with new kitchen recipes.

On Shabbat the ladies' gallery was empty except for two very old women, local poor folk, who sat next to one another and one of whom read to the other in a loud monotonous murmur from a German book of devotions, despite the Hebrew services, which in the meanwhile were taking place in the men's section and which the two old women could not see from their rear seats anyway. When I was a child these two shriveled women and their monotonous murmuring seemed to me to belong inseparably to the inventory of the synagogue. Incidentally, the other women attending the synagogue also made use of said book of devotion, which was called *"techinne."*³ The text was full of exhortations, empty phrases, and impossible sentence structures, and, as the foreword expressed it, was supposed to serve the purpose of "edification of the Jewish woman."

I must not fail to point out the elating impression that the synagogue made on Yom Kippur, when it was filled to the very last seat with earnest worshipers. The men in their white coats formed a humble, classless community divested of every external sign of prestige, and the women bent over their books without chatter. For refreshment during the long day in the unventilated room packed with people, they had brought along an apple studded with cloves, which did, in fact, smell pleasantly and refreshingly and which they used in place of smelling salts.

The quality of Yom Kippur that made everyone equal disappeared with the last sound of the shofar.⁴ In everyday life, class rules were sacrosanct. We had it good because we belonged to the middle class, which represented the broadest section. The "wealthy" had it bad in their isolation, while the poor in their parts of town cultivated neighborly relations in solidarity with the non-Jews. For eternally egalitarian poverty does not have the time or the right to concern itself with differentiations that do not lie within the realm of vital necessities.

For the life of the community it was an advantage that there were poor Jews in our small town. For whereto were the loudly proclaimed, ample donations to flow? One had to be generous. Where else were the *"schlachmones"* packages at Purim to be sent?⁵ My mother, though, took the easy way out. Without considering their religious affiliation, she simply placed such gifts into the skinny hands of the children of the back street, whom she saw from her kitchen window playing around the courtyard of the synagogue. Our Jews really had it good with their poor, for there were also stipends and similar bestowals to distribute. Originating in the capital of the province, they were granted according to a certain scale to the small towns too. I remember a small town in East Prussia where the Jews were in a great predicament because of this, and finally sent for a poor cobbler's family, which was richly blessed with children. After a few years, due to their comfortable start, the generously supported training of the children, and their income, they attainéd such a good economic status that the predicament of the community began anew.

Now back to my hometown and the most important chapter: Jewish education. Recognizing the priority of this task, the governing body engaged a teacher who twice a week, on Wednesday afternoon and Sunday morning, gathered the young people around him for Hebrew lessons. We were ready to sacrifice the afternoon, but we tried to save Sunday with the usual excuses. When we got all that we could out of "headaches" and "nausea," we feigned forgetfulness and sudden recollection if mother came into the children's room on Sunday to admonish us. She quickly helped us get on the way, and if we came too late this was usual and was not at all punished. Herr R., who was employed at the town's primary school, and who wanted to improve his meager pay and help his large family by the extra income from the community, knew exactly whom he had to thank for this privilege and treated the children of the well-to-do accordingly. To make his goodwill perfect, he prefaced every name with the words "my dear little." Thus, there was a dear little Liliental, a dear little Ullendorf, etc. The tardy were politely shown to their seats in the very first rows. In the back sat the poor, and they had nothing to laugh about. My brother, who once in the middle of the lesson let his head fall onto the first row of benches and produced soft sounds of slumber, caused Herr R. to continue instruction in a whisper and, nodding towards the sleeper, to demand this tone from the pupils, too.

How R. succeeded in teaching us the Hebrew letters and to read fluently in a year is a mystery to me, especially since all age groups were put together in one classroom and met at the same time. But after the first year and in the following seven school years there was only the translation of the most important prayers in the same, never-changing sequence. The translation proceeded word by word and was rigorously carried out in favor of the German language and at the expense of Hebrew. The *Schemone Esre*[6] began: *Adonai* = Lord, *sfossai* = my lips, *tiftach* = open, "Lord open my lips." The boredom was agreeably interrupted by the late arrival or early departure of the favored class and by the punishment, to the point of thrashing, of pupils in the rear rows. Foaming at the mouth and with a stick in his hand, Herr R., irritated by the constant coming and going before him, which he did not want to stop for the already mentioned reasons, would suddenly rush at a pupil in the rear rows, in the process of which his voice broke hoarsely and a drizzle poured over us at the front.

That was not the only Jewish education that was offered us. The Gymnasium pupils and the girls from the girls high school received religious instruction from the Herr Rabbi within the framework of the general curriculum. The rabbi of the community, a fine gentleman with sophisticated airs, of course of liberal bent, belonged to the faculty of the secondary schools. He taught us "biblical history," anxiously avoiding all laws and prescriptions and with special emphasis on the universal message of the prophets, which we had to memorize in the German version, of course. Memorization was the core of the instruction for years, and the translation as a rule was so liberal that later I did not always recognize the texts in the original language. The name and face of the rabbi changed every couple of years, since these gentlemen used the dull provincial town only as a steppingstone to more interesting appointments.

Then one day Rabbi Fritz Bernstein appeared on the pulpit of the synagogue. This time it was not only a new name and a new face. It was a new human being. The gentlemen of the governing body, who had liked the sample sermon exceptionally well (and each time that was the decisive criterion for the appointment), did not suspect what a troublemaker—from their point of view—they had loaded upon themselves. Rabbi Bernstein was a Zionist. When he arrived in our small town with a nonterminable contract in his pocket, he brought with him, besides a bride, the elan of his youth, with which he was determined to spread his Zionist ideal and to help it to victory among us. What more promising field of activity could he possibly want than the unspoiled youth of a closely knit Jewish community.

At first he began cautiously, with reforms of the stagnant, monotonous religious ceremonial, which was divested of all living freshness. "Reform" is a poor expression for this undertaking, which rather amounted to a renaissance when Bernstein made it his business to involve the entire congregation in the services, at first through common singing and by having the worshipers join in the chanting with the cantor. In addition, a girls' choir was organized. The rabbi himself took over the rehearsal of the choir, in his residence. In the process, the fruits of many years of lessons in translating Hebrew became apparent, when, for example, the girls, who had the text in Latin script right below the notes, referred to the hymn that began with *"Kohanecko jilbeschu zedek. . ."*[7] as the "Song of the Gilded Shoes." The gentlemen of the community began to prick up their ears. They began to feel uneasy. They regarded any departure from what was traditional and constant as a departure from the firm ground on which their parents and forefathers had taught them to stand in one particular way and no other. When, however, the rabbi had a *sukka* erected in the synagogue courtyard for the Sukkos holiday, they resorted to a—for the time being still silent—protest by simply boycotting this undertaking and unmistakably giving expression to their view by not appearing in the tabernacle.

Then the unthinkable happened: Rabbi Bernstein gathered the youth around him and told them about Zionism. The young people went to the fashionably and tastefully furnished rooms of the rabbi's home. If for no other reason, they went because there they found their first opportunity to be together casually. Unfortunately, the rabbi's enthusiasm did not suffice to counterbalance the influence of their complacent, bourgeois, patriarchal homes. Perhaps it was also not very wise of Bernstein to point to the masses of impoverished Jews from the East, oppressed and degraded by the arbitrariness of the authorities, and also to the pioneer work that the first immigrants were accomplishing under difficult conditions in the Holy Land. The parents had an easy time convincing their offspring, grown soft from their good life, how good they had it here in their comfort and how crazy it would be to load hardships and privations upon themselves. "But besides and above all, we are living here as free citizens of a free, great German fatherland, whose culture is centuries removed from the pogrom countries of the East."

But when from the pulpit, too, the rabbi spoke words that accorded with those with which he intended to "capture" the young people, something had to be done. The governing body convened for a special meeting. In the meanwhile, in his cozy home, Rabbi Bernstein, smiling, was reading his contract, which assured him a permanent appointment, and was playing unconcerned with the little daughter that his wife had borne him after a year of marriage. The gentlemen of the governing body were not ready to take it lying down. At first they forbade the rabbi to speak from the pulpit. But the young people were still available to Bernstein. To be sure, he no longer succeeded in gathering them around him in full force at his home, but his instruction at the higher schools gave him constant opportunity to be in touch with young people, and precisely with the more intelligent among them. Already in some homes Zionist songs were heard and writings were found whose texts made the masters of the houses turn pale. In view of this danger threatening the community, the governing body was ready to go to extremes. To avert the calamity even the sacrifice of money was not too much. Rabbi Bernstein was informed through an official letter that, in accordance with his contract, he would indeed continue to receive his pay, but that he was forbidden to carry out any official duties, for which another gentleman would be engaged as quickly as possible.

This blow, which condemned Bernstein to inactivity and threw charity at his feet, hit him hard, as did his ostracism, which was the natural outcome of said official act. As one says: "He became skin and bones." He went on trips here and there, in order to get a new position through trial sermons. On one such journey, to Silesia, he became ill, and the influenza that raged at that time put an end to his young life, far away from wife and child.

Soon thereupon the community dissolved. Through the treaty of Versailles, Preussisch-Stargard fell to Poland; more precisely, it became part of the Polish Corridor. The members of the community, the majority of whom opted for Germany, dispersed to all directions of the Reich.

Rabbi Bernstein led only me and my brothers and sisters to Zionism, and we landed in Israel. Of the other members of the community not a single one found his way to our land. The widow of Rabbi Bernstein, along with her two children—the second of whom was born after its father's death—also lives in Israel, the country to which her prematurely deceased husband had guided her.

1. Prayerbook.

2. The *Yizkor* service is held on holidays for deceased parents. Children whose parents are alive leave the synagogue during this service.

3. *Techinne* or *techinna* (Hebrew for "to beseech") is the generic term for prayer books that were written in Yiddish and later in German, and were intended exclusively for women.

4. The shofar is a wind instrument made of a ram's horn, which is blown at the end of the services on Yom Kippur and on Rosh Hashana.

5. Gift packages with foodstuffs. According to the instructions in the Book of Esther 9:22, food and alms are given on Purim as a sign of joy.

6. The main prayer, the *Shmone Esre,* which is said three times a day by the orthodox.

7. Psalm 132:16: "Her priests also will I clothe with salvation."

# 30 *Arnold Tänzer*

BORN IN 1871 IN PRESSBURG (AUSTRIA); DIED IN 1937 IN GÖPPINGEN (WÜRTTEMBERG).

Arnold Tänzer, War Memoirs. Undated manuscript, fragment, 49 pages.

*Arnold Tänzer was trained as a rabbi in Pressburg and officiated in Hohenems and Meran until he went to Göppingen (Württemberg) in 1907 as the community rabbi. From 1910 to 1914 he edited the* Israelitische Wochenschrift *and published several works on Jewish history. Filled with great national fervor, he volunteered immediately upon the outbreak of war in 1914 to serve as an army chaplain. His petition was not granted consideration until 1915, and he began his service with the Bug Army. The fragment relates the everyday activities of the army chaplain at the*

*Eastern front in the year 1915. Stationed mainly in Brest Litovsk, Tänzer experienced the reality of war in the destroyed city; he visited the infirmaries and conducted prayer services.*[1]

If only one could faithfully describe that singular feeling of fervid enthusiasm that caused every patriotic German heart to beat faster in those first days of August 1914! That feeling still stirs in me today and remains indelibly engraved in my memory. Countless times since, during the often long and monotonous trips on peasant carts or field-railways through the Russian sands, as well as in hours of the most earnest self-examination after returning to my so sorely tried homeland, I have attempted to fathom the fervent mood of those days. Was it the passion to conquer, the lust for plunder, the desire for war of a generation that after forty-three years of peace did not know the dread seriousness of war and its inevitable sacrifices, and for that reason also did not fear them? No, a thousand times no. There was nothing of that—even if the culture of the twentieth century has been sullied in the most unheard-of way by the infamous Article 231 of the forcibly imposed Peace of Versailles. Despite Germany's official acknowledgment, which was extorted by means of the most dire threats, the allegation of Germany's sole blame for the war is and will remain the most repugnant lie in world history, and it is all the more repugnant as its inventors produced it against their better knowledge in order to veil their own, heavy guilt and at the same time to create a justification for their war aim, which from the very start was the destruction of Germany.

At the outbreak of the war every German knew or felt this very will to destroy on the part of its enemies, who had long since been conspiring to it, and thus it was nothing else but love, devoted love for all things German, which were so gravely threatened, love for the German homeland, for German culture, for the German people, that filled every German heart at that time. The feeling in the collective soul of the German people was at that time holy and pure. Few knew, but all felt that this war had been forced on us by our enemies, that it was a matter of defending the homeland against the threat of destruction. Our experiences in the postwar period confirmed fully, however, that this feeling was only all too warranted. What we all experienced in those first days of August were solemn hours; for they were inspired by the purest performance of duty, by performance of duty toward one's people and fatherland.

It was this alone that likewise inspired me at that time, that also allowed me, a man of forty-three, grown deeply earnest thanks to his profession and experience in life, to recognize only one love, only one concern: the German fatherland. Whatever else so entirely filled my mind—my profession, my scholarly work, my fatherly obligations toward my six children—all that receded into the background, appeared secondary and meaningless in view of the great danger that was threatening the German fatherland and waxing greater day by day. When in the last days of July the prospects of peace were growing ever dimmer, when finally on Friday, July 31st, after the unbearable tension of the preceding days, the Kaiser's decree appeared declaring a "State of Imminent War" for the entire German Reich, I was resolved to take part through military service in any war that might come, even though at my examination I had been declared physically unfit. Now everyone who was honestly willing simply had to be fit. [. . .]

The patriotic mood reached its peak in the late afternoon of August 1st, when the three Göppingen daily papers published the mobilization order in a special edition. Now the die had been cast. A people such as the Germans, whose greatest majority was peaceful through and through, saw itself forced by the destructive will of its enemies into a hard battle for its national existence. Faced with this defensive war, which had been forced upon it, the entire people closed ranks. All political, social, and religious barriers fell. In the eyes of the Kaiser and for the nation everyone was a German.

That fateful August 1st was a Sabbath. At its conclusion, in the late evening, almost my entire congregation had appeared in the synagogue. The prayer service was that of the Ninth of Ab, the yearly day of commemoration and mourning for the destruction of Jerusalem. Even though this day was already stamped with deep earnestness, since it awakened the memory of Israel's thousand-year history of suffering outside its ancestral home, on this particular day an especially serious mood, which expressed itself in heightened devotion, was unmistakable. Every heart was filled with anxious concern over what the immediate future would bring the nation and the individual.

After the the service ended, at about ten o'clock, I wrote my first petition to my immediate superiors, the Israelite High Consistory in Stuttgart, and requested my assignment as a Jewish chaplain. I took the letter to the post office myself at midnight. This haste was superfluous, since my wish was fulfilled only after exactly one year. In order to let no chance pass, in the following days I also registered by letter and telegram with the Verband der Deutschen Juden in Berlin. In the absence of any legal provision, it had taken the commendable initiative of establishing a Jewish field chaplaincy immediately upon the outbreak of war, and the "authorization" of the military rabbis by the War Ministry in Berlin resulted through its intercession. With understandable impatience I looked forward to the quick and favorable decision that I certainly was expecting.

With the first day of mobilization, the scene below my window had also changed. In the big banquet tent, which was now emptied out, the conscripted soldiers gathered before they set out together for the railway station, hundreds every day, all of them in good cheer. Many a one whom I envied in those days because he was marching off has since gone to an early, hero's grave in enemy soil.

For Tuesday, the 4th of August, at ten in the morning I had scheduled a special prayer service to bid farewell and, in parting, to give God's message and blessing to approximately thirty congregation members who were setting out during the first days of mobilization. (In the course of the war, their number rose to ninety-two, of whom six fell in battle.) The entire congregation appeared at this first wartime prayer service, most of those who were marching off in uniform. There was no need for any special exhortation to perform one's duty as faithfully as possible. On every face one could see complete understanding for the earnestness of the situation, and firm determination to give their best for our threatened fatherland. I emphasized the common spirit that bound all together regardless of creed, and the obligation to generously support the families of all soldiers, and this soon met with notable success.

A collection for the Red Cross that I had initiated in my congregation that same day brought in handsome returns, as in general the members of my community contributed most selflessly during the entire war in the continuously organized war aid collections. Upon the suggestion of the Israelite High Consistory, a "War Charity" category was introduced into the list of synagogue donations for the duration of the war. The board of directors regularly channeled the proceeds from it to fitting causes. Also, at my instigation, the members of the Israelite Women's Association and the Israelite Young Women's Association, who participated devotedly in patriotic relief work throughout the war, revived a sewing circle that had existed earlier, in order to assist the Red Cross as much as possible. Several members of these organizations were later distinguished by being awarded the Charlotte Medal.

*[Since at the start of the war only six rabbis were planned for, Tänzer was not called up for the Bug River Army until July 1915. He received identity papers with the following text:]*

"Rabbi Dr. Tänzer of Göppingen is authorized to serve as pastor to the Jewish soldiers in the troop zone assigned to the military high command of the Bug River Army. For his duty in the war theater he is entitled to: the use of a wagon, two horses and a driver, free meals, free quarters, free transportation to the army, rations for the horses, and, given space, shared use of the official motor vehicle. These privileges are subject to the regulations for the Christian Field Division Chaplains. He has no title to further benefits. For issuance of the necessary military transportation tickets, particularly for the trip to Breslau, he is to apply to the appropriate base headquarters. The chief of staff of the command headquarters of the Sixth Army Corps, to which he is to turn for this purpose with these identity papers, will equip him with wagon, horses, and driver. — All military and civilian officials are requested to provide him with all possible support and, when required, the necessary protection and aid in order that he may fulfill his mission. In accordance with Article 20 of the convention of 6 July 1906 for aid to the wounded and sick of combat armies, he is entitled to wear the prescribed emblem, to wit, an armband fastened to his left arm with the red cross on a white field. Upon presenting his identity papers, he is to have this armband stamped by the nearest military office. — Berlin, 29 July 1915. The Royal Prussian Ministry of War."

At that time I experienced personally that there are no insuperable difficulties if one is strong-willed. Although I myself was completely inexperienced in military matters and had no one knowledgeable nearby whom I could have asked for advice, in just a few days I was ready to depart as prescribed. To be sure, the money that had been approved for equipment was insufficient, and I had to add a considerable sum from my own pocket. But I gladly made this little sacrifice, since I was finally to see service. The Stuttgart firm of Bender & Co. satisfactorily supplied me with my entire regulation uniform. The initial feeling of strangeness in my unaccustomed attire was quickly overcome, as in general all external matters were completely secondary for me at that time. As hardly ever before, the life I led in those days was an entirely spiritual one, divorced from my immediate surroundings. My every thought and wish revolved around the question of how and with what means I could prove useful to our fighting men in the field, and indeed, as was my resolve from the very start, regardless of their religious creed.

In order to know at least something about active duty, I had read various pertinent works in the past weeks and had also taken riding lessons in a Stuttgart riding school, in the course of which I achieved respectably sore buttocks. I also acquired a revolver and took instruction in its use, something that later proved very practical.

*[Tänzer travels by way of Cracow to Chelmno in Russian Poland.]*

On the next morning, I first went to the supervisory headquarters behind the lines, where I hoped to receive some sort of instructions about the nature and scope of my duty. Here, as with all of the authorities in the following years, I met with cooperation and complete readiness to further my official task in every possible way. But I was told that, within the framework of the general service regulations, I was to conduct my affairs entirely as I saw fit. The high command alone was competent to issue any kind of instructions, just as it had all further jurisdiction over my military activities. It was to it that I must turn. But the high command, I was told further, was on the way to Brest Litovsk, which had been captured three days earlier.

I wanted to betake myself there as quickly as possible, but saw myself forced to spend three days in Chelmno because my horses needed to rest and my wagon had to be repaired. I therefore immediately took up my work as chaplain there. I got information about the three field hospitals in Chelmno and arranged to hold a camp service in the main synagogue, which was requested of the Jewish community to this end. All units that could be reached were informed through official channels of this camp service, and the Israelite soldiers were ordered to attend it. Since the service was to take place in two days, I devoted the interval to visiting the infirmaries. There I went from bed to bed in all of the sick rooms, as I always did thereafter, and made myself available to my comrades regardless of their creed. In the case of Jewish soldiers, a more or less religious conversation evolved naturally. In Field Infirmaries 7 and 50, both of which were overcrowded, I found many Jewish comrades, some of them wounded, others sick.

In Field Infirmary 7 I had a pleasant experience. Hardly had I entered the sickbay when to my surprise I heard my name called out. It was a comrade from Göppingen, the mechanic B., who had to undergo an appendix operation there. We both rejoiced over our unexpected meeting in enemy territory, and since then we have at times recalled it back home. — Field Infirmary 3 was temporarily set up in a church. Here I had to provide my comrades, at their request, with a lengthy report on the prevailing military situation. I was happy that I could report only good news.

On Sunday, August 29th at 10:00 a.m., I held the scheduled prayer service in the spacious main synagogue, which the Jewish communal authorities had gotten ready for this purpose. Because of the risk of cholera the civilian population had been forbidden to enter the synagogue during worship. All the more eagerly did they crowd outside at the windows. Along with a considerable number of Jewish military, several Christian officers had also appeared for the service. Before the start of prayers I distributed for those present to keep, as I always did later, the little army prayer book that the Verband der Deutschen Juden had published at the outbreak of the war and had made available free of charge. My sermon, "Sense of Duty and Trust in God," was well received by everyone present.

I hardly saw anything of the town at that time. And the little I saw thoroughly displeased me. Just about everything, the streets, the houses, the people, in their filth and decay, showed unmistakable signs of their suffering from the war. The poor, careworn appearance of the almost entirely Jewish civilian population was especially conspicuous. The meals for officers in transit were provided through the resourcefulness of a Jewish couple, who with great dispatch had set up a pleasant restaurant in an empty store, where one could eat well at a reasonable price. And at that time, while on the advance, we were most undemanding.

*[After a short visit to the army high command in Jablon, Tänzer travels to heavily destroyed Brest Litovsk.]*

On the next morning I set out to look for the infirmaries. It was there that I sought and found my most important and dearest work during the time of my service at the front. In those days the infirmaries in Brest Litovsk were easy to find. I needed only to follow the many horse-carts that drove through the town loaded with the sick. During the first weeks, a smaller, little damaged synagogue, the "Blue Church"—a Russian church so designated by our troops because of its blue tower—and, near to it, the large Gymnasium building, which was later occupied by Army Railway Headquarters III, were set up as infirmaries in the most primitive manner. In the synagogue I found only cholera and typhus cases, who were lying on straw on the floor; in the "Blue Church" I also found lying that way only lightly wounded and sick men, and in the Gymnasium men with every sort of sickness. Here there were but few beds, and the building was dreadfully overcrowded from one end to the other. With shocking clarity the horror and ghastliness of war, even in the camp of the victor, revealed itself to me. And I would advise all of those, unfortunately not few, who at home enthusiastically backed the war, in their often quite cheap and convenient patriotism, to expose themselves just once to the impressions of such a field hospital—not even to mention the kinds of impressions that one gained at that time in the large infirmary in Brest Litovsk. The latter soon became the sole infirmary in the town, since all of the occupants of the two already named infirmaries were brought into the Gymnasium. Together with my Christian colleagues, I helped to transport them. We carried our dangerously sick comrades from the wagons into the building and were happy if at least in the corridors we could find a spot for them somewhere in the straw. Packed tightly together, the so admirably patient men filled every corner in every room and hallway. No one there asked about religion or social position. There only the suffering human being mattered and served unwittingly as the most urgent protest against the horror of war. The wounded and sick were constantly borne through the corridors into the operating room, where the work did not cease. Along with the others, I helped wherever possible, since there was such a lack of personnel.

Only late in the evening did I return to my quarters, where a most unpleasant surprise was awaiting me. My two horses and my wagon were gone. In a large courtyard opposite my quarters there were some sturdily built, unused stables. I had put my team in one of them and had secured the door with a padlock. In the courtyard itself there was a guard from the noncombat company, which had been billeted there. In order to tend to the horses, my orderly had possession of the key. According to the testimony of the guard, in the late afternoon a lieutenant had entered the courtyard, asked what was in the locked stables, and after he found out he broke into the stable and drove off with the team of horses. He said only that he needed the wagon for urgent official purposes and hoped that he could soon send it back. Since the wagon did not belong to the noncombat company and the guard had not been specially charged with watching over it, he had not bothered any further about the matter.

Naturally, I filed a report with the local command post and had them issue me an attestation, which I sent to the military high command. A few weeks later the latter sent me another team and wagon. In those days, by the way, the breaking of locks and appropriation of another's property was not uncommon in Brest Litovsk. At about the same time, a fairly large sum of money had been stolen from the locked coffer of the judge advocate at the local command post. And I myself once happened upon a non-commissioned officer who was trying to break into my locked room with the help of a sidearm. The chase, which began immediately with the aid of several comrades, unfortunately failed, since the fellow had jumped from a window and in the darkness easily found hiding in one of the rubble piles.

On the 6th of September I began preparations for the field services on Rosh Hashana, the Jewish New Year festival, which was celebrated on the 9th and 10th of September. First of all, with the generous help of the local commander, Major von Ranke, I had the pertinent orders of the day issued to the units within reach (the Conta Corps, the Beskides Corps, and the 41st Reserve Division). I then went to the main synagogue, the only one that could be considered for prayer services. Situated at the corner of Politseyskaya Street and Sbirogovskaya Street, it was visible from a distance—not only because it towered up as a stately edifice that had suffered little external damage amidst the world of ruins that surrounded it, but also because the bright yellow of its outside walls gleamed from afar. This house of worship, which on the outside was octagonal and rose to a point, was popularly known as the Great Synagogue—in contrast to the second, smaller communal synagogue and the approximately fifty other places of prayer, of which only three had escaped destruction.

The Jewish community in the former city of Brest Litovsk had owned a synagogue that was known far and wide for its beauty and in 1841 was the last building to be torn down. As a result of the many obstacles imposed by the government, the building of a large communal synagogue in the new city could be begun only in 1851. It was completed and inaugurated in 1861. It stands in the middle of a big, open square that is closed off from the street by a wall. The middle main portal leads into the large sanctuary for the men with some 600 seats, while both side entrances lead to the two women's balconies. One could still see that the internal decorations of the high, broad room, made possible in 1878 through the legacy of a certain Ch. J. Schereschewsky, must have been very beautiful. Opposite the entrance, on the eastern wall, dominating the entire view, there towered the Holy Ark, in which the Torah scrolls were housed. Charming paintings, representing bundles of flowers or musical instruments according to their descriptions in the Psalms, adorned the ceiling and walls, which latter also contained built-in cupboards for storing books. Two large marble tablets, bearing prayers for the Tsar in Hebrew and Russian, were located on the north and south walls. Numerous tall arched windows allowed light to fall profusely into the wide room, which was illumined by spirit-lamps in the evening.

When I entered the synagogue through the middle portal on September 6th, I was met with an agonizing sight in the little vestibule. Standing there, nailed shut, were two boxes that had once been full to the brim with Torah scrolls. The fleeing Jews had left them behind, trusting that these ceremonial objects—which, after all, possessed great value for the pious emotions of the Jews alone—would be spared if only because they served a sacred purpose. Now I found the boxes broken open and their contents strewn on the floor, partly in shreds. This was an unspeakably painful sight, since it is a millennia-old Jewish custom to treat Torah scrolls with every sign of reverence. If, during worship, for example, such a Torah scroll ever slipped from its bearer's hand and fell to the floor, all of those present had to atone for this sin by fasting for an entire day. And as in the vestibule, inside, too, I found all of the boxes, which had contained only Torah scrolls and holy books, broken open and their contents scattered about on the floor. In several places the roof and ceiling of the synagogue had holes, so that the rain of the past few days had formed a number of puddles on the floor. The fragments of the window panes, of which not one had remained whole, covered the floor ankle-high. Filth of every kind filled the room. Overturned and piled one on the other, the pews created a desolate chaos. First some sort of order had to be made before one could think about holding a prayer service. With the help of several Russian prisoners of war, who had been assigned to me for the purpose, and assisted by my orderly and a few Jewish comrades, I was more or less able to get the synagogue ready in the next two days.

The same day presented me with another significant experience. The unique sight of this town in ruins, in which there were no civilian inhabitants whatever and in which only soldiers wandered about, was made strangely complete by the fact that one ran into many soldiers who were curiously outfitted with pokers, iron bars, little shovels, and the like, without exception tools with which one could rummage in the debris. Soldiers were digging for treasure. They were searching zealously for valuables that the fleeing civilians might have buried. Not an entirely safe undertaking, since the ruins constantly threatened to cave in, and for that reason this most repulsive and depraving activity was soon strictly forbidden. But in those first weeks it was in full bloom and resulted in the strangest finds. In keeping with orders, these were all to be turned over to the local command post, which at that time still belonged to the Second Army. Books of all kinds were delivered in veritable masses. Mostly Hebrew books, or such in Jewish-German jargon,[2] but also many in Russian, among them German grammar texts and readers. One particular find, which testified to the concern of the Russian military administration for the countless illiterates in its army, had a comical side to it: we found ready-to-mail letters for the soldiers to send their relatives at home, in various versions and printed in type that simulated handwriting, in which they reported that the Russian army was campaigning valorously and triumphantly. Certainly a very convenient method of correspondence, since only the names of the sender and the recipient had to be added. I have saved two such "letters from the front" as a remembrance.

Because of such a find I was summoned that day to the local command post. Piled on a large table I found an impressive quantity of silver synagogue objects of all sorts.

The gentlemen there wished me to inform them about the age of the separate pieces as well as their cash value, as they were to be sold as war spoils. I could determine their age with no difficulty since the year of their manufacture was stated in Hebrew script on each object. On the other hand, it was far more difficult to estimate their value. Besides that, I was thoroughly reluctant to do so because the contemplated use of these ceremonial objects was unauthorized and went against orders. I very candidly explained this to the gentlemen, described the exclusively religious use of each individual piece, and pointed out that this was so-called church property, which by no means came under the category of war spoils. For that reason I urgently requested that each and every object, of which I wanted to make a list, for the time being remain locked in safekeeping at the command post until the high command, to whom I intended to report immediately, gave further instructions. My proposal was unanimously approved with no further ado and immediately carried out with my assistance. I will yet relate how I was later able to place these and still other silver synagogue objects from Brest Litovsk in custody in Germany.

Among the abundance of Hebrew writings of every kind that our soldiers had turned up and that lay about in piles in all of the quarters, I also found a small Torah scroll. Since it was easily transportable, it seemed to me to be well suited for later use in my many field prayer services with the individual army units. The Austrian army chaplains had all been equipped by their military administrations with such little Torahs. With the permission of the local command post I took the one that had been found there, and it served me very well. I later had it acknowledged in writing as my personal property by the governors of the Brest Jewish community, and I retain it to this day as my dearest remembrance of the war.

News of the field service on Rosh Hashana had spread quickly. More and more Jewish comrades called at my quarters. On both holy days I conducted prayer services that lasted several hours, and they were very well attended. P., a hearty comrade from the Diedenhofen Home Guard Company No. 66, who knew how to sing, functioned outstandingly as cantor. I delivered two sermons and strove to transform the homesickness, which filled every heart especially on such holidays, into a mood of piety and joy in discharging one's obligations. Afterward, I spent a few more stimulating hours in my billet with some of my comrades.

No matter what, I wanted to pass the Day of Atonement, the most important Jewish holy day, which was to be celebrated a week later, with the frontline troops. To that end I thought that I could assemble the Jewish soldiers of the 41st Reserve Corps and the Conta Corps at some suitable place between Kobrin and Antopol. Now I deeply regretted the loss of my horses and wagon. But the newly appointed local commander, Baron von Gesevius, was friendly enough to procure me a little, open rack-wagon, a so-called Panje wagon, along with two small but unbelievably steadfast and undemanding horses, with which I laboriously covered the 50-kilometer stretch to Kobrin, arriving there on September 14th. Hovering crazily above the Muchavez River, I rode across on some loosely laid boards, since the bridge had been blown up by the Russians. Awful was the sight of the refugees who were camped in the forests on either side of the road. In their neglected, starved condition they resembled animals more than humans. Everything that could be spared in the way of provisions was given the unfortunate ones by the passing German soldiers. A little girl snatched a bag of zwieback from my hands and ran with it into the woods, where she perhaps made her family quite happy with it.

In Kobrin, where the command post of the Bug River Army was just setting up after Mackensen's retreat, I was informed at the local command post that my plan could not be carried out since the troops were already 120 kilometers from Kobrin and moreover were quickly advancing, which meant that for the time being there could be no thought of assembling for prayers. An immediately telephoned request to the Army Supreme Command produced only the same negative message and, in addition, the order to hold services in Brest Litovsk for those troops who could be reached. After a brief inspection of the little ruined town, in which almost every house bore the ominous signs signifying an epidemic, and after resting miserably during a completely sleepless night, on the next day I had to drive back to Brest Litovsk to make preparations for the prayer services for the Day of Atonement. On the following two days, the 16th and 17th of September, the field hospital in Brest Litovsk was especially crowded. Thus, I had rich opportunity to help, and I remained there almost until the beginning of prayers.

On the Day of Atonement I held three field services with sermons, and Remembrance Services, etc., which were attended by about a hundred comrades and some Russian war prisoners. We all fasted the entire day as prescribed. With my above-mentioned comrade, P., I shared in reciting the prayers, which on this day are particularly extensive, and that induced a most devout atmosphere.

1. During the war Tänzer published the brochure *Brest-Litowsk: Ein Wahrzeichen russischer Kultur im Weltkriege,* Berlin 1917.
2. "Jewish-German jargon" was at that time the customary, denigrating designation in Germany for the Yiddish language. On the other hand, see the memoirs of Sammy Gronemann (28), who, as a Zionist, speaks only of "Yiddish."

# 31  *Bernhard Kahn*

BORN IN 1876 IN OSCARSHAMN, SWEDEN; DIED IN 1955 IN NEW YORK.

Bernhard Kahn, Memoirs 1914–1921. Undated manuscript; written after 1939; 74 pages.

*Bernhard Kahn, Doctor of Law, was Secretary General of the Hilfsverein der Deutschen Juden in Berlin from 1904 to 1921. This welfare organization, founded in 1901, was dedicated to helping the Jews of East Europe and Palestine. When the First World War broke out, Kahn organized a committee for the repatriation of Russian nationals. During the war, with the help of American and German funding, he created a large-scale aid organization that supported the Jews in the occupied areas of Poland and Lithuania. In 1916 Kahn was placed under surveillance by General Ludendorff when they disagreed on the question of emigration for these Jews. — As of 1921 Kahn worked for the Jewish aid organization*

*American Joint Distribution Committee, first in Berlin and Paris, and, starting in 1939, in New York, where he became its vice-president.*

*[The following material has been taken from the original manuscript, written in English.]*

It was vacation time in July and August. Usually hundreds of thousands of Russians, mostly of the wealthy classes, came to German summer resorts or to the big cities, to consult German physicians. About 100,000 of these people were caught in Germany by the war. It seemed to me and to Mrs. Kahn, who is of Russian descent herself, that something must be done immediately for this unfortunate group of people.

When I went to the office of the Hilfsverein der Deutschen Juden, which was on Luetzow Strasse, I found the office surrounded by groups of these Russian people, frightened and not knowing what to do. They had a hard time, badly treated as they were by the general population. We observed a sad scene in the best part of the German capital, on Tiergarten Strasse. Some Russian women had asked the inhabitants of some of the palatial houses for a drink, and the latter brought out water but poured it out on the street rather than give it to the thirsty, our so-called enemies.

Nobody wanted to change any foreign money; soon there were some sharks who asked 100 roubles from these poor Russian people just for a few marks.

I immediately decided to help these unfortunate people, and to put the office at their disposal. Our group was Jewish only, but since there were at least 40 percent non-Jews among the foreigners affected by the war events, I tried to form a nonsectarian committee consisting of groups who might have retained some humane attitude toward these people. We selected one or two socialists, one or two left-wing liberals, and one of the Polish faction of the Reichstag, and formed a nonsectarian committee for the protection of the Russian people.

When it became known among the members of the Hilfsverein that such a committee had been set up, hundreds of overpatriotic Jews protested against it. But when the people learned of the existence of this committee, those in distress flocked to our office, which was swamped by many thousands of men, women, and children. About a dozen mounted policemen with drawn sabres, and a number of other policemen surrounded the crowd. I got in touch with the army administration, which was in command of the situation in Berlin, and after difficult negotiations, we were given permission to act as a committee for these people in distress.

Many of the people seeking assistance had known me and Mrs. Kahn personally before the outbreak of the war, and many knew our names; and so, very soon, our private residence was just as much invaded as the office. With the mounting suspicion of the general population and the rising hatred against the Russians, it was a trying position for us in our apartment.

A few weeks before the outbreak of the war, our children had been visiting their grandparents in a small Bavarian town. There they were given little blue and white Bavarian flags to play with, and they took some of the pennants along with them when they returned to Berlin. The children, seeing that everybody was hoisting flags, got hold of their Bavarian flags and hung them out of the window. Very soon, an angry and dangerous-looking crowd moved toward our apartment, inciting the population against us, claiming that we were displaying Russian flags or signs for the Russian enemy. At that time I had already established so much contact with the Berlin Commandatura that I could telephone them for help. A sergeant with about a dozen men came to our rescue, trying to explain to the excited mob that the pennants flying from our windows were Bavarian flags.

The office of the Hilfsverein was kept open almost day and night. We occupied one floor of a building on Luetzow Strasse, and when two other floors were vacated on account of the war, we seized this good opportunity and rented the three floors for the offices of the Hilfsverein.

Soon the foreign press, particularly French, English, and Russian papers, published accounts of the ill treatment of foreigners in Germany, and of the barbarian attitude of the German population. To counteract these reports, the authorities were glad to be able to point out that we at least took care of these foreigners in need. Soon thereafter, articles in the French and Russian newspapers indicated that the Hilfsverein der Deutschen Juden and I were the only people who still had some human behavior left.

The Chancellor of the German Reichstag informed the authorities by a special decree that the Hilfsverein was the welfare agency to which they should turn with all problems concerning the Russian people. About 60,000 to 80,000 among them were poor people who had been visiting Germany as tourists or to seek relief from illness in summer resorts and sanatoria, and to see German doctors. Then there were many thousands of Russians living permanently in Germany, who were now considered enemies, lost their property, and were restricted in their movement. All of them were economically in a difficult situation, or even entirely ruined.

*[The committee organizes the exchange of these Russians for Germans in Russia.]*

There was another difficult task, with which we were confronted just a few days after the outbreak of the war. The German armies had invaded Russia, which meant at that time the bordering countries of Poland and Lithuania. After a terrible battle, which caused heavy damage to the industrial districts and a great loss of lives, they took the cities of Kalish and Lodz, and then the smaller cities around them. These were areas with a dense Jewish population, and ten thousands of Jews were in great distress.

The Hilfsverein did its best to come to the aid of these victims of the war. Again it was not very easy to persuade the German military authorities to permit this relief work of a German group on behalf of the enemies. But soon the misery became so great that it began to endanger even the advancing army, and we secured permission to come to the rescue of these war victims. It was about two weeks after the outbreak of the war, the middle of August, when we came to the conclusion that the means of the Hilfsverein and the relatively small Jewish community in Germany were not enough to do efficient relief work.

We had always been on friendly terms with some prominent American Jews, especially with Mr. Jacob H. Schiff, of New York.[1] We had already had their cooperation, even though on a small scale, at the time of the Kishinev pogroms in 1903, in the first Balkan war in 1912/13, and in our project of the Technicum in Haifa. [. . .] Thus, we cabled Schiff describing the situation as we found it, and asked whether the Americans could give us some help. We received an immediate reply, in which we were offered a contribution of $100,000. This was the beginning of the American relief work, as far as Poland and Lithuania were concerned. We did not know the source of the $100,000; we did know of an American Jewish relief committee which, at that time, was the same as the American Jewish Committee, or was a branch of it.[2]

Mr. Schiff made the following stipulations: The relief work was not to be done for Jews only; we were to set up a nonsectarian committee; and all activities were to be conducted on a nonsectarian basis. We of course complied with Mr. Schiff's requests. The nonsectarian committee was formed and placed under the protection of the Spanish Embassy. A commission was sent to the districts where the need was very great, and the first funds were distributed on a nonsectarian basis. Soon, however, we found that the real sufferers were the Jews. It was impossible to have a nonsectarian committee; there were so many intrigues involved with such a committee and with nonsectarian relief that it would have been impossible for us to do efficient work on that basis. We cabled all this to New York. The need of the Jewish masses as a result of the war had in the meantime become so well known in the United States that the Americans consented to a "Jewish Relief Committee for Poland and Lithuania." There arose again the great difficulty of securing permission for this Jewish relief work from the German Army, since they, too, wanted to have a nonsectarian committee and wanted the Jewish funds distributed also among the non-Jews. Especially Ludendorff was very stubborn in that respect, and it took me quite some time before I could overcome all objections.

I also handled the executive part of the work of the Jewish Relief Committee for Poland and Lithuania. The Americans had agreed to its establishment under the condition that there be some Zionist and some orthodox representatives. Of course, we had no objections to any Jewish group, and the committee consisted of Dr. Paul Nathan, Justice Waldstein, Captain Melchior, with Dr. James Simon as chairman, Max M. Warburg as treasurer, and myself as executive director.[3] This committee administered the American relief funds and, of course, the funds that were still contributed by the Hilfsverein itself.

We decided that a commission be sent to the accessible parts of Poland, to investigate the situation there. This commission consisted of Dr. Paul Nathan; Dr. Fink, who represented B'nai B'rith; Hermann Struck, a Zionist and an artist; Dr. Eduard Heimann, an economist, who is now professor of economics at the New School for Social Research in New York; and myself. Between February 17 and April 17, 1915, we made four trips to Poland, one to the northern, one to the central, and two to the southern part of Poland.

The commission found that eight of the ten *gouvernements* (governmental districts) had already at that time been wholly or partially occupied by the Austrian or German armies. The number of inhabitants in the occupied areas was 5,190,000, among them 700,000 Jews. The Jews constituted over 13 percent of the population. They were mostly concentrated in the cities, where the misery brought by the war made itself most strongly felt, so that the Jewish population suffered most heavily under the stress of war.

The areas of Wloclawek, Plock, Kutno, Kolo, and Konin, where no great battles had been fought, were the least damaged, and the suffering of the general and Jewish population there was not so great as in other parts of Poland. Kalish, Lodz, and the surrounding cities had suffered severely, and there were at least 100,000 Jews who lacked simply everything. The misery there, however, was still surpassed by conditions in the Dombrova Basin and the industrial district of Czenstochau, where 400,000 people had to be provided with food, and 250,000 were in need of support, among them 75,000 Jews. Special assistance was necessary for Galicia, where the Jewish population was first driven out by the Russian advance, or taken to Russia when part of Galicia was later liberated again by the German armies. The relief activities in this area were conducted by the Israelite Alliance[4] of Vienna in close cooperation with us, since part of the Russian-Polish district, such as Petrikau and surroundings, was occupied by the Austrian Army.

We sent exhaustive reports and findings to our friends in the United States. In the meantime, new organizations had been created in the United States that wanted to help the Jewish people in Poland, Lithuania, and Galicia. Besides the already existing American Jewish Committee, which had no definite character of a relief organization, there was first established, around November 1914, the Central Relief Committee by the orthodox group. At first, the support from the United States came very regularly, but it took quite some time until the relief organization was set up and established. The distress in the Eastern countries increased every day with the progress of the war and with the occupation of more and more territory in Poland, Russia, and Lithuania by the German Army. I had to travel very often to areas which were newly occupied, to get relief to the distressed Jewish victims of the war. [. . .]

Up to 1916, ten tours into the occupied territories were made, to ascertain the need and to organize the relief work. The relief activity consisted in the establishment of loan *kasses*, soup kitchens, tea rooms, consumers' stores, heated shelters, and other public welfare institutions for the needy population, and in the distribution of funds to maintain existing institutions.

We worked hand in hand with the nonsectarian German Central Relief Committee for Poland. America made large funds available. In cooperation with the Frankfurt Relief Committee for Needy Eastern European Jews, and with the Grand Lodge of B'nai B'rith for Germany, we conducted two big drives in Germany proper for a Relief Fund in 1915, the proceeds of which amounted to one million marks by 1916.

In peacetime there were about 1,700,000 Jews in Poland. One-fifth of this population, about 340,000, had voluntarily or forcibly gone to Russia. Thus, about 1,360,000 Jews still remained in Poland at that time. One-third of this population, about 455,000 souls, suffered from hunger and cold; 50,000 of them had been evacuated from the front lines; they were homeless and in a lamentable state. The number of those in need of relief increased from month to month. Since there were hardly any opportunities for earning a livelihood, those who still had some savings at that time were in need soon thereafter.

In Lithuania, the number of Jews was in normal times 700,000. One-fourth of these Jews—175,000—had been driven to Russia. An additional 125,000 went voluntarily back with the Russians, so that there were then about 400,000 Jews in the occupied parts of Lithuania, of whom at least 250,000 were in direst need. Since that territory had always been in a poorer economic condition, the misery of the Jews in Lithuania was even worse than that of the Jews in Poland.

In Courland, there were all in all 50,000 Jews; 40,000 of them had in the most brutal manner been expelled by the Russians, and of the remaining 10,000 Jews there were 8,000 in Libau alone. Relief activities on behalf of the Jews in Courland were at that time not necessary, since four-fifths had been driven away and the small remainder naturally did not require our assistance to such an extent as did the war victims in Poland and Lithuania.

As a whole there were then about 700,000 needy Jews in the occupied territory, whose number was increasing daily.

The Relief Committee for Poland and Lithuania had spent almost 2,000,000 marks for relief. In addition to these funds, about 75,000 marks from the German Central Relief Committee had been spent for the Jews; furthermore, 110,000 marks had been transmitted by the ICA [Jewish Colonization Association],[5] an additional 500,000 marks came directly from America, and 100,000 marks from other neutral countries or from other sources. At that time, relief to Poland and Lithuania amounted to 2,750,000 marks. In the following months the Jewish Relief Committee had to spend 500,000 marks monthly for the alleviation of the worst misery. With 700,000 starving people, this amount was, of course, extremely small; however, we had to provide for a longer period of time, so that larger funds could not be distributed for the time being. With these 500,000 marks, 225 cities and localities in the occupied territories were being supported monthly, including a total of 90 soup kitchens, 25 tea rooms, and many other public institutions from which the starving people benefited.

Besides the funds that had been made available, we aided the destitutes in another effective way. We sent large shipments of clothing, bedding, underwear, and shoes to the occupied territories. In 1915 a total of 150,000 kg of supplies were shipped, of which about 100,000 kg alone came from our very active committee in Koenigsberg. At a later clothing collection the Grand Lodge of B'nai B'rith for Germany participated in an outstanding manner. An important factor of these collections was that with the supply of clean clothing and underwear to the destitute people, the spreading of diseases had been avoided.

With the occupation of larger and larger parts of Russia, we were confronted with very great tasks of ideological as well as material importance. There was the question of reestablishing contact between the inhabitants of the occupied areas and their relatives, particularly in the United States, but also in Russia and other countries. This work had from the beginning been built up on a nonsectarian basis. A letter and information service on the largest scale was established. In the last months of 1915, up to the first part of 1916, more than 120,000 letters and individual inquiries had been conveyed to Poland, Lithuania, and Courland, and 100,000 from there to the United States and other countries.

Our office was considered the central agency for this work, also for letters to non-Jews. The American Embassy, other embassies, and all consulates, as well as Polish Catholic organizations and other non-Jewish institutions, military headquarters, and police authorities were using our intermediary for this service. The following example may show the extent of incoming mail. In one day alone, on March 22, 1915, we received 2,300 letters, among them 900 registered communications. Here I must mention that conveying these letters and news was not mere routine work since, in the interest of German military safety, we could not transmit the correspondence in the original; excerpts had to be made containing only unobjectionable subject matter, which was then translated. With the prevailing restrictions the mailing of the news was also extremely complicated.

The second task which we had to perform was the transmission of funds, a service that was even more responsible, and economically more important, than the transfer of correspondence. These remittances from relatives abroad to their folks in the occupied parts of Russia had also taken on large dimensions. The banking firm M. M. Warburg & Co. in Hamburg served as the main intermediary; it then referred the funds to us, and we expedited the transmissions to Poland, Lithuania and Courland. However, we also received very large funds from America directly. As with our news service, we had also with these activities become known as the agency best fit to handle all money transmissions, so that banks in Germany, America, and elsewhere turned to us to channel the funds received by them to Poland and Lithuania. The moneys passing at that time through our hands in very small amounts every month totaled about 500,000 marks monthly, and increased continuously. Sometimes we received and transmitted in a single day 100,000 marks, in small amounts of ten to one hundred or two hundred marks. I need not emphasize the high value of this material help thus given from relatives to relatives, and the importance of the renewal of torn family ties.

Also in these war times we considered emigration a further relief for the Jews in the occupied territories. It had really never been completely interrupted. During the entire war we had to make expenditures for emigration, although not to the former extent, of course. After order had been established in the occupied territories by the German administration, emigration again set in slowly. At the various conferences which we held with the competent German authorities, particularly at the conference on February 21, 1916 at the Eastern headquarters, under the chairmanship of Lieutenant General Ludendorff, it was declared that there should be no obstacles to emigration, that, on the contrary, it should even be promoted as far as feasible in the existing state of war.

It was a matter of course that emigration could not take on the same dimensions as in peacetime. Anyhow, there were many families who still had the steamship tickets sent to them before the war and, with the cooperation of authorities, we had in most cases been able to have these tickets revalidated and exchanged. Usually, we had to supply the means necessary to pay the difference resulting from the increase in rates during the war.

Furthermore, we received very many prepaid tickets from America, designated for relatives in the occupied territories; also funds were sent to the Hilfsverein for these purposes. In general, the Hilfsverein, on its part, was not to support emigration by advancing funds to destitute persons for their emigration. Those, however, who received money for the passage, or steamship tickets from their relatives, depended on our assistance at that time to a much higher degree than in peacetime. As far as any intervention through the Hilfsverein was concerned, in this field we did not differentiate between religious denominations, and we made our services available to Jews and non-Jews alike (Catholics, Greek Orthodox, and Protestants), who turned to us in great numbers.

Naturally, the extensive activities of the Hilfsverein in the occupied parts of Russia could only be conducted in agreement and closest cooperation with the military and civilian authorities. At first we had to surmount many difficulties, but thanks to the understanding attitude of everyone involved we were able to carry out extensive, fruitful work for Jews and non-Jews, and this also benefited Germany. [. . .]

German military authorities were considering a plan to promote as far as possible the emigration of Jews from the large parts of Lithuania and Poland that were occupied by the German Army.

In February, 1916, Ludendorff called a conference, to be held for that purpose at his Eastern headquarters, in Kovno. Besides the Hilfsverein der Deutschen Juden there participated in this conference the two German steamship companies, the North German Lloyd and the Hamburg America Line, as well as high officers of the German Army. The Hilfsverein and the Relief Committee for Poland and Lithuania were represented by Dr. James Simon, Dr. Nathan, Dr. Franz Oppenheimer,[6] and myself; [. . .] the Hamburg America Line by the director of the emigration department, Mr. Stahmer.

I went to this conference together with Dr. Franz Oppenheimer. We arrived in Kovno early in the morning and, of course, had to register with the military police. To our astonishment they asked us about our religion. It was the first time this had happened to us, since neither in Germany nor in the occupied territories was a German ever asked a question concerning his religion. When we expressed our surprise, the officer was very much embarrassed but explained that this was a rule established a short time ago, and every visitor from Germany had now to state his religion; although he knew that we were invited by Ludendorff to the conference, he could not make an exception.

When we came to our hotel, we met a number of high German officers, who wanted to entertain us until it was time for us to go to the conference. They drove us out to the fortress and showed us how it had been taken by German guns, explaining that the atmospheric pressure produced by these guns had almost blown to pieces the soldiers who were in the fortress. They gave us some more military details, and then drove us around and showed us the sights of the city.

We found quite a number of high German officers present at the conference. Ludendorff addressed the meeting, explained the ideas of the Army, and expressed the opinion that special ships should be used to get as many Jewish emigrants as possible out of Poland and Lithuania. He and the representatives of the steamship companies then went into the details of how this emigration movement was to be conducted. The question arose whether these ships would be safe or not, but it appeared that Ludendorff did not care as much about the safety of the ships as for a large-scale emigration by all means. The Jewish representatives were rather stunned by Ludendorff's ideas, but nobody dared to speak up. I finally got up and spoke against Ludendorff's plan, although rather timidly because I knew that if Ludendorff was displeased it would mean my being called to the front at once, and I certainly would not have been treated with much consideration by the Army. I had the floor for a few minutes, and most of the people present, including the Jewish representatives, were looking rather bewildered at me and listening with great astonishment to what I had to say. They apparently were somewhat surprised that I dared to oppose Ludendorff. After my speech there was a minute of stony silence. Ludendorff did not reply, and since there was no further discussion, he adjourned the meeting.

Before the meeting, the director general of the North German Lloyd had invited all of us and the representatives of both shipping companies for dinner. But before closing the meeting, Ludendorff asked the officers and the representatives of the steamship companies to have dinner with him that night. So our dinner with the director general was called off, but he asked one of his executives who was with him to invite us for dinner, and we refused.

After the meeting was over, everybody went up to say goodbye to Ludendorff. I was, of course, the last one, and I approached him very timidly. He shook hands with me, looked at me very sternly, and there ensued the following questions and answers between us: "When are you leaving, Dr. Kahn?" "Tomorrow morning, at eight o'clock, Your Excellency." "Oh, that's a pity, I would like to have a talk with you before you leave." "Your Excellency, I can, of course, postpone my return. After all, I came here to be at Your Excellency's service for any questions or problems you deem advisable to discuss. I am entirely at your disposal, Your Excellency." "Well, it would be very nice if you could stay over for one day. Are you an early riser?" "I am at your service, at any time, Your Excellency." "Would you come to see me at my headquarters as early as 7:30 in the morning?" "I am entirely at your disposal, Your Excellency." And so ended our conversation.

Our Jewish group had dinner together, and in discussing Ludendorff's ideas about the emigration, we all agreed that I had been right to raise objections to his plans. We had no idea what Ludendorff would have to say to me the next morning, and it was decided that I remain in Kovno for my discussion with Ludendorff. They warned me not to oppose him any further, since we were, after all, entirely dependent on him in this matter.

The next morning, at 7:30, I went to Ludendorff's headquarters. He received me in a very friendly way, and was quite a different person. At official meetings and discussions his face always had a very stern expression, which was the more accentuated on account of his being slightly squint-eyed. On that morning, however, he did not have the usual very martial countenance, and nothing of a wargod-like expression was noticeable. He was even charming, and told me that he had been listening carefully to what I had said the day before, and on second thought he felt that I was not entirely wrong, and that he would not insist on his plan of an almost enforced large-scale emigration. Yet, he would still like to see the emigration of the Jewish people being conducted in some way. When he asked me for my views, I told him that I thought regular emigration should not be enforced, and if the transports were not arranged on ships which were filled with Jewish emigrants only, such emigration would be quite satisfactory.

While we were discussing this I heard a door open behind my back, and when Ludendorff looked up, I turned around and saw Hindenburg coming into the room. Ludendorff introduced me to Hindenburg, and told him in a few words what our discussion was all about. He then said to me that urgent military business made it impossible for him to continue our conversation, and he led me to a second room filled with about a dozen officers of all ranks. He introduced me to them, explaining what he had been discussing with me; he told me that all his officers were at my disposal and that I should further discuss the matter with his staff. For about an hour we went into all details, and all officers went out of their way to be friendly, but I had a feeling that their friendliness was just a mask.

I left for Berlin the next day. When I walked to my office a day after my arrival in Berlin, I met on Kurfuerstendamm Mr. Korfanti,[7] the Polish member of parliament. Mr. Korfanti and his family and mine were quite friendly. They came to see us very often, and we went sometimes to their house. I may tell here in advance that in November 1918, during the so-called revolution, the Korfantis went to Poland. The night before they left he and his wife were at our house. Suddenly there was a terrible shooting in the neighborhood. We kept away from the windows, and even put the little beds of our children behind the chimney in the kitchen, to protect them from possible machine-gun shells. After half an hour the shooting was over, and the next morning the Korfanti family went to Poland. Coming back to my meeting with Mr. Korfanti on Kurfuer-stendamm, he asked me: "What has happened between you and Ludendorff?" "Why," I said, "Ludendorff and I are great friends." He looked around as if afraid of listeners, pulled me to the entrance of an apartment house, looked around again and, seeing that the entrance hall was empty and nobody there, he said: "There certainly must be some great friendship between you and Ludendorff. I have a cousin in the intelligence de-partment who, knowing that you and I are friends, has told me that Ludendorff has given orders to the intelligence department and the post office that all letters addressed to you, or sent by you, are henceforth to be thoroughly scrutinized. They are to be investigated not only as to their contents, but also to see whether any invisible ink or code had been used." I was really surprised. Although I did not truly believe in the friendliness of Ludendorff and his staff, I did not think they would go that far. I said to Korfanti that I was not worried about me, but about the poor Jews in Poland and Lithuania who were always writing letters to me convinced that they can say anything they want in them. Now there will certainly be many caught at making none-too-cautious remarks in their letters. I recalled an incident which occurred early in the war, and to give an example of the kind of letters these people in the Eastern countries wrote to me, I told Mr. Korfanti the story. A Jewish watch dealer in Lodz sent me a letter asking me to order for him parts of a watch movement from Switzerland. On two pages he described, in terms which only a watchmaker could understand, the various parts, talking of works and pinions, and this and that, giving details and figures, etc. And then two detectives came to my house asking me what kind of machines I was sending to Russia via a neutral country. Of course, I could not explain it myself, and only after a watchmaker was called in could it be established that the machines and other things mentioned in the letter were nothing else but parts of a watch movement.

In the afternoon there was a meeting of the Hilfsverein and the Relief Committee for Poland and Lithuania, to review the conference with Ludendorff. I reported on the conversation I personally had with him, how we were interrupted by Hindenburg, and the ensuing discussion with Ludendorff's staff. I did not want to say anything about what Mr. Korfanti had told me of Ludendorff's new orders concerning my mail, as I did not want to frighten the members of the Hilfsverein. They were very patriotic and saw in Ludendorff and Hindenburg the saviors of Germany. I concluded my report with the remark that Ludendorff was a great general and strategist, but that I had the feeling he was politically very reactionary. This remark about the much admired Ludendorff caused a storm of indignation among many of the people present, and especially Professor Soberheim,[8] related by marriage to Mr. Schiff, was very angry. He cried: "It is a shame to say such a thing. You are not a German." So I answered: "Und wenn schon"—and so what!

1. Jacob H. Schiff (1874–1920) was born in Frankfurt am Main, emigrated to America at the age of eighteen, and married into the large industrial bank of Kuhn, Loeb and Co., which he later directed. His many foundations were dedicated primarily to Jewish educational institutions and to the welfare of Russian Jews.

2. The American Jewish Committee was founded in 1906 by prominent American Jews, among them Jacob Schiff, as a self-help organization to protect Jewish rights. Having originated in response to the pogroms in Russia, in its first decades the committee mainly carried on diplomatic and philanthropic activities in behalf of the Jews there.

3. The co-founders of the Hilfsverein der Deutschen Juden in 1901, the textile industrialist Dr. James Simon (1851–1932) and Dr. Paul Nathan (1857–1927), became, respectively, its chairman and its executive director. Max Warburg (1867–1946) was co-owner of the banking house M. M. Warburg and Son, which was founded in Hamburg in 1798. His brother Felix M. Warburg was the son-in-law and partner of Jacob H. Schiff in New York (see note 1). Captain Carl Melchior (1871–1933) was a judge and banker in Hamburg. In 1917 he became a partner in the Warburg bank.

4. The Israelitische Allianz (Israelite Alliance) of Vienna, founded in 1873, was the Austrian aid organization for East European Jews and emigrants. During the First World War it looked after more than 100,000 refugees from Galicia.

5. The Jewish Colonization Association was founded in 1891 by Baron Moritz Hirsch as an international aid organization for emigration and colonization (Argentina, Palestine). It also organized schools and credit cooperatives in East Europe.

6. Dr. Franz Oppenheimer (1864–1933), physician, economist, and sociologist, was a Zionist and a member of the committee to aid the Jews in East Europe.

7. Wojciech (Adalbert) Korfanty (1874–1939) was the leader of the Polish faction in the Reichstag (1903–1912 and 1918) and in the Prussian State Parliament (1904–1918). In 1921 he fought in the "Korfanty Uprising," as plebiscite commissioner, for the annexation of Upper Silesia to Poland.

8. As of 1919 the Orientalist Prof. Moritz Sobernheim (1872–1933) was a legal adviser in the Foreign Office and deputy chairman of the Jüdische Gemeindebund (Union of Jewish Communities).

Rabbi Esriel Hildesheimer (1820–1899) and his brother-in-law, entreprenuer Gustav Hirsch (1822–1898), of the metal firm Aron Hirsch and Son in Halberstadt. The Leo Baeck Institute, New York.

Moritz Daniel Oppenheim (1800–1882): "The Passover Seder."
Lithographs of Oppenheim's "Bilder aus dem juedischen
Familienleben" ("Scenes of Jewish Family Life") decorated many
bourgeois Jewish homes. The Jewish Museum, New York.

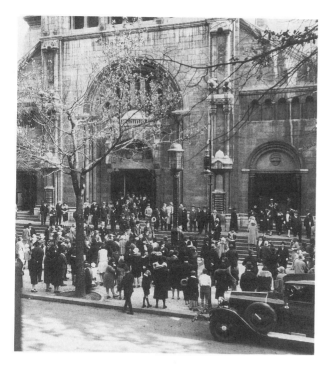

After services, in front of the synagogue on Fasanenstrasse, Berlin Charlottenburg. Landesbildstelle, Berlin.

After services, in front of the synagogue in Breisach/Baden. The Leo Baeck Institute, New York.

Jewish bourgeoisie, Dr. Raphael Silberstein and family. Silberstein, a
social democrat, was both physician and city councilor in Berlin
Neukoeln. Reprinted from Monika Richarz, ed., *Jüdisches Leben in
Deutschland*, Vol. III, 1918–1945, Leo Baeck Institute. Original, Ernst
Silberstein, University Heights, Ohio.

Cartoon showing Samuel
Gronemann (right) and the
Jewish artists Hermann Struck
and Hans Goslar in the editorial
office of the Lithuanian newspaper
*Dabartis*, Kovno, 1916. Sketch
by Magnus Zeller. Reprinted from
Sammy Gronemann, *Hawdoloh
und Zapfenstreich*, Berlin:
Juedischer Verlag, 1924.

Community soup kitchen established for Polish Jews by Rabbi Arnold Tänzer (left, center) while an army chaplain, 1916. The Leo Baeck Institute, New York.

Rabbi Arnold Tänzer, decorated army chaplain in uniform; a Star of David hangs from a chain. The Leo Baeck Institute, New York.

Paul Mühsam (1876–1960), writer. The Leo
Baeck Institute, New York.

Session of the Preussische Landesverband Juedischer Gemeinden
(Prussian Union of Jewish Communities) held in the former Prussian
Parliament, March 1930. The Leo Baeck Institute, New York.

Ottilie Schönewald, neé Mendel (1883–1961),
last chairwomen of the Jüdischer Frauenbund.
The Leo Baeck Institute, New York.

Life in hiding. Identity card for Dr. Hermann Pineas, who lived as
Hans Perger while evading the Nazis. The Leo Baeck Institute, New
York.

Elderly men and women awaiting deportation from Frankfurt am Main to Theresienstadt, fall 1942. The Leo Baeck Institute, New York.

# III ❧

# *Weimar Republic and National Socialism, 1918–1945*

# 32 *Henry Buxbaum*

BORN IN 1900 IN ASSENHEIM (HESSE); DIED IN 1979 IN CANANDAIGUA, NEW YORK.

Henry Buxbaum, Recollections. Manuscript, 1979, Canandaigua; 252 pages.

*Heinrich Buxbaum was the son of a peddler. With the help of a scholarship he was able to attend the Gymnasium in Friedberg. After receiving the special "emergency diploma," he became a soldier in 1917, and from 1919 to 1924 worked his way through the university in Frankfurt am Main. He was graduated as Doctor of Medicine and worked for several years as a temporary replacement for rural physicians. In 1930 he opened his own practice as a country doctor in Griesheim (Hesse). When he was excluded from the health insurance plan in 1933, he worked out a private insurance for his patients and thus was able to continue his practice until 1936. Early in 1938 he emigrated to the United States, where he worked as a male nurse and earned the money needed for his wife and three children to join him. In 1940 he passed the medical board examination in the state of New York. Determined to resume work as a country doctor, he first practiced for four years on an Indian reservation and then in Canandaigua in northern New York.*

*[The following material has been taken from the original manuscript, written in English.]*

In Friedberg[1] the distinction was always there between the old, settled Jews of our community and the newcomers, some of whom had established large businesses. They were rich, they had married native girls, but it was never forgotten by some of our conceited local yokels that their place of origin had been somewhere east of Berlin. The greatest number of Prussian Jews lived in the province of Posen (Poznan), the old Polish province which in the partition of Poland in the 1770s had been annexed by Prussia, as Galicia had been swallowed up by the Austro-Hungarian empire in the same partition. Its numerous Jews consequently had become first Prussian and perforce after 1870 German citizens. But some of our local Jews never forgave them their origin, and if they no longer called them outright Pollaks at least they referred to them as coming from the "Fifth army-corps." Now, everybody in the know would understand what was meant by that. Prussia, and thereafter Germany, using the military yardstick, divided the whole country into twelve districts with each district supplying the men for one of the twelve army corps which together made up the great German army. The Fifth army-corps had its headquarters in Posen, the capital of the province of Posen, and everyone understood at once what was meant in referring to a neighbor as: "He comes from the 'Fifth army-Corps'."

There were other divisions, more of a local coloration, inside the community. The native Friedberger Jews, whose ancestors had been residents in the Jewish quarter of the city for many generations, considered themselves nobility and looked down with contempt and derision at the "yokels," the peasant Jews, who only lately had arrived from the surrounding villages. These old families never fully accepted the newcomers, like ourselves, who had come from Assenheim to Friedberg in 1908 and had not lived there for three hundred years or longer as had some of the older families. They suffered them in their midst but didn't feel they belonged. The "Landjuden," the country Jews, couldn't care less: they had long since become the majority within the Jewish congregation and, anyway, as the old saying went: "Fuer's Gehabte gibt der Jud nix"—"what has been isn't worth a farthing to the Jew."

But the real division, and the one which counted most in the daily life of the community, was the difference between rich and poor, between people of wealth and the others of little means, the group to which we belonged. I never was able to overcome my feelings of inferior status within the social life of the community. Not that it mattered with my friends, some of whom belonged to the rich families in town, but it certainly affected me as soon as I entered their houses. As a boy during our earlier years in Friedberg, each time I was invited to a birthday party, a Bar Mitzvah, or a "Holigrasch"[2] [in German "Holekrasch"] for a newborn brother or sister, I remember with what awe and discomfort I entered such a house. True, I felt the same way when I went to one of the rich and cultured homes of my Gentile friends. It was the same there as in the Jewish homes. I was impressed by the rich furniture, the large, bright rooms, the wide windows hung with silken or velvet curtains, a bathroom full of priceless wonders, with a finely shaped mosaic floor upon which rested a bathtub of marble as large as a sarcophagus, and sitting next to it the most wonderful object, a low toilet of glossy whiteness which to my thinking should have served a higher purpose and which had to be flushed when you were through. There was a roomy kitchen full of light and brightness, not like the always gloomy dark kitchen in our household, with a maid bustling around who chased us out when we got too close. Nothing in their kitchen of a stone sink in one corner with one miserable faucet rising above it, which when turned on ran only a stream of cold water. All the brightness and riches made me feel small and little. I never knew where to turn, where to stand, or where to sit down.

When I got older, and came for a visit to my friends' houses, I was no longer affected by the strangeness which had overwhelmed the small boy. But the feelings, and with it the knowledge that the surroundings and the people I came from belonged to a lower step on the social ladder, never left me. And the sad part is, I doubt that I have ever been able to overcome it. In fact, I am sure it has colored my whole attitude toward life and people. All I know is that whether in Germany or in the States I have always felt more comfortable, more at home, with the people who come from the lower rungs of the social ladder. And this holds true especially in my practice, the same as it was in Germany. I have always been more at ease with patients who come from a background similar to mine. This has nothing to do with Jew or Gentile; its roots spring purely from social relationships. Since I can identify more easily with this type of patient, a result is that I am also a better doctor with them and for them. Here, there is instant rapport, an intimacy of feelings and understanding which includes the ever-present awareness of their economic problems, whereas confronted with upper-class patients, at once some of the old strangeness will creep in and make me less relaxed than I normally am. [. . .]

The time when antisemitic agitation became more than an after-hours entertainment started at the moment of Germany's defeat and the so-called November Revolution. Each segment of German society was severely affected by the two events. But the group which felt the changes more than any other was the German-Jewish community. Suddenly the whole atmosphere of Jewish life inside Germany changed for the worse. You could taste antisemitism everywhere; the air of Germany was permeated by it. All the unavoidable consequences of military defeat, revolution, a ruinous inflation, the Versailles Treaty, the loss of the territories in the east and west, the unsettling social changes following in their wake — each and every thing was blamed on the Jews and/or the Communists, who for the convinced Jew-hater were interchangeable. If we had been an exposed element in the Wilhelminic era before the war, during decades of peace, and then had come under some virulent attack during the strain of war, more than we were used to, now the attacks upon us went beyond bounds. The antisemitic excesses which before could still be dealt with in a civil manner or on an individual basis took on a sinister character, became something different, much more dangerous, an early shadow already approaching the lawlessness of the Hitler period. [. . .]

I was on a train one night on my way home from Frankfurt. The train was pitch-dark. The lights were out, nothing uncommon after the war when the German railroads were in utter disrepair and very few things functioned orderly. It was in either 1919 or 1920, during one of the early periods of violent antisemitic attacks which might occur anywhere, and when a Jew who had the guts to fight could become embroiled in a vicious brawl. It happened often enough on a train and it was difficult not to react to the slander and the smears poured over you. That night, we were seven or eight people in the dark, fourth-class compartment, sitting in utter silence till one of the men started the usual refrain: "Those God-damned Jews, they are at the root of all our troubles." Quickly, some of the others joined in. I couldn't see them and had no idea who they were, but from their voices they sounded like younger men. They sang the same litany over and over again, blaming the Jews for everything that had gone wrong with Germany and for anything else wrong in this world. It went on and on, a cacophony of obscenities, becoming more vicious and at the same time more unbearable with each new sentence echoing in my ears. Finally, I couldn't stand it any longer. I knew very well that to start up with them would get me into trouble, and that to answer them wasn't exactly the height of wisdom, but I couldn't help it. As happened so often during those years when I was confronted with this sort of thing, I had to respond to it. I was burning with rage and told them exactly what I thought of them and their vicious talk. I began naturally with the announcement: "Well, I am a Jew and etc., etc." That was the signal they needed. Now they really went after me, threatening me physically. I didn't hold my tongue as the argument went back and forth. They began jostling me till one of them next to me and near the door, probably more encouraged by the darkness than by his own valor, suggested: "Let's throw the Jew out of the train." Now, I didn't dare ignore this signal, and from then on kept quiet. I knew that silence for the moment was better than falling under the wheels of a moving train. One of the men in our compartment, more vicious in his attacks than the others, got off the train with me in Friedberg. When I saw him under the dim light of the platform I recognized in him a fellow I knew well from our soccer club, V.F.B.[3] I would never have suspected this man of harboring such rabid, antisemitic feelings. [. . .]

Zionism right after the war was already in the German air. It had made no inroads yet in our staid, conservative congregation, but soon, pushed by an active, likeable group of students, it found a small but enthusiastic following among our local youth. [. . .] We organized a group of young people who were animated by the same spirit or became infected enough by our enthusiasm to join us. Our "Bund" — more a small devoted band of fellows my age plus a number of younger boys — was modeled along the lines of our old "Wandervogel" with the one important difference that now its members were all Jews and the old German folksongs we loved so much or the marching rhythms we sang on our hikes were interspersed now with sad and soulful Yiddish tunes and the early, exciting melodies of the *"Chalutzim."*[4] Every Bund, any new organization, needs a flag to march under, a banner to wave in people's faces and a standard to follow. Again, ours, as it had to be, was the "Mogen David." [. . .] We got in trouble only once with it and if our shiny golden ensign was the cause of it, the pole which carried it above us helped us to get out of it again.

We were on our way home from a hike to the Burg-Ruins of Muenzenberg, one of the famous castles from the Hohenstaufer era, built around 1175 to help protect the empire of the Staufen-Kaiser. We had to pass through Gambach, a village which was hostile territory, meaning that the village was very much a citadel of antisemitism. It was full of the followers of Professor Werner[5] from nearby Butzbach, the arch antisemitic preacher of our area and at the same time a state assemblyman. It was a quiet, warm Sunday afternoon when our little group of three grownups and five kids came abreast a big mansion in the center of town. A wide stairway of broad stone steps led from the front entrance of the house—which looked more like a castle—down to the highway— our route home. A small company of young fellows in their Sunday best were lounging on the broad stairway watching us file by. Suddenly they spied our flag. One of the fellows stood up and pointing to the big, yellow-red emblem of the Swastika on the lapel of his coat, he yelled at me: "Hi, that's what you should pin on your pennant." He didn't know who we were and he certainly had never seen a Mogen David. I was familiar with the antisemitic atmosphere inside Professor Werner's territory and should have kept quiet. But my contempt and ever-present hate of this symbol of our defamation flamed up against my will and in a reflex motion I raised my behind against him, patting it to make sure they understood, yelling back, "That thing we will stick on our ass." At once all hell broke loose. They jumped down the stairs and at the same time set the dogs on us. While our younger boys were crying with panic and fear, we started a fast run to get some distance between the villagers and ourselves. They fortunately gave up the chase after a while but kept the dogs at our heels. While I tried to hold the boys in line, Isy, always ready to jump into the breach, kept the pole of the pennant working furiously. With the ensign firmly grasped in his shoemaker's hands, he swung the pole in wide semicircles into the dogs, protecting our rear, all the time encouraging everyone loudly: "Fear not, fear not, they won't get us." We kept up a steady run nearly to the end of the town when the clamour died down. [. . .]

The year 1920 was filled with demonstrations from both sides of the political spectrum, the left and the right. They all took place on the Kaiserstrasse, our wide main street, just as it had been with every important event through its centuries of existence. Discontent was high this year everywhere on the home front. On a gray, drizzly day in November it was the farmers' turn to show their resentment and make their complaints known. This was not one of the regular Saturday or Wednesday market days when our farmers set up their stalls along the street to sell their home-grown vegetables and fruits to the city people, waiting patiently on customers. There was no patience in the thousands of farmers who had descended on our town this dreary November morning to demonstrate against the farm policies of the new Weimar government. It had put the farmer in a straitjacket with its maze of regulations embracing everything produced on the farm and by now had stretched the endurance of the farmer to the breaking point. Each and every farm product had come under rigid controls—the animals he raised, the milk he sold, the crops he grew—but worst of all was a price control which during a period of spiraling inflation left the farmer to starve. [. . .]

The farmers' protest march broke up near the old Hotel Trapp, a block from the Cathedral, and at once a large group of younger men separated from the main body and headed past the church to collect themselves again on the other side of the church and in front of the sprawling property of the biggest cattle dealer in the country, Bernard Rosenthal. Rosenthal was the government appointee who handled the controls in the Viehwirtschaft, the dairy and beef industry. He had been chosen for his knowledge in this field, for his close connections with the farmers, and not the least for his reputation for fairness. But his job was a difficult one at all times and under the best of circumstances. Even with complete fairness, he could never remove the stigma associated with his position as the official who interfered with and intruded upon the freedom of the farmer. There had already been a lot of grumbling about the way he was said to handle his appointment, the loudest complaint being that he played favorite toward the bigger farmers to the detriment of the smaller ones, who were the majority. Now, suddenly, stimulated by the impetus of the rally, all this discontent exploded in front of his house. A huge barn stood on the grounds behind the house inside the wide cobblestone yard, where Bernard Rosenthal could hold at any time 30 to 40 head of cattle ready for trading. The estate was closed off by a wall on one side and in front by the large facade of the house facing the street. Between the high wall and the house was the entrance, which was closed securely toward the street by the solid set of its two heavy, oaken doors. At once a number of young men tried to break down the doors, but they were bolted firmly together and easily withstood the furious attack of bodies who threw themselves against the massive enclosure. They repeated their attack again with might and fury, making the doors reverberate. Suddenly the doors unlocked from the inside, opening wide. At once they were flung back their whole width to their hinges by the onrushing crowd. At the same moment, confused and bewildered, the mob stopped in their rush forward: In the breach between the wide open doors stood two silent figures: Bernard Rosenthal, the father, and, side by side with him, his son Siegfried. They stand there, engraved in my mind's eye forever, two silent people, their heads bowed, ready and with quiet dignity in the helplessness of surrender. The attackers had stopped for some surprised seconds. Part of them rushed forward again toward the barn while others, forming a tight knot around the two men, began to jostle them, swinging their fists in their faces, all assailing them with angry words and gestures. But the onslaught didn't last. At once a number of elderly, courageous farmers pushed their way inside the ring of assailants and, forming a shield around the Rosenthals, with their arms and bodies held off the most violent of the attackers. Fencing with them, they tried at the same time to calm down the crowd, while begging them to desist from their violence. [. . .]

1. The Jewish community of Friedberg (Upper Hesse) was rich in tradition. A ritual bath from the thirteeth century has been preserved. In 1905 the community counted about 550 Jews. By 1925 this number had dropped to 380.

2. Naming celebration, at which the children of the community lift up the newborn child, try to guess its name, and are then rewarded with sweets. This Jewish custom was known only in southern and western Germany, as well as in Alsace and Switzerland.

3. From 1918 to 1933 Jews made up half of the first team of the Friedberg sport club.

4. Pioneers (Hebrew), i.e., members of the Zionist Chalutz organization, which prepared its members for emigration to Palestine.

5. Ferdinand Werner (1876–1961), senior primary school teacher in Butzbach, was twice a representative to the Reichstag, in 1918 for the Deutschsoziale Wirtschaftliche Vereinigung (German Social Economic Union) and from 1924 to 1928 for the Deutschnationale Volkspartei (German National People's Party).

## 33 *Edwin Landau*

BORN IN 1890 IN DEUTSCH-KRONE (WEST PRUSSIA); DIED IN 1975 IN RAMAT GAN, ISRAEL.

Edwin Landau, My Life before and after Hitler. Manuscript. Ramat Gan, 1940, 52 pages.[1]

*Edwin Landau's father was a hardware dealer and plumber in Deutsch-Krone and chairman of the representatives of the Jewish community there. While three of his brothers studied at universities, Edwin Landau became a plumber and later took over his father's business. Brought up orthodox, he was at the same time markedly German in his thinking. Having returned from four years of army service, he founded in Deutsch-Krone a local group of the Reichsbund jüdischer Frontsoldaten with forty members. In 1921 he married, enlarged the plumbing business by accepting public commissions, and became head of the Jewish community. When, after the National Socialists seized power on April 1, 1933, all Jewish businesses were boycotted, Landau's world collapsed. He no longer regarded himself as a German, declared himself a Zionist, and decided to go to Palestine. In November 1934 he emigrated with his wife and two children, and opened a new plumbing business in Ramat Gan.*

I returned home unexpectedly on December 10, 1918, and my family's joy was great. It became even greater when I unpacked all my gifts, which I had brought with me from France and Belgium. They were all things that one had had to do without for a long time at home, as, for example, laundry soap, coffee, chocolate, cocoa, tea, and candles. And then I began my story-telling and the neighbors came and listened. Daily now, soldiers were returning, and I was able to see and speak with many acquaintances, among whom some were officers. And everyone I spoke to was glad that finally, after four years, the war was over, even if not all approved of the Republic. One sensed that many of these people, coming from middle-class circles, would have preferred to see prominent personalities at its head. At heart, I, too, was not a republican, since the monarchy was still too much in my blood. I needed some time to accustom myself to everything and to free myself from old ideas. Interesting for me was the fact that my father was a stalwart republican and my mother constantly defended the kaiser and made no secret of her love for the monarchy, so that occasionally there were political discussions between my parents. [. . .]

Although the greatest part of the Jewish citizens rallied round the left-wing parties, only a single one had the courage to show the black, red, and gold flag on every occasion. After Hitler seized power he had to pay for this act of courage in a concentration camp. At the election rallies which soon began, and at which I also participated regularly, one could soon tell who was a republican and who was an opponent. I had very many Catholic acquaintances and also customers with whom I occasionally had frank conversations. Still, one was not able to be entirely open, since one could not look into the hearts of these people. After all, in those days there was still a certain atmosphere of distrust among the citizens. They were still in a state of ferment, and many didn't know themselves where they belonged. One thing was certain, however: If we Jewish soldiers had thought that by our participation in the war we would gain the love of our fellow citizens, then we were mistaken. Even if there was no open antisemitism, a large part of the people who hated the Republic still opposed the Jews, who, after all, were on the side of the workers. Also, it seemed as if the economic power of these opponents was very strong, and they, too, were soon repeating the slogan that most Jews had been shirkers. And the way things were in my hometown, that is how they were in the whole Reich; and even if the workers constantly defended the Jews, the Jewish frontline soldiers, for whom protection coming from these quarters represented a certain humiliation, nevertheless united under the leadership of former officers to form an organization, the Reichsbund jüdischer Frontsoldaten.

I myself undertook the formation of a local group, which soon counted forty members who, according to the statutes, could prove their identity as frontline soldiers with their military identity cards. My father did not entirely approve of my activities, for he was afraid, perhaps not incorrectly, that we could lose some of our customers. After all, among them were many Junkers, farmers, officials, and architects who, even if they were not German nationalists, nevertheless did belong to the Deutsche Volkspartei and to the Stahlhelm. Soon the Deutschsoziale Partei and its leader, the infamous "Cudgel-Kunze," let themselves be heard from in our town, too.[2] This party held an election rally, at which our frontline soldiers organization and a large part of the workers also participated. A Dr. Veit from Meiningen gave a speech. The speaker told such stupid lies about Jews that I almost wanted to speak up in order to retort. Since my father had strictly advised me not to speak in public, I refrained from doing it. In the further course of events the workers expressed their protest, since they, for one, did not believe the accusations against the Jews. Then the speaker had the nerve to maintain that if he had not spoken the truth then at least one Jew would have asked for the floor in order to rebut him, which, however, had never happened on any of his lecture tours.

At that I could no longer restrain myself and I called out: "Then one is asking for the floor now!" The speaker hesitated at first and then he called out: "It will be a great pleasure for me, afterward," whereupon I answered: "And perhaps not!" After he had finished his lecture I pushed my way to the lectern on the stage, followed by many members of the frontline soldiers organization and some workers who knew me. In a speech that lasted almost an hour and in which I limited myself to defense, through the ardor of my argumentation I had made such an impression on my fellow citizens, who knew me, that I saw that I would win. The opponents, who noticed that, tried to cut me short, especially the pupils of the building trade school, whom I could easily take care of. But the workers took my side, and the result was that the speaker could no longer make his concluding remarks since everything was drowned out in a commotion. Many of my fellow citizens called out to me: "Well, you certainly let him have it!" All that had mattered to me was that we not be called cowardly.

My father did not approve of my conduct, which was mentioned in the newspaper the next day. But the leaders of the Jewish community came to me to express their thanks for my courageous act, which I accepted with a smile. But I was on the blacklist of our opponents. [. . .]

I did not become a member of any political party, but I went to all of the meetings and I learned quite a bit. With great zeal I now devoted myself to the Jüdischer Jugendbund, where my brother, who had returned home from war captivity, gave a lecture about his experiences. I also spoke before the Jewish community and was now elected to its representative council by a great majority. I was also elected to the executive body of the Jewish benevolent society, which had been founded by my grandfather. My father, who previously had been chairman of the representatives for many years, said that, to be sure, every office brought with it much annoyance and animosity if one wanted to carry it out objectively, but I must say that I, the youngest representative, was shown esteem and respect, since I always remained purely objective.

As far as the business was concerned, I had not only made a good impression on my old customers, but had also gained new ones, so that I got the plumbing work for many new buildings in town. I also went to the authorities and soon had good business contacts with the Municipal Construction Office, the County Construction Office, the Prussian Building Construction Office, as well as with the military authorities. Since my younger brother had become an employee in a factory for beer pumps and soda fountains, I took over the representation of this firm, which partially belonged to my oldest brother and which supplied a number of restaurants with new appliances.

One day I received a letter from my girlfriend in Berlin with the news that she had become engaged. (Her brother, my friend, had in the meanwhile become a general practitioner in Berlin.) I received this news with interest, to be sure, but I was not greatly affected by it. In general, I must say that I had changed in the war. I was out of my stormy years and had become more realistic.

My father also thought that it was time for me to think of marrying. And, in the town where she lived, my married sister was friends with a family that had two daughters, the older of whom had just become engaged, while the second, a respectable girl, well-trained in money matters, was still to be had. I, too, liked this girl quite well and, with the consent of her parents, I began a friendly correspondence with her. At the wedding of the older sister our engagement also took place. Among others, many Christian neighbors, and even the nationalist mayor, were present. The town was almost completely Protestant, and in many cases inclined to antisemitism. I married in the year 1921. [. . .]

From the regional postal office administration in Köslin, for which I had done work previously, I also received a fairly large commission in our town in 1932. I was sitting in a restaurant negotiating with the architect in charge (he could drink a great deal) when he said to me: "You see, it's strange, I'm a Nazi, you're a Jew, and still I prefer you for the work because you are a decent, honest human being; yet on account of the party I should not give you the contract. I am an objective person."

For me that was a harbinger of things to come, and I asked myself how often I would again be hearing that kind of talk. Meanwhile, already under the Republic one felt that the country was secretly arming. All around us defense projects were being carried out and camouflaged shelters, secured against gas, were being constructed near the army camps. But there was no work there for me. Maybe they did not consider me trustworthy enough. In the meantime Adolf Hitler spoke for the first time before an election in Schneidemühl, and everyone streamed there to hear this up-and-coming man. The newspapers brought true mystical outpourings about this pilgrimage. From then on, an antisemitically tinged article frequently appeared in the local press. When we lodged a complaint with the owner of the paper, this national party fool answered that not he but rather his editor was responsible for it. Of the latter we knew, of course, that he was a member of the National Socialist Party. Especially worth mentioning, however, is the fact that almost all officials of the revenue office, up to and including the senior executive officer, were correct and accommodating in an exemplary fashion. On the other hand, the mayor switched from the Deutschnationale Volkspartei to the Nazi camp. Some Catholics, too, felt that the time had come to leave the Centrist Party. They did not want to miss out if new positions opened up. Now the antisemitic smearsheet *Der Stürmer* appeared in our town in a small edition, and the personal defilement of Jewish citizens began. The smear campaign increased steadily and brought harm to many Jews. The desecration of cemeteries and the molestation of leftist republican citizens began. [. . .]

We sensed that a volcano was about to erupt. For us the fateful year 1933 began with fear. At the beginning of January, when I happened to be at the director's office of the District Administration, he told me that they had received from the Reichsbund jüdischer Frontsoldaten the memorial book for the Jewish soldiers who had been killed in action in the World War.[3] However, he believed that soon it would be discarded, and he would rather give it to me, because with me it would be in better hands. It would be a great pity if it were desecrated. As is well known, the president of the Reich had written a foreword to it, and the then head of the Department of the Wehrmacht, Lieutenant Colonel Ott, had given the following speech at the formal presentation on November 17, 1932: "Gentlemen, in the name of the Defense Minister of the Reich,

I have the honor, on this solemn occasion, to declare that we shall greatly esteem this memorial book for our Jewish comrades who fell in the World War, as a remembrance of these loyal and true sons of our German people." I accepted the book from the official with thanks, and was very moved by this sign of character.

Often one heard it said in the other parties, even by many Jews, that perhaps it would be good if Hitler joined the government, for soon he would drop his radical ideas, especially since the parties on the right would keep him in check, and then the party would lose voters. It would soon turn out that this was a false conclusion.

Things were soon in a turmoil everywhere, and then the day came on which Papen overthrew Chancellor Schleicher, and the president of the Reich appointed Adolf Hitler to the government as chancellor, a day to be remembered, full of extraordinary tragedy for all times. With their money the leaders of heavy industry, especially Thyssen, Vögler, and Klöckner, had helped to become chancellor a man who they assumed would be a puppet in their hands. (Today, as I am recording this, Thyssen knows from abroad what he has helped to bring about.)[4]

Then, on the radio we heard the big torchlight procession of the Nazis marching past the Chancellery of the Reich, heard the tumultuous jubilation of the multitudes and became very depressed. We did not dare go into the street of our town that evening, for there, too, there was unparalleled jubilation, and outside one heard the shouts of the marching Nazis: "Death to the Jews!"

And on the next day the swastika flags were fluttering from the houses, and next to them also the black, white, and red flags of the monarchy. But now one could tell who of one's aquaintances was a Nazi follower. On the faces of some citizens one saw a look that earlier one had not noticed. Many Catholics were already also joining in. And the youth went marching at the head. Then one heard the great declaration of the new government and the speeches of the new ministers. Herr Hugenberg spoke, and the radio transmitted to us, among other things, a sentence that immediately made me wonder: "We expect that our new chancellor will faithfully keep the promises he has made us." Then new elections were called. The republic had exited ingloriously. Perhaps it had earned this disgraceful exit. Just a week before Hitler came to power, the leader of the Reichsbanner Höltermann said at the Berlin Lustgarten: "Rather dead than a slave." He did not die, nor did he become a slave, but instead, like many others, he was soon out of the country. Shortly before the elections the Reichstag fire occurred and arrests began. The ban of the Communist Party followed. On the Day of Potsdam the factories were closed so that the employees could experience, through loudspeakers, the ceremony and the first meeting of the new Reichstag. Hitler was empowered, and Herr Göring remained president of the Reichstag. To be sure, a few Social Democrats still dared to resist, but it was no more than grasping at a straw before drowning. The war against the Jews was the first item of the agenda that was implemented. Fate took its course.

In our town, too, the Nazi gangs made the streets unsafe. Thus, the first of April, the day of the boycott of the Jews, came nearer. Already early on Friday morning one saw the SA marching through the city with its banners. "The Jews are our misfortune." "Against the Jewish atrocity propaganda abroad." In the morning hours the Nazi guards began to place themselves in front of the Jewish shops and factories, and every shopper was warned not to buy from Jews. In front of our business, also, two young Nazis posted themselves and prevented the customers from entering. To me the whole thing seemed inconceivable. It would not sink in that something like that could even be possible in the twentieth century, for such things had happened, at most, in the Middle Ages. And yet it was the bitter truth that outside, in front of the door, there stood two boys in brown shirts, Hitler's executives.

And for this nation we young Jews had once stood in the trenches in cold and rain, and spilled our blood to protect the land from the enemy. Was there no comrade any more from those days who was sickened by these goings-on? One saw them pass by on the street, among them quite a few for whom one had done a good turn. They had a smile on their faces that betrayed their malicious pleasure. At an earlier time it was once said in exuberance: "The German way will heal the world," but this now was no less than Satanism, and it was just the beginning.

I took my war decorations, put them on, went into the street, and visited Jewish shops, where at first I was also stopped. But I was seething inside, and most of all I would have liked to shout my hatred into the faces of these barbarians. Hatred, hatred—when had it become part of me?—It was only a few hours ago that a change had occurred within me. This land and this people that until now I had loved and treasured had suddenly become my enemy. So I was not a German anymore, or I was no longer supposed to be one. That, of course, cannot be settled in a few hours. But one thing I felt immediately: I was ashamed that I had once belonged to this people. I was ashamed about the trust that I had given to so many who now revealed themselves as my enemies. Suddenly the street, too, seemed alien to me; indeed, the whole town had become alien to me. Words do not exist to describe the feelings that I experienced in those hours. Having arrived at home, I approached the one guard whom I knew and who also knew me, and I said to him: "When you were still in your diapers I was already fighting out there for this country." He answered: "You should not reproach me for my youth, sir . . . , but I've been ordered to stand here." I looked at his young face and thought, he's right. Poor, misguided young people!

In spite of everything, on this day, too, a number of customers came to me, especially Catholics, and among them there was many a person who visited me only out of protest against the happenings outside. The office director of the District Administration also came, simply to shake my hand, as he so kindly put it. When I thankfully told him that he should not risk his position on account of me, and to think of his family, he answered full of pride: "I am party member number twenty of the Deutschnationale Volkspartei; what can happen to me?" The poor idealist, soon he would discover that this party, too, would not count for much. But I was grateful to him from my heart, for I was hurting inside. In the afternoon two Jewish landowners were arrested and the Catholic District Administrator was removed. I ran into the street and went to my Jewish schoolmate who had a uniform-price store next door, and we walked up and down the street. In front of the door of his shop I asked him what he would do if on the next day, too, the SA people were still standing outside. He answered with his cigar in the corner of his mouth: "I would close."

I went home. The new guard didn't want to let me in, and I kicked up a racket, saying that he had no right to refuse me entrance to my business, whereupon several

SA people came up and asked the fifteen-year-old Hitler youth why the Jew was making so much noise. Then I went unmolested into my business, which my wife locked immediately. The employees looked at me sadly and asked whether they should come the next day. I said no . . . they left . . . I was inwardly crushed. Nothing mattered any more.

In the apartment my wife was preparing for the Sabbath. I went to the synagogue like many other Jews. There I saw desperate faces full of the most profound mental anguish—pale and trembling. Never before did Jews pray more ardently than on that evening on which they were experiencing their being Jews so fundamentally. My heart, too, trembled and my soul cried secretly to its God: "My God, why have you forsaken me?" Once Christ, too, had sobbed like this, full of pain on the cross. We, too, were being nailed to the swastika-cross. The prayer gave me little solace, and no less shaken I went home to my wife and children. And when, as always, I consecrated the Sabbath there, in the circle of my family, and came to the passage in the prayer "You who have chosen us from among all the peoples," and saw my children, who were looking at me with innocent and questioning eyes, my composure was at an end. The whole weight of the day's experiences struck me, and I broke down, just barely stammering the last words. The children either did not know or did not understand why I was crying so violently, but I knew: This was my leave-taking from everything German, my inner separation from what had been my fatherland—a burial. I buried forty-three years of my life. And even if this had been merely the one and only day of such an experience, after that I *could not* be a German anymore.

And what was I now? To be sure, I was a religious Jew and yet already quite assimilated. I had become homeless. That night the Nazi hordes marched through the city and rampaged. The next day, Saturday, the house searches of Jews and Social Democrats began. The brown gangs also appeared at the homes of many of my Jewish friends. The whole town was in a turmoil. Again the guards were posted. I could not and did not want to see anything, I was finished. In the evening I was together with some Jewish friends, and one of them suddenly asked how long Hitler would rule, whereupon a friend, the owner of the uniform-price store, said: "Ten years." The others protested and thought three months, or a year. Today this friend is in the U.S.A. and Hitler has already been in power for seven years.

We thought the other countries would not tolerate such barbarism in the twentieth century. Where was England, where was America? What about Christianity? To be sure, John Simon[5] gave several protest speeches at that time, but that did not change anything, and Israel stood completely alone. Was God on its side?

What did the future hold? The following days brought some relief and we, too, began to think more calmly. I made an appointment with the new provisional District Administrator, as the chairman of the representatives of the community. Many Jewish citizens had come to me and said that I was the only one who could achieve anything with him. And that is why I went there and was admitted. I was told that I should calm the other Jews; the campaign had ended, it had only been punishment for the Jewish propaganda abroad. I told this to my fellow sufferers and they were somewhat encouraged. I, however, no longer had faith; I was, to be sure, outwardly courageous and strong, but inwardly disheartened and forsaken. I went to the graves of my parents, grandparents, and great grandparents, and spoke with them. I returned to them every-thing German that I had received from three generations, and had absorbed and cul-tivated. I cried into their graves: "You were mistaken. I, too, have been misled. I now know that I am no longer a German. And what will my children be?" The question remained open . . . the gravestones remained silent. My old teacher also could not answer from the grave.

And the living? My former teacher, who was a popular principal at the girls' Gymnasium and was highly esteemed by the teachers, the pupils, and their parents, soon found out the answer. During the morning hours, as he was teaching, SA men appeared and in the presence of the pupils shouted at him: "You Jew, get out of here right away! You have no right to teach German children!" He became numb. Many girls began to scream and shouted his name. He, however, said to them: "Dear children, I have taught here for over fifteen years. I have always wanted the best for you, have also imparted German culture to you . . . I shall go from you now, because those in power want it thus. Farewell." And so he went, and his colleagues followed him with their eyes. That had been the thanks for his selfless work. But he was still to have one joyous experience. In the afternoon many pupils appeared at his apartment with flowers and other small tokens. It was the judgment of a still unspoiled and unbiased youth. [. . .]

I myself was like a pendulum. I had nothing to hold on to. The community members met frequently at the community house or at the cemetery. It was still peaceful there. But when a Jew was buried, (in contrast to earlier) one no longer saw Christians in the funeral procession. The people had also become cowardly and fearful.

One evening I was invited by my school friend M. to his apartment, where a number of acquaintances and also older Zionists were present. My friend gave a rousing and provocative speech in favor of Zionism, for the purpose of forming a local group there. I sensed that now the Centralverein deutscher Staatsbürger jüdischen Glaubens was finished, because we constitute a race and not a religious community. Had I been asleep all that time, half of my life? Had we not once become a nation and a religious community at Sinai? I saw how many Centralverein members joined the new Zionist local group. I, however, could not decide. I was still too confused by all the events. Right away the Zionist local group had twenty members. I was invited as a guest to the first meeting. The Zionist publication *Jüdische Rundschau* was laid out. There I read captions like "Say yes to Judaism" and "Wear it with pride, the yellow badge."[6] What if one could do that, inwardly transform "the infamy aimed at us" into national pride, the abusive word Jew into a name of honor? Would that not show the way out of the inner devastation and despair? Would one not be able again to hold one's head high as before, in spite of everything?

It turned out to be an interesting evening, during which also some *chaluzim* spoke. We heard the word "Palestine." I thought about my school days. Our teacher, standing by the large map, said: "This is the Holy Land, the land of our fathers." And now it was once more to become the land of our children! Perhaps even our land! At the end, "Hatikva," our national hymn, was sung. I stood up as I once did when "Hail to Thee who wears the victor's laurels" was sung on the kaiser's birthday. On the way home only my friend M., the chairman of the local group, went along with me. We went through the quiet streets in the moonlight. I felt inwardly freer. He spoke and tried to persuade me. His words fell upon me like the early morning dew on the plants and trees. They freed me from my inherited bonds, and eased the pain of my soul. And even late in the night there was a throbbing within me: Palestine . . . *"Altneuland"* . . . Herzl . . . Think of the children.

The business continued to go downhill. Customers withdrew and no new ones came. What was to happen? Whenever we went walking with acquaintances it was more like "sneaking a walk." By roundabout routes, where otherwise few people go, we went to the beech forest, to the lakes, but not to the restaurant. How I have loved you, from my young years on, you lakes and forests of my homeland! How I longed for you when I was far away on the battlefield as a soldier! And now . . . you have become alien, for you no longer belong to me. I have no right anymore to love you. But one thing I can still do—I can thank you for your beauty, for the coolness that you so often afforded me, for the hours of rest that I enjoyed in your midst. And you are not bad. You are nature—a part of God.

After another meeting my friend pressed me to take on a lecture, even without my being a member. He would leave the topic up to me, he said; he could not ask me to give a Zionist lecture. After some hesitation, I agreed. In my library I had a volume of poems by Hugo Zuckermann, the Jewish poet who had fallen in the World War.[7] While reading it, I was very moved by the tragic fate of this man, who had lost his life for his fatherland. I therefore decided to speak about him, and some young people would recite a few of his poems, while at the same time I would supply the appropriate connecting words.

The Sunday afternoon of the lecture arrived. The room was crowded. Young and old were present. Several Zionists from the neighboring group were also there. And as I began, I saw all the faces turned toward me, with a spellbound look. Yes, within me there began a singing, a glowing, and I saw tears in many young eyes. In a vision I saw the land of which the poet had sung. My older boy also recited a poem . . . I was as though in a dream, transported, and the words just flowed from me until I was finished. Everyone came up to me, with enthusiasm, and the chairman, while expressing his thanks, said it was a moving Zionist lecture, that I had become a member of the local group through my speech and no longer had to join, for I was already one of them.

Thus, after years, I became a Zionist. And the members were glad that they had me, for they knew that I am always *active* wherever I am a member. For me personally, however, it was a spiritual elevation. I became calmer and began living anew.

1. Published in part in *Mitteilungen des Verbandes der ehemaligen Breslauer und Schlesier in Israel*, Nos. 45 and 46, Tel Aviv, 1979/80.

2. The Deutschsoziale Partei, a national (*völkisch*) antisemitic splinter group, existed from 1921 to 1928. Its chairman, Richard Kunze, got his nickname from selling truncheons for "intellectual" disputes. In 1930 he joined the National Socialist Party (NSDAP), and between 1933 and 1945 he was a Reichstag delegate.

3. *Die jüdischen Gefallenen des deutschen Heeres, der deutschen Marine und der deutschen Schutztruppen 1914 bis 1918. Ein Gedenkbuch*, published by the Reichsbund jüdischer Front-soldaten, Berlin, 1932. The book contains the names of 10,623 Jewish soldiers killed in action in the First World War. The president of the Reich, von Hindenburg, did not write a foreword,

as Landau claims, but rather it was his letter of thanks to the chairman of the Reichsbund that was printed in the commemorative volume.

4. Fritz Thyssen (1873–1951), the German industrial magnate, was the first and strongest financial supporter of the National Socialist Party. At the beginning of the war he broke with Hitler, emigrated to Switzerland and then to France, where he was arrested and brought back to Germany. From 1941 until 1945 he was detained in camps, and in 1948 he was classified as "lesser implicated." The steel industrialist Albert Vögler (1877–1945), Reichstag delegate of the Deutsche Volkspartei and, from 1933 until 1945, of the National Socialist Party, as well as Peter Klöckner (1863–1940), member of the Centrist Party, until 1933 financed the Deutsche Volkspartei, the Deutschnationale Volkspartei, and the Zentrum.

5. Sir John Simon (1873–1954) was British foreign minister from 1931 until 1935.

6. Robert Weltsch's famous editorial "Tragt ihn mit Stolz, den gelben Fleck!" appeared after the boycott day in the *Jüdische Rundschau* of April 4, 1933.

7. Hugo Zuckermann (1881–1915), Bohemian poet and Zionist, wrote, among others, the "Österreichisches Reiterlied," which was much sung during the First World War.

# 34  *Wolfgang Roth*

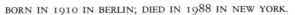

BORN IN 1910 IN BERLIN; DIED IN 1988 IN NEW YORK.

Wolfgang Roth, It All Depends on the Lighting. Manuscript, New York, 1977, 416 pages.[1]

*Roth grew up as the son of a waiter in proletarian Berlin. At the age of sixteen he attended the School of Arts and Crafts and at the same time was learning to be a house painter. In 1928 he became a pupil in the master class of Cesar Klein at the Academy of Art and began to work as a stage designer for political theater groups. He joined the Communist Party and the "Association of Revolutionary Visual Artists." In 1929 Roth was an assistant of Traugott Müller's at the Piscator stage and attended the Piscator studio. At Piscator's he met Brecht, and until 1933 he worked as an assistant to the latter's stage designers Caspar Neher and Teo Otto. Roth was briefly arrested after the Reichstag fire because of his party activities. He fled in March 1933 to Vienna via Prague. Between 1934 and 1938 he lived in Zurich, where he worked for the Corso Theater, and in 1938 he emigrated to New York. After years of barely making ends meet he received his first Broadway assignment in 1943. His greatest success became the setting for* Porgy and Bess *on its world tour in 1952. Internationally known, he was active after 1969 as a guest in the Federal Republic and in Switzerland.*

Whether my parents liked it or not, at the age of fifteen I had had enough of humanistic studies at the Vereinigtes Friedrich-Humboldt Gymnasium in Berlin. I had enough of the old Latin professor Cohn, enough of the Nazi math teacher Schlichter, called "Ajax," enough of the director, Professor von Trendelenburg. I wanted to become an artist! Maybe that was because my school was around the corner from what was then Max Reinhardt's theater, the Deutsches Theater. But actually I had no idea what I wanted; I was merely impressed by certain modern posters and advertisements on the billboards. "I want to design something like that, too," I said to my big sister, who quite often looked after me.

With the help of my clever sister I scoured the art schools, but noticed right away that something like the famous Reimann Schule was not for me. Too much elegance and too many bored girls from good families, and one had to pay quite a bit. No way! But finally I discovered the municipal School of Arts and Crafts, and that was the best thing that could happen to me. I had to pass an exam to be admitted. I was afraid of it, for until then I had scarcely drawn a line. When we children returned to school after the summer vacation, I was never able to depict my "summer's experiences" in drawings or pictures, and I also didn't feel like it. After all, what did children from tenement houses like me experience in the neighborhood of the Schlesischer train station? Maybe seeing how the cheap prostitutes in their high laced boots dragged customers to their dark cellar dwellings on our Müncheberger Strasse, and how the customers stole away again after ten minutes? Or perhaps watching how different gangs disguised as clubs—one was called "Edelweiss"—organized huge booze parties in a tavern, and often also brawls, when they returned from the funeral of one of their members who had been shot dead?

My father was one of the few Jewish waiters at that time in Berlin. He had grown up as an orphan, was actually named Haberkorn, and sometime, somewhere in eastern Germany he had been adopted by people called Roth. He had learned little at school, but thanks to his energy and hard work he had slowly but surely made his way as a good waiter. He went through the whole business: as an apprentice waiter (called a Piccolo), a serving waiter, and finally a headwaiter. When he was a dining-car waiter with "Mitropa" he had even learned a few languages. He told much about it, and when I was still little his stories impressed me a great deal. If he was in a good mood, he performed little skits for us children about things that had happened in the dining car or kitchen. He also showed us tricks, for example how a skillful waiter, balancing ten to twelve plates on one arm, can pretend to be stumbling and falling, but then still catch himself at the last moment. We children cheered him as we would have an acrobat. In the evening we had to tickle the soles of his feet in order to soothe him when, after sixteen hours of work, he plopped himself tired into bed and made up stories for us about how things would be if in his second life he came into the world again.

That was the little waiter Hirsch Roth, a Jew, who allowed himself to be exploited for paltry tips, and knocked himself out in order to support his family of six. Although he never wanted to admit it, he was a proletarian and remained one despite several attempts to improve his situation. Once we even had two real café-restaurants, incidentally with wonderful homemade ice-cream. But all that went to the dogs, because first of all my parents were not good business people, and, second, the whole economic situation in Germany was miserable. My father was going downhill financially and otherwise. He began to drink. Things reached the point where Mamma left us for a time, since she couldn't stand watching her husband have a love affair with a waitress and also go to ruin because of his alcohol addiction. One night, in a delirium he even smashed his restaurant. We children watched, spellbound and frightened to death, until the police came and stuck Papa into a straitjacket.

Mamma was a born Austrian and therefore a good cook. She could even sing a little and waltzed wonderfully. Maybe I inherited my talent for dancing from her. She understood me somewhat better than Papa did as far as my wishes and ambitions were concerned, and often took my part. But she never got over the fact that at the last moment, after everything had already been prepared, I refused to become Bar Mitzva. That is the moment in the life of a thirteen-year-old Jewish boy in which he becomes a man and a full member of the Jewish community. I simply couldn't see why I should give an idiotic speech to the guests, one that a rabbi had hammered into me word by word. I still know it by heart today, after half a century.

Mamma had no idea of what was driving me, but she had a good heart. Long after I had moved away from home she continued to bake me cakes and brought them to me, to my own apartment. She also liked to cry and did it often, with or without reason. Only when I suddenly had to leave in March 1933, in order to flee the Nazis, she did not cry but instead was completely silent and looked worried. I never again saw either Papa or Mamma. Papa died soon after my flight, in May 1933, in Berlin, and is buried there. Mamma was fortunate enough to be able to follow her other children to Palestine, and died there during the war of 1948.

Well then, I took the entrance exam for the School of Arts and Crafts. The result, which really surprised me, was that I was accepted into the preparatory class. After half a year they would see whether I was developing at all, and in what direction. Then, in a revolutionary uprising, I left my parents' home—fourth-floor, rear courtyard. My brothers made fun of me, and my father once again withdrew his support from me. Papa had ambitions for his children. They were not to serve other people all their lives, as he did. My little sister was to become a doctor, I at least a banker, and the twins— university professors. Nothing came of it. "Art is unprofitable," he reproached me.

With the little bit that was in my piggy bank I could pay for the night in the floating youth hostel on the Spree. I thought, somehow things will work out, and they worked out. Upon the good advice of my limping teacher, I also became a painter's apprentice with a house painter in Neukölln. First of all, I could learn a trade in this way, and, second, I could earn some money. And so I slaved away during the day at the house painter's and in the evening at the Arts and Crafts school in order to become an "artist."

The son of my painter boss, Rudi Pieroth, a quarrelsome and quick-witted communist, became my best friend and adviser—not only in painting and mixing colors, but also in politics and the question of what one does with girls, and how it's done. And we did it abundantly, too, on weekend trips with tent and foldboat, often interrupted by fights with Nazi storm troopers or motorcycle gangs. Gerhard Feilchenfeld, a third friend, was also with us. As two Jews, we were the majority in our triad. What became of Gerhard Feilchenfeld, who also studied painting, I don't know. I only know that Rudi was murdered by the Nazis.

I became more and more occupied with politics, wanted to fight for a better world. We lived in a strange blend of absolute desperation and enormous zest for life. The times were actually horrible, and everyone knew that, too. Constantly lurking catastrophes, increasing street battles between communists, socialists, and Nazis! We on the left were not aware in those days that we would lose in spite of all our efforts. We were so young, so enthusiastic, and had answers for everything. And after all, we wanted to help the masses—the same mass of humanity that then, a little later, influenced by Hitler, stabbed us in the back.

*[In 1928 Wolfgang Roth is a pupil in Cesar Klein's master class at the State Academy of Art.]*

There began an intensive time of study. On the side, I also designed sets for political theater groups, built them, and sometimes also acted myself. I joined the "Association of Revolutionary Visual Artists of Germany" and there got to know important people, who had a great influence on me: the creator of photo montages John Heartfield, Georg Grosz, Teo Otto, and many other political artists.[2] I was convinced that the most important purpose of art was to employ it in gaining support for the leftist movement and in educating the masses.

Because of our reputation of being pupils in the master class of Cesar Klein,[3] the six of us in our class had much outside work as a group. We did decorations for balls, costume parties, restaurants, and club rooms, among others, for the club of the Soviet Russian Commercial Agency, which was very progressive at that time. The academy did me much good. I met and often spoke with the kind, warm Käthe Kollwitz, who taught graphics there, and with her husband, a physician, who treated poor people mostly free of charge.

The theater occupied me more and more. I wanted to realize on the stage what until then I had created in graphics with political slogans on posters and banners. I now eagerly attended and admired agitprop groups, which functioned under every imaginable name: "The Red Megaphone," "Column Left," "The Red Blouses," and others. I also saw productions by Piscator[4] and was completely carried away. I wanted to be part of it! I couldn't stand it at the Academy any longer, I wanted to be part of the theater immediately. I felt that you cannot learn theater in school and that the teachers at the Academy were not much interested in political art, or were even against it. The Academy was actually no more than an artistic-esthetic substitute for reality. Besides, my teacher, the honorable Professor Cesar Klein, now and then stage designer himself, rarely came to discuss our work. He also had the bad habit of changing what he saw before him so thoroughly, for example, my design, that one could easily sign it "Cesar Klein." To his great indignation I did just that one day. I wrote his name under my design and left my romantic master-pupil existence at the Academy.

I asked John Heartfield for advice. He encouraged me to apply to Piscator, saying that perhaps he needed someone. So I wrote a timid letter to Traugott Müller,[5] Piscator's stage designer at the theater on Nollendorfplatz. He was a man whose work impressed me very much. I began to occupy myself more intensively with Piscator and his ideas, and I read whatever I could get—books on the theater, reviews, magazines, and Piscator's own works about the theater. I saw his Red revue "In Spite of All That" at Poelzig's Grosses Schauspielhaus, and the controversial *Robbers* at the Berliner Schauspielhaus. I found out about his beginnings at the front theater during the First World War, and about his political plays in halls and taverns. I was angry about the Social Democratic Berlin Volksbühne. It had thrown him out as director since he was politically too radical for it. In order to support him I became a member of the "Young People's Stage," a political organization of theatergoers, made up of young proletarians and intellectuals, who unfortunately comprised only a small part of Piscator's audience. In the season of 1927/1928 Piscator opened his own theater in an elegant, unproletarian part of Berlin on Nollendorfplatz. Piscator's "political" theater audience consisted, to a large extent, of high society in tuxedos and evening gowns, which found it great to be insulted from the stage, while upstairs, on Mount Olympus, the "Young People's Stage" sat in the cheap seats and applauded wildly.

The reply from Traugott Müller's assistant, Hilde Böhm, "Frau Doktor," as he called her, arrived soon. I was supposed to meet Müller at the stage door. For this occasion I put together a nice portfolio with sample designs, in the assumption that I could impress Müller with it. Traugott Müller, curly-haired, roguish, and from the Rhineland, stood by the stage door and looked at my portfolio: "Why this? Everyone can make designs. . . . Why do you want to join the theater? Don't you have anything better to do? Don't you know that the theater is crap and one is only exploited there. Here mainly by Piscator. Yes, he is a communist, but be careful, dear friend. Tell me, can you sing or dance? That's much nicer . . . " And so it went for an hour. Müller was a cynic on a grand scale. He didn't take anything seriously, but he was a great artist and innovator, and—even more important—a great theater man. It occurred to me that I had already seen him once on the stage in *Volpone*. He had created the set for it, but between acts also sang songs to lute accompaniment in front of the curtain. "Why don't you come for dinner in the evening day after tomorrow, and then I'll test you, and then we'll see."

At the appointed time I went to Traugott Müller's apartment, met his beautiful wife, as well as the actress Maria Fein, a few other girls, and an Egyptian stage design student, painter, and actor named Veli El Din Samih, at that time one of Piscator's many vassals. And we began to eat and drink. Müller suddenly got out a guitar and began singing Wedekind songs. I was given a second guitar and sang along; I also sang my old Peasant Wars songs, and it turned into a wonderful evening. Not a word about a "test." Around three o'clock in the morning, having become somewhat more sober, I finally asked as matter-of-factly as possible: "Herr Müller, how about my test?" With a girl on his lap, Traugott smiled: "Listen, what do you want—you passed it!" And so I became his assistant and pupil, engaged by the Piscator stage, naturally at a low salary. That was in 1929.

I was part of everything, brought the coffee to the theater during rehearsals, made sketches and other technical drawings, or better, I was learning to make them. I swept the floor of the painters' workshop, built models, learned proportions, read manuscripts, and made myself useful in general. I learned, studied, and worked myself to death. If we happened not to be working, I sat at night with Müller and others at Schwannecke's and we drank wine and told dirty jokes. I also became an assistant and a pupil at Piscator's studio, which was attached to the theater. I not only learned how to make designs and paint scenery, but also how to fence, act, and stage. People from many parts of the world came to the studio, and I got to know more and more actors, directors, and film makers. Among them were Leopold Lindtberg, Erwin Kalser, Leonhard Steckel, Alexander Granach, Ernst Busch, Curt Oertel, and many others.[6] For me it was a good, valuable, and fascinating time. In the meanwhile, economic and political conditions in Germany were becoming critical, and outside of the theater I was making more and more political drawings and election posters.

In the summer of 1929 Piscator's rehearsals for Walter Mehring's "The Merchant of Berlin" began. This was a political-satiric treatment of the German inflation of 1923, with dialogues, songs, music, projections, and manifold stage devices—devices, however, that were dramaturgically called for. In spite of all his loyalty towards Traugott Müller, Piscator had hired Professor Moholy-Nagy[7] of the Bauhaus for the stage designs. After all, the Bauhaus and Gropius had outfitted his apartment. Along with the countless assistants and experts, whom the professor brought with him from the Bauhaus, I, too, was once again an assistant. It was an excellent staging by Piscator, with stirring music by Hanns Eisler,[8] whom I met and came to love on that occasion. During the rehearsals everything went askew, and not only askew, for the stage ceiling even sagged under the immense weight of the steel platforms that Moholy had hung from the ceiling. And that was the way it worked: with film, projections, conveyor belts, three trapdoors, revolving stage, steel platforms up and down the gridiron. Eisler conducted, balancing his paunch on the piano, and Mehring ran up and down the auditorium like a madman. The play was completely ripped apart by the press: "Partisan theater instead of art." Only a few, not entirely idiotic people supported Piscator; Alfred Kerr,[9] for one, in the *Berliner Tageblatt*: "Piscator triumphs—Klopfer loses" (Ludwig Klopfer was the unknowing producer and financial backer). The last performance was superb and moving. At the end, everyone came onto the stage—actors, stage hands, technical personnel, about one hundred fifty people—and while the stage and the house were enveloped in projected streaming flags, they sang along in the concluding chorale, which was addressed to the audience sitting in the orchestra stalls in their tuxedos and evening gowns: "When will we carry the flag?" And I cried and went home. For the time being, my work with Piscator was over.

After the failure of the "Merchant of Berlin" Piscator no longer wanted to continue, and was very depressed and disappointed. A group of actors set themselves up under the nominal direction of the actor Erwin Kalser. This Piscator collective, of which I was also a member, got together primarily to motivate Piscator to stage plays again, and also in order to find new work for the actors. The collective began with "Paragraph 218" by Crede, a play against the prohibition of abortion. Traugott Müller, who was to do the sets for the play, handed the job over to me: "You can do it alone, I'm sure . . ." With his instruction, I designed a simple, functional scene without conveyor belts, without a revolving stage, without film and orchestra and changes. It was no more than a supporting framework for the play, easy to transport, set up, and disassemble. This staging became one of Piscator's greatest successes.

Piscator had also formed a writers' collective at his theater. That helped him to examine the plays from the artistic and political perspective, rewrite them, and stage them. Among the writers were Franz Jung, Ernst Ottwald, Leo Lania, the old anarchist Erich Mühsam,[10] and also Bertolt Brecht, whom I got to know thanks to Traugott Müller's intercession—Brecht with his leather jacket and cap, the ever-present cigar in his mouth, cynically contradicting himself and convincing others. I applied for an assistant's position with Brecht at the time when he was still planning his *Threepenny*

*Opera,* with Erich Engel as director at the Theater am Schiffbauerdamm. And I was accepted. For me that was the beginning of my collaboration with Brecht. I became the assistant to Caspar Neher, who was Brecht's stage designer.[11] I learned to observe—and to observe Brecht at work was pure joy and an experience. Slowly we also became friends, the Brecht clan and I. I learned from Brecht that stage settings are not window dressings or picture postcards. An experience that developed further what I had already begun to understand while working with Piscator. Stage settings make as much of a statement as the word of the author or a gesture of an actor. They must play a role, not just be there to be admired. My teacher Traugott Müller had lectured me, saying: "For years I have been working to get rid of stage sets." That was very ironic, but it was also true. I noticed that Brecht had learned from Piscator, and Piscator from Brecht as well.

In 1930 I worked with Teo Otto on Brecht's choral work *Measures Taken,* and in 1932 with Casper Neher on Brecht's play *The Mother.* While Hanns Eisler was composing the music for *Measures Taken,* I was nailing together shelves in the same room of his apartment. It didn't bother him, and he didn't bother me. The work on Brecht's first film, *Kuhle Wampe,* also began, a film about massive unemployment and its results in Germany. I spent much time in Brecht's studio high up on Hardenberg-strasse with a view of the "Knie," sat on the couch covered with a heavy, velvet-like cloth, or on rough-hewn chairs, joined in the discussions, and listened. A blackboard—or was it a plywood board?—hung on the wall, and it was much used for drawing, writing, sketching, and composing. This studio was a meeting place, and Brecht, with his ever-present cigar, marched back and forth in the room with sharply accentuated strides, while he spoke on the phone—and he was telephoning constantly—dragging the especially long telephone cord with him. Or he stood behind his tall writing desk and wrote poems. Hanns Eisler composed the music for Brecht's "Lullabies of a Proletarian Mother" on the old pianoforte up there. Kortner was there, and Oskar Homolka, and Peter Lorre, and we discussed *Saint Joan of the Stockyards,* which was performed in 1932 on the Berlin radio as a radio play. It was not performed on the stage until after the war. I began to work with Brecht on a puppet production of his long poem "The Three Soldiers," but Hitler and his Thousand Year Reich put an end to that.

On the evening on which Mackie Winzer of Herzfelde's Malik Publishing House[12] and I were coming from a performance of Wangenheim's *The Mousetrap,* we saw the Reichstag burning. "It's begun," I said to Mackie, "the Nazis have made it. I'm sure there will be mass arrests immediately. I think I'd better not go home today." That night I slept at the apartment of Sonja Wronkow, whom I tracked down at the Romanisches Café and asked for shelter. It was good that I did not return home, for the person living with me, the painter Alois Erbach, and many other artists and writers were arrested that night—some even before the Reichstag fire had started. Göring must have made a slight error in time.

We, the active antifascists, went underground. Meta and I lived in different parts of the city from night to night. We hardly trusted anyone, often not even good friends, for in the meanwhile they could have become Nazi informers. Daily existence had become dangerous for us, and we never knew whether we would live to see the next night, the next day as free people. We wrote and printed manifestos, tracts, and appeals to the public, also short daily newspapers, on primitive hand presses in an apartment, a cellar, or a colony of summer houses. We even printed little books and distributed them by shrewd methods. We took a detective story or a classic, and the first few pages were above suspicion, but if one leafed further, one read indictments of fascism. This literature was often thrown from windows onto the street, blown away by the wind, and soon picked up; and it disappeared as quickly as it appeared. The illegal groups consisted mostly of four to five people, who often hardly knew one another. Some of these cells were busted, since informers were hanging around everywhere. We met in coffeehouses, pretended to be playing chess, without even knowing how. But this made it possible to meet and talk with one another.

The Brecht clan was gone. Many were gone all of a sudden—either to prison, or out of Germany, or dead. Once I went home to put on clean underwear and was immediately picked up and thrown into prison. I was lucky, however, for after a week and some beatings I was released, since, as I heard, some old Social Democratic policemen from our neighborhood had interceded in my behalf. The police even returned my passport, with the somewhat roguish advice to make use of it for a vacation trip abroad. Not everyone fared as well as I. Later, when I was already in safety, my friend Erbach was picked up by the Gestapo again and murdered. After further meetings with my artist and political friends, in March 1933, with a heavy heart, I decided to flee.

1. The text printed here is a slightly edited selection, authorized by the author, from the first 76 pages of the manuscript. Because of numerous chronological inversions it does not contain any elision marks.

2. The "Association of Revolutionary Visual Artists of Germany" (ASSO) was founded in 1928 in Berlin by artists of the graphic studio of the German Communist Party. Until 1933 it comprised over five hundred professional and lay artists in sixteen local associations. — John Heartfield (1891–1968), actually Helmut Herzfelde, became famous through his antifascist photo montages, but also worked for Piscator and later for Brecht as stage designer. Between 1933 and 1950 he lived in exile. In contrast to him, the socio-critical painter Georg Grosz (1893–1959), who lived in the United States after 1933, changed his style there completely. Teo Otto (1904–1968) was stage designer at the Zurich Schauspielhaus during his emigration, from 1933 to 1955.

3. Cesar Klein (1876–1954) taught mural and glass painting at the Academy of Art in Berlin and designed stage sets for Berlin theaters. In 1937 he was deprived of his professorship.

4. Erwin Piscator (1893–1966) was director of the Berlin Volksbühne in the years 1924–1927. Then, until 1931, he headed the Piscator Stage in the Theater am Nollendorfplatz in Berlin. He spent the years 1933–1951 in emigration and in 1962 became director of the Freie Volksbühne in West Berlin.

5. Traugott Müller (1895–1944) developed a new concept of stage setting while working for the Piscator Stage, and after 1933 he worked with the directors Fehling, Gründgens, and Stroux.

6. Leopold Lindtberg became director at the Zurich Schauspielhaus in 1933. Starting in 1933, Erwin Kalser and Leonhard Steckel also played in Zurich, where Alexander Granach also came, by way of Poland and the Soviet Union. Kalser and Granach later emigrated to Hollywood.

7. Laszlo Moholy-Nagy (1895–1946) taught between 1923 and 1928 at the Bauhaus in Weimar and Dessau. Starting in 1937 he headed the New Bauhaus in Chicago.

8. In addition to numerous orchestral, chamber, and choral works, Hanns Eisler (1898–1962) composed some eighty works for the stage and film. His life-long collaboration with Brecht began in 1930. Between 1933 and 1948 he lived in exile.

9. Alfred Kerr (1867–1948) was theater critic with the *Berliner Tageblatt* between 1920 and 1933. In 1933 he emigrated, and in the years 1941 to 1947 he headed the PEN center of German-speaking authors abroad.

10. Erich Mühsam (1878–1934) was sentenced in 1919 for high treason because of his participation in the first Revolutionary Commune in Munich, but was released from prison early, in 1924. In 1933 he was arrested again and was murdered in the Sachsenhausen concentration camp.

11. Caspar Neher (1897–1962) was a close friend and the most important stage designer for Bertolt Brecht until the latter's death.

12. The Malik Publishing House was founded in 1917 in Berlin by Wieland Herzfelde (brother of John Heartfield; cf. note 2), and existed between 1933 and 1939 in Prague and London, as an important exile publishing house for communist and socialist writers.

# 35  *Carl Schwabe*

 BORN IN 1891 IN HANAU; DIED IN 1967 IN PHILADELPHIA.

Carl Schwabe, My Life in Germany before and after January 30, 1933. London, Manuscript, 1939, 90 pages.

*At the age of fifteen Carl Schwabe became an apprentice at the Kahn Department Store in Hanau, run by his father and a partner. After a training period of three years in Duisburg he joined his father's firm, while his two brothers attended the university and became a doctor and a lawyer. From 1916 until 1918 Carl Schwabe was a soldier; one of his brothers fell in the World War. In 1922 he married, and in spite of the inflation and increasing competition he successfully steered the firm through the twenties. From 1933 on, because of frequent harassment the business suffered such decline that in 1935 he greatly reduced it and sold it in 1938. His second brother was driven to his death by the police. After the November pogrom, Schwabe was imprisoned for a month in Buchenwald. Then, in 1939 he emigrated to London with his wife and two children. In 1940 he settled in the United States and earned his living until his old age by tuning and repairing pianos in Philadelphia.*

During the inflation we in Hanau had worked out a basic price table, which was to be multiplied by a key number computed according to the rate of exchange. A cousin of mine who owned a factory for gold wares had access to the financial news broadcasts and he received news every day, transmitted by radio, about the current rates of the dollar. At one o'clock we closed the stores, at two o'clock all retailers gathered behind locked doors in our furniture storehouse, which had another entrance on a side street, and then there followed the announcement of the new rate of exchange and the determination of the key number. As long as the rate of exchange for the mark remained approximately the same, the system worked. However, when the rate of exchange collapsed for good, the race between the increase in price and the devaluation was hopeless. Since the new rate of the dollar was not made known until noon, in the morning one still had to sell at the "old" prices. The public, which, after all, had only marks, was naturally extremely edgy about price increases. At that time, I had a conversation at a party with an associate judge of a district court, who worked at the so-called usury court. It cost me hours of effort to convince the old gentleman that the businessman who—as he told me indignantly—had charged him a higher price for a candle from the same box on the next day nevertheless had not earned more, and most likely was unable to replace his candle from the profit. Instead, for the devalued money he would perhaps get no more than the match to light it with. In this way I succeeded in giving a judge an idea of our difficulties, and by doing so I probably kept many a merchant from punishment. However, the masses, who were deceived and cheated the same as we, saw *us* as the main culprits.

On the other hand, of course, we tried to invest the returns in goods right away. Every morning we went to Frankfurt with a suitcase full of bank notes and returned with purchases, which we had carried back with us—a nice variant of the expression "to be worth its weight in gold." The manufacturers all switched to calculating everything in dollars or Swiss francs only. We sent in our daily receipts, incredible sums, the quickest way, and a few days later received a statement that so and so many dollars and cents were credited to us. Naturally, the goods had cost far more than this sum. No amount of calculating and saving helped; we saw that every day we were losing. Only very late did an acquaintance tell me how he had overcome these difficulties. So we also did it that way. We sent two checks—one with the amount of the value of the bill on the day it was issued, and a blank check. This blank check was filled out by the supplier, with the difference according to the rate of exchange on the day of arrival, and thus the account was settled. When the check arrived at the bank, naturally there were long since enough funds from the earnings to cover it, and now we were the ones to profit from the devaluation. Tremendous transactions were made with drafts. Unbelievable as it may be, the Reichsbank accepted longer-term drafts at a discount. The discount was fantastically high, but we wouldn't have minded if it had been several times higher. At maturity the bill was redeemed at a fraction of the profits from the sale. We businessmen of the old school were timid and were afraid of an increase in the exchange rate. For this reason I made purchases only once or twice paying by draft, and only for such a small amount that I was able to assume the risk. Others, who had nothing to lose because they owned nothing, had fewer doubts, and huge stocks were bought up in this manner. Overnight firms came into being that advertised tens of thousands of meters of wares of all kinds. For us poor wretches, that was completely incomprehensible in those days.

In our private lives, of course, we felt the inflation quite terribly. The main burden was borne by the women. If one discovered a store where one could buy fat, rice, or anything else, friends were informed, and they hurried to get there in time. Often they didn't succeed, and it was hard to manage. Bartering sprang up again. In this way we got a few centners of potatoes and a sack of flour, sometimes even eggs or butter and similar precious items—what great, much envied luck! Matters became more and more unsettled in the city and in the Reich. The growing antisemitic party made rabid propaganda. We didn't take that so seriously; rather, we feared the communist threat and in our city felt more and more clearly the impoverishment and embitterment of the masses. [. . .]

After inflation things at the business were considerably less alarming, and confidence that stabilization would continue grew. Still, in February I had experienced a terrible scare, because for two days the exchange rate of the mark had dropped to ninety-five Swiss francs for one hundred reichsmarks. But that had been the only setback. Now it became evident that the old firms did have considerable advantages, due to their reputation of soundness. We received sufficient offers and credit from our suppliers. One would have thought, now that the mark was stable, that buyers would have refrained from buying, since it was no longer necessary to use money immediately. However, the supply of clothing and household goods in the past years had been so completely inadequate that a tremendous demand for them had built up. Thus, the good wares that appeared on the market were now eagerly bought from us; in those days we had no sales problems.

The improved economic situation brought increased competition. The big department store combines began to expand. They opened new branches, bought old-established firms in places that seemed to them to be advantageous, and everywhere they were renovating and expanding. They were able to do that because they were constantly receiving large foreign loans. The first uniform-price stores appeared. Woolworth started, Tietz and Karstadt followed. We had to exert ourselves in order to hold our own. The clientele became harder to please, expenses rose. The daughter of my partner married; his son-in-law entered the firm. He had been in the banking line. It was not easy for him to get used to our business and to get on good terms with our clientele. Our balance sheet for 1926 showed increased sales but no increase in profit. Still, in 1927 the upswing continued.

In the middle of that year it became known that the Tietz Combine[1] intended to buy a building site in Hanau in order to erect a new department store. There was great agitation in retailer circles. It was known that Tietz had made a bid to the city for a particular plot of land. The association of retailers tried to forestall the combine and to raise the money for the purchase. The city stipulated conditions that could not be met; the chief mayor wanted to speed up this development. Under his regime the city had built a harbor on the Main during the time of inflation. After that it had undertaken big housing projects and granted assistance for the settling of new industries. Now he was trying to give retail business a new look. Finally, the building site was bought by a branch of the Frankfurt department store combine Wronker,[2] which had existed in Hanau for many years. Tietz did not give up. He negotiated with a businessman who, as straw man, bought a number of houses at a good commercial location, and thus, within a year, Hanau was blessed with two department stores, which were much too big for the place. Moreover, a uniform-price store was opened at the same time.

The reaction within the different circles was varied. The development ran parallel to that throughout the Reich. Working-class circles welcomed it, for the greater competition was supposed to bring with it more shopping possibilities and cheaper prices. The small, merchant middle class saw its very existence threatened and was desperate. At that time the so-called Wirtschaftspartei was founded,[3] which recruited its members from among the latter and craftsmen circles, and took up as its cause the battle against the department and chain stores. Its failure promoted the rise of National Socialism. Antisemitism increased greatly, since it was precisely the big department store combines that were under Jewish management. The larger stores tried to take up the fight. There was much rebuilding, expansion, and beautification, and money for interior decoration was spent most generously. In every issue the specialized periodicals printed new discussions on rebuilding and interior design. The business streets of the cities glittered and sparkled. In Hanau the city offered cheap rates for display window illumination, to encourage the consumption of electricity.

We could not escape the spirit of the times. We believed we could maintain our rank by providing better facilities for display and by better furnishing of the salesrooms, as well as through a larger stock. Thus, in the year 1928 we completely rebuilt our main store. I took out a mortgage and thought that in this way I was financially strong enough for any eventuality. My partner suffered a stroke, and thus, unfortunately, just at that time I lost his valuable help and experience. With my new partner, his son-in-law, I did not get along at all. Soon serious disagreements arose and I had to part with him. He left the firm. Since Herr S. was no longer active, I concluded a new contract with him, which assured him a definite income, independent of the progress of business. At the start, all went well. The new display window did, in fact, bring new customers. The department stores opened, prices were lowered, and the stiff competition made itself felt. Despite all, at first sales remained unimpaired. I was considering merger plans with several other firms. Thus passed the year 1929.

In spite of all the struggle, excitement, and worries we had a beautiful family life and felt happy and strong. My wife was healthy. Our little boy lived in his green garden in a child's paradise. The large sandpile we had heaped up for him attracted playmates, and he always had merry company. My brother had established a good practice, which was constantly growing. He was much more content now than earlier. He was especially very popular among the simpler people. They knew that for Dr. Schwabe no hour was too late and no distance too far if he was needed.

A new arts society had formed and brought much stimulation through slide lectures, concerts, and other events. Jewish academicians who had settled in Hanau after the war played a leading role. We bought our first radio: unforgettable the excitement and the delight of hearing an opera from Budapest for the first time—it was Gounod's *Faust*. The radio in those days was still completely unpolitical, and the programs stressed the arts far more than today. The first war novels appeared. Reinhard Wehr published his realistic portrayals in the *Frankfurter Zeitung*. Remarque published his *All Quiet on the Western Front*. Jakob Wassermann's wonderful novels of social criticism appeared; Hermann Hesse, Werfel, the Zweigs, and many others came out with new works and were widely read.

I went to Berlin often, frequently accompanied by my wife. Many new firms had opened, which did not simplify buying. The intention was to offer a constantly greater selection; every firm tried to specialize in a very particular type of wares. Berlin was trying to outdo itself. Besides Max Reinhardt, other theaters, too, presented brilliant performances. Popular writers who were soon forgotten and classics were produced with equal care. Revues, patterned after French and American models, displayed more and more pageantry and scantier and scantier costumes. We had relatives in Berlin and in the summer we frequently went on drives with them to the magnificent Berlin surroundings. I showed Lotte Sanssouci and the Havel lakes; we drove to Wannsee and also to Treptow, where the Berlin workers celebrate their Sundays. A different Berlin, Berlin E. There the furniture industry is located. There, too, I had to do buying. There were no showy streets there, but instead huge factories and warehouses, endless tenement houses with sunless courtyards. Countless children romped about in the street; everywhere there was noise and dust. One felt that there people *worked*. A different tone prevailed than in the West, coarser and more masculine. There was no elegance anywhere. In the stores only the cheapest, simplest selection. When I went back to my hotel, I was once again in another world. [. . .]

I will now try to describe how between the years 1930 and 1933 my personal fate was affected by the general events. First, there came a very sharp recession in sales throughout the retail trade. When cheaper prices are expected, the buyer holds back; when salaries are reduced and the yields from the economy decrease, the standard of living cannot be maintained. Raw material prices were falling, since the world economy was also ruined. Whoever had substantial reserves, lost. The department store combines tried absolutely to maintain their sales by all possible means. Thus, the price level dropped even more rapidly than would have been necessary if business had been conducted sensibly. Firms with large capital bought from ailing manufacturers at giveaway prices and sold the goods more cheaply than they could be purchased under regular circumstances. Capital assets dwindled, salaries were reduced, laborers and white-collar workers were let go. Here, too, the big combines proceeded ruthlessly. "If our display windows get smashed, we are insured," the manager of a central branch in Cologne supposedly said. The smaller businesses, which had a close personal relationship with their help, could not simply turn them onto the street. In this regard I was not firm enough. Later I had to pay dearly for it. The decline of buying power proceeded parallel to the decline in sales and the value of goods. Naturally, the decline did not proceed as rapidly as I am describing it here. I fought as well as I could. Our regular clientele remained loyal to us. To be sure, we now had to grant a good deal of book credit. We had months in which we succeeded in raising sales and in which we hoped that we were over the hump. We tried to reduce expenses wherever we could. [. . .]

On January 30, 1933, Hitler was entrusted by Reichspresident Hindenburg with the office of Chancellor of the Reich. The propaganda increased immediately. The *Hanauer Anzeiger* was suddenly more National Socialist than the party press. Here, as everywhere, fear for one's position, for one's daily bread quickly caused those holding different views to fall into line. There were men, there were honorable people, but on the whole how pitifully, how spinelessly, and in what an undignified manner did the world of commerce, science, officialdom, and justice capitulate. After all, the NSDAP was still in the minority in the government as well as in the parliament. The Deutschnationale and Zentrum parties still held key positions. They had allowed Hitler to come into power only under certain conditions. They did not make use of this position. It was precisely the newly converted, the opportunists, as well as those who occupied positions that they wanted to keep, who were only too ready to renounce their convictions of yesterday.

After the first weeks the tone became noticeably more antisemitic. It was, after all, so easy to denounce and disparage as being Jewish everything that didn't suit one. The *Stürmer*, Streicher's infamous paper,[4] set the trend, the rest of the press followed. A pretext was needed for laws that were already being prepared. The Reichstag fire, the elections, the persecution of the communists had been taken care of. Now it was the turn of the Jews. Suddenly it was discovered that an "atrocity campaign" was being waged by Jews abroad. A cry for revenge: We need a boycott against the Jews to stop the smear campaign. Thus, the boycott of April 1st was organized, just as everything in Germany is organized. Streicher was at its head. The boycott was to last until the goal of stopping the campaign abroad was achieved. The beginning was set for ten o'clock in the morning. We were at the store and waited. In the preceding days we had a greater rush of customers than for years. Everyone told us how little they were in agreement with the boycott and how they sympathized with us. Everyone bought what they needed for the near future, in case the boycott lasted longer.

The boycott lasted one day. I will never forget it. The street was filled with people. Young fellows howling, older people curious, many incensed. In front of each Jewish store the SA men in brown were lined up. The leaders, in snappy new uniforms, checked the guards. I closed up and went home. After all, we were not yet so humbled, so trampled down as not to have been seized by a raging anger and the shame that something like that was possible in Germany. My wife and I went to a nearby forest, and in the evening we visited a district court judge, with whom we were on friendly terms. There we met friends, and a Protestant pastor who came somewhat later said: "Some nice company I'm finding here, a Catholic district court judge, a Social Democratic director, and two Jewish couples! High time that the police put an end to this scandal!" It did so soon enough.

Soon after the boycott the first laws appeared throwing Jews out of the professions that until then they had practiced with the greatest success and to everyone's satisfaction. Lawyers, doctors, and officials who had not worked before 1914 or had not been frontline soldiers in the war had to leave professional life.[5] Physicians lost the right to treat subscribers to the health insurance plan. Since almost every patient was insured by such a plan, those affected lost the basis of their existence because of this ban. My brother-in-law in Stuttgart had worked during the war as a surgeon and orthopedist in the hospital in Canstatt. His superiors had not let him leave the hospital for the front, because they considered him indispensable. Now he lost his main practice. His wife had gone to an epidemic disease hospital at the front as a medical student and had taken her exams after the war. Since she had not worked as a doctor she was not granted the privilege of a frontline soldier. The two emigrated to Palestine.

The Jewish community banded more closely together. The Zionist paper *Jüdische Rundschau* helped much to uplift spirits by its encouraging articles. We tried to establish a Jewish school in Hanau, but the government refused permission. The stores were harassed. Our supplies of flag material were "confiscated" by the union of retailers although there was not the slightest justification for it. The pressure on the clientele to stay away from Jewish businesses became stronger. The NS trade organization was exerting itself.

We spent the 1st of May, which was celebrated as a "day of national labor," with friends in the country, in Schlüchtern. They had a soap factory there and lived in a charming house. Their enterprise provided bread to many, and their charity had helped all poor people as much as possible. The firm had donated the plant flag (under gentle pressure by the negotiating council), and it was now odd to see the Jewish owner presenting the Nazi flag. However, to cry with the pack did no good in this case. Countless times that day we heard the Horst Wessel song and the German national anthem. The organization was perfect.

On the next day the trade unions were dissolved. The NSBO,[6] later called the Arbeitsfront, inherited their ample assets. Then began the bogus trials, which were supposed to justify the measure. Stories about embezzlements, mismanagement, and waste by union officials were reported by the press. The clamor lasted a few weeks, then it was over, its purpose achieved. NSBO: "Nun sind die Bonzen oben,"* that is how the people interpreted the abbreviation. Naturally, business suffered. Previously we had made deliveries to hospitals, public authorities, and the city; now we lost all of that. Officials, teachers, and everyone who was somehow dependent on the state or local government was intimidated. My brother, as a frontline soldier, had retained his practice for members of the health insurance plan and he had more work than ever. The new National Socialist principles of regulating medical treatment apparently did not appeal to his patients so much as to make them leave him. One did not change one's doctor as easily as a store. Health is more important than clothing.

We continued playing music regularly at the H.'s. We had many a conversation about topics of the day. There appeared an issue of the *Stürmer* (the ritual murder issue) that in vileness by far surpassed everything until then. Crying, Frau H. told us how ashamed she was for Germany. Then came a day on which Herr H. appeared at the store. He had had to join the SA. Under these circumstances . . . That was the end! This experience was typical.

A bitter joke from that time: "How many decent Jews are there in Germany?" And the reply: "Sixty million, every Aryan knows at least one."

The ruling on the admission of Jewish pupils and students to secondary schools and universities produced new pressure, new abuse, new degradation. Jewish books were burned in public. Jewish authors and artists were banned.[7] Every day brought new vileness. Every means suited them. Lies, falsified statistics, defamations, everything was used. The 1st of October: "Harvest Festival Day." Fraternization between town and country by official decree. The "workforces" of the individual firms marched with their "leaders"—the Jewish firms naturally without a leader—out to the country for the Harvest Festival. Afterward our people told me how our customers in Mittelbuchen had enjoyed themselves with them and that they all sent me their greetings.

As every year, this time, too, there was supposed to be a joint advertising campaign by the retailers for Christmas. Advertisement papers were published, we were charged the usual fee, the texts were picked up, and our participation in the Christmas raffle was anounced. Suddenly, someone made the terrible discovery that Jews and Aryans were working as equals. Impossible! We were told that we would not be admitted. At that time we were still naive enough to believe in justice. Two gentlemen went with a lawyer to Frankfurt in order to present a complaint to a higher court. We got through a directive to the association that permission was to be given. The result: The event

*"Now the bigshots are on top."

was not held, the advertisement paper, already paid for, did not come out, and for Jewish stores the Christmas trade was "made easy" by boycott pickets. We were thus protected from the rush. [. . .]

I could not maintain my business any longer. I had to carry too many burdens, make too many payments. My nerves were at an end. I put my firm up for settlement. My good name helped me. The negotiations dragged out for some time, the settlement took place, and I was able to meet the terms. In the spring of 1935 I was free. For the most part, I had been able to dismiss the costly personnel, had reduced my expenses to a bearable measure, and hoped to be able to maintain my livelihood on a smaller but more solid basis. I suffered terribly. My wife stood by me faithfully. Without her I would not have made it through. [. . .]

Naturally, we constantly considered the idea of emigration. My brother still had quite a bit of work, but he, too, was suffering, as were we all. Our money was tied up in our real estate, and if in those times it was difficult as it was to find a ready market for real estate, for Jews it was almost impossible even to get a fairly decent price. The period of "Aryanization" had begun. Every day one read in the daily and trade press: Firm X and firm Y and firm Z have been transferred to Aryan hands and have been taken over by Herren . . . I myself had tried to sell my business after it had been restored to financial soundness. The buildings were on the most desirable business street, and before 1933 it would have easily been possible to sell them for a relatively good price. Now, an Aryan who had a couple thousand marks thought he could acquire something worth ten times as much from a Jewish owner. After deduction of expenses, taxes, etc. I would have been left almost without anything. The real estate would hardly have brought in enough to meet the mortgage debt.

In the middle of 1936 the owner of a movie house approached us. A strange creature, somewhat inclined towards swindling, he had opened the movie theater with borrowed money. In 1933 he succeeded in making it the official party movie house and from then on he did well. He had fallen out with his landlord, as, in general, he was constantly quarreling with everyone. His rental lease ran out, and he was looking for another place. In order to save on real estate taxes, which were not charged for vacant buildings, I had transferred my furniture department, which was stored separately in a big house, to my other building. Herr E. was interested in the vacant one. We negotiated with the greatest caution on both sides. Apparently he used our offer as a means of pressuring his landlord. The negotiations proceeded according to the way matters stood at any one time. The pressure that was being exerted on our business increased. I had curbed my expenses and believed that I was secure at least for the immediate future. Developments showed that whenever there was a new propaganda thrust, more customers stayed away. [. . .]

My brother was preparing for his emigration. He supplied himself and his family abundantly and acquired the newest and best medical equipment. He was learning English diligently and was quite confident. On September 10, 1937, he went to Stuttgart with his wife and children in order to fetch the visa. He got it without any difficulty. Immediately after his return we went with Herr E. to the notary to complete the contract. There were still small matters to be discussed, after which Herr E. was to receive the formal permission of the party and the city, which had been promised him, and then the final signing was to take place. My brother made his last dispositions. We had a talk about personal matters in order to settle financial questions. Then, by coincidence, I did not get to his apartment for a few days. I never saw him alive again.

On Monday, the 21st of September, my sister-in-law sent for me. I found her in tears. "Otto has been arrested." I was in a daze. What had happened? My brother had treated a woman patient for years, had helped her, had placed orders several times with her husband, a roofer, to do repairs on our buildings. Thus a kind of an acquaintanceship had developed. The woman had frequently visited my sister-in-law and had played with the children. Now, the couple discovered that my brother was leaving in the near future. Apparently in order to blackmail him, the husband accused him of having become too familiar with his wife and of having performed an abortion. He poured forth threats. My brother consulted with his two best friends. Meetings were arranged that were listened in on by witnesses in the next room. Finally, my brother lodged charges of blackmail with the police. The two were questioned, my brother was told to come the next day, and was arrested. The poor man had believed that a good name and innocence would be enough to protect him. He had his passport and his visa in his pocket, had the exit permit. He could have easily left even on the day before his interrogation by the police if he had had even the slightest doubt about the positive outcome of his case. We do not know what happened to him during the interrogation. I went to the lawyer, consulted with my sister-in-law and friends. On Wednesday, the 23rd of September, in the morning I went to my sister-in-law's on the way from a consultation. The lawyer had tried to give us hope and had suggested certain steps. While I was reporting, an old woman patient came to the apartment crying: "You probably don't even know yet what has happened. Dr. Schwabe has done away with himself." We did not believe her, could not believe her.

I went with my friend to the police. A crowd of people in front of the building. Blood spots on the steps confirmed that a tragedy had happened. In the barracks no one wanted to give us information. Finally we got to the police chief himself, and he told us that after the interrogation was concluded my brother was to be taken to the prosecutor's office. He had waited in the room on the third floor and had conversed calmly with the officials present there, then suddenly he went to the window, flung it open and threw himself out of it. An official who had wanted to hold him back had hurt his hand in the process. We will never be able to ascertain if this story was true. [. . .]

One morning all Jewish stores found on their display windows signs with the inscription "Jew Store." Naturally, we removed them, but the next morning they were there again, now with a small inscription at the bottom: "Whoever tears this off is a betrayer of the people." In Hanau a new district leader had become head of the local organization and had to prove his talents. Easter was around the corner, boycott pickets assembled. This time it was civil servants, teachers, and municipal employees who were chosen for the honorary post. Every adult was assigned a few schoolboys, who naturally enjoyed the whole thing tremendously. To be able to behave insolently towards adults with official sanction, that was something altogether new. If someone stopped in front of the display window of a Jewish store, the little heroes were right on the spot. Signs for "betrayers of the people," who might dare to enter the stores, were readied. Cameras were to immortalize the image of such an *"untermensch"* for the *Stürmer*.

In short, it was a great time for young people. Sometimes they threw fireworks and stink bombs into the stores, all that under the supervision and with the approval of the teachers and dignitaries. Some of the latter had refused to participate, but "an order is an order," and exclusion from the party meant certain loss of livelihood.

At the same time another kind of boycott began. At the entrances of Christian stores signs appeared reading: "No admittance to Jews." At first in one street, then in another; more and more stores were forced to participate. If the businessman refused, he risked denuciation and even worse. With few exceptions every one of them disapproved of the move. After all, the Jews had been good and well-paying customers, and the business situation was not such that the loss would not have been felt. We had no difficulties. We had enough friends who got us everything we needed, and we could go to Frankfurt, but we felt this stupid nuisance as something rotten.

At the beginning of April Herr E. showed up again. He was in a difficult situation. The permit from the motion picture board, necessary for every new construction of a movie house, had run out. Now the board demanded, before it even made a decision, that he present a bill of sale by which he could prove ownership of the property. If the decision turned out against him, then, of course, the property was of no value to him. We concluded a "gentlemen's agreement" that in the latter case I would not consider the contract as signed and would not insist on any rights contained in it. Such an agreement between a party member and a Jew, with the approval of the party lawyer— that was something special. We signed the contract on the 26th of April 1938, and on the 27th there was a decree by Göring that from that day on no Jew was allowed to sell real estate without the permission of the appropriate district president. Later it turned out that these permits took months to get. Things reached the point of dramatic final struggles; both parties went to Berlin to the highest court of justice. Then, at the end of May, a commission of the motion picture board came to inspect the premises and decided in E's favor. He took over the buildings as of April 1st, so that I was spared the considerable additional tax payment.

It was a rescue at the last moment, for hardly a customer was still coming to us. On a side street, in a Jewish-owned house, I rented the ground floor, which on the outside did not look like a store. We moved once more. As soon as their visits to us could no longer be easily checked, the customers came—in greater numbers than they had for many months! In the meantime we had received the affidavit for immigration to the United States and gradually liquidated the business.

1. Starting in the nineties, the family Tietz established two big chains of department stores: the Hermann Tietz Combine and the Leonhard Tietz Corporation. The Hermann Tietz Combine was privately owned by the family and in 1933 had some 14,000 employees.

2. Hermann Wronker (born in 1867; deported in 1942) established a department store in 1891 in Frankfurt am Main.

3. The Wirtschaftspartei, or Reichspartei des deutschen Mittelstandes, founded in 1920, was a rightist interest party of home and real-estate owners, tradesmen, and retailers. In 1928 it had over twenty-three seats in the Reichstag.

4. Julius Streicher (born in 1885; executed in 1946) was NSDAP regional leader in Franconia and in the years 1923–1945 published the National Socialist weekly *Der Stürmer,* which served the propagation of the most fanatical antisemitism and propagandistically paved

the way for the destruction of the Jews. The paper was publicly posted everywhere in the so-called Stürmer cases. See A. Schwerin (44).

5. The Gesetz zur Widerherstellung des Berufsbeamtentums of April 7, 1933 decreed the dismissal of all civil servants of Jewish origin, with the exception of those who had already been civil servants prior to 1914 or had fought at the front during the World War. The same exemption regulation is found in the Gesetz über die Zulassung zur Rechtsanwaltschaft of April 11, 1933, which denied Jewish lawyers admission to the bar, and in the Verordnung über die Zulassung von Ärzten zur Tätigkeit bei Krankenkassen of April 22, 1933, by which Jews were deprived of medical practice involving members of the health-insurance plan.

6. Nationalsozialistische Betriebszellen-Organisation; founded in 1931 in order to gain National Socialism access to the factories. In 1935 it was incorporated into the Deutsche Arbeitsfront (DAF). The DAF, created in May 1933, after the dissolution of the unions, forcibly organized employees and employers.

7. The Gesetz gegen die Überfüllung der deutschen Schulen und Hochschulen of April 25, 1933 limited the number of Jewish students and pupils to 1.5 percent of the total number. The public book burning took place on May 10, 1933 in numerous university towns.

## 36   *Emil Schorsch*

BORN IN 1899 IN HÜNGHEIM (BADEN); DIED IN 1982 IN VINELAND, NEW JERSEY (U.S.A.).

Emil Schorsch, The Twelve Years before the Destruction of the Synagogue in Hannover. Manuscript, Vineland (New Jersey), 1975, 95 pages.

*Although Emil Schorsch first trained as a primary school teacher in Esslingen, affected by his experiences at the front, he decided to become a rabbi. He made up for his Gymnasium diploma, studied between 1922 and 1926 at the Jewish Theological Seminary in Breslau, and attained his Ph.D. Between 1927 and 1938 Schorsch was the assistant local rabbi in Hannover, a congregation with some 5,500 members, of whom almost one third were East European Jews. He devoted himself to youth work and tried to counteract religious indifference. In this he found support above all in the vibrant religiosity of the East European Jews. He was among the founders of a Jüdisches Lehrhaus, whose curriculum was expanded after 1933 by practical courses for emigrants. After the November pogrom in 1938, he was interned in the concentration camp at Buchenwald, but because he possessed an English visa he was freed after ten days. In 1940, with his wife and two children, Schorsch emigrated from England to relatives in the United States. From 1940 until 1964 he was rabbi in Pottstown, Pennsylvania.*

According to my contract, my duties as rabbi in Hannover included the "Department for Religious Instruction," giving sermons in the synagogue, the supervision of *kashrut*,[1] and the directorship of the community library. The supervision of religious instruction at first caused much work but was, for the most part, a clearly defined task. We formed twenty-eight religion classes for the some 650 Jewish pupils of the primary and secondary schools in Hannover. For the primary school classes we had a special religion school on Lützowstrasse, where the community building was located. These pupils had no difficulty attending religious instruction twice during the week and on Sunday morning. For the pupils of the secondary schools it was more difficult because there were relatively few Jewish pupils in each school. Thus we gave up the idea of establishing classes in the different secondary schools, but instead combined these pupils in the afternoon in one of these schools, which had been selected for that purpose.

The result was not good. The pupils had the feeling that the entire matter of religious instruction did not have to be taken seriously. It was very difficult to fight the resulting irregularity of class attendance. We had, of course, worked out a curriculum, and all questions connected with religious instruction were discussed in special teachers' meetings. We even introduced meetings of all teachers of the province of Hannover, and they were very well attended. Nevertheless, there was no use pretending that religious instruction—Hebrew as well as the historical and theoretical components—contributed much to heightening Jewish religious consciousness. The reason was that one can hardly expect to influence the personality if the family life of the pupils is inconsistent with the goal of instruction. And there could be no doubt that only to a small extent did the Jewish religion serve as the model for the parents' life, perhaps only to the degree that seemed necessary to them for the sake of public appearances, although they scarcely gave this much thought. [. . .]

Widespread religious ignorance was a fact. It reached the point where someone who became a member of the community council felt superior to the rabbi because he managed the community's finances. Ignorance in religious matters did not burden him, since materialism ruled the lives of modern people, and a place was made for religion only for political considerations. It was still true that society expected a religious affiliation. Where there were churches, there also had to be synagogues, otherwise the Jewish community would have been labeled as communist. In many cases this attitude did not go beyond paying the community taxes; for the rest, the taxpayer wanted to be left in peace. Perhaps subconsciously they felt that by employing a rabbi something could be done to preserve Judaism as a religion. But that did not make the task of the rabbi any easier. He felt the cold hand of unbelief, of indifference, of hostility towards everything religious to a degree that almost stifled his efforts. Were prayer services more than well meant self-deceptions? This question could not be dismissed from one's heart. When the rabbi sermonized on God, he was turning to many a person in the synagogue who was convinced that God did not exist. How long could the perseverance of tradition withstand an atmosphere that was so destructive of feeling? [. . .]

Such a view and pronounced negative attitude can have only a paralyzing if not fatal effect on religious education. The most that a religion teacher could expect was that a miracle happened and the pupil possessed a heart inclined toward Judaism, which was waiting to be opened by a guide. Against indifference, however, there was in general nothing that one could really call religious influence. It was quite clear that I had to try to create an atmosphere that would open up possibilities for religious education. It had to be something that, like the parental home and family, also exerted an emotional influence. Thus it came about that I developed the idea of a youth congregation.

Since children imitate their parents, it is not surprising that this imitation also extends to the affiliation with a community. Children do not know why father and mother sometimes attend a service, but they are inclined to do the same, especially if they are not of secondary importance but can be at the center of it. It was obvious that a youth congregation would create such an opportunity. Not only would the children and adolescents conduct the service as cantor and rabbi, but they could also be chairmen and distribute honorary posts, and still everything would be without the false intentions that endangered the true nature of the synagogue, since children do not yet actively participate in economic life.

The idea of the youth congregation was a hit. The children and youth were enthusiastic. We created a Saturday afternoon service that was based on the above-mentioned principles. Especially children who came from religious families, and among them were many East European Jewish families, felt at home in this youth congregation. Suddenly the children and youth were organized religiously. The individual child could perhaps be neglected in regard to religion, but not the youth congregation. The executive committee of the synagogue regarded the youth congregation as an unusually valuable innovation and was willing to carry the financial burden after the youth congregation had secured its existence for a few years.

Of course, the Sabbath services were not the only activity of the youth congregation. Youth services for the holidays were also introduced, and a very great surprise was the first *Simchas Tora* service.[2] Until then, on the holidays a few children came to the synagogue with their parents, but for this *Simchas Tora* service, which took place in the afternoon, 300 children gathered in the community's beautiful House of Worship. In the following years their number reached 1,000. Admittedly, it was sometimes difficult to get the quiet necessary to hear the cantor or the rabbi's sermon. But finally we found a way to achieve the necessary silence without giving the children the feeling that they were to be subjugated by strict discipline. Chief cantor Alter, with his voluminous, penetrating voice, sometimes had trouble being heard, but he did not let himself be discouraged. And I discovered very soon that the heart of a child can be opened relatively easily through the telling of a beautiful story. A further activity of the youth congregation was its self-government; it had to elect an executive committee. We established a journal, to which members of the youth congregation contributed, and the Jewish community paper printed a supplement of the youth congregation.

The most important achievement of this youth congregation was the recognition that Jewish youth as a totality could have religious claims. The parents noticed that they could not simply neglect their religious responsibilities without somehow feeling that they were wronging all of Jewish youth. It was important to create not only a youth organization that could demand its rights from the community administration, but rather a Jewish youth organization that placed Jewish religion at its center. It created a basis for Jewish existence that united all Jewish people of the most varied views into a community. That was especially important for the children and youth from East European families. In the youth congregation they were united with all of the others. [. . .]

In the Jewish community of Hannover there were many families that came from Poland, Russia, and other East European countries. I would estimate their number at about 1,700 souls. Many had settled in Hannover decades ago, their children were born in Hannover and received their education in German schools. [. . .]

Most of the East European families in Hannover were orthodox. Their businesses stayed closed on the Sabbath. On Friday they hung a notice on the shop door that read something like: "This store will close on Friday afternoon at 3:00, and will open again on Saturday at 6:00 p.m." I do not believe that the stores suffered losses because of this practice; rather, I often noticed that Christians placed great trust in Jewish business people who took their religion seriously. The East European families had created for themselves three so-called *Stübel,* that is, small prayer houses in which their special religious customs were observed. In the first *Stübel* there gathered the Jewish families from Lithuania, in the second those from Poland, and in the third the Galicians. This separation is not difficult to understand if one considers that in the prayers the small differences in pronunciation, delivery, and melody play an important role. Whenever well-known melodies occur, the entire community hums along with the cantor. Probably the Yiddish language was also used in conversation. These three *Stübel* had appointed one of their members, Raphael Balsam,[3] as their rabbi, whose task was especially to decide over the *kashrut* of poultry. In principle, however, the Jewish families of East European origin in Hannover felt themselves to be members of the synagogue community. On the one hand this can be explained by the fact that there was a law according to which everyone who declared that he belonged to the Jewish religion had to belong to the Jewish community of the town in question and pay community taxes; on the other hand, it was the desire of the East European Jews to join the general German-Jewish community.[4] Complicating matters was the circumstance that German citizenship was regarded as necessary in order to become a full, equal member of the community. Only a few of the East European families were ready or able to bear the costs of naturalization. The result was that most of them could not become full members.[5]

At prayers there were always many East European families present, since they observed the Sabbath strictly. How large the number of the East European Jews attending the synagogue was became almost frighteningly clear when on October 28, 1938, the Nazis had deported the East European Jewish population of Hannover to the no-man's-land on the Polish border. That happened on a Friday; on the following Saturday morning the synagogue was almost empty. It is possible that some German Jews did not come to the synagogue on this Sabbath because of fear. Nonetheless it proved that for the Sabbath morning services one could not depend on a Jewish population that had turned the Sabbath into a workday. [. . .]

Not being a full member had no effect on the fact that all of the services of the synagogue community were available to all Jewish families in Hannover. Everyone could attend worship; only for the High Holy Days were tickets distributed that required membership.[6] But on the other holidays the synagogue was filled with our East European members. The *Simchas Tora* festival was the only exception. After the Torah scrolls had been carried around in the synagogue in a festive joyous procession accompanied by the traditional melodies, when the Torah reading had taken place and the service was finished, I went to the *Stübel* of the East European Jews to participate in their *Simchas Tora* celebration. That was a bit wilder. There, the boys sat high up on the cabinets and loudly sang the melodies for the procession. Real dancing with the Torah scrolls was part of the *hafakot.*[7] In spite of the immense noise it was a heartwarming experience.

All the religious practices of the East European families radiated this particular warmheartedness. One had the feeling that for them religion was reality. Since so many did not have German citizenship, and since they certainly were not proud of their Polish homeland with its never-ending antisemitism, it is perhaps understandable that Judaism, that is, the Jewish religion with all its laws, customs, and traditions, was their real inner home. This warmheartedness, however, cannot be explained only thus, for it was deeply anchored in the personality of the individual. In contrast to this inner emotional warmth, the Judaism of the German Jews was something cold, at best an intellectual-emotional phenomenon, as I knew it especially in the case of my teacher Isaak Heinemann in Breslau.[8] The top hat that the German Jews wore in the synagogue signified more than a custom, more than self-imposed respect before God. It was also a sign of a certain numbness of the heart. The Christian *Shammes,*[9] too, who strolled up and down the hallway of the synagogue during the service, seemed to me always like an embodiment of ossified Judaism. All that was expected in this splendid House of God was decorum, external decorum. Underneath the surface indifference or even opposition could be rampant. I have not found such an inner contradiction among East European Jewish families.

Whenever I visited an East European family on the Sabbath or for a Bar Mitzva, I was always surprised at how many Christian neighbors were present. Obviously, there was a great external difference between the Christian Germans, who spoke Hannover German, and the East European families, who often had a Yiddish intonation. But this difference had no influence on the understanding between the two groups. The East European families lived in the poorest sections of town, and it was especially the simple Christian population that got along well with their Jewish neighbors. I found a much weaker link between the German Jewish families and the Christian population, although both groups spoke German with a Hannover accent. Probably there was less complacency and vanity on the simpler level of the East European Jews than on the so-called higher cultural level of the German Jews.

1. *Kashrut* (noun; adj. "kosher") means the fulfillment of the ritual food laws. The rabbi, for example, supervises the *schächten,* that is, slaughtering according to religious prescription.

2. Prayer service on the festival of Simchat Torah. On this day the yearly reading of the weekly Torah portion is concluded and started anew. In the synagogues adults and children celebrate this festival in exuberant merriment, in the process of which selected members dance with the Torah in their arms.

3. The Talmud scholar Raphael Balsam died in Haifa in 1974; he held the office of rabbi for the East European orthodox community of Hannover between 1912 and 1936, and then emigrated to Palestine.

4. The East European Jews, then, despite their own prayer rooms and their own rabbi, belonged to the so-called unified congregation, and not to the orthodox secession. In Prussia it was legally possible from 1876 on for Jews to withdraw from the Jewish community in order to form separate congregations (orthodox secessionist congregations), something that part of the orthodox community took advantage of.

5. It was less a question of cost that prevented naturalization than the politics of the states that had to approve each naturalization individually without exception before it became valid for the Reich.—According to a decision of 1914 by the Prussian Minister of the Interior, the right to vote in community elections could not be denied to foreigners; however, in the Jewish

community of Hannover in 1929 a property qualification law was still in effect, which excluded the majority of East European Jews as non-taxpayers from voting. Cf. *Jüdisch-liberale Zeitung*, 1929, No. 11.

6. The High Holy Days are the New Year (Rosh Hashana) and the Day of Atonement (Yom Kippur). See Glossary.

7. Processions (Hebrew).

8. Isaak Heinemann (1876–1957) was lecturer at the Jewish Theological Seminary in Breslau between 1919 and 1938, and between 1930 and 1933 also honorary professor for Classical Philology at the University in Breslau. Beginning in 1920, he edited the *Monatsschrift für Geschichte und Wissenschaft des Judentums*. In 1939 he emigrated to Palestine.

9. Caretaker of the synagogue.

# 37   *Ottilie Schönewald, née Mendel*

 BORN IN 1883 IN BOCHUM; DIED IN 1961 IN NEW YORK.

Ottilie Schönewald, Memoirs. Manuscript, New York, 1961, 22 pages.

*The feminist Ottilie Schönewald came from a wealthy family in Bochum. She received a traditional girl's education and married a lawyer early in her life. Through his practice she recognized the legal discrimination of women and became active in the Bochum Office for the Protection of Women's Rights of the Federation of German Women's Organizations. When women received the right to vote with the establishment of the Weimar Republic, she became municipal councilor of the German Democratic Party. Starting in 1926 she was a member of the executive in the Westphalian State Federation of the Jewish Women's Federation. From 1929 on she belonged to the Federation's central governing body in Berlin, where she headed the Committee for Women's Rights. As a representative of Jewish women she was also elected to the main governing body of the Centralverein and to the Prussian State Federation of Jewish Communities. From 1934 until its dissolution in 1938, she was the last president of the Jewish Women's Federation. In 1939 she emigrated with her husband and their daughter by way of Holland to England, and in 1946 to New York, where she remained active in all aspects of social work.*

What great hopes were created by the granting of absolute political equality to German women in 1919, at the end of the World War, which Germany lost! Was gaining the numerically predominant segment of the population for responsible political activity in the work of recovery a compensation for the sustained loss in external power and prestige? Were women able and willing to master this enormous task? Well, at the end of this development came the Hitler period, to the rise of which, according to statistical data, women's suffrage was supposed to have contributed decisively.[1] If that is correct, it would be a devastating answer to my question. But for my report, there lies in between a period of time filled with new tasks, which shall be dealt with in chronological order, as an important chapter in the development of my life.

No wonder that in 1919, when the political declaration of women's majority was made, a declaration for which until then the women's movement had struggled in vain, all political parties looked around for a suitable woman representative. Since, as a woman, I combined the popularity I had gained by my work during the war with the "advantage" of being a representative of Jewish interests, but occupied only *one* place on the candidate list, it was understandable that the offer came from several parties to propose me as candidate at the elections for municipal council. In accordance with my political views, I accepted the offer of the Deutsche Demokratische Partei (later Staatspartei), and until 1926 I was active in the city council, where, at times, I served on fourteen committees, among others the central committee. My co-option to the Committee of the Reichspartei in Berlin occurred soon thereafter. All that, along with my membership in the local party executive committee and extensive engagements as a speaker, especially on local politics and women's interests, would have been more than enough for a full work schedule.

In 1922, however, there also followed the founding of the Prussian Union of Jewish Communities, and now, following the trend of the times, in Jewish circles too they remembered that the participation of women was essential. Until then I had always regretted the exclusion of women from participating in leading Jewish organizations. For that reason I believed that I could not decline the delegate position in the Prussian Union offered to me by the Westphalian Jewish women. In addition, I had also accepted my election to the executive committee of the Centralverein and the Vereinigung für das Liberale Judentum, and was delegated by the latter in 1930 as their speaker to the international congress of the Weltbund für Liberales Judentum in London.[2]

It was a stroke of fate that the year 1919, which was abounding in new duties, also brought me the fulfillment of my heart's desire, indeed the high point of my life, namely the assumption of motherly duties, thanks to the adoption of our beloved, sunny little daughter. The blessing of children had been denied our extremely happy, harmonious marriage. But by no means should one conclude from this that my energetic efforts in social work were a compensation, intended to bridge a certain void in my life. On the contrary, I can certainly say that both—social work and adoption—had their source in an overflowing motherliness and the pronounced sense of duty that compelled me to activate fully the energies that had been granted me. The coincidence in time of voluntarily overtaxing myself with work and the adoption may serve as proof of that. I believe I am able to invalidate the seemingly justified reproach that the tasks of a real mother do not allow such intense involvement outside the home, by pointing out that my body was conditioned to six hours of sleep at night, and that the hours spent by many mothers at kaffeeklatsches, at the bridge table, or at the hairdresser's were devoted to my domestic, motherly duties. The stimulation and experiences of my public life certainly proved useful for the task of child-rearing, just as they enriched our married life. That the latter was the case is due, above all, to my husband's constant support of my interests outside the home, and to his readiness to take upon himself all of the private burdens connected with them. Of this I am fully aware.

When, however, in 1925 my election to the executive board of the Rhenish-Westphalian Verband des Jüdischen Frauenbundes[3] took place, I was glad to be able to decline this new obligation by pointing out that in Bochum we did not have a local group of the organization; thus I was not a direct member and not eligible to be elected. The result was that in 1926 in Cologne, the seat of the executive body of the Rhenish-

Westphalian Verband, the establishment of such a new local group in Bochum was undertaken, namely by Frau Paula Ollendorff (Breslau)[4] and Clara Samuel (Elberfeld). They made me president and the next year repeated my election to the board of the Verband. Luckily, that coincided with the end of my office in the city council, since during the new elections in 1926 several Nazis entered the city parliament, and the party representatives of the Democrats did not want to expose me to personal abuse.

The broad range of Jewish tasks that was opened to me made it easier for me to part from the interesting previous activities of which I had grown fond. That is why I felt justified in describing myself as an example for the assertion of Bertha Pappenheim[5] that the Jewish community had forfeited the interest and the cooperation of the Jewish woman by refusing her the full joint responsibility that alone leads to the fulfillment of duty. My first meeting with Bertha Pappenheim at the big German Women's Conference in 1912 in Berlin determined my later fate. I attended the Congress as an alternate of the Bochum branch of the Bund Deutscher Frauenvereine, and Bertha Pappenheim attended as a representative of the Jüdischer Frauenbund, which had been founded by her in 1904. She was one of the three main speakers, who, before the large audience, dealt with the position of women within the three great religions. Bertha Pappenheim was the clear victor in this contest, in which she often made the critical observation, mentioned by me above, on the connection between rights and sense of public duty, and with superb rhetoric interwove this thought with Lessing's parable of the three rings. We, at that time still young, Jewish women were filled with pride at this success by one of ours, and were enthusiastically determined to face her conclusions and demands. The First World War, with its varied tasks for women, and the paralyzing period of inflation closed the door on any practical consequences.

In the year 1926 there began the chapter in my life for which all that I have reported previously is intended to represent only the background, to create access to it and to promote understanding for it. In 1929 I was elected to the executive body of the Jüdischer Frauenbund in Berlin. Looking back, it seems to me as if from the very start of my participation the leadership of the Jüdischer Frauenbund at that time had in mind the goal of grooming me for the office of First Secretary of the organization. At any rate, they immediately assigned me important tasks, for example, the organizational preparation and advancement of the cooperation of Jewish women in the representative and executive bodies of the Jewish communities, which until then had been purely male. At the international Women's Congress in Hamburg I gave a paper on this important question, which required detailed preliminary studies in the areas of statistics and religion. This congress, which took place in 1930, served above all the formal founding of the Weltbund Jüdischer Frauen. The president at that time, Mrs. Kohut from the U.S.A., presumed to declare: "Today we have made history." This business, to be sure, was brought to a quick end by the advent of the Hitler era and the Second World War, which came in its wake. It remained to me, shortly after my arrival in the United States [1946], to encourage the revival of the Weltbund Jüdischer Frauen, which here calls itself the International Council of Jewish Women (I.C.J.W.). Today it can claim an impressive number of members, among other places, in Israel and Germany. In further preparation for the post in the executive, I was given speaking assignments at meetings, in summer courses, etc., the accomplishment of which forced me to become thoroughly familiar with the fields in question and which at the same time made me known to the membership.

As a result, in 1934, when Bettina Brenner, the First Secretary of the Jüdischer Frauenbund at the time, resigned from her office due to her impending emigration, I was unanimously elected as First Secretary. My Zionist opponent, Frau Dr. Rahel Straus,[6] had in the meanwhile emigrated to Israel.

It was clear to me from the start that a Jewish organization under Nazi rule, even if at the start of 1934 its practices were still relatively bearable, would have to employ new methods in order to be able to do justice to its tasks. Naturally, that had to lead to differences of opinion with the previous leadership, which was attuned to normal conditions. Still, it should be ascribed to the influence of Bertha Pappenheim that we regarded keeping families together as our essential task, and therefore we opposed the sending of children to Palestine, which had already begun in 1934, as long as there was still a prospect for the further existence of our community in Germany. This applied especially to the sending of children who were not yet of school age. When all hope of remaining in Germany dissolved, we put our entire energies, without reservation, at the disposal of the Youth Aliyah, and also established *Hachshara* centers for the older girls to prepare them for the responsibilities awaiting them in Palestine.

Without going further into the details of the work of the Jüdischer Frauenbund, within the framework of these personal memoirs I would like merely to record that our efforts were aimed at inspiring the Jewish women who joined us with the spirit of resistance against the ruling powers and providing them with the necessary capacity for this: in the first place, the recognition that it was necessary to fill all our new institutions, which in Hilter's Germany would be granted only a brief duration, with the belief that they were forever. I believe that my development, depicted above, sufficiently explains the conception of such ideas and duties. [. . .]Here I would also like to recall to memory my closest co-workers in the Jüdischer Frauenbund, Professor Cora Berliner,[7] Second Secretary, and Hannah Karminski,[8] protocolist and secretary-general, because I am aware of how much I have gained from their spiritual strength, their stimulation, and their support, not only in my work but also in human and personal matters. Along with other colleagues from the executive, they both became victims of National Socialism, martyrs because of their devotion to duty and to their Jewish convictions.

1. This popular claim is not supported, but rather refuted by statistics. Precisely because women were conservative voters and preferred parties like the Zentrumspartei and the Deutsch-nationale Volkspartie, they swung over to the NSDAP more slowly than men. For years, starting in 1930, only nine, mostly big-city precincts, were counted by sex and here women still voted for the NSDAP somewhat less frequently than men.

2. The Vereinigung für das Liberale Judentum, founded in 1908, united Jews of that religious orientation that aimed at the progressive development of Judaism, while retaining its central religious content. It joined the World Union for Progressive Judaism (Weltbund für Liberales Judentum), which was founded in London in 1926.

3. The Jüdischer Frauenbund, founded in 1904 and forcibly dissolved in 1938, had local chapters in most of the larger Jewish communities and had as many as 50,000 members. Ottilie Schönewald devoted herself, above all, to the struggle of the Frauenbund for the right to vote

and participation of women in the Jewish communities, which by 1933 had not yet been successful in all of the communities.

4. Paula Ollendorff (1860–1938) founded the local chapter of the JFB in Breslau in 1908 and from 1910 until 1938 was a member of the main executive body of the JFB. Like Ottilie Schönewald, she became municipal councilor of the DDP and was active in the Vereinigung für Liberales Judentum.

5. Bertha Pappenheim (1859–1936) was, as a social worker, co-founder of the JBF and from 1904 until 1924 its First Secretary. Her personality, characterized by her energy and devotion to her duties, shaped the JFB till its end. She dedicated herself above all to the fight against white-slave traffic, to the protection of children, to occupational training for girls, and to the home for girls at risk, founded by her in Neu-Isenburg.

6. The Munich physician Dr. Rahel Straus (1880–1963), member of the executive of the JFB, was one of the few Zionists in the Frauenbund. Although Bertha Pappenheim was an anti-Zionist, she asked her to become a candidate because she appreciated her active Judaism.

7. The economist Dr. Cora Berliner (1890; deported in 1942) was a senior executive officer in the Statistisches Reichsamt and from 1930 until 1933 Professor at the Berufspäda-gogisches Institut in Berlin. She devoted herself in part to the JFB, in part to the executive work in the Reichsvertretung and the Reichsvereinigung. Active in emigration aid, from her sense of duty she declined emigration for herself.

8. Hannah Karminski (1897–1942) trained as a kindergarten teacher and social worker. She worked, after the dissolution of the JFB, in the emigration aid department of the Reichs-vereinigung. At the end of October 1942 she was arrested as a hostage when twenty employees of the community evaded deportation, and was deported with five hundred employees of the Reichsvereinigung. She died during the transport.

# 38 *Alexander Szanto*

BORN IN 1899 IN BUDAPEST; DIED IN 1972 IN MANCHESTER, ENGLAND.

Alexander Szanto, In the Service of the Community. Manuscript, dated Manchester, 1968; 241 pages.

*As a child Alexander Szanto moved with his parents from Budapest to Berlin, received German citizenship, and became a journalist. He was a Social Democrat, a firm opponent of Zionism, and a member of the reform congregation. From 1923 until 1933, as a stenographer he recorded the meetings of the assembly of the representatives of the Berlin Jewish community, and from 1925 until 1930 also of the Preussischer Landesverband jüdischer Gemeinden, until he became a delegate himself in 1930. From 1933 until 1939 he was in charge of the financial section of the "Wirtschaftshilfe," a self-help institution of the Jewish community. In December 1939, having in the meanwhile become stateless, Szanto, using falsified documents, emigrated to his hometown of Budapest, where he was interned, but survived as a forced laborer. Persecuted as a Social Democrat in the People's Republic of Hungary, he participated in the uprising of 1956 and then fled to England. There he worked in law offices and as a journalist.*

My first contacts with the Berlin Jewish community stem from 1923, the year of the great inflation. The grave economic crisis that at that time engulfed Germany was, of course, a turbulent time for the German Jews as well. If previously the Jewish community had to tend solely to religious, charitable, and cultural tasks, now economic and sociopolitical problems entered increasingly into its sphere of work. The executive body of the community had its hands full doing justice to the growing demands that were made on it, and the assembly of representatives, a community parliament chosen by free election, had to hold many more meetings than earlier to manage the work load. Not only did the number of meetings increase, but their agendas also became more extensive and significant. Therefore it was decided in place of the previously customary minutes now to have a verbatim shorthand record made of the meetings, and I was charged with this task. [. . .]

The locale of these meetings was the big Assembly Hall in the administration building of the community, at 29 Oranienburger Strasse. In the huge hall, from whose walls oil paintings of deceased community leaders looked down upon those assembled, there was a big horseshoe-shaped table, at both sides of which the representatives took their seats. In the middle, somewhat elevated, sat the president of the assembly, to his right the orthodox (officially they called themselves conservatives), and next to them the Zionists; on his left sat the liberals. At the open end of the horseshoe was a long table, at which the members of the community executive had their seats. In the background there usually sat or stood some leading community officials. There was no speaker's desk. Every representative who took the floor during the debate rose from his seat and spoke from there. The same was true for the members of the governing body of the community, when they took the floor to give explanations or to answer questions. The horseshoe-shaped table of the representatives was so big that in the space between there was enough room for a smaller round table, at which sat the representatives of the Jewish press, the stenographer, and the secretary responsible for the administrative agendas of the meeting. The last-named post was filled for years by the community official Silberberg, a man who had grown gray in his position and who was much liked by all.

The meetings were public. All around the hall, quite high up, was a balcony, where there were always a number of spectators. The meetings were held at regular intervals, approximately every two to three weeks, mostly on Sunday mornings, but, depending on need, also on weekday evenings. All of the seats were always occupied, for, according to the community statutes, at every election, along with the representative a substitute was elected, who stepped in for the representative if the latter was not available.

The deliberations on the yearly budget of the community were the high point of each session. Besides the expenditures for religious purposes and welfare, new construction of synagogues, establishment and management of old-age homes, orphanages, hospitals, etc., to an increasing degree cultural and economic tasks required large sums of money. The goal, desired by individual speakers at the budget debate, of having some institutions survive on their own revenues could almost never be achieved in practice. Only the cemetery brought in a financial surplus in some years, especially after a community-owned commercial garden had been added to the burial business in Weissensee.

In addition to the institutions belonging to the community, numerous other Jewish societies and organizations were constantly subsidized. In all such cases the assembly of representatives had to give its consent for the approval of the moneys. That did not happen without examining the situation thoroughly, and often only after a careful debate, and yet in most cases the decision was quite generous, as a matter of fact, even when it was a question of institutions whose purview was not limited to the capital of the Reich. In contrast to the Berlin community many small communities in the provinces could not support themselves on their own, and thus, in one way or another, Berlin had to help them in their need. The economic existence of the small communities, the question of the salaries of their rabbis and teachers, etc., were a constant problem, and the calls of distress resounded all the way to the Berlin community office. Not least, the necessity to even out the burdens of the poor and the financially strong communities finally gave the impetus for the creation of the Preussischer Landesverband jüdischer Gemeinden.[1]

The deliberation on the budget took place in such a way that the estimate was discussed in detail in the committees comprised of deputies of the representative and executive bodies of the community. As a rule, it took a very long time for the finished budget to reach the plenum of the assembly of representatives, and mostly by that time a considerable part of the fiscal year had already passed. It was an annually recurring complaint of the representatives that essentially they had to vote on moneys that in reality were already spent. However, this situation did not prevent the budget discussions in the plenum from being used to debate the great ideological differences of opinion. The individual parliamentary parties, the liberals, Zionists, and conservatives, sent forward their most brilliant speakers, and only after these had set off their rhetorical fireworks did a dry, businesslike debate ensue, within whose framework the representatives entrusted with the task reported on the separate items of the budget and on their preliminary discussion in the committees. To be sure, here, too, often lively discussions took place. [. . .]

The year 1926 saw new elections to the assembly of representatives, and on this occasion the liberals lost their majority. They now held only twenty of the forty-one seats. The Zionists, who ran under the name of Jewish People's Party, won fourteen seats, and the remaining seven seats went to the different conservative groups. Still, the liberals had remained the strongest party; they lacked only a single seat for the absolute majority. But the Zionists and the different conservative groups joined forces immediately to form a united front, and they used their majority of one voice achieved in this manner to establish their own regime. Numerous new appointments to leading positions in the community administration were undertaken, and the course was thrown sharply to the right. That led to an intensification of the debates in the assembly. External circumstances contributed to exciting tempers even more: the growing danger of antisemitism, the disputes in world politics over the Palestine question, and still others. The Jewish public took a more lively part in the internal Jewish quarrels than before. The Jewish press, above all the Zionist *Jüdische Rundschau* and the anti-Zionist *Jüdisch-Liberale Zeitung,* now regularly sent their reporters to the meetings of the assembly (which previously had been the case only sporadically), and gave detailed accounts in their columns. Their mutual polemics reached a peak. [. . .]

I was a naturalized, not a native, German, but on the other hand I had lived for many years in Germany and had been educated there, so that I thought I knew the shortcomings as well as the virtues of the Germans rather well. I was also well aware that some advocates of the German-Jewish ideology, in the overloud emphasis of their Germanness, were sometimes led to exaggerations and lack of tact. This was especially true of the men from the Verband nationaldeutscher Juden,[2] but apart from that, on the whole I considered it right that a Jew living in Germany should serve this state, the Weimar Republic, not only with civic loyalty but—in keeping with the spirit of a genuine democracy—with sincere devotion. This republic, engaged in a difficult struggle with reactionary powers, had given itself a democratic constitution, which promised equality and protection to the Jews too; and its leading parties—the Social Democrats, the Centrist Party, and the Democratic Party—fought against antisemitism and reaction, advocated progress and social justice, i.e., made demands that were compatible with the Jewish as well as the Christian religious ethos. Jewish personalities occupied leading government positions, proved their worth, and gained recognition. Under such circumstances, in my eyes a German Jew not only had the right but also the duty to profess his loyalty to this state, to serve its good to the best of his ability, and to feel himself to be a member of the community. Any other consideration, especially one of a double civic loyalty, seemed wrong to me.

There was also the fact that as a socialist I adopted the intellectual ideas of the socialist champions of the old school, according to which nationalistic or racial prejudices would disappear with the worldwide realization of socialism. To the extent that there was a specific Jewish problem at all, it had to be settled within the framework of the overall progress of humanity. As a pupil of the great ideas of the Enlightenment I could not imagine any course other than that of unstoppable progress, the victory of freedom over reaction, humanity over regression, justice over the prejudices of the past. The optimistic belief in progress was for me, as for so many of my generation, the great spiritual symbol in the glow of which we all too gladly and all too joyfully overlooked the threatening shadows.

The Zionist world of ideas remained alien to me. Not that I might have failed to acquaint myself with its doctrines. I read Zionist literature, I also attended Zionist meetings, but I found no inner contact. [. . .]From the perspective of the socialist, the pacifist, the antimilitarist, the humanist in pursuit of cosmopolitan ideas I believed that I could not accept a Jewish nationalism. In the spirit of the Enlightenment there could be only a development forward and upward, away from the egoism of groups and nations, toward more and more universal spheres of humanity. And as far as Jews were concerned, they, as the international group par excellence and as guardians of the old prophetic spiritual heritage, had to fulfill a special mission for humanity within the framework of this progressive development. The Jewish national idea, on the other hand—so it seemed to me—did not proceed from the Enlightenment but rather from Romanticism. The disastrous taint of reaction surrounded it.

*[In the spring of 1933 Alexander Szanto becomes co-worker of the just-established Wirtschaftshilfe of the Berlin Jewish community.]*

The Wirtschaftshilfe began its work at a difficult time and under chaotic conditions. Thousands and thousands of victims of National Socialism turned to the community, its office rooms overflowed with a flood of helpless and desperate people, and no one could quite imagine how our coreligionists, who had overnight lost their sustenance and had found themselves in need, could be offered productive assistance. We had no experience with such an extraordinary situation; there was no ready plan. It speaks for the capability and organizational efficiency of the German Jews that they succeeded, within a relatively short time, in bringing order to the chaos and turning an institution born from the need of the times into a well-functioning organization that brought effective aid to countless fellow Jews.

The necessary financial means were made available without great difficulties by the community, by private donors, and also by foreign organizations (Joint). Later, they were incorporated according to plan into the budget of the community and the newly created Reichsvertretung der deutschen Juden. The offices were made available by the community. At first they consisted of the building at 31 Oranienburger Strasse, directly next to the big synagogue. Earlier, this building had served as an old-age home of the Jewish community for housing old people, and it proved not to be very suitable for its new purpose, so that in the course of the following years a large number of renovations had to be undertaken in the building. In the first months, when thousands upon thousands of people seeking counsel and help virtually stormed the building from early morning until evening, conditions were very bad. It was like a beehive there. In the rooms and hallways a continual swarm of excited people moved about; the stairways were swamped with them, and often it was difficult to get from one floor to the other. With horror I recall the winter of 1933/34, when to make matters worse we also had to house the emigration information center of the Hilfsverein der Deutschen Juden,[3] and the people were crowding, body next to body, in the hallways and on the staircase. At first it was difficult to maintain any kind of order; the heating functioned poorly, ventilation was bad, the air often stiflingly bad. But gradually we succeeded in overcoming these difficulties. [. . .]

In the creation of the Wirtschaftshilfe and throughout its existence, old community officials and newly recruited experts, Zionists and non-Zionists, liberals and orthodox, all worked together compatibly, and the work itself—free of any partisan commitment or bias—was carried out exclusively with a view to the most extensive assistance possible for all coreligionists who found themselves in distress. With a matter-of-factness that was born of the need of the hour, all co-workers, the old as well as the new, carried out their duty under the most difficult conditions. For them, especially during the first, hard times, there was no letup and no limit to their working hours and workload. With unequaled devotion, day after day, often to the limits of one's physical capability, the task of counselling and helping a multitude of often excited and at times desperate fellow Jews seeking aid was mastered. It was honest, respectable, Jewish, and humane work that was accomplished in those years, there in that ancient building on Oranienburger Strasse.

*[One of the departments of the Wirtschaftshilfe was the Commercial Advisory Department.]*

Of the many cases that the Commercial Advisory Department of the Wirtschaftshilfe handled I would like to cite here a few from my memory that demonstrate as vivid examples how many a fellow Jew could be helped in those days.

The Jewish gastronomer X for many years operated a small confectionery, whose patrons consisted mainly of Christians. Although personally he was very well liked by the customers, the latter scarcely dared to enter his business after the day of boycott, especially since that part of town had been turned into one of their strongholds by the Nazis. At the same time, difficulties arose for him with the Christian waiters working at his place, and the authorities plagued him with all sorts of chicanery. He ran into debt, did not find a buyer for his business, and had to close. At that time there were no possibilities of emigration for him. The Wirtschaftshilfe helped him to open an ice-cream parlor in a completely different part of town, in which he sold ice-cream wafers during the summer and sweets during the other seasons. The ice-cream machine was purchased for him by the Wirtschaftshilfe from a Jewish manufacturer. He did not need any employees, since the members of his family helped in the store. Of course, the undertaking was considerably smaller than his previous one; also, it had a distinct seasonal character. But still his earnings were such that he and his family were able to maintain their living standard. The business lasted until the summer of 1938, when the Nazis undertook a smear and boycott campaign against Jewish ice-cream parlors. But at this time, finally, there arose the opportunity for him to emigrate, and he went overseas with his entire family. Earlier he had already paid off his loan to the Wirtschaftshilfe to the very last penny.

The Jewish businessman Y was an able traveling textile salesman. Since he had been very well established among his clientele, Jews and Christians, he could at first continue his trips in the provinces successfully. But he had difficulties with lodgings in the small provincial towns, where the hotels and inns increasingly proceeded to refuse lodgings and food to Jewish persons. The Wirtschaftshilfe got him a car and later a delivery van, whereby he was enabled to arrange his trips independent of the train schedule, so that in the evening he regularly reached a larger town where possibilities for lodgings were still available. When, starting around 1937, this, too, became impossible, he used to sleep over on the highway in his delivery van and eat canned food that he had brought with him. That certainly was no pleasure for him, but in this way he could continue his job until the end of 1938, at which time he emigrated. He, too, paid back his loan in full to the Wirtschaftshilfe.

The press photographer Z was dismissed as a non-Aryan from his well-paying position at a newspaper publisher's. The Wirtschaftshilfe gave him a loan for the purchase of his own photography gear, with high-quality equipment, and set him up in his own studio, in which he was still able to work independently for several years and earn a good income as a technical photographer for industry and advertising. When at the time of his emigration the loan was not yet entirely paid back, he returned to the Wirtschaftshilfe part of his photo equipment, which it could use in its vocational retraining courses.

Countless were the cases in which Jewish business people called upon the Wirtschaftshilfe because they now had to pay cash, but could not raise the liquid funds on their own, for the purchase of wares that until then they had bought on credit from Aryan suppliers. But just as often there were also cases, as the above example of Z illustrates, in which people who previously had been permanently employed and had lost their positions were enabled by the Wirtschaftshilfe to provide for themselves a sufficient basis for survival for several years through self-employment in a related professional field. [. . .]

The physicians organized a kind of self-help by which those able to continue their practice collected money for their less fortunate colleagues. In this way considerable sums were raised, which benefited the doctors who had lost their livelihoods. Besides the regular contributions, which the physicians raised according to a specific scale, until 1938 sizable sums flowed into the doctors' fund from the receipts of the doctors' ball. This was a ball that the doctors organized every winter and that marked *the* social event in the Berlin Jewish circles of those otherwise so dark years. Just as did the physicians, the Jewish dentists and dental surgeons also organized their self-help, as did the Jewish pharmacists and Jewish lawyers. The Wirtschaftshilfe took part in these drives only to the extent that it looked after the administration of the doctors' and the lawyers' fund, that is, it carried out the disbursements and dispositions in accordance with the instructions from the physicians' committee and the lawyers' committee respectively. Of course, this purely administrative function added a significant measure of extra work to our other tasks.

Difficult problems arose for the Jewish organizations in caring for artists who had lost their livelihoods. Actors, musicians, painters, graphic artists, sculptors, and performers were among the first to be completely excluded from public life, and thus they were cut off from any possibility of earning a living. Most of the prominent ones among them emigrated immediately; a few were able to switch to other professions, but the majority remained entrusted to the care of the Jewish agencies.

A large-scale attempt to erect a Jewish cultural sector of its own within Germany was made by the Jüdischer Kulturbund.[4] In Berlin alone, in the years 1933 to 1939, the Jüdischer Kulturbund not only provided the possibility for hundreds of Jewish artists to develop their talents, but at the same time it offered thousands of coreligionists the opportunity for artistic enjoyment in a Jewish milieu, and for entertainment and relaxation. With that it accomplished truly Jewish cultural work in the most difficult of times.

In the cultural area, the Wirtschaftshilfe set itself a more modest goal. For very soon it became apparent that the Jüdischer Kulturbund, as a result of its limited means, was not in a position financially, administratively, and geographically to provide work to all Jewish artists who had become needy. Even if hundreds of them found employment there for a longer or shorter time, or perhaps found only stopgap work, there remained thousands who were without the possibility of work. In order to help them, the "Artists' Aid" department was created within the framework of the Wirtschaftshilfe. On the whole, it was the less prominent ones who turned to this agency for help. But no one asked about that, as little as one asked whether the person in question had previously been aware of his Jewishness, or whether it was only the hour of need that drove him to the Jewish community. Our doors stood open to any fellow Jew affected by the actions of the Nazis, and we sought to help him wherever and in whatever way possible. [. . .]

A large number of vocational retraining courses were established, in which during the years 1935 to 1939 several thousand people, men and women, received training. The Wirtschaftshilfe set up, above all, three big training establishments of its own: a workshop for the building trade (masons, carpenters, fitters), another for the metal-working industry (machinists, welders, etc.), and a third for wood working (joiners, turners, etc.). The training in these community-owned workshops took place under the instruction of experts—engineers, craftsmen, foremen—and with the use of up-to-date machines and implements, and the greatest possible care was taken to truly impart trade skills. The "retrainees," as we termed them, since it would have been somewhat peculiar to use the designation "apprentices" or "pupils" for people between the ages of twenty and forty, worked eight hours daily. The total duration of the courses was, as the case may be, nine to twelve months. The division of labor took place approximately according to the norms that were customary in a corresponding factory.

The costs of these training courses were considerable. Not only did the retrainees, who, after all, had no earnings of their own at this time and mostly no means of existence, have to be supported financially, but the acquisition of machines and material, the salaries of the permanently employed experts, the rent for the premises, lighting, heating, etc., consumed great sums. For my division, Accounts, Bookkeeping, and Statistics, new problems resulted from that. I tried as much as possible to introduce efficient economic measures; for one, by strict control of the inventory and of the materials to be used, and, second, by purchasing whenever possible from Jewish firms and sup-pliers, which were looked after by the Commercial Advisory Department of the Wirt-schaftshilfe anyway, so that here the tendency to create a kind of Jewish economic sector was emphasized. Furthermore, we tried to make use of the products of the training workshops in order to recover part of the costs. Thus, for example, in the joiners workshop the more skilled retrainees made desks and writing tables that could be marketed in Jewish stores or used by the offices of the community itself.

Naturally, however, not all retraining courses were carried out in our training workshops. In the textile branch, for example, it proved to be more efficient and practical to send the retrainees to existing Jewish firms as apprentices, rather than to acquire a great many sewing machines. Still, the instruction there was supervised by us and financially compensated by us in a commensurate manner. In this way, a large number of male and, even more, female tailors, cutters, pressers, sewing machine operators, and linen seamstresses could be trained. The training period in these textile courses was, as a rule, considerably shorter than in our own training shops mentioned above. Other retraining courses that were conducted in the course of these years were photography, bookbinding, auto mechanics, ceramics, chemistry, show-window decoration, kinder-garten teaching, nursing, cosmetics, fashion design, dietary and institutional cooking, weaving, leatherworking, watchmaking, millinery, and still others.

The industrial and occupational retraining was at least equalled, if not surpassed, in significance by agricultural training. In this field, to be sure, the Jewish organizations were in the fortunate position of being able to send the retrainees to Jewish agricultural properties that had already existed for years, where under expert supervision they received thorough training in the different areas of farming, livestock production, and garden-ing. [. . .] The largest and best-known Jewish agricultural training center was the country estate of Neuendorf[5] in the vicinity of Fürstenwalde, some forty kilometers distant from the urban area of the capital of the Reich. Under the supervision of the Jewish agri-culturalist Moch,[6] many hundreds of young Jewish people were trained there to be expert farmers, cattle producers, and gardeners. Neuendorf was a vast farm. There were grain and potato fields, vegetable fields, flower gardens, and hothouses there; furthermore, there were extensive stables, cattle breeding grounds, dairies, poultry farms—indeed, even a pigpen. Director Moch was of the opinion that a perfect farming enterprise also had to engage in pig breeding, and he gained acceptance for his views, supported by expert arguments, over the objections expressed by the Jewish-orthodox side.

As a rule, the training in Neuendorf lasted approximately one year, and thus everyone who persevered through this time—there were relatively few failures—had the opportunity to do or, as the case might be, to learn farm work in all seasons. Alternatively, the apprentices, boys as well as girls, men as well as women, were employed, in a precisely ordered rotation, in the grainfields, at vegetable growing and work with root crops, in the different livestock barns, as well as in the gardens. There was even a cartwright shop, in which one was supposed to acquire adequate skill in the production and repair of agricultural equipment. Of course, Moch could not accomplish the work alone. He had a small staff of agricultural instructors and inspectors with him, among them also two non-Jews. Moch's capable wife took care of the physical well-being of the trainees with respect to meals, clothing, and laundry. In this she was helped by several young people, who after they completed their agricultural training also wanted additional practice in the areas of institutional cooking and housework.

The success of the agricultural training method in Neuendorf was especially obvious. From this training farm numerous capable farmers went to Palestinian settlements such as Yavneh, Hasorea, and smaller kibbutzim, and some to JCA settlements[7] in Argentina.

Another training farm, which also was not too far from the capital of the Reich, was Gross-Gaglow[8] near Cottbus. This agricultural site had been established by Jewish organizations some two years before the Nazi seizure of power, as a community settlement on a cooperative basis, and devoted itself expressly to the retraining of Jews coming from urban professions. Here, above all, they pursued vegetable and fruit growing. Among other things, big asparagus fields were regularly cultivated, and they brought a rich harvest, which was sold to domestic canneries. In this way, Gross-Gaglow worked from time to time very successfully, with a financial profit. The Berlin community or the Wirtschaftshilfe nevertheless paid regular monthly fees for the retrainees it sent to Gross-Gaglow, and thus the continuing operation of the farm was assured even in less productive periods. From Gross-Gaglow many farmers emigrated to Brazil.

1. The Preussischer Landesverband jüdischer Gemeinden, founded in 1922, supported some 250 communities in 1925 that were unable to support themselves.

2. The Verband nationaldeutscher Juden, founded in 1921, was headed by the lawyer Dr. Max Naumann. This small organization of nationalistic German Jews firmly opposed, for example, the immigration of East European Jews.

3. The Hilfsverein der Deutschen Juden, founded in 1901, originally devoted itself to social work among Jews in Eastern Europe and Palestine, as well as emigration assistance for East European Jews. After 1933, emigration aid for German Jews who were not going to Palestine became its main task. Between 1933 and 1938 it assisted the emigration of 31,000 people. On the Wirtschaftshilfe see also the article by A. Szanto, "Economic Aid in the Nazi Era," *Leo Baeck Institute Yearbook IV* (1959,) pp. 208–219.

4. On the origin and history of the Jüdischer Kulturbund, see the memoir (42) of Kurt Baumann.

5. The Jüdische Arbeitshilfe had originally established the training farm of Neuendorf, which occupied 1,500 acres, as a training center for unemployed young Jews. After 1933 it became a place of agricultural retraining for non-Zionist Jews, and in 1938 it was able to accommodate over 135 trainees.

6. Alexander Moch (born in 1889 in Nonnenweier; died in 1977 in Tel Aviv) directed the training farm of Neuendorf from 1933 until 1938, and then an agricultural school (Tythrope House) for Jewish refugees in England. He was a farmer in Kenya, Africa, and finally an agricultural advisor in Israel.

7. The JCA (Jewish Colonization Association), founded in 1891 by Baron Moritz Hirsch, financed Jewish agricultural settlements primarily in Argentina, Brazil, and Canada.

8. The Reichsbund für jüdische Siedlung, founded in 1928 upon the initiative of the Reichsbund jüdischer Frontsoldaten, bought the estate Gross-Gaglow in 1930. Some two dozen Jewish families settled there, mostly as small farmers, until the farm was forcibly dissolved in 1935.

# 39 *Marta Appel, née Insel*

BORN IN 1894 IN METZ; DIED IN 1987(?) IN LOS ANGELES.

Marta Appel, Memoirs. Undated manuscript, 610 pages. Written in 1940/41 in the United States.

*The author grew up in Metz (Alsace-Lorraine), from where her family was expelled by the French authorities in 1918. In the same year she married Dr. Ernst Appel (1884–1973), who at that time was a rabbi in Bingen. The couple had two daughters and lived in Bingen until 1926, at which time Appel received a rabbinical post in Dortmund. The author describes in detail the situation of her family and the Jewish community, which was under constant Gestapo surveillance after 1933. Her daughters were exposed to growing persecution at school, but her husband was attached to Germany and his community, and she was unable to persuade him to emigrate. In April 1937 the two were arrested as co-presidents of the Dortmund B'nai B'rith Lodge, when the Gestapo dissolved it and confiscated its assets. After their release, in May 1937, secretly, with no farewells, they fled with their daughters to Holland and emigrated from there to relatives in the United States. Until 1969 Ernst Appel served as rabbi in Jackson, Tennessee. After his death the author moved to Hollywood, California.*

*[The following material has been taken from the original manuscript, written in English.]*

The children had been advised not to come to school on April 1, 1933, the day of the boycott. Even the principal of the school thought Jewish children's lives were no longer safe. One night they placed big signs on every store or house owned by Jewish people. In front of our temple, on every square and corner, billboards were scoffing at us. Everywhere, and on all occasions, we read and heard that we were vermin and had caused the ruin of the German people. No Jewish store was closed on that day; none was willing to show fear in the face of the boycott. The only building which did not open its door as usual, since it was Saturday, was the temple. We did not want this holy place desecrated by any trouble.

I even went downtown that day to see what was going on in the city. There was no cheering crowd as the Nazis had expected, no running and smashing of Jewish businesses. I heard only words of anger and disapproval. People were massed before the Jewish stores to watch the Nazi guards who were posted there to prevent anyone from entering to buy. And there were many courageous enough to enter, although they were called rude names by the Nazi guards, and their pictures were taken to show them as enemies of the German people in the daily papers. Inside the stores, in the offices of the owners, there was another battle proceeding. Nazis were forcing those Jewish men to send wires abroad to foreign businesses, saying that there was no Jewish boycott and that nothing unusual was happening. Accompanied by two Nazi officials, one of the men was taken even to Holland to convince the foreign customers and businessmen there.

Our gentile friends and neighbors, even people whom we had scarcely known before, came to assure us of their friendship and to tell us that these horrors could not last very long. But after some months of a regime of terror, fidelity and friendship had lost their meaning, and fear and treachery had replaced them. For the sake of our gentile friends, we turned our heads so as not to greet them in the streets, for we did not want to bring upon them the danger of imprisonment for being considered a friend of Jews.

With each day of the Nazi regime, the abyss between us and our fellow citizens grew larger. Friends whom we had loved for years did not know us anymore. They suddenly saw that we were different from themselves. Of course we were different, since we were bearing the stigma of Nazi hatred, since we were hunted like deer. Through the prominent position of my husband we were in constant danger. Often we were warned to stay away from home. We were no longer safe, wherever we went.

How much our life changed in those days! Often it seemed to me I could not bear it any longer, but thinking of my children, I knew we had to be strong to make it easier for them. From then on I hated to go out, since on every corner I saw signs that the Jews were the misfortune of the people. Wherever I went, when I had to speak to people in a store I imagined how they would turn against me if they knew I was Jewish. When I was waiting for a streetcar I always thought that the driver would not stop if he knew I was Jewish. Never did anything unpleasant happen to me on the street, but I was expecting it at every moment, and it was always bothering me. I did not go into a theater or a movie for a long time before we were forbidden to,[1] since I could not bear to be among people who hated me so much. Therefore, when, later on, all those restrictions came, they did not take away from me anything that I had not already renounced. Nevertheless, it meant a new shame. Not to go of my own accord was very different from not being allowed to go.

In the evenings we sat at home at the radio listening fearfully to all the new and outrageous restrictions and laws which almost daily brought further suffering to Jewish people. We no longer visited our friends, nor did they come anymore to see us. Why should we be together, since our minds were upon only one thing and, when we spoke, we heard only one story more cruel than the other? Was it not sufficient to face the cruelty during our day's work? Why should we sacrifice our sleep to hear of more and more atrocities?

Since I had lived in Dortmund, I had met every four weeks with a group of women, all of whom were born in Metz, my beloved home city. We all had been pupils or teachers in the same high school. After the Nazis came, I was afraid to go to the meetings. I did not want the presence of a Jewess to bring any trouble, since we always met publicly in a café. One day on the street, I met one of my old teachers, and with tears in her eyes she begged me: "Come again to us; we miss you; we feel ashamed that you must think we do not want you anymore. Not one of us has changed in her feeling toward you." She tried to convince me that they were still my friends, and tried to take away my doubts. I decided to go to the next meeting. It was a hard decision, and I had not slept the night before. I was afraid for my gentile friends. For nothing in the world did I wish to bring them trouble by my attendance, and I was also afraid for myself. I knew I would watch them, noticing the slightest expression of embarrassment in their eyes when I came. I knew they could not deceive me; I would be aware of every change in their voices. Would they be afraid to talk to me?

It was not necessary for me to read their eyes or listen to the change in their voices. The empty table in the little alcove which always had been reserved for us spoke the clearest language. It was even unnecessary for the waiter to come and say that a lady phoned that morning not to reserve the table thereafter. I could not blame them. Why should they risk losing a position only to prove to me that we still had friends in Germany?

I, personally, did not mind all those disappointments, but when my children had to face them, and were not spared being offended everywhere, my heart was filled with anguish. It required a great deal of inner strength, of love and harmony among the Jewish families, to make our children strong enough to bear all that persecution and hatred. [. . .] My heart was broken when I saw tears in my younger child's eyes when she had been sent home from school while all the others had been taken to a show or some other pleasure. It was not because she was denied going to the show that my little girl was weeping—she knew her Mommy always could take her—but because she had to stay apart, as if she were not good enough to associate with her comrades any longer. It was this that made it hard and bitter for her. .I think that even the Nazi teacher sometimes felt ashamed when she looked into the sad eyes of my little girl, since several times, when the class was going out for pleasure, she phoned not to send her to school. Maybe it was not right to hate this teacher so much, since everything she did had been upon orders, but it was she who brought so much bitterness to my child, and never can I forget it.

Almost every lesson began to be a torture for Jewish children. There was not one subject anymore which was not used to bring up the Jewish question. And in the presence of Jewish children the teachers denounced all the Jews, without exception, as scoundrels and as the most destructive force in every country where they were living. My children were not permitted to leave the room during such a talk; they were compelled to stay and to listen; they had to feel all the other children's eyes looking and staring at them, the examples of an outcast race.

Every day they had to face another degrading and offensive incident. As Mother's Day came near, the children were practicing songs at school to celebrate that day. Every year on that occasion the whole school gathered in a joint festival. It was the day before when my girls were ordered to see the music teacher. "You have to be present for the festival," the teacher told them, "but since you are Jewish, you are not allowed to join in the songs." "Why can't we sing?" my children protested with tears in their eyes. "We have a mother too, and we wish to sing for her." But it seemed the teacher did not want to understand the children's feelings. Curtly she rebuked their protest. "I know you have a mother," she said haughtily, "but she is only a Jewish mother." At that the girls had no reply; there was no use to speak any longer to the teacher, but seldom had they been so much disturbed as when they came from school that day, when someone had tried to condemn their mother.

The only hope we had was that this terror would not last very long. The day could not be far off when this nightmare would cease to hound the German people. How could anybody be happy in a land where "freedom" was an extinct word, where nobody knew that the next day he would not be taken to jail, possibly tortured to death. The Jewish people were not the only ones afraid of a loud spoken word; many others, too, were trembling for fear that somebody might listen even to their thoughts. [. . .]

We were not even allowed to hold meetings of the various organizations of our congregation without the presence of a supervisor sent by the Gestapo. Therefore we sometimes had the members assemble in our house. I always saw to it that the maid was away on such an evening. The telephone was disconnected, and our friends entered the house only singly and at different times. It was strange to see that most of the time those Nazi supervisors became very friendly with the Jews after they had come to the meetings for a while. Very much to our displeasure they liked to stay even after the lectures or the business part to have a cup of tea with us. They apparently felt so pleased in our company that they were not aware how much we wanted to get rid of them. But the Gestapo resented their "conversion." Whenever the reports of those men became too good, they were replaced by a new and better Jew hater. [. . .]

Hanukka [1934], the feast of light, was near. Now that the Jews were suffering the deepest degradation, it was a comfort to be reminded of the glorious deeds of the Maccabees when they freed the Jews from the bondage of the Syrians. We had planned that year to have at least a Hanukka play for our children. The Gestapo had given its permission, but even to the children's play they sent their supervisor. One part of the program was magical art. A boy fourteen years old played the magician. He really was splendid. Everybody liked him; he was so very witty.

At first he demonstrated some simpler tricks, but then he needed some help out of the audience. He had already chosen some of the children, when he decided to have one of the adults, too. He looked around, and his eyes rested on a man who was sitting in the first line with the children. "Well," he said, "I guess you are the nearest and the best one for my experiments."

We never could decide whether it was because this young Gestapo official forgot his mission so completely in watching the show, or because he just did not know what to say. He got up very red and embarrassed, but as the boy had said, he made an excellent medium. The boy went ahead as if he were entirely unaware that this was one of the much feared Gestapo men, and he made him do the funniest things. We laughed so hard that the tears came to our eyes. The Jewish boy and the Gestapo official were the best liked number on the program.

As in all the years before, we were very busy in all the auxiliaries making Hanukka parcels for our poor. The list of needy people had grown out of all proportion, while our contributions had become smaller and smaller. It had become a difficult task for anyone to give an adequate offering. If we wished to be of any real help to our poor, we had to give up all entertainments and lectures by out-of-town people. Prices had become so high that, since Jewish people did not get the same relief from the city as others, many were without heat and food. That winter we had to open a kitchen where we gave warm meals to the poorest of them. Besides that our B'nai B'rith women's auxiliary[2] furnished a lunch for all needy school children. We did all that we could, but the families that we could not help were those to whom the Gestapo brought death and hardships. We were entirely powerless against its actions. The intervention of a Jewish lawyer most of the time was not acknowledged at all, and Christian lawyers were afraid to speak up for Jews.

If God did not help, there was no help at all. And no one was sure that the next day it would not be his turn to disappear behind electrified barbed wire, to come back either in a crematory urn or bearing the marks of pitiless mistreatment on body and soul. It was an almost unbearable pain to see our friends return, their spirit so broken that they did not speak of their experiences even to their wives. Persistently I begged my husband to leave everything and to take us to a country where each day I would not be tormented by the fear of losing the dearest thing that I possessed. I used to watch nervously for my husband whenever he came late from a meeting, or when he was summoned by the secret police. The steady feeling of insecurity and uncertainty began to torture my nerves. Sometimes I was tempted to run away. [. . .]

One day, for the first time in a long while, I saw my children coming back from school with shining eyes, laughing and giggling together. Most of the classes had been gathered that morning in the big hall, since an official of the new *Rasseamt,* the office of races, had come to give a talk about the differences of races. "I asked the teacher if I could go home," my daughter was saying, "but she told me she had orders not to dismiss anyone. You may imagine it was an awful talk. He said that there are two groups of races, a high group and a low one. The high and upper race that was destined to rule the world was the Teutonic, the German race, while one of the lowest races was the Jewish race. And then, Mommy, he looked around and asked one of the girls to come to him." The children again began to giggle about their experience. "First we did not know," my girl continued, "what he intended, and we were very afraid when he picked out Eva. Then he began, and he was pointing at Eva, 'Look here, the small head of this girl, her long forehead, her very blue eyes, and blond hair,' and he was lifting one of her long blond braids. 'And look,' he said, 'at her tall and slender figure. These are the unequivocal marks of a pure and unmixed Teutonic race.' Mommy, you should have heard how at this moment all the girls burst into laughter. Even Eva could not help laughing. Then from all sides of the hall there was shouting, 'She is a Jewess!' You should have seen the officer's face! I guess he was lucky that the principal got up so quickly and, with a sign to the pupils, stopped the laughing and shouting and dismissed the man, thanking him for his interesting and very enlightening talk. At that we began again to laugh, but he stopped us immediately. Oh, I was so glad that the teacher had not dismissed me and I was there to hear it."

When my husband came home, they told him and enjoyed it again and again. And we were thankful to know that they still had not completely forgotten how to laugh and to act like happy children.

"If only I could take my children out of here!" That thought was occupying my mind more and more. I no longer hoped for any change as did my husband. Besides, even a changed Germany could not make me forget that all our friends, the whole nation, had abandoned us in our need. It was no longer the same country for me. Everything had changed, not people alone—the city, the forest, the river—the whole country looked different in my eyes.

*[In the spring of 1935 a Jewish doctor flees from Dortmund, leaving all that he owned behind.]*

A few days after the doctor had left with his family, we were invited to a friend's house. Of course the main subject of the evening was the doctor's flight. The discussion became heated. "He was wrong," most of the men were arguing. "It indicates a lack of courage to leave the country just now when we should stay together, firm against all hatred." "It takes more courage to leave," the ladies protested vigorously. "What good is it to stay and to wait for the slowly coming ruin? Is it not far better to go and to build up a new existence somewhere else in the world, before our strength is crippled by the everlasting strain on our nerves, on our souls? Is not our children's future more important than a fruitless holding out against Nazi cruelties and prejudices?" Unanimously we women felt that way, and took the doctor's side, while the men, with more or less vehemence, were speaking against him.

On our way home I still argued with my husband. He, like all the other men, could not imagine how it was possible to leave our beloved homeland, to leave all the duties which constitute a man's life. "Could you really leave all this behind you to enter nothingness?" From the heavy sound of his voice I realized how the mere thought was stirring him. "I could," I said frankly, and there was not a moment of hesitation on my part. "I could," I said again, "since I would go into a new life." And I really meant it.

Our private life became more and more troublesome. It was not simply that my husband always had difficulties with his sermons. Everywhere they tried to set a trap for him. There were so many regulations always being set up for a large congregation, and the rabbis had to abide by them. Every four weeks from now on we had to send revised typewritten lists of all the members of the different clubs. Whenever some of them were moving, we had to know it and inform "the party" immediately. We had to ask the Gestapo for permission for everything that went on in the temple and in the community house.

Our New Year and the Day of Atonement, the highest Jewish holy days, were approaching [1935]. Carefully my husband and I went through each of his sermons. Word for word we read aloud and considered whether they would pass the scrutiny of the Nazi supervisor who was present at every service. On the other hand, there was so much that my husband wanted to say to his people during these holy hours that he was not permitted to utter. The whole congregation would be there to get new hope out of those sacred days. He had to arrange his words in such a way that without mentioning the facts he could make his meaning clear to his audience. It was a hard task. It was not just a matter of his own safety that made my husband careful, but a case of preventing the Nazis, if possible, from getting a reason out of his sermons for closing the services and arresting the whole board of the congregation.

Two or three days before the holy days the pavement around the temple was besmeared with big white letters, "The Jews are our bad luck," and many similar signs. We cleaned the pavement on the eve of the first holy day, but the next morning it was even worse. That was not the only disturbance; a group of young Hitler Boys in their uniforms were posted at the entrance of the temple to make a deafening noise. When people entered the temple they had to walk though two lines of boys who were beating drums with all their force and sounding their trumpets in dreadful dissonance. A policeman was posted not more than ten steps away at the street corner, but when the ushers asked him to help them send the boys away, his reply was, "There is nothing I can do about it; they are sent on a special order." And the boys stayed until nobody was entering, until the tardiest arrival had come in. The sound of their raucous playing entered into the quiet of our temple, disturbing our prayers.

The next holy day passed without interference. Sometime later we learned that numerous anonymous letters had poured in to the Gestapo expressing the indignation of the Christian citizens at the disturbance of our service. At that time it still may have seemed wiser to the Nazis not to arouse too much sympathy for the Jewish people, and not to show their real intentions toward them too openly.

There were still millions of Germans who did not believe that this treatment was accorded us with the official sanction of the Hitler government. We would hear them say constantly, "If Hitler knew about such cruelty, he never would allow it. He would stop them at once. He does not know about what is going on. This is all illegal, and done by these vile Storm Troopers without his knowledge."

Many eyes were opened only when, in the fall of that year, 1935, the *Nuernberger Gesetze,* the laws of Nuremberg, were proclaimed. Only then did they believe, after reading in every paper and listening to each broadcast, that Jewish people were no longer citizens. Furthermore, the Jews remained subjects of the German Reich, with all the duties of a subject but without any of the rights of a citizen. [. . .]

Whenever we went to a meeting I saw faces which I had never seen before, while many of the old and well known were missing. Our congregation changed its members constantly now. Following the laws of Nuremberg, more and more businesses were forced to close, and the former owners left the country or went to Berlin, where they thought to lose themselves in the great mass of Jews. In spite of that our congregation did not decrease, since, from all smaller places around, Jews came to bigger cities. Life in a small town had become intolerable for Jews. They could not even buy food any longer in an Aryan store, and the Jewish ones had been closed for a long time.

Once my husband had to go to the country for a funeral service. He came back the next day sick from the cruel ordeal he had had to go through on that occasion. They had not been allowed to bring the body to the cemetery until it was dark. All Jews or Gentiles other than the immediate family were forbidden to attend the funeral. Not even a gravedigger was permitted, and members of the family had to dig the grave for the father themselves. Nazi guards were posted outside so that nobody could help.

After the funeral my husband was called before the Nazi official. "How can you dare, you dirty Jew, tell your people that they should hope for a better time to come?" the man shouted at him when my husband entered the police office.

"I was giving an interpretation of the Holy Bible. Do you have any objection to that?" my husband asked very calmly. This mean and common-looking man did not make any impression on him. His shouting did not frighten him. It made him feel only deep contempt and aversion.

"Who reads your Bible?" the man retorted. "Nobody anymore is interested in this Book. The times of the Bible are over. Our Bible is Adolf Hitler's book, 'My Battle.' " With this confession of faith in the Nazi God, he calmed down and released my husband. [. . .]

Again it was spring! [1936] Nature, in its own new strength, was bringing new hope. But, for us, there was no hope. The restrictions were drawn tighter and tighter, strangling the life of the Jewish congregations. The budget of our congregation, which had been 800,000 marks when Hitler came to power, had diminished to 80,000 marks. Where we had had less than a quarter of our people on relief before, we now had more than three-fourths of them on our relief roll. The city relief scarcely provided for Jewish people, and now no religious or private institution was permitted to make a charity drive. The only thing to do for our paupers was to have, as the Nazis had, a weekly "pound" collection of food and another of old clothing. Week after week a truck went around and every Jewish household gave at least one pound of some foodstuff. More than once, those of us on the committee did not know what to do when nothing but sacks of dried peas and lentils came in. Even people with money could not buy what they needed. Fruit, vegetables, butter, eggs, and meat were no longer on the market in sufficient quantities. It was clear that people could give only of what they themselves had plenty. We had the same sad experience with our clothing collection. The new substitutes, which looked very nice in the show windows, did not last long. People would alter their old clothes to make them look like new, so that the wardrobe for the poor in our community house gradually became empty.

Never, in my memory, had we had so much activity in our community house. From the basement to the attic there was not a single space where a group of people was not taking a course of some sort. Men and women, boys and girls came to learn new trades and professions which they hoped would enable them to make a living abroad. Ladies who had never touched a thing in their own homes came now to learn to cook, to sew, to become a milliner, a hairdresser, or to prepare in some other way to make a living abroad. Men who had been retired for several years, or those who had

had big businesses and factories of their own, came to learn to be farmers, shoemakers, or carpenters, or to fit themselves for some other vocation. And, mingled with the sounds of all these trades coming out of the various rooms, there was also a mixture of different languages echoing throughout the building. Spanish, French, English, or Hebrew could be heard whenever one passed a room.

The hardest task I had to do was to arrange for the transportation of children to foreign countries: the United States of America, Palestine, England, and Italy. It was most heartbreaking to see them separate from their parents. Yet the parents themselves came to beg and urge us to send their children away as soon as possible, since they could no longer stand to see them suffer from hatred and abuse. The unselfish love of the parents was so great that they were willing to deprive themselves of their most precious possessions so that their children might live in peace and freedom. [. . .]

Besides all other duties, we had been busy for weeks and weeks outfitting a great number of children for Palestine[3] The enthusiasm was as great among the Jewish children to build up a new homeland in Palestine as among the German youths to build up a new Germany. They came in throngs to enroll and were eager to be the first to go. It was not just the wish to go away from hate and slander which influenced these Jewish boys and girls. The idea of having again a great and holy task to live for made them strong and eager. In no country of the world had the idea of rebuilding Palestine been fought so desperately or caused so much opposition toward its followers as in Germany. Even now most of the older generation were strictly opposed to it. "We are Jews by religion, but our political ideals are German," was a tenet deeply rooted for centuries in the minds of the German Jews. Hatred and persecution could not destroy the love we felt for our homeland. The rising new enthusiasm of the Jewish youth for Palestine caused ill feeling in a great many homes. Often we had to smooth the friction between parents and children. The youth did not want to wait any longer, while the parents' hearts and hopes still belonged to the German fatherland.

One day I left Dortmund with a group of Jewish children to take them to Berlin, where a long train was leaving for Palestine. Our train coming from Dortmund was a little late, and I was hoping with all my heart that there would not be very much time left for me. Because I was still suffering from the tragic scenes of our departure from Dortmund, I felt I could not endure again seeing those heartbreaking farewells. In the great station at Berlin, hundreds of mothers and fathers filled the vast platform, which had been closed to everyone but the accompanying parents. By the time I reached the platform with my group, the train was already filled. All the windows were crowded with the children's shining faces. Pleasure and anticipation were written in their eyes and made them forget the pain of parting. Not so the group of parents who were standing, sad and silent, alongside the train. I tried to avoid looking at those faces. I did not want to see their grief. "What should I feel if my own children were among them?" I thought, while I guided my group to the compartment which was reserved for them.

Scarcely had they taken their seats when the whistle blew and I had barely time for a hasty goodby and the injunction that they be brave, before I descended from the train. "Greet my Mommy! Greet my Dad! They must not worry about me," the children were calling behind me. Before I could close the door, a boy of sixteen came near me and pushed a tiny parcel into my hand, "Please take this to my mother," he begged me, "and tell her to wear it until we see each other again." It was a tiny gold ring. The boy had made it himself, as he was learning to become a goldsmith. This was his first independent work, and he wished to dedicate it as a farewell gift to his beloved mother.

I was standing on the platform again, and as the slowly moving train passed by me, I noticed how quiet the children had become. The beaming light had faded from most of the young faces as they looked for a last time upon their dear ones. I saw many little girls who had been laughing before now stretching out their hands for a last handshake with their mothers and fathers, while the tears were running down their cheeks, and I saw many a boy's face distorted into a twisted smiling one. "We will be brave" and "Sholem Aleichem," the Jewish greeting, was sounded through the vast hall, while hundreds of Jewish children left their German fatherland.

The fluttering handkerchieves had disappeared, and the noise of the departing train had long since faded away, but still the crowd stood motionless, looking ahead where nothing was to be seen. I kept wondering numbly how many of those parents and children would ever see each other again. Suddenly I heard a scream, and when I turned back I saw people crowding together at one point. "A woman fainted," I heard people saying, and the call for a doctor went around. A few minutes of silence passed while a doctor bent down over the poor mother, and again, low and incredible, the message came to the last of the line, where I was standing, "She is dead." She had been strong enough to bring her child to the threshold of a new life, but her heart could not endure more. [. . .]

In 1937 it became more and more difficult for my husband to perform his duties under the supervision of the Gestapo of the city. All this was wearing on my husband's health, and besides, the uncertain, unpromising future of our girls was upon his mind both day and night. I could not help him. What I wished to say was, "Let us go," but I had promised not to urge him anymore, not to make it still harder for him. So what was ever-present in our thoughts lay unspoken between us.

"He has to take a rest," the doctor told me. "He has to go away from home to forget all these troubles for a while." As my husband did not want to go alone I decided to go with him, much as I hated to leave the children alone in such a perilous time.

To make it even more painful for us to leave them in a time when they so greatly needed someone to help them against the cruelty of Nazism, my older girl came home the day before we left with her face pale and stunned and her lips pressed together in a thin line. I knew this expression in my children's faces. They tried with all their willpower not to let us know about their suffering, but the signs of pain in the girl's childlike face were too evident to escape our eyes. I thought I could spare my husband, so I did not ask my daughter anything when she came in to the dinner table. But even my husband, whose mind was absorbed by the hundreds of things that he still had to arrange for his absence from the congregation, was aware of her grief.

"It is nothing, Daddy, but a headache." She tried to divert my husband's attention, but her eyes immediately filled with tears. "No, my dear," my husband said, "it is more than a headache which is bothering you. Please tell me what it is." But it was the younger one who had to tell it, since the child's resistance was now broken and, with the wild sobbing which followed, there was not one word we could understand. "Daddy, they have a new classroom," our little daughter explained, "and the benches are arranged in a different way, so that the teacher has made a new seating arrangement. And you know, Daddy," she said, "until now, sister was sitting beside her best friend, though they had not been allowed to be together on the way home, nor during the recreation hour. But now the teacher said, in the presence of all the girls, that it was no longer possible to have an Aryan girl sitting beside a Jewish girl. This would be a disgrace for an Aryan. And the teacher ordered her to take her seat in the last bench against the wall, and no Aryan girl could take a seat in this row. Now she is sitting alone in the rear of the classroom and is separated even during class from all the pupils."

My husband did not answer, but his face and his lips grew so bloodless, so pale, that even the children in their own grief were frightened.

*[During the vacation trip in April 1937 the parents are arrested for several days in connection with the closing of the B'nai B'rith Lodge. At the end of May the family flees to Holland.]*

1. The ban forbidding Jews to attend the theater, concerts, movie houses, etc. was not effected until November 12, 1938. Three days later Jewish children were expelled from the public schools.

2. The independent Jewish order B'nai B'rith (Sons of the Covenant) was founded in 1843 in New York, and as of 1882 it also existed in Germany. In 1932 there were more than a hundred individual lodges in Germany, which were dedicated to social activities and educational and social work. As of 1897 women were members of the B'nai B'rith Sisterhood, which joined the Jüdischer Frauenbund (Jewish Women's League) in 1929. On April 19, 1937, the B'nai B'rith was dissolved by the Gestapo and its assets were confiscated.

3. From 1934 to the end of 1939 over 18,000 Jewish children and young people emigrated from Germany without their parents, 8,100 to England and 5,300 to Palestine. Emigration to Palestine was organized by the Youth Aliya, which had been initiated by Recha Freier in Berlin. In Palestine the Youth Aliya was directed by Henrietta Szold.

# 40 *Ernst Loewenberg*

 BORN IN 1896 IN HAMBURG; DIED IN 1987 IN BROOKLINE, MASSACHUSETTS.

Ernst Loewenberg, My Life in Germany Before and After January 30, 1933. Manuscript dated Boston (Massachusetts), 1940, 83 pages.

*The author, son of the Hamburg school principal and writer Dr. Jakob Loewenberg, studied Germanic and Romance languages and literatures and, after receiving his doctorate, taught from 1921 until 1934 at the progressive Lichtwark School in Hamburg. After his father's death in 1929, he took over the latter's private girls' school, which, however, he dissolved in 1931. Although he had been a front-line soldier in World War I, in March 1934 he was forced to retire. He joined the staff of the orthodox Talmud-Torah school, which had become a Jewish Gymnasium in 1932. From 1930 until 1938 he was on the executive committee of the CV regional*

*association of northwest Germany. Already a member starting in 1929, and as of
1933 chairman of the assembly of representatives of the Jewish community, he was
elected associate head of the community in 1934. He worked in a leading capacity
on the most important tasks of the community during the Nazi period in the areas of
economic aid, vocational retraining, and the expedition of emigration. In October
1938 he emigrated with his wife and sons to the United States. From 1940 to 1962
he taught at the elite Groton School in Massachusetts and then, until 1965, at
Brandeis University. The three sons of the author became university professors, two in
the United States and one in Israel.*

After my forced retirement, the pupils of the Lichtwark School do not waiver
in their devotion. During that first summer, time and time again I meet several who
tell me how persistently the classes as a whole refuse to join the Hitler Youth. As late
as 1935 there are still classes in which no one is a member of the Hitler Youth. It
seems as if the old spirit were radiating from the walls of the young school. The new
people are not able to bring the school into line. At first they abolish coeducation, then
the entire school—the pupils and the staff are divided among other schools. In April
1937 the Lichtwark School is closed and another school is opened on the grounds by
the city park.

Wherever I see a former pupil, he comes up to me to ask about my well-being
and to tell me about himself. One morning I run into a Labor Service girl who accompanies me home in order to tell me of her new experiences. It does not bother her (in
the fall of 1934) that Aryans and Jews see her conversing with a Jew. — A year later
a Reichswehr soldier asks me: "You know who I am, don't you? How are you doing?"
After a short conversation I say to him: "Dear friend, it is better if you part from me
now. The people passing by are already staring at you. There come some officers. It is
in your own interest not to speak with me." For a moment he looks at me without
comprehending, then he goes.

Two years after my dismissal, girls from my last class bring me flowers for my
birthday. Only one—our little dummy—is in the Bund Deutscher Mädchen. (Even today
we still have egg cozys and mats that she crocheted for me.) When in the summer of
1935 we get a garden plot, the same girls visit us. Out there, by the Alster, I talk with
their parents for hours. There, where they are unobserved, they, too, are their old selves:
"I'm leaving school next year," Helga, a bricklayer's daughter, says to me. "I would
have liked to become a teacher, but then I would have to join the BDM, and I'd rather
go to work in a factory and remain decent than do that."

In November 1934 eight to ten pupils from the two upper classes of the Lichtwark
School come to me and ask me if I could work with them on German. They have Herr
O., and no one can stand it. Since I know O. from my student days, I do not doubt
the validity of this judgment. But why are they coming to me? Only one or two know
me from a French course. "Well, we know about you and would like to work with
you." The boys are in the Hitler Youth. "Are you allowed to come to me?" "Why
not? I even asked my group leader. He is a former Lichtwark pupil, graduated from
the Gymnasium in 1925 and had German with you. He told me: 'Go to L., with him
you'll learn something about German literature.' " We agree to do Rilke. But I ask for

time to think about it. Am I allowed to do it? I confer with friends, get a trade license, which costs twenty marks, and ask the participants to pay a small fee in order to create a clear basis for them, too, which would prevent any political suspicions.

For weeks now, every Wednesday ten boys and girls come to me. We read Rainer Maria Rilke, follow the path of this serene, subtle poet from his beginnings in mystical longing to the final pinnacle of his *Duino Elegies*—celebrations of German poetry. One evening, as I take them down in order to open the door of the apartment house, I see K.—my colleague and neighbor—walking up and down in front of the door, and I know that it's all over. Did a Nazi neighbor in the house report us? It is more likely that word got around in school. Two days later I hear that all participants were ordered to appear before the school principal, who notified them that it was doubtful whether they would be permitted to take the school-leaving examination if they displayed their moral immaturity so flagrantly by working with a Jew. "And I wrote down every word on the last two evenings," says Elsbeth L. "I suspected something. We can answer for every word. Please have the courage, continue working with us." But I refuse. "I cannot work with you knowing that I am endangering you. None of us would feel free any longer. It is better for everyone if we stop. Later you will agree that I was right."

> *[In the following, Ernst Loewenberg tells about his work as associate head of the Hamburg Jewish community]*

On April 2, 1933, the day after the boycott of Jewish businesses, the representatives of the Jewish organizations met with the executive committee and the council of representatives in order to centralize the relief work in one organization uniting all groups. Following the Berlin model, "Hilfe und Aufbau" was founded in Hamburg.[1] The hour of need also gave rise to the name "Beratungsstelle für jüdische Wirtschaftshilfe," called "Beratungsstelle" for short. We thought that economic aid was the main task, but soon vocational retraining, vocational training, and counseling on emigration became more and more predominant. The advisory center, which worked closely with the community as far as substantial matters and the staff were concerned, became the center for all relief work in Hamburg. [. . .]

The fall of 1933 brought the long hoped-for establishment of the Reichsvertretung der deutschen Juden. The large communities, which had had a conference group, and the three large federations, the Reichsbund jüdischer Frontsoldaten, the Centralverein, and the Zionistische Vereinigung für Deutschland, united. On September 17, 1933, the founding took place. Hamburg sent the venerable chairman Alfred Levy and, to assist him, Rudolf Samson and me.[2]

At the center of the negotiations was the relationship of Berlin and the Prussian state federation to the other parts of the Reich. This was thoroughly German particularism, but at the same time it was also an attempt of the Berliners to regulate everything from there on the basis of their numerical strength. In opposition to this there was the fact that the three South German federations—above all Bavaria and Württemberg— were constitutionally more strongly secured as national federations than the voluntary association of the Prussian state federation. Berlin was headed by Director Stahl, and behind him, as the driving force, stood the revisionist Kareski, to whom power was everything, and the Zionist leader Dr. Alfred Klee (later also his son Hans Klee).[3] Bavaria was led by the state supreme court counselor Neumeyer, Baden by Professor Stein. Only when Saxony and Hamburg declared that they would establish a Reichsvertretung with the South Germans alone and would leave it to the Berliners to join or not was a compromise solution in regard to distribution of power, which Samson and I had presented, agreed upon. Only reluctantly did the Berliners approve the election of Rabbi Leo Baeck, the head rabbi of Berlin, as president, and of Assistant Department Head Otto Hirsch as executive chairman.[4] When Hamburg waived representation in the council, we simplified further negotiations. We assumed that in important decisions our voice would be heard—even without an official seat. [. . .]

The Reichsvertretung, with the Zentralausschuss für Hilfe und Aufbau and the Zentralwohlfahrtsstelle,[5] tried to organize the planning of the entire relief work in the Reich. To be sure, that was made more difficult because of the lack of contacts with the appropriate authorities. What was still possible in Hamburg and often in South Germany—establishing personal contacts—was out of the question in Berlin. In addition, there were harassments by the Gestapo and the opposing efforts of the Berlin community and the Reichsvertretung. The subventions for new training workshops, for the preparatory centers for emigration, and the equalization of financial burdens were regulated from Berlin. Jewish schools had been founded anew in some larger communities, such as Munich, Nuremberg, Karlsruhe, Stuttgart, and Hannover. On the whole, however, restraint was exercised. One did not want to relieve the state of a burden that the law still obligated it to bear. This applied, above all, to Berlin itself, where at most one-third of the Jewish pupils were in community schools. Soon there developed a private school system on a large scale. Only hesitantly did the Berlin community establish a secondary school in 1936. In addition to the existing orthodox teachers college in Würzburg, a liberal Jewish teacher's college was established in Berlin under the leadership of Fritz Bamberger.[6] In the small and middle-sized communities the decision was even more difficult. Should a primary school consisting of one class be established and the children thereby be deprived of the advantages of a fully developed school? Thus, this happened only upon the request of the state, as in 1937 in Augsburg, where the community was not allowed to pay on its own for a second teacher. The educational department of the Reichsvertretung, headed by Adolf Leschnitzer,[7] also provided for refresher courses for teachers (in Lehnitz and Karlsruhe), and for new educational materials, since it was impossible to give textbooks full of racial slurs to Jewish pupils. [. . .]

In April 1933 the Jewish lawyers, doctors, and teachers of Hamburg formed special committees to help colleagues affected by the Gesetz zur Wiederherstellung des Berufsbeamtentums (April 7, 1933).[8] Often it was more a matter of advice than of financial help. In 1933 and later, as representative of the teachers, I personally saw probably all of the teachers who had to leave the Hamburg schools. In addition to that, it was a question of situating my Hamburg colleagues in the newly founded Jewish schools, through contacts with the educational department of the Reichsvertretung. Thus a colleague from Hamburg took over the administration of the new Jewish school in Stuttgart. The lawyers and doctors also helped financially, with means raised by those who were still working, to provide members of the middle class with financial assistance that went beyond the welfare center allowances. Above all, it was necessary to help doctors and lawyers who until then had had a predominantly Aryan practice to build up a Jewish one. In the first years economic advice and support for small businesses were possible and justifiable. In this regard the situation in the provinces and small towns soon became untenable, because there the party controlled things too closely. In the big city many an existence could be sustained for some years with sparse means. Later, with each new economic "Gleichschaltung"—at first by the transfer of Jewish firms to Aryans, later by legislative measures (exclusion from foreign currency allocation, revocation of stock exchange cards, exclusion of all brokers)—the constantly changing tasks of initial assistance fell upon the shoulders of the advisory center. Here there was close cooperation with the welfare commission of the community, that is, with the Aid for the Middle Class of the credit bank, which had already existed for years, and with the loan bank. By putting them together in an apartment house, which belonged to the community and soon proved to be too small, and by extensive cooperation, double approvals were avoided. The community was not so large that an overview was not possible.

Of the many visits by colleagues I remember one especially. In the fall of 1933, a haggard, elderly teacher came to me and explained right away that she had never before been at a Jew's, but she did not know what to do. For many years she had been a village school teacher in Schleswig-Holstein in the vicinity of R. She came from a strictly Protestant home; she had lost her father early in life. Thus she grew up in the Deaconesses' Institute in Potsdam, the same institution in which Reich President von Hindenburg had received his education. Now, while establishing proof of her Aryan ancestry, she discovered that her father—himself a pastor's son—was racially a Jew. And thus she had been dismissed. Distant friends had taken in the completely destitute woman. Her brothers were abroad. She could not comprehend that she, a German Protestant, had to be helped by Jews, with whom, after all, she had nothing to do. I advised her to leave Germany as soon as possible since there was no other way out. I gave her the money to go to the advisory center. Her passage to the United States was later paid from a general fund and from Jewish quarters. Until then she received assistance. Sometimes the church, too, gave converts one-half, and the Jews gave the other.

Vocational retraining created completely new tasks. Merchants, students, and academicians wanted to learn a trade before emigrating. The possibilities that were created for retraining were, to start with, a course in metalwork and joinery, and also a course for agricultural retraining. Here it was primarily the members of Hechalutz (the name of the Palestinian workers organization), oriented towards Palestine, who sought an agricultural *Hachschara* (preparation) in order to get a worker's permit for emigration to Palestine. — Those circles that were not Zionist but wanted to put Jewish retraining of every form into practice had established, in the twenties, a Jewish farm in Gross-Gaglow near Cottbus.[9] The same circles now proposed that a non-Zionist agricultural preparatory course be organized in the vacant children's home of the Jewish community in Blankensee. The Reichsbund für jüdische Siedlung supported this plan. A heatable greenhouse was built, half of the tract of land was transformed into a terraced vegetable garden, and fields were leased. An experienced head gardener assumed the direction.

It soon turned out that most of the countries of immigration could not offer agricultural workers from Europe any possibility of making a living. The sole exception was the settlements of the JCA in Argentina,[10] which, however, asked for larger families with agricultural experience. Thus, the participants of this course swung more and more in the Zionist direction. This being the case, the experiment had to be considered unsuccessful and the settlement school was closed. In its place a training course in gardening was established for young people, who could live in the house.

The initial enthusiasm for "retraining" did not last very long. The adults had neither the patience nor the means for proper occupational training. But only that would have been meaningful. We rejected crash courses, such as were frequently advertised privately. In the agricultural training of the Hechalutz, as well as in the trade courses of the advisory center, primary training became more and more important. Important for the older people were the retraining courses in sewing and tailoring, which were under the direction of a master craftswoman. The preparation for Palestine was taken over by the Hebrew language school, which was subsidized by the advisory center. English and Spanish were also given by the advisory center, in courses that provided the opportunity to offer dismissed colleagues some employment. For a time there was also instruction in commercial subjects.

Besides the Jewish trade school for women tailors, the advisory center established, in a building provided by the community, a school of home economics, where teachers who formerly were in the civil service gave instruction. In addition to specialized instruction, there were languages (English, Hebrew) and also religion, for which a compromise was achieved with great difficulty among the different religious branches. For the most part, pupils from other places went as apprentices in home economics to the girls' orphanage Paulinenstift. For formal reasons, both home economics schools later were placed under the direction of the girls' school. In this way it was also possible for the newly established school to receive state recognition and dispensation for its pupils from attendance at the school for compulsory continued education. The Paulinenstift had had this approval for many years. After it became known that many married couples had started as "butlers," there was also in the home economics schools a special course for men in serving.

Individual positions in households were offered, to be sure, but most of the time the girls refused to accept such posts in Germany. The Misrachi (religious Zionists) had an institute in Hamburg for training girls. In the morning they worked in orthodox households—often for food and lodgings—and in the afternoon from two to seven they had instruction. But this remained only a temporary solution, which, in addition, brought with it various legal difficulties such as a migration ban for employees from other places, insurance, taxes, and employment record, which finally led to its discontinuation.

Increasingly, in order to learn a vocation the pupils left school right after completing their compulsory schooling. As throughout Germany, everyone at first streamed to Hechalutz, whose new social ideal, the communal life of the kibbutz, along with a racial self-awareness that went with the national wave, so very much eased the attainment of emotional equilibrium. How many conflicts there were when the parents wanted to go abroad in Europe or to the United States but their children pushed for Palestine! How many parents gave in to the will of the children and are today in the United States, whereas their children helped to build Palestine!

The training became more and more difficult. At every moment commercial apprentices were at risk of losing their position through Aryanization or even more often through the liquidation of the firm. If there were still some favorable decisions at the beginning, whereby contracts of apprenticeship had to be abided by in case Aryanization took place, later there was no permission at all to employ Jewish apprentices.

Thus, vocational counseling at the special office of the community became more and more difficult. In the first years it was still possible to consult the state vocational counseling department, which in Germany, after all, was obligatory; it also had to approve the employment of apprentices after they had passed a qualifying examination. The Jewish vocational counseling office, along with the advisory center, tried to obtain every available position. There still existed a fairly large Jewish machine factory and a Jewish trawler shipping company, which was managed by a Frau Borchard. Through her cooperation Hamburg had the only seafaring *Hachschara,* and many a Jewish boy drowned on a tugboat on the high seas.

For Hechalutz the community made available an apartment house and later, for the younger ones, a private house, where they had their first experiences in communal living. The apprentices in the trades lived in the city, and in the surroundings of Hamburg there were three big agricultural training centers. The cost of living of forty marks per month, with which, however, the entire undertaking had to be maintained, was paid by their home communities and by the Zentralausschuss für Hilfe und Aufbau in Berlin. The accommodations were primitive and, since the young people rejected any influence or control by their elders, order and discipline often left a great deal to be desired. It was especially difficult to provide for sufficient food, because of the sparse means and the frequently insufficient knowledge of the Jewish girls in the management of a large household, although many foodstuffs were donated and the purchasing for Hamburg and vicinity was centrally organized. In later years the advisory center assumed a certain measure of financial control. This had become necessary above all because more and more frequently the "home communities" did not pay the promised contributions and often had to be reminded. Repeatedly the advisory centers and the community gave extra subsidies.

Two experiences growing out of this communal training are noteworthy. On the one hand, the young people regarded it as a natural duty of the communities to provide financially for their training in every way. This aid was the only justification for their elders' existence. But they did not think of somehow showing regard for the property or the feelings of the community whose hospitality and help they accepted. Because of that there repeatedly occurred annoyances that in themselves could have been avoided, as, for example, when the nonreligious members of Hechalutz washed their laundry on Jewish holidays, stood in front of the door smoking, and went for bike rides and thus disturbed the worshipers at the neighboring synagogues. Consideration did not exist.

On the other hand, the solidarity within each community was exemplary. When immigration to Palestine became more difficult, the problem of those who had "exhausted their benefits" arose. What was to happen with those who had completed their occupational training and the time in the "kibbutz" prescribed for Palestine? The subsidies were only for eighteen months. The means had to be stretched. Work could hardly be found. But many boys and girls could not and did not want to return to their parents' home—either because they no longer fitted in there due to their attitudes, or because they did not want to go back to the harassment in their small town, or also because they could not burden their needy parents. And thus it often happened that the staff pooled their sparse means and fed their old friends or went hungry along with them. Before the training period was extended as a result of increasing difficulties with certificates, the aid organizations had to help out.

The general attitude depended to a large degree on the frequently young *Hachschara* leaders who, coming from the Palestinian working class, had been assigned for "front-line duty." Depending on their human and organizational talents, things either went smoothly or not. Their judgment was decisive in issuing certificates, which gave them dangerous power. Since many an older person confronted this undertaking, which was in the hands of young people, in complete ignorance, I, as a friend of both camps, was often asked to conciliate. The state authorities looked upon these training centers altogether favorably and with understanding—in Hamburg always, and in Altona for the most part. If the public health inspectors occasionally issued injunctions, they were thoroughly legitimate or justifiable. For example, that the bathrooms for boys and girls be more strictly separated, or that there be better house entrances for boys and girls.

A difficult problem was the sham marriages that necessarily resulted from the administration of the immigration certificates.[11] It was simply a matter of getting as many *chawerim* and *chaverot* (modern Hebrew expressions for comrades) to Palestine as possible. The risk and the justification of these sham marriages were often debated. In some cases there were marriages of which the parents sending their young children to the Alt-Neuland gladly approved. Here one could observe how often people from entirely assimilatory homes took East European Jewish marriage partners in order to draw closer to the Jewish masses in this way, too.

1. The Zentralausschuss für Hilfe und Aufbau [Central Committee for Aid and Reconstruction] did not originate officially in Berlin until April 13, 1933. In it representatives of the large Jewish organizations came together to better coordinate and finance, supraregionally, economic assistance, welfare work, and help with emigration in the time of need. The Zentralausschuss was a forerunner of the Reichsvertretung der deutschen Juden, which was created in September 1933, and it continued to exist as the financial department of the latter.—Regarding the economic aid of the Berlin community, see A. Szanto (38).

2. Alfred Levy (1854–1939?) was, between 1918 and 1933, the first chairman and, from 1933 until his emigration in 1939, the honorary chairman of the Deutsch-Israelitische Gemeinde in Hamburg. Attorney Rudolf Samson (1897–1938) directed the Hamburg Beratungsstelle für Wirtschaftshilfe, and as of 1934 he was chairman of the CV regional association of northwest Germany and the Hamburg branch.

3. Heinrich Stahl (1868–1942), director of the Victoria Insurance Company, was chairman of the Berlin Jewish community between the years 1933 and 1940. In 1942 he was deported and died in Theresienstadt.—Georg Kareski (1878–1947) was director of the Jewish cooperative bank *Iwria,* which he founded in 1927, and which had to cease payments in 1937. As a member of the executive of the Jüdische Volkspartei and of the Berlin Jewish community, from 1929 to 1931 he was the first and only Zionist head of the community. Expelled from the Zionistische Vereinigung in 1933 because of arbitrary infringements, he founded the rightist Staatszionistische

Organisation. On his collaboration with the Gestapo and his attempt to take over the Reichs-vertretung in 1937, see Herbert Levine, "A Jewish Collaborateur in Nazi Germany: The Strange Career of Georg Kareski 1933–1937" in *Central European History VIII*, No. 3 (1975). — Dr. Alfred Klee (1875–1943), a lawyer, was one of the leading Zionist politicians in the Berlin community. As of 1920 he led the faction of the Jüdische Volkspartei in the assembly of the representatives to the community and became its deputy head. In 1938 he fled to Holland, where he perished in the Westerbork camp in 1943.

4. Dr. Leo Baeck (born in 1873 in Lissa; died in 1956 in London); beginning in 1912 rabbi in Berlin and *Dozent* at the Hochschule für die Wissenschaft des Judentums. As the spiritual leader of German Jewry, he became president of the newly founded Reichsvertretung der Deutschen Juden in 1933 and also formally directed the Reichsvereinigung der Juden in Deutschland, which had been set up in 1939 and was subject directly to the supervision and orders of the Gestapo. He was deported to Theresienstadt in January 1943, survived the camp, and emigrated to England. — Dr. Otto Hirsch (1885–1941), assistant department head in the Württemberg state government. From 1929 to 1933 he was president of the Union of Jewish Communities in Württemberg. He was a member of the main governing body of the Centralverein and from 1933 to 1939 he was the executive director of the Reichsvertretung der Juden in Deutschland. Thereafter, he was a member of the executive of the Reichsvereinigung, was arrested in 1941 while holding this office, and was murdered in the Mauthausen concentration camp.

5. The Zentralwohlfahrtsstelle der deutschen Juden in Berlin was founded in 1917 as an umbrella organization for Jewish welfare work in the German Reich.

6. Dr. Fritz Bamberger (born in 1902 in Frankfurt am Main; died in 1984 in New York); he directed the Jewish teachers college in Berlin from 1933 to 1938. He emigrated to New York in 1938, was active as a publicist, and between 1962 and 1978 he taught at the Hebrew Union College. Bamberger was a cofounder and vice-president of the Leo Baeck Institute in New York.

7. Dr. Adolf Leschnitzer (born in 1899 in Posen; died in 1980 in New York) was dismissed from civil service as a tenured secondary school teacher in 1933; between 1933 and 1938 he was in charge of the educational division of the Reichsvertretung. To provide educational materials, he published the *Jüdische Lesehefte*. He emigrated to New York, taught German language and literature at the City College, and contemporaneously, from 1952 to 1972, the history of the German Jews at the Freie Universität in Berlin.

8. See Karl Schwabe (35), note 5.

9. See Alexander Szanto (38), note 8.

10. See Alexander Szanto (38), note 7.

11. The English mandate government in Palestine permitted emigration only on the basis of allotted certificates. The so-called workers certificates, which members of *Hachschara* received, were greatly reduced in number after the Palestinian disturbances of 1936. The distribution of these certificates was the duty of the Palestine office in Berlin, which therefore was forced to make a selection. A married couple needed only *one* certificate, so that through sham marriages human lives could be saved.

# 41  *Gerhard Bry*

BORN IN 1911 IN BERLIN.

Gerhard Bry, Resistance: Recollections from the Nazi Years. Manuscript dated 1979; West Orange, New Jersey; 273 pages.

*Gerhard Bry, the son of a pharmacist, grew up in Berlin and began the study of law in Heidelberg. Having returned to Berlin, he was recruited by Jewish friends in 1931 for the secret organization "Neu Beginnen" (Fresh Start), which was intended to unite Social Democrats, communists, and trade unionists in the fight against fascism. Bry was a member of the SPD and the KPD, successively. In 1933 he had to give up his studies. He scraped along as a laborer and then began a commercial apprenticeship in the firm of a Jewish electrical engineer. At the same time he continued his underground work for Neu Beginnen and was one of the majority of its members who in 1935 dismissed the old leadership. When several members to whom he had close ties were arrested in September 1935, the organization decided that he should leave Germany. Bry emigrated with his future wife to London, where he worked in business. In 1938 he emigrated by way of Cuba to New York, where he studied economics. He worked for many years in the National Bureau of Economic Research, and was Professor of Economics from 1955 to 1976, his last post being at New York University. He then taught as professor emeritus at Pace University in New York.*

*[The following material has been taken from the original manuscript, written in English.]*

Soon after the coup of the Nazis I stopped going to the University. It was dangerous for Jews to show their faces at the school, and my face looked sufficiently typical to make matters worse. [. . .]

A big question was what to do occupationally. If I wanted to stay in Germany, in connection with my Org work,[1] I obviously had to have an occupation which was innocuous and close to the nonprofessional groups of society. It also had to support me. I decided to become a worker, first an unskilled one, in the hope that I might be able, later, to learn a trade. I worked, successively, as a helper in a large automobile repair shop, as an unskilled worker on a building construction job, and finally as a commercial apprentice in a shop doing electrical installations and repairs. [. . .]

The most important single fact of the Org's history during the Nazis' destruction of the leftist organizations was that it stayed entirely intact. We only lost a single person during the early months of Nazi rampage, even during the first few years. This was, of course, partly due to the underground character and the conspiratorial traditions of the group. Most of our members worked far from home and under assumed names. Also, the publicly exposed members, such as the Socialist Youth leadership group, went into well-prepared hiding. But there were other reasons for this success. What was a severe weakness in the past, the absence of really important public figures in our organization, became an asset in the struggle for survival. Furthermore, the Org decreed immediate withdrawal of its members from the suicidal hyperactivism of communist and other radical groups. [. . .]

During the previous period we had aimed to be the most progressive part of the existing labor organizations. Now that democratic parties and unions were destroyed, where was the new locus for political leverage? Several options were discussed and partially tried. If one took the theory literally that there could be only Nazi organizations, one would have to go into these organizations (obviously a course not open to our Jewish members). I doubt that the Org did anything of this sort, except perhaps for information purposes. It would certainly have discredited these changelings in the eyes of their former socialist comrades. An alternative would have been to use the nonpolitical social aggregates such as trade organizations, civil service, professional organizations, perhaps the Armed Services, as contact groups. Still another possibility was to argue that before any new cataclysmic event, such as a full-blown war, there was no chance to do any meaningful political work, and attempts to do so would only result in useless sacrifices. To my knowledge, this view was not expressed inside the Org until two or more years later. What we finally did was dictated by the form in which opponents of the regime actually congregated—small circles of former union members inside or outside of large enterprises, and small-scale reorganizations of Social Democrats, communists, or members of splinter groups. Obviously, these were aggregations which could be used for collecting and disseminating information, for building an organizational network within and between large cities, for improving the quality of political understanding and technical competence—in short, for performing those tasks to which the victory of the regime had reduced the proud aspirations of the Org. This was the course which the Org, after some wavering, actually followed.

My next job was somewhat better. It started in the early winter of 1933, in a building construction firm which also had a machine shop. For a few weeks I did simple drilling and stamping work in the shop. Then I was put on a team which had to correct a design deficiency on Berlin's first high-rise office building, the Columbus Haus on Potsdamer Platz, designed by the architect Erich Mendelsohn.[3] The building was of modern form, with a number of untried features. Specifically, the windows were metal framed and could, by crank, be rotated vertically around their center. This looked fine and airy, only the fit wasn't tight enough to exclude draft. During the cold winter months it was impossible to sit near the window, particularly on the higher storm-exposed floors. We were told to affix to the windows flexible brass strips which were supposed to press tightly against the frame and thus exclude the draft. This involved drilling holes into the window frame, cutting threads, and affixing the pre-cut brass strips with little screws. Usually we did the drilling early in the morning, the rest later in the day. For drilling the part of the frame which opened outward, one had to lean out and work partly outside the building. This was a bit dangerous, but most of all very cold in the winter mornings. While the drilling was noisy, the threading and affixing was quiet, and one could talk to the people in the offices. I did a lot of that, and it gave me plenty of personal contacts—though most were short-lived. I developed a routine for making these contacts. I was very solicitous about not making a mess, helped to move chairs and desks, and tried to protect the office personnel from cold or draft. In the course of such help I let it be known that I was very new at the job and, as a matter of fact, at this kind of work. That invariably led to inquiries about my previous activities and permitted me to mention that I had studied law but had to give it up because of my faith. Some office workers dropped the conversation at that point, but a larger number expressed sympathy and some were quite open about their thoughts. I was obviously somebody to whom one could talk without fear. (I hoped that the Nazis would never think of such a ploy to ferret out malcontents.) Not that I acquired very important information from these sources, but it was a far cry from the isolation in which I worked at the motor repair shop. [. . .]

I had worked my way across a certain floor, slowly approaching a suite of engineering offices. One night Stefan called me and asked me to meet him. He said that he was instructed to inform me that I was approaching the clandestine headquarters of the Org which operated under the guise of engineering consultants (who also did real engineering work) in the new building. I was told to behave exactly as any strange workman would, not let on that I recognized anyone, and to promptly forget whatever I saw or heard. I did what I was told—that is, almost! I got some broad smiles when I entered, since there were obviously no bona fide customers in the office. I also got a kiss, a hug, and an apple. But we didn't talk and there were absolutely no other signs of recognition! I don't know whether they gave this treatment to all strange workmen. It certainly did not happen to me in any other office.

I worked on the building job for several months. When the window repairs were finished, I quit. From the two work experiences I concluded that my face, language, and mentality would make it impossible for me to ever really merge into the working classes and make manual work the basis for financial support and social contacts. I had to find some kind of white-collar occupation which served these purposes. I heard, around this time, that a small electrical contracting firm was looking for a commercial apprentice who wished to learn the bookkeeping, estimating, buying, and selling aspects of the trade. The proprietor of the enterprise was an electrical engineer, a Jew, with lots of technical knowledge and a jovial disposition. The business affairs of the firm were more or less in the hands of his wife, who was intelligent, parsimonious, and domineering. The firm's quarters consisted of a shop with one highly-skilled worker and several assistants, and of small offices for the owners, a secretary, and me. My education was managed by the lady boss, and I received a very modest salary. During the first year, 1934, I helped to process the voluminous paperwork which is required in the estimating, bidding, buying and selling operations of such a firm. I also learned some basic book-keeping skills and got acquainted with various other phases of office work. Later, in 1935, when the fortunes of the enterprise began to flag—partly in connection with the regime's admonition to give German work to German firms—I was sent around to drum up business. In this process I learned a bit about the art of selling. This activity also gave me some unsupervised time, which I had not enjoyed while doing office work. Furthermore, it provided more contact with outsiders and some opportunity to find out about their thoughts and feelings, an aspect which I liked for both personal and political reasons. I did not know exactly what I would do after my training as a "technical merchant," but I thought I would perhaps be able to fill a position in the offices of a technically-oriented firm and, if present levels of tolerating Jewish employees continued unchanged, I would find such a job. If that wasn't the case, one would have to think anew. It was certainly difficult during those years to make longer-term plans, occupational or other. [. . .]

The Org did many new things in the first two and a half years of the Third Reich. It adapted its internal operations to the repressive environment, expanded its work in Berlin and other cities, established close alliance with a sister organization in Austria and a bureau for representation abroad in Prague; it also organized courier services and frontier posts, and developed communication techniques. Its foreign representative was Karl Frank,[4] who managed to visit the homeland repeatedly. The year 1934 also saw the publication of Miles's book *Neu Beginnen,* which appeared in many translations and gave the group its name.[5] The book was not a straightforward statement of the Org's beliefs. Instead of giving the old Leninist conception of clandestine work in all parties, it presented a left-wing activist socialism and explained the group's clandestine behavior as technically needed for work under Hitler. This line even approximated our actual strategy under the new conditions, since we had pulled out of communist organizations.

It is very difficult to arrive at a meaningful estimate of the numerical strength of our group, because of the problem of including support groups, loosely affiliated contacts, and contacted groups. I thought at the time that, at its most developed stage during 1934, the Org itself might have had up to 200 members in Berlin, perhaps 100 in the remainder of the Reich, and again as many members abroad. The groups with which we had contact and on which we exerted influence, either directly from Berlin or through our centers abroad, could have counted in the high hundreds. Although this may seem a very small size, it is not so small when one considers the need to protect all activities against discovery and prosecution. I could not estimate the total strength of organized socialist and communist groups in Germany. However, in 1934 there was hardly a good-sized city without some such groups, and the total number of members was certainly considerably larger than the number of those with which we had contact. But even if at times the total number of organized resisters might have reached 10,000 members, this would only be a little more than one-tenth of one percent of the German population. There were, of course, millions of unorganized anti-Nazis, Jewish and non-Jewish. Quite a number of them were prepared to help and actually helped those persecuted by the regime for political or racial reasons. I recently discussed these estimates with Eva Jeremias,[6] who was the secretary of the Prague office of the Org during this time. She suggested that I would be nearer to the truth if I cut all my Org figures in half. She said that the Reich leadership of the Org at that time thought it necessary to bolster our morale, and better secure the needed financial support, by intimating a larger size and scope of the organization than actually existed.

Regardless of the size, the group Neu Beginnen was the only centralized and centrally organizing force of socialist underground activities on a national level. We provided information, political guidance, technical advice, and help. We also collected information from inside Germany, which we edited and distributed inside and outside the country. This work was made possible on a relatively broad scale by the fact that the three most important frontier secretaries, the men who supported inland work from abroad, had switched their allegiance from the old Social Democratic Party leadership (Sopade) to our group. This was done because we had considerably more to offer to the inside groups which looked to them for support.[7] [. . .]

Among the activities of the frontier secretaries was also the smuggling into the country of the *Sozialistische Aktion,* a paper published by the Sopade under the guidance of Paul Herz.[8] Herz sympathized with our goals and later joined our group. We contributed to this paper, at least during certain periods. [. . .]

The attitude toward nationhood was probably also one of the few differences between non-Jewish and Jewish members of the Org. I did not talk often about this topic, but when I did I was under the impression that many of the non-Jewish members felt that socialist resistance against the Hitler regime was a noble patriotic duty. They were the real patriots, not the Nazis. My own orientation, and I presume that of Eliasberg, of Rix,[9] and of other Jewish members of the Org, was more internationalist, or, to put it a bit more carefully, lacked the component of patriotic fervor. This attitude cannot be attributed to the fact that Jews in general, as the Nazis were prone to claim, were rootless and loyal to "their own kind" rather than to the nations in which they dwelt. It was, in the case of the Germany of the thirties, a consequence of the antisemitic traditions existing in a large part of the public and of the anti-Jewish policies of the Nazis, which had led to a thorough alienation from specifically German values. [. . .]

Jewish resistance to the Nazis could not be meaningful on an individual basis, but only on an organized basis. The organization could not be purely Jewish, but had to have broader political goals. Resistance had to be planned, not improvised. Participation of Jews in underground anti-Nazi organizations was the most effective way of resistance open to them. It is regrettable that this participation has not been the subject of more thorough inquiry and has not gained the attention which it deserves.

Among the several political strategies open to opponents of Nazism I mentioned the possibility of confining one's activity to information exchange and of maintaining only a small skeleton organization until serious cracks in the monolithic structure of the regime made intervention feasible. The argument was that organized political activity before such time would only result in useless sacrifices of freedom and lives. Actually this was the view which, with some modifications, the Org leadership developed and began to present during the first half of 1935. The modifications were as follows: In view of the assumedly superior insights developed by the Org leadership, annihilation of the Org would also endanger the possibility to use these insights for the progress of the labor movement in the democratic countries. A small group of skillful Marxist revolutionaries—perhaps 20 to 30 people—should be left in Germany for reporting and contact purposes. The remainder of the Org should either be deactivated or should emigrate with the purpose of raising the struggle of fraternal groups abroad to higher levels of political consciousness and effectiveness.

*[Most of the Org members rejected this strategy as defeatist and split with the old leadership.]*

The "split" itself was carefully prepared. A paper by Rix, which traced the new policy of the Org leadership to shortcomings in their basic conception, today still reads like a little classic. Another brief paper, by Stefan, showed how the actual history of the Org reflected these shortcomings. The takeover was accomplished in the middle of 1935. The Org members of my sector assembled in my home under the guise of a birthday party.[10] The takeover took place without a flaw. Only very few people chose to remain with the old Org leadership. From the circle of our close friends, only Heinrich Jacubowicz and the Turkish-born Gurland stayed with the Menz group.[11] I asked Stefan how we could protect the Org and its new leadership against irrational retribution or administrative indiscretion. He assured me that we had enough hold over the old leadership to make such events most unlikely. I should report how large this historically minute event looms in my memory. During the months before the takeover, I had feared that the only successful attempt to maintain a socialist underground organization against Nazi discovery and persecution was doomed to fall victim to a defeatist policy. The takeover of the Org by my activist friends gave new hope. Karl Frank became the Org's official head, Peuke[12] the head of the inland organization, Rix the recognized theoretician, and Stefan became part of the Org's leadership group. The Org founder, Walter Löwenheim, soon emigrated to England. [. . .]

Unfortunately, actual developments did not permit my elation about our victory to last long. Barely two months after the takeover the Gestapo struck. It struck forcefully and close to home. Some of my closest personal friends in the Org were arrested: Stefan Eliasberg by the end of July, and Edith (Ted) Taglicht[13] at the beginning of August. Ted's friend and later husband, Fritz Schmidt, was able to escape to Prague. Also Konrad Frielinghaus, the fellow student of my school days whom I had brought into the Org, was caught at about that time. A little later the Nazis caught up with Edith Jacobsohn, the psychoanalyst, and with Gerhard Dannis. Most tragically, an outstanding young woman, Lisel Paxman, who served as one of our main couriers between Berlin and Prague, was arrested at her re-entry into Germany. She ended her life rather than subjecting herself to the cruelties of Gestapo interrogations and leaving us open to the dangers of whatever she might be forced to reveal.[14] The Org knew that Lisel Paxman was endangered, but an attempt to warn her failed. Apart from political encounters, I knew Lisel socially. We sometimes went for walks, and once we visited my friend Rut in Papenberge. Her death was a terrible event. [. . .]

When I was informed of the arrests of my friends, I left home and changed living and sleeping quarters frequently. Now it really paid off that I had a large circle of personal and political friends who were prepared to help in times of need. There were a number of tasks to be performed under the circumstances. One of the most important was to get some materials out of a hiding place in Stefan and Vera's apartment—the new Org had its own small archive. The trouble was that it was hidden in the home of an arrested Org member, and this home may well have been under constant surveillance. There were several vital reasons for removing the documents. One was for the protection of Stefan and Vera. If the documents were found, as they eventually might be, Stefan would be identified as a member of the new Org leadership. The second had to do with defense strategy. We hoped that the Gestapo did not know about the leadership change and that, therefore, the liquidationist line could be offered as support of the assertion that the Org had de facto dissolved itself. The activist nature of the hidden documents would have made this assertion futile. Finally, the nature of the activist goals, the building of a network of revolutionary anti-Nazis in Germany, would—if known to the authorities—lead to a concentration of the Gestapo on finding and destroying the rest of our Organization.

Franz Carsten[15] and I were given the mission to rescue the documents. Carsten had been renting a room at the Eliasberg's apartment and thus had good reason to have the apartment key. I was to accompany him, for a bottle of wine and a social chat. We were apprised of the location and nature of the hiding place inside a hollowed door which, on its underside, had a snugly fitted cover that could be removed by activating a pin-lock. The pin had to be inserted in a tiny hole the position of which could be found by exact measurement from the edges of the door. Observation of house entrance and windows, and repeated telephone calls made it seem unlikely that the Gestapo was actually waiting in the apartment, but one could never be sure, of course. There were two further complications: The landlord, who knew of Eliasberg's arrests, and was known to be a Nazi sympathizer, lived in the apartment directly under that of Stefan and Vera. Also, a police station was located very close by and could bring policemen to the home in a minute or two. The idea was to enter the apartment as noiselessly as possible, use not more than a few matches for light, and remove the material. Should we be blocked by the landlord on our way out, we hoped to force our exit with the help of two full bottles of wine which could be used as clubs. Finally, we would meet another Org member in a nearby park, hand the archive over, and depart in different directions. We divested ourselves of all identifying papers, and I obtained a firm promise to have my younger brother, Ernst, sheltered and sent abroad immediately in case our mission led us into the hands of the Nazis. Then we left with fervent good wishes by our comrades, who were assembled in Edith Jacobsohn's apartment or office. Compared with the anticipatory anxiety, the mission itself was anticlimactic. We went to the apartment, removed the files, left, and handed the material to the Org member.

There were some other tasks to be performed, partly in connection with our support groups. Basically, I told my group members that all organized contact was to cease and that we would approach them individually, if circumstances warranted. We also agreed on some warning codes in case we thought they had to leave their homes or flee the country, and we rehearsed cover stories in case they should be interrogated about their relationship to one or the other of our members. I remember the goodbys to have been highly emotional.

After reporting my tasks completed, I was advised to leave the country myself. Peuke and Hanna explained: Being such a close friend of several of the arrested persons, I was deemed personally in imminent danger and was regarded as a liability for further political work. Also, inside Germany the scope for political work by Jewish Org members was shrinking; I might be of more use abroad. I assume that this was said as a boost to my morale. The actual message was: Get out!

1. Org (for: Leninist Organization) was the original designation for the socialist group Neu Beginnen, which took on its second name in 1933 when its founder, Walter Löwenheim

(1897–1977), published the programmatic document "Neu Beginnen" under the pseudonym "Miles" (see note 5). Löwenheim broke with the KPD in 1927 and in 1929 created Org as a conspiratively operating underground organization, which was intended to overcome the split in the German workers movement, in order to carry on the fight against National Socialism more effectively. The members came from the KPD (German Communist Party), KPDO (German Communist Party–Opposition), SPD (German Socialist Party), SAJ (Young Socialist Workers), SAP (Socialist Workers Party), and other parties. The group Neu Beginnen was politically close to the left wing of the SPD and for a time was supported financially by the SPD in exile. It was able to operate in Berlin until 1938, and a remainder existed in Bavaria until 1943.

2. Stefan was the cover name of the chemist Dr. George J. Eliasberg (1906–1972), who together with Richard Löwenthal (note 9) came from the communist student faction and belonged to Org from the beginning. Bry had been friends with Eliasberg and his future wife Vera since 1931. The student group Org, whose membership according to Bry was half Jewish, gathered around the Eliasbergs. In July 1935 Eliasberg was arrested and sentenced to four and one-half years in prison. After his release he was expelled as a stateless person. In 1941 he arrived in New York, where he worked as a journalist until his return to Germany. In 1968 he became a staff member of the Friedrich Ebert Foundation in Bonn.

3. Erich Mendelsohn (1887–1953), one of Germany's leading modern architects; among his projects were prestigious administration buildings and department stores in Berlin. He emigrated in 1933, designed buildings in England and Palestine and, after 1940, in the United States.

4. Dr. Karl Frank (1893–1969), a psychologist from Vienna, was active, in succession, in the KPÖ (Austrian Communist Party), KPD, KPDO, SAP, and SPD. He joined Neu Beginnen in 1933, became its representative in Prague, and after the split in 1935 he directed the organization. In 1938 he went to London with its foreign leadership, and in 1939 to New York, where an office of Neu Beginnen was likewise created. In New York Frank became a psychotherapist.

5. See note 1. The precise title of this analysis of fascism was "Neu Beginnen! Faschismus oder Sozialismus: Diskussionsgrundlage zu den Streitfragen unserer Epoche; von Miles" (Fresh Start! Fascism or Socialism: Position Paper on the Conflicts of Our Epoch. By Miles). The brochure appeared in September 1933 with the SPD Party Press in Karlsbad, and it also was published in a disguised edition for Germany, under the title "Arthur Schopenhauer: Über Religion" (Arthur Schopenhauer: On Religion). French and English translations of this much-discussed document appeared in 1934.

6. Eva Jeremias, née Elsa Groneberg, was a secretary and part of the Eliasberg circle. In 1938 she went to Paris, and from there to New York.

7. The frontier secretaries of the SPD executive alluded to here are Erwin Schoettle, Waldemar von Knoeringen, and Franz Bögler.

8. Dr. Paul Hertz (1888–1961) was SPD Reichstag member in the years 1920–1933. From 1933 to 1938 he belonged to the exile executive of the SPD, from which he withdrew when he joined Neu Beginnen. He emigrated to the United States in 1939, and from 1951 to 1961 was councilor for economic affairs in West Berlin.

9. Rix is Richard Löwenthal (born in 1908 in Berlin), whom Bry met as a student in Heidelberg, where Löwenthal belonged to the communist student faction, later KPO. Löwenthal became the leading theoretician of Neu Beginnen and worked for the split of 1935. In August 1935 he emigrated to Prague. There, as well as later in Paris and London, he worked in the foreign office of Neu Beginnen. During the war he lived in London as a political journalist. From 1948 to 1954 he was a British correspondent in Germany, and from 1961 to 1974 he taught courses in foreign policy at the Free University in Berlin, where he now lives as an emeritus. — Löwenthal does not entirely share Bry's opinion, and he commented in 1982: "Internationalism and concern for Germany's future was not a contradiction for me."

10. Bry's birthday was the 29th of June. — The leadership was declared deposed by four city district meetings that took place at the same time. Walter Löwenheim, the founder, declared

in September, for his part, that Neu Beginnen was dissolved. He emigrated to Prague and later to London.

11. Menz is the founder and leader Walter Löwenheim. — Ruben Gurland emigrated to Brussels, and Heinrich Jakubowicz to London, where he adopted the name Hellmann.

12. In 1933–34 Werner Peuke directed the illegal KPD district of Central Berlin, and then joined Neu Beginnen. He was interred in the concentration camp Sachsenhausen from 1936 to 1939.

13. Edith Taglicht is the daughter of the Vienna rabbi David Israel Taglicht (1862–1943).

14. Lisel Paxman committed suicide on September 13, 1935 in the Dresden prison.

15. The historian Franz Carsten (1911–  ) belonged to Bry's Org cell and, like Bry, emigrated to England in 1935. He now lives in London as a retired professor of European History.

# 42  *Kurt Baumann*

BORN IN 1907 IN BERLIN; DIED IN 1983 IN ITHACA, NEW YORK.

Kurt Baumann, Memoirs. Manuscript, 126 pages; written in Ithaca, New York, 1977.

*Kurt Baumann's father was owner of a plumbing business in Berlin. From 1928 until 1932 Kurt Baumann studied theater, was an intern and assistant producer at the Berlin Staatsoper, and in 1932/1933 was dramatic adviser of the Berlin Rotter stages. In view of the dismissal of Jewish artists and the isolation of all Jews, in April 1933 he devised a plan for the founding of a separate Jewish cultural organization. He presented the plan to Dr. Kurt Singer, the director of the City Opera, who intended to do something similar and under whose leadership the plan was realized in a short time. In June 1933, with government approval there was founded the Kulturbund deutscher Juden, which organized theatre, opera, and film presentations as well as concerts and lectures until 1941. Kurt Baumann became director of the opera division and the artists bureau, and starting in 1935 he also became the "self-censor." In August 1939 he emigrated to the United States, and from 1946 until 1972 he was librarian at Cornell University in Ithaca (New York), where he also founded a small opera.*

My idea to found a Jewish cultural circle was based on very simple figures: in 1933 there were 170,000 Jews living in Berlin alone; many other large cities had proportionally similar concentrations. I calculated that a city of 170,000 inhabitants could maintain its own theater, an opera, a symphony orchestra, museums, lectures, indeed even a university, and do that under the economic conditions of a medium-sized city.

It was clear to me from the start that for the time being it was still doubtful whether and how approval of the authorities could be obtained, precisely because it was uncertain which wing of the Nazis held what official positions and what the party program meant to the government offices in question. It was also clear to me that Zionist circles would give their support only if we were to carry out all our cultural endeavors either in Yiddish or in Hebrew. Apart from the fact that, on the whole, German Jewry knew neither Yiddish nor Hebrew well enough, and that translations of Yiddish and Hebrew literature scarcely existed, in those days the Zionists were a minority in the Jewish population. From the majority, which was united in the Centralverein deutscher Staatsbürger jüdischen Glaubens, and from the Reichsbund jüdischer Frontsoldaten I could expect that the proposal for a purely Jewish cultural circle in Germany would be answered with the cry: "We won't go to the ghetto voluntarily!"

At any rate, it was clear to me that there would have to be a plan, worked out exactly to the last detail, with a budget, artistic and intellectual personnel, and an organization of members to prove that such an idea could be realized. I therefore sat down and in approximately two weeks drew up a plan worked out to the last detail. The next consideration was who should assume the management of such an undertaking. I recognized that I, at the age of twenty-six, was known neither among German Jews nor in German official places, nor was I of any significance. It had to be someone who had a good and well-known name in artistic circles and who, if possible, had served both sides so well that the German authorities could not reject him out of hand.

It took only a short while before my mentor, the former director of the City Opera, Dr. Kurt Singer,[1] occurred to me. Not only was he a very well-known musician and organizer, he also had another great advantage: Singer had been a frontline soldier during the First World War, and as conductor of the doctor's choir in Berlin he had done especially valuable work for the German folk song in his writings and on the podium. Because of that he was even very well-known and popular in German nationalist circles, although he himself was a liberal democrat, formerly probably a Social Democrat. I went to him, told him about the general idea, and asked him in strictest confidence to have a close look at my plan. He was immediately very interested and said that he, too, had already considered similar ideas, but that he had not thought about it any further. He promised to study the plan closely.[2] After a very short time Dr. Singer called me and invited me to his place to discuss my plan. There now began an intensive daily collaboration in the course of which some revisions of the plan were undertaken. Dr. Singer had received the idea with enthusiasm and had declared himself willing to take charge of the organization if it succeeded.

*[Kurt Singer gains the support of the Berlin Jewish community and applies for permission at the Prussian Ministry of Culture.]*

Given the confusion that prevailed at the ministries and their unwillingness to answer to their superiors for such an odd organization, it was no wonder that the ambitious young state commissioner Hinkel[3] very soon sensed that by his agreement to negotiate with us, and later perhaps even to supervise us, a great career opportunity was opening up for him. And that was precisely the way things then developed. By May we were that far along. We were allowed to rent an old theater and to found a club in which exclusively Jewish artists and intellectuals could present events of all kinds to an exclusively Jewish audience. The members had to have identification papers with a photograph, and were able to get in only with season tickets. To attend an evening event straight from the street was forbidden even for members. Individual seats could not be had at the box office. In return we were promised that we would receive police protection and that no National Socialist organizations would bother the members when they arrived or departed, or during the performances. Naturally, all texts, the music, and the exhibition items had to be approved beforehand by a security office of the ministry. It should be noted here that we were "urged" to avoid as much as possible works of German culture that were considered to be especially German.

It had become clear to us long ago that to start with we would most likely have to pay for an eventual permit by being allowed to work only under strict official supervision. The greater price, however, was that the Nazis would use us as one of their most powerful means of propaganda whenever, say, anti-Jewish measures would trigger great commotion abroad about "horror tales." We did, in fact, go into the ghetto voluntarily, but to the Jewish public we provided, at least for some time, a place with cultural offerings that they were accustomed to, and in an environment that protected them from any kind of trouble.

The great Jewish artists of international reputation, above all the musicians, had emigrated from Germany right after Hitler had seized power; they had no difficulties finding work and sustenance abroad. But at the beginning there were in Berlin hundreds of highly talented and well-trained artists and intellectuals who were not able to emigrate as easily, because they were not known outside of Germany and no longer got work in Germany.

In the contract that was being drawn up between us and the Prussian government it was made clear to us from the German side that members of the governing body of the Berlin Jewish community would have to be represented in our supervisory board, in order to lend our organization an official status. Thus began our negotiations with the Jewish community of Berlin, which turned out to be more difficult than those with the Nazi authorities. As I have already mentioned, at first the battle within the community between Zionist and non-Zionist forces had to be fought, until finally both wings had come to an agreement and were prepared to send representatives to our board. What Dr. Singer had prophesied to us now happened. The head of the department in which Hans Hinkel was working suggested to Prime Minister Göring that he make Herr Hinkel head of a new department and name him director and supervisor of Jewish cultural affairs in Prussia. We never learned anything officially about the internal negotiations, but in the middle of May 1933, Herr Hinkel informed Dr. Singer that there was nothing to prevent the contract any more, that he, Hinkel, had been named director by Göring and that Dr. Singer had to answer with his head for the smooth implementation of the conditions contained in the contract. It was now necessary only to to to appear before Minister Göring and receive his "blessing." And that did, in fact, happen. Göring tried to be amiable and jovial and said something like: "If you do everything right and do Herr Hinkel's bidding, then everything will be all right, but if you get carried away, then things will start popping, and you know it."

Finally, on May 20, 1933, all was ready. A contract was concluded, which was signed by Dr. Singer for the Kulturbund deutscher Juden, and by the new undersecretary in the Prussian Ministry of Culture, Hans Hinkel. Hermann Göring signed only with his initials. [. . .]

The response among the Berlin Jews was much greater than we had ever imagined. For the first major publicity event in the synagogue on Prinzregentenstrasse, featuring a choir, an orchestra, and an address, two and a half thousand people gathered right in the middle of summer. Half of them became members on the spot, and ninety percent of the others ten days later, after it had become clear that there were no disturbances of any kind and that only light police protection was present, as was usual for all cultural functions, Jewish or non-Jewish. Following events were even more over-crowded than the first and had similar recruitment results.

Each new member received, first of all, a membership card, on which his picture appeared and which bore *our* stamp. The program scheduled the performance of a play for a month and of an opera for the following month. In addition, every month there were two concert performances and two lecture series. The subscriber could select his days himself and had the right to two events that he could choose freely.

*[Kurt Baumann becomes a member of the board of the Kulturbund, and director of the opera division and the artistic bureau.]*

The theater of the Bund was to be opened on October 1, 1933. Since the preparation of a play requires somewhat less time than that of an opera, it was clear that we would open with a play. There had never been a question which play that should be. There was only *one* work that was suited to depict our new situation. It had a Jewish theme, was a German classic, and its author was at the time not officially forbidden, to be sure, but nevertheless not very performable. It was Lessing's *Nathan der Weise,* with Kurt Katsch as Nathan, Sigmund Nunberg as the pater, Fritz Wisten, who also directed it, as the dervish, and Lenart as the templar.[4] It turned out to be a festive opening. The house was sold out, Herr Hinkel came with his staff, there were no disturbances, and the audience was both moved and enthusiastic.

Thus began a series of cultural events which—with the exception of brief inter-ruptions—continued into the year 1941. During the heyday of the Kulturbund sometimes several events took place daily. Lectures and exhibitions were also organized, as well as concerts, matinees, and theater and opera performances. Sometimes the orchestra went on tour, sometimes the theater or the opera were on the road. Later were added the cabaret of Max Ehrlich and Werner Hinzelmann's theater for young people, which performed not only in Berlin but also elsewhere. [. . .] Almost all employees, artists, and administrators had been hired with at least a year's contract. At that time we already were making a conscious effort to present as much Jewish art as was at all possible, but we were still permitted to present German literature and music. That we never played Wagner, nor Richard Strauss, was obvious, since they were considered Hitler's favorite composers. We also never chose Schiller, although at the beginning we probably would have been allowed to. Instead, we presented much foreign literature and music. The difficulty was that in the later years contemporary foreign authors and composers entailed fees and thus foreign currency, and we knew that this did not suit the authorities. For the same reasons, for a long time we were denied a film division, something we were able to add only much later under entirely different circumstances.

*[In numerous other cities there arose Jewish cultural organizations, which in 1935 united into a Reichsverband.]*

At the inaugural meeting of the Reichsverband der jüdischen Kulturbünde in Deutschland, under pressure from the authorities the name "Kulturbund deutscher Juden" was changed to "Jüdischer Kulturbund Berlin." At the same time, at this congress, Hinkel let us know clearly that now we should set about including more Jewish themes into our repertory and that from now on permission for German authors would be handled more strictly.

We had already anticipated that and had asked a group of first-rate Judaists to translate something from classical Yiddish literature, at least for a start. To be sure, it was a slow, difficult task, but two plays and a number of cabaret programs were already finished. In the meantime, some of our artists and employees, as well as a steadily increasing part of our audience, had already emigrated. Membership in the Kulturbund Berlin had reached its peak in the spring of 1936 with 20,000 members, and it was clear to us that this number would quickly drop. This explains our short-term planning. I, too, thought more and more of emigrating.

Then Dr. Singer asked me to take over a new post: the position of self-censor, officially called "reader." All texts, music, etc. that were performed or shown in Jewish cultural circles had to be approved by the authorities. Since this was to take place at the Reich level, it was an absolute necessity that someone read our programs with National Socialist eyes, as it were, in order, as much as possible, to prevent our being forbidden to put something on. Dr. Singer offered me this post in the Reichsverband der jüdischen Kulturbünde. I would remain at the opera of the Kulturbund theater but give up the artistic bureau of the theater. Although I knew that the best days of the Kulturbund were over, I still did not want to leave my post, especially since until then Herr Hinkel had not permitted anyone from the National Socialist offices or organizations to address even a rude letter to us or to threaten us, let alone take other measures.

Starting in 1935, however, the question of censorship became more critical, for the simple reason that we had to work with a new ministry and did not know how it would react to eventual "mistakes" on our part. Also, due to Hinkel's pressure we were given fewer opportunities to present German artistic works. Above all, it was completely unclear which German art would be allowed, and which not. At this point, one has to take a brief look at the so-called National Socialist cultural policies, not only in regard to Jewish cultural circles, but also toward the German ones. The guiding principles for the Jewish cultural organizations seemed to be very simple: German material that was regarded as especially *German,* above all German Romanticism, was more or less forbidden. The German classics, except for Schiller, were, in fact, permitted until the end. Themes of the German Middle Ages and the so-called "heroic age" were taboo from the start. The business with German Romanticism was very peculiar. In music, the entire German Romantic period was allowed for a long time, above all, in its symphonic form, whereas in the question of songs it was a matter of sensibility as to which song texts of which authors would perhaps be permitted and which not. The so-called leftist authors of the Weimar period were, of course, forbidden from the start, not only to the Germans but also to us.

I have already suggested that the question of foreign authors was never made clear in the guidelines. Until 1936 the matter of foreign currency was probably decisive. How very much a Jewish precensorship had to rely on sensitivity, luck, and the diligent reading of newspapers will be shown by a few examples, which today strike us as very funny, but in those days were a most serious matter, since it was possible that because of an error by the precensor one could expect to be sent to a concentration camp or at least to be placed in coercive detention. We planned to put on Shakespeare's *Hamlet*. To be sure, we were not yet certain whether we could cast the play, but we wanted to submit it nonetheless, as it sometimes took a few weeks until permission arrived. In rather short time we received the approval; only the great monologue "to be or not to be" had been excised by the authorities.

Officially we had no possibility of ever inquiring why certain things were allowed or not allowed. Thus, we had to find a way that was somewhat complicated, but often provided us with information that otherwise we could never have gotten. My friend Klaus Jedzek, at just that time, was dramatic adviser at the Prussian State Theater under Gustaf Gründgens. He had the opportunity to approach some of the young people in Hinkel's office, for these young people were the "readers" for our permits and thus had to know on what political grounds refusals and approvals were based. Klaus Jedzek succeeded in inviting one of Hinkel's readers to a wine restaurant and to wrest from the young man, who was in an intoxicated condition, the secret of the Hamlet monologue. It turned out that the line "the oppressor's wrong, the proud man's contumely," spoken on a Jewish stage, could give the impression that the Jews were complaining about their treatment by the Nazis. For this reason they eliminated not only this line, but at the same time the entire monologue. [. . .]

After we had played Gustav Mahler's music for years, suddenly one day his "Songs of a Wayfarer" were forbidden to us. There was great confusion over this in the Jewish Kulturbund, for we could not imagine at all why they wanted to forbid us a Jewish composer. So we once again used our proven round-about maneuvers. This time it turned out that a new young man in the department of music censorship in Hinkel's office was fully convinced that the composer of "The Youth's Magic Horn" had to be Aryan. Once again we had proof that Hinkel himself probably was able to read the things he signed only hastily, for he had always cited Mahler as a special example of what we should perform. Naturally, the error was corrected by Hinkel's office right away. [. . .]

From the end of 1936 on it became clearer and clearer to us that we were leading an increasingly more isolated life—not only in regard to the the German public, but noticeably also in regard to the Jewish community. The economic, political, and legal isolation in which the Jewish community in Germany found itself became greater and greater. We realized that the existence of the Jüdischer Kulturbund was based ever more on the fact that the Nazis were using us as counterpropaganda against the growing pressure of foreign public opinion, and that sooner or later this would be the only reason to continue sanctioning the organization. With growing alarm we saw that the "Gleichschaltung" of public opinion in Germany was gaining success. We had to recognize that the hope of wide circles of seeing moderation in National Socialist politics was in vain. Accordingly, emigration by all Jewish circles, ours included, was pursued more vigorously. For the first time we, too, lost a number of our performing artists and, of course, also our members. Joseph Rosenstock was appointed director of the Imperial

Philharmonic in Tokyo, and Wilhelm Steinberg took his place.[5] That, too, lasted only a short time until Steinberg, upon the recommendation of Toscanini, went to New York. In his place came Rudolf Schwarz, who in 1939 was called to the Stockholm Royal Opera by his mentor Leo Blech.[6] Some of our best singers and actors and several of the prominent reciters also finally succeeded in surmounting the difficult conditions for emigration. Thus passed the year 1937. Finally, at the beginning of 1938, I, too, believed that the Kulturbund had passed its prime and from then on would diminish more and more. Thus, I began to pursue plans for my emigration.

*[After the pogrom of November 9/10, 1938, in the absence of Kurt Singer, his deputy, Dr. Werner Levie, is summoned to Hinkel at the Propaganda Ministry.]*

Hinkel said that it was probably clear to us also that our people and our house had not been kept from destruction without reason. "The Herr Minister gave me the order that at all costs the Jüdischer Kulturbund immediately open its doors again and continue performing." Hinkel repeated that the Minister would have his head if that did not come about. He implored Dr. Levie[7] to speak with us and to see to it that what was needed be done. Besides, he wanted us to try to reach Dr. Singer and to tell him to return as quickly as possible. Herr Hinkel requested an answer on the same afternoon. Having returned to the theater, Dr. Levie asked us to stay together and to consider very carefully what we should now do. The overwhelming majority of us at first insisted that any further cultural work was impossible. It was clear to us that in the most extreme case we would all end up in the concentration camps. Dr. Levie returned from his attempts to reach Dr. Singer and told us that Dr. Singer's ship had just left the harbor in New York; he was on the high seas and would arrive in Rotterdam in approximately six days. We, in turn, told him our opinion and of our apprehensions. In a lengthy discussion the thought crystalized that if Hinkel was truly subjected to such pressure there might perhaps be the possibility to blackmail him. Apparently the outcry of public opinion abroad had become so loud that the continuation of our events had become an important alibi for Goebbels.

Dr. Levie had wisely seen to it already before his meeting with Hinkel that we find out how many active members of the Kulturbund in the Reich had been arrested and how matters stood with the synagogues and other Jewish properties in the provinces. Up to the time of Dr. Levie's afternoon conference with Hinkel we knew that over a hundred active members in the Reich had been arrested and that the number of the other Jewish people who had been deported from Berlin and the Reich amounted to about 30,000. Slowly we came to an agreement. Dr. Levie would present Herr Hinkel with an entire series of demands. We would see how many of our demands Herr Hinkel was ready to grant, and thus the degree of pressure actually being exerted on him would be revealed. Dr. Levie reminded us that the fact that he was a Dutch citizen provided him with a certain protection, so that he would try to wrest as many concessions from Herr Hinkel as possible. In great haste a list was drawn up of two hundred people who had been arrested. We would insist that without these people we could not carry out any Kulturbund work in the Reich, and that they be released immediately. They were all intellectuals and artists; a large number of these people had, in reality, never or almost never been active in our work, but we knew them and wanted to get them out as soon as possible. In addition, a complete list of other demands was drawn up in a great hurry, among them also financial ones that we wanted approved. We waited in great suspense.

Dr. Levie went for his afternoon meeting with Herr Hinkel. When he came back after a long time, he reported that all our demands had been granted without reservations and that the necessary steps would be taken immediately. [. . .] In return, Dr. Levie was to promise to reopen the Kulturbund in three days. It wasn't at all easy to induce Herr Hinkel to extend this period of time to twelve days. Now we no longer had any choice; we had to continue working. Herr Hinkel had promised that extensive explanations would be given in the German press and on the German radio to reassure the Jewish audience that all our events would be protected, as previously, and that there was no danger for any of our members. And that was done in no time. Apart from everything else, the fact that we succeeded in saving two hundred Jewish people from the concentration camp, so that they could emigrate safely, made the founding of a Jewish Kulturbund and its continuation in that critical time worthwhile.

1. Dr. Kurt Singer (1885–1944), neurologist and musicologist, founded and directed the Berlin physician's choir. From 1927 to 1933 he was manager of the Städtische Oper of Berlin. From 1933 to 1938 he was in charge of the Jüdische Kulturbund Berlin as director and was a member of the directorate of the Reichsverband jüdischer Kulturbünde, created in 1935. During the November pogrom he was on his return trip from the United States and remained in Holland. From there he was deported in 1943 to Theresienstadt, where he died in 1944.

2. Excerpts from the handwritten document and the first typed version, countersigned by Dr. Singer, were bequeathed to the Leo Baeck Institute, along with the author's literary estate.

3. Hans Hinkel (1901–1960) had been a member of the NSDAP since 1921. In 1923 he established the Kampfbund für deutsche Kultur, and in 1930 he became a member of the editorial staff of the *Völkischer Beobachter*. On January 30, 1933 he became state commissioner in the Prussian Ministry for Science, Art, and National Education and was in charge of the theater committee. Hinkel used the surveillance and censorship of the Jüdischer Kulturbund as a means of furthering his own career. As of 1935, Reich Cultural Administrator and department head at the Reich Ministry of Propaganda, he increasingly tightened the censorship of the Kulturbund until it was forbidden to perform any works by non-Jews.

4. Kurt Katsch (1893–1958) from Grodno (White Russia); until 1933 he played leading parts on German language stages and in 1934 at the Berlin Kulturbund theater. After that he was director at the Yiddish theater in Warsaw and emigrated to Hollywood in 1938. Cf. K. Katsch (19). — Fritz Wisten (1890–1962); previously at the Schauspielhaus in Stuttgart, he was actor and director at the Jüdischer Kulturbund from 1933 to 1941. Married to a non-Jewish colleague, he survived in Berlin and from 1946 until 1954 he directed the Theater am Schiffbauerdamm and from 1954 to 1962 the Volksbühne in East Berlin.

5. Joseph Rosenstock (born in Cracow in 1895); before 1933 music director in Darmstadt, Wiesbaden, and Mannheim, he was artistic director of the Kulturbund opera until 1936. From 1936 on he directed the Nippon Philharmonic Orchestra in Tokyo, was the general manager of the New York City Opera between 1948 and 1956, and from 1961 to 1969 conductor at the Metropolitan Opera in New York. — Wilhelm Steinberg (1899–1978) was music director in Frankfurt a.M. until 1933. In 1936 he emigrated to Palestine and in 1938 to the United States. After the war he conducted the symphony orchestras in Buffalo, Pittsburgh, London, and Boston.

6. Leo Blech (1871–1958); conductor and composer, he was musical director at the Deutsche Staatsoper in Berlin from 1913 to 1937. He emigrated to Sweden by way of Riga and

in 1953 returned from his position as conductor of the Royal Opera in Stockholm to the Berlin Staatsoper. — Rudolf Schwarz (born in 1905 in Vienna); prior to 1933 conductor at the operas in Düsseldorf and Karlsruhe, he was musical director at the Jüdischer Kulturbund in Berlin between the years 1936 and 1941. He survived the concentration camps of Auschwitz and Bergen-Belsen and in 1945 emigrated to England, where he conducted the orchestra of the BBC and the symphony orchestra of Birmingham.

7. Dr. Werner Levie (1903–1945); economist and journalist with Ullstein, he became administrative director of the Kulturbund in 1933 and from 1935 on general secretary of the Reichsverband jüdischer Kulturbünde. After Singer's departure he was in charge of the Kulturbund for a year, and at the end of 1939 he returned to the country of his birth, Holland. In 1943 he was deported, by way of Westerbork, to Bergen-Belsen, where he died one month after liberation.

# 43   *Hans Berger*

 BORN IN 1898 IN WIESBADEN; DATE OF DEATH UNKNOWN.

Hans Berger, Remembrances of Kristallnacht and My Experiences in the Concentration Camp Buchenwald. Manuscript dated Brussels, January 15, 1939, 10 pages.

*Hans Berger grew up in Wiesbaden, where his father owned a factory for physical therapy appliances. After completing the Gymnasium he attended the school of engineering in Friedberg and entered his father's firm, which he took over in 1930. Active in the Jewish B'nai B'rith lodge, upon its compulsory closing in 1937 Berger was arrested for a time. After the Reich pogrom, on November 11, 1938 he was once again arrested and was brought to the Festhalle in Frankfurt and from there taken to the Buchenwald concentration camp. With some 10,000 other Jews arrested during the pogrom he was exposed to severe maltreatment. When he was released after three weeks, he fled to Brussels. The following report about his arrest and his time in the camp was written there and then sent to Palestine. According to information from two of Berger's siblings, who emigrated to the United States, Berger then lived with his wife and two sons in southern France, where he probably fell victim to deportation.*

On Wednesday, November 9, 1938, we were sitting together in the evening with our English teacher Moses in our cozy home and were talking about the threat that had been pronounced against the German Jews by the government after the death of Ernst vom Rath.[1] None of us believed possible the insane brutality from which we were going to suffer, even to the point of murder, in the very next days.

When on the morning of the 10th of November I was driving my car to work, as I did every day, my route took me past the synagogue, whose dome was ablaze. Fear went right through me. A big crowd of people stood around it silently and the fire department was content with protecting the surrounding houses from catching fire. My way took me to the Jewish school, where I got out to check on my children. There they still did not know about the burning House of Worship, and only in the factory did I hear through telephone reports that all Jewish businesses in the city were completely demolished. The wares were thrown onto the street and set on fire, and all this happened at the hands of only a few juveniles who had been appointed by the party for this purpose. After a short time my children arrived at my office, frightened, and Uncle Maas, who in the meantime had also arrived, took them by car into the city and home. I then received a telephone call from which it became clear that a large number of Jewish men in the city had been arrested. Then Mariechen, my wife, who did not know that Uncle Maas had already taken the children home, came to pick them up, and Liesel, too, arrived pale with fear. After we had learned by telephone that Lotte was at home with the children, Liesel and Mariechen stayed at the factory for the time being.

Toward noon I overheard a telephone conversation of our supervisor[2] with the Labor Front, from which I gathered that our factory was supposed to be protected against destruction, but that I and Maas were to be taken into protective custody. Thereupon we decided to go immediately in two separate cars to Frankfurt in order to escape arrest. I left without delay with Mariechen, and went first to Fritz Duensing, whose wife immediately declared herself willing to take in our children. Since we feared that I might be arrested in the city or at home, Mariechen went alone to our apartment, which I myself could enter freely only after three weeks and under completely changed circumstances. Mariechen fetched the children, and after a brief leave-taking both of us went to Uncle Maas in Frankfurt.

There we missed one another, and we looked for him the entire afternoon until we met up at our common Aryan acquaintances'. In the meantime we made a visit to the Israelitisches Krankenhaus, where we learned that a few hours before our arrival, Dr. Rosenthal,[3] the doctor who had operated on Mariechen two weeks earlier, had escaped arrest by suicide.

When we met up with Maas, we learned that in Frankfurt and Mainz, too, the synagogues had been set on fire, Jewish businesses demolished, Jewish men even arrested on the street, and that already quite a number of Jewish private residences had been destroyed in the most bestial way. We deliberated on how to save what perhaps could still be saved, and came to the decision that I was to return to the factory while Maas, who in contrast to me had a valid passport, should try to get across the border. Like hunted game we had to leave the apartment of our Aryan friend on the sly when two unfamiliar men appeared there, of whom one assumed that they were plainclothes policemen. Since we had also heard that on the highway they were pulling Jews out of cars, Mariechen drove the car back to Wiesbaden alone, and I went by train, strangely enough without being stopped. Mariechen, on the other hand, was stopped on the highway, a short distance outside of Frankfurt, questioned about her racial identity, and released only after some twenty minutes, when it was established that she was traveling without male company. After I had gone the distance from the station to the factory in Wiesbaden on foot, Mariechen caught up with me at night, in the car, and then drove ahead to the factory by herself to find out whether the coast was clear there. After consultation with the foreman Seibel, we ascertained that I could sleep over at his place without danger (as we assumed). Thus, after I had removed a few things from my office, for example my dagger from the war, I went to sleep at Seibel's. Every half-hour during the night I heard guards going through the factory courtyard, who called out to Seibel and asked if everything was all right. If they had known that I myself was sleeping in the lion's den, they would have probably arrested me on that same night.

The next morning I began my work early and took care of the most urgent business matters, signed a check for the salaries and received telephone calls from which I thought I could deduce that the arrests had stopped. At approximately 9:00 a representative of the Labor Front came, sat down in my office, and explained to me that the factory must continue to be run smoothly at all costs, and that it was his duty to see to it that no destruction occur at the plant. Incidentally, he did not disturb me any further at my work. Toward 12:30 two officials of the Gestapo appeared, one of whom I knew. They asked for me and explained that they were going to search for weapons in my office, also that I should go with them for questioning. Since I might possibly have to be away from the factory for a few days, I should entrust someone with the authority in banking matters. In the course of the conversation it then turned out that they were also demanding from me information concerning Aryanization of the firm; further, I had to hand over the correspondence and papers concerning the firm that were still in my possession. My objection that the smooth continued operation of the plant, which the gentlemen wished, was not possible without my work was dismissed with a shrug and the remark that in the following days a change was to be expected anyway. Thus there remained nothing else for me to do but to appoint as trustee as dependable a friend as possible. Fortunately, as it later turned out, I chose Herr Schwerdtfeger, the chairman of our board of trustees and owner of a machine factory in Wiesbaden. During a telephone conversation with this gentleman, which I had in the presence of the Stapo and the people from the Labor Front, Schwerdtfeger did protest against my arrest, but when this protest met with no success, he accepted the mandate. In the meantime Mariechen had arrived outside to check on me, and after a short house search in my office Karl Seibel Jr. drove us together with the two men from the Stapo in one of our Opels to my residence, where I discovered to my joy that nothing had been destroyed. There I was given time to change clothes and to take along a few necessary items of clothing. I was even left alone with Mariechen for a short time. A cursory house search took place, and then the men drove me in my own car, with my wife accompanying me, to the court prison. Mariechen was dropped off earlier. I had 112 reichsmarks with me and knew that Mariechen was in the possession of about 600 reichsmarks in cash.

In the prison the first person I saw was Ernst Springer, with whom I had already experienced the same situation on the occasion of the arrests when the Jewish lodges were dissolved.[4] In the course of the afternoon the cell kept filling up, until we finally stood closely packed, some thirty-five men in a narrow cell, the smallest number of them from Wiesbaden, mostly people they had arrested at the Wiesbaden station, on the street, and in hotels. Among them was an elderly gentleman from Berlin who, while visiting Frankfurt, had made an excursion to Wiesbaden, was not even a professing Jew, and, without a hat and in a light coat, had landed straight from the street in our cell. There was also Herr Kahn from Schierstein, who told us that in Schierstein not only the Jewish businesses but also every apartment had been demolished in the most horrible way. The furniture was smashed to pieces with an ax, drapes and pictures cut, underwear and linen treated the same way, kitchen supplies, jelly, oil, etc., poured into the eiderdowns, and all the china smashed; in short, there was not an undamaged piece left in any apartment. The wretched man did not know where his wife and children were, since he had been surprised at his store by the vandals in the morning, and when he went home to look after things he no longer found his wife and children there but instead had been arrested on the spot. Later I found out that this unfortunately was not an individual case but rather the rule, and that I had escaped this common fate of destruction only through a stroke of luck, of which the time that followed had several more in store for me.

In the evening we were transferred to the police prison, where, among other acquaintances, I also found the lawyer Liebmann.[5] We spent the night there accommodated in a royal manner, compared to what was yet to follow. On the next day, Saturday, November 11th, there followed, among other things, an interrogation by the Stapo about our emigration plans, and Ernst Springer, who in his pocket had his completed ship documents for emigration to America for the 7th of December, was released immediately. Besides him, two others were freed, one with an open wound on his leg, the second a man with severe epilepsy. In the evening, after we had already been told to go to sleep, we were suddenly all released from the prison. Our money and valuables were returned to us. But we were not set free, as we fools had hoped, but instead were sent from the hands of the regular police to the clutches of the Stapo.

Still on the same evening, in severe cold, we were taken in trucks to Frankfurt to the Festhalle, where we arrived at eleven at night. A howling mob received us at the entrance to the Festhalle—abusive shouts, stone-throwing, in short the atmosphere of a pogrom. On the double we went into the hall, where at first we got only a faint idea of what still awaited us. Right opposite the entrance a dead man lay on the floor. He seemed to have succumbed to a heart attack. In the huge hall there were thousands of people divided into small groups, which, under the supervision of SS men in black uniforms and in civilian clothes, were in part exercising and doing gymnastics, in part also sitting on the floor and resting, and in part being registered by policemen or SA men at tables standing in the middle of the hall. The exercises were meant only as something for the new arrivals to do as long as they were not busy with the deposition of personal data and registration. We were lucky not to have arrived until late in the evening, because for others this procedure had already been going on for many hours. When we arrived the sentry squad was apparently already tired of tormenting people and had us ordered about by our own comrades who had been officers or noncommissioned officers, while they themselves only watched, smoking their cigarettes. Only now and then did they pull out one or the other who appeared to them suited as object of their sadistic pleasure, and then this poor person, God knows, had nothing to laugh about. I saw how one had to do knee bends with his face directly against the wall. Naturally, one falls over backward. Then the SS snot stood behind him and each time beat him with a horse whip. This, according to my estimation, was repeated many hundreds of times, until the poor man was hardly able to stand on his feet. Imagine the worst Prussian noncommissioned officer and sadist, magnified many times and let loose in perhaps three hundred copies on a few thousand Jews, who were defenselessly surrendered to their spite, and then you will have an approximate idea of the events in the Festhalle in Frankfurt. In addition, imagine the bellowing that accompanied it, the noise of columns of men exercising, the screams of people being beaten, for it rained blows, and you will have the foretaste of what awaited us in the following days.

Just a small example of the mental anguish. A new *tallis*[6] was found on one of the Jews; another one was called to the front and was supposed to explain what was to be done with it. For this purpose they had picked out a rabbi. He had to put on the *tallis* and explain different customs, in the process of which he was abused in the coarsest manner, and his explanations were accompanied by derision and mockery. In the end the *tallis* itself was used to clean shoes, and then thrown into the rubbish.

The registration work, which continued in the meantime, was also accompanied by the worst abuses and insults of the coarsest kind, not to mention blows and punches. Razors, valuables, and money were taken from us. Of the above-mentioned 112 marks I later saw only 12 again. My housekeys were also taken from me and thrown into the rubbish, with the comment that, after all, I would have no occasion to use them ever again. Those were nice prospects! We were divided into new groups—I ended up with people only from Frankfurt—were lined up anew, and a part had to sweep the Festhalle thoroughly. It was now two o'clock in the morning. A compassionate SS man, I meant to say a humane one—for something like that does still exist outside the concentration camp—allowed us at least to go to the toilet and to rinse down the worst dust from our mouths and throats with a swallow of water.

Then in groups we were driven in busses to the South Station in Frankfurt and there, all the while on the double, we had to run the gauntlet through a howling, stone-throwing crowd. Someone tripped me up and I went sprawling. We were put on an unheated special train there, with carefully locked doors, and after the train was filled, it started moving into the night toward an unknown goal under the guard of the gendarmerie. On the way the order was given: "Remove your coats!"—so that we would be better exposed to the cold. Tobacco and food had been taken from us. In some compartments, in which gendarmes were riding with us, the Jews were especially harassed. Soon we realized the direction, when, without stopping, we passed Erfurt and Eisenach at express-train speed. We were terrified, and the concentration camp of Weimar-Buchenwald, the most notorious of all, appeared before us with its quarries.

At about six o'clock on Sunday morning the train stopped at the station in Weimar, Goethe's city, which for all times will remain most horribly linked in my memory with the following scene in the tunnel between the platforms. We had to get off the train by compartments, and had to run, on the double, accompanied by blows with steel rods and pokes by rifle butts, along the platform, down the stairs, into the tunnel. Woe unto him who tripped or fell down the stairs. The very least was that the ones coming after him had to trample over him, or also fell down and were brought back onto their feet by renewed blows and jabs. In the tunnel itself we had to place ourselves in lines of ten, one behind the other, the first person with his face directly against the wall, and the gendarmes saw to it that we stood crammed together like herrings. The poor people who stood last in the line had to suffer blows and pokes, the effect of which was that the lines pressed closer and closer together. I was standing in the middle; in the end it was hardly possible to breathe. On top of it, whips whistled above our bare heads and the most obscene bellowing and most vile phrases that anyone can imagine poured forth onto the desperate crowd of packed-in Jews. This lasted about two hours. Then, by rows and once again on the double, we had to run further through the tunnel, up the steps, and climb onto waiting trucks, which were equipped with seats, constantly under blows from whips and sticks that were part of all this. In the cars we were told: "Put on your hats and lower your heads!" Woe unto him who did not duck low enough. A blow to his head with the whip or a stick was the least he could expect. Off we went at terrible speed through the forest. After approximately a ten-minute drive the car stopped. Once again on the double, we got out and ran through a gate into a big yard, in which thousands of fellow sufferers were standing lined up in rows of ten. We were in the Buchenwald concentration camp.

It is difficult to describe the first impressions that assailed us there. The description of the violence and agitation at the Festhalle would have to be intensified by a few degrees if what must be depicted here is to be (more or less) accurate. We had not eaten anything for a long time now, and thirst was one of the worst torments that befell us, and this torment would stay with us until our release from the camp. First, all of our hair was cropped. When I looked around while this was being done, I discovered that at one spot of the square there was not one dead person, as in the Festhalle, but no less than four, lying one next to another. Over the camp loudspeaker system, which was installed in such a way that in each camp building one could hear the orders from the central office by loudspeaker, they asked whether anyone knew the dead men, since all identification had been taken away from us in Frankfurt. Immediately each one of us received a number on a slip of paper, on which we had to write our name and put this in our pocket as a means of identification. After hours of waiting, each one of us got a piece of fresh bread, and each group of ten men a container of so-called coffee. Each got a swallow, a mere drop for our parching thirst.

The entire day was spent standing around, setting up lists, taking down personal data and such. We had time to look around. We also saw the people who had arrived on the previous day and of whom we heard that they, too, had not slept, but for the most part had been forced to spend the night outdoors, since the barracks designated for us had not yet been completed. An especially large group of several thousand men was from Silesia, and all day long the names of the Silesians were called out and they were registered. Here I also heard the name of Adolf Mandowsky, without seeing him or even being able to speak with him. To give a hint of the multitude of humanity there, let me mention that in those days, as we discovered later, about 25,000 people were assembled in the camp, among them about 16,000[7] from the operation of the 9th of November alone, several thousand from Austria, who had been interned there since March, others from the June operation, and, in addition, the regular inmates of the camp—Aryans and Jews—professional criminals in security custody, sex criminals, political prisoners, those who had had sexual relations forbidden by the racial laws, and those who had evaded work. Further, there were 3,000 men from the operation in the prison in Weimar, and others in the camps of Dachau, Oranienburg, Sachsenhausen, etc., and in the many prisons of the Reich. It is not possible for me to give even roughly the total number of arrested Jews.[8] At any rate, the Buchenwald camp was not at all able to house or feed this flood of people in a fashion at least somewhat worthy of human beings, even if there had been the intention to do so. At this point I must add that enormous things were actually accomplished to meet these demands at least to some degree, and here I must express my praise and thanks to those thousands of Austrian Jews who not only gave up part of their rations so that we could have them, but also in the following nights and days spared no effort to prevent panic and to maintain calm, order, and discipline among us.

Situated on the Ettersberg near Weimar, the camp consists of two concentric rings, which are separated by barbed wire charged with electricity at night, and by the so-called death zone. The death zone is a ring about twenty meters wide that runs along the inner side of the barbed wire, the entering of which, by day or by night, is punishable by immediate execution. For this purpose, around the entire ring there stand on watch-towers sharpshooters with machine guns, who without warning shoot down anyone who enters the death zone. At night the latter, just as the entire camp, is lit bright as day by hundreds of searchlights. Entering the death zone is suicide and is also considered such by the camp administration. Many made use of it, and if at night one heard two or three brief bursts from the machine guns, one could be sure that, accordingly, the next morning one would see the corpse lying in the death zone. The ring is interrupted at several spots by closely guarded gates that lead to the outer ring. The main gate, an imposing structure that contains the administration offices, is at the same time the command headquarters of the camp. Above this gate, in all their splendor, were the words: "Right or wrong, my fatherland." Erected on the roof of the gate structure is a circle of powerful searchlights that can illuminate the gigantic square before it on the inside as bright as day, and besides, day and night there are guards with machine guns standing on the roof. The square lying inside, in front of the gate, is the parade ground, tarred and covered with pebbles, good for exercises but bad to sit on. From the vantage point of the gate, on the other side of the parade grounds, but still, of course, within the inner ring, are the barracks, the domestic offices, goods storeroom, kitchen, garden, etc. Outside the parade ground, which, in comparison to the area of the big inner ring, is small, lies forest soil; due to the dampness of the November days it had turned into a swamp, for which our street shoes were unsuitable. To the side of the parade ground, thus in the swampy area, there stood, at the time of our arrival, four temporary barracks; they were building a fifth and a sixth. Around the inner ring there runs an even far bigger outer ring, containing an SS training camp, also workshops, a tailor's, a lock-smith's, a joinery, etc. For the most part it is covered with forest and it, too, is watched all day by a chain of guards. At night the prisoners working there are brought back to the inner ring, as well as those working in the more distant quarries under supervision of SS men with guns loaded with live ammunition.

After we had stood around the whole day partly on the parade ground and partly in the swampy area, toward the evening we received food in small bowls from big portable caldrons; in fact, contrary to expectation, we got good goulash and potatoes. There were no spoons, so that we had to eat with our hands, which had not been washed for two days and looked like it. The possibility of washing one's hands in the camp did not exist, and, for most, not only on this first day but for the following weeks as well. This brings me to the greatest torment in the Buchenwald camp, the total lack of water, of which I will say more later.

Soon after the meal we were driven to the temporary barracks to rest. These temporary barracks are a different matter again. Imagine huge huts made of fir boards,

crudely nailed together, without sufficient ventilation, with only a few narrow windows
and a small door scarcely wide enough for two people abreast. On the inside these
barracks consisted essentially of shelves, something like warehouse racks, four tiers, one
above the other, the individual shelves not high enough for one to sit up on, but long
enough, or better, wide enough, for one to lie stretched out on. Here we had to lie
down, without a straw sack, without a blanket, on the bare wood, in the clothes that
we were wearing when we were pulled off the street. As latrine there served a space
directly next to the death zone, a huge dug-out ditch with a pole across it, thus a latrine
of a rather dubious quality, everything constructed poorly and in haste. This latrine
could be used only before the barracks were locked; it was forbidden on penalty of death
to leave the barrack during the night. I immediately climbed to the top tier in the
barrack, where one could at least sit up, and, dead tired I lay down, already quite tightly
wedged in among others; but sleep was impossible. The hard bed, thirst, dust, and the
noise made sleep impossible. Scarcely were we lying down when again columns of our
fellow sufferers were squeezed into the barrack and, at all costs, also had to have a place
to lie down. Lying on one's back became an impossibility. Whenever room was not
made voluntarily by everyone turning on his side and lying close like sardines, the whip
helped things along. Soon lying also became torture. One did not know what to do
with one's arms; one could not turn, the air became stifling, the noise insufferable.

And then came a new, common agony. A large part of the prisoners, certainly far
more than half, suddenly got diarrhea. No one was allowed to get up or go out. The
moaning of the men afflicted by abdominal pains filled the room, and soon thereupon
there was an almost unbearable stench from those who had gotten it and who could
not help but relieve themselves right then and there in their pants. Be it that I had
refused the bread and ate it dry only on the following day, or be it for other reasons,
I, at any rate, was spared this plague. That night the despair of the poor people grew
beyond imagining. Piercing screams resounded through the room, coming from those
who were no longer in control of their nerves and who gave expression to their pain
like animals. Here and there one jumped up and tried to escape from the barrack. Only
some of those who tried this could be held back by force. And, perceptible only to our
ears, each time the following took place: First a rush around the barrack, screams of
fear of a man being pursued, screams of pain of a man being beaten, wilder and wilder,
and then slowly becoming weaker and weaker until they finally died down in a whimper.
We assumed that everyone whose screams we heard found their death, and even today
I still do not know whether this was the case. Later we heard from comrades who lay
near doors and windows that others were dragged outside by force and then suffered
the same fate. During the night some threw themselves down from the highest tier of
the shelf with suicidal intent, others, again, tried to pray loudly, to cry, to give speeches
and call upon everyone at least to go to their deaths together. The madhouse scene from
*Peer Gynt* came into my mind, but the horror was nothing compared to what confronted
us during that night.

Before lying down we were told that anyone found in possession of a lighter would
be immediately shot, and also, since there was no water, if fire broke out it could be
extinguished only with machine guns; and we had no illusions that this was an empty
threat. And then, on this night, one man, whose senses had left him completely, got

up, left the barrack, and dashed around outside, shouting with all his might: "Out, comrades, out! You're lost, they are setting fire to our barracks!" Next to me lay a seventeen-year-old boy who along with others had been driven out of a *Hachshara* in Upper Silesia. He jumped up, and with him many others. With a firm grip I pulled him back onto his bed and I succeeded in calming him. One way or the other we are in the hands of the Philistines; whether we die by fire or a machinegun bullet need not matter to us, but now, a panic of over 2,000 people in a room whose door allows only two at a time to get out, and then only to certain death, would have been the greatest stupidity and our certain end. The danger of a panic was at this moment the greatest, and here it was thanks only to the brave among us and the Viennese Jews, who supervised things inside the barrack, that a bigger disaster did not occur.

This night, too, came to an end. In the morning we went out, and only now did it become clear in what a hell we had landed. Around the latrine were standing hundreds, trying to clean their underwear and clothes. No water, not a drop of water with which to rid oneself of one's own excrement. No animal lives without cleansing itself, and for that we lacked the bare necessities. Packed together, the thousands of Jews stood up to their ankles in the quagmire, dirty, haggard, a picture of misery—doctors, lawyers, scholars, people with the highest level of education, treated worse than the worst cattle. And there were sick people among them, for whom we feared. There was no medical help, there were no medications, there was not even water to quench the parching thirst that this hell had produced. — On this morning I ran into a group of friends and people from my town. Jacob Oppenheimer, Fritz Marx (Sonnenbergerstrasse), Berthold Guthmann,[9] Max Liebmann, Paul Rothbart, and there, in the middle of the quagmire, in the middle of the crowd, a man lay on the ground: Dr. Fackenheim. We from Wiesbaden gathered around him in order to prevent anyone from kicking him, and the only help I could bring him was a bottle of mouthwash that I had in my pocket, a refreshment with which to moisten one's parched lips and the peppermint scent of which one could breathe in. Immediately hands were stretched out all around me, also wanting to get hold of a few drops of the precious liquid. I dispensed it until there were just a few drops in the bottle, which I wanted to save as a precaution for even more urgent situations.

Then the order came to line up. We took the physician Dr. Fackenheim, who had been weakened by diarrhea, under his arms, Jacob Oppenheimer on the right, I on the left, and thus we lined up. Slowly the good doctor recovered and could at least stand on his own again, and we stood for a long time. For hours and hours the one command resounded: "Fall in!" By the thousands we stood there in open ranks; here and there someone collapsed, debilitated by diarrhea, hunger, thirst, and the sleepless night. The words "A doctor!" went from mouth to mouth, and good Dr. Fackenheim, who could scarcely hold himself up, ran with the last drops of my mouthwash as the sole refreshment, as the only medication, from one place to another until that, too, was harshly forbidden him. We stood like that for four hours, and then came the order "Sit down," and we sat in rank and file with our legs drawn up for another four hours, in our civilian clothes, on the pebbles of the parade ground, favored by no one but the weather, for the sun was shining. During these four hours we received food and drink. The food was good. This time we even got spoons, but there was much too little to drink and there was not enough to quench even the worst of our thirst. No one was allowed to go relieve himself. Diarrhea was still raging and Fackenheim, next to me, had to do moaningly what he could not avoid doing. Then someone came like a sleepwalker through the ranks and sat down next to me, right in the middle of the straight ranks. It was Julius Kahn, a man of over sixty, who already some time ago had lived through a serious illness and who begged me urgently to go with him to the gate. His wife was out there with a car, he said, and wanted to fetch him. The old man was no longer in control of his senses; he did not know that no civilian could get near the gate, but rather would have had to wait many kilometers beyond it. He spoke insanely. With great effort we prevailed upon him to return to his place; on his way there, he fell into the hands of an SS man and we saw how the old, confused man received a terrible slap from the young snot. I did not see him again; a few days later he died in the camp.

This day, too, passed; again we went back to the temporary barracks, and again there followed a night like the first; and if it was not quite as alarming, it was still no less torturous. New prisoners had arrived, among them a group from the Bergstrasse with a twelve-year old boy. People who had been driven from house and home. The camp director, a man wearing the Blood Order, gave us the following speech: "The rumor will not subside that you are badly put up here. I shall accommodate you better." And now about 1,000 men of our group, I also among them, were separated and outfitted. It was a blessing to be allowed to take off our dirty civilian clothes, which were taken from us. We received army boots, socks, linen underwear, and a striped prisoner's suit with cap, and were taken out of the temporary barracks and housed in the regular camp barracks. But only about 1,000 men. The many other thousands remained in the temporary barracks, remained in their dirty civilian clothes, and even if, as I was told, gradually more order came into their lives, they remained the whole time without water to wash with and without the possibility of satisfying even the most urgent hygienic needs. We who had been outfitted could not talk to them anymore. A wire fence separated us from them. But we saw them daily standing by the wire fence, from day to day more squalid, with growing beards, a terrible picture; and the rage at this baseness, which turned human beings into animals, made us clench our fists in our pockets. Our lot, that of those who had been outfitted, had changed. Each one of us received a straw sack or two straw sacks for three people, each one two blankets, and from now on our lives went on in a more military fashion, even if with much harassment and brutality from our immediate supervisors, the senior block inmates, who themselves were Aryan prisoners, and from the SS, the masters and tyrants of the camp. Let me not speak of the insulting speeches that they had for us, of the punishments that were inflicted for minor offences, for the least insubordination, for a few words. To stand a whole day with one's face turned to the wall may be a nuisance, to stand with raised arms tied to the wall is a torture that was already known to the Inquisition. Flogging of all degrees is a custom practiced daily. The poor person who, strapped to a sawbuck, has to put up with twenty-five blows from a long stick on his bare rear can neither sit nor lie for weeks, and that is not even the most severe punishment. I had to watch such torture frequently, and I shall never forget that either.

The days passed and no one knew what was to happen with us. No one knew what was happening with his wife and children on the outside. Slowly a prison psychosis set in, and it was necessary again and again to encourage this one or that one in order to keep him from desperation. When we saw our fellow sufferers from the temporary barracks, how they slowly became seedy, stood around without a collar, without a shirt, bearded, and dirty, then our lot seemed the better one, for now at least almost daily we could wash our face and hands once, and we had a regulated life, even if not a pleasant one. At five o'clock in the morning we were awakened. Getting dressed, making beds, getting coffee, and occasionally getting washed, that is, if there was water, took place within the barrack, whose dayroom was heated. Then, at six o'clock we lined up on the parade ground. In thin clothing, in rain and morning fog, that was something that one had first to get used to. From seven to eleven exercising, occasionally also working, but not hard, then drawing rations outside, in front of the barracks, then an hour's break in which one did what one wanted, then again three hours of exercising, gymnastics, etc. At five o'clock general muster, then an evening meal—mostly, to be sure, a very meager one—in the form of a little piece of cheese or sausage, eaten inside the barrack. Then until about eight o'clock a free hour, in which one could sit in the day room of the barrack convivially, to the extent that there was still a place left for sitting. Here we could even be shaved.

This report would never come to an end if I wanted to convey the many lesser and greater tortures to which we were subjected, for example, that as punishment for badly made beds we had to stand all night in front of the beds without sleep, and during the night had to make beds. One person went around and again and again undid the made bed so that it could be made anew. The ancient Greeks, too, must have known this type of punishment. At any rate, today no one can tell me any more how it was with Tantalus and Sisyphus, or in Egypt or in Spain.[10] I experienced it all myself. Worst of all were the nights in which I could not sleep. For I did not know whether Maas had escaped across the border, or what happened at my firm. I had the notion that something was being pinned on me and that I, be it as a hostage or for other reasons, would never again get out of this hell alive.

Slowly the discharges began: at first people over sixty and under eighteen, and people who had their emigration papers complete or who were summoned to appear soon at the American consulate in Stuttgart. We, however, stayed and stayed. [End of fragment.]

1. Ernst vom Rath, secretary at the German Embassy in Paris, was shot on November 7, 1938, by seventeen-year-old Herschel Grynszpan and died two days later. Grynszpan's parents were among the Polish Jews who were forcibly deported from Germany at the end of October. The death of vom Rath served as a pretext for the pogrom of 9/10 November 1938.

2. The German Labor Front was the National Socialist compulsory organization for employers and employees. Its administrators functioned as trustees; in the factories and in Jewish firms they often were informers and instruments of "Aryanization."

3. Dr. Bernhard Rosenthal (1881–1938) was chief of the gynecological department of the Israelitisches Krankenhaus in Frankfurt am Main.

4. In connection with the closing and dissolution of the B'nai B'rith lodges and the seizure of their assets on April 1937, individual lodge presidents were temporarily arrested.

5. Dr. Max Liebmann was a member of the executive body of the Israelitische Kultusgemeinde in Wiesbaden, and later emigrated to London.

6. Prayer shawl.

7. This number is too high. Of those arrested during the pogrom (according to Kogon) 9,815 were imprisoned in Buchenwald, where there already were about 900 Jews, who had been arrested in June 1938 as so-called asocials.

8. The exact number is unknown; today it is estimated that 26,000–35,000 people were arrested during the pogrom.

9. Berthold Guthmann, lawyer and CV chairman in Wiesbaden, was the last chairman of the Jewish community until 1943, when he was deported from Wiesbaden to Theresienstadt and was murdered in Auschwitz.

10. Allusion to the slavery of the Jews in ancient Egypt, and to their persecution by the Spanish Inquisition in the fifteenth century.

# 44  *Alfred Schwerin*

 BORN IN 1892 IN BUCHEN (BADEN); DIED IN 1977 IN CINCINNATI, OHIO.

Alfred Schwerin, Remembrances from Dachau to Basel. Manuscript, dated Basel, 1944, 236 pages; Appendix: Letters from Gurs to the author, 20 pages.

*Alfred Schwerin, son of the teacher of the Jewish community in Buchen (Odenwald), was apprenticed at Schiff's leather goods store in Frankfurt. As a frontline soldier in the First World War, he was wounded several times. Until 1923 Alfred Schwerin was employed by the Schiff firm; then he married, settled in Pirmasens as a leather salesman, and after 1937 lived alone with his daughter, as a widower. During the pogrom in November 1938 he was arrested and taken to the concentration camp of Dachau. After his release he assumed the office of community secretary of the Jewish community in Pirmasens. In the spring of 1939 his ten-year-old daughter was able to emigrate to France with a children's transport. At the beginning of the war the Jews of Pirmasens, which was near the border, were evacuated and Schwerin continued to fulfill his office out of Ludwigshafen. In March 1940 a Gestapo official sent him illegally across the border into Switzerland. From 1940 to 1948 he lived in Basel and then he emigrated with his daughter to the United States. He settled in Cincinnati, where he worked in the office of a shoe firm.*

In Dachau there was a small number of Austrians among us Palatines in Block 18. It was from them that I heard for the first time the derisive and abusive nickname "Piefke," used in Austria for the Germans from the Reich, and applied in the concentration camp of Dachau, of all places, to their fellow Jews from the German Reich. Mostly, the maliciously used word was uttered during drills, in the course of which we often fell into disarray because the Austrians did not keep in step. On the one hand, the result was that it was very difficult to march, and on the other, that there was the danger of being harassed by the Block Leader or by the supervising SS. We were angry about the Austrians, who, in turn, were infuriated about us, because according to them we were playing the Prussian militarists, something, however, that was very far from our minds.

While for me, as I have said, this pronounced difference between Germans and Austrians among Jews in such a situation was surprising and incomprehensible in the extreme, I found most sickening the thefts of bread and other food within our community of deprivation. Certainly, among thousands of people there are always some depraved individuals who will not allow anything to stand in the way of their inborn selfish or even criminal inclinations and actions. Still, for all those affected it was repulsive and disconcerting to find themselves forced to hide at night the bit of bread, synthetic honey, or whatever else they had bought at the canteen, in the straw of their sleeping space so that the next morning they would not have to search vainly for these things in their unlockable chests.

These thefts were something that our Aryan Senior Block and Room Inmates observed uncomprehendingly and that cost us much sympathy and, in many instances, all respect. They, the Aryan inmates, who had been there for years because of their political convictions, who knew why they were holding out and clenching their teeth, formed a spiritual and comradely elite, which was united by a common idea, a common goal, and in which each took responsibility for the other and shared all with his comrade-in-struggle. That one of us, as I myself experienced, refused out of greed to lend another a postage stamp for the letter to his family seemed incomprehensible to them, and justifiably so. They simply believed that being a Jew united us in the same way as, for better or worse, their avowal of socialism or communism united them. As regards the majority of German and Austrian Jews at that time, however, this was a false assumption in every respect, since, if for no other reason, many of them no longer had any inner or external relationship to the Jewish religion and Jewish community and were forcibly returned to it only by Hitler and National Socialism—often against their own will and conviction.

Because of these thefts and nightly quarrels about blankets, as well as similar incidents, our Block Leader often reached such a peak of rage that he unjustly called all of us, without exception, scoundrels and criminals, and sometimes beat individuals as if he were one of the SS. Matters even reached the point where for the least little reason he made us do punitive exercises or, when all the other blocks had already gone inside, he had us squat in front of the barracks, even in the rain. If our Senior Room Inmate had not sometimes intervened and let him know that he mustn't treat his fellow prisoners that way, it could have become dangerous. To be sure, one must make allowances for him, because like many of those imprisoned since 1933, he was at the end of his nerves and no doubt had the so-called camp madness. Besides, he had already been waiting for weeks for the discharge that had been promised him and thus was in a barely endurable state of tension. On the other hand, he possessed the extraordinary decency to virtually force bread and butter from his provisions upon one of our orthodox rabbis, who, whenever there was pork, never wanted to eat anything, and he did not give up until the pious man was more or less full.

Our Senior Room Inmate proved himself outstandingly. I don't know if he was a Social Democrat or a communist. At any rate, he had been imprisoned since 1933. Many an evening, after eight-thirty, when the light was turned off and we lay on our straw mats, this exemplary human being and comrade came to us, at his own risk, despite the existing prohibition, gave us advice on how to behave, pointed out important matters, comforted us, and gave new courage to the hopeless. He was a simple laborer and probably a minor party functionary, but a human being of such steadfast and honest basic convictions, of such clear mind and noble character as one rarely encounters. Unfortunately, I have forgotten his name.

It is eerie when at night one's sleep is disrupted and in the middle of the room; which is half-lit by the lights outside and by the circling of the searchlights, a figure arises and, mentally confused by all he has experienced, begins in a monotonous voice to recite Kaddish, that prayer that all believing Jews say every year in memory of dead family members on the anniversary of their passing. Or when in the washroom a desperate person—who according to strict orders was not to be prevented by us from carrying out his intention, nor taken down by us after death had occurred—hanged himself, and from barrack to barrack, through the silence everywhere, the cry of the Senior Block Inmate resounds to notify the guard at the camp entrance. It is not possible to do it in another way, since there is no telephone and anyone who leaves the barrack at night is shot at with no further ado. Many a person to whom life here became an unbearable burden made use of the prohibition to put an end to himself by running out of the barrack into the fire of the machine-gun towers.

*[After five weeks Alfred Schwerin is discharged from Dachau.]*

Dachau and the experiences prior to and following it brought home to me with extraordinary urgency that it was high time to turn my back on Germany. Above all, my daughter Ellen had to go if there was no possibility for both of us to emigrate together.

Until the year 1937 I had never seriously occupied myself with this problem. There were many reasons for that. In the first place, I had neither relatives nor friends abroad who could have helped me. Furthermore, since 1933 the request had been made again and again by the competent Jewish agencies that as long as one still had the possibility to earn wages and make a living one should stand back and give priority to the young people as well as those coreligionists who for political or economic reasons absolutely had to get out of the Reich. In 1937, however, I became more and more convinced that it would be best to quit the land, which increasingly was becoming inhospitable, as soon as possible. Since, on the one hand, however, I saw no legal way for myself and, on the other hand, was hesitant to flee illegally with Ellen, I signed up the child for a children's transport to America, in order to get her out of the danger zone in this way. This step was by no means easy for me. Ellen, too, at first could not reconcile herself to the idea. Only the gravity of the ensuing events had gradually caused her to change her mind. But time was passing and there was no sign of a transport. America behaved exactly as did all the other big countries with immense settlement areas and sufficient means to help everyone in distress and to save them. Indeed, things reached a stage where the more the National Socialist pressure against its opponents within and the Jews increased, and the more they were persecuted, the more hermetically sealed did the gates become on which they were knocking in vain. [. . .]

After my return from Dachau, still other reasons than the aforementioned ones impelled me to tend to Ellen's departure in a hurry. For I noticed more from day to day how very much the child was suffering under such conditions and how her disposition was darkening. One incident was especially indicative. One evening I was about to go to the third floor to chat some with the people upstairs. For the first time Ellen objected and begged: "Don't go up, stay with me!" Never had she done that; she had always peacefully fallen asleep when I went away for a visit. The unaccustomed tone and the serious expression on her face puzzled me. Since she would not admit why I should not leave her alone, I stayed and also went to bed, about which she was very happy. "Now tell me why I shouldn't go away," I inquired. She did not give me a straight answer, but rather, looking fixedly at the ceiling, said: "If we die, let us die together." For a moment my heart stopped. This child was nine years and ten months old! Then I said to her: "We must not think of death but of life, Ellen! It would suit the others just fine if we despaired and gave up. No, we must gather all our strength and remain strong and have confidence in ourselves. We owe it to ourselves and all those who are in the same situation as we. If we do that, somehow it will work out. And we still have the dear Lord, too. Didn't I always know during the last war that I would return home? Didn't I predict to you my return from Dachau? Soon you will go with a transport somewhere to another country. Perhaps there will be a war again and we will remain separated for years. It doesn't matter what comes, just believe that we will see one another again! And then things will become better once more. We don't want to die together but rather master life together!" "Do you think that the transport will leave soon, Papa?" "Of course, child!" "Oh, I would be so glad!" Her attitude toward emigration had changed thoroughly. Now she could scarcely wait to get away.

A few days after this conversation the Jewish aid organization in Ludwigshafen inquired whether it was all right with me if Ellen were assigned to a transport to France or Holland. Naturally I said yes, for my watchword was, with no qualifications: Out at any cost! And then, on March 4, 1939, we received the important document that said that departure for France was scheduled for March 8th. Ellen jumped with joy when I read it to her. A dear Christian acquaintance insisted on taking care of the child's clothes and underwear. Thereupon Ellen and I did the necessary shopping together. [. . .]

On the next morning the train took us to Kaiserslautern. The express train from Ludwigshafen, with which the others came, arrived two hours later. Thus we had a lot of time left and we went back and forth chatting in the station concourse, for entry to the waiting halls was forbidden to Jews. Later, Ellen sat beside me on the suitcase, serious and pale, and I saw how she was pondering. Suddenly she said: "Papa, if you need the ten marks that you gave me as travel money"—to give more was not permitted by the currency regulations—"then take them back. I don't need them!" The good girl was worried because in her eyes I had spent so much money for new things. "No, child, keep the few marks. I really don't need them. But you know what, we almost forgot the blessing! Come, let's go back there in the corner, by the pay scale; we won't attract attention there." "Oh yes!" She jumped up and we went together to that spot. There I placed my hands on her head and quietly spoke the ancient Jewish blessing: "God bless you like Sarah, Rebecca, Rachel, and Leah!" Then I kissed her. "Now luck will always be with me!" Ellen rejoiced and looked at me with bright eyes.

Finally, we were standing on the platform. We looked silently in the direction from which the train was rushing towards us. I didn't dare say a word. But when the train was already very close, Ellen turned to me, with a determined start and cried out laughing: "But Papa, do say adieu to me!" I knew, and also noted, with what unbelievable energy she forced this smile, and I felt a lump in my throat. But I also smiled and kissed her and said: "Farewell child, stay healthy, and auf Wiedersehen!" Ellen kissed me again, once more gave me her hand, and then got into the train. For a few moments she stood at the window and looked at me. Suddenly, she turned and disappeared in the background. It was all over with her composure. Immediately after that the train left, and I went back to Pirmasens alone.

*[In the spring of 1939 Alfred Schwerin becomes secretary of the Jewish community of Pirmasens.]*

The head of the community, Karl Hahn, and I worked in our office daily from eight-thirty in the morning until six in the evening, except on Saturday and Sunday. Often it was even much later because there was more than enough work. As the only office where our coreligionists of the city and state districts could receive information and aid, the little room was often crowded with people seeking counsel and help.[1] We received all new decrees pertaining to Jews either directly from the authorities and the Gestapo, or through the umbrella organization in Berlin created by the government, the Reichsvereinigung der Juden in Deutschland. This organization was primarily responsible for properly transmitting and carrying out the laws on the Jews and was subject to special supervision by the Gestapo.

Above all, the Reichsvereinigung organized emigration and also the support of the constantly growing number of persons without means, and attended to cultural concerns. Among other things, it regularly had theater performances and concerts organized in the big cities by Jewish artists who had lost their livelihood, and assembled touring groups for the provinces.[2] For attendance at state as well as city cultural institutions was forbidden to Jews throughout the Reich. Expert lectures on pertinent topics such as the possibilities of emigration to various countries or the current situation in Palestine came about in this way. At all of these events only Jewish matters were allowed to be discussed, and only literature and music produced by Jews were to be presented. The presentation of "Aryan" art was permitted reluctantly, even if the subject was purely Jewish. Every program required the express permission of the responsible department head at the Reich government office, Hans Hinkel,[3] who presided over the monitoring headquarters. In addition, each program had to be submitted to the local police, who usually assigned one or two detectives to monitor the performances.

Since many books and documents had been destroyed during the November pogrom, we had no choice but to rebuild the administrative apparatus. Aid for the needy had to be organized, schooling for the remaining thirty children had to be taken care of, and living quarters had to be provided. The work was made more difficult for us in many respects, because all cash in the bank and other deposits of the community were blocked, and for every withdrawal we had first to wait for written permission from the official party economic advisor.

After the synagogue went up in flames in November, we tried from the start to get permission to regularly hold services at the apartment of a community member.

Finally, we did receive permission, but with the reservation that we announce every service beforehand to the police.

The emigration problem demanded our greatest labors. We registered children and adults with the emigration aid agencies, filled out the endless questionnaires, wrote testimonials, and took care of providing funds for the journey and the purchases needed for it. This often entailed quite considerable sums. For instance, the departure from Germany of a family of four, the transportation of its furniture as well as its agricultural equipment overseas, involved significant costs. The Reichsvereinigung did not approve immediately and readily, because it wanted to help as many people as possible and tried to avoid spending too great an amount for any one case.

Individual persons, too, now and then demanded disproportionately high sums. A young man from Pirmasens, for instance, who had served a one-and-one-half-year prison term because of sexual relations with a non-Jew could be saved from the concentration camp only by disappearing from Germany within three days of his release—as the Gestapo always demanded in such cases. No sort of visa could be obtained for him. After many unsuccessful attempts there remained only the alternative of sending him with a steamship that happened to be docked in Triest to Shanghai, the only place in the world where one could still land without a visa. But since steerage and the second-class cabins were sold out, we bought, for better or worse, a first-class ticket for more than two thousand marks—after we had fought a hard battle down to the last moment for the approval of the funds.

Considering the haste with which everything had to be taken care of, and in view of other difficulties that had arisen—at the instigation of the Gestapo, the police had already arrested the young man again on the afternoon of the third day—there wasn't even time for us to get our protégé decent underwear and clothes. He began his journey to the other side of the world with an old, shabby suitcase with even shabbier contents, and on his departure said jokingly that he felt a bit creepy in the presence of the stewards, who would surely take him for a porter and not for a passenger in the first class. [ . . .]

That in such circumstances contact with the Christian population decreased more and more, and especially relationships with previously friendly families also ceased, goes without saying. Spying on and threatening of friends of Jews assumed ever greater dimensions. Finally, we voluntarily broke off our relations with the most loyal ones, since we wanted to spare them any unpleasantness. Besides, it also caused bitter feelings when again and again one experienced how a man who only yesterday had cordially shaken one's hand today passed one by like a stranger, or sent a letter to one's home asking one not to greet him any more and not to enter his apartment, because he had been threatened by the party with fitting reprisals if he did not give up his relations with Jews.

Thus, social life was restricted entirely to visits from Jewish acquaintances. One conversed, played chess or cards, and listened to the radio. [ . . .] But when one met in Jewish company, it meant mostly that there was not the slightest relaxation, because every last person had either his own unpleasant experience or some sort of ill tidings to report from somewhere else.

I tried to counter this oppressive and in the long run unnerving situation by undertaking long hikes on Sundays if conditions and the weather permitted. I put on my knapsack, as I was used to doing from the good old days, and early in the morning rode out to a station in the Western Palatine, from where I climbed through the wide forests up to the mountain tops or strolled through the pleasant vineyards. Here I had the advantage over my coreligionsts, who scarcely dared to leave the house for a walk any more, and it kept me strong. As in the most peaceful times, I sat evenings on the terrace of the castle among cheerful people, drank my wine, and conversed with them uninhibitedly. In this way, I not only sharpened my eye but also saved myself from being swallowed up by apathy and hopeless despondency. And quite often I felt the urge to laugh when my table companions, frequently with the party badge on their lapels, against the background of the many castle ruins crowning the surrounding heights, listened attentively to my lectures on German legend and history, drank to my health, and bid farewell with a respectful "Heil Hitler!" [. . .]

However, on my hikes there were also very specific things that could affect my mood for the moment or make me boil inside, for instance signs placed by order of the party at the entrances to all localities, the prohibition signs at the restaurants, the *Stürmer* display cases, and now and then conversations I overheard. At the main entrances of almost all towns there stood or hung large boards with messages baiting Jews. The most innocuous read: "Jews are unwelcome here!" or "No Jews allowed!" But many Nazis used this opportunity to vent their intellectual and poetic talents. The entrance to the town of Dahn, for example, was decked out with the following words: "If you don't know about the Jews, you'll soon be stripped down to your shoes." In order to discourage Jewish traveling salesmen, Pirmasens had put up a banner above the junction of Zeppelinstrasse with the following inscription: "This is not the road to Palestine!" In Edenkoben it was impressed upon the hiker that the Jews were for humanity what fleas are for a dog. One could find such creations of the intellect by the thousands everywhere in the streets of Germany.

It was much the same with the signs at restaurants and cafés. The owners were compelled to put up the sign: "Jews are unwanted here" on the door or window. Here, too, there were people who tried to shine with their miserable wit and imagination. In Karlsruhe, for example, after much searching I found a café where no sign was to be seen. However, when I closed the outside door behind me, right in front of my nose on the revolving door stood the words: "Juda, back out!"

In the smallest village, at one or several main intersections, there were the *Stürmer* display cases, which always bore the same inscription: "The Jews are our misfortune!" They contained the weekly paper *Der Stürmer,* published by the infamous regional governor Julius Streicher. It was the playground of all the pornographic and sadistic minds of the Third Reich who felt that somehow they had to express their boundless hatred of the Jews in writing. With each issue *Der Stürmer* produced a lasting, igno-minious document of the spiritual and cultural decay of Hitler's Germany and of the crude and brutal mentality that was being implanted into the masses by the party. The articles as well as the pictures abounded in a vile, very dangerous, and unsurpassable incitement against the Jews. Special issues in red print called outright for pogroms. The newspaper contained a regular column of denouncements, with letters from all over the Reich, whose senders claimed to know that in such and such a place a fellow German, whose name was given, was still associating with Jews.

*[At the beginning of the war the Jews are evacuated from Pirmasens, which is near the border. Alfred Schwerin moves the community office to Ludwigshafen.]*

Naturally, the outbreak of the war gave the regime a new opportunity and a new pretext for further oppression and disfranchisement of the Jews. Often they were branded as enemies of the German people, and as spies and helpers of the Allies. They were not allowed to go out after eight o'clock in the evening. In some places it was even forbidden for Jewish families who lived on different floors of the same building to visit one another after this hour. It was forbidden to speak with members of the army. The railway station could not be entered without identification. In some places Jews had to get the permission of the police to leave the city limits.

At the rations offices the ration cards for Jews were issued at separate counters. The cards bore the red stamp "Jew," to inform the merchant in advance of the shopper's racial identity. All coupons for extra rations, as well as those for legumes, were invalidated. The afternoon hours from two to three-thirty were established as the shopping time for Jews. As much as possible, Aryans were supposed to stay away from the stores during this time so that they would not come into contact with Jews. Often, desirable goods were already sold out early in the morning, so that the Jewish housewife had to return home in the afternoon without the wares she had wanted. But there were decent business people everywhere who did not abandon their longstanding Jewish customers and often put aside for them more than the quantity to which they were entitled. I, too, always got almost twice the meat and sausage ration from a woman from Pirmasens who was working at a butcher shop in Mannheim.

With time, the problem of clothing became serious, for we received no coupons for textiles or shoes. We also did not get permission to have our shoes resoled. Only darning yarn was allotted us once every three months, but—would you believe it!—for no more than twenty reichspfennigs. For this reason the communities set up collection centers for clothes and shoes early on, and saw to it that especially those who were emigrating donated part of their supplies to their coreligionists who stayed behind.

During the month of October 1939, I went to Frankfurt to pick up my suitcase on Dahlmannstrasse. To my astonishment, my reception there—in contrast to the kind one that had been extended to me by the daughter of the house a few weeks earlier—was one of the most disgraceful things that happened to me in Germany throughout the entire Hitler period. I had been close friends with this family for thirty-one years. I was the godfather of one son, who was then twenty-five. When my friend and I said goodbye to one another on the first mobilization day in the year 1914, he had embraced me emotionally, had said I should call him "Du," and had asked me to look after his wife and children in case he did not return. Since then we had stuck together in perfect friendship.

Now, as I was going up the stairs to the apartment, my friend, who had just come from the cellar and saw me from above, hurried ahead of me without giving a sign of greeting and alerted his family. His wife asked me from a distance to wait for them in the living room. As I was walking past the kitchen, through the crack of the door I saw the sons and the sons-in-law hide behind the door and move closer together in order not to be seen by me or have to greet me. Then, after a few minutes, the couple, greatly embarrassed, came into the room where I was, and for the moment they were unable to utter a word, although we hadn't spoken with one another for a long time. Also, neither one of the two had the courage to ask me to sit down. Finally, they reported that they had already taken the luggage to the station, supposedly to make it easier for me to transport it; but probably the truth was that out of cowardly fear they had no longer wanted to store Jewish property. Also, from a remark I had to conclude that they had gone through the suitcases to see for themselves that they did not contain any suspicious objects.

To get over the unpleasant situation, my former friend now began to lament that the Germans were now suffering for the misdeeds of the Nazis against the Jews, and his wife declared moaningly that she would take poison if her boys had to go to the front. All the while they hurried back and forth excitedly, without figuring out how to tell me to disappear from the scene as soon as possible. Without saying a word, I observed this sickening spectacle and intentionally did not leave right away, because I did not want to make the couple's wretched role too easy for them. After I had finally taken my leave, I once again could not come to grips with the fact that these last years could have changed the Germans so much.

*[Alfred Schwerin has the following experience in January* 1940, *after a birthday celebration of the families Sauer and Strauss in Ludwigshafen.]*

While I was saying goodbye to the guests, the bell in the hallway rang. Immediately thereupon the host was called from the room. Frau Sauer, who had followed him out of curiosity, returned right away with the muted cry of dismay: "Two policemen are outside!" In total distraction she reached for a plate with nut shells and orange peels that was sitting on a table, and with a hurried, nervous motion she senselessly placed it on the sideboard next to her. Inge, whose birthday it was and who until then had been so happy, cried out loudly, the faces of the guests changed color, and for a moment everyone sat or stood as if petrified. To be sure, the men, after overcoming the initial shock, tried desperately to pick up the thread of the conversation, which had suddenly broken off, and to act as if they attributed no significance to the incident. But the eyes of the women—restlessly wavering, questioning, and wandering back and forth—showed how cruelly one was once again torn from the illusion of a normal middle-class existence, and that one felt suddenly transported into present reality with its barbarity and law-lessness. That more and more each day the Jew was becoming fair game was the devastating realization that underscored every experience of this kind and threatened to turn life into an endless hell. The agonies of the parents, who feared for the future of their children with growing concern and trembling heart, already at that time reached the limits of the endurable.

Once again there was also a crass incongruity between cause and effect. The girl had left the light on in a room that had inadvertently not been blacked out. The policemen had noticed it from the street and had come up in order to point it out. They were satisfied with the explanation that Strauss gave them for the sin of omission. Nevertheless, the older of the two did feel obligated to check the dining room, where the frightened guests were, in order to see for himself that the Jews there were indeed having a small celebration and were not holding a secret gathering threatening to the state. However, when in the expressions of those sitting frozen in silence he read the panic that his unexpected appearance had triggered, he himself became embarrassed to a degree and, without making any further trouble, he and his colleague left.

There were people who drew the right conclusions from such and other incidents and their psychic effects. They saw in them proof of how very much every one of them felt himself at the mercy of the whims of the state and on what perilous ground they were obviously standing. They recognized that with each day it was becoming more urgent to escape from this chaos and to find a way across the border. But because one wasn't immediately placed in a concentration camp for such a paltry offense during a blackout or because a policeman smiled kindly, there were others who concluded that all of the bad times had taken a turn for the better and from then on the sun of National Socialist favor would also shine upon the Jews. Again and again one encountered such foolish people, who pulled the wool over their own eyes and imagined that because for two or three months there had been no special operation against the Jews, one did not have to reckon with any further deterioration of one's own situation and had to regard the present state as the basis on which, for the time being, one had to plan one's future existence. In their stupidity, they worried amazingly little about how they were to accomplish this in the long run, considering that all gainful employment was forbidden.

For these and, of course, also other reasons it came about that of the entire birthday group I was the only one to escape deportation, thanks to a timely departure. All the others, together with all the Jews from the Palatinate and Baden, 6,500 in number, were taken in the fall of the same year [1940] to the ill-famed concentration camps in southern France.[4]

*[In March 1940 Alfred Schwerin illegally crosses the Swiss border.]*

1. The secretariat of the community of Pirmasens, according to Schwerin's accounts, took care of some three hundred Jews from the municipal and rural administrative district.
2. This took place through the Jewish cultural associations that existed in Berlin and other cities, in part until 1941. See Kurt Baumann (42).
3. On Hans Hinkel, see Baumann (42), note 3.
4. On the deportations from Baden and the Palatinate to southern France, on October 22nd and 23rd, 1940, see Miriam Gerber (47).

# 45 *Michael Meyer*

 BORN IN 1881 IN BLANKENBURG; DIED IN 1956 IN BERLIN.

Michael Meyer, A Journey to Eretz Israel in the Year 1940. Manuscript dated August 1941, Tel Aviv; 22 pages.

*Michael Meyer, son of a lottery entrepreneur in Blankenburg in the Harz, grew up in a religiously traditional family, attended the Gymnasium, and studied law.*

*During his internship in Magdeburg, under the influence of his friendship with Arthur Ruppin (later the director of settlement work in Palestine) he turned to Zionism. In 1909 Meyer settled in Berlin as a lawyer and specialized in matters relating to the metal trade, real estate, and rentals. As a frontline soldier of the First World War, he did not have to give up his practice until November 1938. Starting in 1939 he worked in an honorary capacity in the Palestine Office in Berlin, which was in charge of emigration to Palestine. When the latter became more and more difficult, especially after the start of the war, illegal transports to Palestine were organized with the approval of the Gestapo. In August of 1940, Meyer left Berlin with the last of these transports from Germany, and survived the explosion of the* Patria *in the harbor of Haifa. He became an official in the mandate government. Starting in 1952 he was active as a reparations lawyer and died on an official trip to Berlin. He was buried in Israel.*

I decided to make *aliya* in July 1938, immediately after the laws on the exclusion of the Jews from economic life had been passed.[1] I recognized in this act a radical change and also anticipated that Jews would soon be excluded from practicing law. Since genuine capitalist certificates[2] for Palestine were already difficult to obtain in the normal way, I turned to a source that, as I knew from my experience as a lawyer, procured or negotiated capitalist certificates from Basel in exchange for payment of certain sums. Until then this method had always worked smoothly.

*[Despite payment of 2,000 reichsmarks, Michael Meyer does not receive a certificate, because as a result of the November pogrom, the demand increased enormously.]*

Nothing came of the certificate. In the meantime the new war had broken out, and even many of those to whom *regular* certificates had been issued or were a certainty were left behind after the English consulates in Germany had been closed. Apart from very special exceptions, there was now only one way to get to Eretz Israel, a so-called S.H. Journey. S.H. means Special Hachshara. The expression was chosen to disguise the fact that it was a matter of an illegal *aliya*. It is for this same reason that the Palestine Office in Berlin,[3] which together with its subsidiary organizations, Hechalutz and Youth Aliya, organized this illegal *aliya,* also called Aliya Bet, did not officially come to the fore. Preparation and implementation of the transports were officially in the hands of a so-called Committee for Jewish Overseas Transports.

Of course, the transports were illegal only as far as the English were concerned. In Germany they were legal and could only be legal, since all Jewish Offices were under the supervision of the Gestapo and all emigration, apart from rare exceptions, was possible only with the knowledge and consent of the authorities. Before the outbreak of the war two such transports had already been organized by the Berlin Hechalutz, and, in fact, successfully. After all kinds of hardships and dangers, the participants in S.H.1 and S.H.2 had landed without falling into the hands of the English. S.H.3 left after the outbreak of the war in October 1939, and also arrived safely after three months. The participants, however, fell into the hands of the English and were interned in Athlit, where the women were released a short time later, and the men after six months. The participants in this journey also had survived many dangers and hardships. A fire had broken out on the ship, which, although it was put out immediately, cost the life of a young girl.

S.H.4 departed in November 1939. In the severe winter, which had come early that year, it became icebound on the Danube near the Yugoslavian coast. The participants, mostly young people, were taken to a camp in Cladowe, Yugoslavia and had to suffer greatly there because of hunger and cold, as well as poor accommodations. Numerous attempts to help them to continue their journey failed. Not until spring 1941, when the danger from the Nazis also was drawing nearer to Yugoslavia, did the young people reach Palestine with the help of Youth Aliya Certificates, procured by the ever-energetic Miss Szold.[4]

S.H.5 and S.H.6 were not organized in Berlin but rather in Vienna, by the local Committee for Jewish Overseas Transports on Rotenturm Strasse. It was S.H.7 that my wife and I went on. As previously mentioned, after the outbreak of the war there was no other possibility. Therefore we applied for an S.H. transport, fully aware of the dangers and hardships that such an undertaking entailed. I was pretty much informed about it since I had been working in an honorary capacity at the Palestine Office in Berlin since the spring of 1939, and the reports on the previous transports had come to my attention.

It was not easy to get on S.H.7. The demand was immense. The possibility of such transports had previously been known almost only in Zionist circles, especially in the circles of Hechalutz, which basically organized them only for the pioneer youth. Since February 1940, however, this possibility had become known in all of Germany. At that time the Hapag shipping company had approached the Palestine Office in Berlin and had suggested that it place at its disposal ships for illegal transports to Palestine. At first the Palestine Office did not want to accept, because it was afraid that the Gestapo was behind it, and that many undesirable people would be gotten rid of in this way. After some negotiations, however, it was agreed that the applications of those wanting to go along were to be submitted to the Palestine Office and that the selection of the persons to be included was entirely up to it. From all over Germany a torrent of applications now poured into the Palestine Office. In the course of two or three months some 30,000 applied for the "Apala."[5] Apala was the name suggested by Hapag for the transports. It did not want to come out openly under its own name. Some of those who applied probably did not seriously intend to emigrate to Palestine. All that mattered to them was to have proof in their hands for the Gestapo of efforts to emigrate. By far the greatest number, however, was serious about it.

The Palestine Office then appointed committees to examine and decide on the applications, and they set up guidelines for this. According to them, basically only people were to be selected to be taken along who either could prove Zionist service or whose accommodations and support in the country were assured. Further prerequisites for acceptance were suitability for the journey and the country as far as health was concerned, as well as the ability to obtain the cost of the passage in dollars. The dollars were necessary because the participants themselves had to raise $20,000. As a rule, $200 per person were requested from older people. In the case of Zionsts of long service, the *vatikim,*[6] as well as the *chalutzim,* smaller amounts were sufficient, or the requirement for dollars was waived altogether. The dollars, of course, could be acquired only in neutral foreign countries with the aid of relatives and friends. They had to be deposited at a bank in Zurich.

Advising the public, who came to the Palestine Office daily by the hundreds, on all the pertinent questions required an entire staff of workers. I was one of the advisers. I was also a member of the committee that had to decide on final approval. During the consultation hours many false and foolish views had to be corrected and illusions destroyed. There were also droll scenes. One day a little old woman of almost seventy came and expressed the wish to be taken along to Apala; she thought that was some country overseas. Unfortunately, we had to tell her that at her age she was not up to the expected hardship and thus could not be taken along.

Of the tens of thousands who had applied, naturally only a small number could be approved. We knew the difficulties in organizing such transports. We knew especially the difficulty in obtaining ships. We were not confident that Hapag-Apala would succeed in providing ships. Since war had already broken out, only ships of neutral countries came into consideration. In the neutral countries, too, as a result of the many sinkings of ships every space on a ship was precious. In addition, there was the risk of the journey through war zones, and the risk of a considerable punishment that the captain and the crew had to reckon with because of the violation of the Palestine immigration rules.

Our assumption that the Hapag could not supply ships turned out to be correct. The committees for overseas transports in Berlin and Vienna, supported by the Reichs-vereinigung der Juden in Deutschland and by the Joint,[7] therefore made attempts to obtain new means of transportation by the same methods by which they had obtained ships for the earlier S.H. journeys. The patience of those approved for the journeys, however, was sorely tried. My wife and I were among those approved. We were put off from week to week, from month to month. First we were told there were ships, namely Greek ships. But the Greek government had forbidden departure. Then we were told that the departure was in fact granted but no captain could be found. After a captain was engaged, the ship's crew could not be procured. After the ship's crew was also hired, the Greek shipowner demanded an advance payment of $20,000. Only after payment were the ships to leave the port of Piraeus, toward the mouth of the Danube at the Black Sea. No one wanted to venture that. One had no faith in the Greek swindler. After this difficulty was also overcome and the ships actually had arrived at Tulcea at the mouth of the Danube, we were informed that they had not yet been outfitted at all for mass transport.

In the meantime it was already the summer of 1940. Italy had joined the war. The Mediterranean Sea had become a war zone. France had been defeated. Hitler's invasion of England and his dictatorship over Europe threatened to become reality. And many feared that the control of the entire Mediterranean and of Palestine would fall to Mussolini. At any rate, the situation was such that one had to give up hope of even getting out of Germany, let alone of getting to Palestine during the war. Soon the rumor spread that all emigration was blocked. Then, again, it was said that Jews under forty-five were no longer being let out of Germany. But the improbable became reality or, as I said at the beginning: *"Lo yanum velo yischan."*[8] Providence kept vigil and struck the Nazi chieftains with blindness so that they could not recognize how very much they were harming themselves by still allowing Jews, especially the youth, to emigrate.

At the beginning of July 1940 the Gestapo ordered the Palestine Office to select 500 from the number of those approved for the S.H. journeys, and to present the list of those chosen to the Gestapo by nine o'clock the next morning, as well as to carry out the transportation of these 500 with the greatest haste. A commission, to which I did not belong, met immediately, sat the whole night through, and put together the list of the 500. This did not come about without tough debate. The representative of each individual group attempted to push through the approval of as large a number from his group as possible, representatives of the Chalutz Youth, Youth Aliya, Bachad,[9] Vatikim, and other groups. At that time one already had the feeling that this next aliya would be the last from Nazi Germany and that approval or denial could perhaps be a decision between life and death.

My wife and I were among the 500. We had been approved in the group of *vatikim*. Belonging to the *vatikim* alone, however, would not have sufficed. Aside from me there were hundreds of other *vatikim*. The decisive factor was that $200 for the passage costs had been deposited for us in Zurich. All the chosen ones were now requested to sign a letter of indemnity. The letter of indemnity pointed out the dangers and strains of the journey, and ruled out any liability for damages and stressed especially that no liability at all could be assumed for arrival in Palestine. The signing of the letter of indemnity also meant strict acknowledgment of the conditions of transport. On the basis of previous experiences, the latter concentrated on the observance of the strictest discipline and absolute adherence to every instruction of the transport management.

Among the approved there were some few who had apprehensions or other reservations about going along on the journey. In their place others were chosen from the great number of those who had protested not having been considered. On the final list, which was approved by the Gestapo, there were 350 young people and *chalutzim* up to the age of thirty, and 150 older people. The relatively large number of young people and *chalutzim* can be explained by the fact that the S.H. transports were organized mainly for young people, who were naturally more valuable than older ones for the building of the country.

We 500 now prepared for departure. The fact that in the middle of the war a transport with the destination of Palestine was going to leave after all was the sensation and topic of the day among the Berlin Jews. Many were skeptical and thought that the Gestapo would deport us to somewhere or other. Others thought that we would never reach our destination even if we could sail with the ships. We would hit a mine, be bombed by airplanes, or be captured by the Italians and interned, or we would roam about on the seas for months without being able to land, or we would perish in some other way. I was especially warned by my friends because several times I had had influenza with high fever, and, in addition, in July I had also sustained a rib fracture in an accident. However, we did not allow ourselves to be deterred by all these skeptics and pessimists. As is fitting for Jews, we were optimists, and had to be so. There was also no other choice for us after the Gestapo had ordered the emigration of the 500.

First we had to take care of our emigration documents. For that the Gestapo allowed us another few weeks of time. Many obstacles had to be overcome in this matter.

The tax authorities checked once more very carefully to see whether all taxes, especially the Reich emigration tax and the Jews' fine, were duly paid. The Jewish community, too, had to certify that no back taxes were owed, especially that the Jewish emigration tax was paid, which was to serve to support the Jews left behind and who were without means. I also had a problem at the Tax Office, the solution of which was not simple. The Tax Office had demanded a certification from the Reichsbank that it had no objections to issuing a certificate stating that I had no taxes or loans outstanding. As prescribed, I had informed the Reichsbank of claims for fees in foreign currency against persons living abroad, and also of the receipt of such claimed fees. But some could not be redeemed. Lengthy negotiations with the Reichsbank were necessary in order to convince them of their unredeemability. The Reichsbank at first had suspected that I did not redeem the debts only because I wanted to retain them as foreign exchange assets abroad.

After all obstacles were successfully overcome and we had received our passports, we had to turn them in at the Palestine Office for the purpose of procuring the necessary visa. We wanted to go to Palestine; thus the visa of the British consulate would have been necessary. But, first of all, the British consulate was closed because of the war, and, second, it would not have given us a visa since we had no emigration certificates. The Reichsvereinigung, however, had taken precautions. The consulate of Paraguay provided the desired item for a good price, which was paid by the Reichsvereinigung with the help of Joint. Joint also had to assume the guarantee that in reality we would not go to Paraguay.

Now only one thing was missing: the emigration visa of the police headquarters, which, according to legal regulations, was needed for every frontier crossing. It was issued promptly since the police headquarters was, after all, already informed in detail about us and our intentions. Now we should finally have been able to depart if a new difficulty had not emerged. The Greek government suddenly forbade the flying of the Greek flag. Another flag could at first not be obtained. Without a flag we could not cross the seas. The Reichsvereinigung and the Palestine Office, therefore, did not want to take responsibility for the departure. At that point the Gestapo stepped in and on August 3, 1940, issued the order for departure in groups. According to the order of the Gestapo, by the 18th of August not one of the 500 was to be left in the area of the former German Reich. The first group was to leave already on the following day.

Now matters really became serious. The first group, a *chalutz* group from the provinces, departed for Vienna as prescribed. Other groups followed. Before the departure of the Berlin groups, the Reichsvereinigung and the Palestine Office gave a farewell party during which again and again they stressed the calmness and the courage with which the 500 were facing an uncertain, threatening fate. The leader of the Reischsver-einigung, Dr. Paul Eppstein,[10] spoke at the farewell party. Several days after the cele-bration he was arrested temporarily by the Gestapo. He was probably blamed for not sufficiently speeding up the departure of the transport.

My wife and I left with the last group on the evening of August 17, 1940.[11]

1. The Verordnung zur Ausschaltung der Juden aus dem deutschen Wirtschaftsleben (Ordinance for the Exclusion of Jews from German Economic Life) dates only from November

12, 1938. Individual occupations, however, were already forbidden to Jews by the Gesetz zur Änderung der Gewerbeordnung (Law for Changing Trading Regulations) of July 6, 1938. On July 25, 1938 the Vierte Verordnung zum Reichsbürgergesetz (Fourth Ordinance to the Reich Citizenship Law) decreed the termination of the license of Jews to practice medicine. The corresponding prohibition for Jewish lawyers followed on September 27, 1938.

2. The permit to immigrate granted by the British mandate government in Palestine for owners of capital of at least 1,000 pounds (12,000 reichsmarks). In contrast to immigration certificates for workers and students, capitalist certificates were originally available without limitations.

3. In 1918 the Zionist Executive established Palestine Offices in all countries from which Jews emigrated to Palestine. They had the task of selecting and preparing the emigrants, and they also organized the journey itself. Hechalutz (see Glossary) and Youth Aliya (see M. Appel [39], note 3), originally independent, in 1939 constituted only subsections of the Palestine Office, which in turn had become part of the Reichsvereinigung.

4. Henrietta Szold (1860–1945) American Zionist leader; starting in 1935 she directed the Youth Aliya in Palestine.

5. The Venture (Hebrew).

6. Veterans (Hebrew).

7. American Jewish Joint Distribution Committee; see Glossary for "Joint."

8. "Doth neither slumber nor sleep" (Hebrew). Quote from Psalm 121:4: "Behold, He that keepeth Israel/doth neither slumber nor sleep."

9. Religious Zionist youth organization that emerged from the youth movement.

10. Dr. Paul Eppstein (1901–1944), until 1933 *Privatdozent* ("adjunct lecturer") in economics in Mannheim, directed the Verband Jüdischer Jugendvereine Deutschlands from 1934 to 1938, and from 1933 on was a leading staff member of the Reichsvertretung in Berlin in the field of economic welfare, vocational retraining, and emigration. In the Reichsvereinigung he was also liason to its control authority, the Gestapo. In January 1943 he was deported to Theresienstadt, where he was appointed "The Eldest of the Jews," and was shot in September 1944.

11. On November 1, 1940, Meyer reached the port of Haifa on the ship *Pacific*. The British mandate government refused docking permission and reloaded the passengers onto the *Patria* for further transportation. On November 25th the Hagana wanted to disable this ship through a bomb attack, but sank it, and 260 of the passengers drowned. Meyer swam to shore and was interned for eight months in Athlit.

# 46   *Elisabeth Freund, née Freund*

 BORN IN BRESLAU IN 1898; DIED IN 1982 IN ROCHESTER, NEW YORK.

Elisabeth Freund, Forced Labor, Berlin 1941. Undated manuscript, 188 pages; written in Havana (Cuba), December 1941.

*The author grew up in Breslau as daughter of the neurologist Doctor Carl Freund. She studied economics in Breslau and in Berlin, where she lived in the house of her uncle, the Nobel Prize winner Fritz Haber. In 1922 she married her cousin, Doctor juris Rudolf Freund (1877–1959), member of the board of the Upper Silesian Iron Industry Corporation in Gleiwitz. When this company became part of the Central German Steel Works (Flick combine) in 1924, the wealthy family moved to Berlin. In 1933 Rudolf Freund had to leave the Flick combine and until 1938 he worked as a certified public accountant. After the emigration of her three children, Elisabeth Freund retrained as a photographer. From April until September 1941 she had to do*

*forced labor, at first in a large laundry and then in an armaments plant. After*
*futile attempts to leave Germany, the couple succeeded in emigrating to Cuba in*
*October 1941. In 1944 both moved on to the United States, where the author at*
*first worked as a retoucher and later, in Philadephia, created a collection of*
*instructional materials for the blind.*

We were so sure that we would now [May 1941] receive the visas for the
U.S.A., but we still have not heard anything about them. Our brothers and sisters in
America write that we should inquire of the American Consul, that they had taken care
of everything, that our affidavits[1] were at the consulate and were proper and adequate.
Even a bank deposit was made for us, and a certification by the shipping line was sent,
stating that the tickets were already paid for. Our waiting number, which we had
applied for in November 1938, should have come long ago. But it seems like a disaster;
we still do not have the summons to the consulate. If we only knew why we are not
making any progress! Unfortunately, at the consulate no information is given about the
state of matters pertaining to emigration. We are completely at a loss. What if some
day America really enters into a war with Germany—everything does seem threatening
enough—and then all contacts to foreign countries are barred and we have not received
our visas in time! It is simply inconceivable. Then we will not be able to see our children
ever again.

It is really enough to drive one to despair. We've already done so many things in
order to get away from Germany. We have filed applications for entry permits to
Switzerland, Denmark, and Sweden. It was all in vain, though in all these countries we
had good connections. In the spring of 1939, from an agent we obtained an entry permit
for Mexico for 3,000 marks. But we never received the visa, because the Mexican
consulate asked us to present passports that would entitle us to return to Germany, and
the German authorities did not issue such passports to Jews. Then, in August 1939
we did actually get the permit for England. But it came too late, only ten days before
the outbreak of war, and in this short time we were not able to take care of all the
formalities with the German authorities. In the spring of 1940 we received the entry
permit for Portugal. We immediately got everything ready and applied for our passports.
Then came the invasion of Holland, Belgium, and France by the German troops. A
stream of refugees poured to Portugal, and the Portuguese government recalled by wire
all of the issued permits. As it happened, we were lucky that we had not given up our
apartment and not yet sold our furniture. It was also good that in December 1940 we
had not already paid for our Panamanian visas, for we noticed that the visas offered us
did not at all entitle us to land in Panama. Things can again work out for us in such
a way that we will no longer be able to leave.

We are convinced that in reality America wants to help and is receiving the
European refugees in the most generous manner. But they do not know there how
difficult the situation is; otherwise they would permit these poor and tortured people
to get there quickly, while it is still possible. They could lock them up in a camp there
until the situation of every individual is clarified, and the relief committees could bear
the costs for it. But we had better get away from here, and as quickly as possible;
otherwise we will meet the same fate as the unfortunate people who were deported from

Stettin to Poland, or as the Jews from Baden, who were sent to France and who are being held captive there in the Pyrenees.[2]

*[On June 22, 1941, Germany attacks the Soviet Union. Shortly thereupon Elisabeth Freund collapses doing forced labor at the steam press.]*

I was sick for over three weeks and lay in bed practically the whole time. Our old Hedwig looked in on me every few days and tended to me in a touching way. She is an Aryan woman who has been with our family for more than forty years. As a young girl she was a domestic at my parents'. She knows every member of the family, and practically knows more about all of them than I. She also saw my children growing up and worries about them. Her husband works for the postal service and her son is already married. She never lost touch with us and says again and again that she will never forget that without my parents' help her boy would have probably died many years ago from a serious illness. She is such an upright, faithful human being; I can discuss everything with her and confide everything to her.

How she continues to stick by us amid the greatest difficulties is touching. For the risks that she takes upon herself for our sake are actually so great that I myself should dissuade her from coming to us. At the postal authorities all employees, thus also her husband, have just had to declare under oath once again that they no longer have any connections with Jews. Naturally, this declaration also applies to the acquaintanceships of the wife. If it comes out that she visits us, her husband will lose his position and therewith his livelihood. She herself is in a terrible conflict between fear and conviction. On the one hand, she explained to me that it was all the same to her whether a false declaration under oath was made or not: "One is being virtually trained to commit perjury. What things my husband has to constantly swear to, every week something else! One can no longer have any respect for it." On the other hand, she is terribly afraid that she could be caught. She told her Nazi sister-in-law, who asked about us schemingly, that she did not know where we have emigrated. She is very proud of this diplomatic answer. Early in the morning she scurries into the house and is constantly worried that she could be seen, perhaps through the window or when she leaves. When the doorbell rings, she hides. And in spite of this fear and nervous strain she still comes and hauls food, which I cannot even take because I know that she is depriving herself of it, and that it endangers us both. It is admirable how this simple woman has the courage that so many of the "educated" people do not summon. In such a time of distress the true essence of a person proves itself. Unfortunately, we were mistaken about some of our so-called friends. That much the more one must acknowledge old Hedwig's behavior.

She urges us all the time to finally emigrate. As if that were not our most fervent wish. The bystanders, the Aryans here, and probably people abroad can probably not understand at all why we are still here. They don't know that it does not at all depend on us, but rather that unfortunately we simply do not get admission to any other country. There are no more visas for the U.S.A. My husband has made one last attempt and asked our relatives in America by wire for the entry visas for Cuba. That is the only possibility that still exists. No other country gives an entry permit to German Jews any longer, or is still reachable in any way.

Hopefully, we will succeed this time. The difficulties are already piling up again. The costs for such a visa are very high. Large sums of money have to be deposited for us. I hope that my brother-in-law will raise the money for us. The United States has introduced an exchange embargo and, besides, the rush for these Cuban visas is very great at the moment, so that three to four weeks are necessary for transfer of the deposits. At best we can expect the visas by the middle of August. Hopefully, nothing unexpected will again interfere. After our failures we have become very pessimistic about all matters concerning emigration.

*[Elisabeth Freund now has to work in an armaments plant.]*

It is fortunate for me that I have landed here. Here the heat is not so terrible. When I hear how things still are in the laundry, then I have to be most content that I'm no longer there. No doubt the work is difficult everywhere. The worst thing is the situation of our boy workers. We have a large number, starting at the age of fourteen. I often talk with them when I meet them on the way. My own son is also almost fourteen now. I wonder if he is already as tall as these boys here. I hope that he will not be so embittered and serious. After all, he has it good in his English school. He has the chance to learn something and is growing up as an equal in a big group of comrades. For him it is bad only that he has to be separated from his parents.

The poor Jewish boys here in the factory! The worst thing is not the difficult work, it is the hopelessness. There is one fellow, Kurt, a tall and lanky boy in breeches that are much too short; his arms stick way out of his sleeves. Even the young people do not get ration coupons for clothes! Kurt worked for a year in a training center of the Jewish community, is very interested in technology, and wanted so much to become an electrical engineer. "Then isn't it actually quite interesting for you here, isn't there a great deal to learn?" I ask him. "Oh, that's what you think. Only the Aryan boys are apprentices; they are shown things. We Jewish boys are not allowed to learn anything here. At best we are allowed to work at a machine once in a while, and then we're shown the operation that's needed for that one machine. But that's really all. That's just it—we're supposed to remain unskilled workers." [. . .]

The poor fellows. Everything is hopeless for them. No diligence, no energy, no matter how great, helps any; they can learn nothing. They have a terrible youth. Under these conditions, how long will the educational level of the Jews, which until now was always so high, be maintained at all? The door to every possibility is closed to them. They are not allowed to attend either the theater or concerts. Museums, libraries, even the zoo are forbidden to them. The few Jewish schools still existing suffer from an insufficient number of teachers and insufficient teaching materials. In general, there is only one secondary school for Jewish children left in Berlin, and it, too, will probably not exist much longer. The good school buildings have long since been seized by the party.

I'm always hearing so much about all these hardships because I am friends with a Jewish school teacher. The financial means of the community for all its purposes are becoming more and more tight, the need greater and greater, the difficulties and the pressure more and more insurmountable. This summer, for example, one of the greatest problems was what to do with the school children during the vacation. In almost all families the parents are working in the factories; thus the children were unsupervised at home. Where was one to put them, these poor, overly nervous children, who after these last years with their terrible experiences needed a holiday rest especially badly? In earlier years the Jewish school administration had organized excursions for the children to the forest, with immense difficulty, for the Gestapo had declared that the children are allowed on the streetcars or city trains or subways only in small groups of no more than six. Just imagine how hard it is under these conditions to take even only a hundred children anywhere with supervision. Quite apart is the problem of finding a suitable and undisturbed place for playing, where the children will not be assaulted and beaten up by some ruffians.

This year, however, the Gestapo has also strictly forbidden these excursions to the forest. What was left! The parks are also forbidden. Many of the Jewish day nurseries do not even have a yard, let alone a garden, and if they have one, the children are not allowed to play in it—because of the neighbors, who complain about the noise. Finally, the Jewish community hit upon the solution of transforming every free spot in the Jewish cemeteries into playgrounds with sand boxes for the smaller children. And the bigger children, class by class, had the duty to clear the graves and paths of weeds, and to maintain them in good condition. In this way the children were occupied and out in the fresh air, and at the same time the graves were kept in order, which curiously enough the Gestapo had suddenly demanded and for which otherwise, naturally, there would not have been workers or the financial means. That is what things have come to now: In Germany the cemeteries are not only the final resting place for the old people, but also the only spot where Jewish children can play.

*[In September 1941—according to Elisabeth Freund—Jewish women between the ages of eighteen and forty-five are forbidden to emigrate.]*

The Gestapo has permitted me to leave Germany, in spite of the prohibition! We do not even dare to believe it yet. It came about like this: My husband met an old acquaintance quite by chance on the street, an executive in one of the major banks of Berlin, with whom he had worked together a great deal, especially at the time of the uprisings in Upper Silesia after the First World War. At that time, my husband was a senior member of the board of the Upper Silesian Iron Industry Corporation and, in constant danger of his life, he successfully saw to the provision of Upper Silesia with the financial means to pay salaries. Without that, in addition to the bloody uprisings by the Poles, there would have also been unrest among the workers. His clever negotiations with the English and French occupation authorities prevented much misfortune at that time, and have always been recognized. This gentleman, then, asked quite innocently, in a friendly manner, how we were doing, and was absolutely flabbergasted when he heard what difficulties we were having. "But really, that just can't be! These measures are not meant for someone like you!" How often have we and a thousand other Jews heard these words already: "These measures are surely not aimed at you!"

At whom, then? And if they really were not directed against "especially meritorious people"—who has the right to determine whether a man in a "high position" has greater merit than a simple worker, a hardworking merchant, or an academic? [. . .] Well, at any rate, this gentleman was very sympathetic. He asked for exact details and was going to discuss the matter with the management of his company. There they had the necessary connections to the Gestapo and would somehow fix things up for us. When my husband told me about this meeting I was so pessimistic and so tired from work that I scarcely listened. After all, we had experienced so many disappointments already; why should it turn out otherwise this time? We were also very afraid and not at all so pleased by the well-meaning offer, for after all, one does not know what could happen if something like that were passed on to the wrong place.

But the miracle happened. Things turned out well. The general on Kurfürsten-strasse[3] said to the bank that an exception will be made for me. We also do not have to pay anything. The Gestapo man who negotiated the matter, to be sure, would like to have a bed from us when we leave—that's all. And we will leave him this bed with the greatest pleasure. All these things are so scarce and cannot be bought in the normal way.

But we have nothing in writing on this decision. In principle, the Gestapo does not provide anything written in such cases. My husband immediately went to the emigration office of the Jewish Aid Society.[4] He was congratulated there, but no one wants to take the responsibility for placing our names on a departure list. One cannot blame them for that; after all, everything is punishable by immediate deportation to a concentration camp.

There are still so many difficulties to overcome. No, I still will not believe it, otherwise there will again be a greater disappointment. We also must not talk to anyone about it. The one office of the Gestapo may have allowed it, but perhaps another one will put us in a camp for it. I must also continue to do my work in the factory, for how can I explain to the employment office for Jews that my work record can be closed for good. Without papers no one will believe me. But without termination of the work record we cannot be assigned to a departing group. We are still a long way from that.

I must go on with my work in the factory. My hours just fly by. My thoughts fly even faster. Even if I don't quite believe it yet, still, just in case, I must consider how to organize things best. A year and a half ago we were permitted to take along quite a few things as personal and household belongings for Portugal. The permission is still valid. But at that time one could still pay the transportation costs with paper marks. Now, every emigrant is allowed to take along only two small suitcases, and from the German border on one must pay in gold marks or dollars. That determines the size of our luggage. Only the most necessary things can be taken along. We will have to part with our whole household. That is bitter, especially for a woman. But I won't make it hard for myself. Three years ago I had to separate from my children—that was hard. Furniture—that's nothing to get excited about. The main thing is that we get out of Germany alive. I will give the things away to good friends; at least I will get pleasure from that. If only we were at that stage already! After all our experiences, we can give up our apartment and furniture only at the very last moment. It can happen to us again, as it did the other times, that once more at the last moment we can't get away. The best thing is to let the business of emigration simply happen, as if it did not concern us at all, as if we were acting in a film. Otherwise the tension is too difficult to bear. We still have a great deal before us: parting from our friends, leaving our old homeland.

Hitler said of the German Jews: "They are all gypsies, who feel just as well in Paris as in Budapest, London, or New York." We loved Germany as much as one can love only one's own country. We detest Hitler's Germany and everything associated with it. But we must leave the country whose language we speak, with whose songs and poems we grew up, and whose forests and mountains we have crisscrossed. For many generations, our families did their utmost for this country, and we are leaving behind their graves in this soil. Our children can grow into another future. My husband and I are no longer young enough. We are going to a foreign country, and much there will be alien and difficult for us. But once we are outside, when we are received in another country in which we are allowed to live with our children undisturbed, then, happy and grateful, we will take pains to work for this new land faithfully, as our parents and ancestors did for Germany.

Our emigration agent brings the news that there are now a number of cases in which exceptions have been made to the emigration prohibition for women. Unfortunately, not many. I also know of such a case in which the Gestapo demanded 5,000 marks for it. In the main, such a permit was given if there was a gynecological certificate of infertility.

I am still working in the factory. My husband, however, now has assurance from the Aid Society that we will be put on the next departure list. However, the next groups are not leaving for three weeks. If we could only speed up our leaving. We are growing more and more frustrated.

Since last week we have been wearing the Yellow Star.[5] The effect on the population is different from what the Nazis expected. Berlin still has perhaps 80,000 Jews.[6] In some sections of town one sees the Yellow Stars in very large numbers. People of whom one would not have thought on the basis of their appearance that they are Jews are wearing the Star. The population in its majority disapproves of this defamation. Until now, all measures against the Jews occurred in the dark. Now no one can ignore them.

Naturally, there are different kinds of experiences. What I hear from other people, I experience myself: I am greeted on the street with special politeness by complete strangers, and in the streetcar ostentatiously a seat is freed for me, although those wearing a star are allowed to sit only if no Aryan is still standing. But sometimes guttersnipes call out abusive words after me. And occasionally Jews are said to have been beaten up. Someone tells me of an experience in the city train. A mother saw that her little girl was sitting beside a Jew: "Lieschen, sit down on the other bench, you don't need to sit beside a Jew." At that, an Aryan worker stood up, saying: "And I don't need to sit next to Lieschen!"

The Yellow Stars are not popular. That is a failure of the party, and then there are the failures on the eastern front. As the usual diversion, there now follows a terrible wave of antisemitic propaganda. In all parts of the city more than two hundred meetings are held, at which the Jewish question is discussed. In the stairwells, early in the morning, there are fliers in which people are openly called upon to carry out pogroms. In the news that a soldier fell in battle, they say that the Jews are guilty of his death!

A former janitor of ours who is an army guard in a concentration camp in Poland sent his wife to us. We should see to it that we get away as soon as possible. She said that he could not bear the thought that the same could happen to us as to those poor people. Didn't we know what was in store for us? That sounds horrible. What in the world are they doing with the camp inmates? The Nazis just cannot be killing them by the thousands! That is just inconceivable—German people doing this to their fellow citizens, with whom they had fought side by side in 1914. And what is happening with the women and children? In Berlin one knows nothing about their fate. The janitor's letter to his wife does not mention any details. The army mail is probably strictly censored.

Almost every store along the entire Kurfürstendamm now has a sign: "No entrance to Jews" or "No sales to Jews." When one walks along the streets one sees "Jew," "Jew," "Jew" on every house, every windowpane, every store. It is difficult to explain that the Nazis, these fanatical Jew-haters, cover their own city completely with this word, whereas there are so few Jews left in Germany. One cannot look anywhere without coming across this "Jew." And it is not just, say, the luxury shops or cigar stores that are forbidden to Jews in the entire city; now the bakeries, the butcher and vegetable shops are showing these signs. And no coal ration cards were distributed to Jews for the winter. Where will it all end!

And I am still working at the factory. Until now I haven't dared to ask for my discharge there. Perhaps in the factory they know that for my age group emigration is barred. If that is the case, then there will be further inquiries and I have nothing to show from the Gestapo. All these things are so difficult. If we do anything wrong now, then everything can be put at risk.

A few days ago I asked the foreman in the propeller department to be allowed to go home an hour earlier because of emigration matters. He became furious and accused me of wanting only to avoid work; he knew very well that there was no longer any emigration and he would not let me do whatever I liked with him. I won't get anywhere with this man.

Then I am told that I am no longer listed with the propeller department, but have been transferred to the petroleum department. Now I must try it. I present my passport with the visas to my new foreman and ask him for a short leave. After five endless hours the foreman calls for me: "Here are your papers. You are dismissed. Go to the employment office and have your work record canceled."

For the last time I am taken by the Aryan escort to the factory exit. "Is it really true, are you getting away? Where is Cuba anyway? And there is really no war there?" He looks around cautiously: "Then I wish you luck. Then you are better off than all of us here."

I have actually been dismissed! Now I just have to go to the employment office. There they make things difficult for me. For people under forty-five there is no cancellation of the work record. Don't I really know that yet? Nothing helps. I have to go to the Gestapo on Kurfürstenstrasse. That is hardly pleasant, but it is the only possible way. The building of the Jewish Fraternal Society is completely empty. Besides me there does not seem to be another Jew there. I am directed into the former festival hall, along the side walls of which a few niches are fixed up as offices. An official listens to my case, but is not informed. He is very cold and quite obviously does not believe me. But he will ask his highest superior. I am told to wait. However, I may not wait by the wall, but must place myself exactly in the middle of the big hall under the huge chandelier, with strict instructions not to move from the spot. I must remain standing exactly in the middle of the inlaid floor. I had heard tell about this sadism, but had considered everything an exaggeration. But no, it was really done that way. During the three-quarters of an hour that I wait there, I am atoning for all my sins, as one says. It is difficult to stand in the middle of such a huge empty room without swaying, without getting "claustrophobic." But this is now the test: Will the Gestapo stand by the authorization it granted?

I wait. I wait. Finally the man returns. Everything is all right. He calls the employment office and gives the necessary instructions. Now I am free! No, not yet, not by a long shot! I know a young girl who was all ready to depart when the prohibition to leave the country came. She was to go one day later. And now she is working in the factory again; only her parents were able to leave. Only when we are across the border, only then will I be free.

Now there comes a great nervous strain. What if in the last moment we cannot get away for some reason! In the final week, my husband pays out all we own as the Reich emigration tax,[7] as the tax to the Jewish community "for the promotion of the emigration of Jews" (which the community, incidentally, does not receive, but which goes to a blocked account!), and for our ship tickets. The price of these ship tickets is determined by the value of the assets still left us. In a certain respect, I approve of that, for how else should people without assets raise the money for the crossing. In our case, for the tickets we must pay everything that is still left in hard cash after payment of all other fees. Why is there such a great fuss being made with the calculations? Whatever we were not able to turn into money, for example, real estate and mortgages, upon our emigration becomes the property of the state anyway, since we will then be deprived of our citizenship, as "enemies of the state," and everything will be confiscated. In the end, not a penny will be left of our still sizable assets. But if we cannot get away now, we will have paid everything and at best will get a partial sum back in paper marks; we will then be completely penniless. [. . .]

Last week a large number of Jewish families in Berlin received notice to vacate their apartments—not from their landlords, to be sure, but rather on printed forms from the police.[8] They were told not to look around for other apartments. They would be notified about what will happen with them. They were told that all their possessions were confiscated. They could regard only a limited number of things as their own, in the case of a woman, for example, two dresses, three shirts, pants, stockings, etc., and one coat.

The agitation is indescribable. What will happen with these people now? Will they be sent to the province, to barracks, or to Poland? And who has received such notices, anyway? Apparently at first the so-called "previously convicted," that is, people who had not properly observed the blackout rules, or were not at home at eight o'clock, or at whose place something had been found during a house search. Bad news keeps coming from all directions. One can hardly keep up with it anymore. A number of our acquaintances are summoned before the Gestapo and punished, partly with a fine, partly with prison, because in the telephone book they are not listed with the compulsory middle names "Sara" and "Israel." Yet none of us has owned a telephone for more than a year. Despite that, they should have immediately applied for a name change in the telephone book. A good friend of ours receives the notification that his nephew, who was in prison for two years for allegedly having had sexual relations with an Aryan, was transferred from there to a labor camp, where he "died" after two weeks.

I go to the post office to make a call from a telephone booth there. I am scarcely in the booth when a woman rips open the door and drags me out screeching: "We Aryans have to wait. The Jews are always in the booths. Out with the Jews! Out! Out with all Jews from Germany!" It is such a terrible scene that I don't know how I got out onto the dark street again. I was afraid she would rip the clothes from my body.

My husband receives a summons to appear at the Gestapo on Alexanderplatz. That is always very unpleasant. The halls leading to the offices have heavy iron bars at their entrance. Once they have closed behind you, you are never sure whether you will be let out again. Both of us had already been summoned more than once, either alone or together. It was always a question of whether we were finally emigrating. This time my husband can fortunately take along our passports with the exit permits. The official really does ask again why we are still there. When my husband presents the passports, the Gestapo official takes a slip of paper with writing on it from our file and tears it up. My husband asks very politely what this paper meant. "That was your expulsion to Poland," is his answer. "I'm glad that you are getting out of it!" He is glad! So, Gestapo men are sometimes also human beings.

That is on Thursday, and on Sunday we are supposed to go. Now everything is happening like clockwork. In the night between Thursday and Friday the Jews in Berlin are taken from their apartments for the first time. Everyone is allowed to take along only a small suitcase. The police come at night, around eleven. In the dark, just so that the population does not take sides. The poor people are taken to a transit center, the synagogue on Levetzowstrasse. The entire block there is closed off. The Jewish community had to provide nurses, doctors, and aides. In great haste provisions are prepared, for no one was allowed to take food along from home.

It is a terrible night, with rain and thunderstorms. The synagogue is not big enough. The people have to stand in the yard for hours in the rain. The scenes that took place there are supposed to have been indescribable. Families were separated, married couples were torn apart, children dragged away, parents left behind. Already during the arrests, in the apartments, people took their lives. There in the synagogue it goes on. Body searches take place, suitcases are ransacked. All must turn in their identification papers, birth certificates, passports, etc. Everything is taken from them that has monetary value, as well as soap, combs, shaving gear, scissors, brushes, everything that a civilized person needs in order to look clean and neat. They are supposed to become as neglected as the unfortunate Jews of the Polish ghettos, whose caricatures appear in the *Stürmer*.

It was only on the following two days that we heard these dreadful details from eyewitnesses. In the laundry people were picked up from the night shift by the police. So working in the factories does not protect one from deportation. A young girl whose mother was part of the transport ran from one Gestapo office to another in order to be deported together with her mother. Her request was turned down. "You are not going to Poland when *you* feel like it, but when it suits *us*." The fear, the panic everywhere simply cannot be described. Really, we have experienced so many horrible things already. But this, this cannot be compared to anything. It is like hunting helpless animals!

One morning I ride the streetcar crisscross through the city to find out about friends and acquaintances, whether they are still there or have already been hauled off. All of us know nothing of one another; after all, we don't have telephones! Not until the very early hours of Saturday are the poor people taken to the Grunewald Station, in barred police cars. This station is so out of the way that only few people can observe what is happening there. (That is why the hospital trains from the front also always arrive there.) The people are loaded into cattle cars. Word has it that the transports are heading to Poland. Nobody knows for sure.

Acquaintances come to our place. They know that we are supposed to leave. They ask us to convey their last greetings to their relatives abroad. We should please see to it that everything is done to procure them an entry visa. We should describe abroad what is happening here, what is awaiting them. Deportation to Poland, now, in the beginning of winter, that is death by freezing, that is starvation and typhus fever, epidemics, and a miserable death. Do the people abroad suspect what is happening here? Will it be possible for help to come before it is too late? Will it be possible to raise the high sums in dollars for the visas? After all, most of the relatives abroad have no money themselves.

A few of our friends have just received visas for Cuba. They are parents or old mothers. Parting from them is easier. We hope that soon they will be able to follow us. Hopefully, they will. It cannot be that now they may no longer be able to leave, after their children procured the visas after such problems. We have to hope that they will yet succeed!

A university friend of my husband says farewell to us. His sister in Breslau just took her own life as she was about to be deported. He himself is completely calm and composed. "I've never been a coward. Until now I have endured everything and coped with it. I have no possibility of getting out. As long as I can, I will put up with things here. I will not let them torture me. If it has to be, then I will know how to die." An old teacher, who lives with an even older sister and her ninety-year-old mother, comes to us. She, too, is admirably calm. "My sister and I would take this, too, upon ourselves. But our mother! We must not subject her to these tortures. She does not know anything about these deportations yet. When we get our notice to vacate the apartment, then we will sit down in the kitchen with mother and turn on the gas. That is the only act of love that we can still perform for our mother." We dare not contradict. These poor people have to decide that for themselves.

Our seventy-two-year-old friend F. asks us to write to his daughter in Bolivia that he is healthy and doing well. Perhaps she can speed up the visa for Bolivia, which was applied for over a year ago. "But don't alarm my daughter. The poor girl cannot help me anyway." I have never seen this dear person be anything but cheerful and consistently friendly. Now, too, he speaks with us as if it were not a serious matter. "May things go well with you. I am really glad that at least you will be getting away. I am an old person. For me a few years more or less do not matter."

These terrible farewells. Don't cry, just don't cry. Once more I go through our house to take leave of the neighbors. One must not be cowardly. Perhaps they, too, have some sort of message. They can depend on us. We will pass it on immediately, as soon as we can write letters freely. If only it happens in time. I jot down addresses abroad; none of us say much, we just shake hands. Just no tears. One must not start that, otherwise one cannot stop. Who knows what will become of these people. In a situation like this, one can no longer say farewell in a conventional way. [. . .] What right do we have to leave this hell when the others have to endure it? Maybe we are only dreaming all of this. It is impossible that something so horrible exists on this earth.

For the last time we are sitting at our own table for a meal. Then we put on our coats, each one of us takes a knapsack and a small handbag, and we leave the house without looking back.

By city train we go to the Potsdam station. There, in the cellar of the station, the Jewish groups are assembled. After the examination of our papers we are let into the cellar. The door closes behind us. Thank God! The group is leaving today after all. Until the last moment we had been afraid that the journey would not be allowed. There are still many formalities with luggage and passports. We find out that last night the first groups also left Frankfurt am Main. Three hours pass until we are finally led in complete darkness through the unlit station to the train to Paris. A sealed car is designated for our group. We get in, the doors are closed, the train begins to move. We are riding to freedom.

Four days later the German government forbids departure for all Jews, and the army command discontinues the release of freight cars for the journey through France.[9]

But the deportation of Jews to Poland goes on.

1. A guarantee by a U.S. citizen in the form of a statutory declaration in which he vouches for the complete support of the new immigrant in case he gets into serious difficulties.

2. On the 12th and 13th of February 1940 some 1,200 Jews from Stettin and the province of Pomerania were deported to the region of Lublin. The deportation of the Jews from Baden, the Palatinate, and the Saarland to camps in southern France occurred on the 22nd and 23rd of October 1940. See Miriam Gerber (47).

3. At 116 Kurfürstenstrasse, in the former building of the Jewish Fraternal Society, there was the Department for Jewish Matters (Dept. IV, B4) of the Central Security Department of the Reich, directed by Adolf Eichmann.

4. See Alexander Szanto (38), note 3. — This harsh judgment on the Hilfsverein der deutschen Juden probably resulted from the fact that the Hilfsverein itself did not arrange for visas, but primarily provided information and counseling on the possibilities for emigration. For a visa one had to apply individually to the various countries, but the Hilfsverein, together with Jewish organizations abroad, tried in general to increase the opportunities for emigration. In the years 1933–1938 the Hilfsverein supported the emigration of 31,000 persons to European and overseas countries. It was not responsible for emigration to Palestine.

5. In the territory of the Reich the Yellow Star had to be worn as of September 19, 1941.

6. According to the statistics of the Reichsvereinigung, on October 1, 1941 there were still 72,872 "racial Jews" living in Berlin.

7. The Reich emigration tax was introduced for all emigrants in 1931. Originally, however, it affected only fortunes of over 200,000 marks and amounted to 25 percent. In May 1941, for Jews it was set at 80 percent, which does not mean that the rest of the fortune could really be taken out.

8. Here and in the following, reference is to the first deportations of Jews from Berlin, which took place on October 18, 1941. The first groups were sent to the Ghetto of Lodz (at that time, Litzmannstadt). On that same day the last train with emigrants, organized by the Reichsvereinigung, could still leave Berlin in the direction of Paris. The author was on it.

9. Emigration was prohibited on the 23rd of October 1941.

# 47  *Miriam Gerber, née Sondheimer*

 BORN IN 1922 IN WORMS.

Miriam Sondheimer, Diary. Manuscript, 98 Pages. Written in Worms, Heidelberg, Gurs, Marseille, Lisbon, Sosua, 1934–1942.

*Miriam Sondheimer's father ran a grain and forage business in Worms. Miriam attended public school until 1935, and then, until 1938, the Jewish district school in Worms. She began training as an infant nurse while the family sought in vain to emigrate. On October 22, 1940, the Sondheimer family, which had in the meantime moved to Heidelberg, was deported to southern France, along with all Jews from Baden, the Palatinate, and the Saarland. Miriam worked in the sick ward of the Gurs camp under the most difficult living conditions. Through relatives her family succeeded in obtaining an entry permit for the Dominican Republic and arrived in Sosua in July 1941. There some 600 Jewish immigrants settled as farmers, supported by the American Jewish Joint Distribution Committee. Miriam worked in a hospital until 1946, when she moved to New York. She married in 1954, had a son, and worked as a secretary.*

*Camp de Gurs, November 6, 1940.*

I have not written for two years. But if I wanted to describe these years precisely, I could fill a hundred diaries and it still would not be all. I think these are the most difficult years for us Jews since the world began. And now it seems gradually to be coming to a climax. I wish to God that it finally be reached and things become better again. Yesterday elections took place in the U.S.A. Perhaps Roosevelt has once more become president and will help us. We do not know anything here, for we've been gone from home for two weeks, and we are in Camp de Gurs in the Pyrenees in unoccupied France, as refugees or as internees or war prisoners, I don't know which. But from 1938 until now it was a long road and certainly not an easy one.

Above all, there was November 10, 1938, on which every synagogue in Germany was destroyed, and so much happened that it cries out to heaven for revenge. I was in the school of home economics in Frankfurt for just three weeks and had to go home again. When I entered our apartment I was greeted by broken glass, broken glass wherever one looked. Papa was fortunately on a trip and so he evaded the concentration camp. At first we didn't know where he was. During the day we lived at Uncle Albert's, and at night we slept at home, after we had picked up our bedding from the street. From then on our grandparents lived with us, for their apartment was completely destroyed. Aunt Paula Kehr was also with us. Uncle Seppl was in Buchenwald. For a period of time I went to the police every day to take food to L. Kiefer. Otherwise, we dared go out only for the most necessary things.

We were supposed to go to Wohlen in Switzerland with the children's transport. That didn't work out. Uncle Seppl returned from Buchenwald in a very sick condition and was gone for a long time for recuperation. Papa returned from the hospital in Mannheim.[1] On the 10th of November we had received notice to vacate our apartment. In January I was in Heidelberg for a time. On March 21st, Grandma's seventieth birthday, we moved. I had taken a course in the theory of baby care, and was supposed to go to Holland together with Lotti. We turned it down because Switzerland seemed more tempting. Lotti went away. Then emigration to England began. After a long search I received a guarantee. I had everything I needed ready. It would have taken another three weeks. Then the great misfortune struck: war broke out. On September 1, 1939 the invasion of Poland took place. Now things happened one right after the other. Radios were taken away from us. We had house searches, the police came constantly. There were food ration cards. We tried to emigrate to every imaginable and unimaginable country. Almost everything was a hoax. Our number for America, 19823, had no chance of coming up for a long time.[2] [. . .]

And then it is October 22, 1940. We are still in bed. Only Mutti is up. It is seven-thirty. Suddenly I hear unfamiliar men's voices in our hallway. And then I understand what it is they are announcing: "You are to be at the station within an hour. Fifty kilograms of luggage are allowed per person. Food for four days." Then there follow other instructions about things one isn't allowed to take along. Each person is allowed a hundred reichsmarks. Otherwise, only wedding ring, stainless steel watch, and necessities. — I am completely paralyzed with fear, jump out of bed, get dressed in the greatest hurry, heavy underwear. Lorle also gets up, listens, and begins to cry. Then, I don't quite know any more, everyone gets up, my grandparents, Papa. I make coffee, do everything wrong: We start packing. Warm things, we're told. Lublin? In the whole house one hears people scurrying about. Downstairs there is a policeman who doesn't let anyone out or in. We pack in a completely haphazard way. Everyone throws into the suitcase what he happens to find and thinks to be the right thing. I busy myself with the provisions. I pack them into the knapsacks.

Our cleaning woman comes and suddenly has a car and a niece at hand, who helps her take all perishables from our apartment. For she's allowed to do that. *We* have less help from her. E's maid takes a basket with freshly laundered linen, goes out the door with it and says to the policeman: "This belongs to me." She also goes to the linen drawers and does exactly the same. Then we are fetched. A police car drives up. By sixes people get in and are unloaded at the station. We are the last from our house. We stand in the house entrance and wait. The house keys are turned in. I go up once more and in a little pot get Lorle's full-cream milk. We drink it. Then the car comes. Our names are read off and we get in. We remain sitting for about another ten minutes in front of the door in the car and have to wait until the house is sealed off. Many people pass, stand nearby, or look out the window. They all gape, laugh, some are serious. All of us are calm and proud.

At the station we get off and are received by the police and the SS. In one room the last will has to be made, and Papa signs that the Reichsvereinigung will be his property administrator or something like that. Everyone, almost everyone, signs it. Then we go to the train. We board and together with the Wolfs we get an express train compartment to ourselves. It is twelve o'clock, and we hear that the train is not supposed to leave until six. The large luggage is loaded into the baggage cars; only knapsacks, blankets, and small suitcases may be taken along. Will we see our luggage again? There have been unfortunate experiences; for example, with the people from Stettin, who were sent to Lublin.[3] In their case the baggage cars were detached. I help to carry. Gradually they all come. Our best acquaintances and faces that we've never seen before in our lives. From the vicinity of Heidelberg, also. Some are calm and composed, others less so. All are struggling under the weight of their things, which they have gathered up in a great hurry. It is a sad picture. The very old and sick in wheelchairs are driven to the train in a car by two ambulance attendants. — Uncle Seppl was with us on the preceding days and now, thank God, he has received permission to go to his wife. We had already said farewell at home. Others were not so fortunate. Maybe someone was on a trip, didn't know anything yet, and his dear ones, here, were being shipped off, God knows where. Will he ever see them again?

Toward six o'clock everyone is there; we have to board. The train is being switched. The two sections are connected. There are about fifteen to twenty cars full of people who are now homeless, who have the bare necessities and sometimes not even that, and who are now being merged into a much closer community of fate than they have already been. Then we leave the station. On an opposite platform stands Frau F. and her son Hans: She is married to an "Aryan" and therefore doesn't have to go with us. Totally distraught, they call and shout and wave: "Goodbye, all the best, farewell!" On the platform we bought pop and beer and got paper cups for it. Now we are moving. The rumor spreads: France, Belfort. Oh God, just not to Poland! The men are discussing the train routes. We are on our way.

The first stop is Bruchsal. New people get on. Comrades in fate. We hear that the operation is only in Baden and the Palatinate. (We still do not know for certain.) Then we continue on our journey. Night comes. The train stops very often. In Karlsruhe and Freiburg more and more Jews join us. The train becomes terribly full. People are sitting and standing in the corridors with their luggage. The windows have to be closed, and the curtains drawn. The air is unbearable. Someone in uniform and two first-aid attendants hurry through the train and call out: "Is anyone feeling sick, does anyone have difficulty breathing?" It was the first and the last time.

We are traveling into the night, into an unknown region. Still the big question: East or West? If Breisach is next, we are saved, so to speak. Have we already passed it? Finally, already at dawn, we go across the Rhine bridge. France! The picture that presents itself to us now is a very unaccustomed one. For we are traveling through a stretch of the war theater. Everywhere untilled fields, huge holes in them, here and there a bunker, smashed rails, houses riddled with bullets. Horrible.

*Marseille, March 26,* 1941

Worms, Heidelberg, Camp de Gurs, Marseille. Who would have thought that we would be freed from Gurs so suddenly? But we must thank God for it, for what we have experienced there would in itself fill a thick book. On October 25, 1940 we arrived in Gurs, and on February 23, 1941 the gates closed behind us again. In between there was much sorrow but also many beautiful experiences.

The journey through France was very interesting in part, and our joy was especially great when we noticed that we were in the unoccupied zone and that the German train crew was gone. Now we could also get off and fetch water when the train stopped, which we weren't allowed to do earlier under threat of death; in the train there was no water. Twice on the way we were given food and drink, once in Mulhouse, where we received bread, soup, and water, and in addition were threatened: "Whoever has money, precious metals, securities, or other forbidden valuables in their suitcases and doesn't turn them in will be shot." That is said twice, three times, four times. Then cursory spot checks of the hand luggage are made. That is all.

We arrive at night in Oloron, and the train stands still until morning—beside three other trains with the same cargo.[4] Where will we end up? Then we are unloaded and piled into trucks, taken somewhere, presumably to a camp.

*Lisbon, May* 17, 1941
Dear God, I thank you! Dear God, I thank you for leading us out of the bedlam alive. Yes, we are really in Lisbon! We truly are, it is not a dream. We are in paradise! Finally, finally we made it! There were hard struggles enough, and the last weeks and days were terribly nerve-racking and upsetting, but now we are here. On the 10th of May in the evening we got on the train in Marseille, and on May 14th at five o'clock in the afternoon we got off here. The trip was strenuous and tiresome, but interesting and nice. Now I can write as I wish, without having to fear that it could be checked. I will now try to describe everything in sequence from Gurs until today. Unfortunately, it won't be as accurate as it would be if it were freshly experienced, but that won't hold me back.

Our truck stops, men out. This means separation from the men! It moves on, stops again, out. We don't see much of where we are. We drag our luggage and follow the ones who are walking in front of us, somewhere, to something—as we will later find out—called Block I. One wooden barrack next to another. At the entrance to the block, which is surrounded by barbed wire, which, of course, was later tripled, there stands a woman and counts us, and says: "Twenty." That means Barrack 20 and someone takes us there. In what area it is, I don't know; all the barracks look alike and face in the same direction. At one barrack door that we pass, I see L.K. from Heidelberg standing, and she calls out to me. Then comes Number 20. I think that for the rest of my life I shall not forget the moment when we entered the barrack and picked our places. For there was literally nothing inside except walls, a ceiling, and a floor. [. . .]

The majority of the 800 people who died during the winter in Gurs died of dysentery. There were days when there were twenty or more burials in the camp. Dysentery barracks were set up in every block. I myself, of course, also had dysentery, but thank God, not very badly. Probably I had caught it because I worked in the infirmary.

I began my work in the camp with duty in the washroom and with sanitation duties in my barrack. It was horrible, since for all practical purposes we had nothing we needed in the first weeks, not even a bed. Washroom duty I did together with A.F., a dear girl from Number 20, with whom I later became friends. Then I began to do night duty in the infirmary.

When I first got there in the evening and saw the many old sick people lying there, some on wooden frames, which in Gurs were give the wonderful name "bed," some on the floor, figures that, in addition to their blankets, were covered and dressed with everything possible in order to keep away the cold, and then the weak light, and the horrible stench, I felt very peculiar and had to leave the hall for a moment so I would not vomit. But that was the only time. Later everything went smoothly. I learned and saw a lot in the infirmary. I saw people getting well and I also saw people who died when terrible diarrhea took from them the last bit of strength they had. I did night duty eight times, and then I was allowed to work during the day, which was incomparably more pleasant for me and my parents. Because of this work I survived life in the camp better, for without work one couldn't have endured it, one would have gone mad.

Mutti also had a lot to do, especially since Grandma was sick practically the whole winter. Once Mutti and Grandma were sick at the same time and I cared for them. [. . .] Grandma became very sensitive as far as food was concerned. She could eat almost nothing of what there was in the camp, and what one was able to procure otherwise in itself did not suffice in the least. In the camp there was black water, called coffee, in the morning; at noon water with turnips; in the evening water with turnips plus either a sixth of a loaf of bread or a seventh, and by now it is only a ninth. And the loaves have by no means become larger. Now we are becoming acquainted with something we otherwise knew only by its name: hunger. It is worst for the people who have no money and who therefore can't afford anything extra. Now I can understand it well when someone steals food. As a matter of fact, I must even admire those people who are hungry and stand in front of food stores without breaking the windows. But for me personally, the cold was even worse than the hunger. It was especially terrible at night. Then Mutti and I put our mattresses on top of one another so that we weren't lying so much on the floor, and we lay down together on them and wrapped ourselves together in our blankets. That way it was warmer and we didn't freeze so. [. . .]

One day, at the end of December, we received a letter from America, from Uncle Gustav, saying that he would try to get us entry to Santo Domingo. His son Walter, he said, was secretary to David Schweitzer, the head of the Jewish Settlement Organization DORSA.[5] On January 8, 1941 we received a summons from the Dominican consulate in Marseille, which was to issue us a visa. That became the basis for our liberation from Gurs.

1. The father had hidden there to avoid deportation after the November pogrom. The author did not mention this fact for safety reasons.

2. The registration number for potential U.S.A. immigrants who fulfilled the immigration requirements but had to wait until their number was called. Corresponding to their quota system, the United States allowed only about 27,000 people from Germany and Austria to immigrate annually. Because of the great stream of refugees, this quota was by no means sufficient in 1939 and 1940. The American immigration law of 1921, which lay down the quota system, was, however, not changed.

3. See Elisabeth Freund (46), note 2.

4. On the 22nd and 23rd of October, 1940, some 7,000 Jews were deported from Baden, the Palatinate, and the Saarland to unoccupied France. The Vichy government detained them under the most primitive conditions in camp Gurs at the foot of the Pyrenees. A part of those affected succeeded in escaping the camp by emigration or flight; the majority were later deported further to the death camps in Poland.

5. Dominican Republic Settlement Association. DORSA was founded in 1939 in New York with funds from the Jewish Joint Distribution Committee in order to settle Jewish refugees from Europe in the Dominican Republic. President Trujillo, at the international conference of Evian, had agreed to accept refugees and made a corresponding contract with DORSA. Starting in 1940 some 600 immigrants were settled on the north coast in Sosua, where they ran dairy farms and founded a plant for dairy products.

# 48  *Käte Mugdan, née Rosenthal*

 BORN IN 1859 IN MAGDEBURG; DIED IN 1942 IN BERLIN.

Heinrich Mugdan, From My Diary. Manuscript, September 1942, 8 pages. Copied by the author in 1959 and furnished with some explanations (in parentheses).

*Käte Rosenthal was born in Magdeburg as the daughter of the physician Dr. Heinemann Rosenthal. In 1880 she married the Breslau merchant Hugo Mugdan, who owned a dry-goods store on the Ring. In 1893 she was already widowed. Of her five children the three sons died early; the two daughters attended the university, and emigrated with their families in 1938/39. In 1931 Käte Mugdan moved to Berlin. When in August 1942 the eighty-three-year-old woman received her notice of deportation, she prevailed upon her grandson Heinrich Mugdan (a chemistry student) to enable her suicide. She spent her final hours with him, reading the classics and praying, and she died with composure. The following selection from the diary of her grandson depicts the last days of his grandmother. Heinrich Mugdan, born in 1916 as son of the physician Dr. Franz Mugdan and his non-Jewish wife, attained his doctorate in 1944 in Heidelberg, and between 1946 and 1978 he was a Gymnasium teacher in Baden and, finally, in Karlsruhe.*

*[Heinrich Mugdan comes from Heidelberg for a visit to Berlin, and lives with his brother Ernst and the latter's fiancée, Edith.]*

*Wednesday, August 12, 1942:* In the afternoon to Grandmother's. Compared to last year, I found her aged, nervous, volatile. [. . .]

*Tuesday, August 18, 1942:* Grandmother has received notification that she is to be taken away. A lady from the Jewish community wrote down her personal data and left her the number Th. 4069 (interpreted by us, no doubt correctly, as Theresienstadt[1]).— Now everything is taking its inevitable course. We deliberate once more: Neckargemünd? Heidelberg? In the evening and after thinking matters over at night, Brunnengasse seems a possibility, and the best one. (On Brunnengasse in Heidelberg L.N. had lived for years in the home of a landlady who had the great advantage of being deaf.) For dinner at Lutz Heuss's.[2] We pretend to be unaffected.

*Wednesday, August* 19, 1942: Lunch at Grandmother's. She is beginning to get things ready and to pack. I mention Brunnengasse. At first she will scarcely hear of it. Finally I make the suggestion again, more urgently. She seems to grasp at it. Yet, the next morning she rejects it completely: "What if I die?" In the evening, after dinner, a visit to Walter with (my cousin) Liesel. [. . .] Conversation about all kinds of things; in my thoughts only my grandmother.

*August* 20 *and* 21, 1942: At Grandmother's, who continues to be occupied with preparations. These days I get to know different friends at her place: Frau Pascher, Frau Professor Ziegler, later also Fräulein Stapel and Fräulein Gerhardt. Then there are the building caretakers ("Aryan" janitor, furnaceman, etc.), whom, more or less, I pretty much dislike; Herr Remer, who hauls away everything he can get his hands on, Frau Raeder, who gets the china. In the meantime, Ernst continues his efforts with Counselor Bollert to get the authorities to exempt Grandmother from deportation. There is no response. The other way out: illness. It depresses Grandmother that she has to feign sickness, although, again, she does not completely reject it, probably would feel capable of it in a moment of danger. But she "simply cannot, will not" lie in bed.

*Saturday, August* 22: I am not at Grandmother's, but Edith and Ernst probably are. Then the next thing happens: the injunction to vacate the apartment by the 31st of August and to ready everything for the relocation to an "old-age home." Dishes and clothing, as far as they are not a personal necessity, are to be picked up by the Jewish community, and, last, the furniture is to be recorded and confiscated. With that the final deadline is set. The distress is becoming greater and greater.

In the meantime, I went rowing with Liesel in the afternoon out on the Wannsee, in Walter's boat. Dinner in the city at the Fürstenhof. After a brief stop on Carmerstrasse, Liesel leaves. I go to bed before the others return. Then I hear Ernst's report.

*Sunday, August* 23: Bad weather—fortunately—thwarts plans for a Sunday outing. Around noon I arrive at the Mommsens'. The poison. (Just in case, I had potassium cyanide on hand from the lab and had sent Grandmother some of it upon her request.) How suddenly people become so much closer. — Lunch with Edith, Ernst, and Walter in a Chinese restaurant on Kantstrasse. Afterwards to Grandmother's. She is becoming more and more resolute in her basic attitude. It is only a pity that her worries about her things do not allow her any peace. Of course, perhaps it's just as well; this way she doesn't have the chance to think too much—at least during the day, for at night she hardly sleeps at all. I try to distract her, draw her attention to the way things were, memories. I read from the old poems, the chronicle of Joachim Mugdan, the guest book—but she never allows that to divert her for very long before something occurs to her that has to be taken care of. Ernst and Edith come after dinner. We play a game of rummy, drink a glass of wine, which unfortunately has turned sour. — My suggestion to stay the night is not yet accepted this time: "Tomorrow." Early in the afternoon Grandmother sends me with a bundle to the Paschers at 11 Tangastrasse. From the Putlitzstrasse station I wander around in the area, probably for an hour. I find the Paschers to be very nice people. (I already knew her from earlier, thus I mean him and their daughter, who is about twenty). The garden. The dahlia "Susanne." The cherries. Frau Pascher's anxiety. In the meantime, Grandmother is very worried about me, since the others also come too late.

*Monday, August* 24: My trip is somewhat delayed. Between the station and Güldenhofer Ufer (No. 10, Grandmother's apartment) I meet Frau Pascher, who is going home overloaded with things and who greets me very cordially. — In the meantime, the mail brought the next notice. Again written by the Jewish community. For the time being, it speaks of a "Berlin Old-Age Home"—3 Gormannstrasse—of luggage that is to be transported, etc. The pick-up date? Thursday, beginning at one o'clock. I decide to make further inquiries at the place of its origin (the Jewish community), Oranienburgerstrasse, although at first Grandmother stubbornly refused to see the purpose of this undertaking. In the end she proved to be right. At the Central Office for Old-Age Homes, my main question: "Is it a matter of a temporary or a long-term stay?" is answered evasively, but the tone of the answer is telling enough. The attempt to find out more at the Housing Office[3] fails, due to the fact that they don't even let me in. I call. The impatient Herr Adler: "Talk faster, I'm busy." To my question as to whether private accommodations are still possible: "No, officially forbidden. Surely you know that the measure is connected with deportation." Gormannstrasse is only a "stopover." — I take the hopeless news to Ernst in his office and then I go out to Grandmother's again. I stay there overnight. How moving, how old Grandmother is, in her little nightgown, her hair braided into a thin little plait, her mouth, without dentures, terribly sunken, her speech difficult. It's a little disconcerting to her that I am there; she would like to take care of everything in the room herself: black-out, open the window. On the other hand, it is probably also comforting to her. Because very soon I hear her breathing deeply in her sleep. I lie awake for a long time, wake up early in the morning, and cannot keep my thoughts from revolving around the end.

*Tuesday, August* 25: While I'm about to call the Welfare Office[4] for Frau Bernheim (the over-seventy-year-old, gabby, and untidy Frau Bernheim, who was lodged at Grandmother's by order, along with the "mixed," and for that reason temporarily unmolested, Garten couple, had also received the order to move out). — A lady comes to the house, who makes a list of all possessions and, besides, reports good things about Theresienstadt, tells us that the luggage will be picked up and that one is permitted to take along all kinds of personal necessities—except books. "And what do you think about that?" — "That didn't concern me in the least. That's out of the question for me. For you I'll be dead there, and for me that is not life anymore. I would have liked to live a little longer the way it was here lately. I really got much pleasure out of it. It was like a second youth. And I had still planned to read so much. I wanted to read *Faust* and *Hamlet* again, as I do every year. And my needlework: I would have liked so much to finish knitting the angora-wool pullover for Irene. And I also started to net a string bag again (how many she has given away as presents these days!). And I enjoyed cooking so much. Earlier I never did cook. And I think I could have learned to cook very well. I really did have a beautiful life until recently. But to be there—away from my dear ones and not to know anything about one another, that I don't want." That was the gist of many a conversation. More and more clearly she was approaching her end.

She didn't expect anything of the Bollert scheme. And really, it could have brought about only an uncertain postponement. That she did not want: to expose herself to ever new threats. Acting sick would also not have been any better. At best she would have been taken to a hospital, where she would have been no safer. — Now, in retrospect, it seems as if, given the unclear jurisdiction of the individual authorities, it would have been possible for her to stay in the apartment after all. For how long, of course? It is possible that a number of similar, seemingly peaceful, days would have been granted her. But it's not likely, and in this one week she had inwardly advanced so far on her road to death that she would no longer have easily regained her peace of mind, considering that there was no security for her. Her decision became more and more unwavering, no enticement could affect it, notwithstanding her enjoyment of beauty and of life, which remained with her until the very last. But after this upheaval her heart would probably not have been in condition, purely physically, for a hazardous existence, and any continuation of her life would have been just that.

In the evening Ernst came for dinner: "I feel like a common murderer." Grandmother: "On the contrary, the ancients regarded it as the greatest and loftiest act of friendship to help a friend in dire need to die." These days she has been looking for the passage in Socrates' *Apology* where he speaks of death: "People speak of death as if they knew that it is the greatest calamity. But I am not sure whether it is not perhaps the highest good. . . . " Ernst doesn't want to hear of it: Death is a gruesome end, a boundary from beyond which no looking back, no contact with the living is possible.

*Wednesday, August 26:* The day begins early with great anxiety. Frau Bernheim is packing desperately and is probably wondering why we are not doing the same, but is totally absorbed by her own worries. — The first one to come is a young man to pick up the luggage. He is decent, calm, although Aryan. He does this all the time. He simply lets Frau Bernheim finish rummaging about and then takes her luggage away. He would have also taken her along right then and there if she had wanted to. Towards eleven o'clock Edith arrives. I leave the two of them alone, get vinegar essence, call Ernst, which takes impossibly long. [. . .] Soon after my return two people arrived, both very correct, one from the community, the other to pick up the things intended for the community. We had nothing ready. But since the men said clearly that whatever they did not get would go to the Gestapo, Grandmother was willing to give it to them. Thus there was great disorder in the apartment. Edith helped quite a bit, among other things by packing some dishes from the kitchen. Finally that, too, was over. Grandmother had gotten very excited and couldn't quite do anything. Fortunately, she didn't have to cook much, since there were left-overs from the night before. In the afternoon, for a long time she couldn't be convinced to sit down and rest. Only later was I able to read to her a little.

Among the old things we had found the little play that Aunt Berta had written for Grandmother's seventieth birthday and that the Stenzels and their friends had performed: about the ceaseless activities of a grandmother who was needed everywhere by everyone, about the Treuenfels' radio, which through the Paschkes got to the drunkard K., etc. Grandmother was able to get real pleasure from it and had many details to relate. I wanted to make use of this good opportunity to immerse ourselves further in our "chronicle," which last night, after Ernst's departure, had taken us back to the more pleasant past for a little while. — Then Ernst arrived. Right away, Grandmother became anxious again. In the meantime, I saw to the dinner that Frau Garten was going to prepare. And she really did cook us an excellent dish: fried potatoes, vegetables with cutlet—for our last coupons. And for dessert there were canned cherries from Neckargemünd. — After dinner Ernst and I washed the dishes. Meanwhile, Grandmother made preparations for her favorite dish: whipped eggs. Frau Remer had brought her two eggs, which I helped her to beat, the yolk separately with sugar and the whipped egg white along with it. The one egg was golden yellow, the other was pale. And we divided both into three cups, equally by amount and color. "Now you've eaten my favorite dish. I've often made that for my evening meal, along with bread and butter. It's really delicious. But I don't know if you like it. I still wanted to make that for you. — My last meal." — It really was delicious. While I was still tidying up, Grandmother read to Ernst from the Bible: "All is vanity" (Ecclesiastes). Then the three of us sat down at the accustomed table by the cozy light. I brought us something to read. And then I once again read aloud Aunt Berta's play, which had amused Grandmother so and did not fail to have its effect now either. In the meantime, it had turned eleven o'clock and time for Ernst to bid farewell. While he was doing that, I occupied myself in the kitchen.

After he had gone, I went to her feeling like a criminal. She was standing there exhausted. But soon she pulled herself together: "Ernst is too soft. We will be strong till the very end." Unforgettable, the gesture with which she said that: complete classical dignity and strength. — Then we sat for a good hour; she told of earlier days, of her happy childhood, her sweet mother; then she spoke of her own children, of the unruly Franz, who after his father's death nevertheless became so easily tractable; of clever Berta; the charming twins, her favorites. And then again she asked about me. It was comforting for her to hear that in spite of everything I believed in life, that somehow I also had hope. "It is good that you are not as despondent as Ernst." — At one point, Thekla's monologue occurred to her, and we looked for the passage in *Wallenstein,* that is, she looked for it. Amazing how she has retained these things in her memory. She had read *Wallenstein* again just recently. "I used to know a hundred poems by Schiller by heart, and I still know them pretty well." In this, too, she was admirable.

Then, it was close to one o'clock. She wanted to go to bed. She noticed two peaches in the fruit bowl. "Oh, the wonderful peaches. Let's eat them." While we are getting ready to do that at the round table, the siren sounds the alarm. The Gartens are moving about outside and I finally have to tell Grandmother, who heard nothing. At first she becomes restless. Then, however, we sit down and eat our peaches. We put the little light back into the room. — Now Grandmother gets ready for the night. Again and again, she thinks of something among her possessions: "But you know very well who is to get what. Whatever you do will be the right thing." — You dear, good Grandmother. — It was almost two o'clock. Grandmother was just about to go into the bathroom when the all-clear signal came. And then she got washed most thoroughly while the Gartens came back up again from outside and then disappeared. She put on her funeral dress, which she had decided upon earlier, braided her hair, removed her dentures, and lay down on her bed. Before, however, she had struggled with hands raised in prayer for the strength for this final step. "God has always been merciful to me. I have always been able to pray. Even now I can do it." And she prayed long and audibly, while I stood at the window with a bad conscience, raised the shade, and let the full moon shine into the room. "It is so beautiful outside, you can still see the moon." — "Then I have to look at it once more." And she came and one more time she drank fully of the pure air and took in the beauty with her eyes. "One can really say: You fill again bush and valley" . . . "Oh, were you, full moon, looking for the last time on my torment," she had quoted yesterday. Then I led her back to bed. She took a strong dose of sleeping pills and still couldn't fall asleep, as she lay there ready for the final step. "I am still completely awake." — "Are you distressed?" — "No, I am completely calm, I am praying for all of you. I am very sure that it will work. Someday things will be better for you." — "I am not asleep at all." — "But we have so much time, the night is still so long. And I would like you to fall asleep peacefully." — "Why do you want to make it so easy on me? For that I have to give you a kiss." Finally, she lay down on her side, as usual, and fell asleep. What emotions.

*Thursday, August 27:* The vain attempt with inhalation (of hydrogen cyanide gas made with the help of the vinegar). At four o'clock I have to wake her, let her drink. The most horrible moments until 4:13. The last ministrations. The hours until the morning, during which I can still be with her, embrace her. The candle, almost consumed, is still flickering. Finally, when I open my eyes, it is dawning. Across the way people are stirring. Shortly before seven I leave my dear one, call the doctor and Ernst. Then it comes over me. Upstairs Frau Garten . . . "Grandmother is no longer alive." — "There is something funny about that." And the chores of this desolate morning, which forced its way into the room with such bright sunlight. Tidying up. Packing. Ernst. At ten o'clock, Dr. Sonntag. Ernst's careless remark about "suicide," which prevents the conscientious man from writing down something else. — The complications at the police. The detective. The suitcases. The "collectors," whom I meet on the stairs. *They* were fetched already earlier, while I was downstairs. — Frau Bernheim's departure. — Exhausted after further brief tidying-up. Frau Garten makes coffee for me. I eat a few pieces of bread, feel somewhat stronger. We leave. Then it comes over me, terribly. Outside. In broad daylight. At "home," to bed. Sleep. — In the evening Liesel comes for a little while, alone. Piano: Bach.

*Friday, August 28:* Made order out there (Grandmother's apartment).

*Saturday, August 29:* A visit to Frau Heuss:[5] "No scruples—ever."

1. Primarily old people from Germany were deported to the Theresienstadt ghetto. Of almost 42,000 Jews from the former German Reich (of whom 20,000 died in Theresienstadt), 31,000 were over sixty-one years old. Most of those who did not die in the ghetto were then deported to Auschwitz and murdered there.

2. Dr. Ernst Ludwig Heuss (1910–1967); the son of the future president of the Federal Republic, Theodor Heuss.

3. The housing information center of the Jewish community managed all Jewish dwellings, since Jews were now allowed to live only in special "Jews houses." The office was forced to cooperate in the preparation of the deportations. Gradually, it had to make all Jews living in Berlin fill out special questionnaires according to which the Gestapo determined those to be deported.

4. The Welfare Office of the community was at that time still managed by Dr. Fritz Lamm (1876–1942), who was shot as a hostage in October 1942. See Bruno Blau (51), note 3.

5. Elly Heuss-Knapp (1881–1952) freely recreated the events depicted by Heinrich Mugdan in the small prose volume *Schmale Wege* (1946).

# 49  *Camilla Neumann, née Selinger*

 BORN IN 1892 IN BUDAPEST; DIED IN 1955 IN NEW YORK.

Camilla Neumann, Report on My Experiences from the Time of Hitler. Manuscript; 29 pages. Written in Berlin, 1946.

*Camilla Selinger grew up in the town of her birth, Budapest, and in Constantinople, where she attended German schools. In 1913 she married the Berlin bank official Ludwig Neumann and lived from 1913 until 1949 in Berlin. Her husband was a middle-level employee of the Dresdener Bank, where she, too, worked until 1918. When her husband was forced to retire in 1936, the author tried in vain to induce him to emigrate. Her daughter emigrated in 1938 as a nursing teacher to England. Starting in April of 1941, the author had to do forced labor. In the course of the "factory operation" of February 27, 1943, her husband was arrested at his job and deported to Auschwitz. She immediately went underground, for a short time lived with different non-Jewish acquaintances, and then worked for a year and a half as help on an estate in Berlin-Frohnau, where her situation was known and exploited. In the end she survived with false papers, and in 1949 she emigrated to the United States.*

In October 1941 the mass deportations began in Berlin. From then on the mood among the Jews reached rock bottom. Already for weeks before the atmosphere was bleak, for in the smaller towns the Jews had already been rounded up and deported to Lublin and Piaski. In Berlin the Kulturbund and the only Jewish school were dissolved,[1] and prayer services were not allowed to be held even in the most modest setting. At the Jewish community, the members of the Kulturbund, actors, musicians, etc., prepared lists of persons for the Gestapo. In a word, it was the beginning of the end. Here, too, one was ready for the worst, and yet, when the horror came, not really. From then on, one packed and unpacked one's suitcases in panic. Every moment there were new regulations about what one could take along. And yet one saw more and more clearly that all the packing was senseless, for the things were taken away from one anyhow. The poor people on the hours-long marches that took them to their "goal" gradually threw away their things themselves, from exhaustion. One did not know where many of the transports ended up, and if one did know it, one found out at the same time that the people were perishing there.

These deportations were something monstrous and were surpassed only by the mass murders. It was horrible when the dark car with the SS bandits stopped in front of the door and picked up the careworn men and women and the innocent children. The manner of picking-up changed every few weeks. They always wanted to do something new; the main thing was that it happened "suddenly" and "spontaneously."

The first ones received notification that their apartment would be used for other purposes, and that they had to fill out the enclosed list. At first no one suspected the purpose of that, but later one did know what the "list" meant. It was a checklist, on which one was supposed to enter all of one's furnishings, clothes, linen. They were then confiscated with the help of the list, right as the "evacuation" was taking place.—Later the list was dropped, and one received only a notification that one had to stay in the apartment the next day or the day after the next for the purpose of being picked up. The messengers were mostly people from the community. Even the orchestra conductor Schwarz[2] delivered such death sentences, for in reality they were nothing else. The Jewish community was simply nothing more than a department of the Gestapo. Of course, it now happened that individuals fled and went underground somewhere, and thus there were no longer always prior notifications. Now one was no longer sure of one's life even for a minute within one's own four walls, and every meal could be the last.

Since picking up people from their apartments did not go fast enough for the Gestapo, a large number of officials of the Jewish community had to participate in the round-ups. They were authorized by the Gestapo, and one had to go with them. If one resisted, they used force. They said that otherwise it would cost them their own heads. We were very distressed that Jews allowed themselves to be involved in something like that. But it did not stop with that. Finally the Jews were caught like dogs. They were rounded up from the stores, from the waiting rooms of doctors, from the streets, and were loaded onto trucks. If one did not climb on quickly enough, one was shoved on. The last operation, the so-called "factory operation," was on February 27, 1943. Everyone was picked up. Hundreds of trucks with SS drove up to all factories where Jews were working and deported the people as they were, straight from their job. They were sent to two camps, men and women apart, and on the same evening their deportation to Auschwitz began. In open cattle cars, without blankets and coats. Many froze to death on the way. Most of the deportees, it was said, went right to the gas chambers. Only young and very strong people were separated and assigned to the labor camps.

Before I begin to talk about our own fate I want to tell about our relatives and friends. For years already Ludwig had not seen his Stettin relatives, the Flaters; I did not even know them. However, when we heard about the horrible lot of the Jews of Stettin, we got in touch with the Flaters and offered them our help. At that time this was still possible. We then found out from them that Adolf Flater had been picked up under cover of darkness, without previous notification, and deported to Lublin with his wife and child, his two sisters and an aunt. That was at the beginning of the year 1940, in the most bitter cold.[3] From Lublin they had to march for several hours through the deep snow to Belzyce. They called that the "death march," for many collapsed on the way and remained lying, among them also their aunt. They themselves, by exerting all their strength, endured the march, but they threw away all their luggage, little by little, along the way. Behind them drove a big truck, which collected the luggage and took it back to Germany. In Lublin the five people had lived in one room, under the most primitive conditions. Still, Adolf as camp physician fared much better than the others who had to live in the camp. The poor hygienic conditions soon contributed to an outbreak of a typhoid epidemic, and people were dying like flies. We, along with the Flaters, the Oppels, Martin and Grete, helped by sending them everything they needed. Even Julius Hirsch participated. We sent them everything from a kitchen pot to a handkerchief. Every day a package went off to them. After only six weeks they wrote that they already had more than they were able to take along from Stettin. Then we provided them with medications and cheap jewelry from Woolworths, since Flaters could exchange these things for food. The Poles were very keen on such baubles. We were in contact with one another until the spring of 1942. Then, very suddenly, there was no more news. The first transport had to make way for other transports.

The Oppels were among the first to receive a "list," and Felix, in his exceedingly great conscientiousness, did fill out everything most accurately. No one knew what that was all about. The Oppels were afraid that they would have to vacate the apartment and then perhaps would be put up in one room. Unfortunately it turned out to be much worse. Two days after they had handed in the list they were picked up on a Friday evening at nine o'clock. A neighbor from the house happened to be at their place when the doorbell rang. Felix went to the door and asked who was there. Thereupon came the answer: "Open up, in the name of the law!" Frightened, the neighbor escaped through the back door, and the Oppels opened. Within one hour they had to get ready and leave the apartment with the officials. They hardly were able to take anything along, because Rosa had to support Felix and for months Erna had had an inflamed nerve in her arm. A Councilor of Commerce lived at their place, and on the next day he told us of the horrible event. I lack the words to describe how crushed we were. Since Felix's serious illness in the summer of 1938, we had been close friends. Rosa held me up as a model, entirely undeservedly, and told everyone how I had contributed to Felix's recovery. Ludwig, who was still not working, went every day to the Oppels and told me how they were freezing because they wanted to save their few pieces of coal for even more severe cold. But then I scolded and told them that these days one could not plan so far ahead. On Friday they let me know that they had taken my advice to heart and had made a nice fire. And on that day the disaster happened. These first deportees from Berlin, exactly two thousand people, were assembled in the synagogue on Levetzow-strasse.[4] They stayed there several days, because at that time there were still many formalities to be taken care of. Later they did not go to so much trouble with us. Although the Oppels were still in Berlin, we could not see them anymore, for the Gestapo had guards in front of the gates. After this group left, several days later the following notice appeared in the paper: "In recent days many Jews have left Germany in great haste, leaving debts behind."

For weeks we heard nothing from the Oppels. With great effort Ludwig finally succeeded in finding out that the Oppels had been sent to Lodz (Litzmannstadt). Ludwig wrote to them through the "Eldest of the Jews" saying that they should tell us their address by return mail so that we could help them. Finally, the reply came, written by Rosa. They were living there under conditions similar to those of the people from Stettin in Lublin, and upon receipt of Ludwig's letter they had cried bitterly from homesickness. Then a card also arrived from Erna. Unfortunately, it was not possible for us to send even *one* little package to them, because the post office did not accept any packages going to Litzmannstadt. Since the Oppels had been so close to us, it was terrible that we could do so little to help them, of all people, in their direct need. To Martin Reissner, who later was sent away, we were able to send packages, or better, to his wife, for he soon died. It was just different—to Warsaw one could send packages, to Litzmannstadt one was allowed only to send ten reichsmarks per week. Receipt was confirmed to us by standard-form cards. The cards were signed alternately by Felix, Rosa, and Erna. This way we knew that all three of them were still alive. After approximately four months, a cash remittance came back. On the stub it said laconically: "Moved. Address unknown." In addition, however, there were three other remittances on the way, which did not come back.

By chance we learned after only a short time what a horrible end those unfit for work met in Lodz. In our house, 26 Heilbronner Strasse, lived a young married couple. They, too, had their parents and a sister in Lodz. Illegally, through a member of the German army, the sister wrote very long and detailed letters, and so we found out that in Lodz every few weeks a roll call took place for the purpose of "resettlement." The Jews had to line up in rank and file, a commission went through the rows and separated all old people, the weak, and the sick. Sometimes it was even enough if one looked bad. These selected people were loaded onto a truck and were driven to the forest. After some hours the trucks returned—with the clothes, shoes, and underwear of the unfortunates. Horrible!

Once the previously mentioned soldier came to Berlin on leave. I did not see him personally, only heard what he had told. Since that time I know *how* the Oppels died. But there are things about which one simply cannot speak. The Nazi mentality devised methods that are truly unique in their cruelty. These memories shock me again and again. [. . .]

And now I shall tell about our personal fate. We received the "list" for the first time in December 1942. Thereupon I was drafted by the factory, and Spanier, who handled our case at the community, deferred us. Since I was afraid that my being drafted might not protect Ludwig in the long run, we were already considering whether it would not be better if Ludwig were also working. We were saved from this deliberating back and forth when Ludwig received a dispatch from the labor office in January 1942. On the very next day he had to begin work at Fromm's in Köpenick. He had more humane superiors than I, but the work went far beyond his capacity. In the room where he worked there were furnaces on both sides, and the heat was unbearable. All day long frames weighing one and a half centners had to be shoved into and pulled out of these furnaces. Two people lifted the frame, and one maneuvered it in such a way that it went into the furnace in the right position. The frames were extremely heavy because of the full glass forms, which were coated with liquid rubber. More than once it happened that someone fainted because of the extreme effort and the terrible heat. In addition, there was also the poor nutrition, for Jews did not receive meat, fish, eggs, vegetables, or fruit. Whether the same happened to Ludwig I don't know, for he concealed everything unpleasant from me as much as he could. He did, however, grow visibly thinner, and if we had not had my sister's help the whole time, Ludwig would not have been able to bear it. Because Ludwig was working, I had it harder, too, for besides the factory I now also had to take care of the household. Grete helped me by coming once a week and cleaning the apartment thoroughly. Even worse than the additional work was the fact that we could hardly talk to one another anymore. If I had the late shift I did not see Ludwig from Sunday evening until Saturday noon, thus for six days. But every evening there were a few dear lines from Ludwig on my night table, and naturally I, too, put a little note for him on the dinner table every day. When he got up in the morning and left, I was still asleep, and when I came home at twelve midnight, he was sleeping. Before I went to bed I sat and prepared breakfast for Ludwig. Thus I did not go into the room before 1:30 and Ludwig got up already at 4:00. If I worked the early shift, we were at least able to eat together in the evening. Ludwig left before 5:00 in the morning and came home at 6:45 in the evening. The way there itself took four hours, and on top of it the heavy labor! He did this work really by expending all his energy. It was, after all, a matter of one's life.

In the spring of 1942 we received the second order to stand by. This time, too, Blaupunkt drafted me, and the draft also extended to Ludwig. But from that time on we did not have a single happy moment. One transport after another left for Poland and there was always one of our relatives or friends on it, and little by little it also leaked out what awaited us there. The mass executions could not be kept secret in the long run. Above all, one already saw the bestial way in which the deportations took place: in open cattle or freight cars, with a bucket for relieving oneself. No food. One awaited every new day with great anxiety. "Who will it be this time?" was the fearful question. The sword of Damocles hung above us constantly, and that demanded all of our spiritual, emotional, and physical strength.

In the fall of 1942, the Gestapo began to pay hardly any attention to the drafts, and also picked up people who were working. The gaps in the factories became bigger and bigger. Since the armaments plants could no longer fulfill their quotas, the army complained to the Gestapo. The Gestapo promised the firms foreign workers. Until then the Jews were to be sent to a camp set up in December on Auguststrasse and were to go to work from there. The camp was an accommodation unworthy of human beings. One lay on plank beds, and otherwise, too, the hygiene left a great deal to be desired. But also, in other ways, the ones who stayed behind were not to be envied; for the fewer workers that remained, the more work was squeezed out of them. But that no longer mattered either. One had become dispirited. Dispirited and tired of life, tired of fear and of horror.

I now decided to put an end to my life. I went to our good Dr. Lissner and asked him for Veronal. He refused it to me. But he himself took poison a week later. I already had sixteen tablets, but you could not do anything with that, especially since I did not want to leave Ludwig behind alone under any circumstances. In those days, Veronal was a desired item; Jews paid a thousand reichsmarks for thirty tablets. But there were still other possibilities of parting with life, and I spoke with Ludwig about it. Ludwig did not want to and had many objections. At first he said: "It would be paradoxical if one took one's life out of fear of death." And then he said again and again that he would like to see Ursel [their daughter] again and did not want to deprive himself of this possibility by suicide. Ludwig simply did not *want* to take a realistic view and was still waiting for the "miracle." Yet he also suffered terribly, for he simply could not grasp that the German people had let things reach that point. He did not understand that a nation that had produced people like Bach, Beethoven, and Goethe now embraced a Hitler, Himmler, and Goebbels. Ludwig realized that he had been mistaken from the beginning and that this mistake was becoming disastrous for us. He asked my forgiveness that he had not done anything about emigration when it was still possible. I could not bear to see that besides all the suffering we were subjected to, he was also tormenting himself with self-reproaches. Therefore, I comforted him and said that we would not have escaped our fate anywhere. At that time this was not yet my full conviction. I only said that to calm Ludwig. Since 1939, when we were still arguing about emigration, there had never been any discord between us.

Starting in November 1942 we lived constantly with the feeling of approaching catastrophe. The system of extermination by the Nazi criminals functioned in a way that overlooked no one. It is impossible to describe those horrible weeks. Every time the doorbell rang, we were startled and we were afraid to go to the door. When we went to work, we were afraid that the car was already standing in front of the door to get us. When we came home from work, at first we did not quite dare enter the apartment. Our "final solution" had long since been decided. Because of the collapse at Stalingrad it could not go fast enough for these monsters; they had to take revenge for their defeat somehow.

At the beginning of January 1943 I had the day shift and came home at six o'clock. In the pitch-dark yard I noticed people running back and forth. When I got to the stairway I saw three men standing in front of the first-floor apartment, which was occupied by the married couple I mentioned earlier. Immediately, the thought came to me that they could be Gestapo helpers, and I opened my coat so that one could not see my star. So that they would not notice that I was going to my apartment, I went up to the Friedländers. The latter were just about to leave. Thus I went down again with them and took this opportunity to go into my apartment unnoticed. I had not darkened any of the rooms yet, and therefore I did not turn on a light, and I waited. After a few minutes the doorbell rang. Then there was knocking. It went on incessantly, but I did not stir. I had to expect that our tenant, Herr Kurzmann, could come home any moment, and was already considering what I would do then. Only a short time later the door was, in fact, being unlocked, and our tenant, followed by three people, came into the apartment. In the darkness I was able quickly to slip into the pantry. Of course I first pulled out the key from the outside. It took quite a while before the light was turned on in the apartment, because Kurzmann had to first darken all of the windows. When the light was switched on, they went through the whole apartment, and every time they came to the kitchen I could see them through a crack in the pantry door. One of them kicked the pantry door once with his boot and asked if that was a backstairs exit, which Kurzmann naturally denied. Since Kurzmann had to get ready for deportation, he came into the kitchen often and I heard him being asked "on his word of honor" where we were, to which he was not able to answer. During the time that I stood in the pantry, I heard how the door to the first floor apartment was smashed in, and after a while a second door crashed. I peeked from the little window and saw that in the yard people were running back and forth with flashlights. My situation was terrible, but still I thank God that on this evening Ludwig had air raid duties and would not run into the arms of the Gestapo. Then I stood immobile for four full hours.

At ten o'clock the Gestapo left the apartment and took Kurzmann along. When I saw that everything was quiet in the yard, I came out of the pantry.

If the past hours had been terrible, those that followed were to become much worse. Above us there had been living for some time a couple named Klein. They were party members. Nevertheless, sometimes the wife secretly slipped something into our hands. Encouraged by that, I ran upstairs to her. I wanted to call Ludwig from the Klein's and tell him that I intended to leave the house at night, and that he should not come home the next morning. To my great horror, I learned from Frau Klein that Ludwig was already on his way home. A colleague of his, Wilhelm Neumann, who also lived on Heilbronner Strasse, had called him and told him that the Gestapo was picking up everyone from our house and that now they had also been in our apartment for a few hours. Thereupon Ludwig called Frau Klein and asked if all that was true. When she confirmed it, Ludwig said that then he would come home right away. That was at nine o'clock. At eleven o'clock, then, he would be home. While I was pondering that, I heard Frau Friedländer coming home. I pulled her into the Klein's apartment, and Frau Friedländer told me that two people were still standing in front of the door, waiting for Ludwig and me. In addition she said that the first-floor apartment had been forced open. Since the young wife was at home alone, she barricaded herself in the bedroom. This second door was also broken down. In the meantime the young woman had taken poison. However, I was thinking only of Ludwig and that Ludwig would run into the arms of the Gestapo. It was not yet ten-thirty. I asked Frau Friedländer to go with me by way of the attic, and then to accompany me out of the house through the front entrance. At first she did not want to because she was afraid. I begged her and told her that Ludwig's life depended on it. Finally she did it. In general, I must say at this point that Frau Friedländer went through a lot with us and always proved herself wonderfully. When we stepped out of the house door, one of the two people followed us a few steps. But when he heard out laughter and joking, he went back again. Yes, we did laugh and joke, but only in order to mislead the Gestapo lackeys. Frau Friedländer accompanied me to the corner of Hohenstaufenstrasse. There I stood and waited for Ludwig. It was a pitch-black and bitter-cold night, and my fingers and toes hurt so much that tears were running down my cheeks incessantly. But I had only the one thought that Ludwig should not run into the arms of the Gestapo. Every time a figure scurried by I called out: "Ludwig?" Luckily, at this time there were few people still on the street. I waited and waited, and feared that Ludwig had gotten off at Bayrischer Platz while I was expecting him from the direction of Viktoria-Luise Platz. Finally, at quarter to twelve he arrived on the double. He came so late because before he had left the factory he had gotten in touch with a director by telephone. He was very surprised to meet me on the street. I informed him briefly about the situation. Now we stood there and did not know where to go.

> *[They spend the night in a stairwell, decide to commit suicide, but then are once more drafted as laborers.]*

Now began the last part of the tragedy. On February 15, 1943, Ludwig called me at the factory and told me, for God's sake, not to go home. He had just been informed by telephone that a big SS car was in front of our house and several SS men were in our apartment. We arranged to meet at six o'clock on the corner of Hohen-staufenstrasse and Heilbronner Strasse and were going to discuss the rest then. At this time it would already be dark and we would not be seen. Since I was free already at three o'clock, I went to my Christian sister-in-law, Martha, and asked her to come along later to our meeting. At the appointed time we were there. The car was still standing in front of our house. To the front part of the car was affixed a searchlight that lit up the entire street. We had to remain cautiously at the corner in order not to be seen. Now, in front of Martha, I told Ludwig once more that for us there were only two possibilities. Either we had to get into the car now, or put an end to our lives. It would be plain crazy now to hope for another solution. Ludwig only nodded silently. We went along with Martha and stayed the night there. We now decided once more to leave this life. However, since we were very tired, we were going to discuss what was most important the next day.

On the next day we went to the sisters [former neighbors] on Weissenburgerstrasse and asked to be allowed to stay there two days, but did not say what we intended to do then. How peacefully and quietly did the sisters live. A world that had become completely alien to us, almost forgotten, opened up before us once more, and we remembered our happiest years, when Ursel was born, and when she was still a small child. Now all that was gone, and one could not conjure up the past anymore. The dictates of the hour were to deal with the present. We saw that nothing could save us from extermination, and that nothing could be delayed or prevented. And thus we had no other choice but to wait for a favorable opportunity and steal into our apartment in order to carry out our plan. We asked the sisters for paper and pen, to bid farewell to our dear ones. [. . .]

I was very composed and assumed that Ludwig was also. Toward eleven o'clock we were on Heilbronner Strasse, which was quiet and peaceful. Everything behind me was now blotted out, and I thought only of the coming hour. Fortunately, the house door was also open, so that we did not have to unlock it first. Very quietly, and in the dark, we sneaked up the stairs. But when we arrived in front of our door we had to see whether the door was sealed. We switched on the light. Frau Friedländer, who had been waiting for us for days, saw that there was light in the stairwell, and in that very moment she came running down. As she was coming down she called out joyfully: "Where were you? Dr. Gent sent someone looking for you a couple of times. He said you should go back to the factory, *nothing* will happen to you." Ludwig changed immediately. He laughed and cried for joy at the same time. During all those years I had not lost my composure and had dealt with the most difficult situations; now, however, I was bewildered. I asked Ludwig not to rely on that, because this degenerate species would not exactly make an exception of us. But Ludwig said that now he did not want to meddle with his life any longer and would let fate take its course. And fate did take its course.

The next day was Sunday. Ludwig took a bath, put on his best suit and enjoyed being alive (this time in the true sense of the word). In the evening we said goodbye to one another, for it was the week in which we were not going to see one another. As always, we went about our work. On Friday evening a colleague said that she had heard through a brother-in-law who worked at the community that the Gestapo was going to change their round-up procedures and no longer pick up the Jews at home but rather at work. This news disturbed me very much. I never used to awaken Ludwig from his sleep, but on this evening I did it very gently, so that he would not get a scare. I told him what I had heard and wanted him to stay at home the next day. And as always, he tried to calm me and said: "Don't worry so much, it doesn't have to be exactly *tomorrow* that they start, and next week I have vacation anyway." After a goodnight kiss I went to bed with a heavy heart. It was our last goodnight kiss.

Since on Saturday Ludwig worked only until noon, the next day I waited for him with lunch. He did not come, but for me it was already high time to go to work. Just as I opened the apartment door to leave, the doorkeeper's wife (a mean Nazi) came upstairs and told me that Ludwig had been picked up that morning at the factory. I stared at her uncomprehendingly. "Yes," she said, "when you were out shopping today, a Russian worker who had been sent by her husband came to convey this message to you." This news hit me so hard that I was unable to say anything or ask another question, and so the woman went downstairs right away. I felt paralyzed. Then I felt my knees growing weak, and I had to hold on to the door. After I had gotten over my attack of weakness a little, grasping the handrail, I slowly went up to Frau Friedländer and asked her to come with me to make a phone call, because Jews were not allowed to enter telephone booths. She called the Fromm firm and unfortunately the horrible fact that Ludwig, together with everyone else, had been picked up by the SS, was confirmed to us. I went to the apartment again and packed a knapsack with warm things in case a Jewish supervisor should come for the things (which sometimes did happen). Suddenly, on the desk I discovered Ludwig's wedding ring, which he had taken off two days earlier. His fingers had become so thin that he had been afraid to lose the ring. With the sad awareness that I would never take it off again, I put it on my finger. Then I wrote a letter to Ludwig and stuck it in the knapsack, but unfortunately no supervisor came. After I had left the things with Frau Friedländer, I went through our apartment once more, to take leave of the rooms in which I had spent many a beautiful hour, but also the most terrible hours of my life. Ludwig's bed was already turned down for the evening. I pressed my head for the last time into the pillow, but I was not able to cry. I did not take along anything but my purse, and so I left 26 Heilbronner Strasse forever. This took place on February 27, 1943.

A few Nazi women were standing in front of the house door. I noticed immediately that they were speaking about me. Since I had no luggage with me, they did not suspect that I would not return ever again; otherwise they would have surely held me back in order to hand me over to the Gestapo. In a completely indescribable state I now walked along the streets at random. After all, I did not have a goal. Things were going around in circles in my head and my only thought was Ludwig. My whole body trembled and shook, and I felt that Ludwig, too, was with me in all his thoughts. I was considering how I might still help Ludwig, but I saw that I was powerless. This powerlessness made me frantic with rage. And as I was thus walking along the streets in my deepest despair, I suddenly saw an SS man coming toward me. He roared at me that I should get the hell home to be picked up, for "today Berlin was going to become free of Jews!" Only then did I realize that I was walking with the Star showing (mostly I removed the Star when I left Heilbronner Strasse). That was approximately on Prager Platz. I ran into the next house. He did not follow me because he assumed that I lived there. I tore the Star from my coat, and after I had ascertained that this bum was no longer in sight, I came out again. Now I remembered that Frau Friedländer had told me that I ought to go to Küstriner Strasse so that—in case a message came from Ludwig—she could reach me. I went there on foot. Having arrived there, I discovered that Erich and Margot had also not come home. Now I knew for the first time that this operation had been carried out in every factory where Jews were working. Partly incapable of understanding all that, partly in such fierce pain that I could have screamed, I spent the evening and the night at Martha's.

The next day I left the house very early with Martha. We went to Oranienburger Strasse [the Jewish community building]. There I hoped to find out something about Ludwig. Martha was naturally searching for Erich and Margot. On the street one saw only Jews who were wearing a white armband. Those were the "supervisors," who had to help the Gestapo with the transports. The Gestapo itself sat in the offices of the Jewish community. I addressed one of the supervisors, who, however, did not respond to me, and I noticed that informers were in the vicinity. Then we went around the corner to Grosse Hamburger Strasse. In front of the old-age home, which served as a transit center for Jews before deportation, I saw several supervisors, among them also little Pinkus from Hirschgarten. I knew him only slightly but immediately headed toward him. "I am the wife of Ludwig Neumann. Do you know where the Fromm workers have gotten to? Ludwig is among them," I whispered to him. He only shook his head in surprise and said: "I don't know. But I didn't know that Ludwig had a Christian wife." Naturally, he had to assume with certainty that I am a Christian, since otherwise I would not have dared go onto the street, let alone to this area. Then he only let me know quietly that he was forbidden to speak, and he went his way. I could not find out anything about Ludwig. In the afternoon I again roamed the streets aimlessly and was completely desperate in my powerlessness.

The second night I spent at Martha's again, but made up my mind to stay only until I received a message from or about Ludwig. I got up early again and this time went alone to Oranienburger Strasse and to Grosse Hamburger Strasse. No one knew where the Fromm workers had gotten to. (Only much, much later did I find out that Ludwig was in a barracks in Moabit.) What I found out from different people bit by bit was staggering. The Jews had not yet received any food since their arrest. The Jewish community simply no longer had the possibility of providing for the thousands of people or giving them even the least little bit.[5] The transports were to begin on March 1st and leave one right after the other. Transports of men and women left separately; men and women were separated from each other immediately after their arrest. Married couples no longer saw one another at all, since they had been working in different factories. Parents did not see their children again. Children were picked up at home and from institutions and were also sent off separately. All of this was totally devastating, and in addition there was the terrible winter cold.

Without results and without being able to learn anything of Ludwig, I now went to an area where I did not know anyone and where no one knew me. I simply did not know what to do. I was desperate, but something inexplicable within me resisted my putting an end to my life.

*[She finds shelter with acquaintances in Berlin-Schlachtensee.]*

Work was the best distraction for me, and I did it gladly. I was very grateful that I could be there, and Lydia once said in passing that she would keep me there if that caused her no financial burden. I immediately declared myself ready to contribute to the household, and we agreed on five marks a day. In addition, I took over the cooking, sewing, and washing. I also took care of errands outside the house, and the neighbors saw me without giving it a thought. But at night, during the air raids, I never went to the air raid shelter in the house next door. Since I was not registered with the police, no one was supposed to see that I lived there. It was not so easy to get used to the illegality of my existence. But still, at first I had the sense of being safe. It warmed my heart that A. always remembered Ludwig in his prayers. At their place, they prayed after each meal and before going to bed. If A. was at work, Lydia led the prayer, and I envied these people for their faith.

Little by little I noticed, however, that their actions were not always consistent with their prayers. Although it shocked me inwardly, I did not betray my feelings. But then I saw more and more how I had misjudged Lydia and A., and it became difficult for me to be silent. Sometimes Lydia also made remarks that hurt me very much and also amazed me. For example, one day she came home beaming with joy and said that she had been at a relative's who was a cartographer. There she saw the new maps of the future Europe. Half of Europe belongs to Germany! It annoyed me that Lydia talked like that, and when she noticed it she said: "Did you perhaps think that Germany will lose the war?" Or she would suddenly begin to speak of "retribution." Yes, once the new weapon is ready, England would be "erased." The children, too, brought similar views from school. Even if I did not believe that for a moment, these comments did hurt me. In addition Lydia was very greedy. A.'s political opinion was more sensible; as far as greed was concerned, however, he surpassed Lydia. I could not comprehend at all how someone who behaves so devoutly can covet earthly goods like that. I will tell only of one incident here. In order to find out whether they were still looking for me, A. inquired about us of the porter's wife on Heilbronner Strasse. He pretended that he had not heard anything from us for half a year. The porter's wife said: "Herr Neumann was picked up and Frau Neumann is on the run. The Gestapo did not seal off the apartment, in order to set a trap for her; for she often left and then came back again. But this time we will catch her right away." Pleasant to hear something like that. A., however, did not let that frighten him. Without my knowledge, three days later he went to the apartment in the late evening hours with my key and "rescued" for himself whatever was not nailed down. Since he could not carry it all, he left part of the things at Friedländers', who were of the opinion that A. had removed them for me. It would take too long for me to tell here what sorts of other peculiar things I experienced with them. To sum up, I will only say that I suffered greatly when little by little I was forced to discover that A. was not the selfless benefactor that Ludwig and I always thought him to be.

Time passed very slowly, but it passed. And one day spring had come! It was incredibly beautiful out there. The blooming trees all around us, the bright lawns, the sweet smell, the chirping of birds! Everything that I had had to do without for a long time, but I felt no joy at it. The pain because of Ludwig, who could not experience it, was too strong. Otherwise, too, my situation was not such that I could be happy about anything. Even if things between us did not reach the point of open conflict—on the contrary, they were even sugar-sweet to me—I still felt that I would not remain there for long. I already suspected that Lydia and A. were considering *how* they ought to put me out, and I waited. And yet it would have been so simple; they could have told me honestly and openly that they did not want to take upon themselves the risk of having me any longer.

Instead, they did it in a totally devious way. One day, at the beginning of June, A. came back at ten o'clock in the morning, supposedly from the office, and presented me with a letter. I was ironing, and since I knew immediately what was what, I put the iron aside. The letter looked as follows: On the top in one corner it said "Criminal Investigation Department." The text of the letter read: "Dear Herr A.! We are warning you! The Criminal Investigation Department." Everything written on a typewriter, including the letterhead and the signature. A. thought I was so stupid that I would take the letter to be genuine; perhaps because I kept quiet about everything. I returned the rubbish to him and said: "Herr A., the Criminal Investigation Department does not warn, it goes right into action. But I've understood you!" I got dressed immediately and in ten minutes I was out on the street. As I was leaving, A. wanted to put his arm around me. He also squeezed out a few crocodile tears, but I shook him off. To Lydia, too, I bid a cold farewell. I could not take along any of my things, since I did not know where I was going.

I kept walking through the streets down to Schlachtensee. I wanted to sit down there and cry my heart out. It was a Tuesday; only a few people, who were looking for relaxation there, passed. No one bothered me, for a crying woman was not a sensation in those days. It was a radiant summer day. The lake was peaceful and the trees swayed quietly in the mild wind. A picture of peace! All that, however, could not ease my pain. The sorrow over my disappointment was terrible, for during our long acquaintanceship with A., we always had the best opinion of him. Ludwig and I practically revered him. Without exaggeration I can say that A. was the biggest disappointment of my life. And that was without even considering my desperate situation. It was merely the human disappointment that had hurt me so deeply. For hours I sat there, until I felt hunger, and then my misfortune became clear to me in its entire magnitude. Slowly I strolled to the station, and that was my departure from Schlachtensee.

In Berlin—for there was nothing else left for me to do than to make my way back there again—I experienced horrible days. I had experienced the darkness of illegality to the full. Today it is almost incomprehensible to me how I was able to bear my cruel fate.

So I returned to Berlin and went instinctively to Weissenburgerstrasse. However, the sisters were not at home, something that had never been the case before. To my horror, I learned from the neighbors that they had gone out of town and intended to stay away a few days. What was I to do now? I went to Neu-Westend to consult with

[Aunt] Grete. Having arrived in Neu-Westend, I suddenly felt inhibited. It was already approaching evening, and Friedel[6] would naturally have interpreted my visit as my wanting to spend the night there. However, Grete had once asked me expressly never and in no way to call upon her help; because it was already enough that *she* was able to be there. I had promised Grete that she could rely on me and that she would have no inconvenience on account of me. Thus I did not go there, but rather strolled about in the vicinity of Heerstrasse. I had terrible hunger pangs, but worry about where I was to spend the night made all the pain seem insignificant. I went across a bridge and looked down at the tracks. Would it not be better if I were to throw myself in front of a train, I asked myself. Immediately, however, I was seized by horror. No, I did not yet want to take this desperate step. I set myself a goal. One week! If in one week I had not found a place to stay, then it *had* to happen! I would not have been able to bear this life any longer.

Suddenly I discovered several telephone booths standing next to one another. I had found my lodging for the night. I bought myself a few newspapers and waited until it was dark. In the one telephone booth there hung an "out of order" sign. I tied this sign outside to the door handle. Thus it would not occur to anyone to open the door. I spread the newspapers out in the booth and squatted down. There could be no thought of sleep, of course, but at least I would not be seized by the police patrol.

But soon the sirens sounded. An air raid warning! I had not thought of that. Now I was again in a fix. One was not permitted to remain out on the street during an air raid. Staying in the booth was not exactly the right thing either, but I remained inside. I really was not afraid, for even if I did not want to end it all myself, on that day my life was not worth very much to me. For that reason, I remained inside, completely calm, and thought, whatever is to be, will be. It was the first time that I could observe a raid so exactly. Countless British planes flew from the northwest over the city. The roaring of the motors made the air tremble. Immediately there was rapid anti-aircraft fire, seemingly without great success, for soon the heavy bombs were impacting with a crash. It was all taking place quite close, and I had to open the door; otherwise the blast would have shattered the panes.

After the planes had flown off, I was freezing most miserably. It was a cold June night and I was wearing only a thin coat. I could hardly wait for day to come, and with the first rays of the sun I also crawled from my hiding place. But it was still very early. I did not want to be on Westendallee before eleven o'clock under any circumstance, in order not to arrive *too* inconveniently. Besides, I thought I looked very neglected. Thus I went to the hairdresser's and had my hair washed and set. I did have money, but unfortunately I could not buy myself anything to eat, because everything was rationed.

*[The memoir ends shortly hereafter with the prospect for a new job.]*

1. On the history of the Jewish Kulturbund see Kurt Baumann (42). It was forbidden on September 11, 1941. The Jewish schools, of which there still were several in Berlin, were not forced to close until June 30, 1942.

2. On Rudolf Schwarz see Kurt Baumann (42), note 6.

3. In Stettin the first deportation from the Reich took place on February 12/13, 1940.

4. The great synagogue on Levetzowstrasse was erected in 1914 for the large Jewish population of the Hansa quarter and had 2,000 seats. Damaged during the pogrom of November 1938, it was once again used for worship starting in 1939, until the Gestapo demanded the keys during the High Holy Days in 1941 and turned the synagogue into a deportation center. Those held there were supplied with food, clothing, bed linen, and medical aid by the Jewish community.

5. During the "factory operation" of February 27, 1943, some 7,000 Jews were arrested. The Gestapo set up four additional assembly centers, which the decimated community, without sufficient means of transportation, could supply with food only with difficulty.

6. Friedel Landsberger, a Christian who for appearance's sake had divorced her Jewish husband, who emigrated, had hidden Grete Neumann, the author's aunt by marriage, at her apartment.

# 50  *Hermann Pineas*

  BORN IN DÜSSELDORF IN 1892.

Hermann Pineas, Our Fortunes after January 30, 1933. Manuscript, dated Memmingen, May 18, 1945, 53 pages. Pages 11–13 of the manuscript contain a report by Mrs. Herta Pineas.

*Hermann Pineas, the son of a merchant, studied medicine and despite a serious war injury was successful in his profession. From 1920 to 1931 he was an intern and then a senior physician in the Neurology Department of the Hufeland Hospital in Berlin. From 1932 until 1939 he practiced privately as a neurologist (in the end, "case attendant"), and from 1939 until 1943 he was director of the Neuropsychiatric Department of the Berlin Jüdisches Krankenhaus. Pineas also took part in the Reichsbund jüdischer Frontsoldaten and in Jewish welfare work. In 1927 he married his second wife, Herta, née Appel, who was active in the Jewish Women's League. After the family's futile attempts to emigrate, in 1938/39 only the three sons were able to leave. From 1941 until 1943 Herta Pineas worked as a helper in supplying the deportation transports, about which she wrote the account that follows below. On March 5, 1943, the couple went underground and stayed mainly in Swabia with members of the Confessing Church, until in September 1944 Pineas succeeded in acquiring false papers and a job in an arms plant in Memmingen. After liberation Pineas emigrated with his wife to New York, where between 1952 and 1969 he was a neurologist in the outpatient clinic of the Veterans' Administration.*

*[Account by Mrs. Herta Pineas of her work with the food service of the Berlin Jewish community during the deportations in 1942:]*

Frau Berta Falkenberg, president of the Jüdischer Frauenbund[1] in Berlin until its dissolution, managed the preparation of the provisions for the transports—under strict supervision by the Gestapo, which also stringently allotted the foodstuffs. Of some forty women who helped in the beginning, in the end there were only eight; the others had also been deported. The making of sandwiches took place in a Jewish school that was no longer in use, in the center of the city. While we were otherwise forbidden to travel by public transportation, for this purpose we received a written travel permit, which had to be presented to the conductor, who otherwise would not have allowed the Jews, identified by a Yellow Star, to get on. How long the transports would be on the way remained concealed from us. At any rate, the amount of food for a single person was insufficient, for it was barely enough for one day. Each time, for approximately 1,000 people—and later the transports comprised more—we made sandwiches and wrapped them for days, distributed the sandwiches at the train, and poured coffee and soup, for which we procured containers. We brought water and helped search for luggage. Mostly we found only a small portion of it; the Gestapo had already kept most of it in the transit center. If there was a calm moment, the people on the transport told of what they had gone through in the transit center. I also knew it from a friend who was a supervisor in the transit center on Levetzowstrasse, which was, appropriately, in the synagogue.[2] She herself is no longer alive, I'm sure. I saw her leave on the train. I also saw the Jewish community officials, along with Hannah Karminski,[3] being taken away. The moral strength of these people was overwhelming. The others being transported had already been stigmatized by the transit center, dazed, neglected, overtaxed, some of them relieved somehow that they were going on, the least of them clear about their fate. We helped those who couldn't carry anything. There were people who were put on the train on stretchers. I saw a lame man (the president of the Jewish Handicapped) on the shoulders of his old father.

There were constant kicks from behind by the Gestapo and threats regarding money hidden or taken along. A Gestapo man constantly waved a steel hand around, which at the press of a button had sprung from a cane. We members of the provisions group at the train were recognizable in the throng by our white arm bands. Nonetheless, it once happened that a Gestapo official by the train also ordered me to get on and depart. Later I could hardly believe that in spite of my fright, words of protest still occurred to me. Once, a doctor with whom I was friends and who was also being deported asked me to keep his brush, in the hollowed-out wooden part of which valuables were hidden. But I had to decline. The Gestapo had just threatened terribly and had scared everyone. Unfortunately, they found gold hidden in someone's pillow. The feathers flew over the whole platform. We were also not allowed, under pain of death, to accept farewell notes, for they could make known what was happening in the transit centers.

Every transport was assigned a Jewish transport physician. I spoke with a doctor with whom I was acquainted, who well into the winter was traveling in his summer coat and straw hat. He had been sentenced to prison in the summer for having listened to a foreign radio station. From his apartment, he was given a small box with instruments and medication, which now stood beside him. He was a neurologist. If there was no medicine to be had on the platform, how could he have helped when someone fell over from exhaustion? The trains were sealed before departure and not a window was allowed to be opened! At the rear of the train there was a machine gun, and in the middle there were also Gestapo. At the station there was no food even for the smallest children; there was only cold skimmed milk, and too little of that, too. And for us at the train the families with many children were the worst. The children were holding their dolls in their arms, happy to be following their grandparents, who had already "departed" ahead of them. An infant lay in an open cardboard suitcase, because, of all people, the official responsible for this family had considered the baby carriage to be a luxury item and had confiscated it. The children poured out of the closed furniture vans, in which, jammed together, they had been cooped up and transported from the transit center to the station. A woman helper, with whom I was friendly, saw me shake my head. The gesture could have brought me disaster. After that I never again betrayed my "disapproval." With what envy did the poor people look upon us, who remained behind, every time the train set in motion!

The people living around the Putlitzstrasse station observed in masses from the bridge across the rails how these transports arrived at the station and departed from an open platform. When we were going back after the departure of the train, these spectators were still standing there—and supposedly they knew nothing of these things? And if already in the summer of 1942 I knew that they were making soap of Jews, the "Aryans" around us supposedly did not know? Not all, but the majority must have known of the horrors. After all, from my apartment on Levetzowstrasse, which was not far from the transit center in the synagogue, I myself saw how the house owners and storekeepers stepped in front of their doors and observed at great length the loading of the Jews into the furniture vans.

The procedure in the synagogue, the body and luggage searches for valuables, lasted two to four days each time. Many suicides took place there. If not successful, suicide was punishable! Those who recovered in the hospital, in a special ward watched over by the police, were taken along on the next transport with the criminal group. It was expressly marked and very heavily guarded, and we were also not allowed to give them any food. Conspicuous were the young girls whom the Gestapo brought along and only one of whom was occupied each time as a clerk. The others came to look at all the goings-on. The BDM, the female Hitler Youth, children as far as their age was concerned, also helped with the luggage search. This I was told by the aforementioned supervisor, although, like many other things, it carried the death penalty.

At the end of 1942, after food allocations had become more and more tight, and the transports more and more frequent, we were no longer permitted to help with provisions. In February 1943 there took place the largest transport of all. Fourteen thousand people were suddenly rounded up like cattle in the firms where they were doing forced labor, and for five days, until the transport,[4] they were left in five big rooms, without water and toilets. The Berlin Jewish community, with its decimated personnel, had to take over their feeding just as "suddenly." The performance of the community was admirable.

Hermann Pineas:

Even if in Berlin we did not know the details about the crimes against Jews [1941], we did have some information. In our house there lived a former Reichstag delegate, the physician Dr. Julius Moses,[5] who had played an important role in the Weimar Republic. We had become friendly during the Nazi regime. One day he came to our apartment to show me something. It was an original letter of a Social Democratic party functionary who was on the Eastern front as soldier and who was foolhardy enough to send this letter by army mail to the former president of the Reichstag, Paul Löbe.[6] From Löbe it got to Dr. Moses. In this letter the writer reported that Russian war prisoners had been on the road for days in sealed freight cars without food or drink, and that upon unloading they were dead. Further, he had witnessed with his own eyes how, in a Russian provincial town, Jewish women had to dig graves, in front of which they then had to place themselves with their children, and were then shot. While reading the letter Moses burst out crying and was emotionally so upset that he could not go on reading. I translated this letter into English, leaving out the proper names, and through the ophthalmologist Dr. Hirschfeld had it passed on to the American embassy just one day before it was closed because of Pearl Harbor. This was at the beginning of December 1941. At Christmas 1941, when my former assistant, Dr. Erwin Rehwald, visited us in civilian clothes, he confirmed, to my horror, that he himself had also seen the shooting of Jews, as described in the letter cited above.

Then, when the president of the German Federation of Protectors of the Law, to use the widespread, pretentious mode of speech, the future governor-general of Poland and Reichsminister Frank,[7] coined the terse sentence: "Right is whatever benefits the German people," my wife and I slowly and gradually came to the decision not to submit to another's dictate, and if we were to perish, to determine the hour when this was to happen ourselves and not let the Nazis decide it. Before I go on to cite individual circumstances that fortified me in our decision to disappear at the right moment, let me report something about the work in the Jewish Hospital,[8] from which I withdrew suddenly and voluntarily on March 6, 1943.

When I took over the Neurology Department on July 1, 1939, after Professor Schuster's[9] departure, there did not exist a neurology ward separate from others; rather, there was only a "mixed ward" for patients suffering from eye, ear, skin, and nervous diseases. Those suffering from eye diseases were at first taken care of by Dr. Oppenheimer, then by Dr. Fritz Hirschfeld; the ear patients by Dr. Else Levy, who disappeared a few weeks before me and apparently perished in hiding. The patients with skin diseases were treated by Professor Buschke,[10] who died in Theresienstadt, and, after his departure, by Dr. Preiser. For the entire ward there was only one head nurse (Hella) and an equally inadequate number of assistant nurses. The Outpatient Department was open once or twice a week, but was frequented little. Things went on like that until the summer of 1942. By then the Gestapo had decided to collect all the psychiatric cases in Greater Germany in Berlin, that is, to set up a psychiatric ward in the Jewish Hospital. Twice the Gestapo had already had the mental patients from the Jewish mental clinic Sayn,[11] near Koblenz, taken away with destination unknown. The Reichsvereinigung had bought this institution from Dr. Jacoby's heirs. It, and also all state, municipal, and private sanatoriums and mental clinics in all of Greater Germany were vacated, and the patients were brought to the new psychiatric ward of the Jewish Hospital. It became the hospital's largest ward, and had about 120 beds. I was assisted in medical matters by Dr. Hanff. He perished in Auschwitz. The facilities of the ward were extremely primitive, the nursing care, by totally untrained personnel, was completely inadequate. What the situation was regarding nutrition one can easily judge for oneself, given the limitations on food supplies. Still, the most essential examinations, tests of cerebrospinal fluid and Cardiazol treatment in the case of schizophrenics, and Pyrifer treatments in case of paralysis, were carried out. Besides that, I also had numerous cases of nervous diseases in the private ward. To have to work under such inadequate conditions was torture.

Besides the already mentioned wards there were a surgical ward, including urology, an internal medicine ward, a gynecology and obstetrics ward, a radiology and a children's ward, and an isolation ward. To specific rooms in the internal medicine ward on the first floor were confined the suicide cases, which increased enormously when people were being picked up for the transit camps. The "drug of choice" was Veronal or Phandodorm, at any rate barbituric acid, which was in the possession of the ill-fated people in huge quantities. My colleagues in the Department for Internal Medicine were of divided opinion as to whether it was better to save the sick of this category or to allow them to pass away peacefully. The mortality rate was huge in any case. In addition to the mentioned departments, to which there were added a Pathology Department under Ludwig Pick and a chemical-serological-bacteriological laboratory under Hans Hirschfeld, there was also a closed police ward ordered by the Gestapo.[12] Received there were all those sent by the police, and all of the suicide cases, who had wanted to escape their arrest. Head nurse of this ominous ward, which was attended to by the heads of all departments, was Nurse Lori. Director of the health administration, in the end also of the Reichsvereinigung, was the retired senior executive officer and senior medical officer Dr. Dr. Walter Lustig,[13] a capable administrator, who, however, was living in a mixed marriage and was totally unburdened by Jewish awareness. He stayed in Berlin. After the liberation, however, he was arrested by the Russians. In Jewish matters he failed the test. This also holds true for the last president of the Jewish community, Moritz Henschel.[14]

At the end, it was the tactic of the Gestapo to arrest and deport the most capable employees from the departments of the community administration, and thus the level of performance inevitably had to sink. Especially ingenious was the method, introduced later, of having Jews picked up by Jews! Virtually, Jewish bands of bloodhounds had to be formed, and in the winter of 1942/43 my colleagues from the hospital and I were once forced to participate in such roundups. (On the date in question my wife worked through the entire night making sandwiches.) When on the next day I reported this to the then public health officer of the district Wedding, Dr. Brunzer, he was visibly horrified. — As we hear, along with a few nurses, Dr. Helmut Cohen,[15] formerly head of the Internal Medicine Department, was left with his Jewish wife and child at the hospital in Berlin. Dr. Cohen now runs the hospital, whose damaged building is being repaired.

A series of events and circumstances prompted our going underground. On September 14, 1942, with fists clenched in my pocket, I had to watch helplessly as my mother was being deported to Theresienstadt. In January 1943, my teacher, Dr. Baeck, suffered the same fate. Now there was no longer anything to keep me at my post, and it was only a matter of waiting for the right moment to go underground, not too early, but, above all, not too late. How many cases we know of in which people had prepared everything for their disappearance but still could not decide, and because of that fell victim to the roundups! [. . .]

There were two main difficulties for every "diver": adequate personal documents, if at all possible with food ration card registration—the latter an almost unsolvable problem—and a reliable shelter. Just think of how difficult it was even to have passport pictures made. Such a wish, expressed in a photo store by someone wearing a Yellow Star on his coat, would have led to denunciation. Thus one had to proceed in the following manner: Go on foot to a far-away store, on the way leave one's overcoat with the Star with reliable people, go to the photo store with the coat that one had been wearing underneath and that had no Star, and while doing all this, hope that nobody there or on the way knew one. The same was necessary when picking up the photos, and since even then mechanical devices were often out of order, cameras too, each one of us often had to make such journeys no less than four times. Identification papers could be had in Berlin for very high sums. Thus I, too, on an occasion that seemed favorable, made use of an available opportunity. For 3,000 marks I received a blank trade license, and now I waited for the fulfillment of the second condition, the solution of the shelter problem. This, too, was seemingly resolved when a patient living in Vienna said that she would find quarters for me. That in this case it was a matter of a psychotic imagination, we did not yet know at that time. Fortunately, as I can say today. After taking care of the prerequisites, it was now a question of carrying out the plan at the most opportune hour possible.

On Thursday, March 4, 1943, Herta and I, along with my colleagues Herr and Frau Jakobsohn, who lived at our place, and many other doctors who until then had been spared deportation, were taken in the afternoon by the police to the transit center on Levetzowstrasse, and our apartment was sealed. However, after a telephone conversation with Lustig—that is to say, with the Gestapo—on Burgstrasse, conducted in the presence of the police while we were still in our apartment, we were released again after a short time in the synagogue and were escorted by an official, who then unsealed our apartment. During said telephone conversation we asked the officials to enter the consultation room; in the meantime, we were able to get two friends in hiding out the front door. They happened to be visiting us and, frightened to death, had fled to our loggia.

On Friday, the 5th of March, when Gustav Degner[16] (now a mayor in Berlin) happened to be at our place and promised to find Herta a lodging, so that I would not have to worry about her, I received a call from Vienna, whereupon I announced my arrival for Sunday, the 7th of March. On Saturday, March 6th, I wanted to get food ration cards for both of us at our assigned rations office, but my wife was lacking the special ID card, that is, one with a stamp of the Jewish community confirming that one worked for the community and was indispensable and was thus entitled to go about freely on the street in spite of the Yellow Star. To obtain this stamp, I had to have the transit center at the synagogue on Levetzowstrasse certify that I had already been sent to the center once and had been released as indispensable. From the ration card office I was now sent to the Gestapo on Burgstrasse. On that day many were kept at Burgstrasse for deportation. I, on the other hand, was sent back to the rations card office, and finally, at my insistence, I received the food ration cards. They covered, for the first month, the basic food needs at least for Berlin. However, because of the countlessly repeated imprint "Jew," they could be used only in the most circuitous ways. Then I went to the hospital for the last time, took care of my duties as usual, went to Degner, who gave me an important address in Vienna, came home, took care of the last preparations, and at four-thirty in the afternoon I was sitting in the Anhalter station in the night express train to Vienna. I had dared the leap into darkness, but could not know how dark it would be there.

I must still recount our three previous escape plans. In October 1942 we wanted to go to France with French worker passports; in January 1943 I wanted to go to England without my wife, on a Swedish ship; in February we both wanted to go on foot across the Alsatian mountains to Switzerland. The plan for England was no doubt suicidal, but with all our senses we were so intent on achieving the one goal, getting out of the pit, that we didn't realize it then. Also during the vacation trips of the French laborers working in Germany—they had come to Germany voluntarily in response to advertisements—many Jews were caught by the Gestapo checking at the platform barrier or in the train, and were taken away as criminal offenders. Still, in this way, by purchasing vacation passes, a considerable number of German Jews succeeded in getting out of Germany. Our route was to go by way of Paris to the unoccupied south of France, then through Spain to Lisbon, and from there to the U.S.A. [. . .]

When today, on May 18, 1945, I consider my disappearance into illegality back then, I must describe it as reckless. My Viennese patient had written to me that I could live at the place of an artist, who was constantly on trips, and that I would be put up there without food ration cards for two hundred marks per month. It was on the basis of this actually quite unlikely claim that I set out on my journey. Upon my arrival it turned out that my patient had simply wanted to have me there. In reality, I lived with her, in her apartment. That this was bound to lead—putting it mildly—to an unwholesome situation should have been obvious to me even then.

My stay in Vienna gave me great encouragement, something to which various factors contributed. For one, there was the almost entirely unfamiliar city, which I had gotten to know only slightly during a neurologists' conference in 1927, and then the wonderful spring weather, which I used for excursions into nature, something I had sorely missed for years, and finally the complete contrast to my previous life. That in the process I completely overlooked the danger in my situation becomes more incomprehensible to me as time passes.

I was introduced to the talkative subtenant of my patient as her uncle from Berlin. Thus it was obvious that I had to be a Berlin Jew. Frau Friedrich was Jewish, but her husband was Aryan. Very soon there followed a denunciation. A kind fate had ordained that Herr Friedrich had energetically pressed for other quarters. Since Frau Habarth, whose address I had received from Degner, maintained that she could do nothing for me, I was on my own. At short notice I was able to get lodgings in the hotel Römischer Kaiser in Pötzleinsdorf, where one Sunday we had eaten Bohemian crepes. On the day of the house search at the Friedrichs' I was living there and had an appointment with Frau Friedrich at the swimming pool. While otherwise she was punctuality itself, this time, after a two-hour wait, she had not yet appeared. Since in the evening we were going to meet at her acquaintances', I went to the latter. Fortunately, Frau Friedrich also came and reported to me that she was gotten out of bed at seven in the morning, was told straight out about my presence (her earlier telephone calls to my Berlin apartment had obviously been monitored), that they were most thoroughly informed about me, and that they then took her to Morzinplatz, where she was interrogated but, alleging ignorance, she had refused to give any information as to my whereabouts. At any rate, she behaved irreproachably. That on the same Friday morning I picked up a letter from my wife from the mailbox of the Friedrichs' apartment I mention only as a curiosity; also that Frau Friedrich and I went on the following Sunday on an excursion to Neu-Waldeck, which also could have become a disaster for me. On the following Monday, the Gestapo again came to her apartment, this time in the evening. They took along my briefcase with toilet articles, which I had left there, and for the rest were content with cautioning Frau Friedrich and demanding that she report me immediately should I show up again. She was also told that she had been seen in Neu-Waldeck on Sunday. Obviously they had not paid attention to her companion!

From another patient, a woman who had also been living in a mixed marriage and had been in Auschwitz and survived, and—strange coincidence—had met Frau Friedrich there and had spoken with her of me, I know that she later perished in Auschwitz.

These events were likely to make things in Vienna too hot for me, and since I could not find permanent lodgings it was time to pack my bags and go somewhere else. At first I went to Linz, the capital of the region of Oberdonau. Journeys to nowhere in particular were quite familiar to me by then, but never had I undertaken a journey into such uncertainty as this: without reserved lodgings, without food ration cards, and naturally without the possibility of registering my arrival and departure with the police. [. . .] It was fortunate that when I bought my trade authorization papers back then in Berlin I received as an extra a blank form of the I.G.-Farben firm; equipped with a photo and properly filled out by my wife, it was very useful to me in getting hotel accommodations. For the time being, then, I was safe for three days in Linz. My noon meals consisted of SSS: soup, house special, and suds, that is, of everything that was not rationed and thus was without nutrition. On the second day of my stay there I went in the direction of Vienna, to St. Pölten, where I succeeded in getting accommodations at the biggest hotel, again for three days. In the period that followed I traveled back and forth between Vienna, Linz, and St. Pölten, and was always on the way during the day, since I had to feign professional activity. In Vienna I had discovered the hotel Wiener Wald in Salmannsdorf, where, with the help of my company identification card, I could stay up to three weeks. Even in Linz I managed to stay up to two weeks in May, which was especially difficult because of the lack of beds there. [. . .]

What did my "working day" in Vienna, Linz, or St. Pölten look like? After breakfast, which I took by myself—I didn't drink anything except water—I left the respective hotel, bought myself one or several newspapers, preferably the *Frankfurter, Das Reich,* or the *D.A.Z.,* and went to one of the parks, where I spent my time until lunch. Then I roamed about in the park for a while and returned to the hotel toward four o'clock. Then I wrote letters; the typewriter on which I am writing this report has been my constant companion. And around six o'clock there was a rather uniform dinner, which I also mostly prepared myself.

Meanwhile, by way of Stuttgart my wife had reached the parsonage in Heimsheim and had helped in the household of the local parson's wife, Helene Fausel, whose husband at that time had a congregation in Ditzingen. As a precaution (since a Jewish woman in hiding had fallen into the hands of the Gestapo in Frau Fausel's brother's parish), she had suddenly to leave Heimsheim, with a serious knee injury caused by a bicycle accident, and move to Schwenningen on the Neckar. There, the curate Margarete Hoffer offered her domicile and care in the Johannis parsonage on the edge of the city. I, too, was invited there by the curate at the beginning of July 1943. Fräulein Hoffer came from Graz and from an out-and-out Nazi family, whom, as we experienced through her actions in our behalf, she opposed out of Christian conviction. When the letter of invitation, addressed to Frau Habarth, reached me, I was at first speechless with joy. After a separation from my wife of more than four months, I was going to see her again for the first time! On the 13th of July I departed by night express train from Vienna's West Station in the direction of Stuttgart. If I had gone one day later, a set of food ration cards sent to me and already paid for would have still reached me. Instead, it was unfortunately lost.

In Stuttgart I became acquainted with pastor (formerly attorney) Kurt Müller[17] from Bremen, who was the motivating force and organizer of all the efforts of the "Sozietät" that were undertaken to help our people. The "Sozietät" was made up of clergymen who belonged to the Protestant Confessing Church, as it was called. Without exception, they were pupils of Karl Barth and stood in opposition to the clergy that adhered to the Hitler government. Upon my arrival in Schwenningen at 10:00 p.m., my wife almost did not recognize me. That is how thin I had become, which was not in the least bit surprising, considering the regimen that I had to follow. Especially my eyes had suffered badly. If I had already been greatly encouraged by the invitation and by the trip that led me out of my hopeless monotony, and above all by the prospect of reunion with my wife, then thanks to my stay of several weeks in Schwenningen and afterward in Haiterbach near Nagold, I once again became a human being.

*[Hermann Pineas and his wife then live separately again with different hosts of the Confessing Church.]*

For Christmas in 1943 we had an invitation to Schwenningen, to curate Hoffer's, and met there on the 22nd of December. Through fortunate circumstances we were able to overcome the travel restrictions decreed at that time for all civilians. In Schwenningen we had a kind of common household with Fräulein Hoffer. On the 10th of February, just as we were taking our luggage on a sled to the station for our separate further journeys, my wife slipped on the ice and broke her left wrist. Thus our stay together in Schwenningen was extended until the end of April 1944. From then on my wife took a strenuous job at a farmer's family in Gniebel, in the district of Reutlingen, where she was taken for someone fleeing the air raids. Meanwhile, I traveled to the parish pastor Gümbel in Stuttgart-Zuffenhausen. I was received very hospitably there, and, in the same house, also by the pastor's widow Elisabeth Kirschmann, and by the parish pastor Dr. Werner. I spent a lovely time there, not least because of several meetings with my wife in Tübingen. Dr. Werner liked having me inform him about Judaism.

In Schwenningen, my colleague Dr. Hans Kohler, who was connected to the Confessing Church, had helped me to get a post office identification card. In contrast to the one from Linz, through which I had become Dr. Hans Perger, it gave me the name of my wife, whereby I became Dr. Hans Günter, biologist, and at the same time it added fifteen years to my age, so that I would not be subject to the newly decreed compulsory labor. This, then, in some respects secured the possibility of our existence together, which was, after all, the aim of our constant efforts. It was much more difficult officially to cancel a food ration card, which would make new registration possible. This came about for us both in Wankheim near Tübingen, where after my departure from Stuttgart I was received with great hospitality and in a friendly manner in the house of pastor Richard Gölz[18] and his wife, Hilde. In the meantime, I was summoned by Fräulein Hoffer to Schwenningen again, where in the person of Frau Anni Cerny I met a companion in misfortune, who was living in the parsonage and who, unfortunately, could no longer bear the inner loneliness, about which she complained to us, and in February 1945, thus a few weeks before liberation, put an end to her life.

When a Nazi girl in the rations office was on vacation, Fräulein Hoffer managed to get me a stamped blank form of withdrawal from the Schwenningen rations office from her religiously oriented replacement. Fräulein Elisabeth Braun used this form in Gerstetten as a document to have us registered at a rations office there, also by a religiously inclined employee, so that we finally came into possession of regular food rations cards when later, in a small village outside Memmingen, we presented the cancellation that we had gotten for this purpose. It was the village of Lautrach, where the chief magistrate was everything wrapped in one person, police, registration office, rations office, and butcher to boot. There things were done not at all officially, so that, for example, the lack of the change-of-address certification from the police and of the clothing and coal rations cards was not noticed. In the meantime, however, much had happened.

I had moved from the Wankheim parsonage to Kirchheim on Teck, 6 Plochinger Strasse, the house of the former pastor Paul Schempp, who had been disciplined because of his anti-Nazism.[19] There I received the bad news that in Wankheim a policeman from Tübingen had asked about me! Afterward I found out that Pastor Gölz was questioned on the next day about me and said that I was a Jewish doctor from Berlin, and that he regarded giving me shelter as his Christian duty. He said he thought that I had traveled on to Friedrichsroda in Thuringia. In addition, he gave a false description of my person. Incidentally, for reasons of safety the people who put us up never knew our real names. And at Pastor Gölz's we had still joked about the species of the "intellectual beasht"—as it is pronounced in the Württemberg dialect—so hated by the Nazis and which I embodied, so that I would certainly easily attract attention in rural areas. For his "offense" the unfortunate pastor was picked up right before Christmas and transported to a labor camp. This saddened us very much. Later we heard that pastor Gölz was freed in May 1945 and is again in Wankheim.

At any rate, in a quite desperate mood, which my wife at first was not supposed to notice, in the middle of August 1944 I went with her to Lautrach near Memmingen. At that time, because I had been told so, I was under the impression, and expected, that they were looking for me and that I was endangering my wife at the same time. To be sure, we were now in Bavaria and no longer in Württemberg, which in regard to pursuit by the police was in our favor. Also, we were in the process of establishing for ourselves a quasi-legal existence together, since we saw the debacle approaching.

After a truly nerve-racking week, during which I expected to be arrested, on the 1st of September I decided to go to Memmingen and register at the employment office there for the "voluntary honor service." If I was successful then we would officially get an apartment assigned to us because of my duties. That was my reason for taking this risk. Without presenting any kind of identification papers, such as proof of profession or family descent and the like, I, who called myself a biologist, was assigned to the Wilhelm Stehle tool manufacturing plant, where I am still "active" today. At the same time, presiding judge Bächler assigned us two rooms in the largest stone structure of the town, the municipal courthouse, appropriated by the city for armaments workers. Now suddenly we had everything: apartment, registration with the police, food coupons, and work. On September 6, 1944, we moved in in Memmingen, and on the 7th I began my new job.

The agent at the employment office had thought that perhaps I could travel for the company when materials had to be procured, and I suggested that to director Born, the son-in-law of the boss, when I was asked about this on joining them. They agreed to it. When I was not traveling, I was to replace a stockman who had just been called up. For my travels I needed a special certificate, which the Swabian regional Chamber of Commerce issued me on September 8, 1944 and which was going to be valid until June 30, 1945. It entitled me to buy tickets for all routes and to use express trains. I noticed right away that on the whole the company had surprisingly few Nazis. Party members were the boss, the director, the attorney, the manufacturing engineer, and some foremen. The engineer and the director were probably the dyed-in-the-wool Nazis, the former an "old campaigner" from before 1933. The firm, which formerly produced wood-working tools, had been working for the navy since 1939 and was making auxiliary devices for submarines and mines. What it was all about in particular I never found out and it never interested me either. My work as stockman was quite boring, but my travels were that much more interesting.

*[Herman Pineas undertakes several business trips, among others to the Ministry of War Supplies in Berlin.]*

On November 28, 1944, Herta came to the firm and brought me that day's issue of the *Allgäuer Beobachter,* which carried the notice that from now on, contrary to an earlier provision, post office identification cards would no longer be regarded as official personal identification. Given the trip that I was supposed to begin the next morning, this caused us to apply still on the same day for the issuance of an identity card, which I actually received that very day. My wife got hers two days later. Thus we were in possession of the best proof of identity, something we had strived for until then, during all of our preparations for our time in hiding and for its duration, and which had seemed unattainable, and in this instance, too, came about without further documents only because of my believable hurry and the importance of Stehle's company. To be sure, it caused my wife considerable anguish that a duplicate identity card had to be sent to Düsseldorf and another to Hamburg, namely to our birthplaces, and we could only hope that the many air raids, which had brought the mail service to a standstill, would prevent from coming to light the nonexistence of the persons described in detail and fingerprinted on the identity cards. To be sure, that gave us no peace of mind until liberation. Finally, we also applied for and received new clothing coupons in place of our "old ones, destroyed in an air raid." Another official form, the so-called personal identity card at the provisioning office, on which are noted all of the purchase certificates issued for textiles or shoes, had also caused us some headaches. We acquired this document automatically after we had found out that in Gerstetten inquiries had been made about it. We were summoned to the local provisioning office only once and were asked for our Berlin address. Here, too, in contrast to my wife, I remained calm by correctly judging the far-advanced confusion in economic and official dealings.

To sum up, it can be said that the final years had constantly caused us worries about identification papers, and today, too, it remains the same, even if the circumstances are different: We are trying for a permit to emigrate to the U.S.A.

1. About the Jewish Women's Federation see Ottilie Schönewald (37), note 3.

2. See Camilla Neumann (49), note 4.

3. See Ottilie Schönewald (37), note 8.

4. Reference is to the so-called factory operation of February 27, 1943, during which about 7,000 Jewish forced laborers were arrested at their workplaces and taken directly to transit centers for deportation to Auschwitz. At this time, the leaders of the Reichsvereinigung, Leo Baeck and Paul Eppstein, had already been deported. According to the report of Hildegard Henschel, on February 26 the Jewish community received the order to supply first aid personnel and clerks for the next day, but it was not notified directly about any of the planned measures. — The number of 14,000 arrested factory workers is too high; according to the deportation lists, some 7,000 people were involved.

5. Dr. Julius Moses (1868–1942); doctor and social hygienist in Berlin; from 1923 until 1932 editor of the periodical *Der Kassenarzt*. As an SPD politician, he was a member of the Reichstag from 1920 to 1932. He died in Theresienstadt.

6. Paul Löbe (1875–1967); typesetter and editor. As a leading SPD politician, he was president of the Reichstag from 1920 until 1932. He was arrested temporarily in 1933 and in 1944, and from 1949 until 1953 he was a member of parliament.

7. Hans Frank (1900; executed in 1946); founded in 1928 the Bund Nationalsozialistischer Deutscher Juristen, later called the Nationalsozialistischer Rechtswahrerbund. Frank was Bavarian Minister of Justice in 1933/34, then Reichsminister, and from 1939 on governor-general in Poland.

8. The hospital of the Jewish community in Berlin, founded in 1862, received a modern new building in 1914 (270 beds) on Iranische Strasse. It continued to function as a Jewish hospital also from 1939 until 1945; from 1943 until 1945 it was the seat of the Rest-Reichsvereinigung and served various NS authorities. For more on this in detail see the memoir of Bruno Blau (51).

9. Paul Schuster (1867); as of 1921 associate professor, he was in charge of the Neurology Department of the Hufeland Hospital in Berlin until 1933; then, until his emigration in the summer of 1933, of the Neurology Department of the Jewish hospital.

10. Professor Abraham Buschke (1868; died in 1943 in Theresienstadt); he was a well-known dermatologist in Greifswald and Berlin.

11. The private kosher psychiatric hospital in Sayn was founded in 1869 by Meier Jacoby. His grandsons, Dr. Fritz Jacoby and Dr. Paul Jacoby, directed it until their emigration in 1940. In March and June of 1942, the Jewish mental patients assembled there were deported.

12. On the police station, see Bruno Blau (51).

13. Senior Executive Officer and Senior Medical Officer Dr. Dr. Walter Lustig (1891–1945) was in charge of the Medical Department of the police headquarters in Berlin until 1932. Since he was living in a mixed marriage, he was the sole member of the Reichsvereinigung not to be deported. Rather, on its closure in June 1943, he was named head of the Rest-Reichsvereinigung, which had its seat in the Jewish hospital. Reports on Lustig's character and activities as executor of the orders of the Gestapo are unfavorable. He was arrested in 1945 by Soviet soldiers and shot for collaboration with the Gestapo. See Bruno Blau (51).

14. Moritz Henschel, as successor to Heinrich Stahl, was president of the Jewish community in Berlin from 1940 until 1943. He survived deportation to Theresienstadt and died in 1946 in Tel Aviv.

15. Dr. Helmut Cohen survived the NS period as an internist in the Jewish hospital and after the war emigrated to the United States. He worked at the Marlboro State Hospital in Marlboro, New York.

16. Gustav Degner was district mayor of the Berlin district Prenzlauer Berg in 1946.

17. Kurt Müller gave up his practice as lawyer after 1933, studied theology with Karl Barth, and became pastor of the Reformed Congregation in Stuttgart. He was in charge of the relief action for Jews of the "Sozietät," which was a union of all the clergy in Württemberg close to the Confessing Church. According to estimates, he was able to hide over a dozen Jews from Berlin in Swabian parsonages.

18. Richard Gölz, pastor in Wankheim and musical director at the Tübingen Theological Seminary, was arrested shortly before Christmas in 1944 in the Tübingen Stiftskirche because Hermann Pineas's stay in the parsonage had become known to the NS authorities. Gölz was in a labor camp until the end of the war.

19. Pastor Paul Schempp was disciplined not because of anti-Nazism, but rather he was suspended from his clerical duties because of a nonpolitical conflict with the church authorities of Württemberg.

# 51 *Bruno Blau*

BORN IN 1881 IN MARIENWERDER (WESTERN PRUSSIA); DIED IN 1954 IN FREIBURG.

Bruno Blau, Fourteen Years of Misery and Horror. Manuscript, 120 pages. Written in New York in 1952.[1]

*After finishing his studies, in 1908 Bruno Blau settled in Berlin as a lawyer. In addition, he devoted himself to statistical research. Starting in 1909 he published the* Zeitschrift für Demographie und Statistik der Juden *in Berlin and was in charge of the Büro für die Statistik der Juden (Jewish Statistical Bureau) there. He took part in the First World War as a frontline soldier. In 1933 Blau was forced to dissolve his law partnership with a non-Jew, and at the beginning of 1936 he had himself removed from the register of lawyers because of the shrinking number of clients. In his futile search for a new life, in 1937 he arrived in Prague by way of Warsaw and Carlsbad. There he was arrested and because of a serious illness he was taken in October 1942 to the Jewish hospital in Berlin, as a prisoner of the Gestapo. Since he was a cancer patient and married to a non-Jew, he remained there until liberation in 1945. In 1947 Bruno Blau emigrated to New York, was librarian at the YIVO Institute there until 1953, and died shortly after his return to Germany. In the following he reports how he and eight hundred other Jews survived in the hospital ghetto.*

When I arrived at the Jewish hospital in the evening—it was October 22, 1942—the ward physician received me and briefly questioned me about my condition. The next morning the first examination was to take place. It was carried out by the physician in charge of the internal ward; then there followed the other routine examinations, such as blood tests, x-rays, etc. A definite diagnosis, however, could not be made; therefore I was also examined by the neurologist, who likewise could not ascertain anything. The x-ray examinations were then continued, and finally they believed they had found so-called metastases of a tumor on my spine. Thereupon I was turned over for treatment to the radiologist, who ordered a number of radiation treatments by x-ray; in addition I received calcium injections. At that time I was virtually immobile, could only walk with the help of a cane, and when I was lying down I was not able to turn over by myself. The radiation, which was administered in exact doses and was to be done at definite intervals, was supposed to produce a result only after some time. Apparently very powerful rays were used, for after a few treatments a burn occurred, so that the treatment had to be interrupted. Some time after the end of radiation my condition actually did improve slowly, and gradually I regained my ability to move. Apparently the radiologist had hit upon the right thing.

I was one of the last patients to be treated by him. One day he was gone, along with his assistant. He succeeded in reaching the Swiss border. He intended to cross it together with a larger group, and he had already done that when he noticed that one of his companions had remained behind. He then turned back and thereupon, with his assistant, was seized by the border police and was taken back to Berlin. There, at police headquarters, both of them took poison. The doctor died on the spot, while his assistant was taken to the Jewish hospital, where she also died.—At about the same time there was a second such case involving another assistant in the radiation ward, the one who usually administered the radiation treatments, in my case, too. She had a brother who was working at the hospital as a ward attendant (the father of the two was a well-known physician in Berlin) and who had also disappeared. Out of fear of being immediately deported in retaliation, the sister committed suicide. The brother survived the Third Reich. These two instances show what the mood was like among the Jews at that time. [. . .]

I entered the hospital as a prisoner of the Gestapo. In it there was set up a special "police ward," behind bars and locked doors, in which were all those patients who had been sent to the hospital by the Gestapo or the prisons, for Jews were not allowed admittance to public hospitals. The Jews arrested for deportation also were sent to the police ward of the hospital if they were sick. The same happened to patients of the hospital as soon as they were designated for deportation. Even if it was only a matter of a single night, they were put into the police ward in order to prevent escape.

In the ward there were at that time some twenty patients. Their number, however, grew constantly in the course of time, so that finally a second police ward had to be set up, and there was a total of some eighty people as prisoners in the hospital. Among the patients I met there was a young man—his name was Heymann[2]—who had been arrested for taking part in communist activities, and who had tried to take his own life by slitting his carotid artery. As soon as he was able to leave his bed, he was picked up early one morning by two Gestapo officials, who stood at his bed until he had finished dressing. On March 4, 1943, his name, along with eight others, appeared printed on red posters on the poster pillars in Berlin: Nine young Jews had been executed for planning high treason. Allegedly they had banded together to form a communist training group; the matter was reported under the rubric: "Heinz Israel Rotholz and Comrades." Heymann was a trained metalworker (lathe operator) and was especially intelligent and well-read. Another patient was picked up for deportation and had jumped out the window on Levetzowstrasse, where the unfortunate ones were taken at that time. In the course of time many patients were brought in who had attempted suicide for fear of deportation. A number of them became well and then immediately had to set out on their journey to death.

The treatment of the inmates in the police ward was no different from that of the other patients, only they were not allowed to leave the ward and could receive visits only by special permission. From time to time, if they were not confined to bed, they were taken for a walk under guard. If they had to go to another building for treatment or examination, they were guarded by a hospital employee. Packages for them were inspected before they were distributed; their correspondence, too, was subject to check.

Several days before my admission, the hospital had gotten a new administrative head. His predecessor, together with a large number of other community officials, had been marked for deportation, and he and his wife had committed suicide. The new director had been named by the Gestapo, without consulting the community, since the appropriate Gestapo officials liked his nature and demeanor, and he was therefore also saved from deportation. A few people had succeeded in escaping their fate during the so-called community deportation. The consequence of this was that four officials of the community—Dr. Lamm, Dr. Blumenthal, Dr. Goldstein, and Dr. Mendelsohn—as well as four board members of the Reichsvereinigung—Selbiger, Looser, Joseph, and Wolff—were shot although they were totally innocent and were not at all in a position to prevent the disappearance of those people.[3] [. . .]

Gradually all the board members of the Reichsvereinigung—among them the president, Dr. Leo Baeck—had been deported. The only one that remained was the senior executive officer and senior medical officer, Dr. Walter Lustig,[4] who was married to a non-Jew. The Gestapo transferred the presidency of the Reichsvereinigung to him, by which he became its absolute ruler. The hospital employees, transposing his name and title, used to call him "Oberlustrat Gierig."*

The health administration, created by the Reichsvereinigung, also supervised the police ward of the hospital and received its instructions for it from the Gestapo. All orders of the Gestapo that related to Jews went to the Reichsvereinigung, and the latter had to see to it that they were carried out. The *Jüdische Nachrichtenblatt*,[5] in which the orders were usually published, also served this purpose. At times, however, they were only posted on the bulletin board at the community offices, and then referred to in the news bulletins, and it was made every individual's duty to note the contents of the postings. As head of the health administration Dr. Lustig was completely inaccessible and not available either to the police prisoners or to their families. It is said that he

---

*Lustig* means "merry"; its stem, *Lust*, also means "lust." Thus, the play on words can be translated as "Senior Lust Officer Lecher" (one meaning of *gierig* is "lustful").

was not only a willing tool in the hands of the Gestapo but that he also even played into its hands, and by his intervention caused the deportation of the hospital's employees as well as patients. What role he actually played is not clear. At any rate, the fact that he was arrested by the Russian police and, according to reliable reports, was shot points to his collaboration with the Gestapo. In any case, he disappeared and nothing was heard about him after his arrest. It is a fact, however, that neither Dr. Lustig nor his assistant Zwilsky had the least bit of good will toward us, which was evident even in trivial matters. They always claimed to be acting on orders from the Gestapo, the "authorities," which, however, one could often interpret in another way. How far this went is illustrated by the fact that, when the Russians were already in Berlin, and the Gestapo officials had already fled long ago, Dr. Lustig refused to release me from the hospital because supposedly he was not allowed to do that without the consent of the Gestapo, whose officials, however, he was not able to reach by telephone, since, after all, they were no longer there. [. . .]

In April 1943 the Gestapo appropriated the pathology building for use as a prison. Before that, the Jews who had been designated for deportation and had been arrested for that purpose were housed in a building in the center of Berlin, on Grosse Hamburger Strasse. On this site is located the oldest Jewish cemetery in Berlin, with the graves of well-known Jews, for example that of Moses Mendelssohn, for whom a monument had been erected. Naturally, the Gestapo had it removed, and the graves were leveled.[6] The house on Grosse Hamburger Strasse had served as an old-age home and as such had become superfluous since it no longer had any inhabitants. At the start of the deportations, the people taken for this purpose from their homes were put up in the synagogue on Levetzowstrasse. However, since these facilities did not suffice and also were unsuited for a longer stay, the old-age home was set up to receive the unfortunate ones; primarily, that is, bars were affixed to the windows to prevent attempts at escape. Here, then, the Jews were kept under strict surveillance until they could be deported. In April 1943, another change occurred, since the house on Hamburger Strasse was needed for other police prisoners. The Jewish prisoners, the candidates for deportation as well as other Jews who had been arrested by the Gestapo, were now sent to the hospital's pathology building, which had a special entrance on Schulstrasse. Naturally, here, too, bars were put up in front of the windows and the building was separated from the hospital by a barbed-wire fence. The directors of this prison, which had the official name "transit center," were several Gestapo officials, headed by the officer Dobberke. In addition, the camp had a Jewish head, the former teacher Reschke, and further, a number of Jewish "order keepers," who had the task of prison guards. Some of them treated the Jews in their charge badly, beating them, too, especially the assistant leader Blond, who disappeared immediately after the Russians marched in. Also employed in the center were some Jewish craftsmen, such as tailors and cobblers, and a barber.

Besides, a number of Jewish men and women actively served the Gestapo as informers and "catchers." They claimed to have been forced to do it, but it is clear that the Gestapo could not possibly have used them against their will. Rather, the people in question believed that by their activities they would be able to escape their own deportation, and therefore they offered their services to the Gestapo. These creatures have many of their brothers and sisters on their consciences, and some of them did get just punishment for their deeds. To the extent that Russian police got hold of them, they were generally shot immediately, for instance, a young man by the name of K., who had been active as a "catcher," and a certain G. When the latter tried to arrest a Jewish woman, he was seriously wounded with a knife by her non-Jewish friend, and for a long time he hovered between life and death. The efforts of the doctors were successful in restoring him, at least to the extent that he was able to move about. The man who inflicted his wounds is supposed to have been condemned to death, for the Gestapo's Jewish catchers had very far-reaching powers and opposition to them was treated like opposition to the Gestapo itself.

Even worse than these catchers were the informants, who practiced their dirty trade by tracking down, in every possible way, Jews who were successfully hiding from the Gestapo, and turning them in to the Gestapo. If they were especially industrious, some of them actually did succeed in escaping deportation and surviving the Gestapo. Most of them, however, as for instance the lawyer Dr. Kurt J. and the physician Dr. J., who functioned as informants, were themselves deported after some time, since the Gestapo eliminated all persons who could become somehow inconvenient as witnesses. How large the number of victims is who perished because of Jewish informants will never be known.

By the way, Jewish "order keepers" were also seen robbing the Jews in their care before the latter were deported. Several of them committed suicide. According to the unanimous judgment of former center internees, no objections could be made to the treatment of Jewish inmates by the camp director Dobberke. He mistreated the inmates only if he thought that he had been lied to, or if he suspected some other resistance; otherwise, however, to the extent that it was within his power, he eased their lot in many ways, although he had the power to turn life into hell for them. One could get a great deal from him with a bottle of spirits made in the pharmacy of the hospital, and the hospital's director did his best to keep Dobberke in a good mood. At any rate, the inmates of the transit center had it much better than the inmates of the police prisons. On Grosse Hamburger Strasse the food was prepared by a Jewish cook who was housed there; on Schulstrasse, however, the prisoners received the same food as the patients of the hospital. As a matter of fact, frequently they received extras, which the patients did not get. The prisoners could also be outside for a while twice a day, and they were kept busy with tasks that were neither difficult nor unpleasant. In part, they worked in the kitchen of the hospital; in part, they were used for cleaning work in the hospital, on the streets, or also in the Gestapo offices (Französische Strasse).

In the final months of the Thousand Year Reich the Gestapo had set up another big hall of the hospital as a work room, and had children's clothing produced there. The necessary machines and other equipment had been provided. Inmates of the transit center were also employed in this factory, and those who proved themselves to be especially valuable were kept from deportation as long as possible. Some evaded it in this way altogether. The Gestapo official in charge of the clothing factory was especially interested in them, and inspected them almost daily. Seemingly, he had a personal interest in it. The enterprise was extremely profitable, since it did not involve any expenses except for the raw materials. No salaries were paid, nor did rent, light, heat, electricity, etc., cost anything, and work was done in two shifts, including a night shift. When the Nazi Reich collapsed, there was a considerable amount of finished children's clothing on hand. It was then distributed among the Jews in the hospital.

Starting on July 1, 1943, on the basis of the 13th statutory regulation of the Reichsbürgergesetz, Jews who had made themselves liable to prosecution were no longer taken to court, but instead were sentenced by the police, that is, the Gestapo. They were entirely at the mercy of this authority, which was not bound by any law. If it was really a matter of a punishable offense, the perpetrators generally were sent to a concentration camp and, as a matter of fact, with a special notation that either ordered immediate liquidation or designated them for later extermination, so that they could still be used for a time as laborers. In some instances deportation to the extermination camp was dispensed with by murdering the persons in question right then and there. In Berlin this was carried out in the SS barracks in Lichterfelde. These Jews were told to go along "without belongings," which, after all, were no longer needed. The wife of a man who was murdered in this way, and whom I had known, was stalled off for months by the police, without being able to get information about her husband's fate. Finally, after much insistence, she received a death certificate, from which the date of his death could be established; it was the day on which the man had been taken from the hospital.

Besides those to be deported, the transit center housed such people who were persecuted because of so-called "Jew crimes." Among them was, above all, the "aiding and abetting of Jews," that is, the support of, or aid to, Jews who were trying to escape deportation. The mere contact with them sufficed; for example, if one had received them in one's apartment and had served them a cup of coffee. For such crimes, by the way, non-Jews were persecuted all the more and were taken to a concentration camp, since there was no judicial penalty for such a serious crime. Among the "Jew crimes" there were further: prohibited visits to restaurants and movie houses, the use of public transportation without permission, omission of the Jewish middle name, not showing the Jewish identification card, use of public telephones, buying of newspapers, shopping at hours other than the assigned ones, keeping of pets, breaking the curfew, and the like, but, above all, not wearing the Yellow Star. Also, the latter had to be affixed according to regulation, that is, sewn onto the article of clothing, rather than simply pinned on and thus removable at will.

Once, during a visit by Gestapo officials, a young girl of nineteen, who was employed by the Reichsvereinigung, was caught with her Star only loosely attached to her coat. She was immediately taken to the police ward of the hospital, and on the same day to the transit center, from where she was sent to the concentration camp, without being allowed to see her mother again. She never returned. Covering the Star with a package or a briefcase was also punishable. — Incidentally, the intended effect of delivering the Jews up to the fury of the people by making them recognizable as such was achieved only in few, exceptional cases. On the whole, the population did not take notice of the Star; instead, at the beginning, derogatory remarks were made by non-Jews about the measure, and there were even demonstrations of sympathy toward Jews in the form of cigars or sweets for children. [. . .]

Privileged mixed marriages were mixed marriages in which the wife was a Jew, or from which children had issued who did not belong to the Jewish religion or were not regarded as Jews according to the Nuremberg Laws. This privilege came into existence on April 30, 1939. It was introduced by the "Law on Rental Leases with Jews" of this date, and freed the Jews in this category from certain exclusionary provisions (limitation of tenant rights, early notice to vacate, obligatory permit). The Privileged Jews were also exempted from obligatory membership in the Reichsvereinigung, and later from quite a number of other regulations. But their most important and externally conspicuous privilege was their exemption from the provisions of the "Police Regulation on the Identification of Jews" of September 1, 1941. They did not have to affix the Star of David to their clothes, nor, later, to the door of their residences. What this means can be appreciated only by someone who himself was forced to wear the Star, by someone who knows how many tears were shed by old men and small children over it and who knows that some risked and even lost their lives because of it. The exclusionary provisions introduced prior to the invention of the Jews' Privilege applied also to the Jews who were later privileged. For example, they always had to carry with them the identification card stamped with a "J," and show it to every official without being asked, as well as to include the identification card number in any correspondence. They had to use the Jewish middle name, etc. But the Privileged Jews were exempted from all degrading, oppressive, and harmful regulations that were introduced later and that restricted the lives of the other Jews and turned them into a martyrdom. They also received the same foodstuffs as non-Jews, got ration coupons for clothes and tobacco, were permitted to make unlimited use of public transportation, could leave the city, were permitted to retain their property rights, were allowed to use their titles, etc. Their standard of living was scarcely different from that of the non-Jews; they experienced none of the torments that were devised for Jews with genuine sadism.

Decisive for the granting of the privilege was whether the children were entered in the register of the Jewish community on the effective date, September 15, 1935. As it was, the registers were often not kept that accurately, so that not all entries in all instances reflected the facts. On the one hand, it happened that children who had been baptized as Christians were not removed from the register, while on the other hand, due to some kind of oversight, children were not registered although they were never withdrawn from the community by their parents and had a Jewish upbringing in the best sense. Earlier there was no reason to check the entry and therefore hardly anyone was interested in it. Now, however, the entries could be of the greatest significance in practical matters. I know of an old Zionist whose daughter, born of his mixed marriage, was brought up as a Jew but by some mistake or another was not in the register. His marriage, therefore, was regarded as privileged, and he had no reason not to make use of the privilege.

Of course, the Gestapo endeavored to limit the privilege whenever possible. For instance, it interpreted the regulations in such a way that a marriage was not affected if the children were living abroad. Later, this arbitrary interpretation was dropped, but it was expressly decreed that if the privilege had previously not been recognized for the mentioned reason, it was to remain so. It must be said that many Privileged Jews made ample use of the privilege, for which they themselves could take no credit (often having gained it by chance), and felt superior to other Jews. Often they avoided all contact with them and feared to appear in public with them. According to the findings of the

Reichsvereinigung, on April 1, 1943 there were 17,375 Jews in the German Reich who did not wear the Star and only 14,393 who did. In Berlin, too, the number of privileged mixed marriages was greater than that of the others. At the end of the Third Reich there were 3,339 privileged and 1,451 regular mixed marriages there. [. . .]

On the occasion of a mass deportation, contrary to the instructions not to deport Jews living in mixed marriages, the Gestapo had a large number of such Jews arrested, too. In the beginning, until "clarification," they were confined in the former administration building of the Jewish community on Rosenstrasse. The wives of the arrested men went to Rosenstrasse in flocks every day, early in the morning, and demanded the release of their husbands.[7] Without regard for their own safety, they demonstrated throughout the day until they were chased away by the police. By their courageous behavior, their readiness to make sacrifices, and their persistence, they finally succeeded in getting the Gestapo to give in and release the arrested men. The conduct of these women shows that it was not impossible to fight against the Nazis with success. If the relatively small number of wives of Jewish men succeeded in changing their fate for the better, then, if they had seriously wanted to, those Germans who in such great numbers now call themselves opponents of Nazism could also have prevented the atrocities that they supposedly did not want or even abhorred. [. . .]

In the police ward there were a number of well-known personalities, for example Theodor Wolff,[8] the former chief editor of the *Berliner Tageblatt,* who was not only of eminent significance as a writer but, for a time, also had great influence in Germany as a politician. He had emigrated in 1933 and was living in Nizza. There he was arrested and dragged through fourteen prisons until he finally landed in the Berlin police prison. During his stay there he was interrogated twice at the Gestapo headquarters on Prinz-Albrecht-Strasse, without having been given a reason for his arrest. The interrogations took place in the form of a colloquium, whose theme on one occasion was Zionism. During the time of his incarceration Wolff had gotten an inflammation (cellulitis). He was therefore taken to the hospital, and his arm had to be operated on; after the operation, cardiac insufficiency set in, which due to the patient's advanced age—he was 76 years old—led to his death. Altogether Wolff was in the hospital for ten days. His mind was completely unimpaired and his appetite was good. That in the end his heart gave out was no wonder, considering all that he had gone through during the last months. He was buried in the row of honor in the Weissensee Cemetery. As chance would have it, later one of his sons came to Berlin as a member of the American occupying forces and was able to have a worthy monument erected to him.

Another patient was the economist Professor Dr. Franz Eulenburg,[9] who as a young instructor in Leipzig had been my teacher. In the end he taught at the Berlin School of Commerce, of which he was also the president for some time. Having already been baptized in his youth, he no longer had any ties to Judaism. It was even said that he was a pious Christian and an avid church-goer. Since he lived in a mixed marriage he was not deported. However, he employed a Jewish secretary who was in hiding from the Gestapo. Now he was accused of aiding and abetting her and was sent to the police prison for "aiding and abetting Jews." To be sure, he denied having known that the lady had "submerged." He claimed not to have been interested at all in her whereabouts. He said that she always came to work regularly and he had had no reason to ask her where she was coming from and whether a change had occurred in her circumstances. Eulenburg was kept in custody and, if he had stayed well, would have been sent to the concentration camp. He was almost dying when he got to the hospital. I was able to do no more than greet him and introduce myself to him as a former student. He seemed happy about it, but soon lost consciousness and died a short time later. [. . .]

Another police prisoner was the well-known chemist Dr. Ernst Eichengrün,[10] who during his employment at the Bayer works had invented aspirin. His crime consisted in omitting the obligatory middle name "Israel" on an application for a patent that he was taking out not for himself personally but rather for his firm, which was registered. Although he lived in a mixed marriage and thus actually was not supposed to be deported, he—as well as two other prisoners—was taken to Theresienstadt. There a laboratory was set up for him, in which he worked.—I should also mention the director of the big Berlin vaudeville "Scala" and president of the Association of German Vaudeville Directors, Jules Marx, who, after his recovery, was sent to Auschwitz—it is not known whether he survived it—and Ludwig Katzenellenbogen,[11] a well-known industrialist and husband of the great actress Tilla Durieux. He was arrested in Yugoslavia, taken to Berlin, and died in the hospital.

*[In the spring of 1944 Bruno Blau is transferred from the police ward to the public ward.]*

It seems that I owe my life to the false diagnosis made by the doctors. It apparently indicated that I was incurably ill. And the Gestapo's lack of interest in me could have arisen from that. The chief physician later explained to me that my case was either among the five percent of cases in which recovery from the diagnosed illness occurs, or that the diagnosis was incorrect.

I used the time in the hospital to gather material about the Nazi period and had sufficient opportunity to get together with a large number of patients and other people from whom I learned much that I partly also experienced myself or verified. Above all, I also came into contact with many detainees of the transit center and with the officials of the Reichsvereinigung. From the statistician, for instance, I received the entire statistical material of the Reichsvereinigung that was still available at that time; part of it had been lost earlier in bombing raids. Everything that was available I saved and edited. Thus I alone was in possession of those important figures.[12] When Dr. Lustig found out that the official in question had placed the material at my disposal, he was very annoyed and forbade him to entrust anything to me in the future. [. . .]

In the summer of 1943, Jews from Frankfurt am Main, Hamburg, and other places, who were living in mixed marriages, were sent to Berlin to be used there in a labor deployment. They were employed either in construction firms, or similar ones, by the Gestapo. The latter had appropriated, among others, the building of the "Brüderverein" at 116 Kurfürstenstrasse in the west of Berlin. This was an old respected society, in character like a club, whose members were well-to-do Jews. The building was quite new and of good, solid construction. A part of the infamous headquarters of the Security Department was housed there.[13] The Zentralstelle für jüdische Auswanderung had also been there, until the Central Security Department of the Reich took over its tasks. This house was now converted by the Gestapo into a veritable fortress and equipped with shelters, bunkers, etc. Apparently the intention was to entrench themselves there if the Allies approached. But it did not come to that. For when things became dangerous, the Gestapo were the first to disappear. At any rate, they worked several years on the fortification of the building and for this purpose, among others, the Jews who came from outside Berlin also were used.

In the fall of 1944 some three hundred additional Jewish men and women were brought to Berlin from the Rhineland and Westphalia. These were the Jewish partners of mixed marriages, who were separated from their spouses at that time and sent to labor camps outside their town of residence. If they were not fit for work, they were sent to Berlin, and there to the hospital. Here they were put, or rather crowded, together in the office building and partly also in the hospital building. Although it was precisely because of their inability to work that they had been sent to the hospital, they were kept busy with physical work and also employed in the above-mentioned clothes factory. They were not compensated for it, but for their room and board they had to pay a specific sum, which was collected from their families. They were not permitted to leave the hospital and could write only one letter a week. They were allowed to receive visitors only by special permission of the Gestapo, which was granted only as a rare exception. In other words, they were treated like prisoners.

Finally, a number of Jews of Russian citizenship were brought to the hospital. As enemy aliens they should have been taken to an internment camp, but because of illness they were transferred to the hospital. Their freedom, too, was restricted. The Reichs-vereinigung had also received orders from the Gestapo to detain all Jews who for some reason or another came to Berlin from elsewhere. These, too, were housed in the hospital and put to work. Thus the hospital was overcrowded, especially since more and more of it became unusable due to damage from bombing raids. In addition, a number of officials of the Reichsvereinigung were bombed out of their homes and received emergency accommodations in the hospital.

All employees of the Reichsvereinigung and the hospital had to be at the Gestapo's disposal at all times for special tasks. One evening, for example, a certain number of them were requested for an urgent job at the Central Security Department of the Reich on Kurfürstenstrasse. They had to transport from there to the hospital a number of bales of material, which were stored in the cellar rooms. Then it turned out that these bales were actually a million and a half Yellow Stars. Later the Central Security Department demanded the return of some 10,000 of them. Perhaps later, in an emergency, they were to be used to disguise Gestapo officials.

Another time employees of the Reichsvereinigung had to unload railway cars at a station. They contained crates with the inscription: "Caution! Explosives!" The crates, however, were relatively light, so that doubt arose as to whether the inscriptions corresponded to reality. And what do you know, while the crates were being unloaded, one of them opened by chance so that one could see its contents: silver and gold Torah ornaments, which had been plundered from synagogues in Greece.

The Gestapo had pretty much assembled the rest of the Jews remaining in Berlin in the hospital. Only those living in mixed marriages who were not in custody and still had their homes in the different sections of the city were excepted. At the end there were still some 160 Jews in Berlin who were unmarried or married to a Jewish spouse, while in the hospital and the transit center together there were some 800 persons.

In the transit center the Gestapo had set up a Jewish registration office, whose head was a Fräulein Raffael. All information from the various authorities pertaining to Jews was gathered here, for example, reports of deaths by the registries. If it was a matter of the death of a non-Jewish partner in a mixed marriage, then the immediate result was the deportation of the Jewish spouse, who from that moment on was no longer protected. Every month Fräulein Raffael had to report to the Reichsvereinigung the latest statistics on the Jews in Berlin. I owe my knowledge of all details concerning mixed marriages, with and without privilege, people considered as Jews according to the Nuremberg Laws, etc. to these reports.

Here in America it often seems impossible to understand why the Gestapo kept the Jewish hospital in Berlin in operation until the end, although otherwise it was its principle to exterminate sick people as quickly as possible. It should be noted that the hospital did not exist as such in name alone, but rather that the patients were actually treated and cared for in an orderly way. For this purpose even the necessary personnel were left there and thus in part spared deportation. Some of the doctors, to be sure, were living in mixed marriages and would not have been deported anyway. Others, however, as well as the nursing staff and administrative employees, were retained as indispensable. Gradually more and more were deported, but nevertheless there still remained so many that the enterprise could be kept going, even if the manner of care left something to be desired and, above all, insufficient attention was paid to the cleanliness of the institution, which in the past had been exemplary.

Some of the people left in the hospital were designated for the Palestine exchange; that is, from time to time Germans were brought back from Palestine and exchanged for Jews. Technically this was done in the following way: On both sides the required number of people were assembled in a camp that was under Swiss protection. As soon as the necessary number was attained, the transports were routed to Turkey and there waited for one another at a railway station. The exchange occurred there according to an exact head count. This process, which took place through international channels, demanded much time and became more and more difficult as the war progressed. However, as soon as a certificate was issued for a Jew living in Germany, he was exempted from deportation. In this way they wanted to bring back to Germany as many Germans as possible. [. . .]

The president of the Berlin community currently in office, Dr. Hans-Erich Fabian,[14] had been deported to Theresienstadt with his wife and small children. Since he was needed in Berlin for certain tasks in the financial administration, he was brought back from Theresienstadt and put in the transit center. From there he was taken daily by an official to the office where he worked, and in the evening he was returned to the center. This went on until the collapse of the regime.

The Jews who were still living in Germany were, without exception, always in danger and had to constantly reckon with being removed by force. This was the case even if according to prior practice they might have been safe, for there was no guarantee that this practice would continue. Especially endangered, however, were the ones in the hospital, since they were always under the eyes of the Gestapo and had no opportunity to escape their fate by flight if things ever became extreme. Even apart from the general raids, immediate extradition to the Gestapo of any individual could be requested at any time of day or night, something that happened in many instances. Even when the Red Army was already in Berlin, some employees of the hospital living outside it were still picked up by SS people and shot, without their families finding out about it right away. The more critical for the Nazis the military situation became, the more dangerous did the situation become for the Jews.

In the middle of April 1945 the Jewish records of the Gestapo, in its different offices, were destroyed. I saw how the files that were in the transit center were burned in the courtyard of the hospital, in front of the office building, and they were not only the files of the transit center itself, but there were other files among them, too, as I ascertained. They wanted to cover all traces and prevent any future disclosures about the deportations and other operations. But they had forgotten one thing: The Gestapo, in each individual case, had informed the Chief Minister of Finance about the impending deportation and then sent him the records of the seizure of property. To the extent that these files did not fall victim to bombing raids, they still exist, and it can be ascertained what property each person deported had left behind and what happened to it. The lists of the individual transports of deportees from Berlin are also available and can be examined. The original material is presently at the Central Tax Office in Berlin, while the Berlin Office of the American Jewish Joint Distribution Committee possesses copies of it.

It was mentioned above that the wing of the hospital with the synagogue could not be used because of bomb damage. In reality, however, it was already not being used earlier, for Jews were forbidden to hold any kind of gatherings. Nevertheless, from time to time on holidays, on special Sabbaths, and after the fortunate conclusion of a heavy bombing raid, in complete secrecy *minyanim*[15] gathered in the hospital, in director Neumann's apartment, to which ten occupants of the hospital were invited through special, trustworthy people. I, too, had the opportunity to participate in them. We had to go there as inconspicuously as possible, and after the end of the *minyan* return to our rooms separately, in part using the cellar corridors. And we were less afraid of the Gestapo than of the head of the Reichsvereinigung, Dr. Lustig, who saw to it that the orders of the Gestapo were not violated. [. . .]

How in the final days of the Thousand Year Reich the events unfolded; how eight hundred Jews confined to a small space, cut off from the world, without freedom of movement, exposed to all the dangers of the terrible war, lived through these days and awaited the dawning of a new era; how, filled with hope and longing, they looked forward to liberation; how, knowing that salvation was coming, they gladly took upon themselves every trouble and hardship—nowhere else could that be experienced with the same intensity as in the Berlin hospital ghetto. For in no other place were as many Jews crowded together as here, where all the institutions that either positively or negatively affected the continued existence of Jews in Germany could also be found, where everyone without exception was inspired by one and the same thought, where on everyone's lips—whether voiced or not—there lingered the one anxious question: Is the end near? When will it come? Will I live to see it?

As late as March 27, 1945, a time when, one would have thought, every railway car was absolutely needed for military or supply purposes, a deportation transport was dispatched from the transit center. Thus the Gestapo continued working until the last moment to carry out their plan for the Jews. In the middle of April, however, after the signs increased that the Gestapo was also anticipating the speedy end of the Third Reich, three Jews used by it as informants fled from the transit center. One of them, the especially infamous Frau Stella Isaacsohn, née Goldschlag, in her first marriage Kübler, later fell into the hands of the Russians, and probably got her due punishment.

On April 21, 1945, the bombardment of Berlin by the Red Army began. On this day two brothers who worked at the hospital were hit by a grenade on their way home and were badly wounded. One lost an arm and with it his occupation as a gardener. They were among the first victims of the battle for Berlin. In the following days three other employees of the Reichsvereinigung likewise found their death.

The bombardment took on such dimensions that even on its first day all the occupants of the hospital—including the healthy ones, the employees, the internees, the children, etc.—constantly had to be taken to the cellar facilities. Here they were to live for the next two weeks without light, without air, without water, and without heat. This was unavoidable because staying even on the first floor was too dangerous. Aerial bombs, grenades, and machine-gun bullets passed over the building and also hit the walls. In many rooms later one could see where they had struck. At times the barrage lasted many hours without interruption. The area was especially dangerous because barricades had been erected in the immediate vicinity of the hospital and pockets of resistance manned by soldiers and SS were set up. There was constantly shooting over our heads. Continuously, wounded people were being brought in, mostly non-Jews, who were bandaged and in some cases also received for further treatment. A Jewish Russian soldier died of his wounds. In the makeshift operating room, which had already been in use for some time during bombing raids, there now was feverish activity. The doctors had their hands full and did not have a moment's rest day or night.

I still remember how we had to grope our way in the darkness through the cold, damp cellar passages, which were crowded with people lying and sitting. Some had to remain sitting the whole time because there was no place to lie. No one got out of his clothes, hardly anyone had a chance to get washed. In my ears I still hear the languishing patients piercingly crying out for water, which could be brought only in very small quantities from a well, at the risk of one's life. I still hear the thunder of the guns, the whizzing and whipping of the bullets, the rat-a-tat of the machine guns, the whirring of the airplanes, the thunder of exploding bombs. I still see the stretchers with the wounded, I still hear their moans and their cries of pain. I still remember how the scanty meals were canceled or postponed, and we had to starve because it was not possible to get the necessary foodstuffs. All that we bore calmly and patiently. After all, we knew that salvation could not come without it. Finally we saw it close at hand.

After the Gestapo officials had fled on April 22nd, we also knew that we no longer had to fear a massacre. Now the Health Department of the Reichsvereinigung could free the police prisoners and the other detainees without fear of the Gestapo. For most, to be sure, at first this had no practical meaning; because of the bombardment they could not leave the hospital and go home anyway. Only a few who lived in the vicinity dared to set out for home during the night.

In the hospital there were still courageous persons who in spite of the bombardment fetched bread and other foodstuffs, and thus saw to it that eight hundred people had something to eat and did not have to suffer too greatly from hunger. In this way, with fear and anxiety, eight hundred Jews survived the last, difficult days, without losing anyone from their ranks. When we finally came out of our live entombment into the light of day, the Nazi nightmare was over—at least at that time. The commandant of Berlin, General Bersarin, had issued an order of the day whereby the Nazi laws were to be "eradicated." But even without formal arrangements and without further ado the laws pertaining to Jews were regarded in practice as null and void. First we took off the Yellow Star, and the compulsory Jewish middle names disappeared. Once again the Jews were human beings.

At first we could not comprehend the miracle that had happened, although we had waited and hoped for it long enough. The joy of most people was also marred because they were uncertain about the fate of their kin. No one knew whether the others were still alive, where they were, how they had survived the final days, if and when they would see one another again.

Soon it also turned out that the few Jews who had survived the thousand years would necessarily be disappointed in many respects. Actually, we did imagine that liberation from Nazi slavery would be different. In spite of the proclamations of the Russian military command, the Russian soldiers did not shrink from ransacking all of the rooms in the hospital, breaking open closets, and plundering to their heart's content. Even in the cellar the soldiers tried to take valuables away from the sick. It did not help any either if one let them know that one was a "Yevrei." They did not believe that we were Jews; they thought that Hitler had "done in" all the Jews and they took us for Nazis in disguise.

We could consider the Nazi period as finished when in accordance with an old custom we gathered to thank God for deliverance from the greatest tribulation, and to remember the victims claimed by the times. On May 6th, the chief rabbi of the Polish army, Kahane, who had arrived in Berlin with the Red Army, gathered around him a group of Jews in the rooms of the Reichsvereinigung. Although the event was completely improvised, the room was not big enough to hold the deeply moved multitude; part of those who came had to remain in the adjoining rooms and hallways. First the rabbi said the *Mincha* prayer and then he briefly and concisely described the situation. He pointed out that the Nazi regime had cost six million Jews their lives, of them three and a half million in Poland alone. In remembrance of the victims, the *chasan,* who also belonged to the Polish army, sang *El mole rachamim*[16] which was interrupted by the sobs of the stirred listeners.

1. The editor thanks the YIVO Institute in New York for permission to print the manuscript.

2. Reference is to twenty-six-year-old Felix Heymann, member of the Jewish resistance group Baum, who was arrested after the group's attempt to burn down the propaganda exhibition

"The Soviet Paradise," sentenced to death by the People's Court, and executed on March 4, 1943. Altogether twenty-seven members of the group were executed in the years 1942/43.

3. On October 20, 1942, all employees of the Reichsvereinigung and the Berlin Jewish community had to appear at the community building on Oranienburger Strasse, where five hundred were selected for deportation. When twenty of these did not present themselves for deportation, twenty hostages were taken, of whom twelve were deported and eight were shot. Among the latter were Dr. Fritz Lamm, head of the welfare and youth welfare office, Dr. Bruno Mendelsohn, head of the Wirtschaftshilfe, Alfred Selbiger, head of Hachshara and Hechalutz in the Palestine Office, as well as Dr. Julius Blumenthal, contributor to the *Jüdische Nachrichtenblatt*.

4. The offices of the Reichsvereinigung and the Berlin Jewish community were closed on June 10, 1943 and the last employees were deported, provided that they did not live in a mixed marriage. Shortly thereafter Dr. Lustig, at the Jewish hospital, must have been named head of the Rest-Reichsvereinigung which was merely executing the Gestapo's orders. On Lustig see Hermann Pineas (50), note 13. In another part of the manuscript Bruno Blau describes in a disapproving manner Lustig's relationship to individual nurses.

5. The *Jüdische Nachrichtenblatt* was the sole Jewish newspaper that was still permitted. It appeared from the end of 1938 until May 1943, under the strictest Gestapo censorship. More and more, it was allowed to print only anti-Jewish regulations.

6. On Grosse Hamburger Strasse, on the spot of the cemetery consecrated in 1672, there is today a public park with the reconstructed gravestone of Moses Mendelssohn and a commemorative stone for the people deported from the transit center, formerly an old-age home. The building of the old-age home no longer exists.

7. The reference is to Jewish men who were arrested on February 27, 1943, during the "factory operation." (See Camilla Neumann [49], note 5.) The successful demonstration of their non-Jewish wives for their release took place daily from February 27th to March 11th. In 1955 the Jewish community of Berlin was able to ascertain the names of sixty-seven participating women, but the number of the demonstrators was far higher.

8. Theodor Wolff (1868–1943) was chief editor of the *Berliner Tageblatt* in the years 1906–1933, and in 1918 was among the founders of the Deutsche Demokratische Partei. He was one of the most influential liberal publicists in Germany. Shortly after his flight, his writings fell victim to the National Socialist book burning. He died on September 23, 1943.

9. Dr. Franz Eulenburg (1867–1943) taught economics as professor in Leipzig and Aachen, and from 1921 to 1933 at the School of Commerce in Berlin.

10. Dr. Ernst Eichengrün (1867–1949), who had been baptized, developed medicines for Bayer, among them aspirin. He also invented the synthetic Cellon, and between 1908 and 1938 he directed his Cellon Works in Berlin.

11. Ludwig Katzenellenbogen (1877–1943?), also a convert to Christianity, was the founder and general director of the Ostwerke AG (spirits, grain alcohol, yeast), which later formed a combine with the Schultheiss-Patzenhofer brewery. He emigrated to Switzerland in 1933, to Yugoslavia in 1938, and was arrested in Saloniki during the war.

12. Bruno Blau utilized the statistics of the Reichsvereinigung for his still unpublished work *Die Entwicklung der jüdischen Bevölkerung in Deutschland* (New York, 1950), pp.334–380. (The original is at the YIVO Institute in New York.)

13. See Elisabeth Freund (46), note 3.

14. Dr. Hans Erich Fabian (1902–1974) directed the Finance and Property Department of the Reichsvereinigung. Deported to Theresienstadt, he was brought back from there to Berlin in order to conclude the property transactions of the dissolved Jewish organizations. After the war Fabian was Supreme Court judge in Berlin, and from 1946 to 1948 chairman of the new Jewish community. In 1949 he emigrated to the United States, where as a lawyer for the United Restitution Organization he specialized in restitution cases.

15. Meant are prayer services that are possible only if a *minyan* is present, that is, a minimum of ten men who are regarded as adults in the religious sense. Such *minyanim* also gathered from 1943 to 1945 in the Jewish cemetery in Berlin-Weissensee (information from Arthur Brass).

16. The cantor chanted the prayer customary at funerals and memorial services.

# Glossary

ALIYAH "Going Up"; Zionist term for Jewish migration to Palestine/Israel.

BARCHES (also Berches or Challe); braided white bread, over which the blessing is spoken at Sabbath and festival meals.

BAR MITZVAH "Son of the Commandments"; on his thirteenth birthday the boy attains religious majority and is obligated to fulfill the commandments. On the day of his Bar Mitzvah he is called up to read from the Torah for the first time and often delivers a short religious discourse.

BENSCHEN Verb; to recite a blessing; to recite Grace after meals.

BLETT See Plett.

B'NAI B'RITH "Sons of the Covenant"; independent Jewish fraternal order, founded in 1843 in New York. In 1932 in Germany there were more than one hundred individual lodges, which were devoted to social events, education, and charity. On 19 April 1937 the order was forcibly dissolved and its properties confiscated.

BOCHER (Pl. Bocherim, Bachurim, Bochers); Talmud student. The bocher took up residence in the town of his rabbi and was supported by the local Jewish community, or he earned his keep as a private tutor.

BRIS MILO (Brit Milah); "Covenant of Circumcision." On the eighth day after birth, the boy is circumcised as a sign of his acceptance into the Covenant (Gen. 17:10–14).

CENTRALVEREIN (CV) The Centralverein deutscher Staatsbürger jüdischen Glaubens was founded in 1893, primarily as a defense organization against antisemitism. With more than five hundred local chapters, it was the largest Jewish organization in Germany until 1933. As the organ of the liberal Jewish middle class, it advocated the symbiosis of German and Jewish identity and until 1933 was anti-Zionist. The CV was forcibly dissolved in November 1938.

CHALUTZ (Pl. Chalutzim); "Pioneer"; also member of the Zionist organization Hechalutz (see below), which prepared its members for emigration to Palestine.

CHANUKAH Eight-day festival commemorating the rededication of the Temple in Jerusalem in 164 B.C.E. During the holiday, an additional candle is lit daily on the menorah, a nine-branched candelabrum (with the so-called *Shammes,* i.e., "servant," as its ninth candle).

CHASEN (Chazzan); cantor and leader of prayers. During worship, he chants the prayers and reads from the Torah. This office can be filled as a full-time or part-time appointment. In small communities it is often filled by the religion teacher.

CHASNE (Also Chassene); wedding.

CHEWRA KADISCHA (Chevra Kadisha); "Holy Brotherhood." Religious society that among orthodox Jews cares for the gravely ill and buries the dead according to strict ritual laws.

CHUPPA Wedding canopy, under which the wedding ceremony is conducted.

DAJAN (Dayan; Pl. Dayanim); judge who decides cases according to Jewish religious law.

FEAST OF BOOTHS OR TABERNACLES See Sukkos (Sukkoth).

GEMARA See Mishna.

GOY (Pl. Goyim); A non-Jew.

HACHSHARA "Making fit"; training for a working life in Palestine, organized by Hechalutz (see below). Hachshara was mainly carried out through collective instruction on training farms.

HAGGADA The text ordering the ritual for the first night of Passover (Pesach Haggada). In the broader sense, also the narrative and exegetic portion of the Rabbinic teachings, as differentiated from the legal portion, i.e., Halacha.

HECHALUTZ "The Pioneer"; international Zionist organization for preparing young immigrants for settling the land of Palestine (see Hachshara). A German branch of Hechalutz was founded in 1918 and existed independently until 1938, and from then until 1942 as part of the Reichsvereinigung (see below).

HILFSVEREIN Hilfsverein der deutschen Juden; founded in 1901 as a charitable organization for the Jews in East Europe and Palestine. In 1933 it became an aid organization for the emigration of German Jews to all countries except Palestine.

JOINT The American Jewish Joint Distribution Committee was established in 1914 as an aid organization of all North American Jews. Until 1933 it primarily assisted Jews in East Europe and Palestine, and thereafter the Jews of Europe under Nazi persecution. The Joint promoted emigration from Germany and until 1941 covered an increasing portion of the budget for the Reichsvertretung and Reichsvereinigung (see below).

JOM KIPPUR See Yom Kippur.

JONTEW (Yomtov); holiday.

KADDISH Prayer praising God and wishing for peace. Kaddish is also recited by mourners for the deceased, particularly by the son for his parents during the first year of mourning and on the anniversary of their deaths.

KASHRUS (Kashrut); "proper," "suitable"; noun, from Kosher (see below); state of being kosher.

KEHILLA Jewish community.

KOL NIDRE "All Vows"; prayer chanted at start of Yom Kippur (see below). It cancels vows with God that may be made thoughtlessly during the year.

KOSHER ("Fit"); in accordance with the dietary laws. This requires, for example, that the blood be drained from a slaughtered animal, that dairy and meat dishes be strictly separated, and forbids the consumption of pork and shellfish.

KULTURBUND The Jüdische Kulturbund of Berlin was founded in June 1933 as the sponsoring and membership organization of a separate Jewish cultural life. United with similar societies in other cities in 1935 to form the Reichsverband jüdischer Kulturbünde, until 1941 it arranged theater and concert performances as well as lecture series, all under the strict censorship of the Reichspropagandaministerium.

LEINEN Verb; to chant from the Torah aloud and according to prescribed melodic intonations.

MATZAH (Pl. Matzoth); unleavened bread, eaten at Passover in remembrance of the exodus of the Jews from Egypt, when they lacked sufficient time to bake leavened bread.

MESCHORES (Meshores, Mesharet); servant.

MEZUZAH (Pl. Mezuzoth); capsule attached to the doorpost and gateposts containing a strip of parchment with the Torah passages Deut. 6:4–9 and 11:13–21. The mezuzah is intended to remind those entering the house of the basic teachings of Judaism.

MINYAN Quorum of ten men who have attained religious majority; required for worship.

MISHNA Rabbinic code of law compiled by Rabbi Judah Hanassi around 200 C.E. Together, the Mishna and its commentaries, the Gemara, constitute the Talmud.

MISRACH (Mizrach); "East"; a plaque, often decorative, on the east wall of a room that shows the direction in which to turn during prayer.

MIZWO (Mitzvah, Pl. Mitzvoth); in the broader sense, a good deed, e.g., support of the needy or sick. In the strict sense, any biblical injunction.

MOHEL Ritual circumciser; a religious office practiced as a secondary occupation by especially certified men.

OREN Verb; to pray.

PARNAS (Pl. Parnassim); community leader.

PEIES (Payut); long sidelocks worn by orthodox Jews in keeping with the commandment in Lev. 19:27.

PESSACH Passover; festival celebrated at the time of the first spring full moon in commemoration of the exodus of the Jews from Egypt (Exodus 12–14). It begins with the Seder, at which the story of the exodus is read from the Passover Haggadah.

PLETT (Blett); a slip or coupon for free meals at the home of a community member, issued by the community administrator to transient or poor Jews.

PURIM Joyous festival at which the Scroll of Esther is read describing the deliverance of the Jews of Persia from the hands of their enemy Haman. It is often celebrated with masquerades and merriment.

RABBI (Rebbe, Reb, Rav); "Reb" is also used as a respectful form of address (cf. Mister). The rabbi is one who is qualified to render judgments in Jewish law. His presence is not required for worship, nor must a person with rabbinic ordination perform the office of rabbi. It was only with Reform Judaism that the rabbi began to deliver sermons in the vernacular each Sabbath.

REICHSBUND JÜDISCHER FRONTSOLDATEN The Reichsbund jüdischer Frontsoldaten was founded in 1919, as a veterans organization with some 50,000 members. It fought against antisemitism and defended the honor of Jewish soldiers. Decidedly patriotic from the start, after 1933 it attempted, without success, to play a leading role among German Jewry. It was banned in November 1938.

REICHSVEREINIGUNG The Reichsvereinigung der Juden in Deutschland was created by dictate in February 1939, as an organization embracing all "racial Jews," as they were defined in the Nuremberg Laws. It was placed under the direct supervision of the Gestapo. Its leadership, transferred to it from the Reichsvertretung, directed emigration, schooling, and welfare work. It was forced to assist with the deportations, and was dissolved on 10 June 1943.

REICHSVERTRETUNG Reichsvertretung der deutschen Juden (after 1935, Reichsvertretung der Juden in Deutschland); founded in September 1933 and incorporating all of the big Jewish organizations and state federations, it was the largest overall representative body in the history of German Jewry. It ran the self-assistance projects and represented Jewish interests to the National Socialist regime. After the Pogrom of 9/10 November 1938 ("Kristallnacht"), it was turned by government order into the Reichsvereinigung.

ROSH HASHANA New Year, generally in September. A High Holy Day, it is celebrated in the synagogue as the day of divine judgment. It introduces the ten days of repentance leading to Yom Kippur (see below).

SCHABBES (Schabatt, Sabbath); the weekly day of rest beginning on Friday evening in the synagogue and with a Sabbath meal at home. In traditional Judaism, all work (including travel and writing) is forbidden.

SCHABBES GOJ (Shabbes Goy); Christian helper, who performs tasks forbidden to Jews on the Sabbath.

SCHECHITA Slaughter according to the prescriptions of religious law, thus making the slaughtered animal kosher. The slaughterer (Schochet; see below) makes a single deep cut through the jugular vein, which immediately renders the animal unconscious and causes the blood to drain. (The consumption of blood is forbidden.)

SCHIWE (Shiva); "Seven"; the seven-day period of mourning after burial. In the home of mourning, the family sits on the floor or on low stools, recites the daily prayers in a quorum, and receives visits from friends, who bring food and offer consolation.

SCHOCHET (Shochet, Pl. Shochtim); ritual slaughterer. Performance of this office requires special training, with an examination by a rabbi. The Shochet can practice his trade as a full-time or secondary occupation.

SCHUL (Shul); Traditional expression for synagogue, which is also a place of learning (school).

SEDER ("Order"); The order in which the Seder meal on the eve of the Passover festival is conducted (see Pessach). To "hold the Seder" means to conduct the ceremony as head of the household.

SHAVUOT (Schewues, Schawues, Schwuaus); Feast of Weeks, celebrated seven weeks after Passover. Originally a harvest festival, it later became the Festival of the Revelation on Sinai and the Covenant.

SHOFAR A wind instrument made from a ram's horn, which is sounded in the synagogue at Rosh Hashana and Yom Kippur. Its voice reminds the congregants of divine judgment and calls on them to repent.

SIMCHAS TORA (Simchat Torah); festival of "Rejoicing in the Law." It takes place at the conclusion of the Feast of Tabernacles (Sukkoth), when the year's cycle of weekly Torah readings is concluded, then to be begun anew. In traditional synagogues, men dance with the Torah scrolls in their arms.

SUKKOS (Sukkoth); Feast of Tabernacles, celebrated in remembrance of the tabernacles or booths in which the Jews dwelt after the exodus from Egypt (Lev. 23:42ff.). For seven days the family dwells mainly in the festively decorated booth (Sukkah), whose loosely covered roof must be open to the sky.

TALLES (Tallis, Tallith); prayer shawl made of four-cornered cloth with stripes and hanging knotted fringes (in accordance with Num. 15:37–41). It is worn at morning prayers.

TALMUD Compilation of the teachings and traditions of post-Biblical Judaism. The Palestinian Talmud was completed around 375 B.C.E., the Babylonian Talmud around 500 B.C.E.

TEFILIN Phylacteries worn at weekday morning services by men on the arm and forehead, according to the commandment in Deut. 6:8. The two capsules attached to them contain the four Torah texts Ex. 13:1–10 and 11–16, and Deut. 6:4–9 and 11:13–21.

TORAH The Five Books of Moses: Genesis, Exodus, Leviticus, Numbers, and Deuteronomy. Every synagogue owns at least one Torah scroll, which is kept in the Ark. The weekly portion is read from it during worship.

TREFE Not kosher (see above).

YESHIVA (Pl. Yeshivot); talmudic academy.

YESHIVA BOCHER See Bocher.

YISHUV "Settlement"; term for the Jewish settlements and settlers in Palestine prior to the founding of the state of Israel.

YOM KIPPUR Day of Atonement, conclusion of the High Holy Days on which penitential prayers and strict fasting serve to reconcile the individual with God and his or her fellow beings.

ZIONISTISCHE VEREINIGUNG The Zionistische Vereinigung für Deutschland was founded in 1897 as the organization of the German Zionists and was part of the international Zionist movement. It propagated the Jewish national idea and settlement in Palestine. Until 1933 it represented a minority that had to struggle for recognition in the Jewish community, but its significance grew during the years of Nazi rule.

# Index